Gleim Publications, Inc., offers five university-level study systems:

Auditing & Systems Exam Questions and Explanations with Test Prep Software
Business Law/Legal Studies Exam Questions and Explanations with Test Prep Software
Federal Tax Exam Questions and Explanations with Test Prep Software
Financial Accounting Exam Questions and Explanations with Test Prep Software
Cost/Managerial Accounting Exam Questions and Explanations with Test Prep Software

The following is a list of Gleim examination review systems:

CIA Review: Part 1, The Internal Audit Activity's Role in Governance, Risk, and Control
CIA Review: Part 2, Conducting the Internal Audit Engagement
CIA Review: Part 3, Business Analysis and Information Technology
CIA Review: Part 4, Business Management Skills
CIA Review: A System for Success

CMA Review: Part 1, Financial Planning, Performance, and Control
CMA Review: Part 2, Financial Decision Making
CMA Review: A System for Success

CPA Review: Financial
CPA Review: Auditing
CPA Review: Business
CPA Review: Regulation
CPA Review: A System for Success

EA Review: Part 1, Individuals
EA Review: Part 2, Businesses
EA Review: Part 3, Representation, Practices, and Procedures
EA Review: A System for Success

Use the order form provided at the back of this book or contact us at www.gleim.com or (800) 874-5346.

Visit www.gleim.com for the latest updates and information on all of our products.

REVIEWERS AND CONTRIBUTORS

Garrett W. Gleim, B.S., CPA (not in public practice), is a graduate of The Wharton School at the University of Pennsylvania. Mr. Gleim coordinated the production staff, reviewed the manuscript, and provided production assistance throughout the project.

William A. Hillison, Ph.D., CPA, CMA, is a Professor Emeritus of Accounting at Florida State University. His primary teaching duties included graduate and undergraduate auditing and systems courses. Dr. Hillison provided substantial editorial assistance throughout the project.

Grady M. Irwin, J.D., is a graduate of the University of Florida College of Law, and he has taught in the University of Florida College of Business. Mr. Irwin provided substantial editorial assistance throughout the project.

Michael Kustanovich, M.A., CPA, Israeli CPA, is a graduate of Ben-Gurion University of the Negev, Israel. He has worked in the audit department of KPMG, Israel, and as a financial accounting lecturer in the department of Economics of Ben-Gurion University of the Negev. Mr. Kustanovich provided substantial editorial assistance throughout the project.

John F. Rebstock, B.S.A., is a graduate of the Fisher School of Accounting at the University of Florida. He has passed the CPA and CIA exams. Mr. Rebstock reviewed portions of the manuscript.

Stewart B. White, CIA, is a graduate of the School of Business at Virginia Commonwealth University. He has passed the CPA and CISA exams and has worked in the fields of retail management, financial audit, IT audit, COBOL programming, and data warehouse management. Mr. White provided substantial editorial assistance throughout the project.

A PERSONAL THANKS

This manual would not have been possible without the extraordinary effort and dedication of Jacob Brunny, Julie Cutlip, Eileen Nickl, Teresa Soard, Joanne Strong, Candace Van Doren, Jennifer Vann, and Eleanor Wilson who typed the entire manuscript and all revisions, and drafted and laid out the diagrams and illustrations in this book.

The authors also appreciate the production and editorial assistance of Melissa Del Valle, Chris Hawley, Katie Larson, Cary Marcous, Shane Rapp, Drew Sheppard, Katie Wassink, and Martha Willis.

The authors also appreciate the critical reading assistance of Ellen Buhl, Reed Daines, Stephanie Garrison, Devin Grief, Daniela Guanipa, Alyssa Hagerty, Lawrence Lipp, and Jerry Mathis.

Finally, we appreciate the encouragement, support, and tolerance of our families throughout this project.

2013 EDITION

CPA REVIEW

Business

by

Irvin N. Gleim, Ph.D., CPA, CIA, CMA, CFM, RTRP

with the assistance of
Grady M. Irwin, J.D.

The AICPA formal title of this section is *Business Environment and Concepts*, and the AICPA acronym is BEC.

ABOUT THE AUTHOR

Irvin N. Gleim is Professor Emeritus in the Fisher School of Accounting at the University of Florida and is a member of the American Accounting Association, Academy of Legal Studies in Business, American Institute of Certified Public Accountants, Association of Government Accountants, Florida Institute of Certified Public Accountants, The Institute of Internal Auditors, and the Institute of Management Accountants. He has had articles published in the *Journal of Accountancy*, *The Accounting Review*, and *The American Business Law Journal* and is author/coauthor of numerous accounting books, aviation books, and CPE courses.

iv

Gleim Publications, Inc.
P.O. Box 12848
University Station
Gainesville, Florida 32604
(800) 87-GLEIM or (800) 874-5346
(352) 375-0772
Fax: (352) 375-6940
Internet: www.gleim.com
Email: admin@gleim.com

For updates to this 2013 printing of
CPA Review: Business

Go To: www.gleim.com/updates

Or: Email update@gleim.com with
CPA BEC 2013-1 in the subject line.
You will receive our current update
as a reply.

Updates are available until the next edition is
published.

ISSN: 1547-8084

ISBN: 978-1-58194-266-8 *CPA Review: Auditing*
ISBN: 978-1-58194-271-2 *CPA Review: Business*
ISBN: 978-1-58194-272-9 *CPA Review: Financial*
ISBN: 978-1-58194-273-6 *CPA Review: Regulation*
ISBN: 978-1-58194-292-7 *CPA Review: A System for Success*

ACKNOWLEDGMENTS

Material from *Uniform CPA Examination, Selected Questions and Unofficial Answers*, Copyright
© 1974-2012 by the American Institute of Certified Public Accountants, Inc., is reprinted and/or adapted
with permission. Visit the AICPA's website at www.aicpa.org for more information.

The author is indebted to the Institute of Certified Management Accountants for permission to use
problem materials from past CMA examinations. Questions and unofficial answers from the Certified
Management Accountant Examinations, copyright by the Institute of Certified Management
Accountants, are reprinted and/or adapted with permission.

The author is grateful for permission to reproduce Certified Internal Auditor Examination
Questions, Copyright © 1991-2008 by The Institute of Internal Auditors, Inc.

This publication was printed and bound by Corley Printing Company, St. Louis, MO, a registered
ISO-9002 company. More information about Corley Printing Company is available at
www.corleyprinting.com or by calling (314) 739-3777.

TABLE OF CONTENTS

DETAILED TABLE OF CONTENTS

vi

PREFACE FOR CPA CANDIDATES

The purpose of this Gleim *CPA Review* study book is to help YOU prepare to pass the 2013 Business Environment and Concepts (referred to throughout the rest of this text as BEC) section of the CPA examination. Our overriding consideration is to provide an inexpensive, effective, and easy-to-use study program. This book

1. Explains how to optimize your grade by focusing on the BEC section of the CPA exam.

2. Defines the subject matter tested on the BEC section of the CPA exam.

3. Outlines all of the subject matter tested on the BEC section in 20 easy-to-use-and-complete study units.

4. Presents multiple-choice questions from recent CPA examinations to prepare you for questions in future CPA exams. Our answer explanations are presented to the immediate right of each question for your convenience. Use a piece of paper to cover our answer explanations as you study the questions.

5. Presents one written communication task in each study unit to acquaint you with the written communication format. Answer the written communication task in your book. A suggested answer follows each task.

The outline format, the spacing, and the question and answer formats in this book are designed to facilitate readability, learning, understanding, and success on the CPA exam. Our most successful candidates use the entire Gleim CPA Review System,* which includes books, Test Prep Online, Audio Review, Gleim Online, Simulation Wizard, Practice Exam, and access to a Personal Counselor; or a group study CPA review program. (Check our website for live courses we recommend.) This review book and all Gleim *CPA Review* materials are compatible with other CPA review materials and courses that follow the AICPA Content and Skill Specification Outlines (CSOs/SSOs).

To maximize the efficiency and effectiveness of your CPA review program, augment your studying with *CPA Review: A System for Success*. This booklet has been carefully written and organized to provide important information to assist you in passing the CPA examination.

Thank you for your interest in the Gleim *CPA Review* materials. We deeply appreciate the thousands of letters and suggestions received from CIA, CMA, EA, RTRP, and CPA candidates during the past 5 decades.

If you use the Gleim materials, we want YOUR feedback immediately after the exam and as soon as you have received your grades. The CPA exam is NONDISCLOSED, and you will sign an attestation including, "I hereby agree that I will maintain the confidentiality of the Uniform CPA Examination. In addition, I agree that I will not divulge the nature or content of any Uniform CPA Examination question or answer under any circumstance..." We ask only for information about our materials, i.e., the topics that need to be added, expanded, etc. Our approach has AICPA approval.

Please go to www.gleim.com/feedbackBEC to share your suggestions on how we can improve this edition.

Good Luck on the Exam,

Irvin N. Gleim

December 2012

---

*Visit www.gleim.com or call (800) 874-5346 to order.

OPTIMIZING YOUR BUSINESS SCORE

CBT-e Exam

Gleim Section Title	Auditing	Business	Financial	Regulation
AICPA Formal Title	Auditing & Attestation	Business Environment & Concepts	Financial Accounting & Reporting	Regulation
Acronym	AUD	BEC	FAR	REG
Exam Length	4 hours	3 hours	4 hours	3 hours
Testlets:				
Multiple-Choice	3, 30 questions each	3, 24 questions each	3, 30 questions each	3, 24 questions each
Simulations	1 with 7 tasks	0	1 with 7 tasks	1 with 6 tasks
Written Communication	0	1 with 3 tasks	0	0

ALLOW GLEIM TO GUIDE YOU THROUGH THE STUDY PROCESS AND PASS THE EXAM

1. Read this **Introduction** to familiarize yourself with the content and structure of the BEC section of the exam. In the following pages, you will find

   a. An **overview of the BEC section** and what it generally tests, including

      1) The AICPA's Content Specification Outlines (CSOs) for BEC, cross-referenced with the Gleim study units that contain each topic

      2) The AICPA's Skill Specification Outlines (SSOs) for BEC

      3) The AICPA's suggested references for BEC

   b. A detailed plan with **steps to obtain your CPA license**, including

      1) The order in which you should apply, register, and schedule your exam

      2) The studying tactics on which you should focus

      3) How to organize your study schedule to make the most out of each resource in the Gleim CPA Review System (i.e., books, Test Prep Online, Audio Review, Gleim Online, Simulation Wizard, etc.)

   c. Tactics for your **actual test day**, including

      1) Time budgeting so you complete each testlet with time to review

      2) Question-answering techniques to obtain every point you can in both the multiple-choice and written communication testlets

      3) An explanation of how to be in control of your CPA exam

2. Scan the Gleim *CPA Review: A System for Success* booklet and note where to revisit later in your studying process to obtain a deeper understanding of the of the CPA exam.

   a. *CPA Review: A System for Success* has seven study units:

      Study Unit 1: The CPA Examination: An Overview and Preparation Introduction
      Study Unit 2: AICPA Content Specification Outlines and Skill Specification Outlines
      Study Unit 3: Content Preparation, Test Administration, and Performance Grading
      Study Unit 4: Multiple-Choice Questions
      Study Unit 5: Task-Based Simulations and Written Communication Questions
      Study Unit 6: Preparing to Pass the CPA Exam
      Study Unit 7: How to Take the CPA Exam

   b. If you feel that you need even more details on the test-taking experience, watch our **Free Tutorial** at www.gleim.com/accounting/cpa/basics.php.

      1) This tutorial is best for candidates who have little or no experience with the basic computer skills required for the CPA exam (e.g., copy/paste, search, etc.).

   c. Additionally, the AICPA requires that all candidates review the tutorial and sample tests at www.aicpa.org.

3. Before you begin studying, take a **Diagnostic Quiz** at www.gleim.com/cpadiagnosticquiz or use our Gleim Diagnostic Quiz App for iPhone, iPod Touch, and Android.

   a. The Diagnostic Quiz includes a representative sample of 40 multiple-choice questions and will determine your weakest areas in BEC.

   b. When you are finished, one of our **Personal Counselors** will consult with you to better focus your review on any areas in which you have less confidence.

4. Follow the steps outlined on page 9, "How to Study a BEC Study Unit Using the Gleim CPA Review System." This is the **study plan** that our most successful candidates adhere to. Study until you have reached your **desired proficiency level** (e.g., 75%) for each study unit in BEC.

   a. As you proceed, be sure to check any **Updates** that may have been released.

      1) Gleim Online, Simulation Wizard, and Test Prep Online are updated automatically.

2) Book updates can be viewed at www.gleim.com/updates, or you can have them emailed to you. See the information box in the top right corner of page iv for details.

b. **Review the *CPA Review: A System for Success* booklet** and become completely comfortable with what will be expected from you on test day.

5. Shortly before your test date, take a **Practice Exam** (complimentary with the CPA Review System) at www.gleim.com/cpapracticeexam.

a. The Gleim Practice Exam is designed to exactly emulate the CPA test-taking experience at Prometric.

b. This timed, scored exam tests you not only on the content you have studied, but also on the question-answering and time-management techniques you have learned throughout the Gleim study process.

c. When you have completed the exam, consult with your Personal Counselor to discuss where you should **focus your review during the final days before your exam** (question-answering techniques, time management, specific content areas, etc.).

6. **Take and PASS** the BEC section of the CPA exam!

a. When you have completed the exam, please contact Gleim with your **suggestions, comments, and corrections**. We want to know how well we prepared you for your testing experience.

OVERVIEW OF BUSINESS

BEC is scheduled for 3 hours (180 minutes).

AICPA title:	Business Environment and Concepts
AICPA acronym:	BEC
Gleim title/acronym:	Business/BEC
Question format:	72 multiple-choice questions (including 12 ungraded pretest questions) in three testlets of 24 questions each
	Three written communication tasks (including 1 ungraded pretest task)
Areas covered:	I. (18%) Corporate Governance
	II. (18%) Economic Concepts and Analysis
	III. (21%) Financial Management
	IV. (17%) Information Systems and Communications
	V. (12%) Strategic Planning
	VI. (14%) Operations Management

The Business Environment and Concepts section tests knowledge and skills necessary to demonstrate an understanding of the general business environment and business concepts. The topics in this section include knowledge of corporate governance; economic concepts essential to understanding the global business environment and its impact on an entity's business strategy; financial risk management; financial management processes; information systems and communications; strategic planning; and operations management. In addition to demonstrating knowledge and understanding of these topics, candidates are required to apply that knowledge in performing audit, attest, financial reporting, tax preparation, and other professional responsibilities as certified public accountants.

According to the AICPA, candidates will be expected to perform the following inclusive list of tasks to demonstrate such knowledge and skills:

1. Demonstrate an understanding of globalization on the business environment.

2. Distinguish between appropriate and inappropriate governance structures within an organization (e.g., tone at the top, policies, steering committees, strategies, oversight, etc.).

3. Assess the impact of business cycles on an entity's industry or business operations.

4. Apply knowledge of changes in the global economic markets in identifying the impact on an entity in determining its business strategy and financial management policies, including managing the risks of: inflation, deflation, commodity costs, credit defaults, interest rate variations, currency fluctuation, and regulation.

5. Assess the factors influencing a company's capital structure, including risk, leverage, cost of capital, growth rate, profitability, asset structure, and loan covenants.

6. Evaluate assumptions used in financial valuations to determine their reasonableness (e.g., investment return assumptions, discount rates, etc.).

7. Determine the business reasons for and explain the underlying economic substance of transactions and their accounting implications.

8. Identify the information systems within a business that are used to process and accumulate transactional data, as well as provide monitoring and financial reporting information.

9. Distinguish between appropriate and inappropriate internal control systems, including system design, controls over data, transaction flow, wireless technology, and internet transmissions.

10. Evaluate whether there is appropriate segregation of duties, levels of authorization, and data security in an organization to maintain an appropriate internal control structure.

11. Obtain and document information about an organization's strategic planning processes to identify key components of the business strategy and market risks.

12. Develop a time-phased project plan showing required activities, task dependencies, and required resources to achieve a specific deliverable.

13. Identify the business and operational risks inherent in an entity's disaster recovery/business continuity plan.

14. Evaluate business operations and quality control initiatives to understand its use of best practices and the ways to measure and manage performance and costs.

AICPA CONTENT SPECIFICATION OUTLINES (CSOs)

In the Uniform CPA Examination Alert newsletter of Spring 2009, when it was first unveiling the new CBT-e exam, the AICPA indicated that the content specification outlines have several purposes, including

1. *Ensure that the testing of entry-level knowledge and skills that are important to the protection of the public interest is consistent across examination administrations*

2. *Determine what kinds of questions should be included on the CPA Examination so that every version of the examination reflects the required distribution and balance of knowledge and skill components*

3. *Provide candidates preparing for the examination with information about the subject matter that is eligible to be tested*

For your convenience, we have reproduced verbatim the AICPA's BEC CSOs. We also have provided cross-references to the study units and subunits in this book that correspond to the CSOs' coverage. If one entry appears above a list, it applies to all items.

AICPA CONTENT SPECIFICATION OUTLINE

Business Environment and Concepts

I. **Corporate Governance (18%)**

    A. Rights, Duties, Responsibilities, and Authority of the Board of Directors, Officers, and Other Employees - SU 1

        1. Financial reporting
        2. Internal control (including COSO or similar framework)
        3. Enterprise risk management (including COSO or similar framework)

    B. Control Environment - 1.4

        1. Tone at the top – establishing control environment
        2. Monitoring control effectiveness
        3. Change control process

II. **Economic Concepts and Analysis (18%)**

    A. Changes in Economic and Business Cycles – Economic Measures/Indicators - SU 3

    B. Globalization and Local Economies

        1. Impacts of globalization on companies - SU 4
        2. Shifts in economic balance of power (e.g., capital) to/from developed from/to emerging markets - 4.1

    C. Market Influences on Business Strategies - 15.1

    D. Financial Risk Management

        1. Market, interest rate, currency, liquidity, credit, price, and other risks - 5.1-5.3
        2. Means for mitigating/controlling financial risks - 4.3, 5.4

III. **Financial Management (21%)**

    A. Financial Modeling, Projections, and Analysis

        1. Forecasting and trends - SU 6
        2. Financial and risk analysis - 1.5, 9.3
        3. Impact of inflation/deflation - 3.5, 4.2

    B. Financial Decisions

        1. Debt, equity, leasing - 7.1-7.3
        2. Asset and investment management - SU 5, SU 8

    C. Capital Management, including Working Capital

        1. Capital structure - 7.1, 7.2, 7.4, 7.5
        2. Short-term and long-term financing - 7.1, 7.2, 9.1, 9.2
        3. Asset effectiveness and/or efficiency - SU 8, 10.3-10.5

    D. Financial Valuations (e.g., Fair Value)

        1. Methods for calculating valuations - 5.3, 10.3
        2. Evaluating assumptions used in valuations - 10.1, 10.2

    E. Financial Transaction Processes and Controls - 11.4, 11.5

IV. **Information Systems and Communications (17%)**

    A. Organizational Needs Assessment

        1. Data capture - 11.3
        2. Processing - 11.3
        3. Reporting - 11.3
        4. Role of information technology in business strategy - 11.1, 11.4, 11.5

    B. Systems Design and Other Elements

        1. Business process design (integrated systems, automated, and manual interfaces) - 12.5
        2. Information Technology (IT) control objectives - 14.1
        3. Role of technology systems in control monitoring - 14.1
        4. Operational effectiveness - 14.1
        5. Segregation of duties - 12.6
        6. Policies - 14.1

    C.   Security - 14.2

        1.   Technologies and security management features
        2.   Policies

    D.   Internet – Implications for Business

        1.   Electronic commerce - 13.3-13.5
        2.   Opportunities for business process reengineering - 12.5
        3.   Roles of internet evolution on business operations and organization cultures - 13.1

    E.   Types of Information System and Technology Risks - 14.1

    F.   Disaster Recovery and Business Continuity - 14.4

V.   Strategic Planning (12%)

    A.   Market and Risk Analysis - 15.1, 15.2
    B.   Strategy Development, Implementation, and Monitoring - 15.2
    C.   Planning Techniques

        1.   Budget and analysis - 15.3, 15.4
        2.   Forecasting and projection - SU 6
        3.   Coordinating information from various sources for integrated planning - 16.1

VI. Operations Management (14%)

    A.   Performance Management and Impact of Measures on Behavior

        1.   Financial and nonfinancial measures - 10.3, 10.4, 17.2
        2.   Impact of marketing practices on performance - 15.1
        3.   Incentive compensation - 17.2

    B.   Cost Measurement Methods and Techniques - SU 18, SU 19, SU 20

    C.   Process Management - 17.3-17.6

        1.   Approaches, techniques, measures, and benefits to process-management-driven businesses

        2.   Roles of shared services, outsourcing, and off-shore operations, and their implications on business risks and controls

        3.   Selecting and implementing improvement initiatives

        4.   Business process reengineering

        5.   Management philosophies and techniques for performance improvement such as Just in Time (JIT), Quality, Lean, Demand Flow, Theory of Constraints, and Six Sigma

    D.   Project Management - 17.7

        1.   Project planning, implementation, and monitoring
        2.   Roles of project managers, project members, and oversight or steering groups
        3.   Project risks, including resource, scope, cost, and deliverables

AICPA SKILL SPECIFICATION OUTLINES (SSOs)

The SSOs identify the skills that will be tested on the CPA exam. The following table explains the skills tested, the weight range assigned to each skill category (approximate percentage of CPA exam that will use skills in the category) in BEC, the question format that will be used to test the skill in BEC, and the resources that will be available to the candidates to demonstrate proficiency in each skill.

Skills Category	Weight	Question Format	Resource(s)
Knowledge and Understanding	85%	Multiple-choice questions	Calculator
Application of the Body of Knowledge*	--	--	--
Written Communication	15%	Essay questions	Word processor

*The Application category is tested through task-based simulations, which are not present in the BEC section of the CPA exam.

REFERENCES

The AICPA suggests that the following publications will be sources of questions for BEC. Our outlines and answer explanations are based on these publications and are organized into meaningful, easy-to-use, common-sense study units to facilitate your exam preparation via the Gleim Knowledge Transfer System.

1. The Committee of Sponsoring Organizations of the Treadway Commission (COSO):
    - Internal Control – Integrated Framework
    - Enterprise Risk Management

2. Sarbanes-Oxley Act of 2002:
    - Title III, Corporate Responsibility
    - Title IV, Enhanced Financial Disclosures
    - Title VIII, Corporate and Criminal Fraud Accountability
    - Title IX, White-Collar Crime Penalty Enhancements
    - Title XI, Corporate Fraud Accountability

3. Current Business Periodicals

4. Current Textbooks on:
    - Accounting Information Systems
    - Budgeting and Measurement
    - Corporate Governance
    - Economics
    - Enterprise Risk Management
    - Finance
    - Management
    - Management Information Systems
    - Managerial Accounting
    - Production Operations
    - Project Management

5. International Standards for the Professional Practice of Internal Auditing

6. COBIT (The Control Objectives for Information and Related Technology)

STEPS TO BECOME A CPA

1. Become knowledgeable about the exam, and decide which section you will take first.

2. Purchase the Gleim CPA Review System to thoroughly prepare for the CPA exam. Commit to our systematic preparation for the exam as described in our review materials, including *CPA Review: A System for Success*.

3. Communicate with your Personal Counselor to design a study plan that meets your needs. Call (800) 874-5346 or email CPA@gleim.com.

4. Determine the board of accountancy (i.e., state) to which you will apply to sit for the CPA exam.

5. Obtain, complete, and submit your application form, including transcripts, fees, etc., to your State Board or NASBA. You should receive a Notice To Schedule (NTS) from NASBA in 4 to 6 weeks.

    a. Do not apply for a section of the exam until you are ready to take it. An NTS is valid for a specific period established by the boards of accountancy, and you will forfeit any fees you paid for sections not taken.

    b. Remember, the following testing windows are available for test taking: January/February, April/May, July/August, and October/November.

6. Schedule your test with Prometric (online or by calling your local Prometric testing site). Schedule at least 45 days before the date you plan to sit for the exam.

7. Work systematically through the study units in each section of the Gleim CPA Review System (Auditing, Business, Financial, and Regulation).

8. Use the Gleim CPA Test Prep Online: Thousands of questions, all updated to current tax law, Accounting Standards Codification, etc. Listen to CPA Audio Review as a supplement.

9. Sit for and PASS the CPA exam while you are in control.

10. Enjoy your career and pursue multiple certifications (CIA, CMA, EA, RTRP, etc.), recommend Gleim to others who are also taking these exams, and stay up-to-date on your continuing professional education with Gleim CPE.

More specifically, you should focus on the following **system for success** on the BEC section of the CPA exam:

1. **Understand the exam, including its purpose, coverage, preparation, format, administration, grading, and pass rates.**

   a. The better you understand the examination process from beginning to end, the better you will perform.

   b. Study the Gleim *CPA Review: A System for Success.* Please be sure you have a copy of this useful booklet. (*CPA Review: A System for Success* is also available online at www.gleim.com/sfs.)

2. **Learn and understand the subject matter tested.** The AICPA's CSOs and SSOs for the BEC section are the basis for the study outlines that are presented in each of the 20 study units that make up this book.* You will also learn and understand the BEC material tested on the CPA exam by answering numerous multiple-choice questions from recent CPA exams. Multiple-choice questions with the answer explanations to the immediate right of each question are a major component of each study unit.

3. **Practice answering actual exam questions to perfect your question-answering techniques.** Answering recent exam questions helps you understand the standards to which you will be held. This motivates you to learn and understand while studying (rather than reading) the outlines in each of the 20 study units.

   a. Question-answering techniques are suggested for multiple-choice questions and essay questions in Study Units 4 and 5 of *CPA Review: A System for Success.*

   b. Our **CPA Test Prep Online** contains thousands of additional multiple-choice questions that are not offered in our books. Additionally, CPA Test Prep Online has many useful features, including documentation of your performance and the ability to simulate the CBT-e exam environment.

   c. Our **CPA Gleim Online** is a powerful Internet-based program that allows CPA candidates to learn in an interactive environment and provides feedback to candidates to encourage learning. It includes multiple-choice questions and written communication tasks (essay questions) in Prometric's format. Each CPA Gleim Online candidate has access to a Personal Counselor, who helps organize study plans that work with busy schedules.

   d. Additionally, all candidates are required by the AICPA to review the tutorials and Sample Test at www.aicpa.org. According to the AICPA, failure to follow the directions provided in the tutorial and Sample Test, including the directions on how to respond, may adversely affect your scores.

4. **Plan and practice exam execution.** Anticipate the exam environment and prepare yourself with a plan: When to arrive? How to dress? What exam supplies to bring? How many questions and what format? Order of answering questions? How much time to spend on each question? See Study Unit 7 in *CPA Review: A System for Success.*

   a. Expect the unexpected and adjust! Remember, your sole objective when taking an examination is to maximize your score. You must outperform your peers, and being as comfortable and relaxed as possible gives you an advantage!

5. **Be in control.** Develop confidence and ensure success with a controlled preparation program followed by confident execution during the examination.

---

*Please fill out our online feedback form (www.gleim.com/feedbackBEC) IMMEDIATELY after you take the CPA exam so we can adapt to changes in the exam. Our approach has been approved by the AICPA.

PRELIMINARY TESTING: GLEIM CPA DIAGNOSTIC QUIZ

The Gleim CPA Diagnostic Quiz provides a representative sample of 40 multiple-choice questions for each exam part to identify your preliminary strengths and any weaknesses before you start preparing in earnest for the CPA exam. It also provides you with the actual exam experience, i.e., what you will encounter when you take the CPA exam at Prometric.

When you have completed the quiz, one of our Personal Counselors will consult with you to better focus your review on any areas in which you have less confidence. After your consultation, you will be able to access a Review Session, where you can study answer explanations for the correct and incorrect answer choices of the questions you answered incorrectly.

For smart phone users, there is also a Gleim Diagnostic Quiz App for iPhone, iPod Touch, and Android. See our website (www.gleim.com/cpadiagnosticquiz) for more information.

HOW TO STUDY A BEC STUDY UNIT USING THE GLEIM CPA REVIEW SYSTEM

To ensure that you are using your time effectively, we recommend that you follow the steps listed below when using all of the CPA Review System materials together (books, Test Prep Online, Audio Review, Gleim Online, and Simulation Wizard):

1. (30 minutes, plus 10 minutes for review) In the **CPA Gleim Online** course, complete Multiple-Choice Quiz #1 in 30 minutes. It is expected that your scores will be lower on the first quiz in each study unit than on subsequent quizzes.

   a. Immediately following the quiz, you will be prompted to review questions you flagged and/or answered incorrectly. For each question, analyze and understand why you were unsure or answered it incorrectly. This step is an essential learning activity.

2. (30 minutes) Use the online audiovisual presentation for an overview of the study unit. **CPA Audio Review** can be substituted for audiovisual presentations and can be used while driving to work, exercising, etc.

3. (45 minutes) Complete the 30-question online True/False quiz. It is interactive and most effective if used prior to studying the Knowledge Transfer Outline.

4. (60 minutes) Study the Knowledge Transfer Outline, particularly the troublesome areas identified from the multiple-choice questions in the Gleim Online course. The Knowledge Transfer Outline can be studied either online or from the books.

5. (30 minutes, plus 10 minutes for review) Complete Multiple-Choice Quiz #2 in the Gleim Online course.

   a. Immediately following the quiz, you will be prompted to review questions you flagged and/or answered incorrectly. For each question, analyze and understand why you were unsure or answered it incorrectly. This step is an essential learning activity.

6. (60 minutes) Complete two 20-question quizzes while in Test Mode from the **CPA Test Prep Online**. Review as needed.

7. (20 minutes, plus 10 minutes for review) Complete a written communication essay question in the Gleim Online course.

When following these steps, you will complete all 20 study units in about 100 hours. Then spend about 10-20 hours taking customized tests in the CPA Test Prep Online until you approach your desired proficiency level, e.g., 75%+. To get immediate feedback on questions in your problem areas, use Study Sessions. You should also complete all of the written communications in the Simulation Wizard for extra practice on this difficult aspect of the exam.

CPA FINAL REVIEW

Final review is the culmination of all your studies and topics and should occur one week prior to when you sit for your exam. All study units in Gleim Online should be completed by this time.

Step 1: Take the CPA Practice Exam at the beginning of your final review stage. This will help you identify any weak areas for more practice. Discuss your results with your Personal Counselor for additional guidance.

Step 2: Work in Gleim CPA Test Prep Online, focusing on your weak areas identified from your Practice Exam. Also, be sure to focus on all the material as a whole to refresh yourself with topics you learned at the beginning of your studies. View your performance chart to make sure you are scoring 70% or higher.

CPA GLEIM ONLINE

CPA Gleim Online is a versatile, interactive, self-study review program delivered via the Internet. It is divided into four courses (one for each section of the CPA exam).

Each course is broken down into 20 individual, manageable study units. Completion time per study unit will average out to 5 hours. Each study unit in the course contains an audiovisual presentation, 30 true/false study questions, 10-20 pages of Knowledge Transfer Outlines, and two 20-question multiple-choice quizzes. Task-based simulations are also included with each study unit in Auditing, Financial, and Regulation, while written communication tasks are in each study unit of Business. Downloadable PDFs with additional information, such as Core Concepts, are also included with each study unit.

CPA Gleim Online provides you with access to a Personal Counselor, a real person who will provide support to ensure your competitive edge. CPA Gleim Online is a great way to get confidence as you prepare with Gleim. This confidence will continue during and after the exam.

GLEIM SIMULATION WIZARD FOR BEC

The Gleim Simulation Wizard for BEC is a training program that focuses on the questions that appear in the written communication tasks in the BEC section of the CPA exam. This online course provides 20 written communications, one per study unit, as well as test-taking tips from Dr. Gleim to help you stay in control.

GLEIM BOOKS

This edition of the CPA BEC Review book has the following five features to make studying easier:

1. **Examples:** Illustrative examples, both hypothetical and those drawn from actual events, are set off in shaded, bordered boxes.

EXAMPLE

The economy of Spain during the Age of Exploration was almost wrecked by the influx of gold and silver from the Western Hemisphere. The sudden appearance of a vast amount of money drove the aggregate demand curve to the right. Since this was not accompanied by an increase in the amount of goods available, the aggregate supply curve remained fixed, and demand-pull inflation resulted. The end result was simply to drive up the prices of existing goods. This incident demonstrates the principle that the value of money is derived from the wealth that underlies it.

---

2. **Backgrounds:** In certain instances, we have provided historical background or supplemental information. This information is intended to illuminate the topic under discussion and is set off in bordered boxes with shaded headings. This material does not need to be memorized for the exam.

Background

In late 2001 and 2002, massive accounting scandals were reported to the media. They involved such large firms as Enron (hid debt of over $1 billion in improper off-the-books partnerships), Global Crossing (inflated revenues; shredded accounting-related documents), and WorldCom (booked operating expenses as capital assets; made large off-the-books payments to founder). In response to these and many other fraudulent practices, Congress passed the Sarbanes-Oxley Act of 2002, named for its sponsors, Democratic Senator Paul Sarbanes of Maryland and Republican Representative Mike Oxley of Ohio.

---

3. **Gleim Success Tips:** These tips supplement the core exam material by suggesting how certain topics might be presented on the exam or how you should prepare for an issue.

 Remember that internal control systems have inherent limitations. Be able to identify what these limitations are.

---

4. **Memory Aids:** These mnemonics are designed to assist you in memorizing important concepts. See an example of a memory aid below.

   The COSO Risk Management Framework lists four categories of objectives that are applicable to all entities:

   1) <u>S</u>trategic objectives align with and support the entity's mission.
   2) <u>O</u>perations objectives address effectiveness and efficiency.
   3) <u>R</u>eporting objectives concern reliability.
   4) <u>C</u>ompliance objectives relate to adherence to laws and regulations.

   Memory aid: <u>S</u>tudying <u>O</u>bsessively <u>R</u>eally <u>C</u>ounts

5. **BEC Review Checklist:** This appendix to the 20 study units contains a complete listing of all study units and subunits in the Gleim BEC Review for 2013. Use this list as a study aid to mark off your progress and to provide jumping-off points for review.

CPA TEST PREP ONLINE

Twenty-question tests in the **CPA Test Prep Online** will help you to focus on your weaker areas. Make it a game: How much can you improve?

Our CPA Test Prep Online (in Test Mode) forces you to commit to your answer choice before looking at answer explanations; thus, you are preparing under true exam conditions. It also keeps track of your time and performance history for each study unit, which is available in either a table or graphical format.

STUDYING WITH BOOK AND TEST PREP ONLINE*

Simplify the exam preparation process by following our suggested steps listed below. DO NOT omit the step in which you diagnose the reasons for answering questions incorrectly; i.e., learn from your mistakes while studying so you avoid making similar mistakes on the CPA exam.

1. In test mode of CPA Test Prep Online, answer a 20-question diagnostic test before studying any other information.

2. Study the Knowledge Transfer Outline for the corresponding study unit in your Gleim book.

   a. Place special emphasis on the weaker areas that you identified with the initial diagnostic quiz in Step 1.

3. Take two or three 20-question tests in test mode after you have studied the Knowledge Transfer Outline.

4. Immediately following each test, you will be prompted to review the questions you flagged and/or answered incorrectly. For each question, analyze and understand why you were unsure or answered it incorrectly. This step is an essential learning activity.

5. Continue this process until you approach a predetermined proficiency level, e.g., 75%+.

6. Modify this process to suit your individual learning process.

   a. Learning from questions you answer incorrectly is very important. Each question you answer incorrectly is an **opportunity** to avoid missing actual test questions on your CPA exam. Thus, you should carefully study the answer explanations provided until you understand why the original answer you chose is wrong as well as why the correct answer indicated is correct. This learning technique is clearly the difference between passing and failing for many CPA candidates.

   b. Also, you **must** determine why you answered questions incorrectly and learn how to avoid the same error in the future. Reasons for missing questions include

      1) Misreading the requirement (stem)
      2) Not understanding what is required
      3) Making a math error
      4) Applying the wrong rule or concept
      5) Being distracted by one or more of the answers
      6) Incorrectly eliminating answers from consideration
      7) Not having any knowledge of the topic tested
      8) Using a poor educated guessing strategy

   c. It is also important to verify that you answered correctly for the right reasons (i.e., read the discussion provided for the correct answers). Otherwise, if the material is tested on the CPA exam in a different manner, you may not answer it correctly.

   d. It is imperative that you complete the predetermined number of study units per week so you can review your progress and realize how attainable a comprehensive CPA review program is when using the Gleim CPA Review System. Remember to meet or beat your schedule to give yourself confidence.

---

*Gleim does not recommend studying for BEC using only this book and Test Prep Online. Candidates need to practice essays for the written communication tasks in an exam environment, which means on a computer. Use CPA Gleim Online and CPA Simulation Wizard to become an expert on written communication tasks.

GLEIM AUDIO REVIEWS

Gleim **CPA Audio Reviews** provide an average of 30 minutes of quality review for each study unit. Each review provides an overview of the Knowledge Transfer Outline in the *CPA Review* book. The purpose is to get candidates "started" so they can relate to the questions they will answer before reading the study outlines in each study unit.

The audios get to the point, as does the entire **Gleim System for Success**. We are working to get you through the CPA exam with minimum time, cost, and frustration. You can listen to two short sample audio reviews on our website at www.gleim.com/accounting/demos.

FINAL REVIEW: GLEIM CPA PRACTICE EXAM

Take a CPA Practice Exam (complimentary with the CPA Review System) shortly before you take the actual exam to gain experience in the computer-based exam environment. The Practice Exam is 3 hours (180 minutes) long and contains three testlets with 24 multiple-choice questions each and one testlet with three written communication tasks, just like the CPA exam. Therefore, it tests you not only on the content you have studied, but also on the question-answering and time-management techniques you have learned.

For the most realistic practice exam experience, we suggest you complete the entire exam in one sitting, just like the actual CPA exam. Once you have completed the Practice Exam and received your grade, you will be provided with a Review Session that shows which questions were answered incorrectly. Additionally, you will be able to study answer explanations to assist you in learning the topics.

TIME BUDGETING AND QUESTION-ANSWERING TECHNIQUES FOR BEC

Expect three testlets of 24 multiple-choice questions each and one written communication task testlet with three essay questions on the BEC section with a 180-minute time allocation. See Study Units 4 and 5 in *CPA Review: A System for Success* for additional discussion of how to maximize your score on multiple-choice and essay questions.

MULTIPLE-CHOICE QUESTIONS

1. **Budget your time.** We make this point with emphasis. Just as you would fill up your gas tank prior to reaching empty, so too would you finish your exam before time expires.

   a. Here is our suggested time allocation for BEC:

	Minutes	Start Time	
Testlet 1 (MC)	35	3 hours	00 minutes
Testlet 2 (MC)	35	2 hours	25 minutes
Testlet 3 (MC)	35	1 hour	50 minutes
Testlet 4 (WC)	60	1 hour	15 minutes
***Extra time	15	0 hour	15 minutes

   b. Before beginning your first testlet of multiple-choice questions, prepare a Gleim Time Management Sheet as recommended in Study Unit 7 of *CPA Review: A System for Success*.

   c. As you work through the individual items, monitor your time. In BEC, we suggest 35 minutes for each testlet of 24 questions. If you answer five items in 7 minutes, you are fine, but if you spend 10 minutes on five items, you need to speed up.

   ***Remember to allocate your budgeted "extra time," as needed, to each testlet. Your goal is to answer all of the items and achieve the maximum score possible.

2. **Answer the questions in consecutive order.**

   a. Do **not** agonize over any one item. Stay within your time budget.

   b. Flag for review any questions you are unsure of and return to them later as time allows.

      1) Once you have selected either the Continue or Quit option, you will no longer be able to review/change any answers in the completed testlet.

   c. Never leave a multiple-choice question unanswered. **Make your best educated guess in the time allowed.** Remember that your score is based on the number of correct responses. You will not be penalized for guessing incorrectly.

3. **For each multiple-choice question,**

   a. **Try to ignore the answer choices.** Do not allow the answer choices to affect your reading of the question.

      1) If four answer choices are presented, three of them are incorrect. These choices are called **distractors** for good reason. Often, distractors are written to appear correct at first glance until further analysis.

      2) In computational items, the distractors are carefully calculated such that they are the result of making common mistakes. Be careful, and double-check your computations if time permits.

   b. **Read the question** carefully to determine the precise requirement.

      1) Focusing on what is required enables you to ignore extraneous information, to focus on the relevant facts, and to proceed directly to determining the correct answer.

         a) Be especially careful to note when the requirement is an **exception**; e.g., "Which of the following is **not** valid acceptance of an offer?"

   c. **Determine the correct answer** before looking at the answer choices.

   d. **Read the answer choices carefully.**

      1) Even if the first answer appears to be the correct choice, do **not** skip the remaining answer choices. Questions often ask for the "best" of the choices provided. Thus, each choice requires your consideration.

      2) Treat each answer choice as a true/false question as you analyze it.

   e. **Click on the best answer.**

      1) You have a 25% chance of answering the question correctly by guessing blindly; improve your odds with educated guessing.

      2) For many multiple-choice questions, two answer choices can be eliminated with minimal effort, thereby increasing your educated guess to a 50-50 proposition.

4. After you have answered all the items in a testlet, consult the question status list at the bottom of each multiple-choice question screen **before** clicking the "Exit" button, which permanently ends the testlet.

   a. Go back to the flagged questions and finalize your answer choices.

   b. Verify that all questions have been answered.

5. **If you don't know the answer,**

   a. Again, guess; but make it an educated guess, which means select the best possible answer. First, rule out answers that you think are incorrect. Second, speculate on what the AICPA is looking for and/or the rationale behind the question. Third, select the best answer or guess between equally appealing answers. Your first guess is usually the most intuitive. If you cannot make an educated guess, read the stem and each answer and pick the best or most intuitive answer. It's just a guess!

   b. Make sure you accomplish this step within your predetermined time budget per testlet.

WRITTEN COMMUNICATION QUESTIONS

In BEC, testlet 4 is a written communication task consisting of three questions that require a response in the form of a memo or business letter (two graded, one pretest). The following information and toolbar icons are located at the top of the testlet screen.

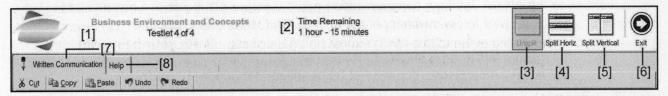

1. **Exam Section and Testlet Number:** For BEC, this part of the toolbar will always show Business Environment and Concepts as the Exam Section and Testlet 4 of 4 as the Testlet Number.
2. **Time Remaining:** This information box displays to the examinee how long (s)he has remaining in the entire exam. Consistently check the amount of time remaining to stay on schedule.
3. **Unsplit:** This icon, when selected, will unsplit the screen between two tabs.
4. **Split Horiz:** This icon, when selected, will split the screen horizontally between two tabs, enabling you to see both the essay question and the help tab, for example, at the same time.
5. **Split Vert:** This icon, when selected, will split the screen vertically between two tabs, enabling you to see both the essay question and the help tab, for example, at the same time.
6. **Exit:** There are three options when you choose this icon.
    *   You may choose Review Testlet to return to the beginning of the testlet to review your answers. You will be able to change your answers.
    *   You may choose Continue Exam to close the current testlet and go on to the next testlet. Once you have chosen Continue, you may not return to that testlet. After choosing Continue, you may choose Break in order to leave the room for a break. The clock will not stop if you choose to take a break. For BEC, the choice to Continue will only be relevant after each multiple-choice testlet, since the written communication is the last testlet.
    *   Finally, you may choose Quit Exam, which means either that you have completed the exam or that you chose not to complete it. Your exam will end and you will not be able to return to any testlet. You will not receive credit for any questions that you have not answered, and you will be required to leave the test center with no re-admittance. If you chose to quit your exam before you have completed it, there are security measures in place to determine that you are intentionally not completing the exam.
7. **Written Communication:** This work tab will contain three written communication questions, each of which will require you to prepare a written memo or business letter as your answer. You will be able to cut, copy, paste, undo, and redo by clicking on the appropriate item.
8. **Help:** This icon, when selected, provides a quick review of certain functions and tool buttons specific to the type of task you are working on. It will also provide directions and general information but will not include information related specifically to the test content.

WRITTEN COMMUNICATION ANSWERING AND GRADING

Remember, on the CPA exam, you will answer three written communication questions, two of which will be graded. Your score on those two responses will make up 15% of your total grade. The other 85% of your grade will be your total score on the multiple-choice testlets.

According to the AICPA, "Written communication responses are scored on the basis of three criteria: (1) organization (structure, ordering of ideas, linking of ideas one to another); (2) development (presentation of supporting evidence); and (3) expression (use of standard business English)." In addition, they advise that all responses "should provide the correct information in writing that is clear, complete, and professional. Only those writing samples that are generally responsive to the topic will be graded. If your response is off-topic, or offers advice that is clearly illegal, you will not receive any credit for the response."

Gleim has expanded the definitions of the AICPA's three criteria below. Note that the italics denote items taken from the AICPA; everything else is further clarification from Gleim.

Organization -- the document's structure, ordering of ideas, and linking of one idea to another

- *Overview/thesis statement:* Inform the reader of the overall purpose of the document; i.e., name the subject about which you are attempting to provide information.
- *Unified paragraphs (topic and supporting sentences):* Make a statement, then use the remainder of the paragraph to back up that statement.
- *Transitions and connectives:* Words such as "because," "although," "however," and "moreover" allow you to connect related topics or shift the reader's attention to a new idea.

Development -- the document's supporting evidence/information to clarify thoughts

- *Details:* Simply asserting a fact, such as that debt on the balance sheet increases risk, is insufficient. The writer must describe the cause-and-effect relationship underlying this fact.
- *Definitions:* Accounting and finance terms, such as solvency and liquidity, may not be understood by the reader. The writer should explain them.
- *Examples:* The description of unfamiliar terms can be enhanced by the use of examples, such as the use of an expert system in the practice of distance medicine.
- *Rephrasing:* Stating an idea twice with different wording can also help the reader understand.

Expression -- the document's use of conventional standards of business English

- *Grammar (sentence construction, subject/verb agreement, pronouns, modifiers):* Adherence to the basic rules of English grammar is essential.
- *Punctuation (final, comma):* A period must be used to bring a complete sentence to a close. Commas should be used to separate items in lists as well as to separate clauses within a single sentence.
- *Word usage (incorrect, imprecise language):* Business readers expect writers to avoid ambiguity and to choose the right word for the situation; for example, not to use the word "bond" where "note" is meant.
- *Capitalization:* The first word of a sentence and all proper names must be capitalized. Concepts and measures, such as liquidity and earnings per share, are not normally capitalized.
- *Spelling:* Business readers have an expectation that writers have a grasp of standard spelling conventions.

To help you gauge your proficiency in constructing a response that excels in all of the AICPA's criteria, Gleim books, CPA Gleim Online, and CPA Simulation Wizard allow you to assign a self-grade to your written communication responses. Self-grading your responses for practice written communication tasks will make you an expert on what the AICPA is looking for, and you will be able to quickly assess your response on the actual exam because you have practiced doing so during your studies.

The self-grading section that appears at the end of each study unit in your book mimics the interactive tools available in CPA Gleim Online and CPA Simulation Wizard. You will grade yourself on a scale of 1 to 5 on each of the AICPA's criteria (organization, development, and expression). An average response is 3. Use 4 for better than average and 5 for outstanding. Use 2 for less than average and 1 for quite poor. Zero is assigned to no response and responses that are off-topic or that give illegal advice.

On the following pages, you will find a written communication question and examples of answers at levels 5 and 1. These examples are intended to provide you with tips about how to structure sentences and state your ideas when answering written communications on the BEC portion. All other suggested responses provided by Gleim throughout your book and online courses are level 5 responses.

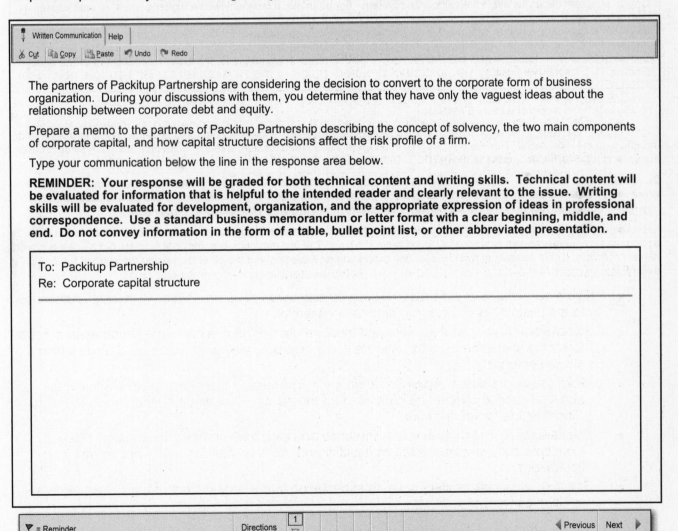

To: Packitup Partnership
Re: Corporate capital structure

Solvency is a firm's ability to pay its noncurrent obligations as they come due and thus remain in business in the long run (this is in contrast to liquidity, which is the ability to remain in business in the short run). The key ingredients of solvency are the firm's capital structure and degree of leverage. A firm's capital structure includes its sources of financing, both long- and short-term. These sources can be in the form of debt (external sources) or equity (internal sources).

Debt is the creditor interest in the firm. The firm is contractually obligated to repay debtholders. The terms of repayment (i.e., timing of interest and principal) are specified in the debt agreement. As long as the return on debt capital exceeds the amount of interest paid, the use of debt financing is advantageous to a firm. The return is often enhanced due to the fact that interest payments on debt are tax-deductible. The tradeoff is that an increased debt load makes a firm riskier (since debt must be paid regardless of whether or not the company is profitable). At some point, either a firm will have to pay a higher interest rate than its return on debt or creditors will simply refuse to lend any more money.

Equity is the ownership interest in the firm. Equity is the permanent capital of an entity, contributed by the firm's owners in the hopes of earning a return. However, a return on equity is uncertain because equity embodies only a residual interest in the firm's assets (residual because it is the claim left over after all debt has been satisfied). Periodic returns to owners of excess earnings are referred to as dividends. The firm may be contractually obligated to pay dividends to preferred stockholders but not to common stockholders.

Capital structure decisions affect the risk profile of a firm. For example, a company with a higher percent of debt capital will be riskier than a firm with a high percentage of equity capital. Thus, when the relative amount of debt is high, equity investors will demand a higher rate of return on their investments to compensate for the risk brought about by the high degree of financial leverage. Alternatively, a company with a relatively larger proportion of equity capital will be able to borrow at lower rates because debt holders will accept lower interest in exchange for the lower risk indicated by the equity cushion.

The above is an example of a Level 5 response.

Organization. The assignment requires that three concepts be explained: solvency, components of the capital structure, and the effect on the risk profile. This memo does that in a logically structured fashion, with the ideas ordered in a way that makes sense, and with each idea leading to the next.

Development. In this memo, debt and equity are presented as having their own risk and reward characteristics. However, this is not simply asserted as a fact to be taken for granted, but is demonstrated by the explanation of tax-deductibility, dividend payments, etc. Thus, the document's supporting evidence/information clarifies the thoughts presented.

Expression. The conventional standards of business English are observed throughout. Overall, use of the semi-colon is limited, and commas are used appropriately to separate clauses. The last sentence is somewhat lengthy, but it is not a run-on sentence; that is, it only consists of two clauses, one containing an assertion and the other containing the support for that assertion.

To: Packitup Partnership
Re: Corporate capital structure

Debt and equity are the two ways that a corporation can raise capital, and they have to stay solvent that way. They are solvent because debt is part of the capital structure and equity is the other part. Debt is from those outside the firm and equity is from those inside.

However, debt which is bonds have to pay interest but the company can deduct interest on bonds. But this is riskier to the firm because they have to pay the interest no matter what.

Equity though is stock which is the ownership of the firm. But the company has to pay a higher return on stockholders than they do on bondholders because these are dividends that they pay to the stockholders but they are not required to pay dividends which they are required to do on bonds and interest. There is also preferred stock.

So you can have:

- Debt
- Common stock
- Preferred stock

BTW If there is more debt there is more risk and there is more leverage.

The above is an example of a Level 1 response. It fulfills the two base requirements (it addresses the topic and does not offer advice that is clearly illegal), but beyond this it does not succeed at its goal of clearly communicating information.

Organization. Relevant ideas are scattered throughout the document with no attempt at creating a flow. For instance, after the three forms of capital are recapped in the bullet list, a new idea is introduced. The run-on sentence in the third paragraph destroys any sense of organization the material might have had.

Development. The second paragraph is an example of how pertinent concepts can be mentioned but not developed. Notice that the writer properly presents two concepts central to the discussion: debt and the associated risk that results from the need to never miss an interest payment. The effectiveness is then immediately diminished by the careless use of connective words: "however" appears once and "but" appears twice in the space of two sentences. Used this way, these words do nothing more than jam the ideas together without actually telling the reader how they relate. Connectors such as "but" and "however" can be useful in establishing a flow or a hierarchy of ideas, but this writer has not done that. Another example of lack of connection is the introduction of the idea of preferred stock at the end of the third paragraph with no attempt to relate it to what has come before.

Expression. The use of standard business English is important to maintaining the proper tone. For example, commas should be used to set off subordinate ideas from the rest of a sentence. In the third paragraph, the sentence that begins, "Equity though is stock..." is a weak sentence made worse by the absence of commas surrounding "though." In the final sentence of the memo, a comma is needed to separate the basic idea, called the premise (if there is more debt), from the result of that idea, called the conclusion (the firm will carry more risk).

Also, the final sentence jams an additional clause on the end ("...and there is more leverage"), connected with nothing more than the word "and." As this demonstrates, a run-on sentence does not have to be long. The last sentence also contains the use of an acronym common to electronic communication (BTW), which is inappropriate for a business memo. Also, the instructions clearly state that bullet points and other list formats should not be used.

IF YOU HAVE QUESTIONS

Content-specific questions about our materials will be answered most rapidly if they are sent to us via email to accounting@gleim.com. Our team of accounting experts will give your correspondence thorough consideration and a prompt response.

Questions regarding the information in this Introduction (study suggestions, studying plans, exam specifics) should be emailed to personalcounselor@gleim.com.

Questions concerning orders, prices, shipments, or payments should be sent via email to customerservice@gleim.com and will be promptly handled by our competent and courteous customer service staff.

For technical support, you may use our automated technical support service at www.gleim.com/support, email us at support@gleim.com, or call us at (800) 874-5346.

HOW TO BE IN CONTROL

Remember, you must be in control to be successful during exam preparation and execution. Perhaps more importantly, control can also contribute greatly to your personal and other professional goals. Control is the process whereby you

1. Develop expectations, standards, budgets, and plans
2. Undertake activity, production, study, and learning
3. Measure the activity, production, output, and knowledge
4. Compare actual activity with expected and budgeted activity
5. Modify the activity, behavior, or study to better achieve the expected or desired outcome
6. Revise expectations and standards in light of actual experience
7. Continue the process or restart the process in the future

Exercising control will ultimately develop the confidence you need to outperform most other CPA candidates and PASS the CPA exam! Obtain our *CPA Review: A System for Success* booklet for a more detailed discussion of control and other exam tactics.

AICPA's NONDISCLOSURE AGREEMENT

The following is taken verbatim from the AICPA's Candidate Bulletin dated June 2012. It is reproduced here to remind all CPA candidates about the AICPA's strict policy of nondisclosure, which Gleim consistently supports and upholds.

Policy Statement and Agreement Regarding Exam Confidentiality and the Taking of Breaks

I hereby agree that I will maintain the confidentiality of the Uniform CPA Examination. In addition, I agree that I will not:

- *Divulge the nature or content of any Uniform CPA Examination question or answer under any circumstance*
- *Engage in any unauthorized communication during testing*
- *Refer to unauthorized materials or use unauthorized equipment during testing; or*
- *Remove or attempt to remove any Uniform CPA Examination materials, notes, or any other items from the examination room*

I understand and agree that liability for test administration activities, including but not limited to the adequacy or accuracy of test materials and equipment, and the accuracy of scoring and score reporting, will be limited to score correction or test retake at no additional fee. I waive any and all right to all other claims.

I further agree to report to the AICPA any examination question disclosures, or solicitations for disclosure of which I become aware.

I affirm that I have had the opportunity to read the Candidate Bulletin and I agree to all of its terms and conditions.

I understand that breaks are only allowed between testlets. I understand that I will be asked to complete any open testlet before leaving the testing room for a break.

In addition, I understand that failure to comply with this Policy Statement and Agreement may result in invalidation of my grades, disqualification from future examinations, expulsion from the testing facility and possible civil or criminal penalties.

STUDY UNIT ONE
CORPORATE GOVERNANCE

(30 pages of outline)

Accounting scandals and concerns about the functioning of financial markets have resulted in greater attention to the means of directing the actions of a corporation (corporate governance). Significant governance tools are internal auditing, other elements of internal control, and enterprise risk management.

1.1 ROLES IN THE GOVERNANCE HIERARCHY

1. **Definition of Corporate Governance**

   a. **Governance** is the combination of people, policies, procedures, and processes (including internal control) that help ensure that an entity effectively and efficiently directs its activities toward meeting the objectives of its stakeholders.

      1) **Stakeholders** are persons or entities who are affected by the activities of the entity. Among others, these include shareholders, employees, suppliers, customers, neighbors of the entity's facilities, and government regulators.

   b. Corporate governance can be either internal or external.

      1) Corporate charters and bylaws, boards of directors, and internal audit functions are internal.

      2) The requirements of the Securities Act of 1933 and the Securities Exchange Act of 1934 administered by the Securities and Exchange Commission (SEC) are external.

2. **Basic Corporate Documents**

   a. Corporations are formed under the laws of the state of incorporation (very few corporations are incorporated under federal law).

      1) Although state laws vary considerably, all are influenced by the Model Business Corporation Act (MBCA), a statement of modern corporate law issued by the American Bar Association. Its purpose is to provide legislators, lawyers, and legal commissions with a basis for drafting and amending state incorporation laws.

      2) The MBCA has been amended frequently, and some of its provisions have been adopted to some degree by every state. The **Revised Model Business Corporation Act of 1984 (RMBCA)** applies to publicly held and closely held corporations.

b. A corporation comes into being when the **articles of incorporation** are filed with the secretary of state of the relevant state. The secretary in turn issues a certificate of incorporation.

  1) The articles ordinarily must include the following:

     a) Corporation's name
     b) Number of authorized shares of stock
     c) Street address of the corporation's initial registered office
     d) Name of the registered agent at that office
     e) Name and address of each incorporator

  2) The articles also may contain optional provisions, such as

     a) Purpose and powers of the corporation,
     b) Internal management, and
     c) Any subject required or allowed to be addressed in the bylaws.

c. The **bylaws** of a corporation may contain any provision for managing the business and regulating the entity's affairs that does not conflict with the law or the articles of incorporation.

  1) The bylaws state such matters as the authority of officers and directors, how they are selected, the lengths of their terms, their compensation, and how the decision to issue new stock will be made.

3. **Shareholders**

a. The common shareholders are those who have contributed the basic capital for the corporation to carry on its business.

  1) Preferred shareholders have an intermediate position between common shareholders and debtholders. They have the contractual right to receive dividends and liquidation distributions ahead of common shareholders but are not always granted voting rights.

b. Generally, shareholders are permitted to act only at a meeting.

  1) They are required to hold an annual meeting. Special meetings may be held for important purposes, such as to approve a merger or other fundamental change.

  2) The most important acts performed by the shareholders at the annual meeting are

     a) Amending the articles of incorporation,
     b) Voting on any matters requiring a general vote, and
     c) Electing or removing directors.

c. Many states permit shareholders to change, by unanimous agreement, the provisions for corporate governance. This flexibility may allow a closely held corporation to function more nearly as a partnership without loss of corporate status.

  1) For example, a shareholder agreement may (a) eliminate the board or restrict its powers, (b) determine who will be officers and directors, or (c) set voting requirements for directors and shareholders.

4. **Board of Directors**

a. All major corporate decisions are made or approved by the board.

  1) The board of directors does not directly manage the day-to-day operations of the entity. That is management's responsibility, with the board playing an oversight role.

  b. Specifically, the board has the following duties:

      1) Selection and removal of officers

      2) Decisions about capital structure (mix of debt and equity, consideration to be received for shares, etc.)

      3) Adding, amending, or repealing bylaws (unless this authority is reserved to the shareholders)

      4) Initiation of fundamental changes (mergers, acquisitions, etc.)

      5) Decisions to declare and distribute dividends

      6) Setting of management compensation (sometimes performed by a subcommittee called the compensation committee)

      7) Coordinating audit activities (most often performed by a subcommittee called the audit committee)

      8) Evaluating and managing risk (sometimes performed by a subcommittee called the risk committee)

  c. Directors (and officers) owe a **fiduciary duty** to the corporation.

 Because of the legislation passed subsequent to the accounting scandals of the early 2000s, Dr. Gleim believes that the AICPA will be testing CPA candidates on the actions required of directors and officers to meet their fiduciary duties.

---

      1) A fiduciary has undertaken a legal duty to act primarily for the benefit of another person in matters related to the undertaking.

          a) A fiduciary is held to a higher standard of care than (s)he would observe in the management of his/her own affairs.

          b) Examples of fiduciaries include an attorney in relation to his/her client, the trustee of a trust, the personal representative of a decedent's estate, and the conservator (legal guardian) of someone legally determined not to be able to manage his/her own affairs.

      2) Fiduciary duty requires directors and officers to

          a) Act in its best interests,
          b) Be loyal,
          c) Use due diligence in carrying out their responsibilities, and
          d) Disclose conflicts of interest.

      3) Controlling or majority shareholders owe similar duties.

          a) However, a conflicting interest transaction (e.g., a personal loan by the corporation to a director or officer) is acceptable if it (1) is fair to the corporation and (2) is approved by informed directors who do not have a conflict of interest.

      4) The Sarbanes-Oxley Act of 2002 generally prohibits personal loans to executives or directors of public companies.

    d.   The **business judgment rule** protects an officer or a director from personal liability for honest mistakes of judgment if (s)he

        1)   Acted in good faith;
        2)   Was not motivated by fraud, conflict of interest, or illegality; and
        3)   Was not grossly negligent.

            a)   To avoid personal liability, directors and officers must (1) make informed decisions (educate themselves about the issues), (2) be free from conflicts of interest, and (3) have a rational basis to support their position.

            b)   Furthermore, a director is entitled to rely on information provided by an officer (or professional specialist) if the director reasonably believes the officer (or specialist) has competence in the relevant area.

    e.   When presented with a **corporate opportunity**, a director's duty of loyalty compels him/her to give the corporation the right of first refusal.

        1)   A corporate opportunity is one in which the corporation has a right, property interest, or expectancy.

        2)   A corporate opportunity arises when

            a)   A director becomes aware of the opportunity in his/her corporate capacity,
            b)   The opportunity is within the scope of corporate activity, or
            c)   Corporate capital, equipment, personnel, or facilities were used to develop the opportunity.

        3)   Generally, a corporate opportunity does not exist if

            a)   Action by the corporation would be beyond its powers,
            b)   The corporation cannot obtain necessary financing or capital to take advantage of the opportunity, or
            c)   The opportunity is rejected by a majority vote of disinterested directors.

5.   **Officers**

    a.   The corporation's officers (i.e., executive management) are responsible for carrying out the entity's day-to-day operations.

    b.   The **chief executive officer (CEO)** is directly selected by, and reports to, the board of directors.

    c.   The CEO in turn usually selects other executives as the chief financial officer (CFO) and chief information officer (CIO). These executives oversee the various functional areas of the entity.

6.   **Other Aspects of Corporate Governance**

    a.   Trusteeship

        1)   The board and senior management act as custodians of corporate assets in the pursuit of positive outcomes for stakeholders.

    b.   Empowerment and Control

        1)   Decision-making should occur at appropriate levels of the organization, and freedom of management should be exercised within a framework of checks and balances.

    c.   Good Corporate Citizenship

        1)   Integrity and ethical values should be reflected by the tone at the top.

    d.   Transparency of Public Disclosures

        1)   Pursuit of transparency may involve accepting a higher cost of capital.

7. Graphical Depiction

Corporate Governance Structure

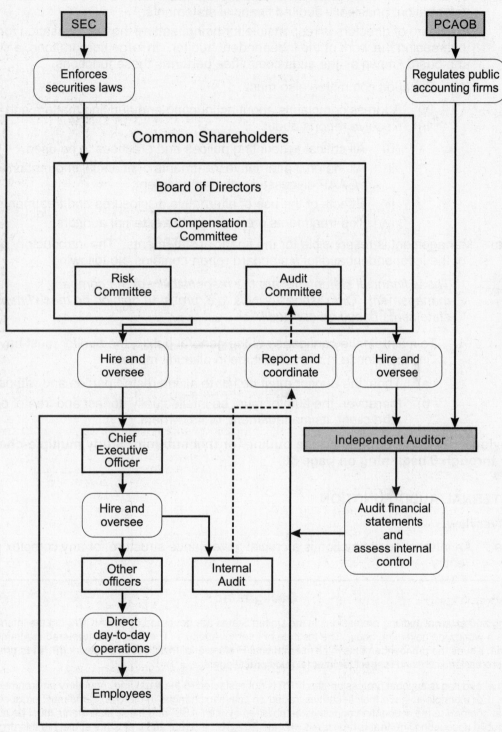

Figure 1-1

8. **Financial Reporting**

   a. A publicly held corporation's annual report to its shareholders must contain certain information, principally audited financial statements.

   b. The board of directors is responsible for hiring, setting the compensation for, and overseeing the work of the independent auditor. In large corporations, a subset of the board known as the audit committee performs these functions.

      1) The audit committee also must

         a) Address complaints about accounting and auditing matters and
         b) Receive reports about

            i) All critical accounting polices and practices to be used,
            ii) All material alternative treatments of financial information within GAAP discussed with management,
            iii) Effects of the use of alternative disclosures and treatments, and
            iv) The treatments preferred by the external auditors.

   c. Management is responsible for the financial statements. The introductory paragraph of the independent auditor's standard report contains the following:

      These financial statements are the responsibility of the company's management. Our responsibility is to express an opinion on these financial statements based on our audit.

      1) To maintain the confidence of the general public, the auditor must have independence in mental attitude in all audit matters.

         a) Thus, the auditor must be fair to all interested parties and without bias.
         b) Moreover, the auditor must be intellectually honest and free of obligation to the client, its management, or its owners.

Stop and review! You have completed the outline for this subunit. Study multiple-choice questions 1 through 6 beginning on page 50.

1.2 THE INTERNAL AUDIT FUNCTION

1. **Overview**

   a. An internal audit function is a crucial governance structure for any complex modern entity.

Background

The accounting and external auditing professions in the United States are governed by the AICPA, but the internal auditing profession has a worldwide governing body. The Institute of Internal Auditors (The IIA), headquartered in Altamonte Springs, Florida, issues the pronouncements in its International Professional Practices Framework (IPPF) to promote competence, professionalism, and respect for internal audit practitioners.

Because internal auditing is a global profession, the IPPF is not restricted to the legal and regulatory environment of any single country. For example, to have their securities traded on active exchanges in the U.S., firms must produce financial statements that conform to the accounting principles established by the FASB, and these statements must be audited by an independent public accounting firm that is registered with the PCAOB. Internal auditing is not subject to this degree of regulation in any country.

---

   b. **Chief Audit Executive (CAE)**

      1) The chief audit executive (CAE) is in a senior position responsible for effectively managing the internal audit activity in accordance with the internal audit charter and the requirements of The IIA.

      2) The specific job title of the chief audit executive varies from entity to entity.

c. **Definition of Internal Auditing**

1) The IIA's Definition of Internal Auditing is the foundation of its International Professional Practices Framework (IPPF):

   Internal auditing is an independent, objective assurance and consulting activity designed to add value and improve an organization's operations. It helps an organization accomplish its objectives by bringing a systematic, disciplined approach to evaluate and improve the effectiveness of risk management, control, and governance processes.

2) The IIA's *International Standards for the Professional Practice of Internal Auditing (Standards)* expand upon this definition.

d. **Independence**

1) Independence is "the freedom from conditions that threaten the ability of the internal audit activity to carry out internal audit responsibilities in an unbiased manner."

   a) Independence is an organizational attribute. An internal audit function is independent if it reports to a level of the organization that can ensure that it receives the resources it needs to carry out the appropriate activities and that the concerns raised in its reports are properly addressed.

2) To achieve the degree of independence necessary to effectively carry out the responsibilities of the internal audit activity, the CAE has direct and unrestricted access to senior management and the board.

   a) The best way to achieve independence is through a dual-reporting relationship in which the internal audit function reports functionally to the board and administratively to the CEO.

e. **Objectivity**

1) Objectivity is a personal attribute. Individual internal auditors must have an unbiased mental attitude. They must (a) believe in their work product, (b) not make quality compromises, and (c) not subordinate their judgment on audit matters to others.

   a) For example, objectivity is presumed to be impaired if an internal auditor provides assurance services for an activity for which (s)he had responsibility within the previous year.

2) The internal auditor's objectivity is not adversely affected when (s)he recommends standards of control for systems or reviews procedures before they are implemented. However, designing, installing, or drafting procedures for operating systems is presumed to impair objectivity.

f. **Assurance Services**

1) Assurance services are an objective examination of evidence for the purpose of providing an independent assessment of governance, risk management, and control processes for the organization. Examples may include financial, performance, compliance, system security, and due diligence engagements.

2) Assurance services are usually requested by the entity's senior management.

g. **Consulting Services**

1) Consulting services are advisory and related client service activities, the nature and scope of which are agreed upon with the client. They are intended to add value and improve an organization's governance, risk management, and control processes without the internal auditor's assumption of management responsibility. Examples include counsel, advice, facilitation, and training.

h. **Risk Management**

1) The internal audit function determines the effectiveness of the entity's risk management processes by assessing whether

a) Organizational objectives support and align with the organization's mission;

b) Significant risks are identified and assessed;

c) Appropriate risk responses are selected that align risks with the organization's risk appetite; and

d) Relevant risk information is captured and communicated in a timely manner across the organization, enabling staff, management, and the board to carry out their responsibilities.

i. **Control**

1) The IIA defines control as follows:

Any action taken by management, the board, and other parties to manage risk and increase the likelihood that established objectives and goals will be achieved. Management plans, organizes, and directs the performance of sufficient actions to provide reasonable assurance that objectives and goals will be achieved.

a) Control is the responsibility of management.

2) Internal audit must evaluate controls in these specific areas:

a) Reliability and integrity of financial and operational information
b) Effectiveness and efficiency of operations and programs
c) Safeguarding of assets
d) Compliance with laws, regulations, policies, procedures, and contracts

3) Except for safeguarding of assets, the control areas listed above are similar to those in the COSO model for internal control that will be described in Subunit 1.4.

j. **Governance**

1) Internal audit must assess and make appropriate recommendations for improving governance to achieve the following objectives:

a) Promoting appropriate ethics and values within the organization

b) Ensuring effective organizational performance management and accountability

c) Communicating risk and control information to appropriate areas of the organization

d) Coordinating the activities of and communicating information among the board, external and internal auditors, and management

2. **The IIA's** *Standards*

a. The Definition of Internal Auditing, The IIA Code of Ethics, and the *Standards* provide **mandatory guidance**.

1) The IIA considers conformance with the principles set forth in the mandatory guidance to be required for anyone engaged in the professional practice of internal auditing.

b. The *Standards* are of three types.

1) Attribute Standards concern the attributes of organizations and individuals providing internal auditing services.

2) Performance Standards describe the nature of internal auditing and quality criteria for evaluation of internal audit performance.

    a) Attribute and Performance Standards apply regardless of the service performed. Thus, they guide for assurance, consulting, and other internal auditing services.

3) Implementation Standards are attribute or performance standards that apply specifically to assurance or consulting services and expand upon the other standards. Each group of Implementation Standards applies only to a major category of engagements.

3. **The IIA's Attribute Standards**

a. In addition to independence and objectivity, the attribute standards require internal audit actions in the following areas:

1) Internal Audit Charter

    a) The purpose, authority, and responsibility of an entity's internal audit activity must be formally defined in an internal audit charter. The charter establishes the internal audit activity's position within the organization.

    b) The chief audit executive must periodically review the internal audit charter and present it to senior management and the board for approval.

2) Impairment of Independence or Objectivity

    a) Impairment of organizational independence and individual objectivity may include, but is not limited to, personal conflict of interest; scope limitations; restrictions on access to records, personnel, and properties; and resource limitations, such as funding.

    b) If independence or objectivity is impaired in fact or appearance, the details of the impairment must be disclosed to appropriate parties. The nature of the disclosure will depend upon the impairment.

3) Proficiency

    a) Internal auditors must possess the knowledge, skills, and other competencies needed to perform their individual responsibilities.

    b) The internal audit activity collectively must possess or obtain the knowledge, skills, and other competencies needed to perform its responsibilities.

        i) Knowledge, skills, and other competencies can be obtained through external service providers in some circumstances.

    c) Internal auditors must have sufficient knowledge to evaluate the risk of fraud and the manner in which it is managed by the organization.

        i) However, internal auditors are not expected to have the expertise of fraud specialists.

4) Due Professional Care

    a) Internal auditors must apply the care and skill expected of a reasonably prudent and competent internal auditor. Due professional care does not imply infallibility.

5) Continuing Professional Development

    a) Internal auditors must enhance their knowledge, skills, and other competencies through continuing professional development.

      6) Quality Assurance and Improvement Program

        a) The chief audit executive must develop and maintain a quality assurance and improvement program that covers all aspects of the internal audit activity.

        b) The quality assurance and improvement program must include both internal and external assessments.

Stop and review! You have completed the outline for this subunit. Study multiple-choice questions 7 through 12 beginning on page 52.

1.3 THE SARBANES-OXLEY ACT OF 2002 (SOX)

Background

In late 2001 and 2002, massive accounting scandals were reported in the media. They involved such large firms as Enron (hid debt of over $1 billion in improper off-the-books partnerships), Global Crossing (inflated revenues; shredded accounting-related documents), and WorldCom (booked operating expenses as capital assets; made large off-the-books payments to founder). In response to these and many other fraudulent practices, Congress passed the Sarbanes-Oxley Act of 2002, named for its sponsors, Democratic Senator Paul Sarbanes of Maryland and Republican Representative Mike Oxley of Ohio.

---

1. **Applicability to Publicly Held Companies (Issuers) and Their Auditors**

    a. Each member of the issuer's audit committee must be an independent member of the board of directors.

      1) To be independent, a director must not be affiliated with, or receive any compensation (other than for service on the board) from, the issuer.

        a) At least one member of the audit committee must be a financial expert.

      2) The audit committee must be directly responsible for appointing, compensating, and overseeing the work of the independent auditor.

        a) The independent auditor must report directly to the audit committee, not to management.

    b. SOX established the **Public Company Accounting Oversight Board (PCAOB)** as a private-sector body to regulate the accounting profession.

      1) The PCAOB (a) issues auditing and related standards; (b) inspects and investigates accounting firms; and (c) enforces compliance with its rules, professional standards, the act, and relevant securities laws.

      2) Public accounting firms that act as independent auditors must register with the PCAOB.

    c. A public accounting firm is prohibited from performing consulting, legal, and internal auditing services (with some exceptions) for the audit client.

      1) Audit firms may, however, provide conventional tax planning and certain other nonaudit services if preapproved by the audit committee.

2. **Section 302 Reporting Requirements**

    a. In every annual or quarterly filing with the SEC, the CEO and CFO must certify

      1) That, to the best of their knowledge, the financial statements are free of material misstatements

      2) That they have taken responsibility for the system of internal control and have evaluated its effectiveness

      3) That they have informed the audit committee and the independent auditors of all significant control deficiencies and any fraud, whether or not material

      4) Whether or not there were significant changes in internal controls, including corrective actions

b. Intentional violations of this section of SOX can result in the forfeiture of

1) Any bonus or other incentive-based compensation received during the previous 12 months and

2) Any profits received from the sale of stock during the previous 12 months.

3. **Section 404 Reporting Requirements**

a. Under current regulations, the annual report must contain a statement by the CEO and CFO that includes the following:

1) A statement that management has taken responsibility for establishing and maintaining an adequate system of internal control over financial reporting

2) The name of the internal control model, if any, used to design and assess the effectiveness of the internal control system (COSO's *Internal Control – Integrated Framework* is the most widely used model in the United States)

3) An assessment as to whether the system is functioning effectively

4) A statement that an independent public accounting firm that is registered with the PCAOB also has assessed the system

4. **Section 407 Financial Expert Requirements**

a. An issuer must disclose whether its audit committee has at least one financial expert.

1) If the audit committee lacks a financial expert, the issuer must disclose the reason(s) why not.

b. To be considered a financial expert, the director must have

1) An understanding of generally accepted accounting principles and financial statements;

2) Experience in –

a) The preparation or auditing of financial statements of generally comparable issuers and

b) The application of such principles in connection with the accounting for estimates, accruals, and reserves;

3) Experience with internal accounting controls; and

4) An understanding of audit committee functions.

5. **Section 802 Criminal Penalties**

a. This section of SOX contains the following wording:

Whoever knowingly alters, destroys, mutilates, conceals, covers up, falsifies, or makes a false entry in any record, document, or tangible object with the intent to impede, obstruct, or influence the investigation or proper administration of any matter within the jurisdiction of any department or agency of the United States or any case filed under title 11, or in relation to or contemplation of any such matter or case, shall be fined under this title, imprisoned not more than 20 years, or both.

Background

The statutory provision above was a direct response to the shredding of documentation by Enron Corporation, an action specifically intended to impede investigation of the company's massive fraud. Enron's independent auditor, Arthur Andersen, also was indicted for shredding literally tons of documents and deleting thousands of emails. Enron eventually declared bankruptcy, and Andersen surrendered its licenses to practice before the SEC.

6. **Section 906 Corporate Responsibility for Financial Reports**

    a. This section of the Act incorporates the requirement that CEOs and CFOs certify financial filings into the U.S. Code.

    b. Separate criminal penalties are provided for unknowingly certifying noncomplying filings and for knowingly certifying such filings.

        1) Unknowingly certifying filings that do not meet the requirements of the Act can result in fines of up to $1,000,000 and/or up to 10 years imprisonment.

        2) Knowingly certifying filings that do not meet the requirements of the Act can result in fines of up to $5,000,000 and/or up to 20 years imprisonment.

7. **Section 1103 Temporary Freeze Authority for the Securities and Exchange Commission**

    a. This section empowers the SEC to petition a federal district court for a temporary order requiring the issuer to place in escrow for 45 days any monies that appear likely to be used to make extraordinary payments to executives.

8. **Section 1107 Retaliation against Informants**

    a. This section of SOX contains the following wording:

        Whoever knowingly, with the intent to retaliate, takes any action harmful to any person, including interference with the lawful employment or livelihood of any person, for providing to a law enforcement officer any truthful information relating to the commission or possible commission of any Federal offense, shall be fined under this title or imprisoned not more than 10 years, or both.

9. **Whistleblowers**

    a. Under SOX and the Dodd-Frank Wall Street Reform Act, the SEC may compensate whistleblowers who provide information other than that from an audit or investigation.

        1) Whistleblowers may sue retaliating employers.
        2) Whistleblower claims may be asserted for up to 180 days.
        3) Trial by jury is allowed.
        4) Whistleblower rights and remedies may not be waived.

10. **Sarbanes-Oxley – Praise and Criticism**

    a. SOX has forced executive management to seriously consider the design and operation of internal controls to a degree it had not prior to the scandals of the early 2000s.

        1) Reexamination of business processes has led to new efficiencies in operations and better design of internal controls in many firms.

    b. At the same time, SOX has been the subject of a great deal of negative reaction.

        1) The original requirement of Section 404 was not simply for the independent auditor to issue a report on internal controls (the fundamental work of which has long been an inherent part of the financial statement audit), but to report on management's system for assessing its own internal control system's effectiveness.

            a) Many in the accounting profession insisted that this "once-removed" type of assurance added no value for the user and was indicative of the fact that legislators are not qualified to issue auditing pronouncements.

            b) In response to this criticism, the SEC revised its rules, changing the requirement for the independent auditor to a straightforward report on the effectiveness of internal control.

2) Any CEO and CFO who are engaged in a serious fraud of the scope of Enron or WorldCom are, by definition, committing multiple crimes simultaneously. They are unlikely to be deterred by the remote possibility of criminal penalties from signing off on statements they know to be not fairly presented.

3) Some have claimed that the benefits of SOX have not been worth the enormous costs in diverted employee hours and documentation, particularly for medium and smaller businesses, which lack sufficient resources to devote to SOX work.

    a) These high compliance costs have also had the effect of discouraging firms from going public.

4) The PCAOB's investigation process has been strongly criticized for excessive secrecy. The names of all accounting firms under investigation are kept secret throughout the entire process, including appeals.

    a) It has been asserted that this gives firms an incentive to simply drag the investigation process out instead of fully cooperating, and that it makes it too easy for accounting firms to avoid the kinds of embarrassing disclosures that are needed to improve the audit process.

Because of numerous accounting scandals, CPA candidates can expect to be tested on the responsibilities imposed by SOX on both the company's audit committee and its management.

Stop and review! You have completed the outline for this subunit. Study multiple-choice questions 13 through 19 beginning on page 54.

1.4 THE COSO MODEL FOR INTERNAL CONTROL

1. **COSO Framework**

    a. *Internal Control – Integrated Framework* has become widely accepted as the standard for the design and operation of internal control systems since its initial publication in 1992.

        1) The COSO document is not the only recognized and credible framework for internal control. Sometimes, regulatory or legal requirements specify the use of a particular control model or design.

            a) COSO has announced its intention to publish a major revision of the framework in the first quarter of 2013.

Background

The Watergate investigations of 1973-74 revealed that U.S. companies were bribing government officials, politicians, and political parties in foreign countries. The result was the Foreign Corrupt Practices Act of 1977. The private sector also responded by forming the National Commission on Fraudulent Financial Reporting (NCFFR) in 1985. The NCFFR is referred to as the Treadway Commission after James C. Treadway, its first chairman.

The Treadway Commission was originally sponsored and funded by five professional accounting organizations based in the United States. This group of five became known as the Committee of Sponsoring Organizations of the Treadway Commission (COSO). The Commission recommended that this group of five organizations cooperate in creating guidance for internal control. The result was *Internal Control – Integrated Framework*, published in 1992 and slightly modified in 1994.

To read the executive summary, see www.coso.org/IC-IntegratedFramework-summary.htm.

2.   **Definition of Internal Control**

a.   The COSO model defines internal control and states three categories of organizational objectives.

Internal control is broadly defined as a process, effected by an entity's board of directors, management and other personnel, designed to provide reasonable assurance regarding the achievement of objectives in the following categories:

- *Effectiveness and efficiency of operations*
- *Reliability of financial reporting*
- *Compliance with applicable laws and regulations*

Memory aid: Everything Really Counts

b.   The board, officers, and employees help to implement internal control.

3.   **Objectives**

a.   **Effectiveness and Efficiency** of Operations

1)   Operations objectives relate to the entity's mission.

2)   Effectiveness and efficiency have traditionally been referred to as "doing the right things" and "doing things right," respectively.

a)   Effectiveness and efficiency in meeting inappropriate goals are not beneficial. Internal controls must be designed so that they focus on the entity's objectives.

b.   **Reliability** of Financial Reporting

1)   To make sound decisions, investors and creditors must have reliable financial information.

2)   In the context of this category of objectives, the Framework makes specific reference to management's assertions described by the AICPA regarding the fair presentation of financial statements (occurrence, completeness, accuracy, cutoff, etc.).

c.   **Compliance** with Applicable Laws and Regulations

1)   Entities are subject to laws at the local, state, and federal levels dealing with such matters as land use, waste disposal, wages and hours, and employee safety. In addition, numerous regulations govern individual industries, such as banking and trucking.

4.   **Reasonable, Not Absolute, Assurance**

a.   No system of internal control can provide absolute assurance of the achievement of objectives for the following reasons:

1)   The costs of internal controls must never exceed their benefits. Absolute assurance can be achieved only at prohibitively great expense.

2)   Any system of internal control has inherent limitations, including faulty human judgment, collusion, and management override.

5. **Aspects of the Framework**

   a. Overlap of Objectives

      1) An objective in one category may overlap or support an objective in another.

      2) An example is a policy to close the monthly books by the fifth working day of the following month. This is an objective for both operations and financial reporting.

   b. Linkage

      1) The entity's overall objectives must link its particular capabilities and prospects with the objectives of its business units.

      2) As conditions change, the objectives (and related internal controls) of subunits must be altered to adapt to changes in the objectives of the entity as a whole.

   c. Achievement of Objectives

      1) An internal control system is more likely to provide reasonable assurance of achieving financial reporting and compliance objectives than operational objectives.

         a) Financial reporting and compliance objectives are responses to standards established by external parties, such as regulators. Thus, achieving these objectives depends on actions almost entirely within the entity's control.

            i) However, operational effectiveness may not be within the entity's control because it is affected by faulty judgments and many external factors.

6. **Components of Internal Control**

   a. The COSO model provides the following definitions of the five interrelated components of a system of internal control:

      1) <u>C</u>ontrol environment

         a) The control environment sets the tone of an organization ... [and] is the foundation for all other components of internal control, providing discipline and structure.

      2) <u>R</u>isk assessment

         a) Risk assessment is the identification and analysis of relevant risks to achievement of the objectives, forming a basis for determining how the risks should be managed.

      3) <u>C</u>ontrol activities

         a) Control activities are the policies and procedures that help ensure management directives are carried out.

      4) <u>I</u>nformation and communication

         a) Pertinent information must be identified, captured, and communicated in a form and timeframe that enable people to carry out their responsibilities.

      5) <u>M</u>onitoring

         a) Internal control systems need to be monitored – a process that assesses the quality of the system's performance over time.

   Memory aid: <u>C</u>arrie <u>R</u>an <u>C</u>attle <u>I</u>n <u>M</u>ontana

7. **Graphical Depiction**

    a.   The COSO model may be viewed as a cube with rows, slices, and columns. The rows are the five components, the slices are the three objectives, and the columns are the activities or units of the entity. The columns also may be viewed as a single dimension depicting the entity as a whole.

        1)   All three objectives should be examined for applicability to every identified activity and operating unit of the entity, and each combination of activity/unit and objective must address each of the five components.

COSO Internal Control Framework

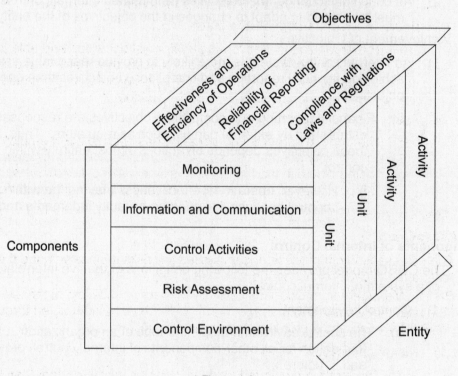

Figure 1-2

8. **The Control Environment**

    a.   The control environment component has the following elements:

        1)   <u>H</u>uman resource policies and practices

            a)   The organization must be committed to hiring individuals who are not just competent but also display evidence of integrity and ethical behavior. Ongoing training is necessary to adapt employees to the shifting control requirements of a changing environment.

        2)   <u>I</u>ntegrity and ethical values

            a)   Through words and actions, management communicates its attitude toward integrity and ethical values. Accordingly, management sets the **tone at the top**. Stated policies are a starting point, but it is the corporate culture that determines what actually happens in practice.

        3)   Organizational <u>s</u>tructure

            a)   The structure of an organization is determined by its size and mission. The entity must be structured to best achieve its objectives, but structure is also, to some extent, a function of size. A large organization probably requires more formal reporting lines than a small one.

    4) Commitment to <u>c</u>ompetence

        a) Internal control is strengthened when management (1) specifies what competencies are required for particular jobs and (2) ensures that employees serving in those jobs have the appropriate knowledge and skills.

    5) Management's <u>p</u>hilosophy and operating style

        a) Regardless of the governing body's involvement, it is management's philosophy and operating style that set the day-to-day tone of the organization, including the entity's attitude toward risk and the degree (formal or informal) of control over routine operations.

    6) Board of directors or <u>a</u>udit committee

        a) The organization's governing body must be willing and able to question management's actions. For this reason, the board should contain at least one, and usually more than one, outside director. The audit committee must be composed of all outside directors.

    7) Assignment of authority and <u>responsibility</u>

        a) The trend in corporate governance has been to allow employees closer to day-to-day operations to make decisions. This greater degree of delegation can lead to faster decision making, but those with increased responsibility also must know that they will be held accountable.

    Memory aid: <u>HIS</u> <u>CPA</u> <u>Responsibility</u>

9. **Risk Assessment**

    a. The risk assessment process encompasses the risks themselves and the need to manage organizational change.

    b. **Risks.** Management must focus carefully on risks at all levels of the entity and take the necessary actions to manage them. Risks must be addressed through a process of identification and a process of analysis (i.e., response).

        1) Risk Identification

            a) The method employed to identify risks is less important than the requirement that all potential risks be considered.

            b) Examples of external risk factors at the entity level include technological changes and changes in customer wants and expectations.

            c) Examples of internal risk factors at the entity level include interruptions in automated systems, the quality of personnel hired, and the level of training provided.

        2) Risk Analysis

            a) This process may be formal or informal. It generally involves

                i) Estimating the significance of an event,
                ii) Assessing the event's likelihood, and
                iii) Considering the means to manage the risk.

            b) In general, the seriousness of a risk and its likelihood are inversely related.

                i) For example, it is highly likely that an improper use of petty cash will be made, but the significance of the impropriety is minimal. A fraud involving bonds is extremely serious, but given the accounting and legal scrutiny of a bond issue, such an event is highly unlikely.

    c)   Each organization must find a suitable method for assessing the relationship between likelihood and significance and designing the appropriate controls.

        i)   Some risks may simply be accepted, but others require the creation of elaborate control structures. For example, the total physical destruction of the data center may be highly unlikely. However, if it were to occur, the ability of the entity to function at all may be questionable. Thus, a contingency plan for such an occurrence is almost a necessity.

  c. **Managing change.** Internal controls must be adapted to the entity's changing circumstances.

    1)   The following examples are typical circumstances requiring special attention:

        a)   Changed operating environment. Changes in the regulatory or economic environment can change the effectiveness of current controls.

        b)   New personnel. A newly hired member of upper management may not share the organization's attitude toward controls.

        c)   New or revamped information systems. Effective controls under the old system may not function under the new system.

        d)   Rapid growth. Controls that were effective under previous conditions may break down under the stresses of increased activity.

        e)   New technology. Any new technology, whether or not computerized, will probably make current controls obsolete. An example is just-in-time inventory, which completely discards traditional methods of tracking and valuing raw materials inventories.

        f)   New lines, products, and activities. Existing controls may be unsuitable for new lines of business. For example, the control system of a commercial bank may be inadequate to the organization's needs when it merges with an investment bank.

        g)   Corporate restructurings. Mass layoffs, or even targeted layoffs of a few key personnel, can render control systems ineffective. The employees remaining may be unable, or too few, to continue executing the old controls.

        h)   Foreign operations. The laws and regulations of the host country may be different from those of the home country. Also, the attitudes of the local personnel toward risk and control are determined by the local culture.

10. Control Activities

  a. Types of Control Activities

    1)   The framework leaves to each organization the designation of control activities as preventive/detective, manual/automated, etc. Instead, it presents the following examples of the matters covered by control activities:

        a)   Top level reviews, e.g., actual versus budget comparisons

        b)   Direct functional or activity management, e.g., day-to-day interaction of managers with line personnel

        c)   Information processing, e.g., general and application controls, described in c. on the following page

        d)   Physical controls, e.g., over equipment, inventories, securities, and cash to prevent theft

                e)   Performance indicators, e.g., the measures of critical success factors, such as daily cash balance and daily sales revenues

                f)   Segregation of duties, e.g., division of job functions among personnel so that the possibility of fraud or error is reduced

    b.   Integration with Risk Assessment

        1)   Once risks have been identified, control activities specifically designed to address those risks must be put in place and relevant personnel trained in their proper function.

                a)   Well-designed controls serve as tools in the pursuit of organizational objectives.

    c.   Controls over Information Systems

        1)   The COSO model distinguishes between general controls and application controls. This distinction has lasted through several generations of information technology development. (These controls will be discussed in more detail in Study Unit 14.)

        2)   **General controls** affect all computer systems in an organization.

                a)   Data center operations controls are controls over the organization's centralized hardware (e.g., "mainframes" or "servers"), the scheduling of batch jobs, and business continuity/disaster recovery planning.

                b)   Systems software controls are controls over the installation of and upgrades to the operating system, database management system, security software, and utility programs.

                c)   Access security controls are controls over (1) who has physical access, i.e., who can gain physical contact with the organization's computer hardware, and (2) who has logical access, i.e., who can view or change the organization's programs and data.

                d)   Application system development and maintenance controls are controls over acquisition of new computer applications, whether purchased from outside vendors or created in-house, and changes to those applications.

        3)   **Application controls** are specific to a given computer application, e.g., payroll processing.

                a)   Completeness and accuracy of transaction processing, authorization, and validity are the goals of application controls. Many specific controls can help to achieve these goals.

                b)   Controls are applied over input, processing, and output of an application.

        4)   Relationship between general and application controls. General controls constitute the environment within which the several sets of application controls function (one set for each application). Thus, poor general controls may mean that application controls are unreliable.

    d.   Entity Specific

        1)   Every entity has a unique set of market, financial, and technological challenges. Every organization must design its system of internal control to fit its particular situation.

11. **Information and Communication**

    a.   Information

        1)   Information systems, in this context, encompass more than just computer-based systems. Information may be financial, such as inventory measurement, or nonfinancial, such as market characteristics.

        2)   Strategic and integrated systems. Information systems are being used to integrate multiple aspects of the organization, such as systems that coordinate marketing efforts with procurement and production. Such systems contribute directly to the degree of success in achieving organizational objectives.

        3)   Information quality. High-quality information is appropriate, timely, current, accurate, and accessible.

    b.   Communication

        1)   Internal

            a)   It is not enough to stress the importance of internal control. The precise function of each employee must be communicated in the form of policies and detailed procedures. Thus, personnel should know exactly what is expected of them.

            b)   Feedback from lower to upper levels is crucial as well, since those closest to frontline operations usually are the best informed about the true state of things.

        2)   External

            a)   Customers and suppliers can provide clues as to the state of an organization's internal control. In addition, external parties must be informed that bribes and kickbacks are not permitted.

        3)   Means of Communication

            a)   Control-oriented communications can take the form of anything from the publication of policy and procedure manuals to one-on-one interaction between management and staff.

12. **Monitoring**

    a.   Just as control systems change over time, the way controls are applied may change as well.

        1)   Procedures that were once adequate and appropriate may become obsolete because of changes in systems or may simply stop being performed through oversight with the passage of time.

        2)   The task of monitoring internal controls is done both continually and through separate evaluations.

    b.   Ongoing Monitoring Activities

        1)   Routine activities that are control-oriented include (a) the periodic reconciliation of operational division data with enterprise-wide financial data, (b) the presence or absence of customer complaints about billing, (c) the reports of internal and external auditors, and (d) training seminars.

c.   Separate Evaluations

1)   The significance of risks will determine the scope and frequency of separate evaluations of internal control.

2)   In some environments, control self-assessment is appropriate. In others, the internal audit function should perform a thorough review.

3)   The evaluation process for a system of internal controls has certain similarities to a financial statement audit. The evaluator must understand how the system is supposed to work and what objectives are being pursued and must perform tests to determine whether the system is working as designed.

d.   A Model for Monitoring

1)   In its 2009 publication *Guidance on Monitoring Internal Control Systems*, COSO describes a three-component model for monitoring. Each component consists of three or four subcomponents.

a)   Establishing a foundation for monitoring consists of

i)   A proper tone at the top,
ii)   An effective organizational structure, and
iii) A baseline understanding of internal control effectiveness.

b)   Designing and executing monitoring procedures that are prioritized based on risks to achieving organizational objectives consists of

i)   Prioritizing risks,
ii)   Identifying controls,
iii) Identifying persuasive information about controls, and
iv) Implementing monitoring procedures.

c)   Assessing and reporting the results, including following up on corrective action where necessary, consists of

i)   Prioritizing findings,
ii)   Reporting results to appropriate levels, and
iii) Following up on corrective action.

2)   To increase the level of success of a system of internal control, COSO recommends a "baseline understanding" [item 1)a)iii) above] as the starting point.

a)   The baseline understanding makes it easier for the organization to make needed changes to the system in real time. The general sequence of steps in this process is as follows:

i)   Control baseline. Establish the starting point to include a supported understanding of the current system's design and operation.

ii)   Change identification. Identify the changes needed to the system of internal control.

iii) Change management. Evaluate the design and implementation of the changes (thereby establishing a new baseline).

iv) Control revalidation/update. Periodically revalidate the proper operation of the system at a time when no known changes have occurred.

e.   Reporting Deficiencies

1)   Whether an internal control deficiency is reportable depends on its effect on the entity's ability to achieve its objectives. If so, the deficiency should be reported to a level of the organization with sufficient authority to correct it.

13. **Inherent Limitations of Internal Control**

a. Internal control, no matter how well designed and operated, provides only reasonable assurance about achievement of the entity's objectives.

1) Some matters are simply beyond management's ability to control. Also, no human system always works perfectly.

Remember that internal control systems have inherent limitations. Be able to identify what these limitations are.

b. The following are basic limitations of any system of internal control:

1) Human judgment is faulty, and controls may fail because of simple errors or mistakes.
2) Controls may fail due to employee misunderstanding, carelessness, or fatigue.
3) Management may inappropriately override internal control, e.g., to fraudulently achieve revenue projections or to hide liabilities.
4) Manual or automated controls can be circumvented by collusion.
5) The costs of a control should not exceed the benefits derived from it.

14. **Foreign Corrupt Practices Act of 1977**

a. The Foreign Corrupt Practices Act (FCPA) was a response to the bribery of foreign government officials by U.S. companies.

b. The FCPA contains two sets of provisions:

1) All issuers must devise and maintain a system of internal accounting control, regardless of whether they have foreign operations.
2) Domestic concerns, whether or not doing business overseas and whether or not registered with the SEC, may not offer or authorize corrupt payments to any foreign official, foreign political party or official thereof, or candidate for political office in a foreign country.

15. **Roles and Responsibilities**

a. **Responsible Parties**

1) Management

a) The chief executive officer (CEO) establishes the "tone at the top." Organizations inevitably reflect the ethical values and control consciousness of the CEO.
b) The chief accounting officer also has a crucial role to play. Accounting staff have insight into activities across and at all levels of the entire organization.

2) Board of Directors

a) The entity's commitment to integrity and ethical values is reflected in the board's selections for CEO and the senior vice president positions.
b) To be effective, board members should be capable of objective judgment, have knowledge of the organization's industry, and be willing to ask the relevant questions about management's decisions.
c) Important subcommittees of the board, in organizations of sufficient size and complexity, include the audit committee, the compensation committee, the finance committee, and the risk committee.

3) Internal Auditors

    a) Although management is ultimately responsible for the design and operation of the system of internal controls, an organization's internal audit function has a consulting and advisory role.

    b) Besides consulting and advising, internal audit also evaluates the system of internal control by performing systematic reviews according to professional standards.

        i) The Institute of Internal Auditors (The IIA) issues the relevant professional standards. The IIA also has established the Certified Internal Auditor Program and awards the Certified Internal Auditor (CIA) designation to qualified applicants.

        ii) The IIA's International Professional Practices Framework includes the following mandatory guidance:

- The Definition of Internal Auditing
- The IIA Code of Ethics
- International Standards for the Professional Practice of Internal Auditing

           ■ **Attribute Standards** address the attributes of organizations and individuals performing internal auditing services.

           ■ **Performance Standards** describe the nature of internal auditing and criteria for measuring its quality.

           ■ **Implementation Standards** are assurance and consulting standards that expand upon and are integrated with the other standards.

    c) To remain independent in the conduct of these reviews, the internal audit function cannot be responsible for selecting and executing controls. This is the sole responsibility of management.

4) Other Entity Personnel

    a) Everyone in the organization must be aware that (s)he has a role to play in internal control, and every employee is expected to perform his/her appropriate control activities.

    b) In addition, all employees should understand that they are expected to inform those higher in the organization of instances of poor control.

b. **External Parties**

1) External Auditors

    a) Traditionally, independent accountants have been required by their professional standards to consider the auditee's system of internal control as part of their audit of the entity's financial statements.

    b) This is no longer simply a good practice self-imposed by the accounting profession. The PCAOB has made it a legal requirement to examine and report on internal control.

2) Legislators and Regulators

    a) Congress passed the Foreign Corrupt Practices Act and the Sarbanes-Oxley Act, both of which set legal requirements with regard to internal control.

3)   Parties Interacting with the Entity

a)   The following are examples of control-related information received from outside sources:

i)   A major customer informs management that a sales representative attempted to arrange a kickback scheme in return for the customer's business.

ii)   A supplier reveals inventory and shipping problems by complaining about incomplete orders.

b)   Parties without a supplier/customer relationship also may provide insight into the functioning of controls.

i)   As a condition for granting a loan, a bank may require that certain ratios be kept above or below specified levels. As a result, management may need to pay closer attention to controls over cash and inventory levels than it did previously.

4)   Financial Analysts, Bond Rating Agencies, and the News Media

a)   The actions of these parties can inform an entity about how it is perceived by the world at large.

Stop and review! You have completed the outline for this subunit. Study multiple-choice questions 20 through 26 beginning on page 56.

1.5 THE COSO MODEL FOR ENTERPRISE RISK MANAGEMENT

1.   **COSO Risk Management Framework**

a.   The **Committee of Sponsoring Organizations (COSO)** published *Enterprise Risk Management – Integrated Framework* in 2004. It describes a model that incorporates the earlier COSO internal control framework while extending it to the broader area of enterprise risk management (ERM). The purpose is to provide a basis for coordinating and integrating all of the entity's risk management activities.

2.   **ERM Definition**

a.   ERM is based on key concepts applicable to many types of entities. The emphasis is on (1) the objectives of a specific entity and (2) establishing a means for evaluating the effectiveness of ERM.

> *Enterprise risk management is a process, effected by an entity's board of directors, management, and other personnel, applied in strategy setting and across the enterprise, designed to identify potential events that may affect the entity, and manage risk to be within its risk appetite, to provide reasonable assurance regarding the achievement of entity objectives.*

3.   **Definitions of Risk and Risk Management**

a.   According to the COSO,

> *Risk is the possibility that an event will occur and adversely affect the achievement of objectives.*

b.   Risk management, at any level, consists of

1)   Identifying potential events that may affect the entity and
2)   Managing the associated risk to be within the entity's risk appetite.

c.   Ultimately, risk management should provide reasonable assurance regarding the achievement of entity objectives.

4. **Responsibilities**

   a. Senior Management

      1) The CEO sets the **tone at the top** of the entity and has ultimate responsibility for ERM.

      2) Senior management should ensure that sound risk management processes are in place and functioning.

      3) Senior management also determines the entity's risk management philosophy. For example, officers who issue definitive policy statements, insist on written procedures, and closely monitor performance indicators exhibit one type of risk management philosophy. Officers who manage informally and take a relaxed approach to performance monitoring exhibit a different philosophy.

         a) If senior management establishes a consistent risk management philosophy, all parts of the entity can respond to risk appropriately.

   b. Board of Directors

      1) The **board has an oversight role**. It should determine that risk management processes are in place, adequate, and effective.

      2) Directors' attitudes are a key component of the internal environment. They must possess certain qualities for them to be effective.

         a) A majority of the board should be outside directors.

         b) Directors generally should have years of experience either in the industry or in corporate governance.

         c) Directors must be willing to challenge management's choices. Complacent directors increase the chances of adverse consequences.

   c. Risk Committee and Chief Risk Officer

      1) Larger entities may wish to establish a risk committee composed of directors that also includes managers, the individuals who are most familiar with entity processes.

         a) A chief risk officer (CRO) may be appointed to coordinate the entity's risk management activities. The CRO is a member of, and reports to, the risk committee.

   d. Internal Auditing

      1) According to The IIA, internal auditors may be directed by the board to evaluate the effectiveness and contribute to the improvement of risk management processes.

      2) The internal auditors' determination of whether risk management processes are effective is a judgment resulting from the assessment that

         a) Entity objectives support and align with its mission
         b) Significant risks are identified and assessed

            i) Appropriate risk responses are selected that align risks and the entity's risk appetite.

            ii) Relevant risk information is captured and communicated in a timely manner across the entity, enabling staff, management, and the board to carry out their responsibilities.

5. **ERM Capabilities**

    a. ERM allows management to optimize stakeholder value by coping effectively with uncertainty and the risks and opportunities it presents. ERM helps management to

    1) Reach objectives,
    2) Prevent loss of reputation and resources,
    3) Report effectively, and
    4) Comply with laws and regulations.

    b. The following are the capabilities of ERM:

    1) Consideration of risk appetite and strategy

        a) **Risk appetite** is the degree of willingness of senior management to accept risk. It should be considered in

            i) Evaluating strategic options,
            ii) Setting objectives, and
            iii) Developing risk management techniques.

    2) Risk response decisions

        a) ERM permits identification and selection of such responses to risk as

            i) Avoidance,
            ii) Reduction,
            iii) Sharing, and
            iv) Acceptance.

    3) Reduction of operational surprises and losses

        a) These are reduced by an improved ability to anticipate potential events and develop responses.

    4) Multiple and cross-enterprise risks

        a) Risks may affect different parts of the entity. ERM allows

            i) Effective responses to interrelated effects and
            ii) Integrated responses to multiple risks.

    5) Response to opportunities

        a) By facilitating the identification of potential events, ERM helps management to respond quickly to opportunities.

    6) Deployment of capital

        a) The risk information provided by ERM permits

            i) Assessment of capital needs and
            ii) Better capital allocation.

6. **Events**

    a. Events with a potential negative impact are risks. Events with a potential positive impact offset risks or create opportunities.

    1) An **opportunity** "is the possibility that an event will occur and positively affect the achievement of objectives, supporting value creation or preservation."

    2) Management makes plans to exploit opportunities, subject to the entity's adopted strategies and objectives.

7. **Entity Objectives**

    a. The COSO Risk Management Framework lists four categories of objectives that are applicable to all entities:

        1) <u>S</u>trategic objectives align with and support the entity's mission.
        2) <u>O</u>perations objectives address effectiveness and efficiency.
        3) <u>R</u>eporting objectives concern reliability.
        4) <u>C</u>ompliance objectives relate to adherence to laws and regulations.

        Memory aid: <u>S</u>tudying <u>O</u>bsessively <u>R</u>eally <u>C</u>ounts

    b. These categories overlap but are distinct. They concern different needs, and different managers may be assigned responsibility for them.

        1) The COSO's ERM framework also defines another category – safeguarding of resources – that may be appropriate for some entities.

    c. Strategic and operational matters are affected by external events that the entity may not control. Hence, ERM should provide reasonable assurance that management and the board receive timely information about whether those objectives are being achieved.

    d. Reporting and compliance are within the entity's control. Accordingly, ERM should provide reasonable assurance of achieving those objectives.

8. **Components of COSO ERM**

    a. The components of ERM are integrated with the management process and may mutually influence each other.

        1) The <u>i</u>nternal environment reflects the entity's (a) risk management philosophy, (b) risk appetite, (c) integrity, (d) ethical values, and (e) overall environment. It sets the tone of the entity.
        2) <u>O</u>bjective setting must be completed before risk events can be identified. ERM ensures that (a) a process is established and (b) objectives align with the mission and the risk appetite.
        3) <u>E</u>vent identification relates to internal and external events affecting the entity. It differentiates between opportunities and risks. Opportunities are referred to the strategy or objective-setting processes.
        4) <u>R</u>isk assessment considers likelihood and impact as a basis for risk management. The assessment considers the inherent risk and the residual risk.

            a) Inherent risk is the risk arising from an activity itself. It is the risk in the absence of a risk response.
            b) Residual risk is what remains after risk responses.

        5) <u>R</u>isk responses should be consistent with the organization's risk tolerances and appetite.
        6) <u>C</u>ontrol activities are policies and procedures to ensure the effectiveness of risk responses.
        7) The <u>i</u>nformation and communication component identifies, captures, and communicates relevant and timely information.
        8) <u>M</u>onitoring involves ongoing management activities or separate evaluations. The full ERM process is monitored.

        Memory aid: <u>I</u> <u>O</u>verlooked <u>E</u>vidence <u>R</u>egarding <u>R</u>espiratory <u>C</u>ontrols <u>I</u>n <u>M</u>edicine

9.   **Graphical Depiction**

    a.   The Framework depicts the interaction of the various elements as a matrix in the form of a cube.

        1)   The four categories of objectives are on one side, the eight interrelated components are on another, and the organizational units of the entity are on the third. The organization can apply the appropriate approach to each intersection of the three elements, such as control activities for reporting objectives at the division level.

COSO ERM Framework

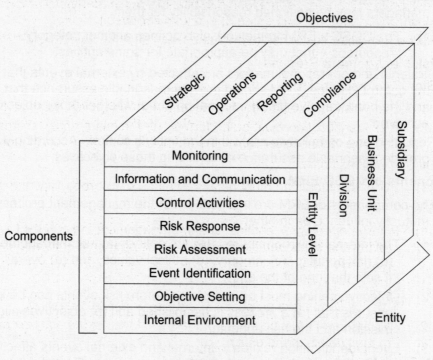

Figure 1-3

    b.   Components should be present and functioning effectively. Consequently, the components are criteria for the effectiveness of ERM.

        1)   "Present and functioning effectively" means that (a) no material weaknesses exist and (b) risk is within the risk appetite.

        2)   When ERM is effective regarding all of the objectives, the board and management have reasonable assurance that (a) reporting is reliable, (b) compliance is achieved, and (c) they know the extent of achievement of strategic and operations objectives.

        3)   The components operate differently in different organizations. For example, they may be applied in a less formal way in smaller organizations.

10.   **ERM Limitations**

    a.   Limitations of ERM arise from the possibility of

        1)   Faulty human judgment,
        2)   Cost-benefit considerations,
        3)   Simple errors or mistakes,
        4)   Collusion, and
        5)   Management override of ERM decisions.

11. **Strategies for Risk Response**

    a.   Risk avoidance ends the activity from which the risk arises. For example, the risk of having a pipeline sabotaged in an unstable region can be avoided by simply selling the pipeline.

    b.   Risk retention accepts the risk of an activity. This term is a synonym for self insurance.

    c.   Risk reduction (mitigation) lowers the level of risk associated with an activity. For example, the risk of systems penetration can be reduced by maintaining a robust information security function within the organization.

    d.   Risk sharing transfers some loss potential to another party. Examples are purchasing insurance, hedging, and entering into joint ventures.

    e.   Risk exploitation seeks risk to pursue a high return on investment.

12. **The Risk Management Process**

    a.   Step 1 – Identify risks.

        1)   Every risk that could affect achievement of objectives must be considered.

        2)   Risk identification must be performed for the entire entity. Some occurrences may be inconsequential for the entity but disastrous for an individual unit.

    b.   Step 2 – Assess risks.

        1)   Every risk identified must be assessed as to its probability and potential effect.

    c.   Step 3 – Prioritize risks.

        1)   In large or complex entities, senior management may appoint a risk committee to review the risks identified by the various operating units and create a coherent response plan.

    d.   Step 4 – Formulate risk responses.

        1)   The risk committee proposes adequate response strategies.

        2)   All personnel must be aware of the importance of the risk response appropriate to their levels of the entity.

    e.   Step 5 – Monitor risk responses.

        1)   The two most important sources of information for ongoing assessments of the adequacy of risk responses (and the changing nature of the risks themselves) are

            a)   Those closest to the activities themselves. The manager of an operating unit is in the best position to monitor the effects of the chosen risk response strategies.

            b)   The audit function. Operating managers may not always be objective about the risks facing their units, especially if they had a stake in designing a particular response strategy. Analyzing risks and responses are among the normal duties of internal auditors.

    Memory aid: I Ate Pie For Money

13. **Event Identification**

    a.   The event identification process should consider past events (looking for trends) as well as future possibilities.

    b.   Specific event identification techniques include the following:

        1)   Event inventories. Certain events are common to particular industries. Software products are available that present the entity with such lists that can be used as a starting point for the event identification process.

        2)   Internal analysis. The entity can consider its own experience with similar risks in the past when planning a response for future occurrences.

3) Escalation or threshold triggers. A certain risk response may be designed to be enacted upon the occurrence of a certain event, such as a dip in cash on hand below a given level or a major price cut by a competitor.

4) Facilitated workshops and interviews. A facilitator leads a discussion group consisting of management, staff, and other stakeholders through a structured process of conversation and exploration about potential events.

5) Process flow analysis. A single business process, such as vendor authorization and payment, is studied in isolation for the events that affect its particular inputs, tasks, responsibilities, and outputs.

6) Leading event indicators. Certain patterns that predict adverse events can be identified and an appropriate response devised. An example is avoiding debtor default by intervention upon the occurrence of a late payment.

7) Loss event data methodologies. The losses associated with adverse events in the past can be used to build a model for predictions. An example is matching workers' compensation claims against the frequency of accidents.

Stop and review! You have completed the outline for this subunit. Study multiple-choice questions 27 through 32 beginning on page 58.

QUESTIONS

1.1 Roles in the Governance Hierarchy

1. Which of the following documents would most likely contain specific rules for the management of a business corporation?

    A. Articles of incorporation.

    B. Bylaws.

    C. Certificate of authority.

    D. Shareholders' agreement.

Answer (B) is correct.
REQUIRED: The document most likely containing corporate management rules.
DISCUSSION: Bylaws govern the internal structure and operation of a corporation. Initial bylaws are adopted by the incorporators or the board. They may contain any provision for managing the business and regulating the affairs of the corporate entity not in conflict with the law or the articles of incorporation.
Answer (A) is incorrect. The articles contain only basic information that must be filed with a designated state official as part of forming the corporation. Answer (C) is incorrect. A certificate of authority is required to do business in a state where the corporation is not incorporated. It is obtained from the secretary of state after paying fees and designating a resident agent. Answer (D) is incorrect. A shareholder agreement governs the exercise of the corporate powers; the management of the business and affairs of the corporation; or the relationship among the shareholders, the directors, and the corporation. For example, it may eliminate the board or restrict its powers. In contrast, bylaws usually address such details as methods of electing directors or the details of scheduling meetings. Also, a shareholder's agreement may be included in the bylaws.

2. In general, which of the following must be contained in articles of incorporation?

    A. Names of states in which the corporation will be doing business.

    B. Name of the state in which the corporation will maintain its principal place of business.

    C. Names of the initial officers and their terms of office.

    D. Number of shares of stock authorized to be issued by the corporation.

Answer (D) is correct.
REQUIRED: The information required in articles of incorporation.
DISCUSSION: Articles of incorporation must contain the name of the corporation, the number of authorized shares, the address of the initial registered office of the corporation, the name of its first registered agent at that address, and the names and addresses of the incorporators. The articles may also include names and addresses of the initial directors, purpose and duration of the corporation, and any provision that may be set forth in the bylaws.
Answer (A) is incorrect. The names of states in which the corporation will be doing business need not be included in the articles. Answer (B) is incorrect. The name of the state in which the corporation will maintain its principal place of business need not be included in the articles. Answer (C) is incorrect. The names of initial officers and their terms of office need not be included in the articles.

3. Which of the following corporate actions is subject to shareholder approval?

    A. Election of officers.

    B. Removal of officers.

    C. Declaration of cash dividends.

    D. Removal of directors.

Answer (D) is correct.
    REQUIRED: The action that must be approved by the shareholders.
    DISCUSSION: A corporation is governed by shareholders (owners) who elect the directors on the corporation's board and who approve fundamental changes in the corporate structure. Directors establish corporate policies and elect or appoint corporate officers who carry out the policies in the day-to-day management of the organization. In most states, the shareholders may by a majority vote remove, with or without cause, any director or the entire board.
    Answer (A) is incorrect. The officers are elected by the directors. Answer (B) is incorrect. Officers are removed by the directors. Answer (C) is incorrect. The board of directors has the discretion to determine the nature, time, and amount of dividends and other distributions.

4. Which of the following actions is required to ensure the validity of a contract between a corporation and a director of the corporation?

    A. An independent appraiser must render to the board of directors a fairness opinion on the contract.

    B. The director must disclose the interest to the independent members of the board and refrain from voting.

    C. The shareholders must review and ratify the contract.

    D. The director must resign from the board of directors.

Answer (B) is correct.
    REQUIRED: The action to ensure the validity of a contract between a corporation and a director.
    DISCUSSION: To protect the corporation against self-dealing, a director is required to make full disclosure of any financial interest (s)he may have in any transaction to which both the director and the corporation may be a party. Under modern corporate law, a transaction is not voidable merely on the grounds of a director's conflict of interest if the transaction is fair to the corporation or has been approved by a majority of (1) informed, disinterested qualified directors or (2) holders of qualified shares. This rule applies even if the director was counted for the quorum and voted to approve the transaction. A qualified director does not have (1) a conflict of interest regarding the transaction or (2) a special relationship (familial, professional, financial, etc.) with another director who has a conflict of interest. Shares are qualified if they are not controlled by a person with (1) a conflict of interest or (2) a close relationship with someone who has a conflict. Thus, the director who contracts with the corporation cannot provide the vote that approves the contract.
    Answer (A) is incorrect. No such requirement exists. However, shareholders who disagree with fundamental corporate changes have appraisal rights to receive the fair value of their shares. Answer (C) is incorrect. Shareholder ratification is unnecessary. However, if the transaction is fair, approval by shareholders prevents it from being voided. Furthermore, unanimous shareholder approval may release the director from liability even if the transaction is unfair. Answer (D) is incorrect. Resignation is not required. Self-dealing transactions are permissible in many cases.

5. The board of directors performs all of the following duties **except**

    A. Managing day-to-day operations.

    B. Selection and removal of officers.

    C. Adding or repealing bylaws.

    D. Initiation of fundamental changes.

Answer (A) is correct.
    REQUIRED: The duty not performed by the board of directors.
    DISCUSSION: The board of directors guides management. It does not directly manage day-to-day operations of the entity. That is management's responsibility, with the board playing an oversight role. All major corporate decisions are made or approved by the board.
    Answer (B) is incorrect. The board has the duty of selection and removal of officers. Answer (C) is incorrect. Adding, amending, or repealing bylaws is a duty of the board. Answer (D) is incorrect. Initiation of fundamental changes, such as mergers or acquisitions, is a duty of the board.

6. The principle that protects corporate directors from personal liability for acts performed in good faith on behalf of the corporation is known as the

- A. Clean hands doctrine.
- B. Full disclosure rule.
- C. Responsible person doctrine.
- D. Business judgment rule.

Answer (D) is correct.

REQUIRED: The principle that protects directors from liability for acts performed in good faith.

DISCUSSION: Courts avoid substituting their business judgment for that of the corporation's officers or directors. The rule protects an officer or a director from personal liability for honest mistakes of judgment if (s)he (1) acted in good faith; (2) was not motivated by fraud, conflict of interest, or illegality; and (3) was not grossly negligent. To avoid personal liability, directors and officers must (1) make informed decisions (educate themselves about the issues), (2) be free from conflicts of interest, and (3) have a rational basis to support their position.

Answer (A) is incorrect. The clean hands doctrine is a principle of equity. A party who seeks an equitable remedy must not have acted improperly regarding the subject of the case. Answer (B) is incorrect. To protect the corporation against self-dealing, a director is required to make full disclosure of any financial interest (s)he may have in any transaction to which both the director and the corporation may be a party. Answer (C) is incorrect. In appropriate circumstances, the corporation (the employer) may be responsible for the acts of its agents (employees).

1.2 The Internal Audit Function

7. The proper organizational role of internal auditing is to

- A. Assist the external auditor to reduce external audit fees.
- B. Help manage operations of the organization.
- C. Serve as the investigative arm of the board of directors.
- D. Serve as an independent, objective assurance and consulting activity that adds value to operations.

Answer (D) is correct.

REQUIRED: The organizational role of internal auditing.

DISCUSSION: An internal audit function is a crucial governance structure for any complex modern entity. As part of its Definition of Internal Auditing, The Institute of Internal Auditors states that internal auditing "is an independent, objective assurance and consulting activity designed to add value and improve an organization's operations."

Answer (A) is incorrect. Reducing external audit fees may be a direct result of internal audit work, but it is not a reason for staffing an internal audit department. Answer (B) is incorrect. Internal auditing has no management responsibilities. Answer (C) is incorrect. Internal auditors serve both the board of directors and management.

8. The reporting structure that is most likely to allow the internal audit activity to accomplish its responsibilities is to report administratively to the

- A. Board and functionally to the chief executive officer.
- B. Controller and functionally to the chief financial officer.
- C. Chief executive officer and functionally to the board of directors.
- D. Chief executive officer and functionally to the external auditor.

Answer (C) is correct.

REQUIRED: The set of relationships that best depicts the appropriate dual reporting responsibility of the internal auditor.

DISCUSSION: Reporting functionally to the board and administratively to the organization's CEO facilitates organizational independence. At a minimum, the CAE needs to report to an individual in the organization with sufficient authority to promote independence and to ensure broad engagement coverage, adequate consideration of engagement communications, and appropriate action on engagement recommendations. Being responsible to the CEO while maintaining a functional relationship with the board satisfies the need for an organizational status sufficient for accomplishment of the internal audit activity's responsibilities.

Answer (A) is incorrect. The reverse arrangement is appropriate. The board is not involved in the routine management of the firm. Answer (B) is incorrect. Reporting administratively to the controller and functionally to the chief financial officer would result in insufficient organizational status for internal auditing. Answer (D) is incorrect. The external auditor is not part of the organizational hierarchy.

9. An internal auditor who had been supervisor of the accounts payable section should **not** perform an assurance review of that area

    A. Because there is no way to measure a reasonable period of time in which to establish independence.

    B. Until at least 1 year has elapsed.

    C. Until after the next annual review by the external auditors.

    D. Until it is clear that the new supervisor has assumed the responsibilities.

Answer (B) is correct.

    REQUIRED: The time when an internal auditor may perform an assurance review of an area where (s)he previously supervised.

    DISCUSSION: Independence and objectivity are incorporated into The IIA's Definition of Internal Auditing. Objectivity is a personal attribute. Individual internal auditors must maintain the ability to make impartial, unbiased judgments. For example, The IIA's professional standards require that no internal auditor who once worked in another area of the entity be allowed to provide assurance services to that area for 1 year.

    Answer (A) is incorrect. The issues are whether (1) objectivity, not independence, has been restored and (2) at least 1 year has elapsed. Answer (C) is incorrect. The external review does not relate to the issue of restoring the internal auditor's objectivity. Answer (D) is incorrect. The new supervisor presumably would have assumed his/her responsibilities immediately. Hence, a year could not have elapsed.

10. The actions taken to manage risk and increase the likelihood that established objectives and goals will be achieved are best described as

    A. Supervision.

    B. Quality assurance.

    C. Control.

    D. Compliance.

Answer (C) is correct.

    REQUIRED: The term for actions taken to manage risk and increase the likelihood that established objectives and goals will be achieved.

    DISCUSSION: Control is any action taken by management, the board, and other parties to manage risk and increase the likelihood that established objectives and goals will be achieved. Management plans, organizes, and directs the performance of sufficient actions to provide reasonable assurance that objectives and goals will be achieved.

    Answer (A) is incorrect. Supervision is just one means of achieving control. Answer (B) is incorrect. Quality assurance relates to just one set of objectives and goals. It does not pertain to achievement of all established organizational objectives and goals. Answer (D) is incorrect. Compliance is adherence to policies, plans, procedures, laws, regulations, contracts, or other requirements.

11. The authority of the internal audit activity is limited to that granted by

    A. The board and the controller.

    B. Senior management and the *Standards*.

    C. Management and the board.

    D. The board and the chief financial officer.

Answer (C) is correct.

    REQUIRED: The source of authority of the internal audit activity.

    DISCUSSION: The purpose, authority, and responsibility of the internal audit activity must be formally defined in a charter. The CAE must periodically review and present the charter to senior management and the board for approval.

    Answer (A) is incorrect. The controller is not the only member of management. Answer (B) is incorrect. The *Standards* provide no actual authority to the internal audit activity. Answer (D) is incorrect. Management and the board, not a particular manager, give the internal audit activity its authority.

12. What is the responsibility of the internal auditor with respect to fraud?

    A. The internal auditor should have sufficient knowledge to identify the indicators of fraud but is not expected to be an expert.

    B. The internal auditor should have the same ability to detect fraud as a person whose primary responsibility is detecting and investigating fraud.

    C. An internal auditor should have sufficient knowledge and training so that (s)he is able to detect fraud.

    D. An internal auditor's primary role is to detect and investigate fraud.

Answer (A) is correct.

    REQUIRED: The internal auditor's responsibility with respect to fraud.

    DISCUSSION: Internal auditors must have sufficient knowledge to evaluate the risk of fraud and the manner in which it is managed by the organization. They are not expected to have the expertise of a person whose primary responsibility is detecting and investigating fraud.

    Answer (B) is incorrect. The internal auditor is not expected to have the expertise of a person whose primary responsibility is detecting and investigating fraud. Answer (C) is incorrect. An internal auditor must have sufficient knowledge to identify the indicators of fraud but is not required to have sufficient knowledge and training to be able to detect fraud. Answer (D) is incorrect. Detecting and investigating fraud is not a primary role of an internal auditor.

1.3 The Sarbanes-Oxley Act of 2002 (SOX)

13. The Sarbanes-Oxley Act of 2002 has strengthened auditor independence by requiring that management

A. Engage auditors to report in accordance with the Foreign Corrupt Practices Act.

B. Report the nature of disagreements with former auditors.

C. Select auditors through audit committees.

D. Hire a different CPA firm from the one that performs the audit to perform the company's tax work.

Answer (C) is correct.
REQUIRED: The Sarbanes-Oxley requirement that strengthened auditor independence.
DISCUSSION: The Sarbanes-Oxley Act requires that the audit committee of a public company hire and pay the external auditors. Such affiliation inhibits management from changing auditors to gain acceptance of a questionable accounting method. Also, a potential successor auditor must inquire of the predecessor auditor before accepting an engagement.
Answer (A) is incorrect. The SEC does not require an audit report in accordance with the FCPA. Answer (B) is incorrect. Reporting the nature of disagreements with auditors has been a long-time SEC requirement. Answer (D) is incorrect. The Sarbanes-Oxley Act does not restrict who may perform a company's tax work. Other types of engagements, such as the outsourcing of the internal audit function and certain consulting services, are limited.

14. Under the Sarbanes-Oxley Act of 2002 (SOX),

A. At least one member of the audit committee must be a financial expert.

B. The chairman of the board of directors must be a financial expert.

C. The audit committee must rotate at least one seat on an annual basis.

D. All members of the audit committee must be financial experts.

Answer (A) is correct.
REQUIRED: The Sarbanes-Oxley requirement relevant to the audit committee.
DISCUSSION: Under the terms of SOX, at least one member of the audit committee must be a financial expert.
Answer (B) is incorrect. The SOX requirement regarding a financial expert does not refer to the chairman of the board. Answer (C) is incorrect. SOX imposes no requirements regarding membership rotation of the audit committee. Answer (D) is incorrect. Under the terms of SOX, only one member of the audit committee need be a financial expert.

15. The Sarbanes-Oxley Act of 2002 (SOX) imposes which of the following requirements?

A. The board of directors must be composed entirely of independent shareholders.

B. At least one member of the audit committee must be a former partner of the independent public accounting firm.

C. The audit committee must be composed entirely of independent members of the board.

D. Once the audit committee has selected the independent public accounting firm, the committee must not interfere with the firm's conduct of the financial statement audit.

Answer (C) is correct.
REQUIRED: The provision required by Sarbanes-Oxley.
DISCUSSION: Under the terms of SOX, each member of the issuer's audit committee must be an independent member of the board of directors. To be independent, a director must not be affiliated with, or receive any compensation (other than for service on the board) from, the issuer.
Answer (A) is incorrect. The SOX requirement regarding independent members refers to the audit committee, not the entire board. Answer (B) is incorrect. SOX does not impose a requirement regarding mandatory former employment with the independent public accounting firm. Answer (D) is incorrect. The audit committee must be directly responsible for appointing, compensating, and overseeing the work of the independent auditor.

16. Which of the following is most likely a violation of the rules of the Public Company Accounting Oversight Board (PCAOB)?

A. An issuer's independent auditor also performs consulting work for the issuer on the design and operation of its internal controls.

B. An issuer offers its common shares and preferred shares on different stock exchanges.

C. An issuer's management is not independent of its board of directors.

D. An issuer uses the same independent auditor in 2 consecutive years.

Answer (A) is correct.
REQUIRED: The action prohibited by Sarbanes-Oxley.
DISCUSSION: Among the PCAOB's rules is the prohibition of a public accounting firm from performing consulting, legal, and internal auditing services (with some exceptions) for an audit client.
Answer (B) is incorrect. The PCAOB regulates public accounting firms, not stock offerings. Answer (C) is incorrect. The PCAOB cannot dictate terms of internal corporate governance. Answer (D) is incorrect. The PCAOB's rules do not prohibit issuers from using the same independent auditor in 2 consecutive years.

17. Section 302 of the Sarbanes-Oxley Act of 2002 (SOX) requires the CEO and CFO, in every annual or quarterly filing with the SEC, to certify all of the following **except**

A. That they have taken every practical step to correct significant control deficiencies identified in the previous audit.

B. That they have evaluated the effectiveness of the system of internal control.

C. That they have taken responsibility for the system of internal control.

D. That to the best of their knowledge, the financial statements are free of material misstatements.

Answer (A) is correct.
   REQUIRED: The provision required by Sarbanes-Oxley.
   DISCUSSION: Whether the issuer has taken sufficient steps to correct significant control deficiencies is a matter of the auditor's professional judgment.

18. Under the reporting requirements of Section 404 of the Sarbanes-Oxley Act of 2002 (SOX), the CEO and CFO must include a statement in the annual report to the effect that

A. The system of internal control has been assessed by an independent public accounting firm that is registered with the PCAOB.

B. The system of internal control has been assessed by an independent public accounting firm that is not currently the subject of any PCAOB investigation.

C. The board of directors has taken responsibility for establishing and maintaining an adequate system of internal control over financial reporting.

D. The issuer has used the COSO model to design and assess the effectiveness of its system of internal control.

Answer (A) is correct.
   REQUIRED: The statement required by Sarbanes-Oxley.
   DISCUSSION: The CEO and CFO must include a statement in the annual report to the effect that the system of internal control has been assessed by an independent public accounting firm that is registered with the PCAOB.
   Answer (B) is incorrect. Section 404 of SOX does not require that the independent auditor not be under investigation by the PCAOB. Answer (C) is incorrect. Section 404 of SOX requires the CEO and CFO to state that they, not the board, have taken responsibility for internal controls. Answer (D) is incorrect. Section 404 of SOX requires that if the issuer used an internal control model, it must be named; it does not have to be the COSO model.

19. Which one of the following is a criticism that has been leveled against the Sarbanes-Oxley Act of 2002 (SOX)?

A. The requirements of Sections 302 and 404 do not provide sufficient guidance for assessing the adequacy of internal control.

B. The remote possibility of criminal prosecution is unlikely to deter an executive management group committed to producing misleading financial statements.

C. The PCAOB's staff find it too easy to bog the process down, keeping public accounting firms and issuers in limbo.

D. The Act transfers too much authority over the audit process to the judicial branch.

Answer (B) is correct.
   REQUIRED: The statement that is a criticism made about the Sarbanes-Oxley Act.
   DISCUSSION: One criticism that has been leveled against SOX is that any CEO and CFO who are engaged in a serious fraud of the scope of Enron or WorldCom are unlikely to be deterred by the remote possibility of criminal penalties from signing off on statements they know to be not fairly presented.
   Answer (A) is incorrect. SOX contains reporting requirements, not criteria for assessing internal control. Answer (C) is incorrect. The PCAOB's investigation process has been strongly criticized for excessive secrecy, which gives accounting firms an incentive to simply drag the investigation process out instead of fully cooperating. Answer (D) is incorrect. SOX does not grant extraordinary power to the judicial branch.

1.4 The COSO Model for Internal Control

20. Internal control is a process designed to provide reasonable assurance regarding the achievement of objectives related to

    A. Reliability of financial reporting.

    B. Effectiveness and efficiency of operations.

    C. Compliance with applicable laws and regulations.

    D. All of the answers are correct.

Answer (D) is correct.
    REQUIRED: The true statement regarding COSO's objectives in relation to internal control.
    DISCUSSION: The COSO model for internal control describes three areas in which control objectives should be established: the effectiveness and efficiency of operations, the reliability of financial reporting, and compliance with applicable laws and regulations.
    Answer (A) is incorrect. The effectiveness and efficiency of operations and compliance with applicable laws and regulations are also correct. Answer (B) is incorrect. The reliability of financial reporting and compliance with applicable laws and regulations are also correct. Answer (C) is incorrect. Reliability of financial reporting and effectiveness and efficiency of operations area also correct.

21. Internal control can provide only reasonable assurance that the entity's objectives and goals will be met efficiently and effectively. One factor limiting the likelihood of achieving those objectives is that

    A. The internal auditor's primary responsibility is the detection of fraud.

    B. The audit committee is active and independent.

    C. The cost of internal control should not exceed its benefits.

    D. Management monitors performance.

Answer (C) is correct.
    REQUIRED: The true statement about the limitation of internal control.
    DISCUSSION: A limiting factor is that the cost of internal control should not exceed the benefits that are expected to be derived. Thus, the potential loss associated with any exposure or risk is weighed against the cost to control it. Although the cost-benefit relationship is a primary criterion that should be considered in designing and implementing internal control, the precise measurement of costs and benefits usually is not possible.
    Answer (A) is incorrect. The internal audit activity's responsibility regarding controls is to evaluate effectiveness and efficiency and to promote continuous improvement. Answer (B) is incorrect. An effective governance function strengthens the control environment. Answer (D) is incorrect. Senior management's role is to oversee the establishment, administration, and assessment of the system of risk management and control processes. Among the responsibilities of the organization's line managers is the assessment of the control processes in their respective areas. Internal auditors provide varying degrees of assurance about the effectiveness of the risk management and control processes in select activities and functions of the organization.

22. Which of the following represents an inherent limitation of internal controls?

    A. Bank reconciliations are not performed on a timely basis.

    B. The CEO can request a check with no purchase order.

    C. Customer credit checks are not performed.

    D. Shipping documents are not matched to sales invoices.

Answer (B) is correct.
    REQUIRED: The inherent limitation of internal control.
    DISCUSSION: Inherent limitations may exist and should be considered by the auditor. Human judgment can be faulty, controls can be circumvented by collusion, and management may inappropriately override controls. Thus, the CEO requesting a check with no purchase order is an inherent limitation. It is an override of the internal control by management, which is possible under any system of internal control.
    Answer (A) is incorrect. Not performing the bank reconciliations on a timely basis relates to the structure and enforcement of the internal control. It is not an inherent limitation of internal control. Answer (C) is incorrect. If a customer credit check is not performed, it relates to a deficiency in an internal control. Its performance should be maintained under internal control. Answer (D) is incorrect. When shipping documents are used to match to sales invoices and the internal control fails, it is a deficiency in the internal control. It can be corrected, and it is not inherent to internal controls.

23. The policies and procedures helping to ensure that management directives are executed and actions are taken to address risks to achievement of objectives are best described as

    A. Risk assessments.

    B. Control environments.

    C. Control activities.

    D. Monitoring activities.

Answer (C) is correct.

    REQUIRED: The definition of control activities.

    DISCUSSION: The COSO model for internal control describes control activities as the policies and procedures helping to ensure that management directives are executed and actions are taken to address risks to achievement of objectives.

    Answer (A) is incorrect. Risk assessment identifies and analyzes external or internal risks to achievement of the objectives at the activity level as well as the entity level. Answer (B) is incorrect. The control environment reflects the attitude and actions of the board and management regarding the significance of control within the organization. Answer (D) is incorrect. Monitoring is a process that assesses the quality of the system's performance over time.

24. Which term best reflects the attitude and actions of the board and management regarding the significance of control within the organization?

    A. Risk assessment.

    B. Control activities.

    C. Control environment.

    D. Monitoring.

Answer (C) is correct.

    REQUIRED: The best term.

    DISCUSSION: According to the COSO model for internal control, the control environment reflects the attitude and actions of the board and management regarding the significance of control within the organization.

    Answer (A) is incorrect. Risk assessment identifies and analyzes external or internal risks to achievement of the objectives at the activity level as well as the entity level. Answer (B) is incorrect. Control activities are the policies and procedures helping to ensure that management directives are executed and actions are taken to address risks achievement of objectives. Answer (D) is incorrect. Monitoring is a process that assesses the quality of the system's performance over time.

25. Management's aggressive attitude toward financial reporting and its emphasis on meeting projected profit goals most likely would significantly influence an entity's control environment when

    A. The audit committee is active in overseeing the entity's financial reporting policies.

    B. External policies established by parties outside the entity affect its accounting practices.

    C. Management is dominated by one individual who is also a shareholder.

    D. Internal auditors have direct access to the board of directors and entity management.

Answer (C) is correct.

    REQUIRED: The instance in which management's attitudes would most likely affect an entity's control environment.

    DISCUSSION: Management's philosophy and operating style is one factor affecting the control environment as described in the COSO model for internal control. Such characteristics as management's attitudes and actions toward financial reporting and its emphasis on meeting budget, profit, and other goals have a significant influence on the control environment, especially when management is dominated by one or a few individuals. When incentives or pressures are present to achieve certain performance goals, the auditor should heighten his/her concern about the possibility of fraud.

    Answer (A) is incorrect. An active audit committee serves to mitigate the risks associated with certain management attitudes. Answer (B) is incorrect. External influences serve to mitigate the risks associated with certain management attitudes. Answer (D) is incorrect. An effective internal audit function serves to mitigate the risks associated with certain management attitudes.

26. Control activities constitute one of the five components of internal control described in the COSO model. Control activities do **not** encompass

    A. Performance reviews.

    B. Information processing.

    C. Physical controls.

    D. An internal auditing function.

Answer (D) is correct.

    REQUIRED: The item not belonging to the control activities component.

    DISCUSSION: The COSO model describes control activities as policies and procedures that help ensure that management directives are carried out. They are intended to ensure that necessary actions are taken to address risks to achieve the entity's objectives. Control activities have various objectives and are applied at various organizational and functional levels. However, an internal auditing function is part of the monitoring component.

    Answer (A) is incorrect. Performance reviews is a category of control activities. Answer (B) is incorrect. Information processing is a category of control activities. Answer (C) is incorrect. Physical controls is a category of control activities.

1.5 The COSO Model for Enterprise Risk Management

27. Enterprise risk management (ERM) helps management achieve all of the following **except**

- A. Reaching objectives.
- B. Reporting on a timely basis.
- C. Preventing loss of reputation and resources.
- D. Complying with laws and regulations.

Answer (B) is correct.
    REQUIRED: The item not a purpose of ERM.
    DISCUSSION: Enterprise risk management (ERM) helps management

1. Reach objectives
2. Prevent loss of reputation and resources
3. Report effectively
4. Comply with laws and regulations

ERM allows management to report effectively, not necessarily on a timely basis.
    Answer (A) is incorrect. ERM helps management reach objectives. Answer (C) is incorrect. ERM helps management prevent loss of reputation and resources. Answer (D) is incorrect. ERM helps management comply with laws and regulations.

28. Which of the following is a category of objectives of ERM?

- A. Compliance.
- B. Control expenses.
- C. Planning.
- D. Information and communication.

Answer (A) is correct.
    REQUIRED: The category of ERM objectives.
    DISCUSSION: ERM has four categories of objectives:

1. Strategic objectives align with and support the entity's mission.
2. Operations objectives address effectiveness and efficiency.
3. Reporting objectives concern reliability.
4. Compliance objectives relate to adherence to laws and regulations.

    Answer (B) is incorrect. Control of expenses is an operations objective of ERM. Answer (C) is incorrect. Planning is not a category of objectives for ERM. It is a means of achieving objectives. Answer (D) is incorrect. Information and communication is a component of ERM.

29. The components of ERM should be present and functioning effectively. What does "present and functioning effectively" mean?

I. No material weaknesses exist.
II. Risk is within the risk appetite.

- A. I only.
- B. II only.
- C. Both I and II.
- D. Neither I nor II.

Answer (C) is correct.
    REQUIRED: The definition of "present and functioning effectively."
    DISCUSSION: "Present and functioning effectively" means that (1) no material weaknesses exist, and (2) risk is within the risk appetite.

30. Inherent risk is

- A. A potential event that will adversely affect the organization.
- B. Risk response risk.
- C. The risk after management takes action to reduce the impact or likelihood of an adverse event.
- D. The risk when management has not taken action to reduce the impact or likelihood of an adverse event.

Answer (D) is correct.
    REQUIRED: The definition of inherent risk.
    DISCUSSION: Inherent risk is the risk when management has not taken action to reduce the impact or likelihood of an adverse event. Thus, it is risk in the absence of a risk response.
    Answer (A) is incorrect. A risk event is a potential event that will affect the entity adversely. Answer (B) is incorrect. A risk response is an action taken to reduce the impact or likelihood of an adverse event, including a control activity. Risk response risk is a nonsense term. Answer (C) is incorrect. The risk after management takes action to reduce the impact or likelihood of an adverse event, including control activities, in responding to a risk is residual risk.

31. Under the COSO's ERM framework, which of the following most accurately describes risk management responsibilities?

    A. In practice, management has primary responsibility.

    B. The internal audit activity has an oversight role.

    C. The board provides assurance about the effectiveness of ERM.

    D. The chief audit executive should serve as chief risk officer.

Answer (A) is correct.

    REQUIRED: The most accurate description of ERM responsibilities.

    DISCUSSION: The board has overall responsibility. However, in practice, the board delegates responsibility for ERM to senior management, which ensures that sound processes are in place and functioning.

    Answer (B) is incorrect. The internal audit activity provides objective assurance that (1) ERM processes are effective and (2) key risks are managed at an acceptable level. Answer (C) is incorrect. The board has overall responsibility. Answer (D) is incorrect. The CAE must not be the CRO because of the impairment of independence and objectivity.

32. Which of the following members of an organization has ultimate ownership responsibility of the enterprise risk management, provides leadership and direction to senior managers, and monitors the entity's overall risk activities in relation to its risk appetite?

    A. Chief risk officer.

    B. Chief executive officer.

    C. Internal auditors.

    D. Chief financial officer.

Answer (B) is correct.

    REQUIRED: The member of the organization with the stated responsibilities.

    DISCUSSION: The chief executive officer (CEO) sets the tone at the top of the organization and has ultimate responsibility for ownership of the ERM. The CEO will influence the composition and conduct of the board, provide leadership and direction to senior managers, and monitor the entity's overall risk activities in relation to its risk appetite. If any problems arise with the organization's risk appetite, the CEO will also take any measures to adjust the alignment to better suit the organization.

    Answer (A) is incorrect. The risk officer works in assigned areas of responsibility in a staff function. The work of a risk officer often extends beyond one specific area because the officer will have the necessary resources to work across many segments or divisions. Answer (C) is incorrect. The internal auditors evaluate the ERM and may provide recommendations. Answer (D) is incorrect. The CFO is subordinate to the CEO.

Use the additional questions in Gleim **CPA Test Prep Online** to create Test Sessions that emulate Prometric!

1.6 PRACTICE WRITTEN COMMUNICATION TASK

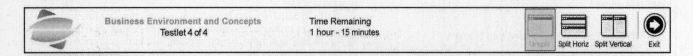

Business Environment and Concepts
Testlet 4 of 4

Time Remaining
1 hour - 15 minutes

Unsplit   Split Horiz   Split Vertical   Exit

DIRECTIONS

Note: If you believe you have encountered a software malfunction, report it to the test center staff immediately.

Navigation

To navigate from task to task, use the controls at the bottom of the screen. Click on the **Next** button to advance to the next task, or the **Previous** button to go to the previous task. To go directly to any task, click on its number.

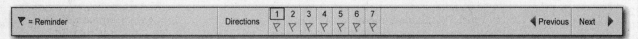

▼ = Reminder   Directions | 1 | 2 | 3 | 4 | 5 | 6 | 7 | ◀ Previous   Next ▶

If you would like a reminder to revisit a task, or want to indicate that you are finished with it, click on the reminder flag below the task number. To clear the flag, click on it again. Reminder flags are for your use only – they do not contribute to your score.

Tabs

In this part of the examination, you will be asked to complete various tasks. Every task has one or more **Work Tabs**. Every task also has a **Help** tab.

Written Communication   Help

Work tab   Help tab

Work Tabs:

- **Work Tabs** are identified with a pencil icon. This is where your responses are expected.
- Each task has one or more **Work Tabs**.
- **Work Tabs** contain directions for completing the task - be sure to read these directions carefully.
- The **Work Tab** name in the example above is for illustration only - yours will differ.
- You must complete all of the **Work Tabs** in each task to receive full credit.

Help Tab:

- The **Help Tab** provides assistance with the exam software that is used in this task. For example, if the task is to compose a memorandum, **Help** will provide information about the word processor.

The Toolbar

The toolbar at the top of the screen shows the amount of time remaining for you to complete the tasks. In addition, the following tools are available. Note that only the **Exit** button is displayed when Directions are visible - the others will appear when you begin the tasks.

Unsplit   Split Horiz   Split Vertical

Click on these buttons to split or unsplit the screen. You can split the screen vertically or horizontally.

Exit

Click on this button to go on to the next part of the examination. You must complete all of the tasks to receive full credit. Once you click on **Exit** and confirm the action, you will NOT be able to return to this testlet.

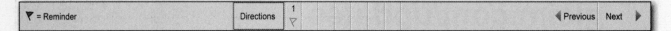

▼ = Reminder   Directions | 1 | ◀ Previous   Next ▶

Snicker Snacks, your client, is a closely held corporation that has been growing rapidly for 5 years. The shareholders, all members of the same family, expect continued profitability in the future and are eager to take the firm public. You are concerned that they are unfamiliar with certain elements of modern corporate governance that are essential for a company of increasing size and complexity.

Prepare a memo to the Board of Directors of Snicker Snacks describing the nature and purposes of an internal audit function. Be sure to define independence and objectivity as they pertain to internal audit, mention the appropriate lines of reporting, and describe the two basic types of internal audit engagements.

Type your communication below the line in the response area below.

REMINDER: Your response will be graded for both technical content and writing skills. Technical content will be evaluated for information that is helpful to the intended reader and clearly relevant to the issue. Writing skills will be evaluated for development, organization, and the appropriate expression of ideas in professional correspondence. Use a standard business memorandum or letter format with a clear beginning, middle, and end. Do not convey information in the form of a table, bullet point list, or other abbreviated presentation.

To: Board of Directors, Snicker Snacks
Re: Aspects of an internal audit function

Unofficial Answer

Written Communication

> To: Board of Directors, Snicker Snacks
> Re: Aspect of an internal audit function
>
> ---
>
> An internal audit function is a crucial governance structure for any complex modern entity.
>
> The company should designate a chief audit executive (CAE) in a senior position responsible for effectively managing the internal audit activity in accordance with the internal audit charter and the requirements of The Institute of Internal Auditors (The IIA). The IIA defines internal auditing as "an independent, objective assurance and consulting activity designed to add value and improve an organization's operations." Internal audit should be specifically charged with evaluating and improving the effectiveness of the entity's risk management, control, and governance processes.
>
> According to The IIA, independence is an organizational attribute. An internal audit function is independent if it reports to a level of the organization that can ensure that it receives the resources it needs to carry out the appropriate activities and that the concerns raised in its reports are properly addressed. In general, the internal audit function should report functionally to the board and administratively to the CEO. Objectivity is a personal attribute. Individual internal auditors must have an unbiased mental attitude. They must (1) believe in their work product, (2) not make quality compromises, and (3) not subordinate their judgment on audit matters to others.
>
> Internal audit performs assurance and consulting services. Assurance services are an objective examination of evidence for the purpose of providing an independent assessment of governance, risk management, and control processes for the organization. Examples may include financial, performance, compliance, system security, and due diligence engagements. Consulting services are advisory and related client service activities, the nature and scope of which are agreed with the client. They are intended to add value and improve an organization's governance, risk management, and control processes without the internal auditor's assumption of management responsibility.

The above depicts a Level 5 answer. See page 16 in the Introduction for a description of the three grading criteria.

Self-Grade

Evaluate each of the following by selecting a 0, 1, 2, 3, 4, or 5. An average response is 3. Use 4 for better than average and 5 for outstanding. Use 2 for less than average and 1 for quite poor. Use zero for no response, if you did not address the topic, or if you gave advice that is clearly illegal.

	0	1	2	3	4	5
Organization	o 0	o 1	o 2	o 3	o 4	o 5
Development	o 0	o 1	o 2	o 3	o 4	o 5
Expression	o 0	o 1	o 2	o 3	o 4	o 5

Your grade for the written communication as a whole is the average of the scores for the three criteria.

Use **CPA Gleim Online** and **Simulation Wizard** to practice more written communication tasks in a realistic environment.

STUDY UNIT TWO
MICROECONOMICS

(26 pages of outline)

Microeconomics is the study of economic activity at the "atomic" level, that is, the actions of individual actors in the marketplace. Covered in this study unit are the external factors affecting the firm (Subunits 1, 2, and 3), internal decision making about the costs of inputs and the prices charged for outputs (Subunits 4 and 5), the cost and profit implications of a firm's competitive environment (Subunits 6, 7, 8, and 9), and the markets where firms must shop for inputs (Subunit 10).

2.1 DEMAND, SUPPLY, AND EQUILIBRIUM

1. **Demand -- the Buyer's Side of the Market**

   a. Demand vs. Quantity Demanded

      1) Demand is a schedule of the amounts of a good or service that consumers are willing and able to purchase at various prices during a period of time. Quantity demanded is the amount that will be purchased at a specific price during a period of time.

Demand Schedule

Price per Unit	Quantity Demanded
$10	0
$9	1
$8	2
$7	3
$6	4
$5	5
$4	6
$3	7
$2	8
$1	9
$0	10

      2) A demand schedule can be graphically depicted as a relationship between the prices of a commodity (on the vertical axis) and the quantity demanded at the various prices (horizontal axis), holding other determinants of demand constant.

b. **The Law of Demand**

1) If all other factors are held constant (ceteris paribus), the price of a product and the quantity demanded are inversely (negatively) related; i.e., the higher the price, the lower the quantity demanded; the lower the price, the higher the quantity demanded.

Movement Along a Demand Curve

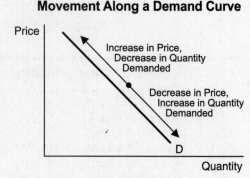

Figure 2-1

a) In other words, a change in price leads to a change in quantity demanded, depicted as movement along a demand curve.

c. Factors Other than Price

1) A change in any of the factors other than price, referred to as the determinants of demand, results in a change in demand, depicted as a shift of the entire demand curve.

Change in Demand

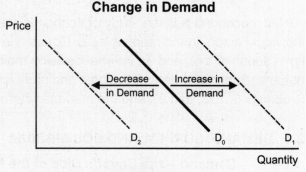

Figure 2-2

2) The determinants of demand are

a) Consumer incomes

i) Most goods are **normal goods**, that is, commodities for which demand is positively (directly) related to income, e.g., steak, new clothes, and airline travel. However, a few goods are **inferior goods**, that is, commodities for which demand is negatively (inversely) related to income, e.g., potatoes, used clothing, and bus transportation.

b) Consumer taste and preference

c) Prices of related goods

i) If a price increase in A results in an increase in demand for B, then A and B are said to be **substitutes**. For example, when beef prices rise, the demand for chicken increases.

ii) If a price increase in A results in a decrease in demand for B, then A and B are said to be **complements**. For example, if the price of bread increases, the demand for jelly decreases.

d) Consumer expectations

e) Number of consumers

i) An increase in the number of consumers shifts the demand curve to the right (increase in demand).

ii) A decrease in the number of consumers shifts the demand curve to the left (decrease in demand).

2. **Supply -- the Seller's Side of the Market**

    a.   Supply vs. Quantity Supplied

        1)   Supply is a schedule of the amounts of a good that producers are willing and able to offer to the market at various prices during a specified period of time. Quantity supplied is the amount that will be offered at a specific price during a period of time.

        2)   A supply schedule can be graphically depicted as a relationship between the prices of a commodity (on the vertical axis) and the quantity offered at the various prices (horizontal axis), holding other determinants of supply constant.

    b.   **The Law of Supply**

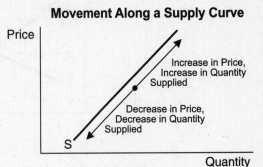

Movement Along a Supply Curve

Figure 2-3

        1)   If all other factors are held constant (ceteris paribus), the price of a product and the quantity supplied are directly (positively) related; i.e., the higher the price, the greater the quantity supplied; the lower the price, the lower the quantity supplied.

    c.   Factors Other than Price

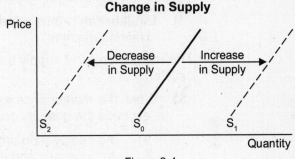

Change in Supply

Figure 2-4

        1)   A change in any of the factors other than price, referred to as the determinants of supply, results in a change in supply, depicted as a shift of the entire supply curve.

        2)   The determinants of supply are

           a)   Costs of inputs

              i)   An increase in the costs of inputs, such as employees' wages and raw material, will shift the supply curve to the left, from S_0 to S_2 (decrease in supply).

              ii)   A decrease in the costs of inputs will shift the supply curve to the right, from S_0 to S_1 (increase in supply).

           b)   A change in efficiency of the production process, e.g., newer technology

              i)   A newer technology that improves the production process will shift the supply curve to the right, from S_0 to S_1 (increase in supply).

           c)   Expectations about price changes

              i)   If firms expect that a product's price will decrease, they will increase their supply before the decrease in prices. The supply curve will shift to the right, from S_0 to S_1.

           d)   Taxes and subsidies

              i)   An increase in taxes or a decrease in subsidies will shift the supply curve to the left, from S_0 to S_2 (decrease in supply).

              ii)   A decrease in taxes or an increase in subsidies will shift the supply curve to the right, from S_0 to S_1 (increase in supply).

3.   **Market Equilibrium**

a.   Market demand is the sum of the individual demand curves of all buyers in the market. Market supply is the sum of the individual supply curves of all sellers in the market.

1)   Market equilibrium is the combination of price and quantity at which the market demand and market supply curves intersect.

Market Equilibrium

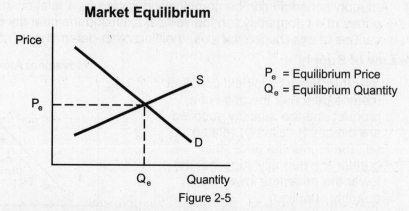

P_e = Equilibrium Price
Q_e = Equilibrium Quantity

Figure 2-5

b.   At the point of intersection of the supply and demand curves, anyone wishing to purchase economic goods at the market price can do so, and anyone offering the goods can sell everything they bring to market.

1)   **Equilibrium** is thus referred to as the market-clearing price and the market-clearing quantity.

c.   The market forces of supply and demand create an automatic, efficient rationing system.

1)   When the market price exceeds the equilibrium price, the quantity supplied exceeds the quantity demanded by consumers, and a surplus results.

a)   The competition among sellers to eliminate their excess inventories leads to price cuts and lower production.

b)   As the price falls, more buyers enter the market. Eventually, the price settles at the equilibrium price, and the surplus is eliminated.

2)   When the market price is lower than the equilibrium price, the quantity demanded by consumers is greater than the quantity supplied, and a shortage results.

a)   Consumers compete for scarce goods by bidding up prices.

b)   As the price rises, new suppliers enter the market. Eventually, the price settles at the equilibrium price, and the shortage is eliminated.

d.   The effects on equilibrium of shifts in the supply and demand schedules are shown below:

	Demand increase	Demand constant	Demand decrease
Supply increase	P_e unknown Q_e up	P_e down Q_e up	P_e down Q_e unknown
Supply constant	P_e up Q_e up	– –	P_e down Q_e down
Supply decrease	P_e up Q_e unknown	P_e up Q_e down	P_e unknown Q_e down

Stop and review! You have completed the outline for this subunit. Study multiple-choice questions 1 through 5 beginning on page 89.

2.2 ELASTICITY

1. **Elasticity of Demand**

   a. Price elasticity of demand (E_d) measures the sensitivity of the quantity demanded of a product to a change in its price.

   $$E_d = \frac{Percentage\ change\ in\ quantity\ demanded}{Percentage\ change\ in\ price} = \frac{\%\Delta Q}{\%\Delta P}$$

   b. Elasticity describes the reaction of demand to a change in price from one level to another. The two common methods to calculate the price elasticity of demand are the point method and the midpoint method.

   1) The **point method** measures the price elasticity of demand for a specific change in the product's price.

   $$\%\Delta Q = \frac{Quantity\ demanded\ \textbf{after}\ the\ change - Quantity\ demanded\ \textbf{before}\ the\ change}{Quantity\ demanded\ \textbf{before}\ the\ change}$$

   $$\%\Delta P = \frac{Price\ \textbf{after}\ the\ change - Price\ \textbf{before}\ the\ change}{Price\ \textbf{before}\ the\ change}$$

   2) The **midpoint method**, also called the arc method, measures the price elasticity of demand of a range for a specific change in the product's price. This method uses averages of the quantities and prices to measure elasticity. The following is the algebraically simplified version of the formula:

   $$E_d = \frac{\%\Delta Q}{\%\Delta P} = \frac{(Q_1 - Q_2) \div (Q_1 + Q_2)}{(P_1 - P_2) \div (P_1 + P_2)}$$

   a) Absolute value is used when calculating the coefficient of elasticity.

EXAMPLE

Roxy's Ice Cream Shoppe sells 100 quarts of chocolate a day at $6 each. If it lowers the price to $3 per quart, it will sell 300 quarts a day.

Point Method

$$\%\Delta Q = \frac{300 - 100}{100} = 2 = 200\%$$

$$\%\Delta P = \frac{3 - 6}{6} = 0.5 = 50\%$$

$$E_d = \frac{\%\Delta Q}{\%\Delta P} = \frac{200\%}{50\%} = 4$$

The elasticity absolute value of 4 indicates that the specific change of the product's price by 50% (from $6 to $3) will increase the demand for the product by 200% (from Q = 100 to Q = 300).

Midpoint (Arc) Method

	Num.	Denom.		Num.	Denom.		Num.	Denom.		Elasticity
$E_d =$	$\dfrac{(100 - 300)}{(100 + 300)}$	$\div \dfrac{(\$6 - \$3)}{(\$6 + \$3)}$	$=$	$\dfrac{200}{400}$	$\div \dfrac{\$3}{\$9}$	$=$	0.500	$\div$ 0.333	$=$	**1.50**

The elasticity absolute value of 1.5 indicates that the range on the demand curve between P = 6 and P = 3 is relatively elastic.

3) When the demand elasticity coefficient is

a) **Greater than one**, demand is in a **relatively elastic** range. The percentage change in the quantity demanded is higher than the percentage change in the price.

$$\%\Delta Q \ > \ \%\Delta P$$

i) For example, a 10% decline in the price of ice cream results in a 20% increase in ice cream demanded.

b) **Equal to one**, demand has **unitary elasticity** (usually a very limited range). The percentage change in the quantity demanded is equal to the percentage change in the price.

$$\%\Delta Q \ = \ \%\Delta P$$

c) **Less than one**, demand is in a **relatively inelastic** range. The percentage change in the quantity demanded is lower than the percentage change in the price.

$$\%\Delta Q \ < \ \%\Delta P$$

i) For example, a 20% decline in the price of ice cream results in a 10% increase in ice cream demanded.

d) **Infinite**, demand is **perfectly elastic** (depicted as a horizontal line).

i) In pure competition, the number of firms is so great that one firm cannot influence the market price. The demand curve faced by a single seller in such a market is perfectly elastic (although the demand curve for the market as a whole has the normal downward slope).

EXAMPLE

Consumers will buy a farmer's total output of soybeans at the market price but will buy none at a slightly higher price. Moreover, the farmer cannot sell below the market price without incurring losses.

---

e) **Equal to zero**, demand is **perfectly inelastic** (depicted as a vertical line).

i) Some consumers' need for a certain product is so high that they will pay whatever price the market sets. The number of these consumers is limited, and the amount they desire is relatively fixed.

EXAMPLE

Addiction to illegal drugs tends to result in demand that is unresponsive to price changes. In this example, existing buyers (addicts) will not be driven out of the market by a rise in price, and no new buyers will be induced to enter the market by a reduction in price.

---

4) The price elasticity of demand of a product can be affected by the availability of substitute products in the market.

a) As more substitute products become available, the demand for the products becomes more elastic. A small increase in the product's price will cause a proportionally larger decrease in the quantity demanded, since the customers can easily find substitute products.

b) As fewer substitute products become available in the market, the demand for the products becomes more inelastic.

5) Price elasticity of demand is useful for a firm wondering how a change in the price of a product will affect total revenue from that product.

Effect on Total Revenue

	Elastic Range	Unitary Elasticity	Inelastic Range
Price increase	Decrease	No change	Increase
Price decrease	Increase	No change	Decrease

2. **Elasticity of Supply**

   a. Price elasticity of supply (E_s) measures the sensitivity of the quantity supplied of a product to a change in its price.

   $$E_s = \frac{Percentage\ change\ in\ quantity\ supplied}{Percentage\ change\ in\ price}$$

   1) The same formulas used in the calculation of price elasticity of demand (see item 1. in Subunit 2.2 for an explanation of these formulas) are used to calculate the price elasticity of supply.

   2) When the supply elasticity coefficient is

      a) **Greater than one**, supply is in a **relatively elastic** range. The percentage change in the quantity supplied is higher than the percentage change in the price.

      $$\%\Delta Q > \%\Delta P$$

      b) **Equal to one**, supply has **unitary elasticity** (usually a very limited range). The percentage change in the quantity supplied is equal to the percentage change in the price.

      $$\%\Delta Q = \%\Delta P$$

      c) **Less than one**, supply is in a **relatively inelastic** range. The percentage change in the quantity supplied is lower than the percentage change in the price.

      $$\%\Delta Q < \%\Delta P$$

      d) **Infinite**, supply is **perfectly elastic** (depicted as a horizontal line).

      e) **Equal to zero**, supply is **perfectly inelastic** (depicted as a vertical line).

         i) A perfectly inelastic supply curve indicates that, in the very short run, a seller cannot change the quantity supplied.

EXAMPLE

A farmer offering a perishable good with no means of storage must sell the entire crop regardless of the price buyers offer. The farmer cannot offer a larger quantity because the harvest has ended for the season.

Stop and review! You have completed the outline for this subunit. Study multiple-choice questions 6 through 8 beginning on page 90.

2.3 GOVERNMENT INTERVENTION IN THE MARKET

1. **Price Controls**

    a. Price controls are attempts by government to remedy perceived unfairness in the marketplace. They are often ineffective.

2. **Price Ceilings**

    a. In an effort to keep essential goods and services affordable to all, sellers are sometimes prohibited from charging the equilibrium price for certain products.

    b. Shortages arise because the market is simply unwilling to supply all that is demanded at the (government-mandated) artificially low price.

    1) The situation can be depicted graphically as follows:

Price Ceiling and Resulting Shortage

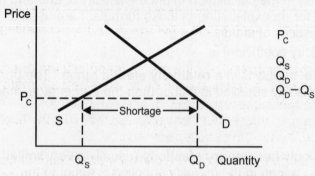

P_C = Artificial ceiling set by government (price not allowed to rise above this ceiling)
Q_S = Quantity supplied at P_C
Q_D = Quantity demanded at P_C
$Q_D - Q_S$ = Amount of shortage

Figure 2-7

    c. Rent controls and usury laws are examples.

3. **Price Floors**

    a. In an effort to compensate certain suppliers perceived to be wrongly treated by market forces, buyers are sometimes required to pay above the equilibrium price for certain products.

    b. Surpluses arise because producers are encouraged by the (government-mandated) artificially high price to generate more than the market is willing to absorb.

    1) The situation can be depicted graphically as follows:

Price Floor and Resulting Surplus

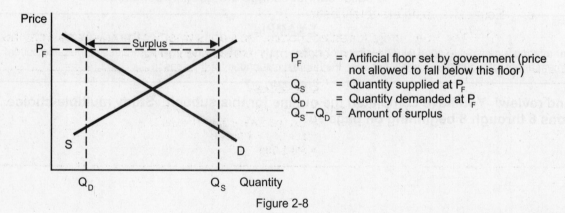

P_F = Artificial floor set by government (price not allowed to fall below this floor)
Q_S = Quantity supplied at P_F
Q_D = Quantity demanded at P_F
$Q_S - Q_D$ = Amount of surplus

Figure 2-8

    c. Price supports for agricultural products and minimum wage legislation are examples.

Stop and review! You have completed the outline for this subunit. Study multiple-choice questions 9 and 10 beginning on page 91.

2.4 PROFITS AND COSTS

1. **Explicit vs. Implicit Costs**

    a. **Explicit costs** are those requiring actual cash disbursements. For this reason, they are sometimes called out-of-pocket or outlay costs.

        1) Explicit costs are **accounting costs**; that is, they are recognized in a concern's formal accounting records.

EXAMPLE

An entrepreneur opening a gift shop has to make certain cash disbursements to get the business up and running.

Inventory	$59,000
Rent	4,000
Utilities	1,000
Total explicit costs	**$64,000**

---

    b. **Implicit costs** are those costs not recognized in a concern's formal accounting records.

        1) Implicit costs are **opportunity costs**, i.e., the maximum benefit forgone by using a scarce resource for a given purpose instead of the next-best alternative.

        2) To measure the true economic success or failure of the venture, the entrepreneur in the example above must tally up more than just the explicit costs that can easily be found in the accounting records.

            a) The entrepreneur's opportunity costs are often important implicit costs. (S)he could have simply gone to work for another company rather than open the gift shop.

            b) The money put into startup costs could have been invested in financial instruments.

            c) A normal profit is a crucial implicit cost.

EXAMPLE

The normal profit is the income that the entrepreneur could have earned applying his/her skill to another venture.

Salary forgone	$35,000
Investment income forgone	3,600
Total implicit costs	**$38,600**

---

    c. Economic costs are total costs.

        1) The true hurdle for an economic decision is whether the revenues from the venture will cover all costs, both explicit and implicit.

EXAMPLE

Economic costs = Total costs
= Explicit costs + Implicit costs
= $64,000 + $38,600
= **$102,600**

---

2.   **Accounting vs. Economic Profit**

    a.   **Accounting profits** are earned when the (book) income of an organization exceeds the (book) expenses.

EXAMPLE

After the first year of operation, the gift shop owner made a tidy accounting profit.

Sales revenue	$100,000
Explicit costs	(64,000)
Accounting profit	**$ 36,000**

    b.   **Economic profits** are a significantly higher hurdle. They are not earned until the organization's income exceeds not only costs as recorded in the accounting records, but the firm's implicit costs as well. Economic profit is also called pure profit.

EXAMPLE

Once total costs are considered, a different picture emerges.

Accounting profit	$ 36,000
Implicit costs	(38,600)
Economic loss	**$ (2,600)**

3.   **Short- vs. Long-Run Costs**

    a.   The **short run** is a time period so brief that a firm cannot vary its fixed costs.

    b.   The **long run** is a time period long enough that all inputs, including those incurred through fixed costs, can be varied.

        1)   Investment in new, more productive equipment results in higher total fixed costs but may result in lower total and per-unit variable costs.

Stop and review! You have completed the outline for this subunit. Study multiple-choice questions 11 through 14 beginning on page 92.

2.5 MARGINAL ANALYSIS

1.   **Marginal Analysis**

    a.   Marginal analysis allows economic decisions to be made based on projecting the results of varying the levels of resource consumption and output production.

        1)   **Total product** is the entire production of a good or service for a given period of time.

        2)   **Marginal product** is the additional output obtained by adding one extra unit of input. It is computed by dividing the change in total output at a given level of input by the change in inputs.

    b.   As inputs are added to a process, each additional unit of input leads to increased production. However, past the point of diminishing marginal returns, the increase is smaller with each unit. The "bang for the buck" steadily diminishes. That is, the benefit of adding input units decreases.

        1)   This principle is the **law of diminishing returns**.

        2)   Eventually, so many inputs are entering the process that efficiency is compromised, and total output actually begins to decrease. This is the point of negative marginal returns. This phenomenon is depicted by the old saying, "Too many cooks spoil the broth."

EXAMPLE

The table below reflects the changes in total product and marginal product as additional units of input are added to the production process.

Units of Input	Total Product	Marginal Product
1	2	2
2	6	4
3	12	6
4	20	8
5	29	9
6	39	10
7	48	9
8	56	8
9	62	6
10	66	4
11	68	2
12	66	−2

At the sixth unit of input, marginal product peaks and then begins to decrease. This is the point of diminishing marginal returns. When the twelfth unit is added, the production process is receiving so much input that the efficiency of the process is actually decreased and total output begins to fall.

c.   These relationships can be depicted graphically as follows:

Marginal Returns

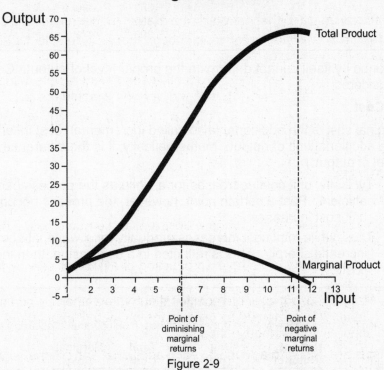

Figure 2-9

2.   **Marginal Revenue**

    a.   Marginal revenue is the additional (also called incremental) revenue produced by generating one additional unit of output. Mathematically, it is the difference in total revenue at each level of output.

        1)   If the product is being sold in a competitive market (i.e., the seller does not have monopoly power), the seller typically must cut its price to sell additional units.

        2)   Thus, while total revenue keeps increasing with the sale of additional units, it increases by ever smaller amounts. This is reflected in a constantly decreasing marginal revenue.

EXAMPLE

A company has the following revenue data for one of its products:

Units of Output		Unit Price		Total Revenue	Marginal Revenue
1	×	$580	=	$ 580	$580
2	×	575	=	1,150	570
3	×	570	=	1,710	560
4	×	565	=	2,260	550
5	×	560	=	2,800	540
6	×	555	=	3,330	530
7	×	550	=	3,850	520
8	×	545	=	4,360	510
9	×	540	=	4,860	500
10	×	535	=	5,350	490
11	×	530	=	5,830	480
12	×	525	=	6,300	470

    b.   Revenue by itself cannot determine the proper level of output. Cost data must also be considered.

3.   **Marginal Cost**

    a.   Marginal cost is the additional (also called incremental) cost incurred by generating one additional unit of output. Mathematically, it is the difference in total cost at each level of output.

        1)   Typically, unit cost decreases for a while as the process becomes more efficient. Past a certain point, however, the process becomes less efficient and unit cost increases.

        2)   Thus, while total cost increases gradually for a while, at some point it begins to increase sharply. This is reflected in a decreasing, then increasing, of marginal cost.

EXAMPLE

A company has the following cost data for the product (for simplicity, each unit of output requires exactly one unit of input):

Units of Output		Unit Cost		Total Cost	Marginal Cost
1	×	$570.00	=	$ 570	$570
2	×	405.00	=	810	240
3	×	340.00	=	1,020	210
4	×	305.00	=	1,220	200
5	×	287.00	=	1,435	215
6	×	279.17	=	1,675	240
7	×	279.29	=	1,955	280
8	×	284.38	=	2,275	320
9	×	295.00	=	2,655	380
10	×	309.50	=	3,095	440
11	×	326.82	=	3,595	500
12	×	347.08	=	4,165	570

4. **Profit Maximization**

    a.   The firm's goal is to maximize profits, not revenues. Thus, marginal revenue data must be compared with marginal cost data to determine the point of profit maximization.

        1)   This occurs where **marginal revenue equals marginal cost**. Beyond this point, increasing production results in a level of costs so high that total profit is diminished.

EXAMPLE

Comparing its marginal revenue and marginal cost data allows the company to determine the point of profit maximization.

Units of Output	Marginal Revenue		Marginal Cost		Marginal Profit	Total Revenue		Total Cost		Total Profit
1	$580	–	$570	=	$ 10	$ 580	–	$ 570	=	$ 10
2	570	–	240	=	330	1,150	–	810	=	340
3	560	–	210	=	350	1,710	–	1,020	=	690
4	550	–	200	=	350	2,260	–	1,220	=	1,040
5	540	–	215	=	325	2,800	–	1,435	=	1,365
6	530	–	240	=	290	3,330	–	1,675	=	1,655
7	520	–	280	=	240	3,850	–	1,955	=	1,895
8	510	–	320	=	190	4,360	–	2,275	=	2,085
9	500	–	380	=	120	4,860	–	2,655	=	2,205
10	**490**	**–**	**440**	**=**	**50**	**5,350**	**–**	**3,095**	**=**	**2,255**
11	480	–	500	=	(20)	5,830	–	3,595	=	2,235
12	470	–	570	=	(100)	6,300	–	4,165	=	2,135

Beyond the output level of 10 units, marginal profit turns negative. Note that this is, by definition, the point of highest total profit.

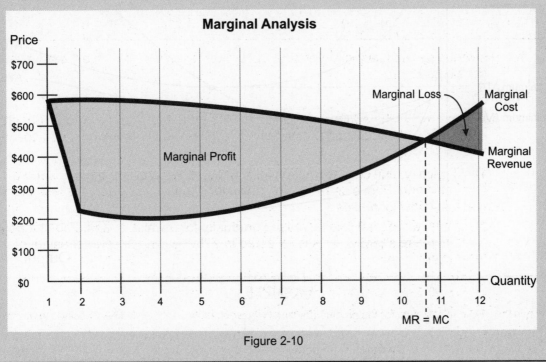

Figure 2-10

---

    b.   Profit is maximized at the output level where marginal revenue equals marginal cost. This is a crucial principle for marginal analysis.

5.   **The Relationship between Marginal Cost (MC) and Average Total Cost (ATC)**

    a.   Total costs of the production (TC) consist of total fixed costs (FC) and total variable costs (VC).

$$TC = FC + VC$$

    b.   Average total cost (ATC = TC ÷ Q) equals the sum of average fixed costs (AFC = FC ÷ Q) and average variable costs (AVC = VC ÷ Q).

    c.   Increase in fixed costs will result in

        1)   An increase in FC and AFC
        2)   An increase in TC and ATC
        3)   No effect on VC or AVC

    d.   The marginal cost curve (MC) will always intersect with the ATC curve and the AVC curve at their minimum points.

Cost Relationships in the Short Run

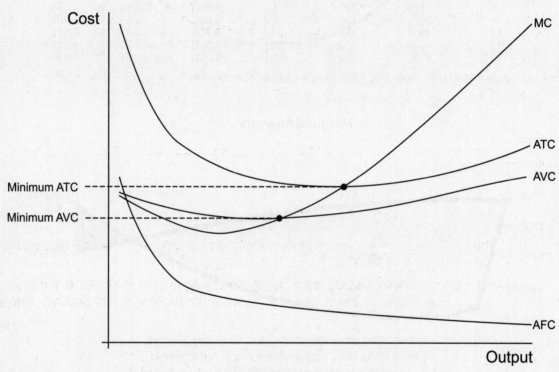

Figure 2-11

6.   **Long-Run Cost Relationships**

   a.   The shape and position of a firm's short-run average total cost (SRATC) curve is determined by the productivity of its current manufacturing plant.

      1)   There are as many SRATC curves as there are possible plant setups. A firm's long-run average total cost (LRATC) curve is therefore extrapolated from all its possible SRATC curves. It represents the lowest average total cost for any level of output that can be produced and is depicted as follows:

Long-Run ATC Curve

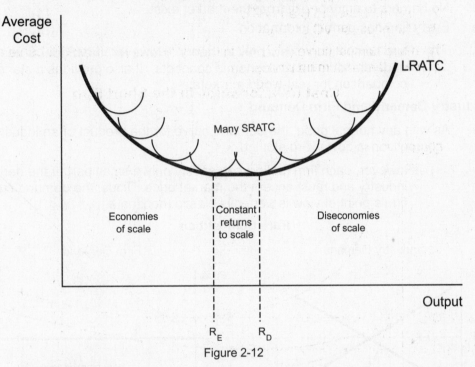

Figure 2-12

   b.   The LRATC curve derives its shape from the phenomenon of economies and diseconomies of scale.

      1)   **Economies of scale**, also called increasing returns to scale. Initially, as production increases, average costs of production tend to decline. Some of the reasons are

         a)   Increased specialization and division of labor
         b)   Better use and specialization of management
         c)   Use of more efficient machinery and equipment

      2)   **Constant returns to scale.** With some plant sizes, an increase in the level of production results in no change in average costs.

      3)   **Diseconomies of scale**, also called decreasing returns to scale. Eventually, as most firms continue to expand output, the marginal cost of production tends to increase.

         a)   The most frequent reason given for diseconomies of scale is the difficulty of managing a large-scale entity.

Stop and review! You have completed the outline for this subunit. Study multiple-choice questions 15 through 18 beginning on page 93.

2.6 MARKET STRUCTURES -- PURE COMPETITION

1. **Defining Characteristics**

    a. A very large number of buyers and sellers act independently. Examples are the stock market and agricultural markets.

    b. The product is homogeneous or standardized. Thus, the product of one firm is a perfect substitute for that of any other firm. The only basis for competition is price.

    c. Each firm produces an immaterial amount of the industry's total output and thus cannot influence the market price.

    d. No barriers to entry or exit from the market exist.

    e. Every firm has perfect information.

    1) Pure competition exists only in theory. However, the model is useful for understanding basic economic concepts. It also provides a standard of comparison for real-world markets.

2. **Industry Demand and Firm Demand**

    a. As with any normal good, the demand curve for the product of an industry in perfect competition is downward sloping.

    1) However, each firm (seller) can satisfy only a small part of the demand facing the industry and must accept the market price. Thus, the demand curve from the firm's point of view is perfectly elastic (horizontal).

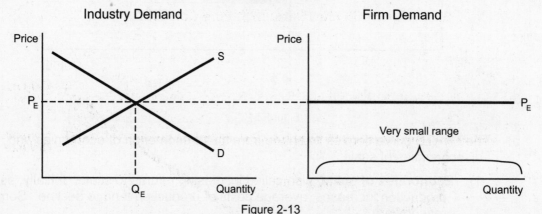

Pure Competition

Figure 2-13

2) The tiny segment of the industry's demand curve occupied by each individual firm is necessarily at the point of market equilibrium.

3) Firms in perfect competition are therefore called price takers because they must sell at the market price.

EXAMPLE

The firm's perfectly elastic demand curve means that marginal revenue, average revenue, and market price are all equal.

Units of Output		Unit Price (Average Revenue)		Total Revenue	Marginal Revenue
1	×	$960	=	$ 960	$960
2	×	960	=	1,920	960
3	×	960	=	2,880	960
4	×	960	=	3,840	960
5	×	960	=	4,800	960
6	×	960	=	5,760	960
7	×	960	=	6,720	960
8	×	960	=	7,680	960

3. **Short-Run Profit Maximization in Pure Competition**

   a. In the short run, a firm should produce (continue to operate) when it can earn a profit or incur a loss smaller than fixed costs.

       1) In the short run, operating at a loss may be preferable to shutting down. This option is indicated when revenues cover all variable costs and some fixed costs (costs incurred even if the firm shuts down).

   b. For all market structures, a firm that does not shut down should produce the level of output at which marginal revenue equals marginal cost **(MR = MC)**.

EXAMPLE

As long as the next unit of output adds more in revenue (MR) than in cost (MC), the firm will increase total profit or decrease total losses. For a purely competitive firm, price = MC is the same as MR = MC. This is noted as 7 units of output in the table below.

Units of Output	Revenue		Cost		Profit	
	Total	**Marginal**	**Total**	**Marginal**	**Total**	**Marginal**
1	$ 960	$960	$1,800	$1,800	$(840)	$(840)
2	1,920	960	2,500	700	(580)	260
3	2,880	960	3,100	600	(220)	360
4	3,840	960	3,600	500	240	460
5	4,800	960	4,200	600	600	360
6	5,760	960	4,980	780	780	180
7	**6,720**	**960**	**5,940**	**960**	**780**	**0**
8	7,680	960	7,060	1,120	620	(160)

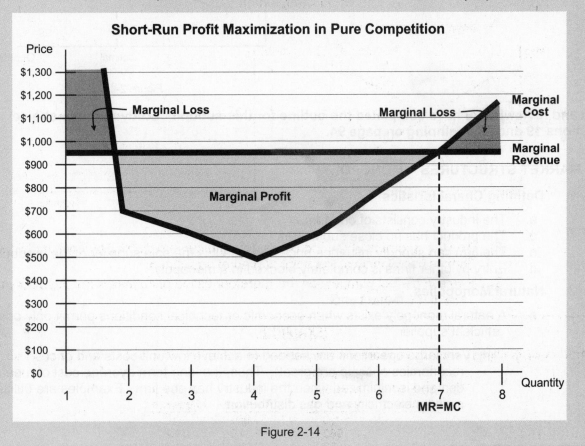

Figure 2-14

4. **Long-Run Equilibrium in Pure Competition**

    a.   Because firms are earning a normal profit, the industry is attractive to new entrants.

        1)   The entry of these new competitors pushes the supply curve to the right. This is because consumers will not absorb the industry's additional output unless price is cut.

        2)   The lower price results in losses for firms with high-cost structures, driving them out of the market. The exit of these firms shifts the supply curve back to the left.

        3)   The amount of output generated by the industry returns to the previous level, and the price can rise again. Equilibrium is restored.

    b.   The surviving firms are those that have achieved the lowest average total cost. Price and quantity settle, as always, at the point where marginal revenue equals marginal cost.

        1)   These relationships are depicted graphically to the right:

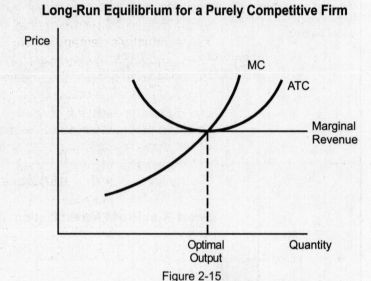

Long-Run Equilibrium for a Purely Competitive Firm

Figure 2-15

Stop and review! You have completed the outline for this subunit. Study multiple-choice questions 19 and 20 beginning on page 94.

2.7 MARKET STRUCTURES -- MONOPOLY

1. **Defining Characteristics**

    a.   The industry consists of one firm.
    b.   The product has no close substitutes.
    c.   The firm can strongly influence price because it is the sole supplier of the product.
    d.   Entry by other firms is completely blocked in a monopoly.

2. **Natural Monopolies**

    a.   A natural monopoly exists when economic or technical conditions permit only one efficient supplier.

        1)   Very large operations are needed to achieve low unit costs and prices (economies of scale are great). Thus, the long-term average cost of meeting demand is minimized when the industry has one firm. Examples are utilities, such as electricity and gas distribution.

3. **Monopoly Pricing Power**

   a. Economists use two terms to describe a monopolist's pricing behavior:

      1) A **price maker** sets prices as high as it likes because it is not limited by competition.

      2) A **price searcher** does not set prices arbitrarily high but seeks the price that maximizes its profits (explained in item 5. below).

4. **Industry Demand is Firm Demand**

   a. The demand curve facing a monopolist is downward sloping because, as with any normal good, the monopolistic firm can sell more product only by lowering price.

      1) However, unlike a competitive firm, which faces only a very small portion of the whole industry's demand curve, the monopolistic firm's demand curve is the entire industry's demand curve.

      2) When a monopolist decreases price to sell more units, the price cut affects all the units sold, not just the additional unit(s). Thus, a monopolist's marginal revenue curve lies below the demand curve.

      3) A monopolist's marginal revenue continuously decreases as it raises output. Past the point where marginal revenue equals $0, the monopolist's total revenue decreases.

EXAMPLE

Units of Output		Unit Price (Average Revenue)		Total Revenue	Marginal Revenue
1	×	$960	=	$ 960	$960
2	×	910	=	1,820	860
3	×	860	=	2,580	760
4	×	810	=	3,240	660
5	×	760	=	3,800	560
6	×	710	=	4,260	460
7	×	660	=	4,620	360
8	×	610	=	4,880	260

5. **Profit Maximization for a Monopolist**

   a. As discussed in Subunit 2.6, the competitive firm must accept the market price and adjust its output to cover its average total costs.

      1) Thus, the competitive firm earns no long-term economic profits.

   b. However, the monopolist has the power to set output at the level at which profits are maximized; that is, **MR = MC**.

      1) The corresponding price is found with reference to the (downward-sloping) demand curve.

         a) Monopoly does **not** result in the highest possible price, and the monopolist does not produce at the lowest average total cost.

EXAMPLE

Price Searching for a Monopolist

Units of Output	Selling Price per Unit	Revenue		Cost		Profit	
		Total	Marginal	Total	Marginal	Total	Marginal
1	$960	$ 960	$960	$ 800	$800	$ 160	$ 160
2	910	1,820	860	1,480	680	340	180
3	860	2,580	760	1,980	500	600	260
4	810	3,240	660	2,320	340	920	320
5	**760**	**3,800**	**560**	**2,800**	**480**	**1,000**	**80**
6	710	4,260	460	3,480	680	780	(220)
7	660	4,620	360	4,420	940	200	(580)
8	610	4,880	260	5,720	1,300	(840)	(1,040)

The monopolist will produce 5 units and sell them at $760 each.

6.   **Economic Consequences of Monopoly**

   a.   Given sufficiently low costs and adequate demand, a monopolist earns an economic profit in the long run. In the graph below, D is the industry demand curve, and MC is the industry supply curve. (The monopolist is the industry.)

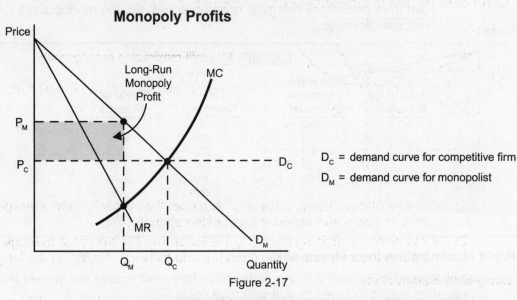

Monopoly Profits

D_C = demand curve for competitive firm

D_M = demand curve for monopolist

Figure 2-17

   b.   In a purely competitive industry, the market price and quantity are P_C and Q_C.

   1)   However, a monopolist restricts output to the profit-maximizing MR = MC level (Q_M). The resulting price is therefore P_M. MR for the monopolist is less than price, and the MR curve is below the demand curve.

   a)   Accordingly, consumers have fewer goods ($Q_M < Q_C$) and pay higher prices ($P_M > P_C$) than under pure competition.

   c.   Allocation of resources is not efficient because fewer resources are used in the production process than is justified by society's interests.

Stop and review! You have completed the outline for this subunit. Study multiple-choice questions 21 and 22 on page 95.

2.8 MARKET STRUCTURES -- MONOPOLISTIC COMPETITION

1. **Defining Characteristics**

   a.   The industry has a large number of firms. The number is fewer than in pure competition, but it is great enough that firms cannot act together to restrict output and fix the price.

   b.   Products are differentiated. In pure competition, products are standardized, so price is the only basis for competition. In monopolistic competition, products can be differentiated on a basis other than price, such as quality, brands, and styles. Thus, advertising may be crucial.

   c.   Few barriers to entry and exit exist. Because firms tend not to be large, great economies of scale do not exist. The cost of product differentiation is the most significant barrier to entry.

2. **Short-Run Profit Maximization**

   a.   As always, the profit-maximizing quantity is found where marginal revenue equals marginal cost. The price is the point on the demand curve corresponding to this quantity.

   Short-Run Profits in Monopolistic Competition

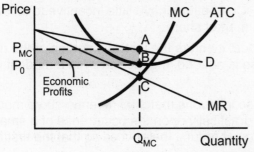

   A = profit-maximizing price/quantity
   B = lowest point on ATC
   C = profit-maximizing quantity (MR = MC)

   Figure 2-18

   1)   If the profit-maximizing price (P_{MC}) is higher than the minimum average total cost, the firm earns an economic profit in the short run.

   2)   If the profit-maximizing price (P_{MC}) is lower than the minimum average total cost, the firm incurs a loss in the short run and exits the industry in the long run.

3. **Long-Run Equilibrium**

   a.   In the long run, the economic profit of all firms is an economic profit of $0 because firms will enter a profitable industry and exit an unprofitable one.

   1)   In a profitable monopolistically competitive industry, the possibility of earning economic profits attracts new entrants to the market.

   2)   The presence of new firms requires all firms to further differentiate their products. This in turn increases the average total costs.

   3)   Higher costs eliminate the economic profits that attracted the new entrants. The firms least able to absorb the higher costs leave the market.

   4)   The remaining firms now have higher costs and steady demand. The economic profits generated earlier are replaced with normal profits.

Stop and review! You have completed the outline for this subunit. Study multiple-choice questions 23 and 24 on page 96.

2.9 MARKET STRUCTURES -- OLIGOPOLY

1. **Defining Characteristics**

    a. The industry has few large firms. Firms operating in an oligopoly are mutually aware and mutually interdependent. Their decisions as to price, advertising, etc., are to a very large extent dependent on the actions of the other firms.

    b. Products can be differentiated (e.g., autos) or standardized (e.g., steel).

    c. Each firm sets price and production level after considering its mutual interdependence with the other firms in the industry.

    d. Entry is difficult because of barriers that can be natural, e.g., an absolute cost advantage, or created, e.g., ongoing advertising or ownership of patents.

2. **Industry Demand**

    a. The price rigidity normally found in oligopolistic markets can be explained in part by the **kinked demand curve** theory. The essence of the theory is that firms will follow along with a price decrease by a competitor but not a price increase.

        1) If price and quantity for the industry are at P and Q, a firm that raises its price will move into the elastic portion of the demand curve.

            a) A small increase in price in this portion of the curve leads to a large decline in quantity demanded. Competitors have little incentive to follow, so the price-raising firm loses market share.

        2) However, if the firm cuts its price, it enters the inelastic portion of the demand curve. A large price decrease is needed to generate even a modest increase in sales.

            a) More importantly, the discontinuous marginal revenue curve means that marginal revenue falls drastically upon the occurrence of a small price cut. Competitors also must reduce their prices so that the first firm gains no market share.

        3) Price and quantity therefore tend to remain at point A on the demand curve.

Kinked Demand for an Oligopoly

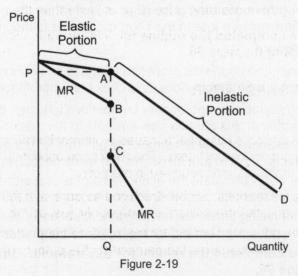

Figure 2-19

    b. To avoid the hazards of the kinked demand curve, price leadership is typical in oligopolistic industries.

        1) Price changes are announced first by a major firm in the industry. Once the industry leader has acted, other firms match its price.

3. **Cartels**

   a. A cartel arises when a group of oligopolistic firms agree to set prices. This practice is illegal except in international markets.

      1) The economic effects are similar to those of a monopoly. Each firm restricts output, charges a higher price, and earns the maximum profit.

      2) Thus, each firm in effect becomes a monopolist, but only because it is colluding with other members of the cartel.

   b. Cohesion within is maintained only if the members maintain their agreed-upon prices and production quotas.

      1) A cartel fails if one member attempts either to increase profits by producing more or to increase market share by cutting prices.

Background

Two real-world examples:

The DeBeers diamond cartel probably has been the most successful example of this market structure in history. Although DeBeers itself does not have a monopoly over the mining of diamonds, it held a monopoly over their distribution for many decades. Anytime a country tried to distribute diamonds outside the cartel's channel, such as Zaire's attempt in the early 1980s, DeBeers could simply flood the market with inventory. The result was the lowering of prices to a ruinous level, driving the would-be independent back into the cartel.

The Organization of Petroleum Exporting Countries (OPEC) for many years held sway over the world's oil markets. The group demonstrated its power to devastating effect in 1973-74 following the "October War" in the Middle East. By reducing the supply of oil available, the resulting rise in prices made record profits for the member nations and almost brought the U.S. economy to its knees. In response, the U.S. and other Western countries were able to reduce their demand for oil by implementing economy measures, such as buying more fuel-efficient vehicles (demonstrating the principle that demand becomes more elastic over time). In addition, the Alaska and North Sea oil fields came online during the 1980s, increasing the petroleum supply from sources not under OPEC control. The cohesion of the OPEC member nations reached a low point during the 1990 invasion of Kuwait by Iraq, but it still remains a potent force in international petroleum markets.

---

4. **Boycotts**

   a. A boycott is a concerted effort to avoid doing business with a particular supplier, forcing a leftward shift in the demand curve faced by that supplier.

      1) Usually, the motivation is moral or ethical rather than purely economic.

Stop and review! You have completed the outline for this subunit. Study multiple-choice questions 25 and 26 beginning on page 96.

2.10 RESOURCE MARKETS AND LABOR

1. **Resource Planning**

   a. Resource planning is essential because profit maximization requires production of the optimal output at the least cost. The resources used in the production process (e.g., labor, raw materials) are acquired in markets.

      1) Resource markets can be structured as pure competition, monopoly, monopolistic competition, and oligopoly, just as the markets for final products.

   b. Derived demand is the demand for the inputs to the production process (sometimes called factors) derived from the demand for the outputs of the process (i.e., final goods).

2.   **Factors Affecting Demand for Resources**

a.   Demand for the final product that the resource produces. Such a change results in a new product price and therefore affects demand.

b.   Productivity of the resource. As the productivity of an input increases, demand for it will increase. This change may occur because

1)   The proportions of the combination of the resource with other resources shift.
2)   Technical improvements are made in those combining resources.
3)   Technical improvements are made in the resource itself.

c.   Prices of other resources.

1)   If the price of a resource that can substitute for another resource falls, the demand for the second resources falls. This is referred to as the substitution effect.

a)   For example, as the price of pens decreases, pens are substituted for pencils, and the demand curve for pencils will shift to the left.

2)   If two resources are complements, a fall in the price of one will lead to an increase in the demand for the other.

a)   For example, as the price of computers decreases, the demand curve for computer technicians will shift to the right.

3.   **Elasticity of Resource Demand**

a.   The elasticity of resource demand concerns movements along, not the shift of, a demand curve. The elasticity of demand for a resource is directly related to the

1)   Elasticity of demand for the final product. Thus, if the demand for chocolate becomes more elastic, the demand for cocoa beans will become more elastic.

2)   Availability of substitutes. For example, as more synthetic chocolates become available, the demand for real chocolate becomes more elastic.

3)   Proportion of total production cost represented by the resource. For example, if sugar is a large proportion of the total production cost of chocolate, an increase in the price of sugar leads to a significant spike in the manufacturer's total cost, and the firm's demand for sugar will become more elastic.

4.   **Wage Determination**

a.   A wage is the amount paid to the factor of production (labor) that includes the efforts of blue-collar and white-collar workers, professionals, and small business owners. The term "wage" customarily relates to amounts paid per unit of time.

b.   **Nominal wages** are the amounts paid (and received), and **real wages** represent the actual purchasing power (goods and services) of nominal wages.

c.   The level of real wages is determined by the productivity (real output ÷ hours worked) of labor.

1)   As productivity increases, the demand for labor also increases. Given a certain supply, greater demand will result in a higher average real wage.

5. **Labor Supply and Demand in a Competitive Market**

   a.   Many firms are competing for a large number of equally skilled workers who provide their services independently, so neither firms nor workers can affect the market rate for labor. Thus, both firms and workers are necessarily price takers.

   b.   Market demand for labor is the total of the individual firms' demand curves, i.e., their marginal revenue product (MRP) curves.

   c.   The market supply curve has a positive slope because, given little unemployment, firms must raise wages to hire additional workers.

      1)   The upward slope reflects the need of firms to match the opportunity costs of workers, such as wages paid in employment alternatives or greater leisure.

   d.   The wage rate and the level of employment in the market are determined by the intersection of the market labor demand curve and the market labor supply curve, i.e., labor market equilibrium.

   e.   Each individual firm must accept the market wage rate as determined by the point of labor market equilibrium. Thus, the supply curve for labor facing a single firm is perfectly elastic, and marginal resource cost (MRC) is therefore the same for all amounts of labor hired.

Supply and Demand for Labor in a Purely Competitive Resource Market

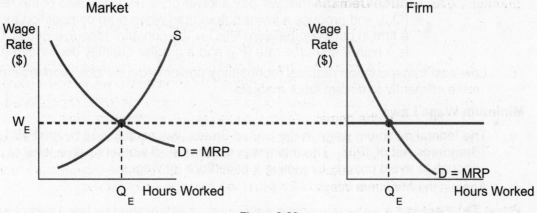

Figure 2-20

6. **Labor Supply and Demand in a Monopsony**

   a.   In some labor markets, workers only have the option of a single employer, as in the case of a company town.

      1)   A market such as this, in which all sellers must sell to a single buyer, is called a **monopsony**.

   b.   For a monopsonist, the marginal resource cost exceeds the current rate for the resource.

      1)   The reason is that, given an upward-sloping supply curve, additional units of the resource can be obtained only by paying a higher rate for all resource units (labor hours).

         a)   In contrast, a firm in perfect competition pays a constant amount per unit because its consumption is not great enough to influence the rate.

      2)   For example, if the first worker may be hired at a rate of $10 but the second must be paid $11, the marginal resource cost (MRC) is $12 ($11 + $1 increase for the first worker), given the need to pay both the same amount to avoid worker dissatisfaction.

3)   To maximize its profits, a buyer of resources in a monopsony uses resources until marginal revenue product equals marginal resource cost.

**Supply and Demand for Labor in
a Monopoly Resource Market**

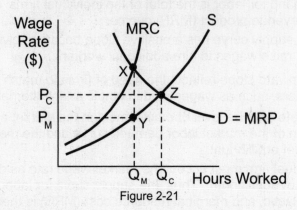

Figure 2-21

4)   The intersection of the upward-sloping MRC curve and the downward-sloping MRP curve (X) determines the equilibrium quantity. The price is determined by reference to the supply curve (Y).

   a)   Thus, a monopsonist will pay a lower price (P_M), buy less of the resource (Q_M), and produce a lower output than when pure competition exists. [For a firm in pure competition, MRC is the constant resource price. The result is a higher resource rate (P_C) and a greater quantity demanded (Q_C).]

c.   Low-cost transportation reduces monopsony power because local workers can travel more efficiently to distant labor markets.

7.   **Minimum Wage Laws**

   a.   The federal minimum wage in the United States was established by the Fair Labor Standards Act of 1938. The intent was to provide all workers with a level of pay high enough to avoid poverty by setting a price floor for wages.

   b.   Against the Minimum Wage

   1)   Because a wage rate above equilibrium is established by law, unemployment is increased. It would be far better for people with marginal skills to have work at some level of pay than to be idle.

   2)   The higher labor cost may drive some firms out of business.

   c.   For the Minimum Wage

   1)   Because many labor markets are monopsonies, minimum wage laws raise pay without increasing unemployment.

   2)   The minimum wage may improve productivity.

   a)   Because firms cannot pay a substandard wage no matter how menial the task, employers may be encouraged to move workers into productive activities.

   b)   A minimum wage may reduce employee turnover, allowing the retention of experienced workers.

Stop and review! You have completed the outline for this subunit. Study multiple-choice questions 27 and 28 on page 97.

QUESTIONS

2.1 Demand, Supply, and Equilibrium

1. Below are the grocers' demand schedules for Palm Valley Grapes. Assuming that John, Towny, and Dorothea are the only three customers of Palm Valley Grapes, which of the following sets of prices and output levels will be on the market demand curve?

Price of Grapes	John Q	Towny Q	Dorothea Q
$6	0	1	0
5	1	2	0
4	2	4	0
3	3	6	1
2	4	8	2
1	5	9	3

A. ($6, 2); ($1, 17)

B. ($5, 3); ($1, 17)

C. ($4, 4); ($2, 12)

D. ($4, 0); ($1, 9)

Answer (B) is correct.
    REQUIRED: The points that will appear on the demand curve for the product.
    DISCUSSION: This type of problem is solved by means of trial and error. Check each of the answer alternatives to determine whether both points represent a level of demand for a given price. Answer (B) is correct because total demand would be 3 at a price of $5, and total demand would be 17 (5 + 9 + 3) at a price of $1.
    Answer (A) is incorrect. Demand would be 1 when the price is $6. Answer (C) is incorrect. Demand would be 6, not 4, when the price is $4, and demand would be 14, not 12, when the price is $2. Answer (D) is incorrect. Demand would be 6 when the price is $4 and 17 when the price is $1.

2. If the average household income increases and there is relatively little change in the price of a normal good, then the

A. Supply curve will shift to the left.

B. Quantity demanded will move farther down the demand curve.

C. Demand will shift to the left.

D. Demand curve will shift to the right.

Answer (D) is correct.
    REQUIRED: The result of an increase in income given little change in the price of a normal good.
    DISCUSSION: The demand schedule is a relationship between the prices of a product and the quantity demanded at each price, holding other determinants of the quantity demanded constant. A movement along an existing demand curve occurs when the price is changed. A shift in the curve itself occurs when any of the determinants changes. Such shifts can be caused by a change in the tastes and preferences of consumers toward a product, for example, as a result of a successful advertising campaign, an increase in consumer income (if a product is a normal good), or changes in the prices of substitute or complementary products. An increase in consumer income would shift the demand curve to the right and result in greater consumption of the product at each price.
    Answer (A) is incorrect. The increase in income shifts the demand, not the supply, curve. Answer (B) is incorrect. Moving down an existing demand curve is the effect of a lower price. The change in income shifts the economy to a new demand curve. Answer (C) is incorrect. A shift to the left means that consumers will buy fewer products at each price. This leftward shift in response to increased income is characteristic of an inferior good, not a normal good. The demand for inferior goods is inversely related to income. Hamburger is an inferior good, and steak is a normal good.

3. A decrease in the price of a complementary good will

A. Shift the demand curve of the other commodity to the left.

B. Increase the price paid for a substitute good.

C. Shift the supply curve of the other commodity to the left.

D. Shift the demand curve of the other commodity to the right.

Answer (D) is correct.
    REQUIRED: The effect of a decrease in the price of a complementary good.
    DISCUSSION: A decrease in the price of a good (e.g., gasoline) will cause the demand curve of a complementary good (e.g., automobiles) to shift to the right (increase). The lower price of the first good results in greater demand for the complementary good at each price level.
    Answer (A) is incorrect. A shift to the left (a decrease in demand) would occur if the price of a complementary product increased. Answer (B) is incorrect. Demand for a substitute would decrease, thereby lowering its equilibrium price. Answer (C) is incorrect. The demand curve will shift to the right, but the supply curve will not change.

4. The demand curve for a normal good is

   A. Upward sloping because firms produce more at higher prices.

   B. Upward sloping because higher-priced goods are of higher quality.

   C. Vertical.

   D. Downward sloping because of the income and substitution effects of price changes.

Answer (D) is correct.
   REQUIRED: The true statement about the demand curve for a normal good.
   DISCUSSION: The demand curve for a normal good is downward sloping to the right. At high prices, the amount demanded is relatively low. As prices decrease, the amount demanded increases. The substitution effect is the change in the cost of a good relative to others that will cause a cheaper good to be substituted for more expensive ones. The income effect is the change in purchasing power experienced by consumers as a result of a price change (real income increases or decreases). Both of these effects cause the price of a product and the quantity demanded to be inversely related.
   Answer (A) is incorrect. An upward-sloping demand curve suggests that consumers purchase more of a product if its price is raised. Answer (B) is incorrect. An upward-sloping demand curve suggests that consumers purchase more of a product if its price is raised. Answer (C) is incorrect. A vertical demand curve signifies that the quantity demanded does not change with price.

5. The situation depicted in the graph below could be caused by

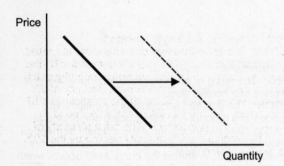

   A. A price cut by all producers.

   B. A price hike by all producers.

   C. A rise in the country's population.

   D. An improvement in manufacturers' productivity.

Answer (C) is correct.
   REQUIRED: The possible cause of a rightward demand curve shift.
   DISCUSSION: A downward-sloping curve relating price to quantity depicts the demand schedule for a normal good. When a country's population grows, producers can sell more of their products at every price level. This is depicted as a rightward shift in the demand curve.
   Answer (A) is incorrect. A price cut by all producers would be depicted as a downward movement along a fixed curve. Answer (B) is incorrect. A price hike by all producers would be depicted as an upward movement along a fixed curve. Answer (D) is incorrect. An improvement in manufacturers' productivity would be depicted by a shift in the (upward-sloping) supply curve, not the (downward-sloping) demand curve.

2.2 Elasticity

6. If the coefficient of elasticity is zero, then the consumer demand for the product is said to be

   A. Perfectly inelastic.

   B. Perfectly elastic.

   C. Unit inelastic.

   D. Unit elastic.

Answer (A) is correct.
   REQUIRED: The applicable term when the coefficient of elasticity is zero.
   DISCUSSION: When the coefficient of elasticity (percentage change in quantity ÷ percentage change in price) is less than one, demand is inelastic. When the coefficient is zero, demand is perfectly inelastic.
   Answer (B) is incorrect. Demand is perfectly elastic when the coefficient is infinite. Answer (C) is incorrect. Unitary inelasticity is a meaningless term. Answer (D) is incorrect. Unitary elasticity exists when the coefficient is exactly one.

7. As the price for a particular product changes, the quantity of the product demanded changes according to the following schedule.

Total Quantity Demanded	Price per Unit
100	$50
150	45
200	40
225	35
230	30
232	25

Using the arc method, the price elasticity of demand for this product when the price decreases from $50 to $45 is

A. 0.20

B. 10.00

C. 0.10

D. 3.80

Answer (D) is correct.
REQUIRED: The price elasticity of demand using the arc method.
DISCUSSION: A product's price elasticity of demand is measured as the percentage change in quantity demanded divided by the percentage change in price. When price falls from $50 to $45, the coefficient is 3.8, calculated as follows:

$$E_d = [(150 - 100) \div (150 + 100)] \div [(\$50 - \$45) \div (\$50 + \$45)]$$
$$= (50 \div 250) \div (\$5 \div \$95)$$
$$= 20.0\% \div 5.26\%$$
$$= 3.8$$

Answer (A) is incorrect. This figure equals the 10% decline in price divided by the 50% change in quantity demanded. Answer (B) is incorrect. This figure assumes a 5% change in price. It also does not calculate the change over the sum of the endpoints of the range. Answer (C) is incorrect. This figure is the percentage change in price.

8. Last week, the quantity of apples demanded fell by 6%. If this was a result of a 10% price increase, what is the price elasticity of demand for apples?

A. 1.67

B. 1.06

C. 0.16

D. 0.60

Answer (D) is correct.
REQUIRED: The price elasticity of demand.
DISCUSSION: The price elasticity of demand is calculated by dividing the percentage change in quantity demanded by the percentage change in price. Thus, the change in quantity of 6% divided by the 10% price increase produces an elasticity of 0.6.

Answer (A) is incorrect. The inverse of the elasticity is 1.67. Answer (B) is incorrect. Adding the 6% quantity decline to 1 results in 1.06. Answer (C) is incorrect. The price elasticity of demand is found by dividing the 6% quantity decline by the 10% price increase, not by adding them.

2.3 Government Intervention in the Market

9. A government price support program will

A. Lead to surpluses.

B. Lead to shortages.

C. Improve the rationing function of prices.

D. Encourage firms to leave the industry.

Answer (A) is correct.
REQUIRED: The effect of a government price support program.
DISCUSSION: A government price support program, which sets a price higher than the market price, will cause producers to supply more goods than can be absorbed by the market. The effect will be surpluses because the amount supplied will exceed the amount demanded. In these cases, the government must buy up the surplus and either destroy it or seek other distribution channels; either is a highly inefficient outcome.

Answer (B) is incorrect. No shortages will occur. Suppliers will be induced by the higher-than-equilibrium price to produce more than the amount demanded. Answer (C) is incorrect. No rationing would occur. Consumers will be able to buy all they desire because supply will exceed demand. Answer (D) is incorrect. Firms will be encouraged to enter the industry by the availability of greater revenue than that provided by consumer demand. In fact, price support programs are often designed with the intention of keeping marginal firms from leaving the industry.

10. A city ordinance that freezes rent prices may cause

    A. The demand curve for rental space to fall.

    B. The supply curve for rental space to rise.

    C. Demand for rental space to exceed supply.

    D. Supply of rental space to exceed demand.

Answer (C) is correct.
    REQUIRED: The effect of freezing rent prices.
    DISCUSSION: Because property owners will not be able to charge a market-driven price, investors will be less likely to invest in housing. In addition, the appeal to renters of frozen rent prices will cause a rise in the quantity of rental units demanded. However, a frozen price will keep the actual quantity supplied lower than demanded. Hence, the result will be a shortage.
    Answer (A) is incorrect. Price changes affect quantity demanded but do not alter the demand curve itself. Answer (B) is incorrect. Investment in housing is less likely due to lower returns, causing quantity supplied to decline. Answer (D) is incorrect. Demand is more likely to increase.

2.4 Profits and Costs

11. The measurement of the benefit lost by using resources for a given purpose is

    A. Economic efficiency.

    B. Opportunity cost.

    C. Comparative advantage.

    D. Absolute advantage.

Answer (B) is correct.
    REQUIRED: The measurement of the benefit lost by using resources for a given purpose.
    DISCUSSION: Opportunity cost is the benefit forgone by using scarce resources in a given way. Thus, it is the benefit that could have been obtained from the best alternative use of the resources.
    Answer (A) is incorrect. Economic efficiency is a comparison measured in dollar terms. Answer (C) is incorrect. Comparative advantage compares the costs of producing products within a single country. Answer (D) is incorrect. Absolute advantage compares input costs among countries.

12. A normal profit is

    A. The same as an economic profit.

    B. The same as the accountant's bottom line.

    C. An explicit or out-of-pocket cost.

    D. A cost of resources from an economic perspective.

Answer (D) is correct.
    REQUIRED: The true statement about normal profit.
    DISCUSSION: Normal profit is the level of profit necessary to induce entrepreneurs to enter and remain in the market. Economists view this profit as an implicit cost of economic activity.
    Answer (A) is incorrect. Economic (pure) profit is the residual return in excess of normal profit. Economic profit equals total revenue minus opportunity costs. These are the sum of explicit and implicit costs, including normal profit. Answer (B) is incorrect. Accounting profit is the excess of total revenue over explicit costs (out-of-pocket payments to outsiders). Answer (C) is incorrect. A normal profit is an implicit cost.

13. A corporation's net income as presented on its income statement is usually

    A. More than its economic profits because opportunity costs are not considered in calculating net income.

    B. More than its economic profits because economists do not consider interest payments to be costs.

    C. Equal to its economic profits.

    D. Less than its economic profits because accountants include labor costs, while economists exclude labor costs.

Answer (A) is correct.
    REQUIRED: The true statement about a corporation's net income.
    DISCUSSION: Economic (pure) profit equals total revenue minus economic costs. Economic costs are defined by economists as total costs, which are the sum of outlay costs, and opportunity costs, which are the values of productive resources in their best alternative uses. The return sufficient to induce the entrepreneur to remain in business (normal profit) is an implicit (opportunity) cost. Net income as computed under generally accepted accounting principles considers only explicit costs, not such implicit costs as normal profit and the opportunity costs associated with not using assets for alternative purposes. Thus, net income will be higher than economic profit because the former fails to include a deduction for opportunity costs, for example, the salary forgone by an entrepreneur who chooses to be self-employed.
    Answer (B) is incorrect. Both economists and accountants treat interest as a cost. Answer (C) is incorrect. Economic profits will be less than net income. Answer (D) is incorrect. Economic profits will be less than net income.

14. In the economic theory of production and cost, the short run is defined to be a production process

    A. That spans a time period of less than one year in length.

    B. In which there is insufficient time to vary the amount of all inputs.

    C. That is subject to economies of scale.

    D. That always produces economic profits.

Answer (B) is correct.
    REQUIRED: The short run in the economic theory of production and cost.
    DISCUSSION: The short run is defined as a period so brief that a firm has insufficient time to vary the amount of all inputs. Thus, the quantity of one or more inputs is fixed. The long run is a period long enough that all inputs, including plant capacity, can be varied.
    Answer (A) is incorrect. The short run can be more or less than a year depending upon a firm's ability to change its inputs. Answer (C) is incorrect. Economies of scale are associated with the long run. Answer (D) is incorrect. Economic profits may be earned, either in the long or short run, when a firm earns more than the profits needed for it to remain in operation.

2.5 Marginal Analysis

15. When long-run average cost is declining over a range of increasing output, the firm is experiencing

    A. Increasing fixed costs.

    B. Technological efficiency.

    C. Decreasing returns.

    D. Economies of scale.

Answer (D) is correct.
    REQUIRED: The condition experienced when long-run average cost declines over a range of increasing output.
    DISCUSSION: When long-run average cost declines as output increases, the firm is experiencing economies of scale. Average cost falls when marginal cost is below it and rises when marginal cost is above it. Average cost reaches its minimum when it equals marginal cost. Some of the reasons for this phenomenon are increased specialization and division of labor, better use and specialization of management, and use of more efficient machinery and equipment.
    Answer (A) is incorrect. An increase in fixed costs could cause average costs to increase. Also, by definition, all long-run costs are variable. Answer (B) is incorrect. Technological efficiency refers to the ratio of physical output of a given technology and the maximum output that is possible. An increase in technological efficiency is only one of the ways that economies of scale can occur. Answer (C) is incorrect. A decline in average cost means the firm is experiencing increasing returns, not decreasing returns.

16. The change in total product resulting from the use of one unit more of the variable factor is known as

    A. The point of diminishing average productivity.

    B. Marginal product.

    C. Marginal cost.

    D. The point of diminishing marginal productivity.

Answer (B) is correct.
    REQUIRED: The term for the change in total product resulting from the use of one additional unit of the variable factor of production.
    DISCUSSION: Marginal product is the output obtained by adding one extra unit of a variable input factor. If the cost of the input factor is constant, a rising marginal product will result in a declining marginal cost of output. If marginal product is falling, marginal cost is rising. Hence, marginal cost is at a minimum when marginal product is at a maximum.
    Answer (A) is incorrect. The point of diminishing average productivity is the point at which average productivity begins to decline as additional units of input are used. Answer (C) is incorrect. Marginal cost is the addition to total cost as a result of increasing production by one unit. Answer (D) is incorrect. The point of diminishing marginal productivity is that point at which marginal productivity begins to decline as additional inputs are added to production.

Question 17 is based on the following information. A company produced the following data (rounded) on its product:

Number of Units Produced	Unit Cost			Marginal Cost	Marginal Revenue
	Fixed	Variable	Total		
1	$100	$85	$185	$ 85	$90
2	50	70	120	55	90
3	33	65	98	55	90
4	25	67	92	73	90
5	20	75	95	107	90

17. How many units should be produced?

A. Two.

B. Three.

C. Four.

D. Five.

Answer (C) is correct.
  REQUIRED: The number of units to be produced given marginal cost and marginal revenue.
  DISCUSSION: Marginal revenue exceeds marginal cost for the fourth but not the fifth unit. Production should continue until marginal cost equals marginal revenue at the minimum average total cost (ATC) point. Accordingly, four units should be produced.
  Answer (A) is incorrect. The highest level of production where marginal revenue exceeds marginal costs is not two units of production. Production should continue up to and until marginal revenue equals marginal cost. Answer (B) is incorrect. A total of four units could be produced and still increase the company's profits. Answer (D) is incorrect. At five units of production, the marginal cost ($107) exceeds the marginal revenue ($90) so the company would lose income by producing this unit.

18. Because of economies of scale, as output from production expands,

A. The short-run average cost of production decreases.

B. The long-run average cost of production increases.

C. The long-run total cost decreases.

D. The slope of the demand curve increases.

Answer (A) is correct.
  REQUIRED: The effect of economies of scale.
  DISCUSSION: When a firm experiences economies of scale, the average unit cost of production decreases as production increases. This phenomenon is attributable to spreading fixed costs over a greater number of units of output. Both the short-run and long-run average costs are lower because of economies of scale.
  Answer (B) is incorrect. Long-run unit production costs decline with economies of scale. Answer (C) is incorrect. Total costs increase with increased production; only the average cost per unit declines. Answer (D) is incorrect. Changes in the supply curve do not affect the demand curve.

2.6 Market Structures -- Pure Competition

19. Which one of the following is **not** a key assumption of perfect competition?

A. Firms sell a homogeneous product.

B. Customers are indifferent about which firm they buy from.

C. The level of a firm's output is small relative to the industry's total output.

D. Each firm can price its product above the industry price.

Answer (D) is correct.
  REQUIRED: The assumption not made about perfect competition.
  DISCUSSION: Perfect competition is characterized by a market structure with many buyers and sellers acting independently, a homogeneous or standardized product, free entry into and exit from the market, perfect information, no control over the industry price, and the absence of nonprice competition. Moreover, customers are indifferent about which firm they buy from because price is the only difference between one seller and the next.
  Answer (A) is incorrect. A homogeneous product is a key assumption of perfect competition. Answer (B) is incorrect. Customer indifference regarding choice of seller is a key assumption of perfect competition. Answer (C) is incorrect. Small firm output relative to the industry is a key assumption of perfect competition.

20. All of the following are true about perfect competition **except** that

    A. There is free market entry without large capital costs for entry.

    B. There are many firms participating in the market.

    C. In the long run, an increase in profit will have no effect on the number of firms in the market.

    D. Firms are price takers.

Answer (C) is correct.
    REQUIRED: The false statement about perfect competition.
    DISCUSSION: Perfect competition assumes a large number of buyers and sellers that act independently, a homogeneous or standardized product, free entry into and exit from the market, perfect information, no nonprice competition, no control over prices (sellers are price takers rather than price setters), and an equilibrium price equal to the average total cost. Given free entry into the market and perfect information, an increase in profits in the industry will attract new firms. This will have the long-run effect of reducing the price to the level at which no economic profits are earned.
    Answer (A) is incorrect. An absence of barriers to entry is a characteristic of pure competition. Answer (B) is incorrect. A large number of firms is a characteristic of pure competition. Answer (D) is incorrect. Firms in pure competition must accept the market price.

2.7 Market Structures -- Monopoly

21. Any business firm that has the ability to control the price of the product it sells

    A. Faces a downward-sloping demand curve.

    B. Has a supply curve that is horizontal.

    C. Has a demand curve that is horizontal.

    D. Will sell all output produced.

Answer (A) is correct.
    REQUIRED: The true statement about a business firm with the ability to control the price of its product.
    DISCUSSION: A firm that can control the price of its product is a monopolist. In a monopoly, the industry demand curve is also the firm's demand curve. The demand curve is downward-sloping since the lower the price, the higher the demand for a product.
    Answer (B) is incorrect. A horizontal supply curve implies that the company will produce any quantity of output at the constant price. The ability to control one's price implies a changing price level. Answer (C) is incorrect. A horizontal demand curve implies an unchanging price. Answer (D) is incorrect. The firm will not be able to sell all of its output if it sets the price higher than what consumers were willing to pay. Also, a monopolist's incentive is not to sell the maximum that can be produced, but to sell the amount that maximizes profits.

22. A characteristic of a monopoly is that

    A. A monopoly will produce when marginal revenue is equal to marginal cost.

    B. There is a unique relationship between the market price and the quantity supplied.

    C. In optimizing profits, a monopoly will increase its supply curve to where the demand curve becomes inelastic.

    D. There are multiple prices for the product to the consumer.

Answer (A) is correct.
    REQUIRED: The characteristic of a monopoly.
    DISCUSSION: A monopoly consists of a single firm with a unique product. Such a firm has significant price control. For profit maximization, it increases production until its marginal revenue equals its marginal cost. In a monopoly, price will be higher and output lower than in perfect competition.
    Answer (B) is incorrect. The monopolist is in control of the quantity supplied. Thus, the supply can be limited to produce the profit-maximizing price. Answer (C) is incorrect. To optimize profits, a monopoly will produce at the point when its marginal revenue equals its marginal cost. Answer (D) is incorrect. There is only one price when a monopoly exists.

2.8 Market Structures -- Monopolistic Competition

23. All of the following are characteristics of monopolistic competition **except** that

    A. The firms sell a homogeneous product.

    B. The firms tend not to recognize the reaction of competitors when determining prices.

    C. Individual firms have some control over the price of the product.

    D. The consumer demand curve is highly elastic.

Answer (A) is correct.
    REQUIRED: The item not a characteristic of monopolistic competition.
    DISCUSSION: Monopolistic competition assumes a large number of firms with differentiated (heterogeneous) products and relatively easy entry into the market. Sellers have some price control because of product differentiation. Monopolistic competition is characterized by nonprice competition, such as advertising, service after the sale, and emphasis on trademark quality. In the short run, firms equate marginal revenue and marginal cost. In the long run, firms tend to earn normal (not economic) profits, and price exceeds marginal cost, resulting in an underallocation of resources. Firms produce less than the ideal output, and the industry is populated by too many firms that are too small in size. Price is higher and output less than in pure competition.
    Answer (B) is incorrect. Responses to competitors' actions are unnecessary if products are sufficiently differentiated to make price competition meaningless. Answer (C) is incorrect. Product differentiation permits some price control. Answer (D) is incorrect. The availability of close substitutes makes the product demand curve elastic.

24. Entry into monopolistic competition is

    A. Blocked.

    B. Difficult, with significant obstacles.

    C. Rare, as significant capital is required.

    D. Relatively easy, with only a few obstacles.

Answer (D) is correct.
    REQUIRED: The true statement about entry into monopolistic competition.
    DISCUSSION: Monopolistic competition is characterized by the existence of a large number of firms, differentiated products, relative ease of entry, some control of price by the firms, and significant nonprice competition (e.g., by advertising). Entry into monopolistic competition is more difficult than entry into pure competition, but it is relatively easy compared with entry into a monopoly.
    Answer (A) is incorrect. Entry is possible and relatively easy. Blocked entry is typical of monopoly. Answer (B) is incorrect. Difficult entry is typical of oligopoly. Answer (C) is incorrect. Given the large number of firms, most are likely to be small, with correspondingly low economies of scale and capital needs.

2.9 Market Structures -- Oligopoly

25. The distinguishing characteristic of oligopolistic markets is

    A. A single seller of a homogeneous product with no close substitute.

    B. A single seller of a heterogeneous product with no close substitute.

    C. Lack of entry and exit barriers in the industry.

    D. Mutual interdependence of firm pricing and output decisions.

Answer (D) is correct.
    REQUIRED: The distinguishing characteristic of oligopolistic markets.
    DISCUSSION: The oligopoly model is much less specific than the other market structures, but there are typically few firms in the industry. Thus, the decisions of rival firms do not go unnoticed. Products can be either differentiated or standardized. Prices tend to be rigid (sticky) because of the interdependence among firms. Entry is difficult because of either natural or created barriers. Price leadership is typical in oligopolistic industries. Under price leadership, price changes are announced first by a major firm. Once the industry leader has spoken, other firms in the industry match the price charged by the leader. The mutual interdependence of the firms influences both pricing and output decisions.
    Answer (A) is incorrect. Oligopolies contain several firms; a single seller is characteristic of a monopoly. Answer (B) is incorrect. Oligopolies contain several firms; a single seller is characteristic of a monopoly. Answer (C) is incorrect. Oligopolies are typified by barriers to entry; that is the reason the industry has only a few firms.

26. An oligopolist faces a "kinked" demand curve. This terminology indicates that

   A. When an oligopolist lowers its price, the other firms in the oligopoly will match the price reduction, but if the oligopolist raises its price, the other firms will ignore the price change.

   B. An oligopolist faces a non-linear demand for its product, and price changes will have little effect on demand for that product.

   C. An oligopolist can sell its product at any price but, after the "saturation point," another oligopolist will lower its price and therefore shift the demand curve to the left.

   D. Consumers have no effect on the demand curve, and an oligopolist can shape the curve to optimize its own efficiency.

Answer (A) is correct.
   REQUIRED: The meaning of an oligopolist's kinked demand curve.
   DISCUSSION: An oligopoly consists of a few firms. Thus, the decisions of rivals do not go unnoticed. Prices tend to be rigid (sticky) because of the interdependence among firms. Because competitors respond only to certain price changes by one of the firms in an oligopolistic industry, the demand curve for an oligopolist tends to be kinked. Price decreases are usually matched by price decreases, but price increases are often not followed. If other firms do not match a lower price, a price decrease by an oligopolist would capture more of the market. If other firms match the price decrease, less of the market will be captured.
   Answer (B) is incorrect. Price changes will have an effect on demand for an oligopolist's product. Answer (C) is incorrect. An oligopolist must essentially match the price of other firms in the industry. A change in price does not shift the demand curve. Answer (D) is incorrect. An oligopolist cannot shape its demand curve.

2.10 Resource Markets and Labor

27. Derived demand can best be described as

   A. The demand derived purely from the market structure of a particular industry.

   B. The demand for a final product generated by the demand for a complementary good.

   C. The demand for an input generated by the demand for the final product.

   D. The demand for a final product generated by an abundant supply of inputs.

Answer (C) is correct.
   REQUIRED: The definition of derived demand.
   DISCUSSION: Derived demand is the demand for the inputs to the production process (sometimes called factors) derived from the demand for the outputs of the process (i.e., final goods).
   Answer (A) is incorrect. Derived demand is the demand for an input generated by the demand for the final product. Answer (B) is incorrect. The demand for complementary goods is not properly referred to as derived demand. Answer (D) is incorrect. Demand for a final product based on the supply of its inputs is not a meaningful economic concept.

28. The amounts paid to laborers are

   A. Real wages.

   B. Nominal wages.

   C. Productivity wages.

   D. Minimum wages.

Answer (B) is correct.
   REQUIRED: The term for wages actually paid to laborers.
   DISCUSSION: Nominal wages are the amounts actually paid (and received), while real wages represent the purchasing power of goods and services that can be acquired by the nominal wages. The level of real wages is determined by the productivity of labor. As productivity increases, the demand for labor also increases.
   Answer (A) is incorrect. Real wages represent the purchasing power of the wages paid. Answer (C) is incorrect. Productivity wages is a nonsense term. Answer (D) is incorrect. A minimum wage is established by law. It is a nominal wage, but all amounts paid to laborers are not minimum wages.

Use the additional questions in Gleim **CPA Test Prep Online** to create Test Sessions that emulate Prometric!

2.11 PRACTICE WRITTEN COMMUNICATION TASK

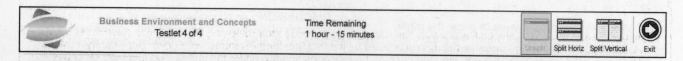

Business Environment and Concepts
Testlet 4 of 4

Time Remaining
1 hour - 15 minutes

Unsplit   Split Horiz   Split Vertical   Exit

DIRECTIONS

Note: If you believe you have encountered a software malfunction, report it to the test center staff immediately.

Navigation

To navigate from task to task, use the controls at the bottom of the screen. Click on the **Next** button to advance to the next task, or the **Previous** button to go to the previous task. To go directly to any task, click on its number.

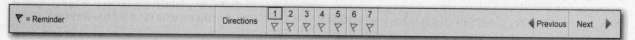

▼ = Reminder   Directions   1 2 3 4 5 6 7   ◄ Previous   Next ►

If you would like a reminder to revisit a task, or want to indicate that you are finished with it, click on the reminder flag below the task number. To clear the flag, click on it again. Reminder flags are for your use only – they do not contribute to your score.

Tabs

In this part of the examination, you will be asked to complete various tasks. Every task has one or more **Work Tabs**. Every task also has a **Help** tab.

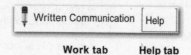

Written Communication   Help

Work tab   Help tab

Work Tabs:

- **Work Tabs** are identified with a pencil icon. This is where your responses are expected.
- Each task has one or more **Work Tabs**.
- **Work Tabs** contain directions for completing the task - be sure to read these directions carefully.
- The **Work Tab** name in the example above is for illustration only - yours will differ.
- You must complete all of the **Work Tabs** in each task to receive full credit.

Help Tab:

- The **Help Tab** provides assistance with the exam software that is used in this task. For example, if the task is to compose a memorandum, **Help** will provide information about the word processor.

The Toolbar

The toolbar at the top of the screen shows the amount of time remaining for you to complete the tasks. In addition, the following tools are available. Note that only the **Exit** button is displayed when Directions are visible - the others will appear when you begin the tasks.

Unsplit   Split Horiz   Split Vertical

Click on these buttons to split or unsplit the screen. You can split the screen vertically or horizontally.

Exit

Click on this button to go on to the next part of the examination. You must complete all of the tasks to receive full credit. Once you click on **Exit** and confirm the action, you will NOT be able to return to this testlet.

▼ = Reminder   Directions   1   ◄ Previous   Next ►

Written Communication | Help

✂ Cut   📋 Copy   📋 Paste   ↩ Undo   ↪ Redo

The owners of Ludicrous Lollipop Partnership came to your office today after reviewing their financial statements for the year just ended. They were surprised and disappointed by the fact that their revenues were down significantly from the prior year. They are considering doubling the price of their lollipops and are under the impression that their revenues will double as a result.

Prepare a memo to the partners explaining the relationship between price and total revenue and why their plan to double price may not have the result they expect.

Type your communication below the line in the response area below.

REMINDER: Your response will be graded for both technical content and writing skills. Technical content will be evaluated for information that is helpful to the intended reader and clearly relevant to the issue. Writing skills will be evaluated for development, organization, and the appropriate expression of ideas in professional correspondence. Use a standard business memorandum or letter format with a clear beginning, middle, and end. Do not convey information in the form of a table, bullet point list, or other abbreviated presentation.

To: Ludicrous Lollipop Partners
Re: Elasticity and total revenue

Unofficial Answer

Written Communication

To: Ludicrous Lollipop Partners
Re: Elasticity and total revenue

Intuitively, a person might conclude that increasing the price of a product would result in an increase in overall revenues. However, the economic laws of supply and demand and the economic phenomenon known as elasticity imply that this is not the case.

The law of supply holds that, the higher the price a supplier of a product can charge, the greater number of that product the supplier is willing to bring to market. This is consistent with Ludicrous Lollipop Partners' desire to sell more units at a higher price. However, the law of demand reveals that the higher the price of a product, the fewer units buyers are willing to buy. This runs counter to the partners' ideas about raising both price and total revenue.

The sensitivity of buyers' willingness to purchase a product based on its price can be quantified with a coefficient known as price elasticity of demand. When the price of a product changes within what is termed an elastic range, a small change in price results in a proportionally greater change in the quantity of the product that buyers are willing to purchase. Likewise, when the price change takes place within an inelastic range, a large price change results in a comparatively small change in the quantity demanded.

Thus, the partners must first establish whether the current price of their lollipops is within an elastic or an inelastic range. If they raise their price within an elastic range, their total revenues will actually decrease (because consumers within an elastic range are resistant to price increases). If they raise their price within an inelastic range, their total revenues will increase (because demand is so strong within an inelastic range that consumers will generally absorb a price increase). In any case, a doubling of prices will almost certainly move price into an elastic range and the partners' total revenue will decrease.

The above depicts a Level 5 answer. See page 16 in the Introduction for a description of the three grading criteria.

Self-Grade

Evaluate each of the following by selecting a 0, 1, 2, 3, 4, or 5. An average response is 3. Use 4 for better than average and 5 for outstanding. Use 2 for less than average and 1 for quite poor. Use zero for no response, if you did not address the topic, or if you gave advice that is clearly illegal.

Organization	○ 0	○ 1	○ 2	○ 3	○ 4	○ 5
Development	○ 0	○ 1	○ 2	○ 3	○ 4	○ 5
Expression	○ 0	○ 1	○ 2	○ 3	○ 4	○ 5

Your grade for the written communication as a whole is the average of the scores for the three criteria.

Use **CPA Gleim Online** and **Simulation Wizard** to practice more written communication tasks in a realistic environment.

STUDY UNIT THREE
MACROECONOMICS

(23 pages of outline)

In the process of attempting to describe (and manage) the economy, macroeconomists require measurements of an economy's performance. Gross domestic product, the most often-used measure of economic activity, can be viewed as the aggregate of demand for an economy as a whole (Subunits 1 and 2). Over time, macroeconomists have noted that economic growth in capitalistic economies has not been constant but has been punctuated by distinct cycles of expansion and contraction (Subunit 3). Macroeconomics is the study of the three interrelated aspects of any economy taken as a whole: growth, inflation, and unemployment (Subunits 4, 5, and 6). If aggregate demand is either too great or too little, the federal government can attempt to stimulate or suppress economic activity (Subunit 7). Money is created by a country's banking system. The level of economic activity in an economy is closely related to the supply of money (Subunit 8). The Federal Reserve Board is the body most responsible for managing the supply of money in the United States. To achieve its goals, the "Fed" deploys the tools of monetary policy (Subunit 9).

3.1 DOMESTIC OUTPUT -- EXPENDITURES APPROACH

1. **Measuring an Economy's Aggregate Output**

    a. **Gross domestic product (GDP)** is the principal measure of national economic performance.

        1) U.S. GDP is

            a) The total market value
            b) Of all final goods and services
            c) Produced within the boundaries of the U.S.
            d) By domestic- or foreign-owned sources
            e) During a specified period of time (usually a year)

        2) GDP is calculated without regard to the ownership of productive resources. Thus, the value of the output of a U.S.-owned factory abroad is excluded, but the output of a foreign-owned factory in the U.S. is included.

Background

The National Economic Accounts are computed by the Bureau of Economic Analysis (an agency of the U.S. Department of Commerce). These can be found at www.bea.gov/national/index.htm.

GDP is contrasted with gross national product (GNP), which is the total market value of all final goods and services produced by U.S.-owned sources, no matter where located. In early 1992, the BEA changed the focus of its national income reporting from GNP to GDP to more closely parallel the reporting of other countries and to reflect the fact that output itself is more important than who owns the factory.

b.   Two approaches to the measurement of GDP are available: the expenditures approach (described below) and the income approach (described in the next subunit).

2.   **Expenditures Approach**

a.   The expenditures approach, the simpler of the two methods, calculates GDP as the sum of all expenditures in the economy.

$$Gross\ domestic\ product = C + I + G + NX$$

b.   Consumer Spending (C)

1)   This is by far the largest component of GDP, and its most important determinant is personal incomes.

2)   Changes in incomes do not affect GDP dollar-for-dollar, however. For every additional dollar consumers receive in income, some portion is spent, and the remainder is siphoned off into savings.

c.   Investment Spending (I)

1)   Business investments are those that create jobs and income, like purchases of equipment and machinery; all construction, including residential since it can be used for rent or lease; and changes in inventory.

2)   While not as large a component of GDP as consumer spending, business investment is by far the most volatile component. This is because investment reflects the level of businesses' optimism about future demand, and business optimism is subject to wide and sudden variations.

3)   The investment demand has an inverse relationship with the real interest rate in the market. In determining whether to invest or deposit the money in the bank, the investor compares the real interest rate in the market and the expected rate of return from the investment. As the interest rate becomes lower, the investor will invest more.

d.   Government Spending (G)

1)   Government's component of total spending consists of outlays for

a)   Goods and services that are consumed by the government in providing public services and

b)   Long-lived public infrastructure assets, such as schools, bridges, and military bases.

i)   Transfer payments (e.g., Social Security benefits) to its citizens are not included since they will be spent on final goods and services by consumers.

e.   Net Exports (NX)

1)   GDP attempts to capture all spending on American-made goods, no matter who purchases them, and excludes the American expenditure on goods and services produced abroad (import).

$$Net\ exports\ (NX) = Exports\ (X) - Imports\ (M)$$

Note that this can be positive or negative.

Memory aid: Creativity Increases Germany's Net eXports

EXAMPLE

Expenditures Approach

	In Billions
Consumption by households (C)	$6,000
Investment by businesses (I)	1,200
Government purchases (G)	2,020
Net exports (NX)	(400)
Gross domestic product	**$8,820**

3. **Graphical Depiction of Expenditures Approach**

Aggregate Expenditures and Equilibrium GDP

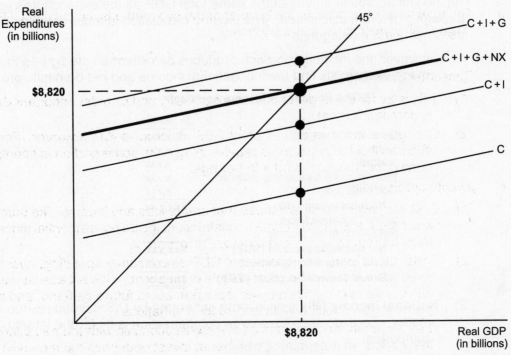

Figure 3-1

a. By definition, total expenditures equal real GDP. Thus, equilibrium is at any point on the 45° line (along which the values on the x and y axes are equal).

b. A shift in any of the four expenditure functions causes equilibrium GDP to rise or fall.

1) Consumer spending (C). If consumers increase their spending, for example, because they expect incomes to rise or because taxes have been lowered, the consumption function shifts up, reflecting a rise in national output.

2) Investment spending (I). If businesses increase their spending on productive facilities, for example, because a new generation of technology is available or because real interest rates have fallen, the investment function shifts up, reflecting a rise in national output.

3) Government spending (G). If government increases its spending, for example, because of a military buildup, the government function shifts up, reflecting a rise in national output.

4) Net exports (NX). If American firms sell more products overseas, the net exports function shifts up, reflecting a rise in national output. If exports eventually exceed imports, this will become a positive number.

a) In the illustration above, the net exports is negative.

Imports > Exports

Stop and review! You have completed the outline for this subunit. Study multiple-choice questions 1 through 3 on page 123.

3.2 DOMESTIC OUTPUT -- INCOME APPROACH

1.   **Components of the Income Approach**

   a.   The income approach arrives at the same total GDP as the expenditures approach through a different calculation. The income calculation is more complex because it uses many more categories.

   1)   However, the income approach produces two intermediate figures that macroeconomists find useful: national income and net domestic product.

GDP Calculation -- Income Approach

	In Billions
Salaries and wages	$ x,xxx
Rents	x,xxx
Interest	x,xxx
Proprietor and partnership incomes	x,xxx
Corporate profits	x,xxx
National income (NI)	**$xx,xxx**
Indirect business taxes	x,xxx
Net foreign factor income	x,xxx
Net domestic product (NDP)	**$xx,xxx**
Capital consumption allowance	x,xxx
Gross domestic product (GDP)	**$xx,xxx**

   2)   **National income (NI)** is all income generated by U.S.-owned resources, no matter where located. Employee compensation is by far the largest component.

   Memory aid for national income: Stalin's Red Influence Promoted Communism

   3)   **Net domestic product (NDP)** measures income generated in the U.S., no matter who owns the resources that generated it. The following two additions are made to NI:

   a)   Indirect business taxes (sales taxes, excise taxes, etc.), which are collected by businesses and passed on to some level of government.

   b)   Net foreign-factor income, which is the excess of income generated in the U.S. from foreign-owned resources over income generated in other countries from U.S.-owned resources.

   i)   NDP can also be calculated as GDP minus the capital consumption allowance (depreciation).

   Memory aid for net domestic product: I Bought Two Nets For Fishing Income

   4)   **Gross domestic product (GDP)** is arrived at by adding to net domestic product an allowance for the amount of capital stock that was consumed in the process of generating the income (depreciation of capital).

   a)   Even though it is merely an accounting convention and not an exact engineering measurement, depreciation is used as the capital consumption allowance.

   Memory aid for gross domestic product: Corn Chowder Associates

---

EXAMPLE

	In Billions
Salaries and wages	$3,200
Rents	500
Interest	500
Proprietor and partnership incomes	200
Corporate profits	2,400
National income	**$6,800**
Indirect business taxes	320
Net foreign factor income	200
Net domestic product	**$7,320**
Capital consumption allowance	1,500
Gross domestic product	**$8,820**

---

2. **Two Other Income Measures**

    a. **Personal income (PI)** is all income received by individuals, whether earned or unearned.

    b. **Disposable income (DI)** is the income of individuals after taxes have been taken out.

        1) Disposable income is divided between (a) consumption and interest payments and (b) savings.

EXAMPLE

	In Billions
National income (NI)	**$6,800**
Social Security contributions	(600)
Corporate income taxes	(100)
Undistributed corporate profits	(100)
Transfer payments	1,400
Personal income (PI)	**$7,400**
Personal taxes	(1,600)
Disposable income (DI)	**$5,800**

---

3. **Graphical Depiction**

Flow of National Income

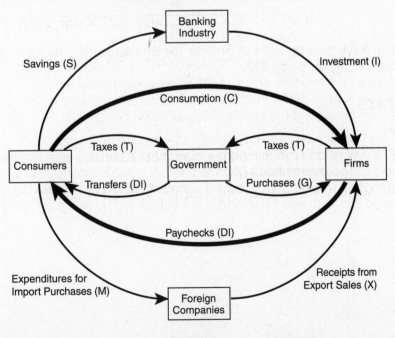

Figure 3-2

4. **Aspects of GDP**

    a. Challenges Inherent in the Calculation of GDP

        1) Calculating GDP requires aggregating an enormous amount of data, some of which (from privately held companies, for instance) may be difficult to acquire.

        2) GDP is a monetary measure; therefore, comparing GDP over time requires adjustment for changes in the price level (see "Nominal GDP" and "Real GDP" under item 5. below).

    b. Limitations of GDP

        1) GDP includes only final goods and services. Much economic activity involves the trading of intermediate goods, such as when a tire company buys rubber.

            a) The exchange of intermediate goods is not captured in GDP since that would involve double counting some goods.

        2) Increases in GDP often involve environmental damage such as noise, congestion, or pollution.

            a) Also, some economic activity takes place as a result of disasters. Following a hurricane, home improvement stores experience a boom in sales. While this benefit is reflected in GDP, the devastating financial loss of the customers is not included in the calculation.

            b) A huge amount of economic activity in developing countries takes place in the underground economy. None of this is captured in GDP.

            c) The value placed by the consumers on leisure time is not included in GDP.

5. **Price Level Accounting**

    a. **Nominal GDP.** The basic GDP calculation involves adding the total market value of all final goods and services in current dollars.

        1) This is clearly unsatisfactory when trying to compare the output of one year with that of another since the general price level is constantly fluctuating.

    b. **Real GDP.** To facilitate year-to-year comparisons, nominal GDP is adjusted for changes in the general price level so it can be reported in constant dollars (the CPI will be defined in Subunit 3.5).

$$Real\ GDP = \frac{Nominal\ GDP}{Price\ index\ (in\ hundredths)}$$

Stop and review! You have completed the outline for this subunit. Study multiple-choice questions 4 and 5 beginning on page 123.

3.3 BUSINESS CYCLES

1. **Overview**

    a. Over the very long run, economic growth in capitalistic economies has not been steady. The overall trend of growth is periodically interrupted by periods of instability. This tendency toward instability within the context of overall growth is termed the business cycle and can be depicted by the graph on the following page.

The Business Cycle

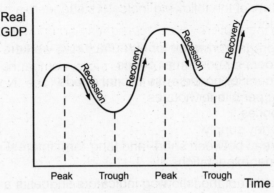

Figure 3-3

1) At a **peak**, the economy is

   a) At or near full employment and

   b) At or near maximum output for the current level of resources and technology.

2) A **recession** is defined as a period during which real GDP falls and unemployment rises.

   a) If the recession is severe enough, prices will fall and the phase will be considered a **depression**.

3) In a **trough**, economic activity reaches its lowest ebb.

4) During a **recovery**, output and employment rise. Eventually, the price level rises also.

In addition to identifying the phases of the business cycle, be able to assess the business cycle's impact on an entity's operations and its industry.

---

b. Possible Causes of Recessions or Troughs

   1) When consumer confidence declines, i.e., when consumers become pessimistic about the future, they spend less. Unsold inventory starts to build. Businesses respond by cutting back production and laying off workers.

   2) The introduction of major innovations, such as railroads and airlines, can have a destabilizing effect on an economy since such major innovations that have great impact on investments and consumption occur irregularly.

   3) A miscalculation in fiscal or monetary policy by the government may be sufficient to induce a recession or a boom.

c. Economists use leading economic indicators to help them forecast future economic trends (by the same token, lagging indicators report past economic activity).

   1) The best-known sets of economic indicators are those prepared by The Conference Board, a private research group.

   2) These indicators in isolation are not meaningful. It is the composite index that has predictive capability. This index has historically been useful but not infallible.

2. **Leading Economic Indicators**

    a. A change in any of the following indicators suggests a future change in real GDP in the same direction:

        1) The average workweek for manufacturing workers
        2) New orders for consumer goods
        3) New orders for nondefense capital goods
        4) Building permits for houses
        5) Stock prices
        6) The money supply
        7) The spread between short- and long-term interest rates
        8) Consumer expectations

    b. A change in either of the following indicators suggests a future change in real GDP in the opposite direction:

        1) Initial claims for unemployment insurance (because more people out of work indicates slowing business activity)
        2) Vendor performance (because vendors have slack time and are carrying high levels of inventory)

You do not need to memorize all of these leading economic indicators. If you were to see one of these economic indicators in the stem of a multiple-choice question, you would need to be able to recall how it may indicate future growth or contraction of the economy. It is possible to see a written communication question on these economic indicators, but if you can remember a few of these indicators, you should be fine. Most of these you should already know from being an accounting major or watching the evening news coverage of stock prices (e.g., the Dow Jones Industrial Average), unemployment claims, interest rates, etc.

Stop and review! You have completed the outline for this subunit. Study multiple-choice questions 6 and 7 on page 124.

3.4 ISSUES IN MACROECONOMICS -- GROWTH

1. **Economic Growth as a Measure of a Country's Prosperity**

    a. The change in real per capita GDP over a period of time is one of the ways to measure economic growth and the accompanying improvement in a country's standard of living.

        1) If real GDP (i.e., adjusted for inflation) rises at a faster rate than the population, the country is experiencing a rising standard of living.

    b. Economic growth also can be measured as an increase in real GDP over a period of time.

2. **Aggregate Supply and Demand**

    a. Just as individual firms face supply and demand curves, an economy as a whole can be described by using the same graphical tools.

    b. Aggregate demand is a schedule reflecting all the goods and services that consumers are willing and able to buy at various price levels. The curve thus reflects the relationship between the price level and real GDP.

Aggregate Demand

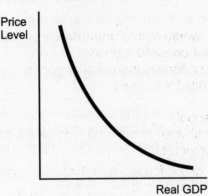

Figure 3-4

1) Aggregate demand is downward sloping.
2) No distinction is made between a short-run and long-run aggregate demand curve.

c.   Aggregate supply is a schedule reflecting all the goods and services an economy is willing and able to produce at various price levels.

Aggregate Supply

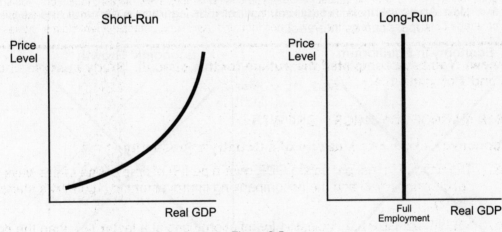

Figure 3-5

1) In the short run, changes in the price level induce firms to adjust their output in an attempt to earn excess profits. Plenty of unused productive capacity is available, and workers are willing to work for the prevailing wage. This is represented in the leftmost portion of the short-run aggregate supply curve, pictured above. The curve rises gradually as more inputs are added to the production process.

2) Over the long run, in an economy in full employment, any change in the price level is matched by a change in wages (and other input prices). Thus, there is no change in firms' real profits, and no additional output is produced.

    a)   Because the change in the price level has no effect on output produced, the long-run aggregate supply curve settles as a vertical line at the level of full-employment GDP.

3.   **Shifts in Aggregate Supply and Demand**

a.   **Growth** is a major macroeconomic goal.

1)   Usually, when an economy grows, workers earn higher real wages and have access to a richer variety and greater quantity of goods and services. This is the essence of a rising standard of living.

b.   One of the most important factors that shifts the aggregate supply curve (AS) is the change in productivity.

1)   Productivity is usually measured by worker productivity, that is, the total real GDP produced during the year divided by the total number of hours worked in the economy. The more a worker can produce in an hour of work, the more productive (s)he is.

2)   Productivity consists of three factors:

a)   Amount of capital. The more an economy has invested in plant and machinery, the higher its productivity will be (more automation = higher productivity).

b)   State of technology. The more technologically advanced an economy's plants and machinery are, the higher its productivity will be.

c)   Workforce competence. The more educated and trained an economy's workers are, the higher its productivity will be.

c.   The following is one possible scenario for economic growth:

1)   An economy is in equilibrium where the aggregate demand and aggregate supply curves intersect.

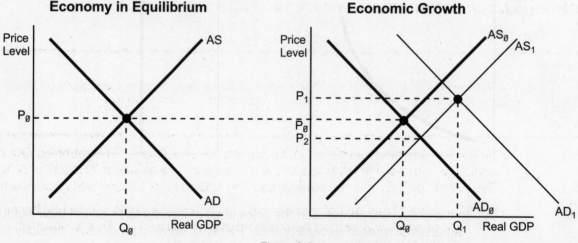

Figure 3-6

2)   The deployment of new technology increases productivity, depicted as a shift of the aggregate supply curve to the right (AS_1).

3)   Such an increase generates additional income for workers and businesses. This additional income shifts the aggregate demand curve to the right (AD_1).

a)   The growth can be depicted as the increase in real GDP from Q_0 to Q_1.

4)   The increase in the price level from P_0 to P_1 (growth may or may not be accompanied by a rise in the price level) depends on the extent to which aggregate demand increases relative to aggregate supply.

a)   If demand does not change, the rightward shift of the aggregate supply curve would result in a lowering of the price level from P_0 to P_2.

4. **Factors in Economic Growth**

    a.   Supply Factors

        1) Increase in productivity

        2) Increase in the quantity and quality of natural resources

    b.   Demand Factors

        1) Increase in total spending (someone has to buy the additional output produced)

    c.   Efficiency Factor

        1) Efficient allocation of resources

5. **Policies for Economic Growth**

    a.   **Demand-side policies.** In modern economies, actors in a free market are not the only parties to the determination of aggregate demand.

        1) The government can deploy the tools of fiscal policy and monetary policy to either stimulate or suppress demand (depending on whether a recessionary or inflationary environment looms, respectively).

            a) To encourage economic growth, stimulative policies are required.

    b.   **Supply-side policies.** The government can also implement policies to increase the country's stock of investment capital. Businesses use this capital to increase their productive capacity, thereby stimulating aggregate supply.

Stop and review! You have completed the outline for this subunit. Study multiple-choice questions 8 through 10 beginning on page 124.

3.5 ISSUES IN MACROECONOMICS -- INFLATION

1. **Overview**

    The AICPA has tested topics related to inflation on recent CPA exams. Multiple-choice questions have asked about how inflation is measured and about inflation's effects on the economy.

    a.   Inflation is a sustained increase in the general level of prices. The reported rate of inflation is therefore an average of the increase across all prices in the economy. This simple definition is not sufficient to fully understand inflation's impact, however.

        1) The value of any unit of money (e.g., the U.S. dollar) is measured by how many goods and services can be acquired in exchange for it. This is referred to as money's purchasing power.

    b.   The rate of inflation is stated in percentage terms, calculated using a price index.

        1) A price index is a measure of the price of a market basket of goods and services in one year compared with the price in a designated base year. By definition, the index for the base year is 100.

            a) The rate of inflation is calculated by comparing the change in the 2 years' indexes.

$$\frac{\textit{Current-year price index} - \textit{Prior-year price index}}{\textit{Prior-year price index}}$$

EXAMPLE

If the price index of the market basket was 10% higher than the base year in Year 3 and was 15% higher in Year 4, the inflation rate for Year 4 is

$$\frac{115 - 110}{110} = 4.55\%$$

---

2) The Consumer Price Index (CPI) is the most common price index for adjusting nominal GDP.

$$CPI = \frac{Cost\ of\ market\ basket\ in\ current\ year}{Cost\ of\ market\ basket\ in\ base\ year} \times 100$$

Background

The CPI is computed monthly by the Bureau of Labor Statistics (an agency of the U.S. Department of Labor). It measures changes in the general price level by a pricing of items on a typical urban household shopping list. According to the agency's website (www.bls.gov/cpi/), prices for the goods and services used to calculate the CPI are collected in 87 urban areas throughout the country and from about 23,000 retail and service establishments. Data on rents are collected from about 50,000 landlords or tenants. The base period for the CPI (i.e., the period for which the index equaled 100) is the period 1982-1984.

---

a) Although the terminology may sound conflicting, the CPI is also a relevant tool in business analysis. For instance, rising prices can lower a business' buying power, which can lead to new challenges in maintaining margins.

b) To compare monetary amounts in constant dollars, both amounts must first be deflated using the appropriate price index, then the difference divided by the prior period's amount.

EXAMPLE

A law firm is analyzing its revenue history. This year's billings amounted to $1,080,000, and last year's were $950,000. This year's CPI is 115, and last year's was 107.

	Nominal Dollars		CPI		Constant Dollars
This year's billings:	$1,080,000	÷	1.15	=	$939,130
Last year's billings:	950,000	÷	1.07	=	887,850
Difference	$ 130,000				$ 51,280

Thus, while in nominal terms billings increased by 13.7% ($130,000 ÷ $950,000), after adjusting for inflation, they increased by only 5.8% (51,280 ÷ $887,850).

---

2. **Real Income vs. Nominal Income**

   a. Nominal income is the amount of money received by a consumer as wages, interest, rent, and profits. For example, a systems analyst might have an annual salary, and therefore a nominal income, of $64,000.

   b. Real income is the purchasing power of the income received, regardless of how it is denominated. Purchasing power relates directly to the consumer's standard of living.

   c. Real income shrinks when nominal income does not keep pace with inflation.

3. **Macroeconomic Effects of Inflation**

   a. When inflation is unexpected, it can cause economic chaos.

   b. The efficiency of business relationships is reduced. Such efficiency relies on stable pricing.

4. **Effects on Financial Reporting**

    a.   The two principal effects of inflation on financial reporting are in the areas of inventory and depreciation.

        1)   Under a last-in, first-out (LIFO) inventory accounting system, the most recently purchased goods are expensed first. In a period of rapidly rising prices, this increases cost of goods sold and decreases operating income, thereby reducing income tax liability.

            a)   If the entity uses first-in, first-out (FIFO) inventory accounting, cost of goods sold consists of older, less costly inventory during times of inflation, thereby boosting operating income.

        2)   The depreciable base of a long-lived asset is its historical cost. During a period of rising prices, the amounts reported as depreciation expense are thus considerably lower than they would be if they were stated in terms of replacement cost. Reported operating income is higher in the current period, but replacing such assets as they are retired is more expensive.

5. **Two Types of Inflation**

    a.   **Demand-pull inflation** is generated by demand outpacing the supply of goods to satisfy it.

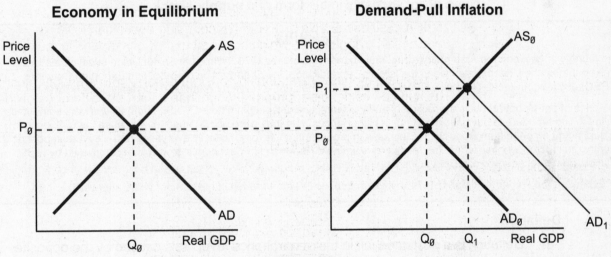

Figure 3-7

        1)   Since the economy cannot produce enough to keep up with demand, the prices of existing goods are bid up. This kind of inflation is depicted by the phrase, "Too many dollars chasing too few goods."

EXAMPLE

The economy of Spain during the Age of Exploration was almost wrecked by the influx of gold and silver from the Western Hemisphere. The sudden appearance of a vast amount of money drove the aggregate demand curve to the right. Since this was not accompanied by an increase in the amount of goods available, the aggregate supply curve remained fixed, and demand-pull inflation resulted. The end result was simply to drive up the prices of existing goods. This incident demonstrates the principle that the value of money is derived from the wealth that underlies it.

---

        2)   In a modern economy, demand-pull inflation arises when the economy approaches full employment and demand continues to increase.

b. **Cost-push inflation** is generated by increased per-unit production costs, which are passed on to consumers in the form of higher prices.

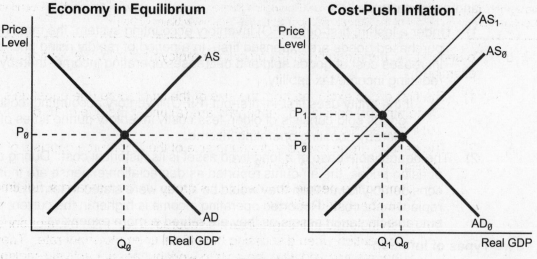

Figure 3-8

1) Increases in raw materials costs are the principal cause, particularly when they come about suddenly in the form of a **supply shock**.

EXAMPLE

The fourth war between the Arab nations and Israel began in October 1973. While the Soviet Union supplied aid to the Arab countries, the United States aided the Israelis. In retaliation, the Organization of Petroleum Exporting Countries (OPEC) declared an embargo of oil shipments to the U.S. The supply curve for petroleum suddenly shifted far to the left.

The price of petroleum products skyrocketed, and the quantity available plummeted. U.S. automobile drivers sometimes waited in line for hours to buy gasoline at much higher prices than they were accustomed to. Because the U.S. economy is so dependent on petroleum products, the increase in production costs for practically everything had a severe impact on the country. In macroeconomic terms, the result was stagflation, in which slow economic growth is accompanied by high inflation, an unprecedented condition at the time.

OPEC ended the embargo in March 1974, but the economic effects were felt in the U.S. for years afterward.

---

6. **Deflation**

   a. Deflation is a sustained fall in the general price level. It is caused by the opposite situations from those described on the previous page and above for demand-pull and cost-push inflation.

      1) A fall in demand unaccompanied by a contraction of supply is depicted by a leftward shift of the aggregate demand curve. Firms liquidate inventory even if they incur losses. Prices and output both fall.

      2) An increase in output unaccompanied by an increase in demand is depicted by a rightward shift of the aggregate supply curve. Prices fall as output increases.

Stop and review! You have completed the outline for this subunit. Study multiple-choice questions 11 through 13 beginning on page 125.

3.6 ISSUES IN MACROECONOMICS -- UNEMPLOYMENT

1. **Overview**

   a. Unemployment is the failure of the economy to fully employ its labor force. The **unemployment rate** is stated in percentage terms.

$$\frac{Number\ of\ unemployed}{Size\ of\ labor\ force} \times 100$$

Background

The unemployment rate is generated from the Current Population Survey, a monthly survey of households conducted by the U.S. Census Bureau on behalf of the Bureau of Labor Statistics (see www.bls.gov/cps/).

---

    b.   To understand the meaning of the official unemployment rate, the contents must be examined.

       1)   The first group excluded from the size of the labor force (the equation's denominator) consists of those who are (a) under the age of 16 or (b) incarcerated or institutionalized.

       2)   The second group excluded from the size of the labor force consists of those classified as not in the labor force.

           a)   Among the people counted in this group are homemakers, full-time students, and retirees.

           b)   Also included in this group are discouraged workers, a major bone of contention when discussing the official unemployment rate. These are the unemployed who are able to work but are not actively seeking work.

       3)   Among those who remain in the size of the labor force, no distinction is made between full- and part-time workers. They are all considered equally employed.

       4)   The number of unemployed (the equation's numerator) consists of those who are willing and able to work and who are seeking employment.

    c.   The official statistics can be distorted by

       1)   Discouraged workers who falsely claim to be seeking work

       2)   Those employed in the underground economy (e.g., cash-only-basis workers)

2. **Three Types of Unemployment**

    a.   **Frictional unemployment** is the amount of unemployment caused by the normal workings of the labor market.

       1)   This group can include those moving to another city, those ceasing work temporarily to pursue further education and training, and those who are simply between jobs.

       2)   This definition acknowledges that a "normal" amount of unemployment exists at any given time in a dynamic economy.

    b.   **Structural unemployment** results when

       1)   The composition of the workforce does not match the need. It can be a result of changes in consumer demand or technology.

           a)   The computer revolution has drastically changed the skills required for many jobs and completely eliminated others.

       2)   The available jobs are not in the location where unemployed workers live.

    c.   **Cyclical unemployment** is directly related to the level of an economy's output. It is likely to occur in the recession phase of the business cycle. For this reason, it is sometimes called **deficient-demand unemployment**.

       1)   As consumers slow their spending, firms cut back production and lay off workers.

       2)   The Great Depression was a period of low prices, low demand, and extremely low industrial output. During the worst of this period (ca. 1933), as much as 25% of the American labor force was unemployed.

3.   **"Full" Employment**

a.   The **natural rate of unemployment** consists of frictional and structural unemployment combined.

1)   Economists consider the economy to be at full employment when all unemployed workers fall into only these two categories (cyclical unemployment is omitted).

2)   The rate varies over time because of demographic and institutional changes in the economy.

b.   The economy's potential output is the real (i.e., inflation-adjusted) domestic output that could be achieved if the economy sustained full employment.

1)   This concept illustrates the importance of providing all interested workers with productive jobs.

4.   **Macroeconomic Effects of Unemployment**

a.   Lost value to the economy is the primary economic cost of unemployment. The goods not produced and services not provided by idle workers can never be regained.

1)   This loss is called the **GDP gap**. (GDP, or gross domestic product, is a measure of national output; it was covered in Subunit 3.1.)

b.   Unemployment has social costs, including loss of skills, personal and family stress, violence and other crime, and social upheaval.

Stop and review! You have completed the outline for this subunit. Study multiple-choice questions 14 and 15 on page 126.

3.7 DEMAND MANAGEMENT THROUGH FISCAL POLICY

1.   **Overview**

a.   Even in capitalistic countries, government plays a very large role in the workings of the economy.

1)   The first major area in which government participates is called fiscal policy, that is, the government as one of the players in the marketplace, taking in revenues (taxes) and making purchases (the annual budget).

2)   The other major area is called monetary policy and is discussed in Subunit 3.9.

b.   Fiscal policies can be discretionary or nondiscretionary.

1)   Discretionary fiscal policy involves spending that is under the control of individuals within the government, such as contracting for new weapons systems.

2)   Nondiscretionary fiscal policy is that which is enacted in law. Certain outlays, e.g., Social Security, must be made regardless of their consequences or source of funding because Congress has made them a legal requirement. No individual bureaucrat or group can choose to withhold (or increase) these expenditures.

c.   The following tools of fiscal policy are deployed by the government:

1)   Tax policy
2)   Government spending (highway maintenance, military buildup, etc.)
3)   Transfer payments (welfare, food stamps, unemployment compensation, etc.)

2. **Deploying Fiscal Policy**

    a.   In the graph below, the economy's full employment output is $8.82 trillion.

Recessionary Gap and Demand Stimulus

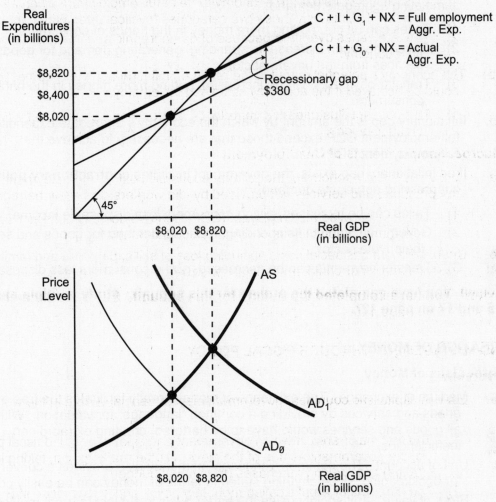

Figure 3-9

    1)   A change in consumer expectations leads to a decrease in consumption, causing the aggregate demand curve to shift to the left from AD_1 to AD_0 (assuming that prices can go down).

    2)   Recession and unemployment follow since real GDP decreased from $8,820 billion to $8,020 billion.

        a)   The $380 billion recessionary gap causes an $800 billion negative GDP gap.

    3)   In an attempt to promote growth and reduce unemployment, the federal government may deploy the tools of fiscal policy and increase its spending (G_1) by $380 billion ($G_1 = G_0 + $380 billion).

        a)   Because of the multiplier effect, an increase in government spending of $320 billion is sufficient to increase real GDP by $800 billion.

    4)   The increase in government spending will shift the economy's aggregate demand curve to the right (from AD_0 to AD_1). The recessionary gap of $800 billion ($8,820 billion − $8,020 billion) will be closed, and unemployment will be reduced.

    b.   **Keynesian theory** calls for expansionary fiscal policy during times of recession (to stimulate aggregate demand) and contractionary policy during boom times (to prevent inflation).

    c.   If a recessionary gap exists, the government institutes **expansionary policies**, stimulating aggregate demand.

        1)   Taxes can be cut, putting more money in the hands of consumers.

        2)   Government can increase its spending, generating demand for goods and services from the private sector.

        3)   Transfer payments can be increased, putting more money in the hands of consumers.

    d.   Inflationary gap is the amount by which the economy's aggregate expenditures at the full-employment GDP exceed those that are necessary to achieve the full-employment GDP.

    e.   If an inflationary gap exists, the government institutes **contractionary policies,** suppressing aggregate demand.

        1)   Taxes can be increased, giving consumers less disposable income.

        2)   Government can cut its spending, reducing demand for goods and services from the private sector.

        3)   Transfer payments can be decreased, giving consumers less disposable income.

Stop and review! You have completed the outline for this subunit. Study multiple-choice questions 16 and 17 on page 127.

3.8 THE CREATION OF MONEY

  1. **Three Uses of Money**

    a.   Medium of exchange. The existence of money greatly facilitates the free exchange of goods and services by providing a common "language" for valuation. Without money, all goods and services would have to be bartered, creating extraordinary inefficiencies.

    b.   Unit of account. The common "language" of money also provides a convenient basis for bookkeeping, since anything stated in terms of money can be easily compared.

    c.   Store of value. Any society using the barter basis is subject to great inefficiencies because many objects of great value, such as foodstuffs, spoil, making them worthless. The value of a unit of money is determined by the quantity of goods and services it can be exchanged for.

  2. **Interest Rates**

    a.   When money is borrowed, the debtor pays the lender back an amount in addition to the sum that was borrowed, which is termed "interest."

        1)   The two major determinants of the interest rate on a loan are

           a)   Overall economic conditions as reflected in the prime rate, which is the rate to the most credit-worthy customers, and

           b)   The creditworthiness of the borrower.

    b.   Economists draw a crucial distinction between real and nominal interest rates.

        1)   The **nominal interest rate** is the stated rate on a loan.

        2)   The **real interest rate** equals the nominal rate minus the rate of inflation that the lender expects will be prevalent over the life of the loan.

            a)   The lender must charge this "inflation premium" in order to compensate for the purchasing power that will be lost while the loan is at the borrower's disposal.

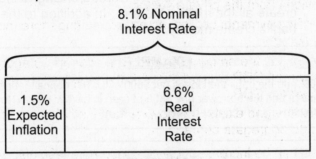

Figure 3-10

    c.   Misunderstandings over the difference between real and nominal interest rates can lead to distortions in the economy.

        1)   For example, a loan bearing 10% interest may seem exorbitant to a borrower, but if inflation is 8%, the borrower is only paying a real rate of 2%.

        2)   By the same token, a loan bearing 6% interest may seem like a bargain on the surface, but if inflation is 1%, the borrower is actually paying 5% interest on the loan in real terms.

3.   **The Supply of Money**

    a.   The Federal Reserve System (see Background at the bottom of this page) tracks and reports the amount of money in circulation.

        1)   The metrics used by the Fed are called M1 and M2. M1 includes only the most liquid forms of money. M2 includes M1 and less-liquid forms of money.

EXAMPLE

The following is a hypothetical money supply calculation for an economy the approximate size of the U.S.:

	In Billions
Currency (paper money + coins)	$ 600
Checking accounts	700
M1 money supply	**$1,300**
Savings accounts, including money market accounts	2,900
Small time deposits (< $100,000)	1,400
Money market mutual funds	800
M2 money supply	**$6,400**

Background

Although they need not be memorized for the CPA exam, the Federal Reserve's latest Money Stock Measures can be found at www.federalreserve.gov/releases/h6/current/h6.htm.

4.   **Banks and the Creation of Money**

   a.   An examination of the example M1 money supply calculation on the previous page illustrates that paper money and coins (collectively referred to as currency) make up less than half the total.

   1)   How can there be double the amount of money in the economy than there is currency to represent it?

   a)   The answer is that the U.S. Bureau of Engraving and Printing does not create all the money there is. In addition to the federal government, banks create money.

EXAMPLE

A bank customer deposits $1,000, and the bank then loans out $800 of it. The depositor has a statement showing that (s)he has a claim on $1,000 of cash, and the borrower has $800 of cash in his/her hand. Now, $1,800 exists where there was only $1,000 previously. The bank has just created $800.

Background

From its founding, the United States tended to view a central bank as an anti-democratic institution. Thus, instead of having a single central bank like many other countries, the United States has 12 regional Federal Reserve Banks. The Federal Reserve, established in 1913, is independent of the rest of the federal government. This independence, and the long terms of its members, insulate the Fed's decisions from political pressures. The Board of Governors is responsible for overseeing the operations of the Federal Reserve System. The Federal Open Market Committee (FOMC) is responsible for administering monetary policy.

In today's world, the actions taken by the Federal Reserve receive heavy media coverage. Be prepared to answer questions regarding policies pursued by the Federal Reserve for different economic situations.

---

5.   **Bank Reserves**

   a.   Fractional reserve banking is the practice of prohibiting banks from lending out all the money they receive on deposit.

   b.   The reserve ratio is the percentage of each dollar deposited that a bank is required to either (1) keep on hand in its vault or (2) deposit with the Federal Reserve Bank in its district.

   1)   This bare minimum that must be held by law is called required reserves.

Background

For example, the Fed recently required medium-sized banks to keep 3% in reserve (i.e., in the vault or on deposit with the district Fed). An explanation and a complete table of the current reserve requirements can be found at www.federalreserve.gov/monetarypolicy/reservereq.htm.

---

   a)   The amount of customer deposits that exceeds required reserves is termed **excess reserves**. It is from excess reserves that the bank makes loans.

   2)   Fractional reserves are obviously not sufficient to prevent a bank's collapse in the event of a run (that purpose is fulfilled by the Federal Deposit Insurance Corporation).

   a)   The real purpose of required reserves is to provide the Fed with another tool for controlling the money supply.

c. The amount of money banks potentially can create can be approximated by using the monetary multiplier.

$$Monetary\ multiplier = \frac{1}{Required\ reserve\ ratio}$$

EXAMPLE

If the Fed required reserves of 4% on all deposits, a bank with $10 million on deposit would be able to create $250 million of new money [$10,000,000 × (1.0 ÷ .04)]. Because the multiplier is an inverse, it clearly shows that the money supply will decrease as required reserves are raised.

Stop and review! You have completed the outline for this subunit. Study multiple-choice questions 18 through 21 beginning on page 127.

3.9 MONETARY POLICY

1. **Goals and Tools of Monetary Policy**

   a. The Fed attempts to balance the goals of gradual, steady economic growth and price stability (manageable inflation).

   1) The Fed has three tools of monetary policy at its disposal to achieve these goals:

      a) Open-market operations,
      b) The required reserve ratio, and
      c) The discount rate.

   2) Fiscal and monetary policy can be combined to influence aggregate demand.

   b. Open-market operations are the Fed's most valuable tool. The Fed can choose a range of potential impacts from large to small, and the effect is immediate.

   1) U.S. Treasury securities are traded on the open market. The Fed can either purchase them from, or sell them to, commercial banks.

      a) When the Fed wishes to loosen the money supply, it purchases Treasury securities; i.e., it takes securities off the market and injects money.

      b) When the Fed wishes to tighten the money supply, it sells Treasury securities; i.e., it takes money out of the economy and gives securities in exchange.

   2) The Federal funds rate is the rate banks charge each other for overnight loans.

      a) Banks with excess reserves do not have to leave these funds idle. They can lend them on a short-term basis to banks that are in danger of dipping below the required reserve ratio.

         i) The relationship between the money supply (M1) and the interest rate (r) is shown in the following graph:

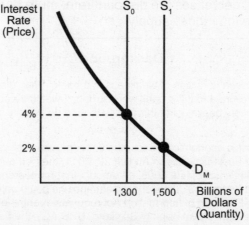

Figure 3-11

       b)   When the Fed buys Treasury securities, the money supply increases and the Federal funds rate falls. When the Fed sells Treasury securities, the money supply decreases and the Federal funds rate rises.

   3)   This chain of cause and effect is summarized in the following table:

To Loosen Money Supply	To Tighten Money Supply
1. Fed sees **recession** looming	1. Fed fears **inflation** heating up
2. Fed **buys government securities** on the open market	2. Fed **sells government securities** on the open market
3. Fed **credits cash to reserve accounts** of banks selling securities	3. Fed **decreases cash in reserve accounts** of banks buying securities
• Increase in supply of cash **creates excess reserves**; banks now willing to lend	• Decrease in supply of cash **reduces excess reserves**; banks unable to lend
• Greater availability of cash for overnight loan causes **decline in Federal funds rate**	• Lower availability of cash for overnight loan causes **increase in Federal funds rate**
4. Fall in interest rates stimulates investment spending by businesses (I in the aggregate expenditures calculation) (see Subunit 3.1)	4. Rise in interest rates depresses investment spending by businesses (I in the aggregate expenditures calculation) (see Subunit 3.1)
5. Rise in investment spending increases aggregate demand (i.e., a shift to the right), which increases real GDP and reduces unemployment	5. Fall in investment spending reduces aggregate demand (i.e., a shift to the left), which decreases the price level and reduces inflation

  c.   Changes in the required reserve ratio are used less frequently. Requiring banks to retain more funds in reserve accounts has a dramatic effect on profits. (In October 2008, the Fed began paying interest on required and excess reserves, but a bank could make more by lending monies out.)

     1)   When the Fed wishes to loosen the money supply, it lowers the required reserve ratio.

        a)   If banks are allowed to retain less money on hand, they have more available to lend out.

     2)   When the Fed wishes to tighten the money supply, it raises the required reserve ratio.

        a)   If banks are required to retain more money on hand, they have less available to lend out.

  d.   The discount rate has come to reflect, rather than enact, changes the Fed wishes to make. The discount rate is the rate Federal Reserve banks charge to commercial banks receiving short-term loans from the Fed's discount window facility.

     1)   If the Fed increases the discount rate, fewer banks will borrow money, and it will decrease the money supply.

     2)   If the Fed decreases the discount rate, more banks will borrow money, and it will increase the money supply.

Background

Use of the discount window is widely seen as a sign of weakness in a bank. This "discount window stigma" is based on the belief that the Fed is a lender of last resort, and if the bank were strong, it would be able to get the funds it needs on the open market. Because of this perception, banks using this facility tend to do so only in emergencies and prefer that the Fed keep their identities secret.

Even when applied in times of nationwide economic distress, the direct provision of cash by the Federal Reserve is not publicized. As reported in *Bloomberg Businessweek* on August 22, 2011, the Fed quietly loaned $669 billion to the 10 largest U.S. banks during the market crisis of late 2008, an amount that far overshadowed the widely discussed $160 billion in bailout money provided by the U.S. Treasury. The magazine could only bring this fact to light after "compilation of data obtained through Freedom of Information Act requests, months of litigation, and an act of Congress." Including both U.S. and foreign banks (e.g., Royal Bank of Scotland, UBS AG), the Fed had $1.2 trillion in loans outstanding on December 5, 2008.

Stop and review! You have completed the outline for this subunit. Study multiple-choice questions 22 through 26 beginning on page 128.

QUESTIONS

3.1 Domestic Output -- Expenditures Approach

1. Which of the following is **not** included in the gross domestic product (GDP)?

A. Purchase of a new home.

B. Investment in new computers.

C. A doctor's fee.

D. Purchase of common stock.

Answer (D) is correct.

REQUIRED: The transaction not included in GDP.

DISCUSSION: GDP is the value of all final goods and services produced in the U.S., whether by domestic or foreign-owned sources, during a specified period. A common stock purchase is not a new good or service. It is instead a claim to ownership of property that already exists.

Answer (A) is incorrect. A new home is a productive good and is included in GDP. Answer (B) is incorrect. An investment in productive assets is part of GDP. Answer (C) is incorrect. The doctor's services were produced during the year. His/her fee is part of GDP.

2. The level of aggregate demand will decline if the level of

A. Imports decreases.

B. Investment spending decreases.

C. Consumption spending increases.

D. Government spending increases.

Answer (B) is correct.

REQUIRED: The activity that will cause aggregate demand to decline.

DISCUSSION: A decrease in investment spending, as well as decreases in consumption and/or government spending, will cause overall demand to decline.

Answer (A) is incorrect. A decrease in imports results in an increase in aggregate demand. Answer (C) is incorrect. An increase in consumption spending will result in an increase in aggregate demand. Answer (D) is incorrect. An increase in government spending will increase aggregate demand.

3. Which one of the following components of gross domestic product (GDP) has the greatest fluctuation from year to year?

A. Personal consumption expenditures.

B. Gross domestic private investment.

C. Government spending.

D. Net exports.

Answer (B) is correct.

REQUIRED: The component of gross domestic product (GDP) showing the most fluctuation from year to year.

DISCUSSION: By far the most volatile component of gross domestic product (GDP) is business investment. This is because investment reflects the level of businesses' optimism about future demand, and business optimism is subject to wide and sudden variations.

Answer (A) is incorrect. Personal consumption, while the largest component of GDP, is not the most volatile. Answer (C) is incorrect. Government spending is not as volatile a component of GDP as business investment. Answer (D) is incorrect. Net exports are subject to less variability from year to year than gross domestic private investment.

3.2 Domestic Output -- Income Approach

4. Personal income is equal to

A. Gross domestic product minus net national product.

B. Net domestic product plus transfer payments to individuals.

C. Disposable income minus personal tax payments.

D. Disposable income plus personal tax payments.

Answer (D) is correct.

REQUIRED: The factors calculated in personal income.

DISCUSSION: Personal income is all income received by individuals, whether earned or unearned. This would be disposable income plus taxes.

Answer (A) is incorrect. Gross domestic product minus net domestic product equals depreciation (the capital consumption allowance). Answer (B) is incorrect. Net domestic product plus transfer payments to individuals does not define a meaningful national income concept. Answer (C) is incorrect. Disposable income equals personal income minus personal income taxes. Thus, adding personal taxes back to disposable income results in personal income.

5. Each of the following is a limitation of GDP's usefulness as a measure of a nation's prosperity **except**

    A. No practical means are available to compare real GDP from different time periods.

    B. GDP leaves out intermediate goods.

    C. Increases in GDP often involve environmental damage.

    D. Cash-only economic activity is not counted in GDP.

Answer (A) is correct.
    REQUIRED: The item not a limitation on GDP's usefulness as a measure of a nation's prosperity.
    DISCUSSION: Comparing GDP over time is a challenge, but it is by no means insurmountable. Various price indexes, such as the Bureau of Labor Statistics' Consumer Price Index and the GDP deflator, are suitable for converting nominal GDP amounts from different years to comparable amounts in terms of a base year.
    Answer (B) is incorrect. GDP only counts final goods and services; economic activity that leads to intermediate goods is left out. Answer (C) is incorrect. Increases in GDP often involve environmental damage, such as noise, congestion, or pollution. Answer (D) is incorrect. Cash-only economic activity is not counted in GDP.

3.3 Business Cycles

6. Which of the following may provide a leading indicator of a future increase in gross domestic product?

    A. A reduction in the money supply.

    B. A decrease in the issuance of building permits.

    C. An increase in the timeliness of delivery by vendors.

    D. An increase in the average hours worked per week of production workers.

Answer (D) is correct.
    REQUIRED: The leading indicator of a future increase in gross domestic product.
    DISCUSSION: An economic indicator is highly correlated with changes in aggregate economic activity. A leading indicator changes prior to a change in the direction of the business cycle. The leading indicators included in the Conference Board's index are average weekly hours worked by manufacturing workers, unemployment claims, consumer goods orders, stock prices, orders for fixed assets, building permits, timeliness of deliveries, money supply, consumer confidence, and the spread between the yield on 10-year Treasury bonds and the federal funds rate. An increase in weekly hours worked by production workers is favorable for economic growth.
    Answer (A) is incorrect. A falling money supply is associated with falling GDP. Answer (B) is incorrect. A decline in the issuance of building permits signals lower expected building activity and a falling GDP. Answer (C) is incorrect. An increase in the timeliness of delivery by vendors indicates slacking business demand and a potentially falling GDP.

7. All of the following are stages of the business cycle **except**

    A. Boom, or peak.

    B. Trough.

    C. Recovery.

    D. Acceleration.

Answer (D) is correct.
    REQUIRED: The item that is not a stage in the business cycle.
    DISCUSSION: A business cycle has four stages: the trough, recovery, peak, and recession. Acceleration is not one of the stages.

3.4 Issues in Macroeconomics -- Growth

8. One of the measures economists and economic policy makers use to gauge a nation's economic growth is to calculate the change in the

    A. Money supply.

    B. Total wages.

    C. General price level.

    D. Real per capita output.

Answer (D) is correct.
    REQUIRED: The measure used by economists to gauge economic growth.
    DISCUSSION: Real per-capita output is defined as the gross domestic product of a nation adjusted for changes in the general price level and divided by the population. It is often used to measure a country's standard of living.
    Answer (A) is incorrect. The change in the money supply is not a direct measure of the nation's output. Answer (B) is incorrect. The change in total wages is not a direct measure of the nation's output. Answer (C) is incorrect. The change in the general price level is not a direct measure of the nation's output.

9. Which one of the following factors would cause the aggregate supply curve shown below to shift from AS_1 to AS_2?

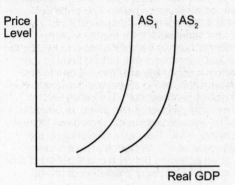

A. An improvement in technology.

B. A higher resource price.

C. An increase in the expected rate of inflation.

D. A decrease in productivity.

Answer (A) is correct.

REQUIRED: The factor causing a rightward shift in the aggregate supply curve.

DISCUSSION: A shift of the entire aggregate supply curve as opposed to a movement along a given curve is caused by any of three determinants of aggregate demand: a change in input prices, a change in productivity, or a change in the legal-institutional environment in which the industry operates. An improvement in technology leads to greater productivity and thus to an outward shift in aggregate supply.

Answer (B) is incorrect. Higher resource prices lead to a leftward shift of aggregate supply. Answer (C) is incorrect. An increase in the expected rate of inflation leads consumers to purchase more goods now before prices go up. This is represented as a movement along the aggregate demand curve. Answer (D) is incorrect. A decrease in productivity would mean a loss of efficiency by businesses, reflected in a leftward shift in aggregate supply.

10. An improvement in technology that in turn leads to improved worker productivity would most likely result in

A. A shift to the right in the supply curve and a lowering of the price of the output.

B. A shift to the left in the supply curve and a lowering of the price of the output.

C. An increase in the price of the output if demand is unchanged.

D. A decrease in real wages.

Answer (A) is correct.

REQUIRED: The result of improved technology and improved worker productivity.

DISCUSSION: Enhanced technology and worker productivity would cause the supply curve to shift to the right, where it would intersect with the demand curve at a lower price level. The shift is caused by the producer's ability to lower costs and produce more at a given market price.

Answer (B) is incorrect. The increased productivity would cause a rightward shift in the supply curve. Answer (C) is incorrect. The rightward shift would result in an intersection with the demand curve at a lower price. Answer (D) is incorrect. Improved productivity leads to lower prices, which constitute an increase in real wages.

3.5 Issues in Macroeconomics -- Inflation

11. Chihuahua Bank is willing to lend a business firm $1 million at an annual real interest rate of 6%. What is the nominal rate Chihuahua Bank will charge the firm if the rate of inflation is anticipated to be 2%?

A. 2%

B. 4%

C. 6%

D. 8%

Answer (D) is correct.

REQUIRED: The interest rate a bank will charge at a given rate of inflation.

DISCUSSION: If Chihuahua Bank requires a real return of 6%, a 2% inflation rate will result in an 8% nominal rate.

12. Demand-pull inflation occurs when

A. Incomes rise suddenly.

B. There are excessive wage increases.

C. There are rapid increases in raw materials prices.

D. There are substantial changes in energy prices.

Answer (A) is correct.

REQUIRED: The cause of demand-pull inflation.

DISCUSSION: When incomes rise suddenly, consumers demand more of everything, driving up the price level.

Answer (B) is incorrect. Excessive wage increases describe the condition known as cost-push inflation. Answer (C) is incorrect. A rapid increase in raw materials prices is termed a supply shock and can be the cause of stagflation but not of demand-pull inflation. Answer (D) is incorrect. Changes in the prices of an important input like energy can be either up or down and so cannot be said to predictably cause inflation.

13. Which of the following concepts compares the price of goods in a given year to a base year?

A. Consumer price index.

B. Consumer confidence index.

C. Gross national product.

D. Net national product.

Answer (A) is correct.

REQUIRED: The economic measure of the price of goods.

DISCUSSION: The CPI measures inflation by a monthly pricing of items on a typical household shopping list. The current index uses a base year as a reference point. The price in the current year of a market basket of goods and services is determined relative to the same basket for the base year.

Answer (B) is incorrect. Consumer confidence measures the amount of confidence that consumers (the public) have in the present and future performance of the economy. Consumer confidence is a key determinant of the aggregate demand curve and a source of business-cycle instability. Answer (C) is incorrect. The gross national product (GNP) is the value of the output produced with U.S.-owned resources, regardless of their location. Answer (D) is incorrect. Net national product is the measure of the market value of all final goods and services produced by citizens of an economy during a given period of time (usually a year) after adjusting for the depreciation of capital.

3.6 Issues in Macroeconomics -- Unemployment

14. The rate of unemployment caused by changes in the composition of employment opportunities over time is referred to as the

A. Frictional unemployment rate.

B. Cyclical unemployment rate.

C. Structural unemployment rate.

D. Full employment unemployment rate.

Answer (C) is correct.

REQUIRED: The rate of unemployment caused by changes in the composition of employment opportunities over time.

DISCUSSION: Economists define full employment as occurring when cyclical unemployment is zero. Hence, the natural rate of unemployment (the full employment unemployment rate) equals the sum of structural and frictional unemployment. Cyclical unemployment is caused by insufficient aggregate demand. Frictional unemployment occurs when both jobs and the workers qualified to fill them are available. This definition acknowledges that there will be changing of jobs, temporary layoffs, etc. Structural unemployment exists when aggregate demand is sufficient to provide full employment, but the distribution of the demand does not correspond precisely to the composition of the labor force. This form of unemployment arises when the required job skills or the geographic distribution of jobs change.

Answer (A) is incorrect. Frictional unemployment results from imperfections in the labor market. Answer (B) is incorrect. Cyclical unemployment is caused by a deficiency of aggregate spending. Answer (D) is incorrect. The full employment unemployment rate is the sum of frictional and structural unemployment.

15. Below are the recent monthly unemployment figures for an economy:

Persons moving to a new city and seeking work	100,000
Persons out of work because their industry has just been rendered obsolete by technological change	12,000
Persons in all industries laid off due to general economic slowdown	120,000
Persons taking 2 months off from work to pursue education	100,000

Applying the Bureau of Labor Statistics' guidelines for calculating the official unemployment statistics, what is the "natural" level of unemployment for this economy?

A. 200,000

B. 212,000

C. 232,000

D. 320,000

Answer (B) is correct.

REQUIRED: The total number of persons included in the natural level of unemployment.

DISCUSSION: The "natural" level of unemployment includes the frictionally unemployed (those moving to another city, those ceasing work temporarily to pursue further education and training, those who are simply between jobs) and the structurally unemployed (those put out of work by changes in consumer demand, technology, and geographical location of industries). The remainder are the cyclically unemployed, that is, those who are out of work because of the generally low output of the economy as a whole (called deficient-demand unemployment for this reason). In this example, frictional unemployment amounts to 200,000 (100,000 + 100,000), and structural unemployment amounts to 12,000, for a total natural level of unemployment of 212,000.

Answer (A) is incorrect. The figure of 200,000 fails to include the former workers in the obsolete industry who are among the structurally unemployed. Answer (C) is incorrect. The figure of 232,000 improperly includes the 120,000 cyclically unemployed. Answer (D) is incorrect. The figure of 320,000 improperly excludes the 12,000 structurally unemployed former workers in the obsolete industry and improperly includes the 120,000 cyclically unemployed.

3.7 Demand Management through Fiscal Policy

16. If a government were to use only fiscal policy to stimulate the economy from a recession, it would

- A. Raise consumer taxes and increase government spending.
- B. Lower business taxes and government spending.
- C. Increase the money supply and increase government spending.
- D. Lower consumer taxes and increase government spending.

Answer (D) is correct.
REQUIRED: The actions taken if a government were to use only fiscal policy to stimulate the economy.
DISCUSSION: According to Keynesian economics, fiscal policy should be expansionary when the economy is in recession. Increases in government spending, decreases in taxation, or both will have a stimulative effect. To achieve this effect, the increase in spending should not be matched by a tax increase, the effect of which is contractionary. Thus, deficit spending is the result of pursuing an expansionary fiscal policy.
Answer (A) is incorrect. Raising consumer taxes would be contractionary. Answer (B) is incorrect. Lower government spending would be contractionary. Answer (C) is incorrect. Increasing the supply of money involves monetary, not fiscal, policy.

17. During a recession, the goal of government fiscal policy is to raise equilibrium output. An appropriate governmental action in this situation is to

- A. Decrease government spending.
- B. Increase government taxes.
- C. Increase government spending.
- D. Increase government taxes and decrease government spending by equal amounts.

Answer (C) is correct.
REQUIRED: The governmental action to increase domestic output.
DISCUSSION: According to Keynesian economics, the sum of personal after-tax consumption expenditures, gross investment, net exports, and government spending equals gross domestic product (GDP) at equilibrium. At this output level, aggregate expenditures equal real aggregate domestic output. Thus, an increase in government spending, with other factors held constant, increases equilibrium GDP, that is, equilibrium output.
Answer (A) is incorrect. A decrease in government spending by itself decreases equilibrium output. Answer (B) is incorrect. An increase in government taxes by itself decreases personal consumption and equilibrium output. Answer (D) is incorrect. An increase in government taxes by itself decreases personal consumption and equilibrium output. A decrease in government spending by itself decreases equilibrium output.

3.8 The Creation of Money

18. The creation of deposit money by U.S. commercial banks increases the

- A. Real wealth of the United States.
- B. Real U.S. national income.
- C. U.S. money supply.
- D. Purchasing power of the U.S. dollar.

Answer (C) is correct.
REQUIRED: The effect of the creation of deposit money by U.S. commercial banks.
DISCUSSION: As money is deposited with banks, the banks lend the money to qualified customers. Banks may only lend a certain percentage of their funds because of the reserve requirement. The more funds they have, the more they can lend. Thus, as the amount of money deposited increases, the amount and number of loans and the money supply increase.
Answer (A) is incorrect. Real wealth is not directly affected by the creation of deposit money. Answer (B) is incorrect. National income is not directly affected by the creation of deposit money. Answer (D) is incorrect. The purchasing power of the dollar (amount of goods that can be bought with a dollar) may well be decreased by the expansion of the money supply.

19. The Federal Reserve System's reserve ratio is the

- A. Specified percentage of a commercial bank's deposit liabilities that must be deposited in the central bank or kept on hand.
- B. Rate that the central bank charges for loans granted to commercial banks.
- C. Ratio of excess reserves to legal reserves that are deposited in the central bank.
- D. Specified percentage of a commercial bank's demand deposits to total liabilities.

Answer (A) is correct.
REQUIRED: The definition of the reserve ratio.
DISCUSSION: The reserve ratio is the percentage of the customer deposits that banks must keep on hand or deposit with the Fed. These deposits are required by law to ensure the soundness of the bank and also serve as a tool for monetary policy; i.e., changes in the reserve ratio affect the money supply.
Answer (B) is incorrect. This description refers to the discount rate: the amount that the Fed charges for loans granted to commercial banks. Answer (C) is incorrect. Excess reserves is a term referring to amounts in excess of the reserve ratio. Answer (D) is incorrect. The reserve ratio is the ratio of required reserves to demand deposits.

20. A bank with a reserve ratio of 20% and reserves of $1,000,000 can increase its total demand deposits by

A. $5,000,000

B. $1,000,000

C. $800,000

D. $200,000

Answer (A) is correct.
   REQUIRED: The amount by which a bank can increase its total demand deposits given the reserve ratio and the amount of reserves.
   DISCUSSION: The amount of new money a bank can create equals actual reserves times the monetary multiplier (or divided by the required reserve ratio). This bank can thus increase total demand deposits by $5,000,000 ($1,000,000 ÷ 0.2).
   Answer (B) is incorrect. Reserves need to be only 20% of deposits; thus, an increase in reserves will support a five-fold increase in deposits. Answer (C) is incorrect. The amount of $800,000 equals the increase in net lendable funds, assuming a $1,000,000 increase in deposits. Answer (D) is incorrect. The reserve is 20% of deposits, not the reverse.

21. The money supply in a nation's economy will decrease following

A. Open-market purchases by the nation's central bank.

B. A decrease in the discount rate.

C. An increase in the reserve ratio.

D. A decrease in the margin requirement.

Answer (C) is correct.
   REQUIRED: The item that causes a decrease in the money supply.
   DISCUSSION: The reserve ratio is the minimum percentage of its deposits that a bank must keep on deposit with the Federal Reserve or in its vault. When the reserve ratio increases, banks must maintain larger reserves, and less money is available for lending and investment. Consequently, the money supply decreases.
   Answer (A) is incorrect. Open-market purchases by the central bank increase the money supply by increasing commercial banks' reserves. Answer (B) is incorrect. A decrease in the rate charged to member banks for loans by the Federal Reserve (the discount rate) increases the money supply by increasing bank reserves. Answer (D) is incorrect. A decrease in the margin requirement decreases the minimum down payment that purchasers of stock must make. This credit control affects the stock market and has no direct impact on the money supply.

3.9 Monetary Policy

22. Providing an adequate supply of money to accommodate the needs of U.S. business is the task of the

A. United States Treasury.

B. Controller of the Currency.

C. Bureau of Printing and Engraving.

D. Federal Reserve System.

Answer (D) is correct.
   REQUIRED: The entity responsible for providing an adequate money supply.
   DISCUSSION: The Federal Reserve Board (the Fed) controls the money supply independently of the federal government. Any policy designed by the Fed to affect the money supply, and thus the economy, is monetary policy. Control of the growth of the money supply by the Fed is viewed as essential to control the availability of credit, spending, and inflation. One reason is that the money supply must grow at the same rate as the economy for the economy to be completely healthy.
   Answer (A) is incorrect. The Treasury is responsible for governmental receipts and expenditures. Answer (B) is incorrect. The Controller of the Currency regulates and charters banks. Answer (C) is incorrect. The Bureau of Engraving and Printing prints money as authorized by the Fed.

23. All of the following actions are valid tools that the Federal Reserve Bank uses to control the supply of money, **except**

A. Buying government securities.

B. Selling government securities.

C. Changing the reserve ratio.

D. Printing money when the level of M1 appears low.

Answer (D) is correct.

REQUIRED: The item that is not a valid tool of the Fed in controlling the money supply.

DISCUSSION: The amount of money to print is a decision for the Department of the Treasury (an executive branch agency), not the Federal Reserve (an independent agency). Besides, paper currency and coins make up only about half of the M1 money supply. The Fed has other, more complex tools for enacting monetary policy.

Answer (A) is incorrect. Buying government securities is one method the Fed uses to control the money supply. Answer (B) is incorrect. Selling government securities is one method the Fed uses to control the money supply. Answer (C) is incorrect. Changing the reserve ratio is one method the Fed uses to control the money supply.

24. The primary mechanism of monetary control of the Federal Reserve System is

A. Changing the discount rate.

B. Conducting open market operations.

C. Changing reserve requirements.

D. Using moral persuasion.

Answer (B) is correct.

REQUIRED: The primary mechanism of monetary control of the Fed.

DISCUSSION: The conduct of open market operations (buying and selling government securities) is the primary means used by the Fed to control the money supply. Fed purchases are expansionary; they increase bank reserves and the money supply. Fed sales are contractional (because money is paid into the Federal Reserve, taking it out of circulation, reducing bank reserves, and "contracting" the money supply).

Answer (A) is incorrect. Changing the discount rate is a less important tool of monetary policy. Answer (C) is incorrect. Changing reserve requirements is a less important tool of monetary policy. Answer (D) is incorrect. Moral persuasion is not a means of manipulating the money supply.

25. In order for the Federal Reserve System to increase the money supply, the appropriate policy is to

A. Encourage banks to increase their holdings of excess reserves.

B. Increase the discount rate.

C. Engage in open-market purchases of government securities.

D. Raise margin requirements on stock market purchases.

Answer (C) is correct.

REQUIRED: The Fed's policy to increase the money supply.

DISCUSSION: Open-market purchases of government securities put more money into circulation. Vault cash that was previously unavailable to the public for circulation is placed into the hands of the public by the open-market purchase of government securities.

Answer (A) is incorrect. An increase in excess reserves or reserve requirements means that member banks could make fewer loans. Thus, less money is introduced into the economy. Answer (B) is incorrect. If the discount rate is raised, member banks will borrow less from the Fed to lend to their customers. Answer (D) is incorrect. An increase in margin requirements means that investors would borrow less.

26. Which of the following results could be expected from an open market operation of the Federal Reserve?

A. A sale of securities would lower interest rates.

B. A purchase of securities would raise interest rates.

C. A purchase of securities would lower security prices.

D. A sale of securities would raise interest rates.

Answer (D) is correct.

REQUIRED: The expected result from the given open market operation.

DISCUSSION: A sale of securities would remove dollars from the economy and reduce bank reserves. Thus, banks could not lend as much as previously, and higher interest rates would follow. Money supply and interest rates are inversely proportional.

Answer (A) is incorrect. A sale would increase interest rates. Answer (B) is incorrect. A purchase of securities would provide greater reserves, allow banks to make more loans, and result in lower interest rates. Answer (C) is incorrect. A purchase of securities would remove securities from the economy, which would increase securities prices.

Use the additional questions in Gleim **CPA Test Prep Online** to create Test Sessions that emulate Prometric!

3.10 PRACTICE WRITTEN COMMUNICATION TASK

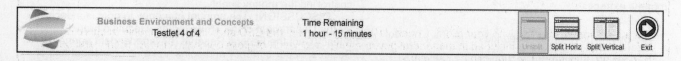

Business Environment and Concepts
Testlet 4 of 4

Time Remaining
1 hour - 15 minutes

Unsplit   Split Horiz   Split Vertical   Exit

DIRECTIONS

Note: If you believe you have encountered a software malfunction, report it to the test center staff immediately.

Navigation

To navigate from task to task, use the controls at the bottom of the screen. Click on the **Next** button to advance to the next task, or the **Previous** button to go to the previous task. To go directly to any task, click on its number.

▼ = Reminder   Directions   1 2 3 4 5 6 7   ◀ Previous   Next ▶

If you would like a reminder to revisit a task, or want to indicate that you are finished with it, click on the reminder flag below the task number. To clear the flag, click on it again. Reminder flags are for your use only – they do not contribute to your score.

Tabs

In this part of the examination, you will be asked to complete various tasks. Every task has one or more **Work Tabs**. Every task also has a **Help** tab.

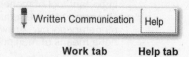

Written Communication   Help

Work tab   Help tab

Work Tabs:

- **Work Tabs** are identified with a pencil icon. This is where your responses are expected.
- Each task has one or more **Work Tabs**.
- **Work Tabs** contain directions for completing the task - be sure to read these directions carefully.
- The **Work Tab** name in the example above is for illustration only - yours will differ.
- You must complete all of the **Work Tabs** in each task to receive full credit.

Help Tab:

- The **Help Tab** provides assistance with the exam software that is used in this task. For example, if the task is to compose a memorandum, **Help** will provide information about the word processor.

The Toolbar

The toolbar at the top of the screen shows the amount of time remaining for you to complete the tasks. In addition, the following tools are available. Note that only the **Exit** button is displayed when Directions are visible - the others will appear when you begin the tasks.

Unsplit   Split Horiz   Split Vertical

Click on these buttons to split or unsplit the screen. You can split the screen vertically or horizontally.

Exit

Click on this button to go on to the next part of the examination. You must complete all of the tasks to receive full credit. Once you click on **Exit** and confirm the action, you will NOT be able to return to this testlet.

▼ = Reminder   Directions   1   ◀ Previous   Next ▶

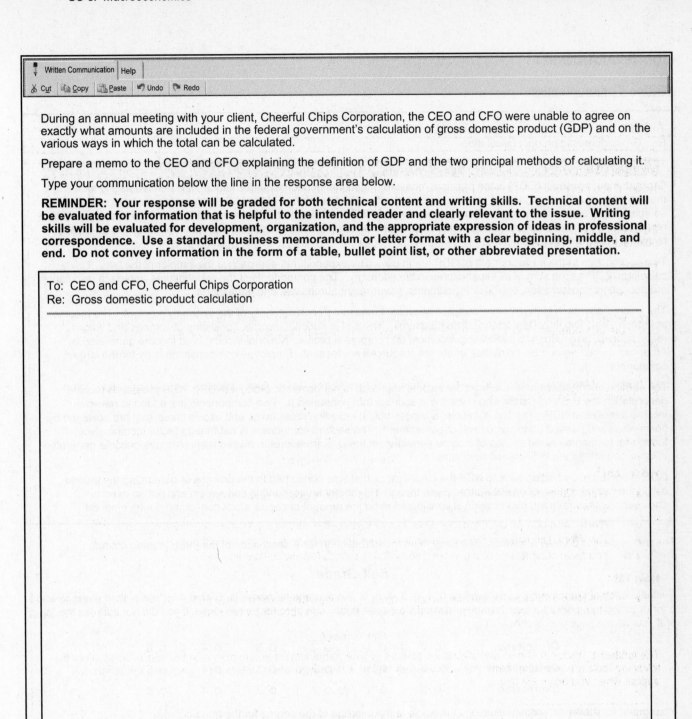

Written Communication | Help

✂ Cut | 📋 Copy | 📋 Paste | ↶ Undo | ↷ Redo

During an annual meeting with your client, Cheerful Chips Corporation, the CEO and CFO were unable to agree on exactly what amounts are included in the federal government's calculation of gross domestic product (GDP) and on the various ways in which the total can be calculated.

Prepare a memo to the CEO and CFO explaining the definition of GDP and the two principal methods of calculating it.

Type your communication below the line in the response area below.

REMINDER: Your response will be graded for both technical content and writing skills. Technical content will be evaluated for information that is helpful to the intended reader and clearly relevant to the issue. Writing skills will be evaluated for development, organization, and the appropriate expression of ideas in professional correspondence. Use a standard business memorandum or letter format with a clear beginning, middle, and end. Do not convey information in the form of a table, bullet point list, or other abbreviated presentation.

To: CEO and CFO, Cheerful Chips Corporation
Re: Gross domestic product calculation

Unofficial Answer

<u>Written Communication</u>

To: CEO and CFO, Cheerful Chips Corporation
Re: Gross domestic product calculation

Gross domestic product (GDP) is the principal measure of national economic performance. It is defined as the total market value of all final goods and services produced within the boundaries of the U.S. by domestic- or foreign-owned sources during a specified period of time (usually a year). GDP is calculated without regard to the ownership of productive resources. Thus, the value of the output of a U.S.-owned factory abroad is excluded, but the output of a foreign-owned factory in the U.S. is included.

Two approaches to the measurement of GDP are in use. The expenditures approach is the simpler of the two. It calculates GDP as the sum of all expenditures in the economy. The components of the expenditures approach calculation are household consumption, business investments, government purchases, and net exports.

The income approach is much more complex because it measures each category of the economy's output. The income approach yields two important intermediate measures. The first is national income, consisting of salaries and wages, rents, interest, proprietor and partnership incomes, and corporate profits. National income is all income generated by American-owned resources, no matter where the resources are located. Employee compensation is by far the largest component.

The second intermediate measure from the income approach is net domestic product (NDP). NDP measures income generated in the U.S., no matter who owns the resources that generated it. Two components are added to national income to arrive at NDP. The first is indirect business taxes, including sales taxes and excise taxes, that are collected by businesses and passed on to some level of government. The second component is net foreign-factor income. Net foreign-factor income is the excess of income generated in the U.S. from foreign-owned resources over income generated in other countries from U.S.-owned resources.

GDP is arrived at by adding back to NDP the capital stock that was consumed in the process of generating the income, called the capital consumption allowance. Even though it is merely an accounting convention and not an exact engineering measurement, depreciation is considered to be the amount of capital stock consumed during a period.

The above depicts a Level 5 answer. See page 16 in the Introduction for a description of the three grading criteria.

Self-Grade

Evaluate each of the following by selecting a 0, 1, 2, 3, 4, or 5. An average response is 3. Use 4 for better than average and 5 for outstanding. Use 2 for less than average and 1 for quite poor. Use zero for no response, if you did not address the topic, or if you gave advice that is clearly illegal.

Organization	o 0	o 1	o 2	o 3	o 4	o 5
Development	o 0	o 1	o 2	o 3	o 4	o 5
Expression	o 0	o 1	o 2	o 3	o 4	o 5

Your grade for the written communication as a whole is the average of the scores for the three criteria.

Use **CPA Gleim Online** and **Simulation Wizard** to practice more written communication tasks in a realistic environment.

STUDY UNIT FOUR
GLOBALIZATION

(13 pages of outline)

As the world economy becomes more interconnected, aspects of conducting business across borders grow in importance. This study unit covers the reasons why some countries raise barriers to trade (Subunit 1) and the challenges inherent in currency exchange (Subunits 2 and 3).

Globalization is driven by the **digital revolution** that facilitates international commerce by providing capabilities that did not exist relatively few years ago. It is also driven by such **political events** as the fall of the Soviet Union, the participation of China in the world economic system, the emergence of the European Union, and the creation of other regional free trade zones.

These technological and political factors are intertwined with **social changes**, for example, greater concern for the rights of women and minorities; the advance of multilingualism; and the convergence of tastes in fashion, music, and certain other cultural factors.

Accordingly, these factors favor globalization by reducing trade barriers, reducing costs of coordination, increasing economies of scale, and encouraging standardization and global branding.

4.1 PROTECTIONISM

1. **Overview**

   a. Even though individuals (on the whole) are best off under free trade, governments often establish policies designed to interfere in the workings of the marketplace. **Protectionism** is any measure taken by a government to protect domestic producers.

Background

Until economists such as Adam Smith and David Ricardo gave life to the free-trade movement in the late 18th and early 19th centuries, it was the policy of governments around the world to actively impede trade. The belief was that exports were to be promoted and imports discouraged in all cases because exports led people in other countries to owe domestic producers money. This theory went by the name of mercantilism. Certain aspects of mercantilism survive in modern protectionist practices.

2. **Forms of Protectionism**

   a. **Tariffs** are taxes imposed on imported goods.

      1) Tariffs can be designed to discourage consumption of foreign goods, raise revenue, or both.

      2) If both goals are intended, the government must set the tariff rate very carefully. If the rate is set too high, demand for the good will be suppressed to the point that revenues decline.

Background

Until the income tax was enacted in 1913, the U.S. government raised most of its revenue from tariffs.

b. **Import quotas** set fixed limits on different products.

1) In the short run, import quotas will help a country's balance of payments position by decreasing foreign outflow payments, but the prices of domestic products will increase.

a) A country's **balance of payments** is the sum of all transactions between domestic and foreign individuals, firms, and governments.

2) An **embargo** is a total ban on some kinds of imports. It is an extreme form of the import quota.

c. Domestic content rules require that at least a portion of any imported product be constructed from parts manufactured in the importing nation.

1) This rule is sometimes used by capital-intensive nations. Parts can be produced using idle capacity and then sent to a labor-intensive country for final assembly.

d. A **trigger price** mechanism automatically imposes a tariff barrier against unfairly cheap imports by levying a duty (tariff) on all imports below a particular reference price (the price that "triggers" the tariff).

e. **Antidumping** rules prevent foreign producers from "dumping" excess goods on the domestic market at less than cost to squeeze out competitors and gain control of the market.

f. Exchange controls limit foreign currency transactions and set exchange rates. The purpose is to limit the ability of a firm selling in a country to repatriate its earnings.

g. Export subsidies are payments by the government to producers in certain industries in an attempt to increase exports.

1) A government may impose "countervailing duties" on imported goods if those goods were produced in a foreign country with the aid of a governmental subsidy.

h. Certain exports may require licenses. For example, sales of technology with military applications are limited by western nations that are members of the Coordinating Committee for Multilateral Export Controls. The related U.S. legislation is the Export Administration Act of 1979.

3. **Economic Effects of Tariffs and Quotas**

a. Workers are shifted from relatively efficient export industries into less efficient protected industries. Real wages decline as a result, as does total world output.

b. Under a tariff, the excess paid by the customer for an imported good goes into government coffers where it can be spent on domestic concerns.

1) Under a quota, prices also are driven up (by the induced shortage), but the excess goes to the exporter in the foreign country.

c. A tariff is laid on all importers equally; thus, the more efficient ones will still be able to set their prices lower than the less efficient ones.

1) An import quota, on the other hand, does not affect foreign importers equally, and import licenses can be assigned as much for political favoritism as on any other grounds.

4. **Three Basic Arguments in Favor of Protectionism**

a. Reducing imports protects domestic jobs.

1) This argument is compelling because the costs of cheaper imports are direct and concentrated (people lose jobs and firms go out of business), but benefits of unrestricted trade are less noticeable and occur in the future (lower prices, higher wages, more jobs in export industries).

2) However, many of the ill effects of job loss can be ameliorated by government programs to help in displaced-worker transition. Such measures are not protectionist.

   b. Certain industries are essential to national security.

1) This is a sound argument up to a point. The counterargument is that it becomes easy for companies only peripherally related to national defense to claim that they are crucial to a country's security.

2) It is in this context that the opposite of protectionism sometimes arises: the U.S. government actually forbids exports of, for instance, nuclear technology and certain weapons to countries such as Cuba, Iran, and North Korea. Domestic exporters are hurt by government policies because of overriding concerns about national security.

   c. Infant industries need protection in the early stages of development.

1) An extension of the infant-industry argument is the "strategic trade policy argument," which contends that a government should use trade barriers strategically to reduce the risk of product development borne by domestic firms, particularly for products involving advanced technology.

2) Two counterarguments are usually offered. One is that, if the company really has sound long-term prospects, venture capital would rush in to sustain it until it becomes profitable. Also, some companies begin their lives dependent on special government protections, then never seem able to wean themselves off.

NOTE: Special-interest groups advocating one or more of these arguments are strong and well-organized, and they lobby effectively for legislation that is harmful to free trade.

5. **Global Capital Flows**

   a. Accompanying the flow of goods and services in international trade is the flow of capital. The rise of high-speed electronic communications makes the flow of capital much faster than in earlier eras.

   b. Emerging-market countries can attract capital with much greater ease than before, thereby exploiting their particular comparative advantages. The economic balance of power can thus shift rapidly back and forth between developed and developing nations.

Stop and review! You have completed the outline for this subunit. Study multiple-choice questions 1 through 10 beginning on page 146.

4.2 CURRENCY EXCHANGE RATES

 The AICPA has been testing the topic of currency exchange rates on recent CPA exams. Since international standards and international topics in general are now eligible to be tested, CPA candidates should have a solid understanding of currency exchange rates as well as the impact of globalization on the business environment.

1. **The Market for Foreign Currency**

   a. When an entity buys merchandise, a capital asset, or a financial instrument from another country, the seller wishes to be paid in his/her domestic currency. Thus, in general, when the demand for a country's merchandise, capital assets, and financial instruments rises, demand for its currency rises.

   b. For international exchanges to occur, the two currencies involved must be easily converted at some prevailing exchange rate. The exchange rate is the price of one country's currency in terms of another country's currency.

Background

The gold standard prevailed from 1876 to 1913, when countries pegged one unit of their currencies to a specified amount of gold. The gold standard was suspended during World War I. Following the war and during the Great Depression, the gold standard's reimplementation did not achieve universal success. In 1944, during World War II, the United States convened a meeting of delegates from all 45 allied nations in Bretton Woods, New Hampshire.

Under the resulting Bretton Woods Agreement, the U.S. guaranteed convertibility of the dollar into a certain quantity of gold, and all other nations in turn pegged their currencies to the dollar. This fixed exchange rate system ended in 1971 when it was agreed that the U.S. currency was pegged too high and that the dollar should be devalued. By 1973, it was clear that any governmental intervention in currency markets was unworkable, and a managed float exchange rate system was established.

---

2.   **Fixed vs. Floating Exchange Rate Systems**

   a.   **Fixed Exchange Rate System**

   1)   In a fixed exchange rate system, the value of a country's currency in relation to another country's currency is either fixed or allowed to fluctuate only within a very narrow range.

   2)   The one significant advantage to a fixed exchange rate is that it makes for a high degree of predictability in international trade because the element of uncertainty about gains and losses on exchange rate fluctuations is eliminated.

EXAMPLE

Since July 1986, the Saudi government has allowed its currency to trade within an extremely narrow band surrounding the ratio of 3.75 riyals to 1 U.S. dollar. Because the U.S. buys a tremendous amount of petroleum from Saudi Arabia, this system has the advantage of adding a degree of stability to the U.S. oil market.

---

   3)   A disadvantage is that a government can manipulate the value of its currency.

EXAMPLE

One of the complaints of authorities in the U.S. with respect to its enormous trade deficit with China is the belief that the Chinese government has held the value of the yuan in an artificially low range in order to make its exports more affordable. (After years of urging by the U.S. government, China allowed its currency to rise almost 18% between 2005 and 2008. After further negotiations, China agreed in April 2012 to allow the value of the yuan to fluctuate by as much as 1.0% against the value of the dollar on any given day; this doubled the size of the previous "trading band" of 0.5%.)

---

   b.   **Freely Floating Exchange Rate System**

   1)   In a freely floating exchange rate system, the government steps aside and allows exchange rates to be determined entirely by the market forces of supply and demand.

   2)   The advantage of such a system is that it tends to automatically correct any disequilibrium in the balance of payments.

   3)   The disadvantage is that a freely floating system makes a country vulnerable to economic conditions in other countries.

Background

The dominant exchange rate system in use today among the world's largest economies is the "managed float" system, which lies between the two extremes described above. Under a managed float, the government allows market forces to determine exchange rates until they move too far in one direction or another. The government will then intervene to maintain the currency within the broad range considered appropriate. The advantage of managed float is that it has the market-response nature of a freely floating system while still allowing for government intervention when necessary.

3.   **Exchange Rates and Purchasing Power**

    a.   The graph below depicts the relationship between the supply of and demand for a foreign currency by consumers and investors who use a given domestic currency.

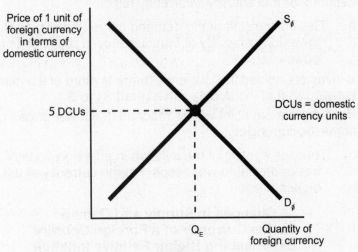

Exchange Rate Equilibrium

Figure 4-1

        1)   The demand curve for the foreign currency is downward sloping because, when that currency becomes cheaper, goods and services denominated in that currency become more affordable and domestic consumers need more of that currency.

        2)   The supply curve for the foreign currency is upward sloping because, when that currency becomes more expensive, domestic goods and services become more affordable to users of the foreign currency, leading them to inject more of their currency into the domestic market.

    b.   When one currency can be exchanged for more units of another currency, the first currency is said to have **appreciated** with respect to the second currency. By the same token, the second currency is said to have **depreciated** against the first.

        1)   This phenomenon has definite implications for international trade. The currency that appreciates is gaining purchasing power. Any financial instrument denominated in that currency is becoming more valuable (expensive).

EXAMPLE

A U.S. company buys merchandise from an EU company for €1,000,000, due in 60 days. On the day of the sale, $0.795 is required to buy a single euro. By the 60th day, $0.812 is required to buy a euro. The dollar has thus weakened against the euro, and the euro has strengthened against the dollar; i.e., the dollar has lost purchasing power with respect to the euro. The U.S. firm only needed $795,000 to pay off a €1,000,000 debt on the date of sale but must now use $812,000 to pay off the €1,000,000 debt.

---

    c.   The five factors that affect currency exchange rates can be classified as three trade-related factors and two financial factors. Each is discussed in detail in items 4. and 5. on the following pages.

        1)   Trade-related factors

            a)   Relative inflation rates

            b)   Relative income levels

            c)   Government intervention

        2)   Financial factors

            a)   Relative interest rates

            b)   Ease of capital flow

4.   **Trade-Related Factors That Affect Exchange Rates**

a.   **Relative Inflation Rates**

  1) When the rate of inflation in a given country rises relative to the rates of other
      countries, the products of that country become relatively expensive and the
      demand for that country's currency falls.

  a) This inward shift of the demand curve (from $D_{\emptyset}$ to D_1) results from the
      lowered desirability of that currency, a result of its falling purchasing
      power.

  2) As investors unload this currency, there is more of it available, reflected in an
      outward shift of the supply curve (from $S_{\emptyset}$ to S_1).

  3) A new equilibrium point will be reached at a lower price in terms of investors'
      domestic currencies.

  a) Thus, as a result of the inflation in a foreign country, the domestic currency
      has appreciated with respect to the currency of the foreign country with
      higher inflation.

**Changes in Supply and Demand
for the Currency of a Foreign Country
Experiencing Higher Relative Inflation**

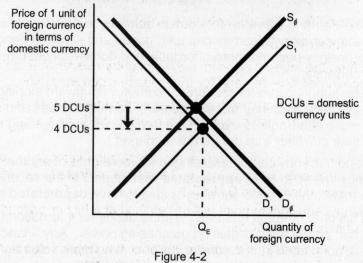

Figure 4-2

  b) The difference between the countries' inflation rates is approximately equal
      to the change in the currency exchange rate between the two countries.

  i)   For example, Japan experiences a period of 3% inflation and the
       U.S. experiences a 7% rate. Because of the difference in the
       inflation rates, the yen will appreciate against the dollar by
       approximately 4% (7% − 3%).

b.   **Relative Income Levels**

  1) Citizens with higher incomes look for new consumption opportunities in other
      countries, driving up the demand for those currencies and shifting the demand
      curve to the right.

  a) Thus, as incomes rise in one country, the prices of foreign currencies rise
      as well, and the local currency will depreciate.

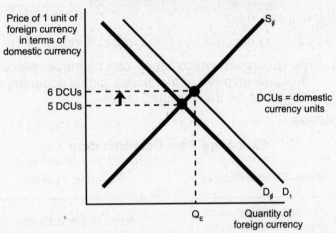

Figure 4-3

c. **Government Intervention**

1) Actions by national governments, such as trade barriers and currency restrictions, complicate the process of exchange rate determination.

5. **Financial Factors That Affect Exchange Rates**

a. **Relative Interest Rates**

1) When the interest rates in a given country rise relative to those of other countries, the demand for that country's currency rises.

a) This outward shift of the demand curve (from $D_\emptyset$ to D_1) results from the influx of other currencies seeking the higher returns available in that country.

2) As more and more investors buy up the high-interest country's currency to make investments, there is less of it available, reflected in an inward shift of the supply curve (from $S_\emptyset$ to S_1).

3) A new equilibrium point will be reached at a higher price in terms of investors' domestic currencies.

a) An investor's domestic currency has depreciated against the currency of a foreign country with higher interest rates.

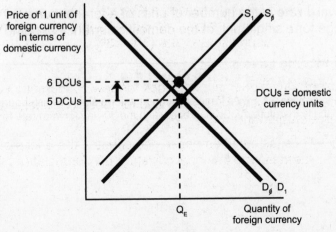

Figure 4-4

b.   **Ease of Capital Flow**

1)   If a country with high real interest rates loosens restrictions against the cross-border movement of capital, the demand for the currency will rise as investors seek higher returns.

2)   This factor has become by far the most important of the five factors listed.

a)   The speed with which capital can be moved electronically and the huge amounts involved in the "wired" global economy easily dominate the effects of the trade-related factors.

6.   **Graphical Depiction**

Exchange Rate Determination

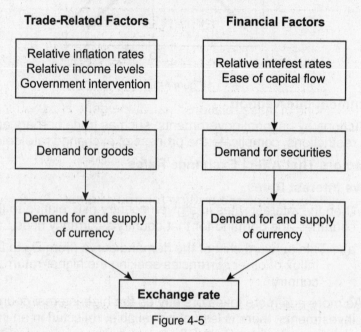

Figure 4-5

7.   **Exchange Rate Basics**

a.   The **spot rate** is the number of units of a foreign currency that can be received today in exchange for a single unit of the domestic currency.

EXAMPLE

A currency trader is willing to give 1.6 Swiss francs today in exchange for a single British pound. Today's spot rate for the pound is therefore 1.6 Swiss francs, and today's spot rate for the franc is £0.625 (1 ÷ F1.6).

---

b.   The **forward rate** is the number of units of a foreign currency that can be received in exchange for a single unit of the domestic currency at some definite date in the future.

EXAMPLE

The currency trader contracts to provide 1.8 Swiss francs in exchange for a single British pound 30 days from now. Today's 30-day forward rate for the pound is therefore 1.8 Swiss francs, and the 30-day forward rate for the franc is £0.555 (1 ÷ F1.8).

---

c. If the domestic currency fetches more units of a foreign currency in the forward market than in the spot market, the domestic currency is said to be trading at a **forward premium** with respect to the foreign currency.

EXAMPLE

Since the pound is fetching more francs in the forward market than in the spot market (F1.8 > F1.6), the pound is currently trading at a forward premium with respect to the franc. This reflects the market's belief that the pound is going to increase in value in relation to the franc.

---

d. If the domestic currency fetches fewer units of a foreign currency in the forward market than in the spot market, the domestic currency is said to be trading at a **forward discount** with respect to the foreign currency.

EXAMPLE

Since the franc is fetching fewer pounds in the forward market than in the spot market (£0.555 < £0.625), the franc is currently trading at a forward discount with respect to the pound. This reflects the market's belief that the franc is going to lose value in relation to the pound.

---

e. The implications of these relationships can be generalized as follows:

If the domestic currency is trading at a forward	Then it is expected to
Premium	Gain purchasing power
Discount	Lose purchasing power

Stop and review! You have completed the outline for this subunit. Study multiple-choice questions 11 through 22 beginning on page 148.

4.3 MITIGATING EXCHANGE RATE RISK

1. **Exchange Rate Fluctuations**

   a. Fluctuations in currency exchange rates can have a significant impact on a firm's profitability.

   b. Review the example of exchange rate/purchasing power interaction in Subunit 4.2, item 3., on page 137. Note that a firm with a payable denominated in a foreign currency would prefer that the foreign currency depreciate by the settlement date, requiring fewer units of its domestic currency to pay off the debt.

      1) The firm on the receivable side of this transaction is indifferent to fluctuations in the exchange rate of the two currencies; the settlement amount is fixed in terms of its domestic currency.

   c. By the same token, a firm with a receivable denominated in a foreign currency would prefer that the foreign currency appreciate by the settlement date. When the firm converts the foreign currency into its domestic currency, the conversion will result in more units of the domestic currency.

      1) The firm on the payable side of this transaction is indifferent to fluctuations in the exchange rate of the two currencies; the settlement amount is fixed in terms of its domestic currency.

d.   These effects can be summarized in the following table:

As of the Settlement Date	A Domestic Firm with Foreign Currency	
	Net Inflows	Net Outflows
	Will Experience a	
If the domestic currency has appreciated and the foreign currency has depreciated	(Loss)	Gain
If the domestic currency has depreciated and the foreign currency has appreciated	Gain	(Loss)

2.   **Three Types of Exposure to Exchange Rate Risk**

   a.   Transaction Exposure

      1)   Transaction exposure is the exposure to fluctuations in exchange rates between the date a transaction is entered into and the settlement date.

   b.   Economic Exposure

      1)   Economic exposure is the exposure to fluctuations in exchange rates resulting from overall economic conditions.

   c.   Translation Exposure

      1)   Translation exposure is the exposure to fluctuations in exchange rates between the date a transaction is entered into and the date that financial statements denominated in another currency must be reported.

3.   **Transaction Exposure**

   a.   Transaction exposure is the exposure to fluctuations in exchange rates between the date a transaction is entered into and the settlement date.

      1)   Multinational corporations enter into hundreds and even thousands of individual cross-border transactions in the course of a year. Each of these transactions is subject to exchange rate variations between the transaction date and the settlement date.

      2)   To address transaction exposure, a firm must

         a)   Estimate its net cash flows in each currency for impacted transactions.

            i)   If inflows and outflows in a given currency are nearly equal, transaction exposure in that currency is minimal, even if the currency itself is quite volatile.

         b)   Measure the potential effect of exposure in each currency.

            i)   A range of possible rates for each currency must be estimated, reflecting that currency's volatility.

         c)   Use hedging tools to mitigate exposure to exchange rate fluctuations (see the next page).

4. **Hedging in Response to Transaction Exposure**

    a. Hedging as a Tool against Uncertainty

        1) When hedging, some amount of possible upside is forgone in order to protect against the potential downside. Hedging thus embodies the old saying, "A bird in the hand is worth two in the bush."

    b. Basic Hedging Principles

        1) When a debtor is to pay a foreign currency at some point in the future, the risk is that the foreign currency will appreciate in the meantime, making it more expensive in terms of the debtor's domestic currency. The hedge is to purchase the foreign currency forward to lock in a definite price.

EXAMPLE

A U.S. company knows that it will need 100,000 Canadian dollars in 60 days to pay an invoice. The firm thus hedges by purchasing 100,000 Canadian dollars 60 days forward. The company is essentially buying a guarantee that it will have C $100,000 available for use in 60 days. The 60-day forward rate for a Canadian dollar is US $0.99. Thus, for the privilege of having a guaranteed receipt of 100,000 Canadian dollars, the company will commit now to paying $99,000 in 60 days.

The counterparty to the hedge just described (i.e., the seller of Canadian dollars) might also be hedging, but could be speculating or simply making a market in the instrument. The two parties are indifferent to each other's goals.

---

        2) When a creditor is to receive a foreign currency at some point in the future, the risk is that the foreign currency will depreciate in the meantime, making it worth less in terms of the creditor's domestic currency. The hedge is to sell the foreign currency forward to lock in a definite price.

EXAMPLE

A U.S. company knows that it will be receiving 5,000,000 pesos in 30 days from the sale of some equipment at one of its facilities in Mexico. The spot rate for a peso is $0.77, and the 30-day forward rate is $0.80. The firm wants to be sure that it will be able sell the pesos it will be receiving in 30 days for $0.80 each. The firm thus hedges by selling 5,000,000 pesos 30 days forward. The company is buying a guarantee that it will be able to sell 5,000,000 pesos in 30 days and receive $4,000,000 (5,000,000 × $0.80) in return.

The spot rate on day 30 turns out to be $0.82. Thus, the U.S. company could have made more money by forgoing the hedge and simply waiting to convert the pesos on day 30. However, this possibility was not worth the risk that the peso might have fallen below $0.80.

The counterparty to the hedge just described (i.e., the buyer of pesos) might also be hedging but could be speculating or simply making a market in the instrument. The two parties are indifferent to each other's goals.

---

    c. The four most common tools for addressing transaction exposure are as follows:

        1) **Money Market Hedges**

           a) The least complex tool for hedging exchange rate risk is the money market hedge.

           b) A firm with a payable denominated in a foreign currency can buy a money market instrument denominated in that currency that is timed to mature when the payable is due. Exchange rate fluctuations between the transaction date and the settlement date are avoided.

           c) A firm with a receivable denominated in a foreign currency can borrow the amount and convert it to its domestic currency now, then pay off the foreign loan when the receivable is collected.

2) **Forward Contracts**

    a) Large corporations that have close relationships with major banks are able to enter into contracts for individual transactions concerning large amounts.

    b) The bank guarantees that it will make available to the firm a given quantity of a certain currency at a definite rate at some point in the future. The price charged by the bank for this guarantee is called the premium.

EXAMPLE

A large U.S. firm purchases equipment from a Korean manufacturer for 222,000,000 won, due in 90 days. The exchange rate on the date of sale is $1 to 1,110 won. The U.S. firm suspects that the won may appreciate over the next 90 days and wants to lock in a forward rate of 1-to-1,110. The firm negotiates a contract whereby its bank promises to deliver 222,000,000 won to the firm in 90 days for $200,000. In return for this guarantee, the firm will pay the bank a 2% premium ($200,000 × 2% = $4,000).

---

    c) Clearly, the use of any mitigation strategy carries an opportunity cost. The firm must execute its part of the contract whether the exchange rate with the won has fluctuated or not. If the won falls in value or rises less than the 2% premium with respect to the dollar, the firm has incurred an economic loss on the transaction.

3) **Futures Contracts**

    a) Whereas forward contracts are negotiated individually between the parties on a one-by-one basis, futures contracts are essentially commodities that are traded on an exchange, making them available to more parties. The clearinghouse underwrites the contract, removing the risk of nonperformance by either party.

    b) Futures contracts are only available for generic amounts (e.g, 62,500 British pounds, 100,000 Brazilian reals, 12,500,000 Japanese yen) and with specific settlement dates (typically the third Wednesday in March, June, September, and December). This rigidity makes them less flexible than forward contracts because forward contracts are customized for the parties.

Background

The largest market in the world for trading currency futures is the Chicago Mercantile Exchange. Information about the sizes and prices of various actively traded futures contracts is available at www.cmegroup.com/trading/fx/.

---

4) **Currency Options**

    a) A currency option differs from a currency futures contract in that a futures contract is, as the name implies, a binding contract; both parties must perform. An option is exercised only if the party purchasing the option chooses to.

    b) Two types of options are available:

        i) A **call option** gives the holder the right to buy (i.e., call for) a specified amount of currency at a specified price at a predetermined date in the future. Call options are among the many tools available to **hedge payables**.

        ii) A **put option** gives the holder the right to sell (i.e., put onto the market) a specified amount of currency at a specified price at a predetermined date in the future. Put options are among the many tools available to **hedge receivables**.

5. **Economic Exposure**

    a. Economic exposure is the exposure to fluctuations in exchange rates resulting from overall economic conditions.

    ### EXAMPLES

    An exporter may require all of its customers to pay their invoices in the exporter's domestic currency, placing all the transaction risk of exchange rate variation on the customers. If the exporter's currency strengthens beyond a certain point, the exporter's products will no longer be price-competitive, and the customers will take their business to local firms, reducing the exporter's cash inflows.

    A manufacturer establishes operations in a low-wage country. As that country's economy strengthens, its currency appreciates and real wages increase. The manufacturer's cash outflows have thus risen, wiping out the original cost advantage.

    ---

    b. Estimating Economic Exposure

        1) The degree of exposure can be estimated using either of two approaches:

            a) Sensitivity of earnings. The entity prepares a pro forma income statement for operations in each country.

            b) Sensitivity of cash flows. The entity performs a regression analysis, weighting each net cash flow by the prevalence of that currency in the firm's portfolio.

        2) Next, the entity constructs multiple scenarios (i.e., performs a sensitivity analysis) using various estimated exchange rates and determines the ultimate impact of each scenario on accrual-basis earnings or cash flows.

    c. Mitigating Economic Exposure

        1) A high level of economic exposure may require restructuring the entity's operations using the following general guidelines:

	Actions to be Taken when Foreign Currency	
Reliance on	Inflows are Greater	Outflows are Greater
Sales to foreign customers	Reduce foreign sales	Increase foreign sales
Purchases from foreign suppliers	Increase foreign orders	Reduce foreign orders

6. **Translation Exposure**

    a. Translation exposure is the risk that a foreign subsidiary's balance sheet items and result of operations, denominated in a currency different from the parent's consolidated financial statements currency, will change in value as a result of exchange rate fluctuations.

    b. The degree of a firm's exposure to translation risk is determined by three factors:

        1) Proportion of Total Business Conducted by Foreign Subsidiaries

            a) A firm with half of its revenues derived from overseas subsidiaries has a high degree of exposure to translation risk. A 100% domestic firm has none.

            b) Note that a 100% domestic firm with foreign customers or suppliers still has transaction and economic risk.

        2) Locations of Foreign Subsidiaries

            a) A firm with a subsidiary in a country with a volatile currency has more translation risk than a firm with a subsidiary in a country with a stable currency.

        3) Applicable Accounting Method

Stop and review! You have completed the outline for this subunit. Study multiple-choice questions 23 through 29 beginning on page 151.

QUESTIONS

4.1 Protectionism

1. Which of the following is a tariff?

A. Licensing requirements.

B. Consumption taxes on imported goods.

C. Unreasonable standards pertaining to product quality and safety.

D. Domestic content rules.

Answer (B) is correct.
REQUIRED: The example of a tariff.
DISCUSSION: Tariffs are excise taxes on imported goods imposed either to generate revenue or protect domestic producers. Thus, consumption taxes on imported goods are tariffs.
Answer (A) is incorrect. Licensing requirements limit exports, e.g., of militarily sensitive technology. Answer (C) is incorrect. Unreasonable standards pertaining to product quality and safety are nontariff trade barriers. Answer (D) is incorrect. Domestic content rules require that a portion of an imported good be made in the importing country.

2. Which of the following is a direct effect of imposing a protective tariff on an imported product?

A. Lower domestic prices on the imported item.

B. Lower domestic consumption of the item.

C. Reduced domestic production of the item.

D. Higher sales revenues for foreign producers of the item.

Answer (B) is correct.
REQUIRED: The direct effect of imposing a protective tariff on an imported product.
DISCUSSION: A protective tariff adds to the purchase price of imported goods. If an imported good's sales price is higher than a comparable, less expensive domestic good, consumers will purchase the domestic good. Thus, the direct effect of imposing a protective tariff on an imported good is lower domestic consumption.
Answer (A) is incorrect. A protective tariff can only increase the domestic price of the imported item. Answer (C) is incorrect. As the imported item's domestic price increases, demand for domestic goods will increase. Thus, domestic production will increase, not decrease. Answer (D) is incorrect. As the imported item's domestic price increases, demand for the item decreases. Lower sales revenues will result.

3. Import restrictions for purposes of creating domestic employment

A. Are likely to increase the number of export jobs.

B. May lead to lower prices for consumers.

C. Will lead to lower sales tax collections.

D. May lead to retaliation by other countries.

Answer (D) is correct.
REQUIRED: The true statement about the effect of import restrictions for creating domestic employment.
DISCUSSION: Protectionism in the form of import restrictions can lead to a variety of economic and social costs, including higher prices to consumers for both domestic and imported goods, higher taxes, and retaliation by other countries.
Answer (A) is incorrect. Export jobs may decline due to retaliation by other countries. Answer (B) is incorrect. Consumers will have to pay higher prices for the protected domestic goods and may have to pay higher prices for foreign goods as well. Answer (C) is incorrect. Depending on the price elasticity of demand for the product, sales tax revenues may or may not fall.

4. Which of the following is an economic rationale for government intervention in trade?

A. Maintaining spheres of influence.

B. Protecting infant industries.

C. Preserving national identity.

D. Dealing with friendly countries.

Answer (B) is correct.
REQUIRED: The best economic rationale for government intervention in trade.
DISCUSSION: The infant-industry argument contends that protective tariffs are needed to allow new domestic industries to become established. Once such industries reach a maturity stage in their life cycles, the tariffs can supposedly be removed.

5. Which of the following results in a complete elimination of trade?

   A. Voluntary export restraints.

   B. Domestic content requirements.

   C. Embargoes.

   D. Import quotas.

Answer (C) is correct.
   REQUIRED: The item that results in a complete elimination of trade.
   DISCUSSION: An embargo is a total ban on some kinds of imports. It is an extreme form of the import quota (i.e., the quota is zero).
   Answer (A) is incorrect. A voluntary restraint can be waived. Answer (B) is incorrect. Domestic content rules require that at least a portion of the imported product be constructed from parts manufactured in the importing nation. As long as this requirement is met, trade is not limited. Answer (D) is incorrect. Import quotas set fixed limits on the quantity of certain goods that can be imported. They limit but do not eliminate trade.

6. The appropriate remedy for the dumping of products by a foreign firm in the U.S. market would be to

   A. Pass "buy American" laws.

   B. Impose restrictions on U.S. exports to the offending country.

   C. Impose countervailing duties or tariffs.

   D. Deny "most favored nation" treatment to exporters of the offending country.

Answer (C) is correct.
   REQUIRED: The appropriate remedy for the dumping of products by a foreign firm in the U.S. market.
   DISCUSSION: Dumping is the practice of supporting exports by selling products at a lower price in foreign markets than in the domestic market. The result is that foreign goods (such as certain items produced in the Far East) can be purchased in the U.S. at a price much lower than would be charged by a U.S. manufacturer. Since dumping lowers the price of foreign goods, the appropriate remedy would be for the importing nation to impose a tariff that would reduce the price differential.
   Answer (A) is incorrect. The passing of "buy American" laws could result in a decline in overall domestic consumption, higher prices, and retaliatory foreign action. Answer (B) is incorrect. A country does not benefit from restricting its exports. Answer (D) is incorrect. Denying "most favored nation" treatment would make trade with a country more difficult and would be a more extreme remedy than necessary.

7. Domestic content rules

   A. Tend to be imposed by capital-intensive countries.

   B. Tend to be imposed by labor-intensive countries.

   C. Exclude products not made domestically.

   D. Restrict demand for affected products.

Answer (A) is correct.
   REQUIRED: The description of domestic content rules.
   DISCUSSION: Domestic content rules require that at least a portion of any imported product be constructed from parts manufactured in the importing nation. This rule is sometimes used by capital-intensive nations. Parts can be produced using idle capacity and then sent to a labor-intensive country for final assembly.
   Answer (B) is incorrect. Labor-intensive exporters are more likely to assemble final products. Answer (C) is incorrect. Domestic content rules place limits on, but do not exclude, imports. Answer (D) is incorrect. Supply is restricted.

8. An exemption from U.S. antitrust law is provided by

   A. The Export Trading Company Act of 1982.

   B. The Export Administration Act of 1979.

   C. Antidumping rules.

   D. The Foreign Corrupt Practices Act.

Answer (A) is correct.
   REQUIRED: The source of exemption from U.S. antitrust law.
   DISCUSSION: The Export Trading Company Act of 1982 permits competitors to form export trading companies without regard to U.S. antitrust legislation.
   Answer (B) is incorrect. This act requires licensing of certain technology. Answer (C) is incorrect. Antidumping rules prevent foreign producers from "dumping" excess goods on the domestic market at less than cost to squeeze out competitors and gain control of the market. Answer (D) is incorrect. The FCPA prohibits bribery of foreign officials.

9. What is the most likely economic effect of tariffs and quotas?

   A. Workers are shifted into more efficient export industries.

   B. Tariffs but not quotas affect all importers of the affected goods equally.

   C. Total world output increases.

   D. The price increase is received by exporters in foreign countries.

Answer (B) is correct.
   REQUIRED: The effect of tariffs and quotas.
   DISCUSSION: A tariff has an equal effect on all goods on which it is applied. Import licenses, however, may be awarded based on political favoritism.
   Answer (A) is incorrect. The effect is to shift workers into relatively inefficient domestic protected industries. Answer (C) is incorrect. Total world output decreases. Answer (D) is incorrect. A tariff increases the domestic government's general tax revenues.

10. The return to the home country of income earned by a domestic firm in a foreign country is

   A. Expropriation.

   B. Bankruptcy.

   C. Repatriation.

   D. Reinvestment.

Answer (C) is correct.
   REQUIRED: The return to the home country of income earned in a foreign country.
   DISCUSSION: Many firms have business operations abroad. Repatriation is conversion of funds held in a foreign country into another currency and remittance of these funds to another nation. A firm must often obtain permission from the currency exchange authorities to repatriate earnings and investments. Regulations in many nations encourage a reinvestment of earnings in the country.
   Answer (A) is incorrect. Expropriation is a foreign government's seizure (nationalization) of the assets of a business for a public purpose and for just compensation. Answer (B) is incorrect. Bankruptcy occurs when a person's liabilities exceed assets or (s)he cannot meet obligations when they are due. Answer (D) is incorrect. Reinvestment in the foreign country is a purpose of restrictions on repatriation.

4.2 Currency Exchange Rates

11. What is the effect when a foreign competitor's currency becomes weaker compared to the U.S. dollar?

   A. The foreign company will have an advantage in the U.S. market.

   B. The foreign company will be disadvantaged in the U.S. market.

   C. The fluctuation in the foreign currency's exchange rate has no effect on the U.S. company's sales or cost of goods sold.

   D. It is better for the U.S. company when the value of the U.S. dollar strengthens.

Answer (A) is correct.
   REQUIRED: The effect of a weakening of a competitor's currency.
   DISCUSSION: If the foreign currency weakens compared with the U.S. dollar, the U.S. dollar will have more buying power in the foreign company's country. Thus, the foreign company will be able to sell more products than the U.S. company for the same amount of dollars.
   Answer (B) is incorrect. A weakening foreign currency makes foreign-produced products cheaper per U.S. dollar. Answer (C) is incorrect. A weakening of the foreign currency will decrease the foreign company's prices relative to the U.S. company's. Answer (D) is incorrect. A strengthening U.S. dollar can buy more of a weakening foreign currency (i.e., products produced in that country), effectively increasing the price of U.S.-produced products in the foreign market.

12. If a U.S. firm can buy £20,000 for $100,000, the rate of exchange for the pound is

   A. $.20

   B. $5

   C. $20

   D. $50

Answer (B) is correct.
   REQUIRED: The rate of exchange.
   DISCUSSION: An exchange rate of $5 to the pound is produced by dividing $100,000 by £20,000.
   Answer (A) is incorrect. The exchange rate for the dollar, not the pound, is $.20. Answer (C) is incorrect. The exchange rate is $5 to the pound. Answer (D) is incorrect. The exchange rate is $5 to the pound.

13. If the value of the U.S. dollar in foreign currency markets changes from $1 = .75 euros to $1 = .70 euros,

    A. The euro has depreciated against the dollar.

    B. Products imported from Europe to the U.S. will become more expensive.

    C. U.S. tourists in Europe will find their dollars will buy more European products.

    D. U.S. exports to Europe should decrease.

Answer (B) is correct.
    REQUIRED: The effect of a depreciation in the value of the dollar.
    DISCUSSION: The dollar has declined in value relative to the euro. If an American had previously wished to purchase a European product that was priced at 10 euros, the price would have been about $13.33. After the dollar's decline in value, the price of the item has increased to about $14.29. Hence, imports from Europe should decrease and exports increase.
    Answer (A) is incorrect. The euro has appreciated (increased in value) relative to the dollar. Answer (C) is incorrect. Dollars will buy fewer European products. Answer (D) is incorrect. U.S. exports should increase because the euro has appreciated with respect to the dollar.

14. The U.S. dollar has a freely floating exchange rate. When the dollar has fallen considerably in relation to other currencies, the

    A. Trade account in the U.S. balance of payments is neither in a deficit nor in a surplus because of the floating exchange rates.

    B. Capital account in the U.S. balance of payments is neither in a deficit nor in a surplus because of the floating exchange rates.

    C. Fall in the dollar's value cannot be expected to have any effect on the U.S. trade balance.

    D. Cheaper dollar helps U.S. exporters of domestically produced goods.

Answer (D) is correct.
    REQUIRED: The true statement about the fall in the price of the dollar relative to other currencies.
    DISCUSSION: A decline in the value of the dollar relative to other currencies lowers the price of U.S. goods to foreign consumers. Thus, exporters of domestically produced goods benefit. A low value of the dollar also decreases imports by making foreign goods more expensive.
    Answer (A) is incorrect. The net export will increase as a result of dollar depreciation. Answer (B) is incorrect. The capital account benefits from the cheaper dollar. Foreigners can buy more dollars with fewer yen, marks, etc. Moreover, foreign capital inflow increases because of the federal government's budget deficits. Hence, the U.S. experiences a net capital inflow. Answer (C) is incorrect. The fall in the dollar has a positive effect on the nation's trade deficit. Exports increase and imports decrease.

15. If the U.S. dollar declines in value relative to the currencies of many of the U.S. trading partners, the likely result is that

    A. Foreign currencies will depreciate against the dollar.

    B. The U.S. balance of payments deficit will become worse.

    C. U.S. exports will tend to increase.

    D. U.S. imports will tend to increase.

Answer (C) is correct.
    REQUIRED: The true statement about the decline in the value of the U.S. dollar.
    DISCUSSION: The decline in the value of the dollar reduces the prices of U.S. goods to foreigners and should increase exports. Also, foreign goods will be higher priced (in dollars) and imports from foreign countries should decrease, thus helping the U.S. balance of payments.
    Answer (A) is incorrect. The dollar has depreciated against foreign currencies. Answer (B) is incorrect. The U.S. trade balance of payments should improve. Answer (D) is incorrect. U.S. imports will decline. Foreign goods will be higher priced than before.

16. If the central bank of a country raises interest rates sharply, the country's currency will likely

    A. Increase in relative value.

    B. Remain unchanged in value.

    C. Decrease in relative value.

    D. Decrease sharply in value at first and then return to its initial value.

Answer (A) is correct.
    REQUIRED: The effect on a country's currency if its central bank raises interest rates sharply.
    DISCUSSION: Exchange rates fluctuate depending upon the demand for each country's currency. If a country raises its interest rates, its currency will appreciate. The demand for investment at the higher interest rates will shift the demand curve for the currency to the right. The reverse holds true for a decrease in interest rates.

17. Given a spot exchange rate for the U.S. dollar against the pound sterling of $1.4925 per pound and a 90-day forward rate of $1.4775 per pound,

A. The dollar is at a discount against the pound and undervalued in the forward market.

B. The dollar is at a premium against the pound and overvalued in the forward market.

C. The forward dollar is at a premium against the pound.

D. The forward dollar is at a discount against the pound.

Answer (C) is correct.
    REQUIRED: The true statement about the given spot exchange rates.
    DISCUSSION: The exchange rate for the pound sterling is lower in the forward market than the spot market. Thus, the pound sterling is trading at a forward discount relative to the U.S. dollar, which is trading at a forward premium.
    Answer (A) is incorrect. The facts do not indicate whether the rates are over- or undervalued. Answer (B) is incorrect. The facts do not indicate whether the rates are over- or undervalued. Answer (D) is incorrect. The dollar is at a forward premium relative to the pound sterling, not a discount.

18. The accompanying graph depicts the supply of and demand for U.S. dollars in terms of euros at a moment in time. Currently, the equilibrium exchange rate is $1 to 0.65 €. If inflation of the dollar exceeds that of the euro, the new equilibrium exchange rate would most likely settle at

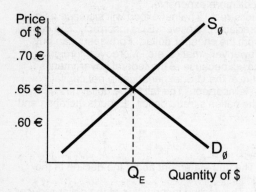

	Quantity	Price
A.	Indeterminate	0.70 €
B.	Lower than Q_E	0.70 €
C.	Higher than Q_E	0.60 €
D.	Indeterminate	0.60 €

Answer (D) is correct.
    REQUIRED: The graphic depiction of inflation of a base currency against a foreign currency.
    DISCUSSION: The graph depicts the supply of and demand for a particular foreign currency by holders of euros; i.e., the euro is the domestic currency. When the foreign currency inflates faster than the domestic currency, the foreign currency loses purchasing power. The weakening foreign currency is less attractive, and demand for it falls (its demand curve shifts to the left). Whether the supply curve for dollars remains the same or shifts to the right, the new equilibrium price for it will be lower (takes fewer euros to buy $1). The new equilibrium quantity could be higher, lower, or the same as the old one.
    Answer (A) is incorrect. The new equilibrium price will be lower. Answer (B) is incorrect. The new quantity cannot be determined, and the new price will be lower. Answer (C) is incorrect. The new equilibrium quantity cannot be determined.

19. The spot rate for one Australian dollar is $0.92685 and the 60-day forward rate is $0.93005. Which one of the following statements is consistent with these facts?

A. The U.S. dollar is trading at a forward discount with respect to the Australian dollar.

B. The U.S. dollar is trading at a forward premium with respect to the Australian dollar.

C. The U.S. dollar has lost purchasing power with respect to the Australian dollar.

D. The U.S. dollar has gained purchasing power with respect to the Australian dollar.

Answer (A) is correct.
    REQUIRED: The statement that can be concluded from the information given about a forward exchange rate.
    DISCUSSION: The exchange rate for the Australian dollar is higher in the forward market than the spot market; the Australian dollar is therefore trading at a forward premium. From this, it follows that the U.S. dollar is trading at a forward discount.
    Answer (B) is incorrect. The U.S. dollar is trading at a forward discount with respect to the Australian dollar. Answer (C) is incorrect. No conclusion about purchasing power changes can be drawn without information about past exchange rates. Answer (D) is incorrect. No conclusion about purchasing power changes can be drawn without information about past exchange rates.

20. Which one of the following statements supports the conclusion that the U.S. dollar has gained purchasing power against the Japanese yen?

    A. Inflation has recently been higher in the U.S. than in Japan.

    B. The dollar is currently trading at a premium in the forward market with respect to the yen.

    C. The yen's spot rate with respect to the dollar has just fallen.

    D. Studies recently published in the financial press have shed doubt on the interest rate parity (IRP) theory.

Answer (C) is correct.
    REQUIRED: The statement that supports the conclusion that the U.S. dollar has gained purchasing power against the Japanese yen.
    DISCUSSION: If the yen's spot rate has just fallen, then more yen are required to buy a single dollar. The yen has therefore depreciated, i.e., lost purchasing power. At the same time, the dollar has gained purchasing power.
    Answer (A) is incorrect. This statement reflects a loss, not a gain, of purchasing power for the dollar. Answer (B) is incorrect. No conclusion can be drawn about changes in purchasing power simply from a statement about forward rates. Answer (D) is incorrect. No conclusion can be drawn about changes in purchasing power simply from evidence for or against the interest rate parity (IRP) theory.

21. A shift of the demand curve for a country's currency to the right could be caused by which of the following?

    A. A foreign government placing restrictions on the importation of the country's goods.

    B. A fall in the country's interest rates.

    C. Domestic inflation worsens.

    D. A rise in consumer incomes in another country.

Answer (D) is correct.
    REQUIRED: The condition that could cause a rise in demand for a country's currency.
    DISCUSSION: Citizens with higher incomes look for new consumption opportunities in other countries, driving up the demand for those currencies. Thus, as incomes rise in one country, the prices of foreign currencies rise as well.
    Answer (A) is incorrect. A shift to the right would be caused by a foreign government removing, not placing, restrictions on the importation of the country's goods. Answer (B) is incorrect. A shift to the right would be caused by a rise, not a fall, in the country's interest rates. Answer (C) is incorrect. As a country's inflation rate rises, its currency loses purchasing power and investors move their capital elsewhere, driving demand for the country's currency down.

22. All of the following are trade-related factors affecting currency exchange rates **except**

    A. Relative interest rates.

    B. Trade barriers.

    C. Relative incomes.

    D. Relative inflation rates.

Answer (A) is correct.
    REQUIRED: The factor affecting exchange rates that is not trade related.
    DISCUSSION: Relative interest rates is a financial, not a trade-related, factor affecting currency exchange rates.

4.3 Mitigating Exchange Rate Risk

23. An American importer of English clothing has contracted to pay an amount fixed in British pounds 3 months from now. If the importer worries that the U.S. dollar may depreciate sharply against the British pound in the interim, it would be well advised to

    A. Buy pounds in the forward exchange market.

    B. Sell pounds in the forward exchange market.

    C. Buy dollars in the futures market.

    D. Sell dollars in the futures market.

Answer (A) is correct.
    REQUIRED: The action to hedge a liability denominated in a foreign currency.
    DISCUSSION: The American importer should buy pounds now. If the dollar depreciates against the pound in the next 90 days, the gain on the forward exchange contract would offset the loss from having to pay more dollars to satisfy the liability.
    Answer (B) is incorrect. Selling pounds would compound the risk of loss for someone who has incurred a liability. However, it would be an appropriate hedge of a receivable denominated in pounds. Answer (C) is incorrect. The importer needs pounds, not dollars. Answer (D) is incorrect. Although buying pounds might be equivalent to selling dollars for pounds, this is not the best answer. This choice does not state what is received for the dollars.

24. A U.S. manufacturer sold a piece of equipment to an engineering firm in New Zealand. The New Zealand firm must pay the invoice in U.S. dollars in 30 days and would like to mitigate the risk that the New Zealand dollar will depreciate against the U.S. dollar in the meantime. The type of exchange rate risk contemplated by the New Zealand firm is known as

A. Transition exposure.

B. Economic exposure.

C. Transaction exposure.

D. Translation exposure.

Answer (C) is correct.

    REQUIRED: The type of exchange rate exposure embodied in a sale transaction.

    DISCUSSION: Transaction exposure is the exposure to fluctuations in exchange rates between the date a transaction is entered into and the settlement date.

    Answer (A) is incorrect. Economists do not recognize "transition exposure." Answer (B) is incorrect. Economic exposure is the exposure to fluctuations in exchange rates resulting from overall economic conditions. Answer (D) is incorrect. Translation exposure is the risk that a foreign subsidiary's balance sheet items and the result of operations denominated in a currency different from the parent's consolidated financial statements currency will change in value as a result of exchange rate changes.

25. A massive inflation across the entire economy of one of a firm's trading partners has benefited the firm greatly by making its fixed amount of payables denominated in that country's currency much cheaper. This exemplifies exchange rate risk stemming from

A. Transition exposure.

B. Economic exposure.

C. Transaction exposure.

D. Translation exposure.

Answer (B) is correct.

    REQUIRED: The type of exchange rate exposure embodied in a foreign country's deflation.

    DISCUSSION: Economic exposure is the exposure to fluctuations in exchange rates resulting from overall economic conditions.

    Answer (A) is incorrect. Economists do not recognize "transition exposure." Answer (C) is incorrect. Transaction exposure is the exposure to fluctuations in exchange rates between the date a transaction is entered into and the settlement date. Answer (D) is incorrect. Translation exposure is the risk that a foreign subsidiary's balance sheet items and the result of operations denominated in a currency different from the parent's consolidated financial statements currency will change in value as a result of exchange rate changes.

26. A Chinese conglomerate owns a construction subsidiary that is building a port in Mozambique. The firm pays its workers in the Mozambique currency but keeps its books for the project in the South African rand. At the end of the fiscal year, the conglomerate must report consolidated financial statements denominated in the yuan. The exchange rate risk encountered by the conglomerate in the currency conversions leading up to its consolidated financial statements is known as

A. Transition exposure.

B. Economic exposure.

C. Transaction exposure.

D. Translation exposure.

Answer (D) is correct.

    REQUIRED: The type of exchange rate exposure embodied in converting the books of foreign subsidiaries.

    DISCUSSION: Translation exposure is the exposure to fluctuations in exchange rates between the date a transaction is entered into and the date that financial statements denominated in another currency must be reported.

    Answer (A) is incorrect. Economists do not recognize "transition exposure." Answer (B) is incorrect. Economic exposure is the exposure to fluctuations in exchange rates resulting from overall economic conditions. Answer (C) is incorrect. Transaction exposure is the exposure to fluctuations in exchange rates between the date a transaction is entered into and the settlement date.

27. A company based in West Palm Beach, Florida, is building a resort in Jamaica. The Jamaican property owners must make a progress payment of US $1 million in 30 days. The spot rate for the U.S. dollar is 88 Jamaican dollars (J $), and the 30-day forward rate is J $90. The most likely hedge in response to the transaction exposure inherent in this situation is

A. The contractor will purchase J $88,000,000 in the spot market.

B. The contractor will sell J $90,000,000 in the 30-day forward market.

C. The property owners will purchase US $1,000,000 in the 30-day forward market.

D. The property owners will sell US $1,000,000 in the 30-day forward market.

Answer (C) is correct.

    REQUIRED: The most likely hedging transaction in response to a receivable/payable.

    DISCUSSION: This receivable/payable is denominated in the currency of the creditor; the creditor thus lacks an incentive to hedge. The debtors (the property owners) want to hedge against the possibility that their domestic currency will depreciate against the U.S. dollar in the next 30 days. The typical mitigation strategy would be to purchase the amount needed to pay the debt such that the funds will be available at the time they are needed.

    Answer (A) is incorrect. The party on the receivable side of this transaction has no need to hedge; the debt is denominated in its domestic currency. Answer (B) is incorrect. The party on the receivable side of this transaction has no need to hedge; the debt is denominated in its domestic currency. Answer (D) is incorrect. The debtors need US $1,000,000 in 30 days to pay the invoice. Thus, they would purchase, not sell, the U.S. dollar in the forward market.

28. A company headquartered in Vancouver, British Columbia, is building a pipeline in Russia. The invoice amount is due in 90 days and is denominated at 28 million rubles. The Canadian dollar is trading for 28 rubles currently and 29 rubles 90 days forward. Which of the following strategies will the Canadian firm most likely pursue in the 90-day forward market to hedge the transaction exposure inherent in this situation?

A. Sell 29,000,000 rubles.

B. Purchase 28,000,000 rubles.

C. Purchase 29,000,000 rubles.

D. Sell 28,000,000 rubles.

Answer (D) is correct.
    REQUIRED: The most likely hedging transaction in response to a foreign-denominated receivable.
    DISCUSSION: The Canadian company knows that it will be receiving 28,000,000 rubles in 90 days. The firm wants to be sure that it will be able sell these rubles at that time for a certain number of Canadian dollars. The Canadian firm thus hedges by selling 28,000,000 rubles in the 90-day forward market. The company is buying a guarantee that it will be able to sell a definite number of rubles in 90 days and receive a definite number of Canadian dollars in return, regardless of fluctuations in the exchange rate in the meantime.
    Answer (A) is incorrect. The creditor firm will receive only 28 million rubles. Answer (B) is incorrect. The creditor firm wants to sell, not purchase, forward rubles. Answer (C) is incorrect. The creditor firm wants to sell, not purchase, forward rubles; also, the firm will receive only 28 million rubles.

29. A company with significant sales in a particular foreign country has recently been subjected to extreme variations in the exchange rate with that country's currency. These variations are expected to continue. To mitigate the resulting economic exposure, a likely strategy for the company to implement would be to

A. Reduce sales to that country.

B. Increase sales to that country.

C. Reduce orders from suppliers in other foreign countries.

D. Increase orders from suppliers in other foreign countries.

Answer (A) is correct.
    REQUIRED: The most likely strategy to mitigate economic exposure to exchange rate variation.
    DISCUSSION: When cash inflows from a country with a volatile currency exceed cash outflows to that country, the appropriate strategy to mitigate economic exposure is to decrease sales to that country.
    Answer (B) is incorrect. The appropriate strategy to mitigate this economic exposure is to decrease, not increase, sales to that country. Answer (C) is incorrect. Reducing orders from suppliers in other foreign countries will not address this economic exposure. Answer (D) is incorrect. Increasing orders from suppliers in other foreign countries will not address this economic exposure.

Use the additional questions in Gleim **CPA Test Prep Online** to create Test Sessions that emulate Prometric!

4.4 PRACTICE WRITTEN COMMUNICATION TASK

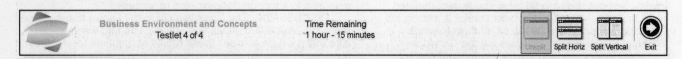

| Business Environment and Concepts | Time Remaining | | | |
| Testlet 4 of 4 | 1 hour - 15 minutes | Unsplit | Split Horiz | Split Vertical | Exit |

DIRECTIONS

Note: If you believe you have encountered a software malfunction, report it to the test center staff immediately.

Navigation

To navigate from task to task, use the controls at the bottom of the screen. Click on the **Next** button to advance to the next task, or the **Previous** button to go to the previous task. To go directly to any task, click on its number.

| ⚑ = Reminder | | Directions | 1 2 3 4 5 6 7 | | ◀ Previous   Next ▶ |

If you would like a reminder to revisit a task, or want to indicate that you are finished with it, click on the reminder flag below the task number. To clear the flag, click on it again. Reminder flags are for your use only – they do not contribute to your score.

Tabs

In this part of the examination, you will be asked to complete various tasks. Every task has one or more **Work Tabs**. Every task also has a **Help** tab.

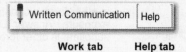

| | Written Communication | Help |

| Work tab | Help tab |

Work Tabs:

- **Work Tabs** are identified with a pencil icon. This is where your responses are expected.
- Each task has one or more **Work Tabs**.
- **Work Tabs** contain directions for completing the task - be sure to read these directions carefully.
- The **Work Tab** name in the example above is for illustration only - yours will differ.
- You must complete all of the **Work Tabs** in each task to receive full credit.

Help Tab:

- The **Help Tab** provides assistance with the exam software that is used in this task. For example, if the task is to compose a memorandum, **Help** will provide information about the word processor.

The Toolbar

The toolbar at the top of the screen shows the amount of time remaining for you to complete the tasks. In addition, the following tools are available. Note that only the **Exit** button is displayed when Directions are visible - the others will appear when you begin the tasks.

Click on these buttons to split or unsplit the screen. You can split the screen vertically or horizontally.

Click on this button to go on to the next part of the examination. You must complete all of the tasks to receive full credit. Once you click on **Exit** and confirm the action, you will NOT be able to return to this testlet.

| ⚑ = Reminder | | Directions | *1 | | | | | | | ◀ Previous   Next ▶ |

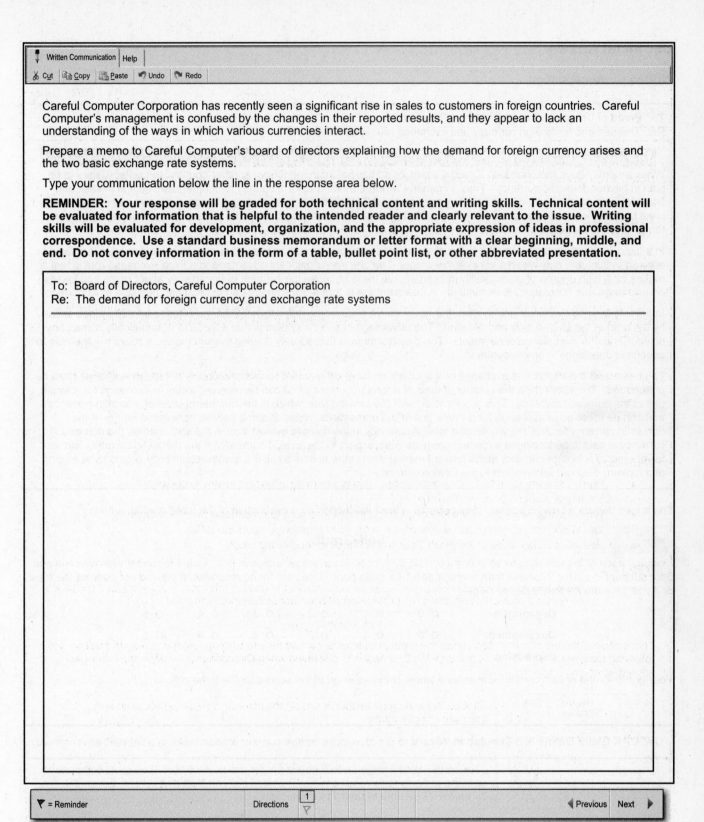

Unofficial Answer

Written Communication

To: Board of Directors, Careful Computer Corporation
Re: The demand for foreign currency and exchange rate systems

When an entity buys merchandise, a capital asset, or a financial instrument from another country, the seller wishes to be paid in his/her domestic currency. Thus, in general, when the demand for a country's merchandise, capital assets, and financial instruments rises, demand for its currency rises. For international exchanges to occur, the two currencies involved must be easily converted at some prevailing exchange rate. The exchange rate is the price of one country's currency in terms of another country's currency.

In a fixed exchange rate system, the value of a country's currency in relation to another country's currency is either fixed or allowed to fluctuate only within a very narrow range. The one very significant advantage to a fixed exchange rate is that it makes for a high degree of predictability in international trade because the element of uncertainty about gains and losses on exchange rate fluctuations is eliminated. A disadvantage is that a government can manipulate the value of its currency.

In a freely floating exchange rate system, the government steps aside and allows exchange rates to be determined entirely by the market forces of supply and demand. The advantage of such a system is that it tends to automatically correct any disequilibrium in the balance of payments. The disadvantage is that a freely floating system makes a country vulnerable to economic conditions in other countries.

To understand the effects that exchange rate fluctuations have on reported results, the basics of foreign exchange must be understood. The spot rate is the number of units of a foreign currency that can be received today in exchange for a single unit of the domestic currency. This is contrasted with the forward rate, which is the number of units of a foreign currency that can be received in exchange for a single unit of the domestic currency at some definite date in the future. If the domestic currency fetches more units of a foreign currency in the forward market than in the spot market, the domestic currency is said to be trading at a forward premium with respect to the foreign currency. If the domestic currency fetches fewer units of a foreign currency in the forward market than in the spot market, the domestic currency is said to be trading at a forward discount with respect to the foreign currency.

The above depicts a Level 5 answer. See page 16 in the Introduction for a description of the three grading criteria.

Self-Grade

Evaluate each of the following by selecting a 0, 1, 2, 3, 4, or 5. An average response is 3. Use 4 for better than average and 5 for outstanding. Use 2 for less than average and 1 for quite poor. Use zero for no response, if you did not address the topic, or if you gave advice that is clearly illegal.

Organization	O 0	O 1	O 2	O 3	O 4	O 5
Development	O 0	O 1	O 2	O 3	O 4	O 5
Expression	O 0	O 1	O 2	O 3	O 4	O 5

Your grade for the written communication as a whole is the average of the scores for the three criteria.

Use **CPA Gleim Online** and **Simulation Wizard** to practice more written communication tasks in a realistic environment.

STUDY UNIT FIVE
FINANCIAL RISK MANAGEMENT

(11 pages of outline)

Every investment carries the expectation of a return while also carrying some amount of risk (Subunit 1). Mathematical formulas can be used to precisely measure the degree of volatility and relative risk of a particular investment security (Subunit 2). An investing entity can receive an adequate return on its investments while minimizing the accompanying risk by understanding the principles of portfolio management (Subunit 3). Derivative financial instruments are those whose price is based on the price of some other instrument and are used for more specialized activities, such as hedging (Subunit 4).

5.1 RISK AND RETURN

1. **Rate of Return**

   a. A return is the amount received by an investor as compensation for taking on the risk of the investment.

   $$Return\ on\ investment = Amount\ received - Amount\ invested$$

   ### EXAMPLE

   An investor paid $100,000 for an investment that returned $112,000. The investor's return is $12,000 ($112,000 – $100,000).

   b. The rate of return is the return stated as a percentage of the amount invested.

   $$Rate\ of\ return = \frac{Return\ on\ investment}{Amount\ invested}$$

   ### EXAMPLE

   The investor's rate of return is 12% ($12,000 ÷ $100,000).

2. **Distributed Interest vs. Compound Interest**

   a. The interest generated by an investment can either be disbursed periodically in the form of cash or rolled into the investment principal in a process known as **compounding**.

EXAMPLE

A mutual fund offers its investors an annual 4% return. This can be taken in the form of cash or it can be compounded. The following tables illustrate the difference in cash flows under the two methods.

	Using Distributed Interest				Using Compound Interest			
	Beginning Balance	Annual Return	Cash Disbursed	Added to Balance	Beginning Balance	Annual Return	Added to Balance	Cash Disbursed
Year 1	$10,000.00 ×	4% =	$400.00	--	$10,000.00 ×	4% =	$400.00	--
Year 2	10,000.00 ×	4% =	400.00	--	10,400.00 ×	4% =	416.00	--
Year 3	10,000.00 ×	4% =	400.00	--	10,816.00 ×	4% =	432.64	--
Year 4	10,000.00 ×	4% =	400.00	--	11,248.64 ×	4% =	449.95	--
Year 5	10,000.00 ×	4% =	400.00	--	11,698.59 ×	4% =	467.94	--

At the end of 5 years, the investor who took periodic disbursements had the use of $400 cash every year but only has his/her original $10,000 balance in the account. An investor who chose compounding got no periodic cash flow but has a balance of $12,166.53 ($11,698.59 Year 5 beginning balance + $467.94 Year 5 return) in the account.

---

3. **Two Basic Types of Investment Risk**

   a. **Systematic risk**, also called **market risk**, is the risk faced by all firms. Changes in the economy as a whole, such as inflation or the business cycle, affect all players in the market.

      1) For this reason, systematic risk is sometimes referred to as **undiversifiable risk**. Since all investments are affected, this risk cannot be offset through diversification.

   b. **Unsystematic risk**, also called **unique risk**, is the risk inherent in a particular investment. This type of risk is determined by the firm's industry, products, customer loyalty, degree of leverage, management competence, etc.

      1) For this reason, unsystematic risk is sometimes referred to as **diversifiable risk**. Since individual investments are affected by the particular strengths and weaknesses of the firm, this risk can be offset through diversification (see item 3. in Subunit 5.2 for an explanation of diversification).

4. **Types of Investment Risk**

   a. **Credit default risk** is the risk that the borrower will default and will not be able to repay the principal or interest that it is obligated to pay. This risk can be gauged by the use of credit-rating agencies.

   b. **Liquidity risk** is the risk that a security cannot be sold on short notice for its market value.

   c. **Maturity risk**, also called **interest rate risk**, is the risk that an investment security will fluctuate in value between the time it was issued and its maturity date. The longer the time until maturity, the greater the degree of maturity risk.

   d. **Inflation risk** is the risk that purchasing power will be lost while the loan is at the borrower's disposal (see Study Unit 3, Subunit 5 for a description of the causes and effects of inflation).

   e. **Political risk** is the probability of loss from actions of governments, such as from changes in tax laws or environmental regulations or from expropriation of assets.

   f. **Exchange rate risk** is the risk of loss because of fluctuation in the relative value of foreign currency.

   g. **Business risk** (or **operations risk**) is the risk of fluctuations in earnings before interest and taxes or in operating income when the firm uses no debt. It is the risk inherent in its operations that excludes **financial risk**, which is the risk to the shareholders from the use of financial leverage. Business risk depends on factors such as demand variability, sales price variability, input price variability, and amount of operating leverage.

5. **Relationship Between Risk and Return**

  a.   Whether the expected return on an investment is sufficient to entice an investor depends on its risk, the risks and returns of alternative investments, and the investor's attitude toward risk.

    1)   Most investors (and people in general) are **risk averse**. Their utility of a gain does not outweigh the disutility of a potential loss of the same amount.

EXAMPLE

This can be illustrated with the actions of people in a casino. Many people are willing to bet $1 on one of the numbers on a roulette table because the chance of a gain of multiple dollars versus the loss of $1 is acceptable. However, as the minimum amount of a bet increases (from $1 to $100 to $1,000), the number of willing casual gamblers decreases because the chance for earning hundreds or thousands of dollars versus the probability of losing $100 or $1,000 is not acceptable.

---

      a)   Because of risk aversion, risky securities must have higher expected returns. These higher expected returns entice investors to take on the additional risk. In the example above, if a casino were to provide better odds (i.e., a higher expected return) for higher bet amounts, more casual gamblers may be enticed to play with higher minimum bets.

    2)   A **risk-neutral** investor adopts an expected value approach because (s)he regards the utility of a gain as equal to the disutility of a loss of the same amount.

      a)   In the case of a roulette gambler, a risk-neutral person would be as willing to gamble if the table minimum were $1, $100, or $1,000. Since the individual is comfortable with the risk, it does not matter what amount the wager is.

    3)   A **risk-seeking** investor has an optimistic attitude toward risk. (S)he regards the utility of a gain as exceeding the disutility of a loss of the same amount.

      a)   In the case of a roulette gambler, a risk-seeking person would be more willing to gamble if the table minimum were higher.

  b.   The greater the risk of the investment, the higher the rate of return required by the investor. For each type of investment risk, the investor requires additional risk premium that compensates him/her for bearing that risk.

    1)   **Risk premium** is the excess of an investment's expected rate of return over the risk-free interest rate.

    2)   The **risk-free rate** is the interest rate on the safest investment. The stated interest rate on U.S. Treasury bills is considered to be the risk-free interest rate.

      a)   A holder of U.S. Treasury bills is generally exposed only to inflation risk. Thus, the market rate of interest on U.S. Treasury bills is equal to the risk-free rate of interest plus the inflation premium.

    3)   **Required rate of return** is the return that takes into account all the investment risks that relate to a specific security.

EXAMPLE

Real risk-free rate	3%
Inflation premium	1%
Risk-free rate	4%
Liquidity risk premium	1%
Default risk premium	2%
Maturity risk premium	1%
Required rate of return	8%

---

6.   **Investment Securities**

   a.   Financial managers may select from a wide range of financial instruments in which to invest and with which to raise money.

   1)   An inverse relationship holds between the safety of an investment and its potential return. The following is a short list of widely available investment securities:

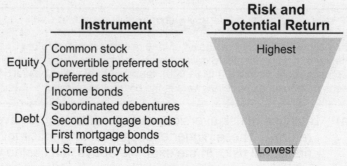

Figure 5-1

   b.   The reasons for the varying risk and potential return of these securities can be summarized as follows:

   1)   Equity securities are necessarily riskier than debt because an entity's owners are not legally guaranteed a return.

   a)   Common shareholders are the residual owners of a corporation; they stand last in order of priority during liquidation, but they have the right to receive distribution of excess profits.

   b)   Preferred shareholders stand ahead of common shareholders in case of liquidation, but their potential returns are capped by the board of directors.

   2)   Issuers of debt securities are legally obligated to redeem them. Because these returns are guaranteed, they are lower than those for equity investments.

   a)   Income bonds pay a return only if the issuer is profitable.

   b)   Debentures are unsecured.

   c)   Mortgage bonds are secured by real property.

   d)   U.S. Treasury bonds are backed by the full faith and credit of the United States Government.

   3)   Normally, precious metals are considered a risky investment because their prices are highly volatile. During periods of high inflation, however, currency loses purchasing power rapidly, and precious metals may offer a safe haven to investors.

Stop and review! You have completed the outline for this subunit. Study multiple-choice questions 1 through 8 beginning on page 167.

5.2 QUANTIFYING INVESTMENT RISK

1.   **Probability and Standard Deviation**

   a.   Probability provides a method for mathematically expressing doubt or assurance about the occurrence of a chance event.

   b.   A **probability distribution** is the set of all possible outcomes of a decision, with a probability assigned to each outcome. For example, a simple probability distribution might be defined for the possible returns on a stock investment. A different return could be estimated for each of a limited number of possible states of the economy, and a probability could be determined for each state. Such a probability distribution is **discrete** because the outcomes are limited.

2. **Measures of Risk – Standard Deviation and Variance**

   a. The **expected rate of return ($\overline{R}$)** on an investment is determined using an expected value calculation. It is an average of the possible outcomes weighted according to their probabilities.

   Expected rate of return ($\overline{R}$) = $\sum$ (Possible rate of return × Probability)

EXAMPLE

A company is considering investing in the common stock of one of two firms, Xatalan Corp. and Yarmouth Co. The expected rates of return on the two securities based on the weighted-averages of their probable outcomes are calculated as follows:

Xatalan Corporation Stock						Yarmouth Company Stock				
Rate of Return %		Probability %		Weighted Average		Rate of Return %		Probability %		Weighted Average
80 %	×	60%	=	48 %		30 %	×	70%	=	21 %
(50)%	×	40%	=	(20)%		(10)%	×	30%	=	(3)%
Expected rate of return ($\overline{R}$)				**28 %**		**Expected rate of return ($\overline{R}$)**				**18 %**

The expected rate of return on Xatalan Corporation stock is higher, but the risk of each investment also should be measured.

---

   b. Risk is the chance that the actual return on an investment will differ from the expected return. One way to measure risk is with the standard deviation (variance) of the distribution of an investment's return.

   Standard deviation (σ) = $\sqrt{\sum [(R_i - \overline{R})^2 \times Probability]}$ = $\sqrt{Variance}$

   Where: R_i = Possible rate of return
   $\overline{R}$ = Expected rate of return

   1) The **standard deviation** measures the tightness of the distribution and the riskiness of the investment.

      a) A large standard deviation reflects a broadly dispersed probability distribution, meaning the range of possible returns is wide. Conversely, the smaller the standard deviation, the tighter the probability distribution and the lower the risk.

      b) Thus, the following general statement can be made: The greater the standard deviation, the riskier the investment.

EXAMPLE

The following measures the risk of the investments from the previous example using standard deviation.

Xatalan Corporation Stock

Standard deviation (σ) = $\sqrt{[(80\% - 28\%)^2 \times 60\%] + [(-50\% - 28\%)^2 \times 40\%]}$ = $\sqrt{4,056}$ = **63.69%**

Yarmouth Company Stock

Standard deviation (σ) = $\sqrt{[(30\% - 18\%)^2 \times 70\%] + [(-10\% - 18\%)^2 \times 30\%]}$ = $\sqrt{336}$ = **18.33%**

Although the investment in Xatalan stock has a higher expected return than the investment in Yarmouth stock (28% > 18%), it also is riskier than Yarmouth because its standard deviation is greater (63.69% > 18.33%). Therefore, to determine which investment is the better choice in terms of the risk-return tradeoff, we must measure the **coefficient of variation (CV)** of the expected returns on the two investments.

---

c.   The **coefficient of variation (CV)** is useful when the rates of return and standard deviations of two investments differ. It measures the **risk per unit of return**.

$$Coefficient\ of\ variation\ = \frac{Standard\ deviation}{Expected\ rate\ of\ return}$$

$$CV = \sigma \div \overline{R}$$

The lower the ratio, the better the risk-return tradeoff is.

EXAMPLE

The coefficients of variation for the expected return of the two potential investments are calculated as follows:

		Coefficient of Variation
Xatalan Corporation Stock: $\sigma \div \overline{R} = 63.69\% \div 28\%$ =		**2.275**
Yarmouth Company Stock: $\sigma \div \overline{R} = 18.33\% \div 18\%$ =		**1.018**

The investment in Yarmouth has a better risk-return tradeoff since its coefficient of variation (CV) is lower than that of the investment in Xatalan (1.018 < 2.275).

---

3.   **Diversification**

a.   The metrics presented thus far have concerned the risk and return for individual securities. However, very few investors hold only one security.

   1)   The goal of portfolio management is to construct a basket of securities that generates a reasonable rate of return without the risks associated with holding a single security.

   a)   Expected portfolio **return** is simply the weighted average of the returns on the individual securities.

   b)   Portfolio **risk**, on the other hand, is usually less than a simple average of the standard deviations of the component securities. This is one of the benefits of diversification.

b.   As described in Subunit 5.1, specific risk (also called diversifiable risk, unsystematic risk, residual risk, and unique risk) is the risk associated with a single investment security. Specific risk is the risk that can be potentially eliminated by diversification.

   1)   Diversification reduces aggregate volatility.

   a)   Some stocks move in the same direction as other stocks in the portfolio but by a smaller amount. Some stocks move in the opposite direction from other stocks.

   b)   Thus, by combining imperfectly correlated securities into a portfolio, the risk of the group as a whole is less than the average of their standard deviations.

   2)   Intuitively, diversifiable risk should continue to decrease as the number of different securities held increases.

   a)   In practice, however, the benefits of diversification become extremely small when more than about 20 to 30 different securities are held. Moreover, commissions and other transaction costs increase with greater diversification.

c.   Market risk, also called undiversifiable risk and systematic risk, is the risk of the stock market as a whole. Ideally, this is the only risk associated with a well-diversified portfolio.

    d.   The **coefficient of correlation (r)** measures the degree to which any two variables, e.g., the prices of two stocks, are related.

        1)   The coefficient of correlation has a range from 1.0 to –1.0 (see Study Unit 6, Subunit 2 for a fuller discussion of correlation).

            a)   Perfect positive correlation (1.0) means that the two variables always move together.

            b)   Perfect negative correlation (–1.0) means that the two variables always move in the opposite direction.

            c)   If a pair of securities has a coefficient of correlation of 1.0, the risk of the two together is the same as the risk of each security by itself. If a pair of securities has a coefficient of correlation of –1.0, all specific (unsystematic) risk has been eliminated.

        2)   The ideal portfolio, then, is one consisting of securities with a wide enough variety of coefficients of correlation that only market risk remains.

            a)   The normal range for the correlation of two randomly selected stocks is .50 to .70.

Stop and review! You have completed the outline for this subunit. Study multiple-choice questions 9 through 14 beginning on page 169.

5.3 CAPITAL ASSET PRICING MODEL

    1.   **Capital Asset Pricing Model (CAPM)**

        a.   As described in the previous subunit, investors want to reduce their risk and therefore take advantage of diversification by holding a portfolio of securities. In order to measure how a particular security contributes to the risk and return of a diversified portfolio, investors can use the **capital asset pricing model (CAPM)**.

        b.   The CAPM quantifies the required return on an equity security by relating the security's level of risk to the average return available in the market (portfolio).

        c.   The CAPM formula is based on the idea that the investor must be compensated for his/her investment in two ways: time value of money and risk.

        1)   The time value component is the **risk-free rate** (denoted R_F in the formula). It is the return provided by the safest investments, e.g., U.S. Treasury securities.

        2)   The risk component consists of

            a)   The **market risk premium** (denoted $R_M - R_F$), which is the return provided by the market over and above the risk-free rate, weighted by

            b)   A measure of the security's risk, called **beta** (β).

                i)   The effect of an individual security on the volatility of a portfolio is measured by its sensitivity to movements by the overall market. This sensitivity is stated in terms of a stock's beta coefficient (β).

                ii)   Thus, the beta of the market portfolio equals 1, and the beta of U.S. Treasury securities is 0.

CAPM Formula

$$Required\ rate\ of\ return = R_F + \beta(R_M - R_F)$$

Where: R_F = Risk-free return
          R_M = Market return
          β = Measure of the systematic risk or volatility of the individual security in comparison to the market (diversified portfolio)

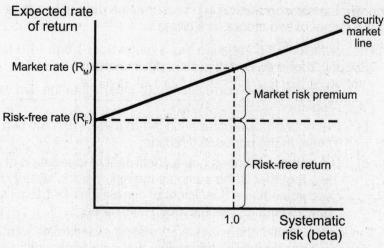

Figure 5-2

d.   The market risk premium varies in direct proportion to beta. Therefore, all investments (securities) must lie on the security market line.

EXAMPLE

An investor is considering the purchase of a stock with a beta value of 1.2. Treasury bills are currently paying 8.6%, and the average return on the market is 10.1%. (Remember, U.S. Treasuries are considered as close to a risk-free investment as there can be.) To be induced to buy this stock, the return that the investor must receive is calculated as follows:

$$\text{Required rate of return} = R_F + \beta(R_M - R_F)$$
$$= 8.6\% + 1.2(10.1\% - 8.6\%)$$
$$= 8.6\% + 1.8\%$$
$$= 10.4\%$$

Stop and review! You have completed the outline for this subunit. Study multiple-choice questions 15 through 23 beginning on page 171.

5.4 DERIVATIVES

1.   **Overview**

   a.   A **derivative instrument** is an investment transaction in which the parties' gain or loss is derived from some other economic event, for example, the price of a given stock, a foreign currency exchange rate, or the price of a certain commodity.

      1)   One party enters into the transaction to speculate (incur risk) and the other enters into it to hedge (avoid risk).

   b.   Derivatives are a type of financial instrument, along with cash, accounts receivable, notes receivable, bonds, preferred shares, etc.

2.   **Hedging**

   a.   Hedging is the process of using offsetting commitments to minimize or avoid the impact of adverse price movements. To hedge the investment, the entity takes a position in a financial instrument that is almost perfectly correlated with the original asset but in the opposite direction.

   b.   An entity has a **long position** in an asset whenever the entity owns the asset. An entity with a long position therefore benefits from a rise in the asset's value.

EXAMPLE

An investor buys 100 shares of Collerup Corporation stock. The investor now has a long position in Collerup Corporation; in financial market terminology, this is referred to as being "long Collerup."

   c.   An entity has a **short position** in an asset when the entity sells an asset that it does not own at the time of the sale. Entities take short positions when they believe the value of the asset will decrease.

       1)   Typically, the entity with the short position must borrow the asset from an entity that owns it before the "short sale" takes place.

EXAMPLE

Money Management Fund A believes that the share price of Collerup Corporation will decrease (perhaps due to a future poor earnings announcement). Fund A thus seeks out Fund B and borrows a block of Collerup shares, which Fund A then sells on the appropriate stock exchange. Fund A is selling short because the fund is selling shares it does not actually own.

- If the price of Collerup decreases, Fund A can repurchase the shares at the lower price and return them to Fund B, thereby making a profit.
- If Fund A guessed wrong and the share price of Collerup remains the same or increases, then, to fulfill its obligation to return the borrowed shares to Fund B, Fund A must purchase the shares on the stock exchange (at the higher price), thus incurring a loss.

---

3. **Options**

   a.   A party who buys an option has bought the right to demand that the counterparty (the seller or "writer" of the option) buy or sell an underlying asset on or before a specified future date. The buyer holds all of the rights and the seller has all of the obligations. The buyer pays a fee to be able to dictate – in the future – whether the seller buys or sells the underlying asset from or to the buyer.

Many CPA candidates become intimidated when studying options. An option is merely a very standardized legal contract that requires two parties to comply with its terms. These contracts are really no more complicated than the legal contract a person has with his/her cell phone carrier. Individuals pay the cellular phone company money, and in return the cell phone provider is obligated to supply the individual with telephone service when the individual wants to place a phone call. Furthermore, some cell phone carriers charge on the basis of pay-as-you-go while others charge a fixed amount for a fixed amount of minutes. There are many terms associated with cell phone providers, and, similar to cell phones, options have their own terminology. The terms below and on the next page are useful for people in finance because they indicate how a contract is standardized, allowing people to communicate quickly and succinctly when discussing options.

       1)   A **call option** gives the buyer (holder) the right to purchase (i.e., the right to "call" for) the underlying asset (stock, currency, commodity, etc.) at a fixed price.

       2)   A **put option** gives the buyer (holder) the right to sell (i.e., the right to "put" onto the market) the underlying asset (stock, currency, commodity, etc.) at a fixed price.

       3)   The asset that is subject to being bought or sold under the terms of the option is referred to as the **underlying**.

       4)   The party buying an option is referred to as the **holder**. The seller is referred to as the **writer**.

       5)   The exercise of an option is always at the discretion of the option holder (the buyer) who has, in effect, bought the right to exercise the option or not. The seller of an option has no choice; (s)he must perform if the holder chooses to exercise.

       6)   An option has an expiration date after which it can no longer be exercised.

4. **Components of Option Price**

   a.   The price of an option (the option premium) consists of two components, intrinsic value and the time premium, also called extrinsic value.

Option premium = Intrinsic value + Time premium

b.   The **exercise price** is the price at which the holder can purchase (in the case of a call option) or sell (in the case of a put option) the asset underlying the option contract.

c.   The **intrinsic value of a call option** is the amount by which the exercise price is less than the current price of the underlying.

1)   If an option has a positive intrinsic value, it is said to be in-the-money.

EXAMPLE

An investor holds call options for 200 shares of Locksley Corporation with an exercise price of $48 per share. Locksley stock is currently trading at $50 per share. The investor's options have an intrinsic value of $2 each ($50 – $48).

---

2)   If an option has an intrinsic value of $0, it is said to be out-of-the-money.

EXAMPLE

An investor holds call options for 200 shares of Locksley Corporation with an exercise price of $48 per share. Locksley stock is currently trading at $45 per share. The investor's options are out-of-the-money (they have no intrinsic value).

---

d.   The **intrinsic value of a put option** is the amount by which the exercise price is greater than the current price of the underlying.

1)   If an option has a positive intrinsic value, it is said to be in-the-money.

EXAMPLE

An investor holds put options for 200 shares of Locksley Corporation with an exercise price of $48 per share. Locksley stock is currently trading at $45 per share. The investor's options have an intrinsic value of $3 each ($48 – $45).

---

2)   If an option has an intrinsic value of $0, it is said to be out-of-the-money.

EXAMPLE

An investor holds put options for 200 shares of Locksley Corporation with an exercise price of $48 per share. Locksley stock is currently trading at $50 per share. The investor's options are out-of-the-money (they have no intrinsic value).

---

e.   Time Premium

1)   The more time that exists between the writing of an option and its expiration, the riskier any investment is. Since the buyer's loss of an option is limited to the option premium, an increase in the term of an option (both calls and puts) will result in an increase in the time premium.

5.   **Forward Contracts**

a.   One method of mitigating risk is the simple forward contract. The two parties agree that, at a set future date, one of them will perform and the other will pay a specified amount for the performance.

1)   A common example is that of a retailer and a wholesaler who agree in September on the prices and quantities of merchandise that will be shipped to the retailer's stores in time for the winter holiday season. The retailer has locked in a price and a source of supply, and the wholesaler has locked in a price and a customer.

b.   Note the significant difference between a forward contract and an option: In a contract, both parties must meet their contractual obligations, i.e., to deliver merchandise and to pay. Neither has the option of nonperformance.

1)   Forward contracts are heavily used in foreign currency exchange.

6. Futures Contracts

a. A futures contract is a commitment to buy or sell an asset at a fixed price during a specific future period; unlike with a forward contract, the counterparty is unknown.

b. Futures contracts are actively traded on futures exchanges.

1) The clearinghouse randomly matches sellers who will deliver during a given period with buyers who are seeking delivery during the same period.

c. Because futures contracts are actively traded, the result is a **liquid market** in futures that permits buyers and sellers to net out their positions.

d. Another distinguishing feature of futures contracts is that the market price is posted and netted to each person's account at the close of every business day. This practice is called **mark-to-market**.

1) A mark-to-market provision minimizes a futures contract's chance of default because profits and losses on the contracts must be received or paid each day through a clearinghouse (and because the clearinghouse guarantees the transactions).

Stop and review! You have completed the outline for this subunit. Study multiple-choice questions 24 through 28 beginning on page 174.

QUESTIONS
5.1 Risk and Return

1. A company is evaluating its experience with five recent investments. The following data are available:

Investment	Cost of Investment	Amount Received
A	$ 8,500	$ 8,390
B	4,200	4,610
C	12,100	12,400
D	7,900	8,220
E	11,000	11,400

Rank the investments in order from highest rate of return to lowest.

A. C, E, A, D, B.

B. B, D, E, C, A.

C. B, E, D, C, A.

D. A, C, D, E, B.

Answer (B) is correct.

REQUIRED: The order of investments from highest rate of return to lowest.

DISCUSSION: Rate of return is equal to the return on an investment (the amount received minus the amount invested) divided by the amount invested. The calculation for these five investments can be performed as follows:

Investment	Cost of Investment	Amount Received	Return	Rate of Return
A	$ 8,500	$ 8,390	$(110)	(1.3%)
B	4,200	4,610	410	9.8%
C	12,100	12,400	300	2.5%
D	7,900	8,220	320	4.1%
E	11,000	11,400	400	3.6%

Answer (A) is incorrect. This ranking is in order by amount received, not rate of return. Answer (C) is incorrect. This ranking is in order by return, not rate of return. Answer (D) is incorrect. This ranking is from lowest rate of return to highest.

2. Dr. G invested $10,000 in a lifetime annuity for his granddaughter Emily. The annuity is expected to yield $400 annually forever. What is the anticipated annual rate of return for the annuity?

A. Cannot be determined without additional information.

B. 4.0%

C. 2.5%

D. 8.0%

Answer (B) is correct.

REQUIRED: The internal rate of return.

DISCUSSION: A return is the amount received by an investor as compensation for taking on the risk of the investment. The rate of return is the return stated as a percentage of the amount invested. In this case, it is 4% ($400 ÷ $10,000).

Answer (A) is incorrect. The rate of return can be calculated. Answer (C) is incorrect. This percentage results from reversing the numerator and denominator. Answer (D) is incorrect. This percentage results from treating the return as semi-annual rather than annual.

3. At the beginning of Year 1, $10,000 is invested at 8% interest, compounded annually. What amount of interest is earned for Year 2?

    A. $800.00

    B. $806.40

    C. $864.00

    D. $933.12

Answer (C) is correct.
    REQUIRED: The amount of interest earned for Year 2.
    DISCUSSION: Compounded interest is the practice of adding interest to the carrying amount of the principal rather than disbursing it in cash. In this case, the $800 ($10,000 principal × 8% stated rate) of interest earned in Year 1 is added to the principal, resulting in a Year 1 ending balance of $10,800 ($10,000 + $800). Interest earned in Year 2 is therefore $864 ($10,800 principal × 8% stated rate).
    Answer (A) is incorrect. The amount of $800 is Year 1 interest. Answer (B) is incorrect. The amount of $806.40 is calculated using the wrong rate. Answer (D) is incorrect. The amount of $933.12 is Year 3 interest.

4. The risk of loss because of fluctuations in the relative value of foreign currencies is called

    A. Expropriation risk.

    B. Multinational beta.

    C. Exchange rate risk.

    D. Undiversifiable risk.

Answer (C) is correct.
    REQUIRED: The risk of loss because of fluctuations in the relative value of foreign currencies.
    DISCUSSION: When amounts to be paid or received are denominated in a foreign currency, exchange rate fluctuations may result in exchange gains or losses. For example, if a U.S. firm has a receivable fixed in terms of units of a foreign currency, a decline in the value of that currency relative to the U.S. dollar results in a foreign exchange loss.
    Answer (A) is incorrect. Expropriation risk is the risk that the sovereign country in which the assets backing an investment are located will seize the assets without adequate compensation. Answer (B) is incorrect. The beta value in the capital asset pricing model for a multinational firm is the systematic risk of a given multinational firm relative to that of the market as a whole. Answer (D) is incorrect. Undiversifiable risk is risk that cannot be offset through diversification.

5. Prior to the introduction of the euro, O & B Company, a U.S. corporation, is in possession of accounts receivable denominated in Deutsche marks. To what type of risk are they exposed?

    A. Liquidity risk.

    B. Political risk.

    C. Exchange-rate risk.

    D. Price risk.

Answer (C) is correct.
    REQUIRED: The risk to which a business is exposed when accounts receivable are denominated in a foreign currency.
    DISCUSSION: Exchange-rate risk is the risk that a foreign currency transaction will be negatively exposed to fluctuations in exchange rates. Because O & B Company sells goods to German customers and records accounts receivable denominated in Deutsche marks, O & B Company is exposed to exchange-rate risk.
    Answer (A) is incorrect. Liquidity risk is the possibility that an asset cannot be sold on short notice for its market value. Answer (B) is incorrect. Political risk is the probability of loss from actions of governments. Answer (D) is incorrect. Price risk is a component of interest-rate risk.

6. Which of the following is **not** a political risk of investing in a foreign country?

    A. Rebellions could result in destruction of property.

    B. Assets could be expropriated.

    C. Foreign-exchange controls could limit the repatriation of profits.

    D. A foreign customer might default on its debt.

Answer (D) is correct.
    REQUIRED: The item that is not a political risk of investing in foreign-based assets.
    DISCUSSION: Political risks include the threat of expropriation of company assets, destruction of assets in rebellions in third-world nations, and limitations on the repatriation of profits (or even initial investments). Default by a foreign customer is not a political risk, but a risk of doing business either locally or internationally.

7. Catherine & Co. has extra cash at the end of the year and is analyzing the best way to invest the funds. The company should invest in a project only if the

A. Expected return on the project exceeds the return on investments of comparable risk.

B. Return on investments of comparable risk exceeds the expected return on the project.

C. Expected return on the project is equal to the return on investments of comparable risk.

D. Return on investments of comparable risk equals the expected return on the project.

Answer (A) is correct.
REQUIRED: The rule for deciding whether to invest in a project.
DISCUSSION: Investment risk is analyzed in terms of the probability that the actual return on an investment will be lower than the expected return. Comparing a project's expected return with the return on an asset of similar risk helps determine whether the project is worth investing in. If the expected return on a project exceeds the return on an asset of comparable risk, the project should be pursued.

8. The marketable securities with the **least** amount of default risk are

A. Federal government agency securities.

B. U.S. Treasury securities.

C. Repurchase agreements.

D. Commercial paper.

Answer (B) is correct.
REQUIRED: The marketable securities with the least default risk.
DISCUSSION: The marketable securities with the lowest default risk are those issued by the federal government because they are backed by the full faith and credit of the U.S. government and are therefore the least risky form of investment.
Answer (A) is incorrect. Securities issued by a federal agency are backed first by that agency and second by the U.S. government. Agency securities are issued by agencies and corporations created by the federal government, such as the Federal Housing Administration. Answer (C) is incorrect. Repurchase agreements could become worthless if the organization agreeing to make the repurchase goes bankrupt. Answer (D) is incorrect. Commercial paper is unsecured.

5.2 Quantifying Investment Risk

9. To assist in an investment decision, Gift Co. selected the most likely sales volume from several possible outcomes. Which of the following attributes would that selected sales volume reflect?

A. The midpoint of the range.

B. The median.

C. The greatest probability.

D. The expected value.

Answer (C) is correct.
REQUIRED: The attribute reflected by the selected sales volume.
DISCUSSION: Probability is important to management decision making because of the uncertainty of future events. Probability estimation techniques assist in making the best decisions in the face of uncertainty. Consequently, the most likely sales volume is the one with the greatest probability.
Answer (A) is incorrect. The midpoint of the range is the point halfway between two points. Answer (B) is incorrect. Half the values are greater and half are less than the median. Answer (D) is incorrect. The expected value is a weighted average using probabilities as weights.

10. Standard deviation and expected return information for four investments selling for the same price is as follows:

Investment	Standard Deviation	Expected Return
A	25%	20%
B	20%	18%
C	12%	8%
D	10%	10%

What investment is the best choice in terms of the risk/return relationship?

A. Investment A.

B. Investment B.

C. Investment C.

D. Investment D.

Answer (D) is correct.
REQUIRED: The calculation of the best investment.
DISCUSSION: The coefficient of variation is useful when the rates of return and standard deviations of two investments differ. It measures the risk per unit of return because it divides the standard deviation by the expected return. Thus, the risk per unit of return for Investment D is 1.00 (.10 ÷ .10), which is the lowest of the given investments.
Answer (A) is incorrect. Investment A has a risk per unit of return of 1.25 (.25 ÷ .20), which is higher than that of Investment D. Answer (B) is incorrect. Investment B has a risk per unit of return of 1.11 (.20 ÷ .18), which is higher than that of Investment D. Answer (C) is incorrect. Investment C has a risk per unit of return of 1.50 (.12 ÷ .08), which is higher than that of Investment D.

11. Konstans Corp. is considering purchasing an investment security with the following information:

Likelihood	Return on Investment
50%	2%
40%	4%
10%	14%

The expected return on this investment is

A. 2%

B. 4%

C. 25%

D. 50%

Answer (B) is correct.
REQUIRED: The expected return on an investment.
DISCUSSION: The expected return on this investment is 4% [(50% × 2%) + (40% × 4%) + (10% × 14%)].
Answer (A) is incorrect. The expected return is a weighted-average. Answer (C) is incorrect. This return is a nonsense answer. Answer (D) is incorrect. This percentage is a likelihood, not a return.

12. The expected rate of return for the stock of Cornhusker Enterprises is 20%, with a standard deviation of 15%. The expected rate of return for the stock of Mustang Associates is 10%, with a standard deviation of 9%. The stock with the worse risk/return relationship is

A. Cornhusker because the return is higher.

B. Cornhusker because the standard deviation is higher.

C. Mustang because the standard deviation is higher.

D. Mustang because the coefficient of variation is higher.

Answer (D) is correct.
REQUIRED: The riskier stock.
DISCUSSION: The coefficient of variation is useful when the rates of return and standard deviations of two investments differ. It measures the risk per unit of return by dividing the standard deviation by the expected return. The coefficient of variation is higher for Mustang (.09 ÷ .10 = .90) than for Cornhusker (.15 ÷ .20 = .75).
Answer (A) is incorrect. The existence of a higher return is not necessarily indicative of high risk. Answer (B) is incorrect. The level of standard deviation by itself is not enough for determining the stock's risk/return relationship. Answer (C) is incorrect. Mustang does not have the higher standard deviation.

13. If two projects are completely and positively linearly dependent (or positively related), the measure of correlation between them is

A. 0

B. +.5

C. +1

D. −1

Answer (C) is correct.
REQUIRED: The measure of correlation when two projects are positively linearly dependent.
DISCUSSION: The measure of correlation when two projects are linearly dependent in a positive way will be +1.0.
Answer (A) is incorrect. A zero correlation indicates no relationship. Answer (B) is incorrect. This figure does not indicate linearity. Answer (D) is incorrect. A −1 would indicate a negative correlation.

14. In theory, which of the following coefficients of correlation would eliminate unsystematic risk in an investment portfolio?

A. 1.0

B. 0.0

C. −1.0

D. No theoretical coefficient exists for the elimination of risk in a portfolio context.

Answer (C) is correct.
REQUIRED: The coefficient of correlation that would eliminate risk in an investment portfolio.
DISCUSSION: The correlation coefficient measures the degree to which any two variables, e.g., two stocks in a portfolio, are related. Perfect negative correlation (−1.0) means that the two variables always move in the opposite direction. Given perfect negative correlation, unsystematic risk would, in theory, be eliminated.
Answer (A) is incorrect. A coefficient of correlation of 1.0 indicates perfect positive correlation. Given perfect positive correlation, risk for a two-stock portfolio with equal investments in each stock would be the same as that for the individual assets. Answer (B) is incorrect. A coefficient of correlation of 0.0 indicates no correlation at all. Answer (D) is incorrect. The coefficient of correlation that would, in theory, eliminate unsystematic risk in an investment portfolio is −1.0.

5.3 Capital Asset Pricing Model

15. A market analyst has estimated the equity beta of Modern Homes, Inc., to be 1.4. This beta implies that the company's

A. Systematic risk is lower than that of the market portfolio.

B. Systematic risk is higher than that of the market portfolio.

C. Unsystematic risk is higher than that of the market portfolio.

D. Total risk is higher than that of the market portfolio.

Answer (B) is correct.
REQUIRED: The implications of a beta greater than 1.
DISCUSSION: Systematic risk, also called market risk and undiversifiable risk, is the risk of the stock market as a whole. Some conditions in the national economy affect all businesses, which is why equity prices so often move together. The effect of an individual security on the volatility of a portfolio is measured by its sensitivity to movements by the overall market. This sensitivity is stated in terms of a stock's beta coefficient. An average-risk stock has a beta of 1.0 because its returns are perfectly positively correlated with those on the market portfolio.
Answer (A) is incorrect. A beta of less than 1.0 means that the market, or systematic, risk is lower than that of the market portfolio. Answer (C) is incorrect. Unsystematic risk is the risk that is influenced by an individual firm's policies and decisions. The beta does not concern unsystematic risk. Answer (D) is incorrect. Only a portion of the risk, not the total risk, is higher than that of the market portfolio.

16. If Dexter Industries has a beta value of 1.0, then its

A. Return should equal the risk-free rate.

B. Price is relatively stable.

C. Expected return should approximate the overall market.

D. Volatility is low.

Answer (C) is correct.
REQUIRED: The result when the beta value is 1.0.
DISCUSSION: The effect of an individual security on the volatility of a portfolio is measured by its sensitivity to movements by the overall market. This sensitivity is stated in terms of a stock's beta coefficient. If the beta coefficient is 1.0, then the price of that stock tends to move in the same direction and to the same degree as the overall market. The expected return can be calculated from the CAPM model formula.

$$\text{Expected return} = R_F + \beta(R_M - R_F)$$
$$R_F = \text{Risk-free rate}$$
$$R_M = \text{Market return}$$

When $\beta = 1$, expected return is equal to the market return.
Answer (A) is incorrect. Return is equal to the risk-free rate when $\beta = 0$. Answer (B) is incorrect. A beta value of 1.0 only means the price of the stock moves in concert with that of the overall market; if the market is not stable, the stock price will not be either. Answer (D) is incorrect. A beta value of 1.0 only means the price of the stock moves in concert with that of the overall market; if the market is volatile, the stock price will be also.

17. Using the capital asset pricing model (CAPM), the required rate of return for a firm with a beta of 1.25 when the market return is 14% and the risk-free rate is 6% is

A. 6.0%

B. 7.5%

C. 17.5%

D. 16.0%

Answer (D) is correct.
REQUIRED: The required rate of return using the capital asset pricing model.
DISCUSSION: The CAPM adds the risk-free rate to the product of the beta coefficient and the difference between the market return and the risk-free rate. The market-risk premium is the amount above the risk-free rate for which investors must be compensated to induce them to invest in the company. The beta coefficient of an individual stock is the correlation between volatility (price variation) of the stock market and the volatility of the price of the individual stock. Thus, the required rate is 16% [6% + 1.25 (14% − 6%)].

18. An analyst covering Guilderland Mining Co. common stock estimates the following information for next year.

Expected return on the market portfolio	12%
Expected return on Treasury securities	5%
Expected beta of Guilderland	2.2

Using the CAPM, the analyst's estimate of next year's risk premium for Guilderland's stock is closest to

A. 7.0%

B. 10.4%

C. 15.4%

D. 21.4%

Answer (C) is correct.
REQUIRED: The expected risk-adjusted premium of a stock based on the capital asset pricing model.
DISCUSSION: According to the capital asset pricing model, the risk premium of a particular stock is the excess of the market rate of return over the risk-free rate weighted by the stock's beta coefficient. For Guilderland Mining, this calculation is:

$$\begin{aligned}\text{Stock's risk premium} &= 2.2 \times (12\% - 5\%) \\ &= 2.2 \times 7\% \\ &= 15.4\%\end{aligned}$$

19. If the return on the market portfolio is 10% and the risk-free rate is 5%, what is the effect on a company's required rate of return on its stock of an increase in the beta coefficient from 1.2 to 1.5?

A. 3% increase.

B. 1.5% increase.

C. No change.

D. 1.5% decrease.

Answer (B) is correct.
REQUIRED: The effect on a company's required rate of return on its stock of an increase in the beta coefficient.
DISCUSSION: The required rate of return on equity capital can be estimated with the capital asset pricing model (CAPM). CAPM consists of adding the risk-free rate (i.e., the return on government securities, denoted R_F) to the product of the beta coefficient (a measure of the issuer's risk) and the difference between the market return and the risk-free rate (denoted $R_M - R_F$, referred to as the risk premium). Below is the basic equilibrium equation for the CAPM:

$$Required\ rate\ of\ return = R_F + \beta (R_M - R_F)$$

In this situation, the risk premium is 5% (10% − 5%). Thus, the required rate of return when the beta coefficient is 1.2 is 11% [5% + (1.2 × 5%)], and when the beta coefficient is 1.5, the required rate is 12.5% [5% + (1.5 × 5%)]. This is an increase of 1.5% (12.5% − 11%).

20. Using the capital asset pricing model (CAPM), the required rate of return for a firm with a beta of 1.5 when the market return is 10% and the risk-free rate is 8% is

A. 5%

B. 8%

C. 10%

D. 11%

Answer (D) is correct.
REQUIRED: The required rate of return using the capital asset pricing model.
DISCUSSION: The CAPM quantifies the required rate of return on a security by relating the security's level of risk to the average return available in the market. The required rate of return is calculated as follows:

$$\begin{aligned}\text{Required rate of return} &= R_F + \beta(R_M - R_F) \\ &= 8\% + [1.5 \times (10\% - 8\%)] \\ &= 8\% + (1.5 \times 2\%) \\ &= 11\%\end{aligned}$$

Answer (A) is incorrect. The required rate of return cannot be lower than the risk-free rate. Answer (B) is incorrect. The required rate of return for the safest investments (U.S. Treasury securities) is the risk-free rate of 8%. Answer (C) is incorrect. The required rate of return is the same as the market return only if beta is equal to 1.

21. According to the capital asset pricing model (CAPM), which of the following statements is true regarding the required rate of return for a security with a beta of 1?

A. The required rate of return is lower than the risk-free rate.

B. The required rate of return is equal to the risk-free rate.

C. The required rate of return is higher than the market return.

D. The required rate of return is equal to the market return.

Answer (D) is correct.

REQUIRED: The true statement regarding a beta value of 1.

DISCUSSION: The CAPM quantifies the required rate of return on a security by relating the security's level of risk to the average return available in the market. When beta equals 1, the required rate of return is equal to the market return, as shown below:

$$
\begin{aligned}
\text{Required rate of return} &= R_F + \beta(R_M - R_F) \\
&= R_F + [1 \times (R_M - R_F)] \\
&= R_F + (R_M - R_F) \\
&= R_M
\end{aligned}
$$

Answer (A) is incorrect. The required rate of return cannot be lower than the risk-free rate. Answer (B) is incorrect. The required rate of return for a security is equal to the risk-free rate when the beta of the security is equal to 0. Answer (C) is incorrect. When the beta of a security is greater than 1, the required rate of return for a security will be higher than the market return.

22. The betas and expected returns for three investments being considered by Sky, Inc., are given below.

Investment	Beta	Expected Return
A	1.4	12%
B	0.8	11%
C	1.5	13%

The return on the market is 11% and the risk-free rate is 6%. If the capital asset pricing model (CAPM) is used for calculating the required rate of return, which investments should the management of Sky make?

A. B only.

B. A and C only.

C. B and C only.

D. A, B, and C.

Answer (A) is correct.

REQUIRED: The investment(s) that should be made based on the CAPM.

DISCUSSION: The required rate of return on equity capital can be estimated with the capital asset pricing model (CAPM). CAPM consists of adding the risk-free rate (i.e., the return on government securities, denoted R_F) to the product of the beta coefficient (a measure of the issuer's risk) and the difference between the market return and the risk-free rate (denoted $R_M - R_F$, referred to as the risk premium). Below is the basic equilibrium equation for the CAPM:

$$\text{Required rate of return} = R_F + \beta(R_M - R_F)$$

The risk premium is 5% (11% – 6%).

The CAPM can be thus applied to each of the three investments as follows:

Investment A: 6% + (1.4 × 5%) = 13.0%
Investment B: 6% + (0.8 × 5%) = 10.0%
Investment C: 6% + (1.5 × 5%) = 13.5%

These required rates of return can be compared to the expected rates to evaluate which investments should be accepted and which should be rejected.

	Required Rate		Expected Rate	Decision
Investment A:	13.0%	>	12%	Reject
Investment B:	10.0%	<	11%	Accept
Investment C:	13.5%	>	13%	Reject

Answer (B) is incorrect. The required rates of return for Investment A and Investment C exceed their expected returns. Answer (C) is incorrect. R for Investment C exceeds its expected return. Answer (D) is incorrect. The required rates of return for Investment A and Investment C exceed their expected returns.

23. The common stock of Wisconsin's Finest Cheese has a beta coefficient of 1.7. The following information about overall market conditions is available.

Expected return on U.S. Treasury bonds	6%
Expected return on the market portfolio	8.5%

Using the capital asset pricing model (CAPM), what is the risk premium on the market?

A. 10.3%

B. 4.3%

C. 2.5%

D. 1.7%

Answer (C) is correct.

REQUIRED: The risk premium on the market using CAPM.

DISCUSSION: The risk premium on the market is the return on the market portfolio (8.5%) minus the risk-free return as measured by the return on U.S. Treasury securities (6%), or 2.5%.

Answer (A) is incorrect. This figure is the expected return on the stock. Answer (B) is incorrect. This figure is the risk premium on the stock, not the market. Answer (D) is incorrect. The stock's beta coefficient and the risk premium on the market are not the same in this case.

5.4 Derivatives

24. The use of derivatives to either hedge or speculate results in

A. Increased risk regardless of motive.

B. Decreased risk regardless of motive.

C. Offsetting risk when hedging and increased risk when speculating.

D. Offsetting risk when speculating and increased risk when hedging.

Answer (C) is correct.

REQUIRED: The effects on risk of hedging and speculating.

DISCUSSION: Derivatives, including options and futures, are contracts between the parties who contract. Unlike stocks and bonds, they are not claims on business assets. A futures contract is entered into as either a speculation or a hedge. Speculation involves the assumption of risk in the hope of gaining from price movements. Hedging is the process of using offsetting commitments to minimize or avoid the impact of adverse price movements.

Answer (A) is incorrect. Hedging decreases risk by using offsetting commitments that avoid the impact of adverse price movements. Answer (B) is incorrect. Speculation involves the assumption of risk in the hope of gaining from price movements. Answer (D) is incorrect. Speculating increases risk while hedging offsets risk.

25. Which one of the following is **not** a determinant in valuing a call option?

A. Exercise price.

B. Expiration date.

C. Forward contract price.

D. Underlying asset price.

Answer (C) is correct.

REQUIRED: The item not a determinant in valuing a call option.

DISCUSSION: The price of an option is equal to its intrinsic value (exercise price less underlying asset price) plus the time premium that depends on the expiration date of an option.

Answer (A) is incorrect. Exercise price is one of the determinants on which the value of a call option is based. Answer (B) is incorrect. The call option's expiration date is used in determining the call option's value. Answer (D) is incorrect. The underlying asset price is one of the determinants of the value of a call option.

26. A forward contract involves a commitment today to purchase a product

A. On a specific future date at a price to be determined some time in the future.

B. At some time during the current day at its present price.

C. On a specific future date at a price determined today.

D. Only when its price increases above its current exercise price.

Answer (C) is correct.

REQUIRED: The terms of a forward contract.

DISCUSSION: A forward contract is an executory contract in which the parties involved agree to the terms of a purchase and a sale, but performance is deferred. Accordingly, a forward contract involves a commitment today to purchase a product on a specific future date at a price determined today.

Answer (A) is incorrect. The price of a future contract is determined on the day of commitment, not some time in the future. Answer (B) is incorrect. Performance is deferred in a future contract, and the price of the product is not necessarily its present price. The price can be any price determined on the day of commitment. Answer (D) is incorrect. A forward contract is a firm commitment to purchase a product. It is not based on a contingency. Also, a forward contract does not involve an exercise price (exercise price is in an option contract).

27. A distinguishing feature of a futures contract is that

   A. Performance is delayed.

   B. It is a hedge, not a speculation.

   C. The parties know each other.

   D. The price is marked to market each day.

Answer (D) is correct.
  REQUIRED: The distinguishing feature of a futures contract.
  DISCUSSION: A distinguishing feature of futures contracts is that their prices are marked to market every day at the close of the day. Thus, the market price is posted at the close of business each day. A mark-to-market provision minimizes a futures contract's chance of default because profits and losses on the contracts must be received or paid each day through a clearinghouse.
  Answer (A) is incorrect. Both a forward contract and a futures contract are executory. Answer (B) is incorrect. A futures contract may be speculative. Answer (C) is incorrect. In a forward contract, the parties know each other. In a future contract, the counterparty is unknown.

28. If on the expiration day a put option is "in-the-money,"

   A. The price of the underlying asset is lower than the exercise price.

   B. The option is not worth exercising.

   C. The exercise price is lower than the price of the underlying asset.

   D. The option has a negative intrinsic value.

Answer (A) is correct.
  REQUIRED: The meaning of a put option being "in-the-money."
  DISCUSSION: A put option gives the holder the right to sell (i.e., put onto the market) the underlying asset at a fixed price, called the exercise or strike. A put option is said to be "in-the-money" when it has a positive intrinsic value, i.e., when the exercise price is greater than the price of the underlying.
  Answer (B) is incorrect. When an option is in-the-money, its intrinsic value is positive and it is worth exercising. Answer (C) is incorrect. When the exercise price of a put option is lower than the price of the underlying asset, the intrinsic value of the option is $0 and the option is out-of-the-money. Answer (D) is incorrect. A put option is said to be "in-the-money" when it has a positive intrinsic value, i.e., when the exercise price is greater than the price of the underlying.

Use the additional questions in Gleim **CPA Test Prep Online** to create Test Sessions that emulate Prometric!

Success story!

I passed all 4 sections with scores greatly exceeding 75. The main thing I liked about Gleim Review Systems for passing the CPA exam was how the information was broken down into 20 separate sub-units. Each unit covered a small selection of material at a time which made it easier to study it. I felt my personal counselor was a useful asset. There was one instance when I do not think I would have been able to get past my issue without my counselor's guidance. I have already recommended Gleim to others.

-Kyle Boehnlein, CPA

5.5 PRACTICE WRITTEN COMMUNICATION TASK

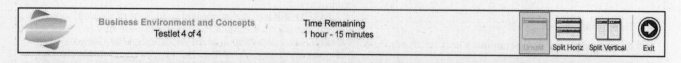

| Business Environment and Concepts Testlet 4 of 4 | Time Remaining 1 hour - 15 minutes | Unsplit Split Horiz Split Vertical Exit |

DIRECTIONS

Note: If you believe you have encountered a software malfunction, report it to the test center staff immediately.

Navigation

To navigate from task to task, use the controls at the bottom of the screen. Click on the **Next** button to advance to the next task, or the **Previous** button to go to the previous task. To go directly to any task, click on its number.

| ▽ = Reminder | | Directions | 1 2 3 4 5 6 7 ▽ ▽ ▽ ▽ ▽ ▽ ▽ | ◀ Previous   Next ▶ |

If you would like a reminder to revisit a task, or want to indicate that you are finished with it, click on the reminder flag below the task number. To clear the flag, click on it again. Reminder flags are for your use only – they do not contribute to your score.

Tabs

In this part of the examination, you will be asked to complete various tasks. Every task has one or more **Work Tabs**. Every task also has a **Help** tab.

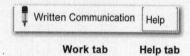

Written Communication   Help

Work tab   Help tab

Work Tabs:

- **Work Tabs** are identified with a pencil icon. This is where your responses are expected.
- Each task has one or more **Work Tabs**.
- **Work Tabs** contain directions for completing the task - be sure to read these directions carefully.
- The **Work Tab** name in the example above is for illustration only - yours will differ.
- You must complete all of the **Work Tabs** in each task to receive full credit.

Help Tab:

- The **Help Tab** provides assistance with the exam software that is used in this task. For example, if the task is to compose a memorandum, **Help** will provide information about the word processor.

The Toolbar

The toolbar at the top of the screen shows the amount of time remaining for you to complete the tasks. In addition, the following tools are available. Note that only the **Exit** button is displayed when Directions are visible - the others will appear when you begin the tasks.

Unsplit   Split Horiz   Split Vertical

Click on these buttons to split or unsplit the screen. You can split the screen vertically or horizontally.

Exit

Click on this button to go on to the next part of the examination. You must complete all of the tasks to receive full credit. Once you click on **Exit** and confirm the action, you will NOT be able to return to this testlet.

| ▽ = Reminder | | Directions | 1 ▽ | ◀ Previous   Next ▶ |

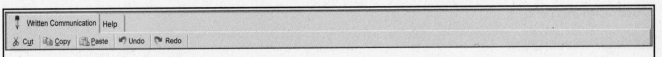

Mr. Smith came to your office today to discuss his tax return, which you have just completed. During the course of your conversation, it became clear that all of Mr. Smith's retirement money is invested in his two favorite foods, a potato chip maker and an ice cream distributor. You attempted to explain to Mr. Smith the issues relating to investing in only two stocks, but he did not have time to listen, so he asked you to write him a memo.

Prepare a memo to Mr. Smith explaining the issues relating to security risk, portfolio risk, and diversification.

Type your communication below the line in the response area below.

REMINDER: Your response will be graded for both technical content and writing skills. Technical content will be evaluated for information that is helpful to the intended reader and clearly relevant to the issue. Writing skills will be evaluated for development, organization, and the appropriate expression of ideas in professional correspondence. Use a standard business memorandum or letter format with a clear beginning, middle, and end. Do not convey information in the form of a table, bullet point list, or other abbreviated presentation.

To: Mr. Smith
Re: Investments, risks, and implications

Unofficial Answer

Written Communication

To: Mr. Smith
Re: Investments, risks, and implications

An investment portfolio is inherently exposed to risk: A market is volatile, so a loss in one security should ideally be offset by a gain in another. Prior to investing, an understanding of the risks involved will make for a stronger portfolio; these risks are security and portfolio risks. Also, the mitigating effect on risk of a diversified portfolio is critical.

Security risk is the risk associated with the individual securities making up a portfolio; the portfolio risk is the combined effect of the individual security risks. Ideally, the portfolio should be composed of offsetting risks, providing a check to the risk posed by investing in one company, industry, or commodity. This is the critical benefit provided by diversifying. An example contrary to an ideal portfolio would be one consisting entirely of stocks in restaurants, even if those restaurants are different brands. An effect on the restaurant market would affect that investor's entire portfolio; there would be no counter-balance.

The effect of an individual security on the volatility of a portfolio is measured by its sensitivity to movements in the overall market; this is called its beta coefficient. The beta is derived from the equation for regressing the return of an individual security to the overall market return; the beta is the slope of the regression line. The beta of a portfolio is the weighted average of the betas of the individual securities.

Another risk directly addressed by diversification is specific risk, also called unique risk. This is the risk associated with a specific investee's operations: new products, patents, acquisitions, competitors' activities, etc. In principle, diversifiable risk should continue to decrease as the number of different securities held increases; however, in practice, the benefits of diversification become extremely small when more than about 20 to 30 different securities are held. These concepts need to factor into any investor's decisions pertaining to portfolio composition.

The above depicts a Level 5 answer. See page 16 in the Introduction for a description of the three grading criteria.

Self-Grade

Evaluate each of the following by selecting a 0, 1, 2, 3, 4, or 5. An average response is 3. Use 4 for better than average and 5 for outstanding. Use 2 for less than average and 1 for quite poor. Use zero for no response, if you did not address the topic, or if you gave advice that is clearly illegal.

Organization	O 0	O 1	O 2	O 3	O 4	O 5
Development	O 0	O 1	O 2	O 3	O 4	O 5
Expression	O 0	O 1	O 2	O 3	O 4	O 5

Your grade for the written communication as a whole is the average of the scores for the three criteria.

Use **CPA Gleim Online** and **Simulation Wizard** to practice more written communication tasks in a realistic environment.

STUDY UNIT SIX
FORECASTING ANALYSIS

(9 pages of outline)

The complex modern organization cannot be administered without forecasts about future activity. The demand for goods, the prices of inputs, the efficiency of a production process, the need for cash, and the trends in interest rates are among the factors about which predictions must be made to adequately prepare for the future, both immediate and long-term. This study unit covers the principal forecasting techniques used in a business setting.

Forecasts are the basis for business plans. Forecasts are used to project product demand, inventory levels, cash flow, etc. **Qualitative methods** of forecasting rely on the manager's experience and intuition. **Quantitative methods** use mathematical models and graphs. When some factor in the organization's environment is plotted on the x axis, the technique is causal relationship forecasting. When time periods are plotted on the x axis, the technique is time-series analysis.

6.1 LINEAR REGRESSION ANALYSIS

1. **Simple Regression**

   a. Regression analysis is the process of deriving the linear equation that describes the relationship between two variables.

      1) Simple regression is used when exactly one independent variable is involved, and multiple regression is used when there is more than one.

   b. The simple regression equation is, obviously, the algebraic formula for a straight line.

$$y = a + bx$$

   Where: y = the dependent variable
   a = the y intercept
   b = the slope of the regression line
   x = the independent variable

      1) The best straight line that fits a set of data points is derived using calculus.

   c. Regression analysis is particularly valuable for budgeting and cost accounting purposes.

      1) One extremely common application of simple regression in a business setting is the estimation of a mixed cost function, i.e., one with a fixed component and a variable component.

      2) The y-axis intercept is the fixed portion, and the slope of the regression line is the variable portion.

EXAMPLE

A firm has performed a linear regression analysis and determined that total manufacturing costs (y) consist of fixed costs of $420,000 and variable costs of $32 per unit of output. This relationship can be stated mathematically as follows:

y = $420,000 + $32x

If the firm is planning to produce 12,000 units of output, its forecast for total manufacturing costs is $804,000 = $420,000 + $32 × 12,000.

EXAMPLE

The firm has collected the following observations on units of output (independent variable) and total manufacturing costs (dependent variable) to support its linear regression analysis:

Units of Output (000s)	Total Manufacturing Costs ($000s)
5	$620
8	$640
14	$850
17	$1,010

The observations are graphed as follows:

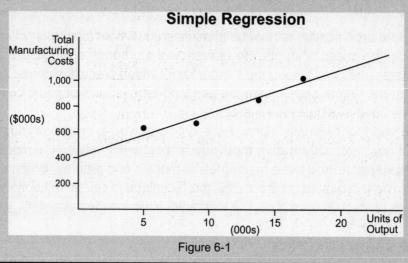

Figure 6-1

2. **Multiple Regression**

    a. Multiple regression is used when there is more than one independent variable.

        1) Multiple regression allows a firm to identify many factors (independent variables) and to weight each one according to its influence on the overall outcome.

        $$y = a + b_1x_1 + b_2x_2 + b_3x_3 + b_4x_4 + etc.$$

3. **Aspects of Regression Analysis**

    a. The linear relationship established for x and y is only valid across the relevant range. The user must identify the relevant range and ensure that (s)he does not project the relationship beyond it.

    b. Regression analysis assumes that past relationships can be validly projected into the future.

    c. Regression does not determine causality.

        1) Although x and y move together, the apparent relationship may be caused by some other factor. For instance, car wash sales volume and sunny weather are strongly correlated, but car wash sales do not cause sunny weather.

4. High-Low Method

    a.   The high-low method is used to generate a regression line by basing the equation on only the highest and lowest of a series of observations.

EXAMPLE

A regression equation covering electricity costs could be developed by using only the high-cost month and the low-cost month. If the lowest costs were $400 in April when production was 800 machine hours and the highest costs were $600 in September when production was 1,300 hours, the equation would be determined as follows:

High month	$600 for	1,300 hours
Low month	400 for	800 hours
Increase	$200	500 hours

Because costs increased $200 for 500 additional hours, the variable cost is $.40 per machine hour ($200 ÷ 500 hours). For the low month, the total variable portion of that monthly cost is $320 ($.40 × 800 hours). Given that the total cost is $400 and $320 is variable, the remaining $80 must be a fixed cost. The regression equation is $y = 80 + .4x$.

---

        1)   The major criticism of the high-low method is that the high and low points may be abnormalities not representative of normal events.

Stop and review! You have completed the outline for this subunit. Study multiple-choice questions 1 through 6 beginning on page 187.

6.2 CORRELATION ANALYSIS

1. Correlation

    a.   Correlation is the strength of the linear (straight-line) relationship between two variables, expressed mathematically in terms of the **coefficient of correlation (r)** (often called the correlation coefficient).

        1)   The coefficient r can be graphically depicted by plotting the values for the variables on a graph in the form of a scatter diagram.

    b.   The value of r ranges from 1 (perfect direct relationship) to –1 (perfect inverse relationship). The more the scatter pattern resembles a straight line, the greater the absolute value of r.

        1)   Perfect direct relationship ($r = 1$)

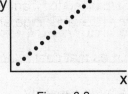

Figure 6-2

        2)   Perfect inverse relationship ($r = -1$)

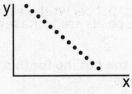

Figure 6-3

3)   Strong direct relationship (*r* = 0.7)

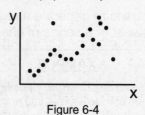

Figure 6-4

4)   No linear relationship (*r* = 0)

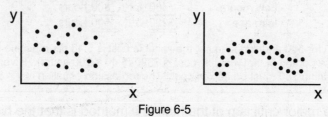

Figure 6-5

a)   Note from the right-hand graph of the pair above that a coefficient of correlation of zero does not mean there is no relationship at all between the two variables, only that what relationship they may have cannot be expressed as a linear equation.

b)   The data points in Figure 6-1 show a very strong direct relationship, reflected in an *r* value close to 1.

2.   **Determination**

a.   The **coefficient of determination (r^2)**, or the coefficient of correlation squared, is a measure of how good the fit between the independent and dependent variables is.

1)   Mathematically, the coefficient of determination is the proportion of the total variation in the dependent variable that is accounted for by the independent variable.

2)   The value of r^2 ranges from 0 to 1. The closer the value of r^2 is to 1, the more useful the independent variable (x) is in explaining or predicting the variation in the dependent variable (y).

EXAMPLE

A car dealership determines that new car sales are a function of disposable income with a coefficient of correlation of .8. This is equivalent to stating that 64% ($.8^2$) of the variation of new car sales from the average can be explained by changes in disposable income.

---

3.   **Standard Error**

a.   Standard error measures how well the linear equation represents the data. It is the vertical distance between the data points in a scatter diagram and the regression line.

1)   The closer the data points are to the regression line, the lower the standard error.

Stop and review! You have completed the outline for this subunit. Study multiple-choice questions 7 and 8 beginning on page 189.

6.3 LEARNING CURVE ANALYSIS

1. **Overview**

   a. Learning curve analysis reflects the increased rate at which people perform tasks as they gain experience.

      1) The time required to perform a given task becomes progressively shorter during the early stages of production.

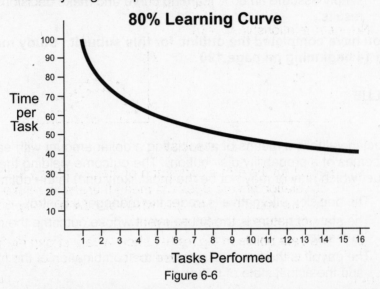

80% Learning Curve

Time per Task

Tasks Performed

Figure 6-6

   b. The curve is usually expressed as a percentage of reduced time to complete a task for each doubling of cumulative production. The most common percentage used in practice is 80%. An 80% learning curve indicates that a doubling of production will reduce the cumulative average unit completion time by 20%.

      1) The following table illustrates this phenomenon for a product whose first unit takes 100 minutes to produce:

Cumulative Units Produced	Total Time	Cumulative Average Time per Unit	The Learning Rate %
1	100	100	–
2	160	80 = (160 ÷ 2) = (100 × 80%)	80 = % [160 ÷ (100 × 2)]
4	256	64 = (256 ÷ 4) = (80 × 80%)	80 = % [256 ÷ (160 × 2)]
8	409.6	51.2 = (409.6 ÷ 8) = (64 × 80%)	80 = % [409.6 ÷ (256 × 2)]
16	655.36	40.96 = (655.36 ÷ 16) = (51.2 × 80%)	80 = % [655.36 ÷ (409.6 × 2)]

      2) With more sophisticated quantitative techniques, a more accurate average can be calculated of the units within each "batch."

         a) With the completion of the final batch (units 9 - 16), the average had come down to 40.96 minutes.

         b) For it to reach this level from the 51.2 minutes it had reached at the end of the fourth batch (units 5 - 8), the average of the units in the fifth batch alone must have been 30.72 minutes [(40.96 minutes × 2) – 51.2 minutes], or [(655.36 minutes – 409.6 minutes) ÷ (16 units – 8 units)].

Candidates need to be alert as to the nature of the question being asked. Sometimes the question might ask, "What is the average time per unit after two units?" From the table above, you can see that the answer is 80. Alternatively, sometimes the question asks, "What is the time to produce the second unit?" The answer would be 60. Since the first unit took 100 minutes and the average for the two units is 80 minutes (a total of 160), then the second unit must have taken only 60 minutes.

2.   **Limitation**

a.   The limitation of the learning curve in practice is the difficulty in knowing the shape of the learning curve.

1)   The existence of the learning curve effect is widely accepted, but companies often do not know what percentage they should use in calculations until after it is too late to use the information effectively. As a result, many companies simply assume an 80% learning curve and make decisions based on those results.

Stop and review! You have completed the outline for this subunit. Study multiple-choice questions 9 through 14 beginning on page 190.

6.4 EXPECTED VALUE

1.   **Overview**

a.   Expected value is a means of associating a dollar amount with each of the possible outcomes of a probability distribution. The outcome yielding the highest expected value (which may or may not be the most likely one) is the optimal alternative.

1)   The decision alternative is under the manager's control.

2)   The state of nature is the future event whose outcome the manager is attempting to predict.

3)   The payoff is the financial result of the combination of the manager's decision and the actual state of nature.

b.   The expected value of an event is calculated by multiplying the probability of each outcome by its payoff and summing the products. This calculation is often called a payoff table.

EXAMPLE

An investor is considering the purchase of two identically priced pieces of property. The value of the properties will change if a road, currently planned by the state, is built.

The following are estimates that road construction will occur:

Future State of Nature (SN)	Event	Probability
SN 1	No road is ever built.	.1
SN 2	A road is built this year.	.2
SN 3	A road is built more than 1 year from now.	.7

The following are estimates of the values of the properties under each of the three possible events:

Property	SN 1	SN 2	SN 3
Bivens Tract	$10,000	$40,000	$35,000
Newnan Tract	$20,000	$50,000	$30,000

The expected value of each property is determined by multiplying the probability of each state of nature by the value under that state of nature and adding all of the products.

		Expected Value
Bivens Tract:	.1($10,000) + .2($40,000) + .7($35,000) =	$33,500
Newnan Tract:	.1($20,000) + .2($50,000) + .7($30,000) =	$33,000

Thus, the Bivens Tract is the better investment.

---

    c.   A criticism of expected value is that it is based on repetitive trials, whereas many business decisions ultimately involve only one event.

EXAMPLE

A company wishes to launch a communications satellite. The probability of launch failure is .2, and the value of the satellite if the launch fails is $0. The probability of a successful launch is .8, and the value of the satellite would then be $25,000,000. The expected value is thus

$$.2(\$0) + .8(\$25,000,000) = \$20,000,000$$

But $20,000,000 is not a possible value for a single satellite; either it flies for $25,000,000, or it crashes for $0.

---

    d.   The difficult aspect of constructing a payoff table is, of course, the determination of all possible outcomes of decisions and their probabilities. Thus, a probability distribution must be established.

        1)   The assigned probabilities may reflect prior experience with similar decisions, the results of research, or highly subjective estimates.

    e.   Expected value is likely to be used by a decision maker who is risk neutral. However, other circumstances may cause the decision maker to be risk averse or even risk seeking.

EXAMPLE

A dealer in luxury yachts may order 0, 1, or 2 yachts for this season's inventory.

The dealer projects demand for the season as follows:

Demand	Probability
0 yachts	10%
1 yacht	50%
2 yachts	40%

The cost of carrying each excess yacht is $50,000, and the gain for each yacht sold is $200,000. The profit or loss resulting from each combination of decision and outcome is thus as follows:

				Expected Value		
Decision	**State of Nature** **Demand = 0**			**Stock** **0 Yachts**	**Stock** **1 Yacht**	**Stock** **2 Yachts**
Stock 0 yachts	$ 0	× 10%	=	$ 0		
Stock 1 yacht	(50,000)	× 10%	=		$ (5,000)	
Stock 2 yachts	(100,000)	× 10%	=			$ (10,000)
	Demand = 1					
Stock 0 yachts	$ 0	× 50%	=	$ 0		
Stock 1 yacht	200,000	× 50%	=		$ 100,000	
Stock 2 yachts	150,000	× 50%	=			$ 75,000
	Demand = 2					
Stock 0 yachts	$ 0	× 40%	=	$ 0		
Stock 1 yacht	200,000	× 40%	=		$ 80,000	
Stock 2 yachts	400,000	× 40%	=			$ 160,000
All expected values				**$ 0**	**$ 175,000**	**$ 225,000**

In this example, a risk-averse decision maker may not wish to accept the risk of losing $100,000 by ordering two yachts, even though that decision has the highest expected value.

        1)   The benefit of expected value analysis is that it allows a manager to apply scientific management techniques to applications that would otherwise be guesswork.

            a)   Although exact probabilities may not be known, the use of expected value analysis forces managers to evaluate decisions in a more organized manner. At the least, managers are forced to think of all of the possibilities that could happen with each decision.

Expected value calculations and analysis may appear difficult. However, you are simply multiplying the probability of each outcome by its payoff and summing the products.

Stop and review! You have completed the outline for this subunit. Study multiple-choice questions 15 through 26 beginning on page 192.

6.5 SELECTING THE FORECASTING TECHNIQUE

1.   **Sensitivity Analysis**

    a.   Sensitivity analysis reveals how sensitive expected value calculations are to the accuracy of the initial estimates. It asks the question, "What if?" It is thus useful in determining whether expending additional resources to obtain better forecasts is justified.

        1)   If a change in the probabilities assigned to the various states of nature results in large changes in the expected values, the decision maker is justified in expending more effort to make better predictions about the outcomes.

        2)   The benefit of sensitivity analysis is that managers can see the effect of changed assumptions on the final objective.

    b.   The trial-and-error method inherent in sensitivity analysis is greatly facilitated by the use of computer software.

        1)   A major use of sensitivity analysis is in capital budgeting, where small changes in prevailing interest rates or payoff amounts can make a great difference in the profitability of a project.

2.   **Simulation Analysis**

    a.   This method represents a refinement of standard profitability theory. The computer is used to generate many examples of results based upon various assumptions.

    b.   Project simulation is frequently expensive. Unless a project is exceptionally large and expensive, full-scale simulation is usually not worthwhile.

3.   **Monte Carlo Technique**

    a.   This technique is often used in simulation to generate the individual values for a random variable.

        1)   The performance of a quantitative model under uncertainty may be investigated by randomly selecting values for each of the variables in the model (based on the probability distribution of each variable) and then calculating the value of the solution.

    b.   If this process is performed a large number of times, the distribution of results from the model will be obtained.

4. **Delphi Technique**

    a. The Delphi technique solicits opinions from experts, summarizes the opinions, and feeds the summaries back to the experts (without revealing participants to each other).

        1) The process is repeated until the opinions converge on an optimal solution.

5. **Time Series Analysis**

    a. Time series analysis (also called trend analysis) is the process of projecting future trends based on past experience. It is a regression model in which the independent variable is time.

Some of the forecasting-related questions on the CPA exam require the candidate to read about a forecasting situation and then choose the appropriate method. Thus, candidates should be as comfortable recognizing when to use the different forecasting methods as they are in working through the details of applying them.

Stop and review! You have completed the outline for this subunit. Study multiple-choice questions 27 through 29 beginning on page 197.

QUESTIONS

6.1 Linear Regression Analysis

1. In the standard regression equation $y = a + bx$, the letter b is best described as a(n)

    A. Independent variable.

    B. Dependent variable.

    C. Y-intercept.

    D. Slope of the regression line.

Answer (D) is correct.
    REQUIRED: The meaning of the letter b in the standard regression equation.
    DISCUSSION: In the standard regression equation, b represents the slope of the regression line. For example, in a cost determination regression, y equals total costs, b is the variable cost per unit, x is the number of units produced, and a is fixed cost.
    Answer (A) is incorrect. The independent variable is x. Answer (B) is incorrect. The dependent variable is y. Answer (C) is incorrect. The y-intercept is a.

2. In order to analyze sales as a function of advertising expenses, the sales manager of Smith Company developed a simple regression model. The model included the following equation, which was based on 32 monthly observations of sales and advertising expenses with a related coefficient of determination of .90.

    Sales = $10,000 + (2.5 × Advertising expenses)

If Smith Company's advertising expenses in 1 month amounted to $1,000, the related point estimate of sales would be

    A. $2,500

    B. $11,250

    C. $12,250

    D. $12,500

Answer (D) is correct.
    REQUIRED: An estimate of expenses using linear regression.
    DISCUSSION: The simple regression equation can be solved as follows:

    Sales = $10,000 + (2.5 × Advertising expenses)
         = $10,000 + (2.5 × $1,000)
         = $10,000 + $2,500
         = $12,500

    Answer (A) is incorrect. The amount of $2,500 includes only the advertising expense. Answer (B) is incorrect. The amount of $11,250 results from improperly multiplying the answer by the coefficient of determination. Answer (C) is incorrect. The amount of $12,250 results from improperly applying the coefficient of determination to the advertising expense.

Question 3 is based on the following information.

In preparing the annual profit plan for the coming year, Wilkens Company wants to determine the cost behavior pattern of the maintenance costs. Wilkens has decided to use linear regression by employing the equation $y = a + bx$ for maintenance costs. The prior year's data regarding maintenance hours and costs, and the results of the regression analysis, are given below and in the opposite column.

	Hours of Activity	Maintenance Costs
January	480	$ 4,200
February	320	3,000
March	400	3,600
April	300	2,820
May	500	4,350
June	310	2,960
July	320	3,030
August	520	4,470
September	490	4,260
October	470	4,050
November	350	3,300
December	340	3,160
Sum	4,800	$43,200
Average	400	$ 3,600

Average cost per hour	$9.00
a	684.65
b	7.2884
Standard error of a	49.515
Standard error of b	.12126
Standard error of the estimate	34.469
r^2	.99724

3. If Wilkens Company uses the high/low method of analysis, the equation for the relationship between hours of activity and maintenance cost would be

A. $y = 400 + 9.0x$

B. $y = 570 + 7.5x$

C. $y = 3,600 + 400x$

D. $y = 570 + 9.0x$

Answer (B) is correct.
   REQUIRED: The equation for the relationship between activity and maintenance cost.
   DISCUSSION: First, determine the months with the highest (520 hours in August) and lowest (300 hours in April) levels of activity.

	Hours	Dollars
August	520	$ 4,470
April	300	2,820
Difference	220	$ 1,650

As the hours increased by 220, cost increased by $1,650, which is $7.50 per hour. Thus, at 300 hours of activity, the total variable costs are $2,250 ($7.50 × 300 hours). Since the total cost was $2,820, the $570 above the variable costs must be fixed costs. Substituting into the standard regression equation of $y = a + bx$ gives $y = $570 + $7.50x$.
   Answer (A) is incorrect. The fixed cost and variable cost are wrong. Answer (C) is incorrect. Both fixed and variable costs are wrong. Answer (D) is incorrect. The variable cost is wrong.

Questions 4 through 6 are based on the following information. Jackson Co. has the following information for the first quarter of this year:

	Machine Hours	Cleaning Expense
January	2,100	$ 900
February	2,600	1,200
March	1,600	800
April	2,000	1,000

4. Using the high-low method, what is Jackson's fixed cost?

A. $160

B. $320

C. $640

D. $1,040

Answer (A) is correct.
   REQUIRED: The fixed cost using the high-low method.
   DISCUSSION: The fixed cost using the high-low method can be found by multiplying the variable cost per machine hour, $.40, by the number of machine hours of either month. This number is then subtracted from the total cost of that respective month. Therefore, using the month of February, it would be:

Total cost	$1,200
Less: Variable cost (2,600 hours × $.40)	(1,040)
Fixed cost	$ 160

   Answer (B) is incorrect. The fixed cost is not $320. Answer (C) is incorrect. The fixed cost is not $640. Answer (D) is incorrect. The variable cost at 2,600 machine hours is $1,040.

5. Using the high-low method, what is Jackson's variable cost of cleaning per machine hour?

A. $.40

B. $.48

C. $2.00

D. $2.50

Answer (A) is correct.
 REQUIRED: The variable cost in the high-low method.
 DISCUSSION: The high-low method is used to generate a regression line by basing the equation on only the highest and lowest of a series of observations. In this problem, March was the lowest and February the highest.

February	$1,200	for	2,600 hours
March	(800)	for	(1,600) hours
Increase	$ 400	for	1,000 hours

Thus, it costs $400 for 1,000 hours, or $.40 for an hour.
 Answer (B) is incorrect. The average of the high and low months is $.48. Answer (C) is incorrect. The March machine hours divided by the March cost is $2.00. Answer (D) is incorrect. The increase in hours divided by the increase in cost is $2.50.

6. Jackson's management expects machine hours for the month of May to be 1,400 hours. What is their expected total cost for the month of May using the high-low method?

A. $560

B. $650

C. $720

D. $760

Answer (C) is correct.
 REQUIRED: The expected total cost using the high-low method.
 DISCUSSION: The expected total cost, using the high-low method, can be found as follows:

Expected total cost = Expected fixed cost + Expected variable cost
 = $160 + (1,400 hours × $.40 per hour)
 = $160 + $560
 = $720

Answer (A) is incorrect. The variable cost is $560, not the total cost. Answer (B) is incorrect. The expected total cost for May is not $650. Answer (D) is incorrect. The expected total cost for May is not $760.

6.2 Correlation Analysis

Question 7 is based on the following information. Alpha Company produces several different products and is making plans for the introduction of a new product.

Overhead costs have not been established for the new product, but monthly data on total production and overhead cost for the past 24 months have been analyzed using simple linear regression. The results below were derived from the simple regression and provide the basis for overhead cost estimates for the new product:

Dependent variable (y) -- Factory overhead costs
Independent variable (x) -- Direct labor hours

Computed values:

y intercept	$40,000
Coefficient of independent variable	$2.10
Coefficient of correlation	0.953
Standard error of estimate	$2,840
Standard error of regression coefficient	0.42
Mean value of independent variable	$18,000
Coefficient of determination	0.908

7. What percentage of the variation in Alpha's overhead costs is explained by the independent variable?

A. 90.8%

B. 42%

C. 48.8%

D. 95.3%

Answer (A) is correct.
 REQUIRED: The percentage of cost variation explained by the regression equation.
 DISCUSSION: The coefficient of determination (r^2) is the square of the coefficient of correlation (r). The coefficient of determination may be interpreted as the percent of variation in the dependent variable "explained" by the variation in the independent variable. Here, $r = 0.953$, and $r^2 = 0.908$. Thus, 90.8% of the variation in overhead costs can be explained by direct labor hours.
 Answer (B) is incorrect. This percentage is the standard error of the regression coefficient. Answer (C) is incorrect. This percentage is an incorrect calculation. Answer (D) is incorrect. This percentage is the square root of the correct answer.

8. Correlation is a term frequently used in conjunction with regression analysis and is measured by the value of the coefficient of correlation, *r*. The best explanation of the value *r* is that it

A. Is always positive.

B. Interprets variances in terms of the independent variable.

C. Ranges in size from negative infinity to positive infinity.

D. Is a measure of the relative relationship between two variables.

Answer (D) is correct.
   REQUIRED: The best explanation of the coefficient of correlation (*r*).
   DISCUSSION: The coefficient of correlation (*r*) measures the strength of the linear relationship between the dependent and independent variables. The magnitude of *r* is independent of the scales of measurement of x and y. The coefficient lies between −1.0 and +1.0. A value of zero indicates no linear relationship between the x and y variables. A value of +1.0 indicates a perfectly direct relationship, and a value of −1.0 indicates a perfectly inverse relationship.
   Answer (A) is incorrect. The coefficient is negative if the relationship between the variables is inverse. Answer (B) is incorrect. The coefficient relates the two variables to each other. Answer (C) is incorrect. The size of the coefficient varies between −1.0 and +1.0.

6.3 Learning Curve Analysis

9. Learning curves are most often used to predict

A. Unit material costs.

B. Overhead variances.

C. Total unit costs.

D. Unit direct labor costs.

Answer (D) is correct.
   REQUIRED: The type of cost best predicted by learning curves.
   DISCUSSION: Learning curves reflect the increased rate at which people perform tasks as they gain experience. Thus, they are useful in predicting unit direct labor costs.
   Answer (A) is incorrect. Unit material costs typically do not decline as workers learn their jobs. Answer (B) is incorrect. Variances are by definition unpredictable. Otherwise, the standards would be changed to avoid the variance. Answer (C) is incorrect. Learning curves apply only to labor efficiency and are not effective predictors of total unit costs or unit variable costs.

Questions 10 through 12 are based on the following information. Aerosub, Inc., has developed a new product for spacecraft that includes the production of a complex part. The manufacture of this part requires a high degree of technical skill. Management believes there is a good opportunity for its technical force to learn and improve as they become accustomed to the production process. The production of the first unit requires 10,000 direct labor hours. Management projects an 80% learning curve and wants to produce a total of eight units.

---

10. Upon completion of the eighth unit, Aerosub's cumulative direct labor hours will be

A. 29,520 hours.

B. 40,960 hours.

C. 64,000 hours.

D. 80,000 hours.

Answer (B) is correct.
   REQUIRED: Calculation of the cumulative direct labor hours using an 80% learning curve.
   DISCUSSION: The underlying assumption of learning curve analysis is that workers gain productivity at a predictable rate as they gain experience with a new process. A common assumption is that the number of hours required for each doubling of output will be 80% of the hours required for the previous doubling. The effects of Aerosub's projected learning curve on this product can be calculated as follows:

Batch	Cumulative Units Produced	Cumulative Average Labor Hours	Cumulative Total Labor Hours
1	1	10,000	10,000
2	2	8,000 (10,000 × 80%)	16,000
3	4	6,400 (8,000 × 80%)	25,600
4	8	5,120 (6,400 × 80%)	40,960

Answer (A) is incorrect. The figure of 29,520 results from improperly summing the cumulative average labor hour figures. Answer (C) is incorrect. The figure of 64,000 results from improperly multiplying the cumulative number of units produced by the 10,000 hours spent on the first batch, then multiplying by the learning curve percentage. Answer (D) is incorrect. The figure of 80,000 results from improperly multiplying the cumulative number of units produced by the 10,000 hours spent on the first batch.

11. After completing the first unit, the estimated total direct labor hours Aerosub will require to produce the seven additional units will be

A. 30,960 hours.

B. 40,960 hours.

C. 56,000 hours.

D. 70,000 hours.

Answer (A) is correct.

REQUIRED: Calculation of the cumulative direct labor hours using an 80% learning curve.

DISCUSSION: The cumulative total hours spent on the units can be calculated as follows:

Batch	Cumulative Units Produced	Cumulative Average Labor Hours	Cumulative Total Labor Hours
1	1	10,000	10,000
2	2	8,000 (10,000 × 80%)	16,000
3	4	6,400 (8,000 × 80%)	25,600
4	8	5,120 (6,400 × 80%)	40,960

Since it took a total of 40,960 hours to complete all eight units and 10,000 to complete the first one, units 2 through 8 took 30,960 hours (40,960 – 10,000).

Answer (B) is incorrect. The figure 40,960 is the number of hours to complete all eight units. Answer (C) is incorrect. The figure 56,000 results from improperly multiplying the seven units by the 8,000 average labor hours consumed in producing the second batch. Answer (D) is incorrect. The figure 70,000 results from improperly multiplying the seven units by the 10,000 average labor hours consumed in producing the first unit.

12. Upon completion of the eighth unit, Aerosub's cumulative average direct labor hours required per unit of the product will be

A. 5,120 hours.

B. 6,400 hours.

C. 8,000 hours.

D. 10,000 hours.

Answer (A) is correct.

REQUIRED: The calculation of the cumulative average hours with an 80% learning curve.

DISCUSSION: The underlying assumption of learning curve analysis is that workers gain productivity at a predictable rate as they gain experience with a new process. A common assumption is that the number of hours required for each doubling of output will be 80% of the hours required for the previous doubling. The effects of Aerosub's projected learning curve on this product can be calculated as follows:

Batch	Cumulative Units Produced	Cumulative Average Labor Hours
1	1	10,000
2	2	8,000 (10,000 × 80%)
3	4	6,400 (8,000 × 80%)
4	8	5,120 (6,400 × 80%)

Answer (B) is incorrect. The projected number of hours after four units is 6,400. Answer (C) is incorrect. The projected number of hours after two units is 8,000. Answer (D) is incorrect. The number 10,000 results from failing to take the learning curve effect into account at all.

13. A learning curve of 80% assumes that direct labor costs are reduced by 20% for each doubling of output. What is the incremental cost of the 16th unit produced as an approximate percentage of the 1st unit produced? All units within a batch are considered to have the average completion time for that batch.

A. 41%

B. 31%

C. 51%

D. 64%

Answer (B) is correct.

REQUIRED: The cost of the last unit produced.

DISCUSSION: With an 80% learning curve, the average cost after eight units is 51.20% of the cost of the first unit (100% × 80% × 80% × 80%). After 16 units, the average cost is 40.96% (51.20% × 80%). Thus, the average cost of units in the last batch (units 9 through 16) must have been 30.72% [(40.96% × 2) – 51.20%].

Answer (A) is incorrect. This percentage is the average time required for the 16th unit. Answer (C) is incorrect. This percentage is the time required for the 8th unit. Answer (D) is incorrect. This percentage is the time required for the 4th unit.

14. A particular manufacturing job is subject to an estimated 80% learning curve. The first unit required 50 labor hours to complete. If the learning curve is based on a cumulative average time per unit assumption, what is the time required to complete the second unit?

A. 30.0 hours.

B. 40.0 hours.

C. 45.0 hours.

D. 50.0 hours.

Answer (A) is correct.
  REQUIRED: The time required to complete the second unit.
  DISCUSSION: The learning curve reflects the increased rate at which people perform tasks as they gain experience. The time required to perform a given task becomes progressively shorter. Ordinarily, the curve is expressed in a percentage of reduced time to complete a task for each doubling of cumulative production. One common assumption in a learning curve model is that the cumulative average time (and labor cost) per unit is reduced by a certain percentage each time production doubles. Thus, an 80% learning curve indicates that a doubling of production will reduce the cumulative average unit completion time by 20%. For example, if the first unit required 50 hours to complete, the average completion time after two units will be 40 hours (50 hours × 80%). If total production time is 80 hours (2 × 40 cumulative average time), and the first unit required 50 hours, the time to produce the second unit must be 30 hours.
  Answer (B) is incorrect. This figure is based on the assumption that the time to produce the last unit (the incremental unit-time assumption) is reduced by 20%. Answer (C) is incorrect. This figure is based on a 90% learning curve and the incremental unit-time assumption. Answer (D) is incorrect. The completion time for the first unit is 50.0 hours.

6.4 Expected Value

Questions 15 and 16 are based on the following information. The probabilities shown in the table below represent the estimate of sales for a new product.

Sales (Units)	Probability
0-200	15%
201-400	45%
401-600	25%
601-800	15%

15. What is the probability of selling between 201 and 600 units of the product?

A. 0%

B. 11.25%

C. 70%

D. 25%

Answer (C) is correct.
  REQUIRED: The probability of selling between 201 and 600 units of the new product.
  DISCUSSION: The probability of selling between 201 and 400 units is 45%, and the probability of selling between 401 and 600 units is 25%. Hence, the probability of selling between 201 and 600 units is the sum of these probabilities, or 70%.

16. Using the midpoint of each range as the best estimate for that range, what is the best estimate of the expected sales of the new product?

A. 480

B. 380

C. 400

D. 800

Answer (B) is correct.
  REQUIRED: The best estimate of the expected sales of the new product.
  DISCUSSION: The expected sales levels should be weighted by the individual probabilities of their occurrence. The midpoint of each sales level is used as the estimate for that level. Thus, sales are expected to be 380 units.

$$
\begin{array}{rcl}
100 \times 15\% & = & 15 \\
300 \times 45\% & = & 135 \\
500 \times 25\% & = & 125 \\
700 \times 15\% & = & \underline{105} \\
& & \underline{380}
\end{array}
$$

  Answer (A) is incorrect. The figure of 480 is based on the maximum value in each range. Answer (C) is incorrect. The maximum value in the modal range is 400. Answer (D) is incorrect. The highest estimate is 800.

17. During the past few years, Wilder Company has experienced the following average number of power outages:

Number per Month	Number of Months
0	3
1	2
2	4
3	3
	12

Each power outage results in out-of-pocket costs of $800. For $1,000 per month, Wilder can lease a generator to provide power during outages. If Wilder leases a generator in the coming year, the estimated savings (or additional expense) for the year will be

A. $(15,200)

B. $(1,267)

C. $3,200

D. $7,200

Answer (C) is correct.

REQUIRED: The estimated savings or additional expense from leasing the generator, given expected levels of occurrence.

DISCUSSION: Each outage costs $800, but this expense can be avoided by paying $1,000 per month ($12,000 for the year). The expected-value approach uses the probability distribution derived from past experience to determine the average expected outages per month.

$$3 \div 12 \times 0 = 0.0$$
$$2 \div 12 \times 1 = 0.16667$$
$$4 \div 12 \times 2 = 0.66667$$
$$3 \div 12 \times 3 = \underline{0.75000}$$
$$\underline{1.58334}$$

The company can expect to have, on average, 1.58334 outages per month. At $800 per outage, the expected cost is $1,266.67. Thus, paying $1,000 to avoid an expense of $1,266.67 saves $266.67 per month, or $3,200 per year.

Answer (A) is incorrect. The annual amount the company will lose without a generator is $(15,200). Answer (B) is incorrect. The monthly amount the company will lose without a generator is $(1,267). Answer (D) is incorrect. The savings amount if two outages occur per month is $7,200.

18. Expected value in decision analysis is

A. A standard deviation using the probabilities as weights.

B. An arithmetic mean using the probabilities as weights.

C. The square root of the squared deviations.

D. A measure of the difference between the best possible outcome and the outcome of the original decision.

Answer (B) is correct.

REQUIRED: The true statement about expected value.

DISCUSSION: Expected value analysis is an estimate of future monetary value based on forecasts and their related probabilities of occurrence. The expected value is found by multiplying the probability of each outcome by its payoff and summing the products. Expected value is thus an arithmetic mean using probabilities as weights.

Answer (A) is incorrect. The standard deviation is a measure of dispersion of a population. Answer (C) is incorrect. This is a nonsense answer. Answer (D) is incorrect. Expected value is a prospective measure.

19. In decision theory, those uncontrollable future events that can affect the outcome of a decision are

A. Payoffs.

B. States of nature.

C. Probabilities.

D. Nodes.

Answer (B) is correct.

REQUIRED: The term describing uncontrollable future events.

DISCUSSION: Applying decision theory requires the decision maker to develop an exhaustive list of possible future events. All possible future events that might occur must be included, even though the decision maker will likely be very unsure as to which specific events will occur. These future uncontrollable events are referred to as states of nature.

Answer (A) is incorrect. Payoffs are outcome measures such as profit or loss. Answer (C) is incorrect. Probabilities are the likelihood of occurrence of the states of nature. Answer (D) is incorrect. Nodes (junction points) are decision points.

20. The expected monetary value of an event

A. Is equal to the conditional value or profit of the event.

B. Is equal to the payoff of the event times the probability the event will occur.

C. Is the profit forgone by not choosing the best alternative.

D. Is the absolute profit from a particular event.

Answer (B) is correct.

REQUIRED: The true statement about the expected monetary value of an event.

DISCUSSION: For decisions involving risk, the concept of expected value provides a rational means for selecting the best alternative. The expected value of a decision is found by multiplying the probability of each outcome by its payoff, and summing the products. The result is the long-term average payoff for repeated trials.

Answer (A) is incorrect. The conditional value is the return given a certain condition or state of nature. Answer (C) is incorrect. The profit forgone by not choosing the best alternative is the opportunity cost. Answer (D) is incorrect. Expected value represents the long-run average profit from an event.

21. Pongo Company's managers are attempting to value a piece of land they own. One potential occurrence is that the old road bordering the land gets paved. Another possibility is that the road does not get paved. A third outcome is that the road might be destroyed and completely replaced by a new road. Based on the following future states of nature, their probabilities, and subsequent values of the land, what is the expected value of the land?

Future States of Nature (SN)	Probability
SN 1: Current road gets paved	.5
SN 2: Road does not get paved	.4
SN 3: Current road destroyed and replaced with new road	.1

Estimates of land value under each possible future state of nature:

Value if SN 1: $200,000
Value if SN 2: $100,000
Value if SN 3: $550,000

A. $133,333

B. $195,000

C. $225,000

D. $283,333

Answer (B) is correct.

REQUIRED: The expected value of the land.

DISCUSSION: The expected value of the land is determined by multiplying the probability of each state of nature by the value under that particular state of nature and adding all of the products. Thus, the land's expected value is $(0.5)(\$200,000) + (0.4)(\$100,000) + (0.1)(\$550,000) = \$195,000$.

Answer (A) is incorrect. The amount of $133,333 places too much weight on the second option. Answer (C) is incorrect. The amount of $225,000 gives too much weight to the third option. Answer (D) is incorrect. The amount of $283,333 uses a simple unweighted average of the returns from the three options.

Question 22 is based on the following information. The College Honor Society sells hot pretzels at the home football games. The pretzels are sold for $1.00 each, and the cost per pretzel is $.30. Any unsold pretzels are discarded because they will be stale before the next home game.

The frequency distribution of the demand for pretzels per game is presented as follows:

Unit Sales Volume	Probability
2,000 pretzels	.10
3,000 pretzels	.15
4,000 pretzels	.20
5,000 pretzels	.35
6,000 pretzels	.20

22. The estimated demand for pretzels at the next home football game using an expected value approach is

A. 4,000 pretzels.

B. 4,400 pretzels.

C. 5,000 pretzels.

D. Some amount other than those given.

Answer (B) is correct.

REQUIRED: The estimated demand using an expected value approach.

DISCUSSION: The calculation using an expected value approach weights each possible sales volume by its probability. Thus, the estimated demand is 4,400 pretzels.

Volume		Probability		Result
2,000	×	.10	=	200
3,000	×	.15	=	450
4,000	×	.20	=	800
5,000	×	.35	=	1,750
6,000	×	.20	=	1,200
Expected value				4,400

Answer (A) is incorrect. The figure of 4,000 pretzels assumes each outcome is equally likely. Answer (C) is incorrect. The estimated demand using a deterministic approach based on the most likely outcome is 5,000 pretzels. Answer (D) is incorrect. The figure of 4,400 pretzels is among the responses given.

Question 23 is based on the following information. Stan Berry is considering selling peanuts at the Keefer High School football games. The peanuts would cost $.50 per bag and could be sold for $1.50 per bag. No other costs would be incurred to sell the peanuts. All unsold bags can be returned to the supplier for $.30 each. Berry estimated the demand for peanuts at each football game and constructed the payoff table that follows.

Demand (Bags)	Probability of Demand	Action (Bags to Stock)			
		20	30	40	50
20	.2	$20	$18	$16	$14
30	.4	$20	$30	$28	$26
40	.3	$20	$30	$40	$38
50	.1	$20	$30	$40	$50

23. The optimum number of bags of peanuts for Stan Berry to stock is

A. 20

B. 30

C. 40

D. 50

Answer (C) is correct.

REQUIRED: The optimum number of bags to stock for each game.

DISCUSSION: Expected value analysis is a means of selecting the best option when decisions involve risk. The expected value equals the sum of the products of the various payoffs and their respective probabilities. Stan Berry can calculate the expected value of each of his four possible actions as follows:

Bags Stocked		Expected Value
20	.2($20) + .4($20) + .3($20) + .1($20) =	$20.00
30	.2($18) + .4($30) + .3($30) + .1($30) =	27.60
40	.2($16) + .4($28) + .3($40) + .1($40) =	30.40
50	.2($14) + .4($26) + .3($38) + .1($50) =	29.60

The action with the highest expected payoff is to stock 40 bags.

Answer (A) is incorrect. The figure of 20 units does not have the greatest expected value. Answer (B) is incorrect. The figure of 30 units does not have the greatest expected value. Answer (D) is incorrect. The figure of 50 units does not have the greatest expected value.

Question 24 is based on the following information. The Booster Club at Blair College sells hot dogs at home basketball games. The group has a frequency distribution of the demand for hot dogs per game and plans to apply the expected value decision rule to determine the number of hot dogs to stock.

24. The Booster Club should select the demand level that

A. Is closest to the expected demand.

B. Has the greatest probability of occurring.

C. Has the greatest expected opportunity cost.

D. Has the greatest expected monetary value.

Answer (D) is correct.

REQUIRED: The demand level that should be selected.

DISCUSSION: The Booster Club should select the demand level that maximizes profits, that is, the level with the greatest expected monetary value. This level may not include the event with the highest conditional profit because this profit may be accompanied by a low probability of occurrence. Alternatively, the event with the highest probability of occurrence may not be selected because it does not offer a high conditional profit.

Answer (A) is incorrect. Stocking an amount equal to expected demand (the sum of the products of the possible amounts demanded and their respective probabilities) does not necessarily maximize expected profits. Answer (B) is incorrect. The number of bags to stock is not necessarily the same as the amount demanded with the highest probability. The inventory decision should be based on the relation of the probability distribution to the monetary outcomes. Answer (C) is incorrect. The greatest opportunity cost is not factored into the expected value analysis.

Questions 25 and 26 are based on the following information. A company is considering three alternative machines to produce a new product. The cost structures (unit variable costs plus avoidable fixed costs) for the three machines are shown as follows. The selling price is unaffected by the machine used.

Single purpose machine $.60x + $20,000
Semiautomatic machine $.40x + $50,000
Automatic machine $.20x + $120,000

The demand for units of the new product is described by the following probability distribution.

Demand	Probability
200,000	0.4
300,000	0.3
400,000	0.2
500,000	0.1

25. Ignoring the time value of money, the expected cost of using the semiautomatic machine is

A. $170,000

B. $130,000

C. $210,000

D. $250,000

Answer (A) is correct.
  REQUIRED: The expected cost of using the semiautomatic machine.
  DISCUSSION: The expected demand is 300,000 units [(.4 × 200,000) + (.3 × 300,000) + (.2 × 400,000) + (.1 × 500,000)]. Total expected cost is therefore $170,000 [$50,000 fixed cost + ($.40 × 300,000) variable cost].
  Answer (B) is incorrect. The amount of $130,000 is calculated by using demand of 200,000 units. Answer (C) is incorrect. The amount of $210,000 is calculated by using demand of 400,000 units. Answer (D) is incorrect. The amount of $250,000 is calculated by using demand of 500,000 units.

26. Using the expected value criterion,

A. The single purpose machine should be used because of the low expected demand.

B. The automatic machine should be used because of the high expected demand.

C. The semiautomatic machine should be used because it has the lowest expected cost.

D. The automatic machine has the lowest expected cost.

Answer (C) is correct.
  REQUIRED: The machine to be used and why.
  DISCUSSION: The semiautomatic machine has an expected cost of $170,000 based on an expected demand of 300,000 units [(.4 × 200,000) + (.3 × 300,000) + (.2 × 400,000) + (.1 × 500,000)]. The single purpose machine has an expected cost of $200,000 [($.60 × 300,000) + $20,000]. The automatic machine has an expected cost of $180,000 [($.20 × 300,000) + $120,000)]. Hence, the semiautomatic machine has the lowest expected cost at the expected level of demand.
  Answer (A) is incorrect. The single purpose machine is not the best choice based on the expected demand level. Answer (B) is incorrect. The automatic machine is not the best choice based on the expected demand level. Answer (D) is incorrect. The automatic machine has the second lowest expected cost.

6.5 Selecting the Forecasting Technique

27. Through the use of decision models, managers thoroughly analyze many alternatives and decide on the best alternative for the company. Often the actual results achieved from a particular decision are **not** what was expected when the decision was made. In addition, an alternative that was **not** selected would have actually been the best decision for the company. The appropriate technique to analyze the alternatives by using expected inputs and altering them before a decision is made is

- A. Expected value analysis.
- B. Linear programming.
- C. Program evaluation review technique (PERT).
- D. Sensitivity analysis.

Answer (D) is correct.
 REQUIRED: The technique that involves altering expected inputs during the decision process.
 DISCUSSION: After a problem has been formulated into any mathematical model, it may be subjected to sensitivity analysis. Sensitivity analysis examines how the model's outcomes change as the parameters change.
 Answer (A) is incorrect. Expected value analysis is used to determine an anticipated return or cost based upon probabilities of events and their related outcomes. Answer (B) is incorrect. Linear programming optimizes a function given certain constraints. Answer (C) is incorrect. PERT is a network technique used to plan and control large projects.

28. A widely used approach that managers use to recognize uncertainty about individual items and to obtain an immediate financial estimate of the consequences of possible prediction errors is

- A. Expected value analysis.
- B. Learning curve analysis.
- C. Sensitivity analysis.
- D. Regression analysis.

Answer (C) is correct.
 REQUIRED: The approach that gives an immediate financial estimate of the consequences of possible prediction errors.
 DISCUSSION: After a problem has been formulated into any mathematical model, it may be subjected to sensitivity analysis. Sensitivity analysis examines how the model's outcomes change as the parameters change.
 Answer (A) is incorrect. Expected value is the probabilistically weighted average of the outcomes of an action. Answer (B) is incorrect. Learning curve analysis quantifies how labor costs decline as employees learn their jobs through repetition. Answer (D) is incorrect. Regression, or least squares, analysis determines the average change in the dependent variable given a unit change in one or more independent variables.

29. A company experiences both variable usage rates and variable lead times for its inventory items. The probability distributions for both usage and lead times are known. A technique the company could use for determining the optimal safety stock levels for an inventory item is

- A. Queuing theory.
- B. Linear programming.
- C. Decision tree analysis.
- D. Monte Carlo simulation.

Answer (D) is correct.
 REQUIRED: The quantitative technique used to determine safety stock given variable usage rates and lead times.
 DISCUSSION: Simulation is a technique for experimenting with mathematical models using a computer. Monte Carlo simulation is a technique to generate the individual values for a random variable. A random number generator is used to produce numbers with a uniform probability distribution. The second step of the Monte Carlo process then transforms the random numbers into values consistent with the desired distribution. The performance of a model under conditions of uncertainty may be investigated by randomly selecting values for each of the variables in the model based on the probability distribution of each variable and then calculating the value of the solution. Advantages of Monte Carlo simulation are that time can be compressed, alternative policies can be considered, and complex systems can be analyzed.
 Answer (A) is incorrect. Queuing theory is used to minimize the costs of waiting lines. Answer (B) is incorrect. Linear programming is used to minimize a cost function or maximize a profit function given constraints. Answer (C) is incorrect. Decision trees are diagrams that analyze sequences of probabilistic decisions, the events that may follow each decision, and their outcomes.

Use the additional questions in Gleim **CPA Test Prep Online** to create Test Sessions that emulate Prometric!

6.6 PRACTICE WRITTEN COMMUNICATION TASK

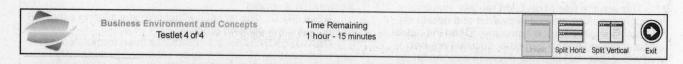

| | Business Environment and Concepts | Time Remaining | |
| | Testlet 4 of 4 | 1 hour - 15 minutes | Unsplit   Split Horiz   Split Vertical   Exit |

DIRECTIONS

Note: If you believe you have encountered a software malfunction, report it to the test center staff immediately.

Navigation

To navigate from task to task, use the controls at the bottom of the screen. Click on the **Next** button to advance to the next task, or the **Previous** button to go to the previous task. To go directly to any task, click on its number.

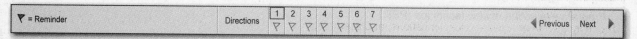

| ▼ = Reminder | | Directions | 1 2 3 4 5 6 7 | ◀ Previous   Next ▶ |

If you would like a reminder to revisit a task, or want to indicate that you are finished with it, click on the reminder flag below the task number. To clear the flag, click on it again. Reminder flags are for your use only – they do not contribute to your score.

Tabs

In this part of the examination, you will be asked to complete various tasks. Every task has one or more **Work Tabs**. Every task also has a **Help** tab.

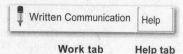

Work tab   Help tab

Work Tabs:

- **Work Tabs** are identified with a pencil icon. This is where your responses are expected.
- Each task has one or more **Work Tabs**.
- **Work Tabs** contain directions for completing the task - be sure to read these directions carefully.
- The **Work Tab** name in the example above is for illustration only - yours will differ.
- You must complete all of the **Work Tabs** in each task to receive full credit.

Help Tab:

- The **Help Tab** provides assistance with the exam software that is used in this task. For example, if the task is to compose a memorandum, **Help** will provide information about the word processor.

The Toolbar

The toolbar at the top of the screen shows the amount of time remaining for you to complete the tasks. In addition, the following tools are available. Note that only the **Exit** button is displayed when Directions are visible - the others will appear when you begin the tasks.

Click on these buttons to split or unsplit the screen. You can split the screen vertically or horizontally.

Click on this button to go on to the next part of the examination. You must complete all of the tasks to receive full credit. Once you click on **Exit** and confirm the action, you will NOT be able to return to this testlet.

| ▼ = Reminder | | Directions | 1 | ◀ Previous   Next ▶ |

Written Communication | Help

✂ Cut | 📋 Copy | 📋 Paste | ↶ Undo | ↷ Redo

The CFO of Oak Corporation noticed that his sales revenue changes depending on the amount of advertising money spent, and he would like to quantify the relationship precisely.

Prepare a memo to the CFO discussing regression analysis and its limitations and assumptions.

Type your communication below the line in the response area below.

REMINDER: Your response will be graded for both technical content and writing skills. Technical content will be evaluated for information that is helpful to the intended reader and clearly relevant to the issue. Writing skills will be evaluated for development, organization, and the appropriate expression of ideas in professional correspondence. Use a standard business memorandum or letter format with a clear beginning, middle, and end. Do not convey information in the form of a table, bullet point list, or other abbreviated presentation.

To: CFO, Oak Corporation
Re: Regression analysis – uses, limitations, and assumptions

Unofficial Answer

Written Communication

To: CFO, Oak Corporation
Re: Regression analysis – uses, limitations, and assumptions

Quantitative techniques are available to model information that will help a user determine possible outcomes and, thus, preferred courses of action. A common technique is regression analysis. This analysis can be beneficial, but it does have some inherent limitations. In addition, some assumptions need to be made for an effective analysis.

Regression analysis is the process of deriving the linear equation that describes the relationship between two variables. Simple regression is used when there is one independent variable. When there is more than one independent variable, multiple regression is used. The best straight line that fits a set of data points is derived using calculus.

This analysis is particularly valuable for budgeting and cost accounting purposes. For example, one extremely common application of simple regression in a business setting is the estimation of a mixed cost function, i.e., one with a fixed component and a variable component.

However, a limitation of regression analysis is that it does not determine causality. Even if x and y move together, the apparent relationship may be caused by some other factor. This limitation does not outweigh the benefits of the analysis, but it does need to be understood so that the information gathered can be relied upon only to a reasonable degree.

The linear relationship established for x and y is only valid across the relevant range, which must be identified by the user; this is a key assumption of the linear regression model. Also, regression analysis assumes that past relationships can be validly projected into the future. Another assumption is that the distribution of y around the regression line is constant for different values of x; this is called constant variance.

After obtaining an understanding of the aforementioned information, the analysis may be performed and the results applied to improve one's understanding and expectations of sales performance.

The above depicts a Level 5 answer. See page 16 in the Introduction for a description of the three grading criteria.

Self-Grade

Evaluate each of the following by selecting a 0, 1, 2, 3, 4, or 5. An average response is 3. Use 4 for better than average and 5 for outstanding. Use 2 for less than average and 1 for quite poor. Use zero for no response, if you did not address the topic, or if you gave advice that is clearly illegal.

Organization	o 0	o 1	o 2	o 3	o 4	o 5
Development	o 0	o 1	o 2	o 3	o 4	o 5
Expression	o 0	o 1	o 2	o 3	o 4	o 5

Your grade for the written communication as a whole is the average of the scores for the three criteria.

Use **CPA Gleim Online** and **Simulation Wizard** to practice more written communication tasks in a realistic environment.

STUDY UNIT SEVEN
CORPORATE CAPITAL STRUCTURE

(12 pages of outline)

The balance sheet of a corporation can be depicted as the perfect balance between the firm's resources and its capital structure. The resources consist of the assets the firm deploys in its attempts to earn a return. The capital structure consists of the amounts contributed by outsiders (Subunit 1) and insiders (Subunit 2) to make the use of these assets possible.

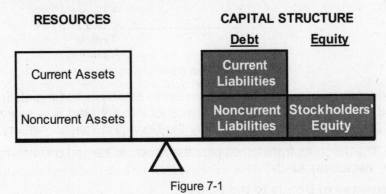

Figure 7-1

Leasing is a means of obtaining the use of plant assets while managing the related liability (Subunit 3).

Arriving at the appropriate mix of debt and equity in the capital structure is a challenge all corporations face. Each component of the capital structure bears a cost that changes as economic conditions change and as more or less of that component is deployed. Finding the right balance of these ingredients is the subject of Subunits 4 and 5.

7.1 BONDS

1. **Aspects of Bonds**

    a. Bonds are the principal form of long-term debt financing for corporations and governmental entities.

    1) A bond is a formal contractual obligation to pay an amount of money (called the par value, maturity amount, or face amount) to the holder at a certain date, plus, in most cases, a series of cash interest payments based on a specified percentage (called the stated rate or coupon rate) of the face amount at specified intervals.

    2) All of the terms of the agreement are stated in a document called an **indenture**.

b.   Bringing a bond issue to market requires extensive legal and accounting work. The expense of this process is rarely worthwhile for bonds with maturities of less than 5 years.

1)   In general, the longer the term of a bond, the higher the return (yield) demanded by investors will be to compensate for increased risk.

2)   This relationship is referred to as the **term structure of interest rates** and is depicted graphically by the yield curve.

Positive (Normal) Yield Curve

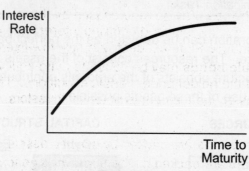

Figure 7-2

c.   A bond indenture may require the issuer to establish and maintain a **bond sinking fund**. The objective of making payments into the fund is to segregate and accumulate sufficient assets to pay the bond principal at maturity.

1)   The amounts transferred plus the revenue earned on investments provide the necessary funds.

d.   **Advantages of Bonds to the Issuer**

1)   Interest paid on debt is tax deductible. This is by far the most significant advantage of debt. For a corporation facing a 40%-50% marginal tax rate, the tax savings produced by the deduction of interest can be substantial.

2)   Basic control of the firm is not shared with debtholders.

e.   **Disadvantages of Bonds to the Issuer**

1)   Unlike returns on equity investments, the payment of interest and principal on debt is a legal obligation. If cash flow is insufficient to service debt, the firm could become insolvent.

2)   The legal requirement to pay debt service raises a firm's risk level. Shareholders will consequently demand higher capitalization rates on retained earnings, which may result in a decline in the market price of the stock.

3)   Bonds may require some collateral that restricts the entity's assets.

4)   The amount of debt financing available to the individual firm is limited. Generally accepted standards of the investment community will usually dictate a certain debt-equity ratio for an individual firm. Beyond this limit, the cost of debt may rise rapidly, or debt may not be available.

2.   **Types of Bonds**

a.   Maturity Pattern

1)   A **term bond** has a single maturity date at the end of its term.

2)   A **serial bond** matures in stated amounts at regular intervals.

    b.   Valuation

        1) **Variable (or floating) rate bonds** pay interest that is dependent on market conditions.

        2) **Zero-coupon or deep-discount bonds** bear no stated rate of interest and thus involve no periodic cash payments; the interest component consists entirely of the bond's discount.

        3) **Commodity-backed bonds** are payable at prices related to a commodity such as gold.

    c.   Redemption Provisions

        1) **Callable bonds** may be repurchased by the issuer at a specified price before maturity. During a period of falling interest rates, this allows the issuer to replace old high-interest debt with new low-interest debt.

        2) **Convertible bonds** may be converted into equity securities of the issuer at the option of the holder under certain conditions. The ability to become equity holders is an inducement to potential investors.

    d.   Securitization

        1) **Mortgage bonds** are backed by specific assets, usually real estate.

        2) **Debentures** are backed by the borrower's general credit but not by specific collateral.

    e.   Ownership

        1) **Registered bonds** are issued in the name of the holder. Only the registered holder may receive interest and principal payments.

        2) **Bearer bonds** are not individually registered. Interest and principal are paid to whomever presents the bond.

    f.   Priority

        1) **Subordinated debentures** and second mortgage bonds are junior securities with claims inferior to those of senior bonds.

    g.   Repayment Provisions

        1) **Income bonds** pay interest contingent on the issuer's profitability.

        2) **Revenue bonds** are issued by governmental units and are payable from specific revenue sources.

3. **Bond Ratings**

    a.   Investors can judge the creditworthiness of a bond issue by consulting the rating assigned by a credit-rating agency. The higher the rating, the more likely the firm is to make good its commitment to pay the interest and principal.

    b.   This field is dominated by the three largest firms: Moody's, Standard & Poor's, and Fitch.

        1) **Investment-grade bonds** are considered safe investments and thus have the lowest yields. The highest rating assigned is "triple-A." Some fiduciary organizations (such as banks and insurance companies) are only allowed to invest in investment-grade bonds.

        2) **Non-investment grade bonds**, also called speculative-grade bonds, high-yield bonds, or junk bonds, carry high risk.

4.   **Bond Valuation**

a.   Of primary concern to a bond issuer is the amount of cash that (s)he will receive from investors on the day the bonds are sold.

   1)   This amount is equal to the present value of the cash flows associated with the bonds (principal at maturity and periodic interest) discounted at the interest rate prevailing in the market at the time (called the market rate or effective rate).

   2)   Use of the effective rate ensures that the bonds' yield to maturity (that is, their ultimate rate of return to the investor) is equal to the rate of return prevailing in the market at the time of the sale.

b.   This present value calculation can result in cash proceeds equal to, less than, or greater than the face amount of the bonds, depending on the relationship of the bonds' stated rate of interest to the market rate.

   1)   If the bonds' stated rate happens to be the same as the market rate at the time of sale, the present value of the bonds will exactly equal their face amount, and the bonds are said to be sold "at par." It is rare, however, for the coupon rate to precisely match the market rate at the time the bonds are ready for sale.

   2)   If the bonds' **stated rate is lower than the market rate**, investors must be offered an incentive to buy the bonds, since the bonds' periodic interest payments are lower than those currently available in the market.

      a)   In this case, the issuer receives less cash than the par value and the bonds are said to be sold at a **discount**.

EXAMPLE

On January 1, Year 1, a firm issues 100 bonds with a face amount of $1,000 maturing in 5 years and bearing 6% annual interest. At the time the bonds are issued, the interest rate prevailing in the market is 8%. The proceeds received by the issuer can be calculated as follows:

Face amount:		
Present value of a single payment of		
$100,000 discounted at 8% for 5 years	$100,000 × .68058 =	$68,058
Interest payments:		
Present value of an ordinary annuity of		
$6,000 discounted at 8% for 5 years	$6,000 × 3.99271 =	23,956
Total proceeds received		$92,014

The issuer thus receives cash of $92,014 and records a discount on bonds payable of $7,986 ($100,000 – $92,014).

---

   3)   If the bonds' **stated rate is higher than the market rate**, investors are willing to pay more for the bonds since their periodic interest payments are higher than those currently available in the market.

      a)   In this case, the issuer receives more cash than the par value and the bonds are said to be sold at a **premium**.

EXAMPLE

On January 1, Year 1, a firm issues bonds like the ones above, except that the stated rate is 8% and the effective rate is 6%. In this case, the present value of the face amount is $74,726 ($100,000 × .74726), and the present value of the interest payments is $33,699 ($8,000 × 4.21236). The issuer thus receives cash of $108,425 ($74,726 + $33,699) and records a premium on bonds payable of $8,425.

    c.   Using the effective rate to determine the bonds' present value ensures that, upon maturity, they will be carried on the books at their face amount.

    d.   When bonds are traded among investors in the secondary market, the issuer is not a party to the transaction and receives no infusion of cash.

        1)   The amount that changes hands between the old and new bondholders is determined by a risk assessment and the interest rate prevailing in the market at the time of the trade; i.e., the bonds are priced to achieve a new yield.

5. Leverage

    a.   Leverage is the relative amount of fixed cost in a firm's overall cost structure. Leverage creates risk because fixed costs must be covered, regardless of the level of sales.

        1)   A firm's total leverage consists of an operating leverage component and financial leverage component.

    b.   **Operating leverage** is the extent to which a firm's costs of operating are fixed as opposed to variable. A firm's degree of operating leverage (DOL) is a ratio that measures the effect that a given level of fixed operating costs has on the earnings of the firm.

$$DOL = \frac{\%\ change\ in\ earnings\ before\ interest\ and\ taxes\ (EBIT)}{\%\ change\ in\ sales}$$

        1)   For instance, if the firm's EBIT increased by 24% as a result of an increase in sales of 12%, the firm's DOL is 2 (24% ÷ 12%).

        2)   The DOL can help the firm to determine the most appropriate level of operating leverage that maximizes the firm's EBIT.

        3)   A firm with a high percentage of fixed costs is more risky than a firm in the same industry that relies more on variable costs, but by the same token, it will generate more earnings by increasing sales.

    c.   **Financial leverage** is the degree of debt (fixed financial costs) in the firm's financial structure. A firm's degree of financial leverage (DFL) is a ratio that measures the effect that a particular amount of fixed financing costs has on a firm's earnings per share (EPS).

$$DFL = \frac{\%\ change\ in\ earnings\ per\ share\ (EPS)}{\%\ change\ in\ earnings\ before\ interest\ and\ taxes\ (EBIT)}$$

        1)   For instance, if the firm's EPS increased by 12% as a result of an increase in EBIT of 6%, the firm's DFL is 2 (12% ÷ 6%).

        2)   When a firm has a high percentage of fixed financial costs, the firm takes more risk to increase its EPS.

    d.   **Degree of total (combined) leverage (DTL)** is the product of the degrees of operating and financial leverage.

$$DTL = DOL \times DFL = \frac{\%\ change\ in\ EBIT}{\%\ change\ in\ sales} \times \frac{\%\ change\ in\ EPS}{\%\ change\ in\ EBIT} = \frac{\%\ change\ in\ EPS}{\%\ change\ in\ sales}$$

        1)   For instance, if the firm's EPS increased by 10% as a result of an increase in sales of 2%, the firm's DTL is 5 (10% ÷ 2%).

        2)   A firm with a higher DTL has a higher return to the investors, but it is also more risky.

6.   **Debt Covenant**

    a.   Debt covenants are restrictions that are imposed on a borrower by the creditor in a formal debt agreement or an indenture.

    b.   Examples of debt covenants

        1)   Limitations on issuing long-term or short-term debt
        2)   Limitations on dividend payments
        3)   Maintaining certain financial ratios
        4)   Maintaining specific collateral that backs the debt

    c.   The more restrictive the debt covenant, the lower the risk that the borrower will not be able to repay its debt. The less risky the investment is for creditors, the lower the interest rate on the debt (since the risk premium is lower).

    d.   If the debtor breaches the debt covenant, the debt becomes due immediately.

Stop and review! You have completed the outline for this subunit. Study multiple-choice question 1 through 6 beginning on page 213.

7.2 EQUITY

1.   **Common Stock**

    a.   The common shareholders are the owners of the corporation, and their rights as owners, although reasonably uniform, depend on the laws of the state in which the firm is incorporated.

        1)   Equity ownership involves risk because holders of common stock are not guaranteed a return and are last in priority in a liquidation. Shareholders' capital provides the cushion for creditors if any losses occur on liquidation.

    b.   **Advantages to the Issuer**

        1)   Common stock does not require a fixed dividend; dividends are paid from profits when available.
        2)   Common stock carries no fixed maturity date for repayment of the capital.
        3)   The sale of common stock increases the creditworthiness of the firm by providing more equity.

    c.   **Disadvantages to the Issuer**

        1)   Cash dividends on common stock are not tax-deductible and must be paid out of after-tax profits.
        2)   New common stock sales dilute earnings per share available to existing shareholders.
        3)   Underwriting costs are typically higher for common stock issues.
        4)   Too much equity may raise the average cost of capital of the firm above its optimal level.

    d.   Common shareholders ordinarily have preemptive rights. Preemptive rights give common shareholders the right to purchase any additional stock issuances in proportion to their current ownership percentages.

    e.   As the corporation's owners, the common shareholders have voting rights; they select the firm's board of directors and vote on resolutions.

    f.   **Common stock valuation** based on dividend payout models

        1)   When the dividend per share of common stock is constant and expected to be paid continuously, the price per share is calculated as follows:

$$P_0 = D \div r$$

            P_0 = Price per share now
            D = Dividend per share (constant)
            r = Required rate of return

        2)   The constant growth model (dividend discount model) assumes that dividend per share and price per share grow at the same constant rate. The price per share can be calculated as follows:

$$P_0 = \frac{D_0(1 + g)}{r - g} = \frac{D_1}{r - g}$$

            P_0 = Price per share now
            D_0 = Dividend per share now
            D_1 = Dividend per share expected next year
            r = Required rate of return
            g = Growth rate (constant)

EXAMPLE

Today a company paid dividends of $10 per share. The dividends are expected to grow at a constant rate of 5% per year. If the investors' required rate of return is 8%, the current market value of the company's share will be $350.

$$P_0 = \frac{D_0(1 + g)}{r - g} = \frac{\$10(1 + 5\%)}{8\% - 5\%} = \$350$$

---

        3)   The required rate of return (the cost of common stock) can be derived from the dividend growth model.

$$r = \frac{D_1}{P_0} + g$$

2. Preferred Stock

    a.   Preferred stock is a hybrid of debt and equity. It has a fixed charge, but payment of dividends is not an obligation.

        1)   Also, preferred shareholders stand ahead of common shareholders in priority in the event of corporate bankruptcy.

    b.   **Advantages to the Issuer**

        1)   It is a form of equity and therefore builds the creditworthiness of the firm.
        2)   Control is still held by common shareholders (preferred stock rarely carries voting rights).
        3)   Superior earnings of the firm are usually still reserved for the common shareholders.
        4)   Since preferred stock does not require periodic payments, failure to pay dividends will not lead to bankruptcy.

    c.   **Disadvantages to the Issuer**

        1)   Cash dividends on preferred stock are not deductible as a tax expense and are paid with taxable income. The result is a substantially greater cost relative to bonds.
        2)   In periods of economic difficulty, accumulated unpaid dividends (called dividends in arrears) may create major managerial and financial problems for the firm.

d. **Typical Provisions of Preferred Stock Issues**

1) Priority in assets and earnings. If the firm goes bankrupt, the preferred shareholders have priority over common shareholders.

2) Accumulation of dividends. If preferred dividends are cumulative, dividends in arrears must be paid before any common dividends can be paid.

3) Convertibility. Preferred stock issues may be convertible into common stock at the option of the shareholder.

4) Participation. Preferred stock may participate with common stock in excess earnings of the company. For example, 8% participating preferred stock might pay a dividend each year greater than 8% when the corporation is extremely profitable, but nonparticipating preferred stock will receive no more than is stated on the face of the stock.

5) Par value. Par value is the liquidation value, and a percentage of par equals the preferred dividend.

e. **Preferred stock valuation** employs the same method used in valuing a bond that was shown in item 4.a. in Subunit 7.1.

1) The present value of future cash flows associated with the security discounted at the prevailing interest rate (investor's required rate of return) can also be used for preferred stock.

2) Unlike the future cash flows from bonds, which consist of principal at maturity and periodic interest, the future cash flows from the preferred stock are assumed to consist only of the estimated future annual dividends (D_p).

$$D_p = Par\ value\ of\ preferred\ stock\ \times\ Preferred\ dividend\ rate$$

3) The discount rate used is the investor's required rate of return (r).

4) Unlike a bond, which has a specific maturity date, preferred stock is assumed to be outstanding in perpetuity.

$$Preferred\ stock\ price\ (P_p) = \frac{D_p}{r}$$

For example, the value of a share of preferred stock with a par value of $100 and a dividend rate of 5% to an investor with a required rate of return of 10% is $50 [($100 × 5%) ÷ 10%].

3. **Initial Public Offering**

a. A firm's first issuance of securities to the public is an initial public offering, or IPO. The process by which a closely held corporation issues new securities to the public is called **going public**. When a firm goes public, it issues its securities on a new issue or **IPO market** (a primary market).

b. **Advantages of Going Public**

1) The ability to raise additional funds
2) The establishment of the firm's value in the market
3) An increase in the liquidity of the firm's stock

c. **Disadvantages of Going Public**

1) Costs of the reporting requirements of the SEC and other agencies
2) Access to the firm's operating data by competing firms
3) Access to net worth information of major shareholders
4) Limitations on self-dealing by corporate insiders
5) Pressure from outside shareholders for earnings growth
6) Stock prices that do not accurately reflect the true net worth of the firm
7) Loss of control by management as ownership is diversified
8) Increased shareholder servicing costs

d. The main differences between debt financing (which entails the payment of interest) and equity financing (which entails the payment of dividends) can be summarized as follows:

	Equity Financing	Debt Financing
Effect on company's control	Yes	No
Cost of issuing	Higher	Lower
Effect on net income	No	Yes
Dilution of EPS	Yes	No
Effect on solvency risk	No	Yes
Tax deductibility of payments	No	Yes

Stop and review! You have completed the outline for this subunit. Study multiple-choice questions 7 through 10 beginning on page 214.

7.3 LEASING

1. **Overview**

   a. A lease is a long-term, contractual agreement in which the owner of property (the lessor) allows another party (the lessee) the right to use the property for a stated period in exchange for a stated payment.

      1) The fundamental issue is whether the lease is a purchase-and-financing arrangement (a capital lease) or merely a long-term rental contract (an operating lease).

   b. Discounting the present value of the cash flows associated with a lease using the time value of money allows a firm to determine the type of lease that is most beneficial.

   c. Lease financing must be analyzed by comparing the cost of owning to the cost of leasing. Leasing is a major means of financing because it offers a variety of tax and other benefits.

      1) If leases are not accounted for as installment purchases, they provide off-balance-sheet financing. Thus, under an operating lease, the lessee need not record an asset or a liability, and rent expense is recognized.

2. **Types of Leases**

   a. A **sale-leaseback** is an alternative method for raising capital. It allows firms to acquire capital from the sale of an asset while retaining use of the asset.

   b. **Service or operating leases** usually include both financing and maintenance services.

   c. **Financial leases**, which do not provide for maintenance services, are noncancelable and fully amortize the cost of the leased asset over the term of the basic lease contract. They are installment purchases.

3. **Lease Classification**

   a. A **capital lease** is, in substance, the purchase of an asset and should thus be treated in a manner similar to a purchase. For a lease to be classified as a capital lease, it must meet at least one of the following four criteria:

      1) Title passes to the lessee at the end of the lease.

      2) The lease contains a bargain purchase option.

      3) Present value of the minimum lease payments (payments to be made during the lease term) equals 90% or more of the fair value of the leased property.

      4) The lease term is 75% or more of the useful economic life of the property.

   Memory aid to remember these criteria: Terry Buys Purple Tricycles

    b.   An **operating lease** (off-balance-sheet financing) is a rental contract and is accounted for as such.

        1)   No entry is made to record the lease. Lease payments are expensed as incurred.

        2)   Expense is recognized as the services are used; if lease payments are not reasonably aligned with service obtained, accruals or deferrals must be used.

Stop and review! You have completed the outline for this subunit. Study multiple-choice questions 11 through 14 beginning on page 215.

7.4 COMPONENT COSTS OF CAPITAL

    1.   **Overview**

        a.   Investors provide funds to corporations with the understanding that management will deploy those funds in such a way that the investor will ultimately receive a return.

            1)   If management does not generate the investors' required rate of return, the investors will sell their stock on the secondary market, causing the value of the stock to drop. Creditors will then demand higher rates on the firm's debt.

            2)   For this reason, the investors' required rate of return (also called their opportunity cost of capital) becomes the firm's cost of capital.

        b.   A firm's cost of capital is typically used to discount the future cash flows of long-term projects, since investments with a rate of return higher than the cost of capital will increase the value of the firm, i.e., shareholders' wealth. (The cost of capital is not used in connection with working capital since short-term needs are met with short-term funds.)

            1)   Providers of equity capital are exposed to more risk than are lenders because

                a)   The firm is not legally obligated to pay them a return and

                b)   In case of liquidation, creditors have priority.

            2)   To compensate for this higher risk, equity investors demand a higher return, making equity financing more expensive than debt.

    2.   **Component Costs of Capital**

        a.   A firm's financing structure consists of three components: long-term debt, preferred equity, and common equity (retained earnings are treated as part of common equity in this analysis for reasons given below).

            1)   The rate of return demanded by holders of each is the component cost for that form of capital.

        b.   The component cost of **long-term debt** is the after-tax interest rate on the debt (interest payments are tax-deductible by the firm).

$$Effective\ rate \times (1.0 - Marginal\ tax\ rate)$$

        c.   The component cost of **preferred stock** is computed using the dividend yield ratio.

$$Cash\ dividend\ on\ preferred\ stock \div Market\ price\ of\ preferred\ stock$$

            1)   The market price of preferred stock upon issuance equals the net proceeds from the issuance (gross proceeds – floatation costs). Floatation costs, also called issuance costs, reduce the net proceeds received, thereby raising the cost of capital.

        d.   The component cost of **retained earnings** is considered to be the same as that for common stock (if the firm cannot find a profitable use for retained earnings, it should be distributed to the common shareholders in the form of dividends so that they can find their own alternative investments).

EXAMPLE

A company has outstanding bonds with a coupon rate of 7% and an effective rate of 5%. The company's 9%, $67.50 par value preferred stock is currently trading at $63 per share, while its $1 par value common stock trades at $1.40 per share and pays a 14% dividend. The applicable tax rate is 35%.

The company's component costs of capital are calculated as follows:

Long-Term Debt	Preferred Equity	Common Equity
Cost = Effective rate × (1.0 – Tax rate)	Cost = Cash dividend ÷ Market price	Cost = Cash dividend ÷ Market price
= 5% × (1.0 – .35)	= ($60 × 9%) ÷ $67.50	= ($1 × 14%) ÷ $1.40
= 5% × .65	= $5.40 ÷ $67.50	= $.14 ÷ $1.40
= 3.25%	= 8%	= 10%

Stop and review! You have completed the outline for this subunit. Study multiple-choice questions 15 through 17 on page 217.

7.5 WEIGHTED-AVERAGE COST OF CAPITAL

The weighted-average cost of capital has been recently tested with both general conceptual questions and calculation questions.

1. **Weighted-Average Cost of Capital (WACC)**

   a. Corporate management usually designates a target capital structure for the firm, i.e., the proportions that each component of capital should comprise in the overall combination.

      1) An example might be 10% debt, 20% preferred stock, and 70% common stock.

   b. A firm's WACC is a single, composite rate of return on its combined components of capital. The weights are based on the firm's target capital structure.

EXAMPLE

The company has set a target capital structure of 20% long-term debt, 30% preferred equity, and 50% common equity. The weighted-average cost of capital can thus be calculated as follows:

	Target Weight		Cost of Capital		Weighted Cost
Long-term debt	20%	×	3.25%	=	0.65%
Preferred equity	30%	×	8%	=	2.40%
Common equity	50%	×	10%	=	5.00%
					8.05%

---

   c. Another way to calculate the weighted-average-cost of capital (WACC) is by using the following formula:

$$WACC = \left(\frac{E}{V} \times R_e \right) + \left[\frac{D}{V} \times R_d \times (1 - T) \right]$$

R_e	=	Cost of equity
R_d	=	Cost of debt
E	=	Market value of the firm's equity
D	=	Market value of the firm's debt
T	=	Corporate tax rate
V = D + E	=	Capital used to generate profits

EXAMPLE

The firm provides the following information:

Capital used to generate profits
50% debt, 50% equity $1,200
Cost of equity   15%
Cost of debt   5%
Corporate tax rate   40%

$$WACC = \left[\frac{(1,200 \times 50\%)}{1,200} \times 15\% \right] + \left[\frac{(1,200 \times 50\%)}{1,200} \times 5\% \times (1 - 40\%) \right] = 0.09 = 9\%$$

---

2. **Optimal Capital Structure**

    a. Standard financial theory provides a model for the optimal capital structure of every firm. This model holds that shareholder wealth-maximization results from **minimizing the weighted-average cost of capital**. Thus, the focus of management should not be only on maximizing earnings per share (EPS can be increased by taking on more debt, but debt increases risk).

        1) The relevant relationships are depicted below:

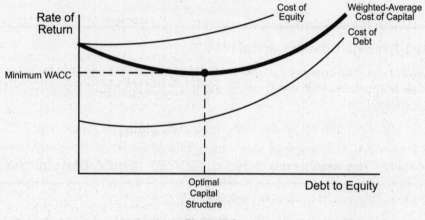

Figure 7-3

        Ordinarily, firms cannot identify this optimal point precisely. Thus, they should attempt to find an optimal range for the capital structure.

3. **Modigliani-Miller and Capital Structure Irrelevance**

    a. The Modigliani-Miller theorem asserts that there is no optimal capital structure for a firm. Thus, whether the firm finances with all debt, all equity, or some combination of the two is of no consequence to shareholders' wealth.

        1) Their reasoning is that any increase in expected return resulting from the use of debt financing is exactly offset by an increase in the required rate of return on equity necessitated by the risk that accompanies leverage.

        2) Thus, such measures as degree of leverage and the debt-to-equity ratio should be of no use to shareholders.

Stop and review! You have completed the outline for this subunit. Study multiple-choice questions 18 through 24 beginning on page 217.

QUESTIONS

7.1 Bonds

1. If Brewer Corporation's bonds are currently yielding 8% in the marketplace, why is the firm's cost of debt lower?

   A. Market interest rates have increased.

   B. Additional debt can be issued more cheaply than the original debt.

   C. There should be no difference; cost of debt is the same as the bonds' market yield.

   D. Interest is deductible for tax purposes.

Answer (D) is correct.
   REQUIRED: The reason a firm's cost of debt is lower than its current market yield.
   DISCUSSION: Because interest is deductible for tax purposes, the actual cost of debt capital is the net effect of the interest payment and the offsetting tax deduction. The actual cost of debt equals the interest rate times (1 – the marginal tax rate). Thus, if a firm with an 8% market rate is in a 40% tax bracket, the net cost of the debt capital is 4.8% [8% × (1.0 – .40)].
   Answer (A) is incorrect. The tax deduction always causes the market yield rate to be higher than the cost of debt capital. Answer (B) is incorrect. Additional debt may or may not be issued more cheaply than earlier debt, depending upon the interest rates in the market place. Answer (C) is incorrect. The cost of debt is less than the yield rate given that bond interest is tax deductible.

2. The term structure of interest rates is the relationship of

   A. Interest rates over different structures of bonds.

   B. Interest rates over different structures of securities.

   C. Interest rates over time.

   D. The maturity dates of an issuance of bonds.

Answer (C) is correct.
   REQUIRED: The relationship found in the term structure.
   DISCUSSION: The term structure of interest rates is the relationship of interest rates and years to maturity. Corporate CFOs use the term structure to decide whether to borrow short-term debt or long-term debt. Investors use the term structure to decide whether to buy short-term or long-term bonds.
   Answer (A) is incorrect. Term structure is the relationship of interest rates over time, not different structures of bonds. Answer (B) is incorrect. Term structure is the relationship of interest rates over time, not different structures of securities. Answer (D) is incorrect. Maturity dates refer to the time element, but the interest rate element is missing.

3. Debentures are

   A. Income bonds that require interest payments only when earnings permit.

   B. Subordinated debt and rank behind convertible bonds.

   C. Bonds secured by the full faith and credit of the issuing firm.

   D. A form of lease financing similar to equipment trust certificates.

Answer (C) is correct.
   REQUIRED: The true statement about debentures.
   DISCUSSION: Debentures are unsecured bonds. Although no assets are mortgaged as security for the bonds, debentures are secured by the full faith and credit of the issuing firm. Debentures are a general obligation of the borrower. Only companies with the best credit ratings can issue debentures because only the company's credit rating and reputation secure the bonds.
   Answer (A) is incorrect. Debentures must pay interest regardless of earnings levels. Answer (B) is incorrect. Debentures are not subordinated except to the extent of assets mortgaged against other bond issues. Debentures are a general obligation of the borrower and rank equally with convertible bonds. Answer (D) is incorrect. Debentures have nothing to do with lease financing. Debentures are not secured by assets.

4. Serial bonds are attractive to investors because

   A. All bonds in the issue mature on the same date.

   B. The yield to maturity is the same for all bonds in the issue.

   C. Investors can choose the maturity that suits their financial needs.

   D. The coupon rate on these bonds is adjusted to the maturity date.

Answer (C) is correct.
   REQUIRED: The reason serial bonds are attractive to investors.
   DISCUSSION: Serial bonds have staggered maturities; that is, they mature over a period (series) of years. Thus, investors can choose the maturity date that meets their investment needs. For example, an investor who will have a child starting college in 16 years can choose bonds that mature in 16 years.
   Answer (A) is incorrect. Serial bonds mature on different dates. Answer (B) is incorrect. Bonds maturing on different dates may have different yields, or they may be the same. Usually, the earlier date maturities carry slightly lower yields than the later maturities. Answer (D) is incorrect. The coupon rate is the same for all bonds; only the selling price and yield differ.

5. If a $1,000 bond sells for $1,125, which of the following statements are true?

I.   The market rate of interest is greater than the coupon rate on the bond.

II. The coupon rate on the bond is greater than the market rate of interest.

III. The bond sells at a premium.

IV. The bond sells at a discount.

   A. I and III.

   B. I and IV.

   C. II and III.

   D. II and IV.

Answer (C) is correct.
   REQUIRED: The true statement(s) about a bond that sells at more than its face value.
   DISCUSSION: The excess of the price over the face value is a premium. A premium is paid because the coupon rate on the bond is greater than the market rate of interest. In other words, because the bond is paying a higher rate than other similar bonds, its price is bid up by investors.
   Answer (A) is incorrect. If a bond sells at a premium, the market rate of interest is less than the coupon rate. Answer (B) is incorrect. A bond sells at a discount when the price is less than the face amount. Answer (D) is incorrect. A bond sells at a discount when the price is less than the face amount.

6. This year, Nelson Industries increased earnings before interest and taxes (EBIT) by 17%. During the same period, earnings per share increased by 42%. The degree of financial leverage that existed during the year is

   A. 1.70

   B. 4.20

   C. 2.47

   D. 5.90

Answer (C) is correct.
   REQUIRED: The degree of financial leverage.
   DISCUSSION: If earnings before interest and taxes increased by 17%, and earnings per share income was up 42%, the firm is using leverage effectively. The degree of financial leverage is the percentage change in earnings per share divided by the percentage change in EBIT. Accordingly, Nelson's degree of financial leverage is 2.47 (.42 ÷ .17).

7.2 Equity

7. Each share of nonparticipating, 8%, cumulative preferred stock in a company that meets its dividend obligations has all of the following characteristics **except**

   A. Voting rights in corporate elections.

   B. Dividend payments that are not tax deductible by the company.

   C. No principal repayments.

   D. A superior claim to common stock equity in the case of liquidation.

Answer (A) is correct.
   REQUIRED: The item that is not characteristic of nonparticipating, cumulative preferred stock.
   DISCUSSION: Dividends on cumulative preferred stock accrue until declared; that is, the book value of the preferred stock increases by the amount of any undeclared dividends. Participating preferred stock participates with common shareholders in excess earnings of the company. In other words, 8% participating preferred stock might pay a dividend each year greater than 8% when the corporation is extremely profitable. Therefore, nonparticipating preferred stock will receive no more than is stated on the face of the stock. Preferred shareholders rarely have voting rights. Voting rights are exchanged for preferences regarding dividends and liquidation of assets.
   Answer (B) is incorrect. A corporation does not receive a tax deduction for making dividend payments on any type of stock. Answer (C) is incorrect. Preferred stock normally need not be redeemed as long as the corporation remains in business. Answer (D) is incorrect. Preferred shareholders do have priority over common shareholders in a liquidation.

8. In general, it is more expensive for a company to finance with equity capital than with debt capital because

- A. Long-term bonds have a maturity date and must therefore be repaid in the future.
- B. Investors are exposed to greater risk with equity capital.
- C. Equity capital is in greater demand than debt capital.
- D. Dividends fluctuate to a greater extent than interest rates.

Answer (B) is correct.
REQUIRED: The reason equity financing is more expensive than debt financing.
DISCUSSION: Providers of equity capital are exposed to more risk than are lenders because the firm is not obligated to pay them a return. Also, in case of liquidation, creditors are paid before equity investors. Thus, equity financing is more expensive than debt because equity investors require a higher return to compensate for the greater risk assumed.
Answer (A) is incorrect. The obligation to repay at a specific maturity date reduces the risk to investors and thus the required return. Answer (C) is incorrect. The demand for equity capital is directly related to its greater cost to the issuer. Answer (D) is incorrect. Dividends are based on managerial discretion and may rarely change; interest rates, however, fluctuate daily based upon market conditions.

9. Unless the shares are specifically restricted, a holder of common stock with a preemptive right may share proportionately in all of the following **except**

- A. The vote for directors.
- B. Corporate assets upon liquidation.
- C. Cumulative dividends.
- D. New issues of stock of the same class.

Answer (C) is correct.
REQUIRED: The item that is not a right of common shareholders.
DISCUSSION: Common stock does not have the right to accumulate unpaid dividends. This right is often attached to preferred stock.
Answer (A) is incorrect. Common shareholders have the right to vote (although different classes of shares may have different privileges). Answer (B) is incorrect. Common shareholders have the right to share proportionately in corporate assets upon liquidation (but only after other claims have been satisfied). Answer (D) is incorrect. Common shareholders have the right to share proportionately in any new issues of stock of the same class (the preemptive right).

10. Which one of the following statements is correct regarding the effect preferred stock has on a company?

- A. The firm's after-tax profits are shared equally by common and preferred shareholders.
- B. Control of the firm is now shared by the common and preferred shareholders, with preferred shareholders having greater control.
- C. Preferred shareholders' claims take precedence over the claims of common shareholders in the event of liquidation.
- D. Nonpayment of preferred dividends places the firm in default, as does nonpayment of interest on debt.

Answer (C) is correct.
REQUIRED: The effect of preferred stock on a firm.
DISCUSSION: Preferred stockholders have preference over common stockholders with respect to dividend and liquidation rights, but payment of preferred dividends, unlike bond interest, is not mandatory. In exchange for these preferences, the preferred stockholders give up the right to vote. Consequently, preferred stock is a hybrid of debt and equity.
Answer (A) is incorrect. The share of profits available to preferred stockholders is normally limited to a percentage of the stock's par value. Thus, they may get more or less than the common shareholders. Answer (B) is incorrect. Preferred stockholders ordinarily do not have voting rights. Answer (D) is incorrect. The passing of preferred dividends does not put the corporation into default. For this reason, preferred stock is sometimes viewed more favorably than debt by corporate management. If the preferred stock is cumulative (which most is), the corporation may not pay dividends to common shareholders until the arrearages to preferred stockholders have been paid.

7.3 Leasing

11. If a company uses off-balance-sheet financing, assets have been acquired

- A. For cash.
- B. With operating leases.
- C. With financing leases.
- D. With a line of credit.

Answer (B) is correct.
REQUIRED: The nature of off-balance-sheet financing.
DISCUSSION: With an operating lease, no long-term liability need be reported on the face of the balance sheet.
Answer (A) is incorrect. No liability arises if the assets were paid for with cash. Answer (C) is incorrect. The long-term liability for financing leases must be reported on the face of the balance sheet. Answer (D) is incorrect. The liability associated with a line of credit is reported on the face of the balance sheet.

12. Neary Company has entered into a contract to lease computers from Baldwin Company starting on January 1. Relevant information pertaining to the lease is provided below.

Lease term	4 years
Useful life of computers	5 years
Present value of future lease payments	$100,000
Fair value of leased asset on date of lease	$105,000
Baldwin's implicit rate	10%

At the end of the lease term, ownership of the asset transfers from Baldwin to Neary. Neary has properly classified this lease as a capital lease on its financial statements and uses straight-line depreciation on comparable assets. At January 1, the leased equipment would be reported on Neary's books as a(n)

A. Asset only.

B. Asset and a liability.

C. Liability only.

D. Expense and a liability.

Answer (B) is correct.
   REQUIRED: The proper classification of leased equipment.
   DISCUSSION: A capital lease is, in substance, the purchase of an asset, thus both the leased asset and the related liability are reported in the balance sheet.
   Answer (A) is incorrect. Neary will also report the lease liability. Answer (C) is incorrect. Neary will also report the computers under assets. Answer (D) is incorrect. Neary will also report the computers under assets.

13. Which one of the following statements with respect to leases is correct?

A. An operating lease is treated like a rental contract between lessor and lessee.

B. A lease that does not transfer ownership from the lessor to the lessee by the end of the lease is automatically an operating lease.

C. Sales and direct financing leases pertain more to lessees than lessors.

D. Unpredictability of lease revenues or expenses can transform what would otherwise be a capital lease for the lessee to an operating lease for the lessee.

Answer (A) is correct.
   REQUIRED: The true statement with respect to leases.
   DISCUSSION: An operating lease is treated like a rental contract between lessor and lessee.
   Answer (B) is incorrect. The transfer of ownership test is only one of four tests that are used to determine whether a lease is classified as a capital lease. Answer (C) is incorrect. Sales-type leases and direct financing leases are reported by lessors, not lessees. Answer (D) is incorrect. The degree of unpredictability of lease revenues or expenses is not a factor in the classification of the lease as a capital or operating lease.

14. Lease A does not contain a bargain purchase option, but the lease term is equal to 90% of the estimated economic life of the leased property. Lease B does not transfer ownership of the property to the lessee by the end of the lease term, but the lease term is equal to 75% of the estimated economic life of the leased property. How should the lessee classify these leases?

	Lease A	Lease B
A.	Operating lease	Capital lease
B.	Operating lease	Operating lease
C.	Capital lease	Capital lease
D.	Capital lease	Operating lease

Answer (C) is correct.
   REQUIRED: The proper classification of leases.
   DISCUSSION: For a lease to be classified as a capital lease by the lessee, any one of four criteria must be met. One of these criteria is that the lease term equal 75% or more of the estimated remaining economic life of the leased property. Both leases meet the 75% criterion and should be properly classified as capital leases.

7.4 Component Costs of Capital

15. The capital structure of a firm includes bonds with a coupon rate of 12% and an effective interest rate is 14%. The corporate tax rate is 30%. What is the firm's net cost of debt?

A. 8.4%

B. 9.8%

C. 12%

D. 14%

Answer (B) is correct.

REQUIRED: The firm's net cost of debt.

DISCUSSION: Because of the tax deductibility of interest payments, the cost of debt equals the effective interest rate times one minus the marginal tax rate. The effective rate is used rather than the coupon rate (stated rate) because the effective rate is the actual cost of the amount borrowed. Thus, the net cost of debt is 9.8% [14% × (1.0 − .30)].

Answer (A) is incorrect. The effective rate is used to determine the cost of debt, not the coupon rate (stated rate). Answer (C) is incorrect. The figure of 12% is the coupon rate. Answer (D) is incorrect. The figure of 14% ignores the tax effect.

16. Maloney, Inc.'s $1,000 par value preferred stock paid its $100 per share annual dividend on April 4 of the current year. The preferred stock's current market price is $960 a share on the date of the dividend distribution. Maloney's marginal tax rate (combined federal and state) is 40%, and the firm plans to maintain its current capital structure relationship. The component cost of preferred stock to Maloney would be closest to

A. 6%

B. 6.25%

C. 10%

D. 10.4%

Answer (D) is correct.

REQUIRED: The component cost of preferred stock in the firm's capital structure.

DISCUSSION: The component cost of preferred stock is equal to the dividend yield, i.e., the cash dividend divided by the market price of the stock. (Dividends on preferred stock are not deductible for tax purposes; therefore, there is no adjustment for tax savings.) The annual dividend on preferred stock is $100 when the price of the stock is $960. This results in a cost of capital of about 10.4% ($100 ÷ $960).

Answer (A) is incorrect. There is no tax deductibility of preferred dividends. Answer (B) is incorrect. There is no tax deductibility of preferred dividends. Answer (C) is incorrect. The denominator is the current market price, not the par value.

17. Global Company Press has $150 par value preferred stock with a market price of $120 a share. The organization pays a $15 per share annual dividend. Global's current marginal tax rate is 40%. Looking to the future, the company anticipates maintaining its current capital structure. What is the component cost of preferred stock to Global?

A. 4%

B. 5%

C. 10%

D. 12.5%

Answer (D) is correct.

REQUIRED: The cost of preferred stock.

DISCUSSION: The component cost of preferred stock is the dividend divided by the market price (also called the dividend yield). No tax adjustment is necessary because dividends are not deductible. Since the market price is $120 when the dividend is $15, the component cost of preferred capital is 12.5% ($15 ÷ $120).

Answer (A) is incorrect. The preferred stock dividend is not deductible for tax purposes. Answer (B) is incorrect. The preferred stock dividend is not deductible for tax purposes. Answer (C) is incorrect. The denominator is the market price, not the par value.

7.5 Weighted-Average Cost of Capital

18. Scrunchy-Tech, Inc., has determined that it can minimize its weighted-average cost of capital (WACC) by using a debt-equity ratio of 2/3. If the firm's cost of debt is 9% before taxes, the cost of equity is estimated to be 12% before taxes, and the tax rate is 40%, what is the firm's WACC?

A. 6.48%

B. 7.92%

C. 9.36%

D. 10.80%

Answer (C) is correct.

REQUIRED: The firm's weighted-average cost of capital.

DISCUSSION: A firm's weighted-average cost of capital (WACC) is derived by weighting the (after-tax) cost of debt of 5.4% = 9% × (1 − 40%) and cost of equity of 12%. The tax rate does not affect the cost of equity. Scrunchy-Tech's WACC can be calculated as follows:

Component	Weight		Component Cost		Totals
Debt	40%	×	5.4%	=	2.16%
Equity	60%	×	12.0%	=	7.20%
	100%				9.36%

Answer (A) is incorrect. Improperly subtracting the effect of taxes from the cost of equity results in 6.48%. Answer (B) is incorrect. Improperly subtracting the effect of taxes from equity, but not from debt, results in 7.92%. Answer (D) is incorrect. Improperly using the before-tax cost of debt results in 10.80%.

19. A firm's target or optimal capital structure is consistent with which one of the following?

    A. Maximum earnings per share.

    B. Minimum cost of debt.

    C. Minimum risk.

    D. Minimum weighted-average cost of capital.

Answer (D) is correct.
    REQUIRED: The true statement about a firm's target or optimal capital structure.
    DISCUSSION: Ideally, a firm will have a capital structure that minimizes its weighted-average cost of capital. This requires a balancing of both debt and equity capital and their associated risk levels.
    Answer (A) is incorrect. EPS is based on the relationship between costs and revenues, whereas the capital structure is related only to the cost of capital. Answer (B) is incorrect. The cost of equity capital must also be considered when optimizing capital structure. Answer (C) is incorrect. The minimum risk may be associated with high costs.

20. An accountant for Stability, Inc., must calculate the weighted average cost of capital of the corporation using the following information.

		Component Cost
Accounts payable	$35,000,000	-0-
Long-term debt	10,000,000	8%
Common stock	10,000,000	15%
Retained earnings	5,000,000	18%

What is the weighted average cost of capital of Stability?

    A. 6.88%

    B. 8.00%

    C. 10.25%

    D. 12.80%

Answer (D) is correct.
    REQUIRED: Calculation of the weighted-average cost of capital.
    DISCUSSION: Since the effect of income taxes is ignored in this situation, the stated rate on Stability's long-term debt is considered to be its effective rate. The weighted-average cost of capital (WACC) can thus be calculated as follows:

	Carrying Amount	Weight		Cost of Capital		Weighted Cost
Long-term debt	$10,000,000	40%	×	8%	=	3.2%
Common stock	10,000,000	40%	×	15%	=	6.0%
Retained earnings	5,000,000	20%	×	18%	=	3.6%
Totals	$25,000,000	100%				12.8%

    Answer (A) is incorrect. This percentage results from improperly ignoring the weighted cost of common stock. Answer (B) is incorrect. This percentage is the component cost of debt. Answer (C) is incorrect. This percentage results from improperly performing a simple average on the four balance sheet items listed.

21. Kielly Machines, Inc., is planning an expansion program estimated to cost $100 million. Kielly is going to raise funds according to its target capital structure shown below.

Debt	.30
Preferred stock	.24
Equity	.46

Kielly had net income available to common shareholders of $184 million last year of which 75% was paid out in dividends. The company has a marginal tax rate of 40%.

Additional data

- The before-tax cost of debt is estimated to be 11%.
- The market yield of preferred stock is estimated to be 12%.
- The after-tax cost of common stock is estimated to be 16%.

What is Kielly's weighted average cost of capital?

    A. 12.22%

    B. 13.00%

    C. 13.54%

    D. 14.00%

Answer (A) is correct.
    REQUIRED: Calculation of the weighted-average cost of capital.
    DISCUSSION: The effective rate for Kielly's debt is the after-tax cost [11% × (1.0 – .40 tax rate) = 6.6%] The weighted average cost of capital (WACC) can thus be calculated as follows:

	Carrying Amount	Weight		Cost of Capital		Weighted Cost
Debt	$ 30,000,000	30%	×	6.6%	=	1.98%
Preferred stock	24,000,000	24%	×	12.0%	=	2.88%
Common equity	46,000,000	46%	×	16.0%	=	7.36%
Totals	$100,000,000	100%				12.22%

    Answer (B) is incorrect. This percentage results from performing a simple average cost calculation on the individual components of capital. Answer (C) is incorrect. This percentage results from improperly using the before-tax cost of debt. Answer (D) is incorrect. This percentage results from performing a simple average on just the preferred stock and common equity components.

22. Following is an excerpt from Albion Corporation's balance sheet.

Long-term debt (9% interest rate)	$30,000,000
Preferred stock (100,000 shares, 12% dividend)	10,000,000
Common stock (5,000,000 shares outstanding)	60,000,000

Albion's bonds are currently trading at $1,083.34, reflecting a yield to maturity of 8%. The preferred stock is trading at $125 per share. Common stock is selling at $16 per share, and Albion's treasurer estimates that the firm's cost of equity is 17%. If Albion's effective income tax rate is 40%, what is the firm's cost of capital?

   A. 12.6%

   B. 13.0%

   C. 13.9%

   D. 14.1%

Answer (B) is correct.

   REQUIRED: Calculation of the weighted-average cost of capital

   DISCUSSION: The effective rate for Albion's debt is the after-tax cost [9% × (1.0 – .40 tax rate) = 5.4%]. The weighted-average cost of capital (WACC) can thus be calculated as follows:

	Carrying Amount	Weight		Cost of Capital		Weighted Cost
Long-term debt	$ 30,000,000	30%	×	5.4%	=	1.6%
Preferred stock	10,000,000	10%	×	12.0%	=	1.2%
Common stock	60,000,000	60%	×	17.0%	=	10.2%
Totals	$100,000,000	100%				13.0%

   Answer (A) is incorrect. This percentage results from performing a simple average on the face rate of the bonds, the face rate of the preferred stock, and the estimated cost of equity. Answer (C) is incorrect. This percentage results from using the bonds' yield rather than the after-tax interest cost. Answer (D) is incorrect. This percentage results from improperly using the before-tax cost of debt.

23. Thomas Company's capital structure consists of 30% long-term debt, 25% preferred stock, and 45% common equity. The cost of capital for each component is shown below.

Long-term debt	8%
Preferred stock	11%
Common equity	15%

If Thomas pays taxes at the rate of 40%, what is the company's after-tax weighted average cost of capital?

   A. 7.14%

   B. 9.84%

   C. 10.94%

   D. 11.90%

Answer (C) is correct.

   REQUIRED: Calculation of the weighted-average cost of capital.

   DISCUSSION: The effective rate for Thomas' debt is the after-tax cost [8% × (1.0 – .40 tax rate) = 4.8%]. The weighted-average cost of capital (WACC) can thus be calculated as follows:

	Weight		Cost of Capital		Weighted Cost
Long-term debt	30%	×	4.8%	=	1.44%
Preferred stock	25%	×	11.0%	=	2.75%
Common equity	45%	×	15.0%	=	6.75%
Totals	100%				10.94%

   Answer (A) is incorrect. This percentage results from improperly applying the tax effect to the rates on preferred stock and common equity. Answer (B) is incorrect. This percentage results from improperly applying the tax effect to the rate on preferred stock. Answer (D) is incorrect. This percentage results from failing to adjust the rate on debt for the tax effect.

24. Joint Products, Inc., a corporation with a 40% marginal tax rate, plans to issue $1,000,000 of 8% preferred stock in exchange for $1,000,000 of its 8% bonds currently outstanding. The firm's total liabilities and equity are equal to $10,000,000. The effect of this exchange on the firm's weighted average cost of capital is likely to be

   A. No change, since it involves equal amounts of capital in the exchange and both instruments have the same rate.

   B. A decrease, since a portion of the debt payments are tax deductible.

   C. A decrease, since preferred stock payments do not need to be made each year, whereas debt payments must be made.

   D. An increase, since a portion of the debt payments are tax deductible.

Answer (D) is correct.

   REQUIRED: The effect on WACC of the replacement of bonds with preferred stock.

   DISCUSSION: The payment of interest on bonds is tax-deductible, whereas dividends on preferred stock must be paid out of after-tax earnings. Thus, when bonds are replaced in the capital structure with preferred stock, an increase in the cost of capital is likely, because there is no longer a tax shield.

   Answer (A) is incorrect. While the dollar amounts may be equal, the different effective rates on the two instruments will cause a change in the cost of capital. Answer (B) is incorrect. The cost of capital will increase (debt is being replaced by preferred stock, not the other way around). Answer (C) is incorrect. The preferred stock has a higher effective rate, leading to an increase in the cost of capital.

7.6 PRACTICE WRITTEN COMMUNICATION TASK

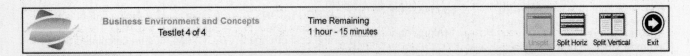

Business Environment and Concepts
Testlet 4 of 4

Time Remaining
1 hour - 15 minutes

Unsplit   Split Horiz   Split Vertical   Exit

DIRECTIONS

Note: If you believe you have encountered a software malfunction, report it to the test center staff immediately.

Navigation

To navigate from task to task, use the controls at the bottom of the screen. Click on the **Next** button to advance to the next task, or the **Previous** button to go to the previous task. To go directly to any task, click on its number.

| ▼ = Reminder | | Directions | 1 ▽ | 2 ▽ | 3 ▽ | 4 ▽ | 5 ▽ | 6 ▽ | 7 ▽ | | ◀ Previous | Next ▶ |

If you would like a reminder to revisit a task, or want to indicate that you are finished with it, click on the reminder flag below the task number. To clear the flag, click on it again. Reminder flags are for your use only – they do not contribute to your score.

Tabs

In this part of the examination, you will be asked to complete various tasks. Every task has one or more **Work Tabs**. Every task also has a **Help** tab.

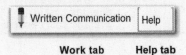

Written Communication   Help

Work tab   Help tab

Work Tabs:

- **Work Tabs** are identified with a pencil icon. This is where your responses are expected.
- Each task has one or more **Work Tabs**.
- **Work Tabs** contain directions for completing the task - be sure to read these directions carefully.
- The **Work Tab** name in the example above is for illustration only - yours will differ.
- You must complete all of the **Work Tabs** in each task to receive full credit.

Help Tab:

- The **Help Tab** provides assistance with the exam software that is used in this task. For example, if the task is to compose a memorandum, **Help** will provide information about the word processor.

The Toolbar

The toolbar at the top of the screen shows the amount of time remaining for you to complete the tasks. In addition, the following tools are available. Note that only the **Exit** button is displayed when Directions are visible - the others will appear when you begin the tasks.

Unsplit   Split Horiz   Split Vertical

Click on these buttons to split or unsplit the screen. You can split the screen vertically or horizontally.

Exit

Click on this button to go on to the next part of the examination. You must complete all of the tasks to receive full credit. Once you click on **Exit** and confirm the action, you will NOT be able to return to this testlet.

| ▼ = Reminder | | Directions | 1 ▽ | | | | | | | | ◀ Previous | Next ▶ |

Written Communication | Help

✂ Cut | 📋 Copy | 📋 Paste | ↩ Undo | ↪ Redo

During a meeting helping your closely held client, Simple Corporation, the shareholders mentioned that they wanted to increase the firm's capital without contributing more of their own money.

Prepare a memo to the shareholders of Simple Corporation explaining the use of debt by a firm and how financial leverage can be a useful tool.

Type your communication below the line in the response area below.

REMINDER: Your response will be graded for both technical content and writing skills. Technical content will be evaluated for information that is helpful to the intended reader and clearly relevant to the issue. Writing skills will be evaluated for development, organization, and the appropriate expression of ideas in professional correspondence. Use a standard business memorandum or letter format with a clear beginning, middle, and end. Do not convey information in the form of a table, bullet point list, or other abbreviated presentation.

To: Shareholders, Simple Corporation
Re: Corporate debt and financial leverage

Unofficial Answer

Written Communication

To: Shareholders, Simple Corporation
Re: Corporate debt and financial leverage

The balance sheet of a corporation can be depicted as the perfect balance between the firm's resources and its capital structure. The resources consist of the assets the firm deploys in its attempts to earn a return. The capital structure consists of the amounts contributed by outsiders (represented by debt) and insiders (represented by equity) to make the use of these assets possible.

Bonds are the principal form of long-term debt financing for corporations and governmental entities. A bond is a formal contractual obligation to pay an amount of money (called the par value, maturity amount, or face amount) to the holder at a certain date, plus, in most cases, a series of cash interest payments based on a specified percentage (called the stated rate or coupon rate) of the face amount at specified intervals. All of the terms of the agreement are stated in a document called an indenture.

The principal advantage of bond financing for the issuer is that interest paid on debt is tax deductible. For a corporation facing a 40%-50% marginal tax rate, the tax savings produced by the deduction of interest can be substantial. Also, basic control of the firm is not shared with debtholders.

Certain disadvantages are also inherent in of bond financing. Unlike returns on equity investments (called dividends), the payment of interest and principal on debt is a legal obligation. If cash flow is insufficient to service debt, the firm could become insolvent. This legal requirement to pay debt service raises a firm's risk level. Shareholders will consequently demand higher capitalization rates on retained earnings, which may result in a decline in the market price of the stock.

The burden placed on a firm by the use of debt is measured in terms of financial leverage. The degree of financial leverage (DFL) is a ratio that measures the effect that a particular amount of fixed financing costs has on a firm's earnings per share (EPS).

The above depicts a Level 5 answer. See page 16 in the Introduction for a description of the three grading criteria.

Self-Grade

Evaluate each of the following by selecting a 0, 1, 2, 3, 4, or 5. An average response is 3. Use 4 for better than average and 5 for outstanding. Use 2 for less than average and 1 for quite poor. Use zero for no response, if you did not address the topic, or if you gave advice that is clearly illegal.

Organization	o 0	o 1	o 2	o 3	o 4	o 5
Development	o 0	o 1	o 2	o 3	o 4	o 5
Expression	o 0	o 1	o 2	o 3	o 4	o 5

Your grade for the written communication as a whole is the average of the scores for the three criteria.

Use **CPA Gleim Online** and **Simulation Wizard** to practice more written communication tasks in a realistic environment.

STUDY UNIT EIGHT
WORKING CAPITAL

(17 pages of outline)

All firms must hold a certain amount of current assets simply to carry on day-to-day operations. Owing to the existence of various types of inventory, manufacturing and distribution companies often have as many as half of their total assets held in the form of current assets. The proper management of current assets is thus crucial to a firm's efficient operation.

Working capital management is the process of determining the optimum level and mix of these assets (Subunits 1, 4, 5, 6, and 8). The measures employed to assess the level of success achieved in this process are also addressed (Subunits 2, 3, 7, 9, and 10).

8.1 WORKING CAPITAL MANAGEMENT

1. **Working capital**, as used by accountants, is calculated as follows:

   Working capital = Current assets − Current liabilities

   a. **Current assets** are the most liquid assets. They are expected to be converted to cash, sold, or consumed within 1 year or the operating cycle, whichever is longer. Ratios involving current assets thus measure a firm's ability to continue operating in the short run.

      1) Current assets include, in descending order of liquidity: cash and equivalents, marketable securities, receivables, inventories, and prepaid items.

   b. **Current liabilities**, by the same token, are ones that must be settled the soonest. Specifically, they are expected to be settled or converted to other liabilities within 1 year or the operating cycle, whichever is longer.

      1) Current liabilities include accounts payable, notes payable, current maturities of long-term debt, unearned revenues, taxes payable, wages payable, and other accruals.

2. **Permanent and Temporary Working Capital**

   a. Trying to apply a simple rule such as "current assets should be financed with current liabilities" is not appropriate to the practice of working capital management.

      1) Some level of liquid current assets must be maintained to meet the firm's long-term minimum needs regardless of the firm's level of activity or profitability. This is termed permanent working capital.

      2) As the firm's needs for current assets change on a seasonal basis, temporary working capital is increased and decreased.

b.   Both of these elements tend to increase over time with the growth of the firm.

Working Capital

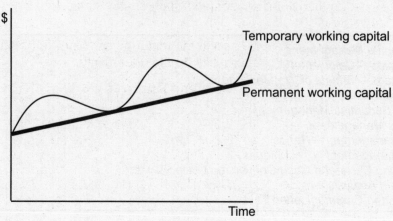

Figure 8-1

3.   **Spontaneous Financing**

a.   Spontaneous financing is the amount of current liabilities, such as trade payables and accruals, that arises naturally in the ordinary course of business without the firm's financial managers needing to take deliberate action.

b.   Trade credit arises when a company is offered credit terms by its suppliers.

EXAMPLE

A vendor has delivered goods and invoiced the company for $160,000 on terms of net 30. The company has effectively received a 30-day interest-free $160,000 loan.

---

c.   Accrued expenses, such as salaries, wages, interest, dividends, and taxes payable, are another source of (interest-free) spontaneous financing.

1)   For instance, employees work 5, 6, or 7 days a week but are only paid every 2 weeks. A company carries on operations constantly but must only remit federal income taxes every quarter.

2)   Accruals have the additional advantage of fluctuating directly with operating activity, satisfying the matching principle.

d.   The portion of capital needs that cannot be satisfied through spontaneous means must be the subject of careful financial planning.

4.   **Short-Term vs. Long-Term Financing**

a.   The firm's temporary working capital usually cannot be financed only by spontaneous financing. Therefore, the firm must decide whether to finance it with short-term or long-term financing.

1)   The interest rate on long-term debt is higher than on the short-term, as will be explained later in this study unit. Therefore, long-term financing is more expensive than short-term.

2)   On the other hand, the shorter the maturity schedule of a firm's debt obligation, the greater the risk that the firm will be unable to meet principal and interest payments. This can lead to insolvency.

b.   In general, short-term financing is more risky and less expensive than long-term financing.

c.   The appropriate way to finance the firm's working capital depends on management's attitude to the trade-off between profitability and risk.

5. **Maturity Matching**

    a.   Ideally, a firm would be able to offset each element of its temporary working capital with a short-term liability of similar maturity. For example, a short-term loan could be taken out as the winter season approached and repaid with the collections made from holiday sales.

         1)   This ideal situation is termed the maturity matching, or hedging, approach. It is rarely achievable in practice due to uncertainty.

Maturity Matching Approach

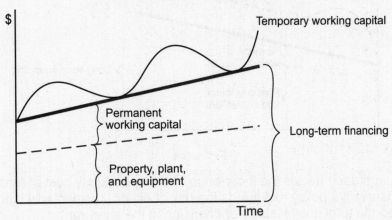

Figure 8-2

6. **Conservative Policy**

    a.   A firm that adopts a conservative financing policy seeks to minimize liquidity risk by financing its temporary working capital mostly with long-term debt.

Conservative Financing Policy

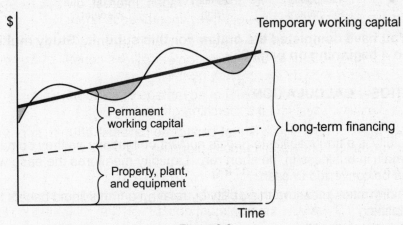

Figure 8-3

    b.   This approach takes advantage of the certainty inherent in long-term debt.

         1)   The locked-in interest rate mitigates interest rate risk (the risk that rates will rise in the short run), and the distant maturity date mitigates liquidity risk (the inability to repay a current obligation when due).

    c.   The drawbacks are

         1)   That working capital sits idle during periods when it is not needed, indicated by the shaded areas in Figure 8-3. This can be mitigated to some extent by investing in short-term securities (discussed in Subunit 8.5).

         2)   That long-term debt is more expensive.

7.   **Aggressive Policy**

a.   An aggressive financing policy involves reducing liquidity and accepting a higher risk of short-term cash flow problems in an effort to increase profitability.

Aggressive Financing Policy

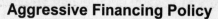
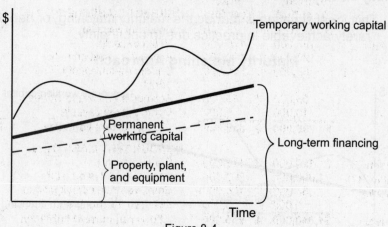

Figure 8-4

b.   This approach avoids the incurrence of the opportunity cost of funds tied up by the conservative policy, but it runs the risk of either unexpectedly high interest rates or even the total unavailability of financing in the short run.

8.   **Summary**

Risk and Profitability in Relation to Financing

Working Capital Component	Financed with	
	Short-Term Debt	Long-Term Debt
Temporary	Medium	Low
Permanent	High	Medium

Stop and review! You have completed the outline for this subunit. Study multiple-choice questions 1 through 4 beginning on page 239.

8.2 LIQUIDITY RATIOS -- CALCULATION

1.   **Liquidity**

a.   Liquidity is a firm's ability to pay its current obligations as they come due and thus remain in business in the short run. Liquidity measures the ease with which assets can be converted to cash.

b.   Liquidity ratios measure this ability by relating a firm's liquid assets to its current liabilities.

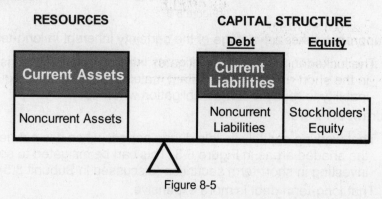

Figure 8-5

EXAMPLE

Example of a balance sheet (used in this subunit as well as Subunits 8.6 and 8.7).

RESOURCES			FINANCING		
CURRENT ASSETS:	**Current Year End**	**Prior Year End**	**CURRENT LIABILITIES:**	**Current Year End**	**Prior Year End**
Cash and equivalents	$ 325,000	$ 275,000	Accounts payable	$ 150,000	$ 75,000
Available-for-sale securities	165,000	145,000	Notes payable	50,000	50,000
Accounts receivable (net)	120,000	115,000	Accrued interest on note	5,000	5,000
Notes receivable	55,000	40,000	Current maturities of L.T. debt	100,000	100,000
Inventories	85,000	55,000	Accrued salaries and wages	15,000	10,000
Prepaid expenses	10,000	5,000	Income taxes payable	70,000	35,000
Total current assets	$ 760,000	$ 635,000	Total current liabilities	$ 390,000	$ 275,000
NONCURRENT ASSETS:			**NONCURRENT LIABILITIES:**		
Equity-method investments	$ 120,000	$ 115,000	Bonds payable	$ 500,000	$ 600,000
Property, plant, and equipment	1,000,000	900,000	Long-term notes payable	90,000	60,000
Less: accum. depreciation	(85,000)	(55,000)	Employee-related obligations	15,000	10,000
Goodwill	5,000	5,000	Deferred income taxes	5,000	5,000
Total noncurrent assets	$1,040,000	$ 965,000	Total noncurrent liabilities	$ 610,000	$ 675,000
			Total liabilities	$1,000,000	$ 950,000
			STOCKHOLDERS' EQUITY:		
			Preferred stock, $50 par	$ 120,000	$ 0
			Common stock, $1 par	500,000	500,000
			Additional paid-in capital	110,000	100,000
			Retained earnings	70,000	50,000
			Total stockholders' equity	$ 800,000	$ 650,000
Total assets	$1,800,000	$1,600,000	Total liabilities and stockholders' equity	$1,800,000	$1,600,000

GLEIM SUCCESS TIPS

Know the formulas and how to calculate the various financial ratios as well as how to analyze the ratio results. Numerous prior CPA exams have included questions on both the calculation and analysis of financial ratios. In ratio calculation, the numbers necessary to calculate a ratio often will not be given directly. You will have to determine these numbers using information given in the question and then calculate the ratio.

Note: This Tip also applies to Subunit 8.7 and Study Unit 10, Subunits 3 and 4.

2. **Liquidity Ratios**

   a. **Net working capital** reports the resources the company would have to continue operating in the short run if it had to liquidate all of its current liabilities at once.

   Current assets − Current liabilities

EXAMPLE

Current year: $760,000 − $390,000 = $370,000
Prior year: $635,000 − $275,000 = $360,000

Although the company's current liabilities increased, its current assets increased by $10,000 more.

b.   The **current ratio** (working capital ratio) is the most common measure of liquidity.

$$\frac{Current\ assets}{Current\ liabilities}$$

EXAMPLE

Current year: $760,000 ÷ $390,000 = 1.95
Prior year: $635,000 ÷ $275,000 = 2.31

Although working capital increased in absolute terms ($10,000), current assets now provide less proportional coverage of current liabilities than in the prior year.

---

     1)   A low current ratio indicates a possible liquidity problem. An overly high ratio indicates that management may not be investing idle assets productively.

c.   The **quick (acid-test) ratio** excludes inventories and prepaids from the numerator, recognizing that those assets are difficult to liquidate at their stated values. The quick ratio is thus a more conservative measure than the basic current ratio.

$$\frac{Cash\ and\ equivalents + Marketable\ securities + Net\ receivables}{Current\ liabilities}$$

EXAMPLE

Current year: ($325,000 + $165,000 + $120,000 + $55,000) ÷ $390,000 = 1.71
Prior year: ($275,000 + $145,000 + $115,000 + $40,000) ÷ $275,000 = 2.09

In spite of its increase in total working capital, the company's position in its most liquid assets deteriorated significantly.

---

     1)   This ratio measures the firm's ability to easily pay its short-term debts and avoids the problem of inventory valuation.

Stop and review! You have completed the outline for this subunit. Study multiple-choice questions 5 through 8 beginning on page 240.

8.3   LIQUIDITY RATIOS -- EFFECTS OF TRANSACTIONS

The previous subunit discussed the mechanics of calculating the standard liquidity ratios as well as their basic interpretation. Given the importance placed on these measures by financial analysts and lending institutions. It is important for the accountant to recognize the efforts that various accounting transactions have on the ratios.

Stop and review! You have completed the outline for this subunit. Study multiple-choice questions 9 through 12 beginning on page 242.

8.4   CASH MANAGEMENT

1.   **Managing the Level of Cash**

     a.   As part of his theory of money demand, English economist John Maynard Keynes (1883-1946) outlined three motives for holding cash:

         1)   The transactional motive, i.e., to use as a medium of exchange

         2)   The precautionary motive, i.e., to provide a cushion for unexpected contingencies

         3)   The speculative motive, i.e., to take advantage of unexpected opportunities

     b.   The goal of cash management is to determine and maintain the firm's optimal cash balance.

         1)   This is not the same as "maximizing cash"; since ready cash does not earn a return, only the amount needed to satisfy current obligations as they come due should be kept. Striking this balance is the essence of cash management.

    c.   The firm's optimal level of cash should be determined by a cost-benefit analysis.

        1)   The need to satisfy the three motives listed on the previous page must be balanced against the opportunity cost of missed investments in marketable securities.

    d.   A **compensating balance** is a minimum amount that the bank requires the firm to keep in its demand (checking) account. Compensating balances are noninterest-bearing and are meant to compensate the bank for various services rendered, such as unlimited check writing. These funds are obviously unavailable for short-term investment and thus incur an opportunity cost.

2. **Speeding Up Cash Collections**

    a.   The period of time from when a payor puts a check in the mail until the funds are available in the payee's bank is called float. Companies use various strategies to reduce the float time on receipts (and to stretch the float time on payments, discussed in item 3. below and on the following page).

    b.   A **lockbox** system is the single most important strategy for expediting the receipt of funds.

        1)   Customers submit their payments to a post office box rather than to the company's offices. Bank personnel remove the envelopes from the mailbox and deposit the checks to the company's account immediately. The remittance advices must then be transported to the company for entry into the accounts receivable system. The bank generally charges a flat monthly fee for this service.

        2)   For firms doing business nationwide, a lockbox network is appropriate. The country is divided into regions according to customer population patterns. A lockbox arrangement is then established with a bank in each region.

    c.   A firm employing a lockbox network will usually engage in concentration banking. The regional banks that provide lockbox services automatically transfer their daily collections to the firm's principal bank, where they can be used for disbursement and short-term investment.

3. **Slowing Cash Disbursements**

    a.   A **draft** is a three-party instrument in which one person (the drawer) orders a second person (the drawee) to pay money to a third person (the payee).

        1)   A check is the most common form of draft. A check is an instrument payable on demand in which the drawee is a bank. Consequently, a draft can be used to delay the outflow of cash.

        2)   A draft can be dated on the due date of an invoice and will not be processed by the drawee until that date, thereby eliminating the necessity of writing a check earlier than the due date or using an electronic funds transfer (EFT). Thus, the outflow is delayed until the check clears the drawee bank.

    b.   A **payable through draft** (PTD) differs from a check in that (1) it is not payable on demand and (2) the drawee is the payor, not a bank. After the payee presents the PTD to a bank, the bank in turn presents it to the issuer. The issuer then must deposit sufficient funds to cover the PTD. Use of PTDs thus allows a firm to maintain lower cash balances.

        1)   Drawbacks are that vendors obviously prefer to receive an instrument that will be paid on demand, and banks generally impose higher processing charges for PTDs.

c.   A **zero-balance account** (ZBA) carries, as the name implies, a balance of $0. At the end of each processing day, the bank transfers just enough from the firm's master account to cover all checks presented against the ZBA that day.

   1)   This practice allows the firm to maintain higher balances in the master account from which short-term investments can be made. The bank generally charges a fee for this service.

d.   **Disbursement float** is the period of time from when the payor puts a check in the mail until the funds are deducted from the payor's account. In an effort to stretch disbursement float, a firm may mail checks to its vendors while being unsure that sufficient funds will be available to cover them all.

   1)   For these situations, some banks offer overdraft protection, in which the bank guarantees (for a fee) to cover any shortfall with a transfer from the firm's master account.

Background

Sometimes having too *much* cash can create a finance challenge. During the summer of 2011, large U.S. firms were awash in cash. They were unwilling to spend in the highly uncertain economic environment, and banks thus found themselves with huge U.S. dollar deposits on their books. This sudden influx of cash greatly raised the banks' interest payouts and made them subject to more stringent ratio and reserve requirements. To compensate, Bank of New York Mellon, the largest custody bank, announced that it would start charging fees to clients whose cash balances exceeded $50 million.

Stop and review! You have completed the outline for this subunit. Study multiple-choice questions 13 through 15 beginning on page 243.

8.5 MARKETABLE SECURITIES MANAGEMENT

1.   **Idle Cash and Its Uses**

   a.   Idle cash incurs an opportunity cost. To offset this cost, firms invest their idle cash balances in marketable securities.

   b.   Beyond earning a modest return, the most important aspects of marketable securities management are liquidity and safety. Marketable securities management thus concerns low-yield, low-risk instruments that are traded on highly active markets, commonly referred to as money market instruments.

   c.   The money market is the market for short-term investments where companies invest their temporary surpluses of cash. The money market is not formally organized but consists of many financial institutions, companies, and government agencies offering a wide array of instruments of various risk levels and short- to medium-range maturities.

2.   **Money Market Instruments**

   a.   U.S. Treasury obligations are the safest investment. In addition, they are all exempt from state and local taxation and are highly liquid.

   1)   **Treasury bills** (T-bills) have maturities of 1 year or less. Rather than bear interest, they are sold on a discount basis.

   2)   **Treasury notes** (T-notes) have maturities of 1 to 10 years. They provide the lender with a coupon (interest) payment every 6 months.

   3)   **Treasury bonds** (T-bonds) have maturities of 10 years or longer. They provide the lender with a coupon (interest) payment every 6 months.

Background

The U.S. government stopped issuing the famous 30-year Treasury bond (the "long bond") in October 2001 as efforts to pay off the national debt accelerated. The long bond became available again starting in February 2006.

b. **Repurchase agreements** (repos) are a means for dealers in government securities to finance their portfolios. When a company buys a repo, the firm is temporarily purchasing some of the dealer's government securities. The dealer agrees to repurchase them at a later time for a specific (higher) price. In essence, the company is providing the securities dealer a secured short-term loan. Maturities vary from overnight to a few days.

c. **Federal agency securities** come in two types: those backed by the full faith and credit of the U.S. government and those that are backed only by the issuing agency.

   1) Obligations of the Federal Housing Administration (FHA) and the Government National Mortgage Association (Ginnie Mae) are backed by the U.S. Treasury.

   2) Obligations of such government-sponsored enterprises (GSEs) as the Federal National Mortgage Association (Fannie Mae) and the Federal Home Loan Mortgage Corporation (Freddie Mac), which issue mortgage-backed securities, are officially backed only by the agency themselves. They do, however, carry an implied guarantee by the federal government.

d. **Bankers' acceptances** are drafts drawn by a nonfinancial firm on deposits at a bank. The acceptance by the bank is a guarantee of payment at maturity. The payee can thus rely on the creditworthiness of the bank rather than on that of the (presumably riskier) drawer. Because they are backed by the prestige of a large bank, these instruments are highly marketable once they have been accepted.

e. **Commercial paper** consists of short-term, unsecured notes payable issued in large denominations ($100,000 or more) by large corporations with high credit ratings to other corporations and institutional investors, such as pension funds, banks, and insurance companies.

   1) Maturities of commercial paper are at most 270 days. No general secondary market exists for commercial paper. Commercial paper is a lower-cost source of funds than bank loans. It is usually issued at below the prime rate.

f. **Certificates of deposit** (CDs) are a form of savings deposit that cannot be withdrawn before maturity without a high penalty. CDs often yield a lower return than commercial paper because they are less risky. Negotiable CDs are traded under the regulation of the Federal Reserve System.

g. **Eurodollars** are time deposits of U.S. dollars in banks located abroad.

h. Others

   1) Money-market mutual funds invest in short-term, low-risk securities. In addition to paying interest, these funds allow investors to write checks on their balances.

   2) State and local governments issue short-term securities exempt from taxation.

Stop and review! You have completed the outline for this subunit. Study multiple-choice questions 16 and 17 on page 244.

8.6 RECEIVABLES MANAGEMENT

1. **Overview**

   a. The goal of receivables management is to offer the terms of credit that will maximize profits, not sales.

      1) Maximizing sales could be easily accomplished by raising discount percentages, offering longer payment periods, and taking on riskier customers, but this strategy could lead to cash flow problems.

Background

In 1969, in a desperate attempt to boost sales, the department store chain W.T. Grant drastically lowered its credit standards. As a result, sales boomed. However, during the economic downturn of 1970-71, cash inflows dried up as customer accounts began to turn delinquent. The company finally collapsed in 1974. Grant's creditors were caught completely unawares because the company's accrual-basis income statement had shown consistently positive results, and Grant had never stopped paying a dividend. The inadequacy of the traditional income statement for assessing liquidity was made glaringly obvious by the Grant bankruptcy. This incident was one of the driving forces behind the adoption of the statement of cash flows by the FASB.

---

    2) At the same time, default risk can be minimized by raising credit standards, but this could starve the company of sales. The entity must strike the proper balance.

  b. A common set of credit terms offered are 2/10, net 30. This is a convention meaning that the customer may either deduct 2% of the invoice amount if the invoice is paid within 10 days or pay the entire balance by the 30th day.

  c. Factoring is an arrangement in which an entity sells its accounts receivable, at a discount, to another entity, called a factor, that usually specializes in collections.

    1) The selling entity generates cash while simultaneously eliminating bad debts from its balance sheet. Also, it is relieved of the need to maintain a credit department and accounts receivable staff.

2. **Basic Receivables Formulas**

EXAMPLE

Excerpt from an income statement:

	Current Year	Prior Year
Net sales	$1,800,000	$1,400,000
Cost of goods sold	(1,650,000)	(1,330,000)
Gross profit	$ 150,000	$ 70,000

---

  a. The **accounts receivable turnover ratio** is the number of times in a year the total balance of receivables is converted to cash.

$$\text{Accounts receivable turnover} = \frac{\text{Net credit sales}}{\text{Average balance in receivables}}$$

EXAMPLE

All of the company's sales are on credit (see example of a balance sheet on page 227). Net trade receivables at the balance sheet date of the second prior year were $105,000.

Current year: $1,800,000 ÷ [($120,000 + $115,000) ÷ 2] = 15.3 times
Prior year: $1,400,000 ÷ [($115,000 + $105,000) ÷ 2] = 12.7 times

The company turned over its trade receivables balance 2.6 more times during the current year, even as receivables were growing in absolute terms. Thus, the company's effectiveness at collecting accounts receivable has improved noticeably.

---

  b. The **average collection period** (also called the **days' sales in receivables**) measures the average number of days that pass between the time of a sale and receipt of the invoice amount.

$$\text{Days' sales in receivables} = \frac{\text{Days in year}}{\text{Accounts receivable turnover ratio}}$$

EXAMPLE

Current year: 365 days ÷ 15.3 times = 23.9 days
Prior year: 365 days ÷ 12.7 times = 28.7 days

Since the denominator (calculated in item a. on the previous page) increased and the numerator is a constant, days' sales will necessarily decrease. In addition to improving its collection practices, the company also may have become better at assessing the creditworthiness of its customers.

Stop and review! You have completed the outline for this subunit. Study multiple-choice questions 18 through 20 on page 245.

8.7 INVENTORY MANAGEMENT -- RATIOS

1. **Inventory Ratios**

   a. Two measures are calculated that report the efficiency of the entity's management of inventory.

   b. **Inventory turnover** measures the number of times in a year the total balance of inventory is converted to cash or receivables.

      1) Generally, the higher the inventory turnover rate, the more efficient the inventory management of the firm. A high rate may imply that the firm is not carrying excess levels of inventory or inventory that is obsolete.

$$Inventory\ turnover = \frac{Cost\ of\ goods\ sold}{Average\ balance\ in\ inventory}$$

EXAMPLE

The balance in inventories at the balance sheet date of the second prior year was $45,000.

Current year: $1,650,000 ÷ [($85,000 + $55,000) ÷ 2] = 23.6 times
Prior year: $1,330,000 ÷ [($55,000 + $45,000) ÷ 2] = 26.6 times

The company did not turn over its inventories as many times during the current year. This is to be expected during a period of growing sales (and building inventory level) and so is not necessarily a sign of poor inventory management.

---

2) As with receivables turnover, if a business is highly seasonal, a simple average of beginning and ending balances is inadequate. The monthly balances should be averaged instead.

3) Since cost of goods sold is in the numerator, higher sales (i.e., higher cost of goods sold) without an increase in inventory balances will result in better turnover.

   a) Since inventory is in the denominator, reducing inventory levels results in a higher turnover ratio.

4) The ratio of a firm that uses LIFO may not be comparable with that of a firm with a higher inventory valuation.

   c. **Days' sales in inventory** measures the average number of days that pass between the acquisition of inventory and its sale.

$$Days'\ sales\ in\ inventory = \frac{Days\ in\ year}{Inventory\ turnover\ ratio}$$

EXAMPLE

Current year: 365 days ÷ 23.6 times = 15.5 days
Prior year: 365 days ÷ 26.6 times = 13.7 days

Since the numerator is a constant, the decreased inventory turnover calculated meant that days' sales tied up in inventory would increase. This is a common phenomenon during a period of increasing sales.

Stop and review! You have completed the outline for this subunit. Study multiple-choice questions 21 and 22 beginning on page 246.

8.8 INVENTORY MANAGEMENT -- TECHNIQUES

1. **Overview**

    a. Costs related to inventory. Minimizing the total cost of inventory involves constant re-evaluation of the tradeoffs among the four components of the total:

        Purchase costs + Carrying costs + Ordering costs + Stockout costs

        1) **Purchase costs** are the actual invoice amounts charged by suppliers. This is also referred to as investment in inventory.

        2) **Carrying costs** is a broad category consisting of all those costs associated with holding inventory: storage, insurance, security, depreciation or rent of facilities, interest, obsolescence and spoilage, and the opportunity cost of funds tied up in inventory. This is sometimes stated as a percentage of investment in inventory.

        3) **Ordering costs** are the fixed costs of placing an order with a vendor, independent of the number of units ordered. For internally manufactured units, these consist of the **set-up costs** of a production line.

        4) **Stockout costs** are the opportunity cost of missing a customer order. These can also include the costs of expediting a special shipment necessitated by insufficient inventory on hand.

    b. The challenge inherent in minimizing total inventory cost is illustrated in the following diagram:

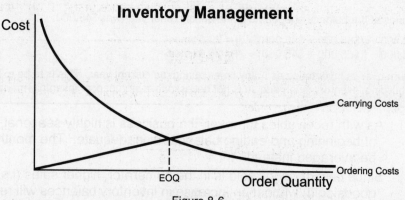

Figure 8-6

    c. Stockout costs can be minimized only by incurring high carrying costs. Carrying costs can be minimized only by incurring the high fixed costs of placing many small orders. Ordering costs can be minimized but only at the cost of storing large quantities. [The economic order quantity (EOQ) model, discussed on the following page, is a widely used aid in meeting this challenge.]

2. **Inventory Replenishment Factors**

    a. **Lead time** is the amount of time expected to pass between placing an order with a supplier and receipt of the goods.

        1) When lead time is known and demand is uniform, the goods can be timed to arrive just as inventory on hand is exhausted. This is the foundation of the just-in-time model, discussed later in this subunit.

b. **Safety stock** is an inventory buffer held as a hedge against contingencies.

    1) Determining the appropriate level of safety stock involves a probabilistic calculation that balances the variability of demand with the level of risk the firm is willing to accept of having to incur stockout costs.

c. The **reorder point** is the amount of inventory on hand indicating that a new order should be placed. It is calculated with the following equation:

(Average daily demand × Lead time in days) + Safety stock

3. **The Economic Order Quantity Model**

a. The economic order quantity (EOQ) model is a mathematical tool for determining the order quantity that minimizes the sum of ordering costs and carrying costs.

$$EOQ = \sqrt{\frac{2OD}{c}}$$

    Where: O = **o**rdering cost per purchase order
                   D = periodic **d**emand in units/usage of units
                   c = periodic **c**arrying costs per unit

b. The assumptions underlying the EOQ model are that

    1) Demand or production is uniform.
    2) Order (setup) costs and carrying costs are constant.
    3) No quantity discounts are allowed.

c. Note how a change in any of the variables changes the EOQ solution. If demand or ordering costs rise, each order must contain more units. If carrying costs rise, each order will contain fewer units.

EXAMPLE

A firm plans to use 2,500 inventory units (D) during the 180-day period. The ordering cost per order is $30 (O). The carrying costs per inventory unit is $15 (c). In order to minimize the total inventory cost for the 180-day period, the firm should order 100 inventory units (EOQ) in each order.

$$EOQ = 100 = \sqrt{\frac{2 \times 2,500 \times 30}{15}}$$

The firm should make 25 orders during that period (2,500 ÷ 100).

---

4. **Advantages of a Perpetual Inventory System**

a. A perpetual system is used by an entity that requires accurate inventory information at all times. Under a perpetual system, every item received is individually recorded in the tracking system. Inventory and cost of goods sold are updated after every sale transaction.

    1) However, even in a perpetual system, a full inventory count must be performed at least annually to correct errors in the tracking system (as well as to derive an appropriate ending balance for financial reporting).

    2) A perpetual system obviously requires very intensive bookkeeping, but the rapid, continuous increases in computer storage and processing power experienced over the last three decades have made such systems more practical and affordable.

b. Use of a perpetual system makes the employment of replenishment models such as EOQ more practical.

1) Under a periodic system (the alternative to a perpetual system), determining the optimal reorder point is extremely difficult. Since item quantities are not continuously monitored, reordering can be haphazard.

2) By contrast, the continuous monitoring inherent in a perpetual system allows reorder points for all items to be preprogrammed. The system can then initiate a reorder automatically. Safety stock levels and stockout costs can be minimized simultaneously.

c. Thus, the added expense of a perpetual inventory system can pay off in terms of the reduced order and carrying costs made possible by modern replenishment techniques.

5. **Value-Added Costs/Activities**

a. A **value-added cost** is the cost of an activity that increases the value of a product or service to the customer. Any reduction in value-added costs will decrease the utility derived from the product and will cause the customer to pay less for the product. Examples of value-added costs are

1) Standard costs of direct material and direct labor that are necessary to produce the product and product-specific features desired by the customers

b. A **non-value-added cost** is the cost of an activity that does not increase the value of a product or service to the customer. The reduction of these costs does not affect the customer's valuation of the product. Examples of non-value-added costs are

1) Costs of moving, handling, and storage of inventory
2) Rework costs on defective products

c. Some costs may relate to activities that include both value-added and non-value-added aspects. Examples of such costs are

1) Costs of indirect labor and indirect materials that cannot be traced to any individual product
2) Testing and inspection costs

d. A **value chain analysis** looks at the entire production process to identify the activities that add value to a product or service and reduce to a minimum the non-value-added costs.

6. **Just-in-Time Inventory**

a. In a just-in-time (JIT) inventory system, the moving, handling, and storage of inventory are treated as non-value-adding activities.

1) Not just safety stock but all raw materials inventories (and their associated carrying costs) are reduced or eliminated entirely. Binding agreements with suppliers ensure that materials arrive exactly when they are needed and not before.

a) These practices are also integral aspects of lean operation (described in item 3.b. in Study Unit 17, Subunit 3).

2) JIT is a pull system, meaning it is demand-driven: In a manufacturing environment, production of goods does not begin until an order has been received. In this way, finished goods inventories are also eliminated.

3) The purpose of the JIT inventory system is to minimize the cost associated with inventory control and maintenance by reducing the lag time between inventory's arrival and use.

b. A backflush costing system is often used in a JIT environment. Backflush costing eliminates the traditional sequential tracking of costs. Instead, entries to inventory may be delayed until as late as the end of the period.

1) For example, all product costs may be charged initially to cost of sales, and costs may be flushed back to the inventory accounts only at the end of the period. Thus, the detail of cost accounting is decreased.

7. Kanban

a. Another method of improving inventory flow is the kanban system, developed by the Toyota Motor Corporation (kanban is not characteristic of Japanese industry as a whole).

1) Kanban means ticket. Tickets (also described as cards or markers) control the flow of production or parts so that they are produced or obtained in the needed amounts at the needed times.

b. Kanban is essentially a visual workflow management system.

1) When a worker sees a kanban, it acts as authorization to release inventory to the next step. Work cannot move to the next stage until a kanban indicates that stage is ready for it.

2) A basic kanban system includes a withdrawal kanban that states the quantity that a later process should withdraw from its predecessor; a production kanban that states the output of the preceding process; and a vendor kanban that tells a vendor what, how much, where, and when to deliver.

8. MRP and MRP II

a. Materials requirements planning (MRP) is a computer-intensive system for driving raw materials through a production process according to a predetermined schedule.

1) MRP embodies the principle of dependent demand (also called derived demand; defined in item 1.b. in Study Unit 2, Subunit 10).

a) Demand-dependent goods are components of other goods. Their demand is driven by the demand for the final goods of which they are a part.

2) MRP is a push system; i.e., the demand for raw materials is driven by the forecasted demand for the final product as programmed into the system.

a) MRP, in effect, creates schedules of when items of inventory will be needed in the production departments.

b) If an outage of a given item is projected, the system automatically generates a purchase order on the proper date (considering lead times) so that deliveries will arrive on time.

3) MRP consists of three essential components:

a) The master production schedule (MPS) is a table of the projected demand for end products along with the dates they are needed.

b) The bill of materials (BOM) is a table of every component part required by every end product (and by every subassembly).

c) Perpetual inventory records must be employed to ensure that a true count of every component, subassembly, and finished good is available at all times.

   b.   Manufacturing resource planning (MRP II) does not replace an MRP system; it simply extends the scope.

   1)   Materials requirements planning is driven by programmed demand, regardless of capacity considerations or changes in the market for the end product.

   2)   Manufacturing resource planning adds a feedback loop (hence the designation of MRP II as a closed-loop system) to allow a manufacturer to take all these considerations into account.

Stop and review! You have completed the outline for this subunit. Study multiple-choice questions 23 through 28 beginning on page 247.

8.9 THE OPERATING CYCLE AND CASH CONVERSION CYCLE

   1.   **Inventory to Receivables to Cash**

   a.   A firm's **operating cycle** is the amount of time that passes between the acquisition of inventory and the collection of cash on the sale of that inventory.

Operating cycle = Days' sales in receivables + Days' sales in inventory

---

EXAMPLE

Current year: 23.9 days + 15.5 days = 39.4 days
Prior year: 28.7 days + 13.7 days = 42.4 days

The company has managed to slightly reduce its operating cycle, even while increasing sales and building inventories.

---

   b.   The following diagram depicts the phases of the operating cycle:

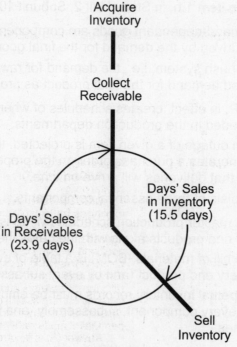

**Operating Cycle
39.4 Days**

Acquire
Inventory

Collect
Receivable

Days' Sales
in Inventory
(15.5 days)

Days' Sales
in Receivables
(23.9 days)

Sell
Inventory

Figure 8-7

2. **Cash Conversion Cycle**

a. A firm's cash conversion cycle is the amount of time that passes between the actual outlay of cash for inventory purchases and the collection of cash from the sale of that inventory.

Cash conversion cycle = Average collection period + Days' sales in inventory – Average payables period

1) The accounts payable turnover ratio is the number of times during a period that the firm pays its accounts payable.

$$Accounts\ payable\ turnover\ = \frac{Cost\ of\ goods\ sold}{Average\ balance\ in\ accounts\ payable}$$

2) The average payables period (also called payables turnover in days, or payables deferral period) is the average time between the purchase of inventories and the payment of cash.

$$Average\ payable\ period = \frac{Days\ in\ year}{Accounts\ payable\ turnover}$$

b. The difference between the operating cycle and the cash conversion cycle arises from the fact that the firm's purchases of inventory are made on credit. Thus, the cash conversion cycle is equal to the operating cycle minus the average payables period.

Stop and review! You have completed the outline for this subunit. Study multiple-choice question 29 on page 249.

8.10 MULTIPLE RATIO ANALYSIS

Some multiple-choice questions require the candidate to combine his/her knowledge of the different categories of ratios. This subunit consists entirely of such questions. Please review Subunits 8.2 and 8.7 before answering these questions.

Stop and review! You have completed the outline for this subunit. Study multiple-choice question 30 on page 249.

QUESTIONS

8.1 Working Capital Management

1. As a company becomes more conservative in its working capital policy, it tends to have a(n)

A. Decrease in its acid-test ratio.

B. Increase in the ratio of current liabilities to noncurrent liabilities.

C. Increase in the ratio of current assets to current liabilities.

D. Increase in funds invested in common stock and a decrease in funds invested in marketable securities.

Answer (C) is correct.
   REQUIRED: The effect of a more conservative working capital policy.
   DISCUSSION: A conservative working capital policy minimizes liquidity risk by increasing net working capital (current assets – current liabilities). The result is that the company forgoes the potentially higher returns available from using the additional working capital to acquire long-term assets. A conservative working capital policy is characterized by a higher current ratio (current assets ÷ current liabilities) and acid-test ratio (quick assets ÷ current liabilities). Thus, the company will increase current assets or decrease current liabilities. A conservative policy finances assets using long-term or permanent funds rather than short-term sources.
   Answer (A) is incorrect. A decrease in the acid-test ratio suggests an aggressive policy. A conservative company wants a higher acid-test ratio, that is, more liquid assets relative to liabilities. Answer (B) is incorrect. A conservative company wants working capital to be financed from long-term sources. Answer (D) is incorrect. A conservative company seeks more liquid (marketable) investments.

2. Which one of the following provides a spontaneous source of financing for a firm?

A. Accounts payable.

B. Mortgage bonds.

C. Accounts receivable.

D. Debentures.

Answer (A) is correct.
REQUIRED: The item that provides a spontaneous source of financing.
DISCUSSION: Trade credit is a spontaneous source of financing because it arises automatically as part of a purchase transaction. Because of its ease in use, trade credit is the largest source of short-term financing for many firms, both large and small.
Answer (B) is incorrect. Mortgage bonds and debentures do not arise automatically as a result of a purchase transaction. Answer (C) is incorrect. The use of receivables as a financing source requires an extensive factoring arrangement and often involves the creditor's evaluation of the credit ratings of the borrower's customers. Answer (D) is incorrect. Mortgage bonds and debentures do not arise automatically as a result of a purchase transaction.

3. Net working capital is the difference between

A. Current assets and current liabilities.

B. Fixed assets and fixed liabilities.

C. Total assets and total liabilities.

D. Shareholders' investment and cash.

Answer (A) is correct.
REQUIRED: The definition of net working capital.
DISCUSSION: Net working capital is defined by accountants as the difference between current assets and current liabilities. Working capital is a measure of liquidity.
Answer (B) is incorrect. Working capital refers to the difference between current assets and current liabilities; fixed assets are not a component. Answer (C) is incorrect. Total assets and total liabilities are not components of working capital; only current items are included. Answer (D) is incorrect. Shareholders' equity is not a component of working capital; only current items are included in the concept of working capital.

4. Determining the appropriate level of working capital for a firm requires

A. Changing the capital structure and dividend policy of the firm.

B. Maintaining short-term debt at the lowest possible level because it is generally more expensive than long-term debt.

C. Offsetting the benefit of current assets and current liabilities against the probability of technical insolvency.

D. Maintaining a high proportion of liquid assets to total assets in order to maximize the return on total investments.

Answer (C) is correct.
REQUIRED: The requirement for determining the appropriate level of working capital.
DISCUSSION: Working capital finance concerns the determination of the optimal level, mix, and use of current assets and current liabilities. The objective is to minimize the cost of maintaining liquidity while guarding against the possibility of technical insolvency. Technical insolvency is defined as the inability to pay debts as they come due.
Answer (A) is incorrect. Capital structure and dividends relate to capital structure finance, not working capital finance. Answer (B) is incorrect. Short-term debt is usually less expensive than long-term debt. Answer (D) is incorrect. Liquid assets do not ordinarily earn high returns relative to long-term assets, so holding the former will not maximize the return on total assets.

8.2 Liquidity Ratios -- Calculation

5. Given an acid-test ratio of 2.0, current assets of $5,000, and inventory of $2,000, the value of current liabilities is

A. $1,500

B. $2,500

C. $3,500

D. $6,000

Answer (A) is correct.
REQUIRED: The value of current liabilities given the acid-test ratio, current assets, and inventory.
DISCUSSION: The acid test or quick ratio equals the ratio of the quick assets (cash, net accounts receivable, and marketable securities) divided by current liabilities. Current assets equal the quick assets plus inventory and prepaid expenses. This question assumes that the entity has no prepaid expenses. Given current assets of $5,000, inventory of $2,000, and no prepaid expenses, the quick assets must be $3,000. Because the acid-test ratio is 2.0, the quick assets are double the current liabilities. Current liabilities therefore are equal to $1,500 ($3,000 quick assets ÷ 2.0).
Answer (B) is incorrect. Dividing the current assets by 2.0 results in $2,500. Current assets includes inventory, which should not be included in the calculation of the acid-test ratio. Answer (C) is incorrect. Adding inventory to current assets rather than subtracting it results in $3,500. Answer (D) is incorrect. Multiplying the quick assets by 2 instead of dividing by 2 results in $6,000.

Questions 6 through 8 are based on the following information.

Tosh Enterprises reported the following account information:

Accounts receivable	$400,000	Inventory	$800,000
Accounts payable	160,000	Land	500,000
Bonds payable, due in 10 years	600,000	Notes payable, due in 6 months	100,000
Cash	200,000	Prepaid expense	80,000
Interest payable, due in 3 months	20,000		

The company has a normal operating cycle of 6 months.

6. The current ratio for Tosh Enterprises is

A. 1.68

B. 2.14

C. 5.00

D. 5.29

Answer (D) is correct.
REQUIRED: The current ratio.
DISCUSSION: The current ratio equals current assets divided by current liabilities. Current assets consist of accounts receivable, cash, inventory, and prepaid expenses, a total of $1,480,000 ($400,000 + $200,000 + $800,000 + $80,000). Current liabilities consist of accounts payable, interest payable, and notes payable, a total of $280,000 ($160,000 + $20,000 + $100,000). Hence, the current ratio is 5.29 ($1,480,000 ÷ $280,000).
Answer (A) is incorrect. The figure of 1.68 includes long-term bonds payable among the current liabilities. Answer (B) is incorrect. The figure of 2.14 is the quick ratio. Answer (C) is incorrect. The figure of 5.00 excludes prepaid expenses from current assets.

7. What is Tosh Enterprises' quick (acid test) ratio?

A. 0.68

B. 1.68

C. 2.14

D. 2.31

Answer (C) is correct.
REQUIRED: The quick ratio.
DISCUSSION: The quick ratio equals quick assets divided by current liabilities. For Tosh, quick assets consist of cash ($200,000) and accounts receivable ($400,000), a total of $600,000. Current liabilities consist of accounts payable ($160,000), interest payable ($20,000), and notes payable ($100,000), a total of $280,000. Hence, the quick ratio is 2.14 ($600,000 ÷ $280,000).

8. Tosh Enterprises' amount of working capital is

A. $600,000

B. $1,120,000

C. $1,200,000

D. $1,220,000

Answer (C) is correct.
REQUIRED: The amount of working capital.
DISCUSSION: Working capital equals current assets minus current liabilities. For Tosh Enterprises, current assets consist of accounts receivable, cash, inventory, and prepaid expenses, a total of $1,480,000 ($400,000 + $200,000 + $800,000 + $80,000). Current liabilities consist of accounts payable, interest payable, and notes payable, a total of $280,000 ($160,000 + $20,000 + $100,000). Accordingly, working capital is $1,200,000 ($1,480,000 – $280,000).
Answer (A) is incorrect. The amount of $600,000 includes long-term bonds payable among the current liabilities.
Answer (B) is incorrect. The amount of $1,120,000 excludes prepaid expenses from current assets. Answer (D) is incorrect. The amount of $1,220,000 excludes interest payable from current liabilities.

8.3 Liquidity Ratios -- Effects of Transactions

9. Farrow Co. is applying for a loan in which the bank requires a quick ratio of at least 1. Farrow's quick ratio is 0.8. Which of the following actions would increase Farrow's quick ratio?

A. Purchasing inventory through the issuance of a long-term note.

B. Implementing stronger procedures to collect accounts receivable at a faster rate.

C. Paying an existing account payable.

D. Selling obsolete inventory at a loss.

Answer (D) is correct.
   REQUIRED: The action to increase the quick ratio.
   DISCUSSION: The quick (acid-test) ratio equals the sum of (1) cash and cash equivalents, (2) marketable securities, and (3) net receivables, divided by current liabilities. Inventory is not included in the numerator of the quick ratio. Receiving cash from the sale of inventory, even at a loss, increases quick assets without affecting current liabilities. The effect is to increase the quick ratio.
   Answer (A) is incorrect. Inventory and long-term liabilities are not included in the quick ratio calculation. Answer (B) is incorrect. Cash and accounts receivable are included in the numerator of the quick ratio. Exchanging one for the other has no net effect. Answer (C) is incorrect. When the quick ratio is less than 1, equal decreases in the numerator and denominator decrease the ratio.

10. Windham Company has current assets of $400,000 and current liabilities of $500,000. Windham Company's current ratio will be increased by

A. The purchase of $100,000 of inventory on account.

B. The payment of $100,000 of accounts payable.

C. The collection of $100,000 of accounts receivable.

D. Refinancing a $100,000 long-term loan with short-term debt.

Answer (A) is correct.
   REQUIRED: The transaction that will increase a current ratio of less than 1.0.
   DISCUSSION: The current ratio equals current assets divided by current liabilities. An equal increase in both the numerator and denominator of a current ratio less than 1.0 causes the ratio to increase. Windham Company's current ratio is .8 ($400,000 ÷ $500,000). The purchase of $100,000 of inventory on account would increase the current assets to $500,000 and the current liabilities to $600,000, resulting in a new current ratio of .83.
   Answer (B) is incorrect. This transaction decreases the current ratio. Answer (C) is incorrect. The current ratio would be unchanged. Answer (D) is incorrect. This transaction decreases the current ratio.

11. Peters Company has a 2-to-1 current ratio. This ratio would increase to more than 2 to 1 if

A. A previously declared stock dividend were distributed.

B. The company wrote off an uncollectible receivable.

C. The company sold merchandise on open account that earned a normal gross margin.

D. The company purchased inventory on open account.

Answer (C) is correct.
   REQUIRED: The transaction that would increase a current ratio that is greater than one.
   DISCUSSION: The current ratio is current assets divided by current liabilities. Thus, an increase in current assets or a decrease in current liabilities, by itself, increases the current ratio. The sale of inventory at a profit increases current assets without changing liabilities. Inventory decreases, and receivables increase by a greater amount. Thus, total current assets and the current ratio increase.
   Answer (A) is incorrect. The distribution of a stock dividend affects only stockholders' equity accounts (debit common stock dividend distributable and credit common stock). Answer (B) is incorrect. Writing off an uncollectible receivable does not affect total current assets. The allowance account absorbs the bad debt. Thus, the balance of net receivables is unchanged. Answer (D) is incorrect. The purchase of inventory increases current assets and current liabilities by the same amount. The transaction reduces a current ratio in excess of 1.0 since the numerator and denominator of the ratio increase by the same amount.

12. Rice, Inc., uses the allowance method to account for uncollectible accounts. An account receivable that was previously determined uncollectible and written off was collected during May. The effect of the collection on Rice's current ratio and total working capital is

	Current Ratio	Working Capital
A.	None	None
B.	Increase	Increase
C.	Decrease	Decrease
D.	None	Increase

Answer (A) is correct.

REQUIRED: The effect on the current ratio and working capital of collecting an account previously written off to the allowance account.

DISCUSSION: The entry to record this transaction is to debit receivables, credit the allowance, debit cash, and credit receivables. The result is to increase both an asset (cash) and a contra asset (allowance for bad debts). These appear in the current asset section of the balance sheet. Thus, the collection changes neither the current ratio nor working capital because the effects are offsetting. The credit for the journal entry is made to the allowance account on the assumption that another account will become uncollectible. The company had previously estimated its bad debts and established an appropriate allowance. It then (presumably) wrote off the wrong account. Accordingly, the journal entry reinstates a balance in the allowance account to absorb future uncollectibles.

8.4 Cash Management

13. A consultant recommends that a company hold funds for the following two reasons:

Reason #1: Cash needs can fluctuate substantially throughout the year.

Reason #2: Opportunities for buying at a discount may appear during the year.

The cash balances used to address the reasons given above are correctly classified as

	Reason #1	Reason #2
A.	Speculative balances	Speculative balances
B.	Speculative balances	Precautionary balances
C.	Precautionary balances	Speculative balances
D.	Precautionary balances	Precautionary balances

Answer (C) is correct.

REQUIRED: The correct classifications for the reasons for a firm to hold cash.

DISCUSSION: The three motives for holding cash are as a medium of exchange, as a precautionary measure, and for speculation. Reason #1 can be classified as a precautionary measure, and Reason #2 can be classified as holding cash for speculation.

Answer (A) is incorrect. Reason #1 is fulfilled by precautionary balances. Answer (B) is incorrect. This combination results from reversing the correct balances. Answer (D) is incorrect. Reason #2 is fulfilled by speculative balances.

14. A lockbox system

A. Reduces the need for compensating balances.

B. Provides security for late night deposits.

C. Reduces the risk of having checks lost in the mail.

D. Accelerates the inflow of funds.

Answer (D) is correct.

REQUIRED: The true statement about a lockbox system.

DISCUSSION: A lockbox system is one strategy for expediting the receipt of funds. Customers submit their payments to a mailbox controlled by the bank rather than to the company's offices. Bank personnel remove the envelopes from the mailbox and deposit the checks to the company's account immediately. The remittance advices must then be transported to the company for entry into the accounts receivable system. The bank generally charges a flat monthly fee for this service.

Answer (A) is incorrect. A lockbox system is not related to compensating balances; a compensating balance may be required by a covenant in a loan agreement that requires a company to maintain a specified balance during the term of the loan. Answer (B) is incorrect. A lockbox system is a process by which payments are sent to a bank's mailbox, which is checked during normal post office hours. Answer (C) is incorrect. The use of a lockbox system entails sending checks through the mail to a post office box. Thus, it does not reduce the risk of losing checks in the mail.

15. A working capital technique that delays the outflow of cash is

    A. Factoring.

    B. A draft.

    C. A lockbox system.

    D. Electronic funds transfer.

Answer (B) is correct.

    REQUIRED: The working capital technique that delays the outflow of cash.

    DISCUSSION: A draft is a three-party instrument in which one person (the drawer) orders a second person (the drawee) to pay money to a third person (the payee). A check is the most common form of draft. It is an instrument payable on demand in which the drawee is a bank. Consequently, a draft can be used to delay the outflow of cash. A draft can be dated on the due date of an invoice and will not be processed by the drawee until that date, thereby eliminating the necessity of writing a check earlier than the due date or using an EFT. Thus, the outflow is delayed until the check clears the drawee bank.

    Answer (A) is incorrect. Factoring is the sale of receivables and therefore concerns cash inflows, not outflows. Answer (C) is incorrect. A lockbox system is a means of accelerating cash inflows. Answer (D) is incorrect. An electronic funds transfer results in an immediate deduction from the payor's bank account, thereby eliminating float.

8.5 Marketable Securities Management

16. When managing cash and short-term investments, a corporate CFO is primarily concerned with

    A. Maximizing rate of return.

    B. Minimizing taxes.

    C. Investing in Treasury bonds since they have no default risk.

    D. Liquidity and safety.

Answer (D) is correct.

    REQUIRED: The primary concern when managing cash and short-term investments.

    DISCUSSION: Cash and short-term investments are crucial to a firm's continuing success. Sufficient liquidity must be available to meet payments as they come due. At the same time, liquid assets are subject to significant control risk. Therefore, liquidity and safety are the primary concerns of the treasurer when dealing with highly liquid assets. Cash and short-term investments are held because of their ability to facilitate routine operations of the company. These assets are not held for purposes of achieving investment returns.

    Answer (A) is incorrect. Most companies are not in business to earn high returns on liquid assets (i.e., they are held to facilitate operations). Answer (B) is incorrect. The holding of cash and cash-like assets is not a major factor in controlling taxes. Answer (C) is incorrect. Investments in Treasury bonds do not have sufficient liquidity to serve as short-term assets.

17. All of the following are alternative marketable securities suitable for short-term investment **except**

    A. U.S. Treasury bills.

    B. Eurodollars.

    C. Commercial paper.

    D. Convertible bonds.

Answer (D) is correct.

    REQUIRED: The item that is not a marketable security.

    DISCUSSION: Marketable securities are near-cash items used primarily for short-term investment. Examples include U.S. Treasury bills, Eurodollars, commercial paper, money-market mutual funds with portfolios of short-term securities, bankers' acceptances, floating rate preferred stock, and negotiable CDs of U.S. banks. A convertible bond is not a short-term investment because its maturity date is usually more than 1 year in the future and its price can be influenced substantially by changes in interest rates or by changes in the investee's stock price.

8.6 Receivables Management

Question 18 is based on the following information.
The following inventory and sales data are available
for the current year for Volpone Company. Volpone
uses a 365-day year when computing ratios.

	November 30, Year 2	November 30, Year 1
Net credit sales	$6,205,000	
Gross receivables	350,000	320,000
Inventory	960,000	780,000
Cost of goods sold	4,380,000	

18. Volpone Company's average number of days to
collect accounts receivable for Year 2 is

A. 18.82

B. 19.43

C. 19.71

D. 20.59

Answer (C) is correct.
REQUIRED: The average collection period.
DISCUSSION: The average collection period equals
365 days divided by the receivables turnover (net credit sales ÷
average accounts receivable). Turnover is 18.52 times
{$6,205,000 sales ÷ [($350,000 + $320,000) ÷ 2]}. Hence, the
average collection period is 19.71 days (365 ÷ 18.52).
Answer (A) is incorrect. The number of 18.82 days is based
on receivables of $320,000. Answer (B) is incorrect. The
number of 19.43 days is based on a 360-day year. Answer (D) is
incorrect. The number 20.59 days is based on receivables of
$350,000.

19. Yonder Motors sells 20,000 automobiles per
year on credit for $25,000 each. The firm's average
receivables are $30,000,000 and average inventory is
$40,000,000. Yonder's average collection period is
closest to which one of the following? Assume a
365-day year.

A. 17 days.

B. 22 days.

C. 29 days.

D. 61 days.

Answer (B) is correct.
REQUIRED: The average collection period given relevant
data.
DISCUSSION: The average collection period, also called
the days' sales outstanding in receivables, is calculated as the
number of days in the year over the receivables turnover ratio.
Yonder's can thus be calculated as follows:

Average collection = Days in year ÷ Accounts receivable
period turnover
= 365 ÷ (Net credit sales ÷ Average net
receivables)
= 365 ÷ [(20,000 × $25,000) ÷
$30,000,000]
= 365 ÷ ($500,000,000 ÷ $30,000,000)
= 365 ÷ 16.667
= 21.9 days

Answer (A) is incorrect. The figure results from improperly
using the turnover rate (16.667) as the number of days.
Answer (C) is incorrect. This figure results from improperly using
average inventory instead of average receivables. Answer (D) is
incorrect. This figure results from improperly adding together the
average collection period and the average number of days that
inventory is held.

20. Green, Inc., a financial investment-consulting
firm, was engaged by Maple Corp. to provide
technical support for making investment decisions.
Maple, a manufacturer of ceramic tiles, was in the
process of buying Bay, Inc., its prime competitor.
Green's financial analyst made an independent
detailed analysis of Bay's average collection period to
determine which of the following?

A. Financing.

B. Return on equity.

C. Liquidity.

D. Operating profitability.

Answer (C) is correct.
REQUIRED: The item determined by an analysis of the
average collection period.
DISCUSSION: Liquidity is a firm's ability to pay its current
obligations as they come due. The average collection period is
the average number of days between the time of a sale and the
receipt of the invoice amount. Thus, the average collection
period is an asset management ratio measuring an entity's use of
assets to generate cash flows. It indicates when proceeds from
sales are available to pay debts.
Answer (A) is incorrect. Financing relates to the firm's use of
debt and equity to obtain resources. Answer (B) is incorrect.
Return on equity is a profitability ratio, not an asset management
ratio. Answer (D) is incorrect. The average collection period
measures the efficiency of receivables management and the
availability of cash, not operating profitability.

8.7 Inventory Management -- Ratios

Question 21 is based on the following information.

Lisa, Inc.
Statement of Financial Position
December 31, Year 2
(in thousands)

Assets	Year 2	Year 1
Current assets:		
Cash	$ 30	$ 25
Trading securities	20	15
Accounts receivable (net)	45	30
Inventories (at lower of cost or market)	60	50
Prepaid items	15	20
Total current assets	170	140
Long-term investments:		
Securities (at cost)	25	20
Property, plant, & equipment:		
Land (at cost)	75	75
Building (net)	80	90
Equipment (net)	95	100
Intangible assets		
Patents (net)	35	17
Goodwill (net)	20	13
Total long-term assets	330	315
Total assets	$500	$455
Liabilities & shareholders' equity		
Current liabilities:		
Notes payable	$ 23	$ 12
Accounts payable	47	28
Accrued interest	15	15
Total current liabilities	85	55
Long-term debt:		
Notes payable 10% due 12/31/Year 9	10	10
Bonds payable 12% due 12/31/Year 8	15	15
Total long-term debt	25	25
Total liabilities	$110	$ 80
Shareholders' equity:		
Preferred -- 5% cumulative, $100 par, non-participating, 1,000 shares authorized, issued and outstanding	$100	$100
Common -- $10 par 20,000 shares authorized, 15,000 issued and outstanding shares	150	150
Additional paid-in capital - common	75	75
Retained earnings	65	50
Total shareholders' equity	$390	$375
Total liabilities & equity	$500	$455

21. Assume sales and cost of goods sold for Year 2 were $300,000 and $220,000, respectively. Lisa, Inc.'s inventory turnover for Year 2 was

A. 3.7 times.

B. 4.0 times.

C. 4.4 times.

D. 5.0 times.

Answer (B) is correct.

REQUIRED: The inventory turnover.

DISCUSSION: The inventory turnover is computed by dividing cost of goods sold by the average balance in inventory. Consequently, the turnover is 4 times {$220,000 ÷ [($60,000 + $50,000) ÷ 2]}.

Answer (A) is incorrect. This ratio is based on the ending inventory. Answer (C) is incorrect. This ratio is based on the beginning inventory. Answer (D) is incorrect. Sales divided by ending inventory equal 5.0.

Question 22 is based on the following information. The following inventory and sales data are available for the current year for Volpone Company. Volpone uses a 365-day year when computing ratios.

	November 30, Year 2	November 30, Year 1
Net credit sales	$6,205,000	
Gross receivables	350,000	320,000
Inventory	960,000	780,000
Cost of goods sold	4,380,000	

22. Volpone Company's average number of days to sell inventory for Year 2 is

A. 51.18

B. 65.00

C. 71.51

D. 72.56

Answer (D) is correct.
    REQUIRED: The average days to sell inventory.
    DISCUSSION: The average days to sell inventory equals 365 days divided by the inventory turnover (cost of goods sold ÷ average inventory). Thus, turnover is 5.03 times {$4,380,000 COGS ÷ [($960,000 + $780,000) ÷ 2]}. Average days to sell inventory is 72.56 days (365 ÷ 5.03).
    Answer (A) is incorrect. The number of 51.18 days is based on sales, not cost of sales. Sales are recorded at retail prices. Answer (B) is incorrect. The number of 65.00 days is based on the beginning inventory. Answer (C) is incorrect. The number of 71.51 days is based on a 360-day year, not a 365-day year.

8.8 Inventory Management -- Techniques

23. The Stewart Co. uses the economic order quantity (EOQ) model for inventory management. A decrease in which one of the following variables would increase the EOQ?

A. Annual sales.

B. Cost per order.

C. Safety stock level.

D. Carrying costs.

Answer (D) is correct.
    REQUIRED: The variable for which a decrease will lead to an increase in the economic order quantity (EOQ).
    DISCUSSION: The EOQ model minimizes the total of ordering and carrying costs. The EOQ is calculated as follows:

$$\sqrt{\frac{2 \times Periodic\ demand \times Ordering\ costs\ per\ order}{Carrying\ costs\ per\ unit}}$$

Increases in the numerator (demand or ordering costs) will increase the EOQ, whereas decreases in demand or ordering costs will decrease the EOQ. Inversely, a decrease in the denominator (carrying costs) will increase the EOQ.
    Answer (A) is incorrect. A decrease in demand (annual sales), which is in the numerator, will decrease the EOQ. Answer (B) is incorrect. A decrease in ordering costs, which is in the numerator, will encourage more orders, or a decrease in the EOQ. Answer (C) is incorrect. A decrease in safety stock levels will not affect the EOQ, although it might lead to a different ordering point.

24. Which of the following assumptions is associated with the economic order quantity formula?

A. The carrying cost per unit will vary with quantity ordered.

B. The cost of placing an order will vary with quantity ordered.

C. Periodic demand is known.

D. The purchase cost per unit will vary based on quantity discounts.

Answer (C) is correct.
    REQUIRED: The assumption associated with the economic order quantity formula.
    DISCUSSION: The economic order quantity (EOQ) model is a mathematical tool for determining the order quantity that minimizes the sum of ordering costs and carrying costs. The following assumptions underlay the EOQ model: (1) Demand is uniform, (2) order (setup) costs and carrying costs are constant, and (3) no quantity discounts are allowed.
    Answer (A) is incorrect. An assumption of the EOQ model is that the carrying cost per unit is constant. Answer (B) is incorrect. The cost of placing an order is constant when using the EOQ formula. Answer (D) is incorrect. An assumption of the EOQ model is that no quantity discounts are allowed.

25. In inventory management, the safety stock will tend to increase if the

    A. Carrying cost increases.

    B. Cost of running out of stock decreases.

    C. Variability of the lead time increases.

    D. Variability of the usage rate decreases.

Answer (C) is correct.
    REQUIRED: The factor that will cause safety stocks to increase.
    DISCUSSION: A company maintains safety stocks to protect itself against the losses caused by stockouts. These can take the form of lost sales or lost production time. Safety stock is necessary because of the variability in lead time and usage rates. As the variability in lead time increases, a company will tend to carry larger safety stocks.
    Answer (A) is incorrect. An increase in inventory carrying costs makes it less economical to carry safety stocks. Answer (B) is incorrect. If the cost of stockouts declines, the incentive to carry large safety stocks is reduced. Answer (D) is incorrect. A decline in the variability of usage makes it easier to plan orders, and safety stocks will be less necessary.

26. A company serves as a distributor of products by ordering finished products once a quarter and using that inventory to accommodate the demand over the quarter. If it plans to ease its credit policy for customers, the amount of products ordered for its inventory every quarter will be

    A. Increased to accommodate higher sales levels.

    B. Reduced to offset the increased cost of carrying accounts receivable.

    C. Unaffected if safety stock is part of the current quarterly order.

    D. Unaffected if the JIT inventory control system is used.

Answer (A) is correct.
    REQUIRED: The effect on the quantity of products ordered as a result of relaxing the credit policy.
    DISCUSSION: Relaxing the credit policy for customers will lead to increased sales because more people will be eligible for more credit. As sales increase, the amount ordered on each purchase order will increase to accommodate the higher sales levels.
    Answer (B) is incorrect. Inventory should be increased to accommodate higher sales levels. Answer (C) is incorrect. Safety stock is based on expected sales, which are expected to rise. Answer (D) is incorrect. A just-in-time system is not used when a company orders inventory once a quarter.

27. In Belk Co.'s just-in-time production system, costs per setup were reduced from $28 to $2. In the process of reducing inventory levels, Belk found that there were fixed facility and administrative costs that previously had not been included in the carrying cost calculation. The result was an increase from $8 to $32 per unit per year. What were the effects of these changes on Belk's economic lot size and relevant costs?

	Lot Size	Relevant Costs
A.	Decrease	Increase
B.	Increase	Decrease
C.	Increase	Increase
D.	Decrease	Decrease

Answer (D) is correct.
    REQUIRED: The effect of a JIT production system on economic lot size and relevant costs.
    DISCUSSION: The economic lot size for a production system is similar to the EOQ. For example, the cost per setup is equivalent to the cost per order (a numerator value in the EOQ model). Hence, a reduction in the setup costs reduces the economic lot size as well as the relevant costs. The fixed facility and administrative costs, however, are not relevant. The EOQ model includes variable costs only.

28. Bell Co. changed from a traditional manufacturing philosophy to a just-in-time philosophy. What are the expected effects of this change on Bell's inventory turnover and inventory as a percentage of total assets reported on Bell's balance sheet?

	Inventory Turnover	Inventory Percentage
A.	Decrease	Decrease
B.	Decrease	Increase
C.	Increase	Decrease
D.	Increase	Increase

Answer (C) is correct.
    REQUIRED: The expected effects of changing to JIT.
    DISCUSSION: A JIT system is intended to minimize inventory. Inventory should be delivered or produced just in time to be used. Thus, JIT increases inventory turnover (cost of sales ÷ average inventory) and decreases inventory as a percentage of total assets.
    Answer (A) is incorrect. Changing to JIT will result in increased inventory turnover. Answer (B) is incorrect. Changing to JIT will increase inventory turnover and decrease inventory as a percentage of total assets. Answer (D) is incorrect. One of JIT's advantages is less stored raw materials inventory, resulting in decreased inventory as a percentage of total assets.

8.9 The Operating Cycle and Cash Conversion Cycle

29. To determine the operating cycle for a retail department store, which one of the following pairs of items is needed?

A. Days' sales in accounts receivable and average merchandise inventory.

B. Cash turnover and net sales.

C. Accounts receivable turnover and inventory turnover.

D. Asset turnover and return on sales.

Answer (C) is correct.

REQUIRED: The pair of items needed to determine the operating cycle for a retailer.

DISCUSSION: The operating cycle is the time needed to turn cash into inventory, inventory into receivables, and receivables back into cash. For a retailer, it is the time from purchase of inventory to collection of cash. Thus, the operating cycle of a retailer is equal to the sum of the number of days' sales in inventory and the number of days' sales in receivables. Inventory turnover equals cost of goods sold divided by average inventory. The days' sales in inventory equals 365 (or another period chosen by the analyst) divided by the inventory turnover. Accounts receivable turnover equals net credit sales divided by average receivables. The days' sales in receivables equals 365 (or other number) divided by the accounts receivable turnover.

Answer (A) is incorrect. Cost of sales must be known to calculate days' sales in inventory. Answer (B) is incorrect. These items are insufficient to permit determination of the operating cycle. Answer (D) is incorrect. These items are insufficient to permit determination of the operating cycle.

8.10 Multiple Ratio Analysis

30. Which of the following ratios is(are) useful in assessing a company's ability to meet currently maturing or short-term obligations?

	Acid-Test Ratio	Debt-to-Equity Ratio
A.	No	No
B.	No	Yes
C.	Yes	Yes
D.	Yes	No

Answer (D) is correct.

REQUIRED: The ratio(s) useful in assessing a company's ability to meet currently maturing obligations.

DISCUSSION: Liquidity ratios measure the ability of a company to meet its short-term obligations. A commonly used liquidity ratio is the acid-test, or quick, ratio, which equals quick assets (net accounts receivable, current marketable securities, and cash) divided by current liabilities. The debt-to-equity ratio is a leverage ratio. Leverage ratios measure the impact of debt on profitability and risk.

Answer (A) is incorrect. The acid-test ratio is useful in assessing a company's ability to meet currently maturing or short-term obligations. Answer (B) is incorrect. The acid-test ratio is useful in assessing a company's ability to meet currently maturing or short-term obligations, but the debt-to-equity ratio does not exclude long-term obligations. Answer (C) is incorrect. The debt-to-equity ratio includes long-term obligations.

Use the additional questions in Gleim **CPA Test Prep Online** to create Test Sessions that emulate Prometric!

8.11 PRACTICE WRITTEN COMMUNICATION TASK

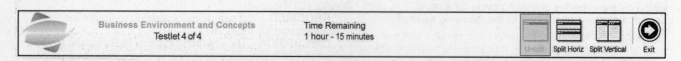

DIRECTIONS

Note: If you believe you have encountered a software malfunction, report it to the test center staff immediately.

Navigation

To navigate from task to task, use the controls at the bottom of the screen. Click on the **Next** button to advance to the next task, or the **Previous** button to go to the previous task. To go directly to any task, click on its number.

If you would like a reminder to revisit a task, or want to indicate that you are finished with it, click on the reminder flag below the task number. To clear the flag, click on it again. Reminder flags are for your use only – they do not contribute to your score.

Tabs

In this part of the examination, you will be asked to complete various tasks. Every task has one or more **Work Tabs**. Every task also has a **Help** tab.

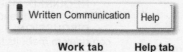

Work tab   Help tab

Work Tabs:

- **Work Tabs** are identified with a pencil icon. This is where your responses are expected.
- Each task has one or more **Work Tabs**.
- **Work Tabs** contain directions for completing the task - be sure to read these directions carefully.
- The **Work Tab** name in the example above is for illustration only - yours will differ.
- You must complete all of the **Work Tabs** in each task to receive full credit.

Help Tab:

- The **Help Tab** provides assistance with the exam software that is used in this task. For example, if the task is to compose a memorandum, **Help** will provide information about the word processor.

The Toolbar

The toolbar at the top of the screen shows the amount of time remaining for you to complete the tasks. In addition, the following tools are available. Note that only the **Exit** button is displayed when Directions are visible - the others will appear when you begin the tasks.

Click on these buttons to split or unsplit the screen. You can split the screen vertically or horizontally.

Click on this button to go on to the next part of the examination. You must complete all of the tasks to receive full credit. Once you click on **Exit** and confirm the action, you will NOT be able to return to this testlet.

Written Communication | Help

Cut Copy Paste Undo Redo

Clara Cleanup, LLC, is a local maid service that has begun experiencing liquidity problems. The owners have come to you for advice and, during your study of their financial operations, you discovered that they were unfamiliar with the principles of sound cash management. One of the owners even suggested they could sell some of their equipment to pay bills, then replace it when their cash flow improved.

Prepare a memo to the owners of Clara Cleanup explaining the concept of working capital, the difference between temporary and permanent working capital, and the various working capital policies.

Type your communication below the line in the response area below.

REMINDER: Your response will be graded for both technical content and writing skills. Technical content will be evaluated for information that is helpful to the intended reader and clearly relevant to the issue. Writing skills will be evaluated for development, organization, and the appropriate expression of ideas in professional correspondence. Use a standard business memorandum or letter format with a clear beginning, middle, and end. Do not convey information in the form of a table, bullet point list, or other abbreviated presentation.

To: Clara Cleanup, LLC
Re: Working capital policy

= Reminder   Directions   1   ◀ Previous   Next ▶

Unofficial Answer

Written Communication

To: Clara Cleanup, LLC
Re: Working capital policy

Working capital is the excess of current assets over current liabilities. Trying to apply a simple rule such as "current assets should be financed with current liabilities" is not appropriate to the practice of working capital management. Some level of liquid current assets must be maintained to meet the firm's long-term minimum needs regardless of the firm's level of activity or profitability. This is termed permanent working capital. As the firm's needs for current assets change on a seasonal basis, temporary working capital is increased and decreased.

Spontaneous financing is the amount of current liabilities, such as trade payables and accruals, that arises naturally in the ordinary course of business without the firm's financial managers needing to take deliberate action. However, the firm's temporary working capital usually cannot be financed only by spontaneous financing. Therefore, the firm must decide whether to finance it with short-term or long-term financing.

Ideally, a firm would be able to offset each element of its temporary working capital with a short-term liability of similar maturity. For example, a short-term loan could be taken out as the winter season approached and repaid with the collections made from holiday sales. This ideal situation is termed the maturity matching, or hedging, approach. It is rarely achievable in practice due to uncertainty.

A firm that adopts a conservative financing policy seeks to minimize liquidity risk by financing its temporary working capital mostly with long-term debt. This approach takes advantage of the certainty inherent in long-term debt.

An aggressive financing policy involves reducing liquidity and accepting a higher risk of short-term cash flow problems in an effort to increase profitability. This approach avoids the incurrence of the opportunity cost of funds tied up by the conservative policy, but it runs the risk of either unexpectedly high interest rates or even the total unavailability of financing in the short run.

The above depicts a Level 5 answer. See page 16 in the Introduction for a description of the three grading criteria.

Self-Grade

Evaluate each of the following by selecting a 0, 1, 2, 3, 4, or 5. An average response is 3. Use 4 for better than average and 5 for outstanding. Use 2 for less than average and 1 for quite poor. Use zero for no response, if you did not address the topic, or if you gave advice that is clearly illegal.

Organization	o 0	o 1	o 2	o 3	o 4	o 5
Development	o 0	o 1	o 2	o 3	o 4	o 5
Expression	o 0	o 1	o 2	o 3	o 4	o 5

Your grade for the written communication as a whole is the average of the scores for the three criteria.

Use **CPA Gleim Online** and **Simulation Wizard** to practice more written communication tasks in a realistic environment.

STUDY UNIT NINE
SHORT-TERM FINANCING
AND CAPITAL BUDGETING I

(11 pages of outline)

All entities require financing from outside sources to carry on day-to-day operations. These usually take the form of either spontaneous financing in the form of trade credit offered by vendors, or bank loans. Organizations must continually decide whether to invest in new product lines or means of production. The process involves identifying appropriate projects, determining the level of resources they will require, predicting the expected amounts and timing of returns, and ranking the desirability of alternative projects.

9.1 TYPES AND COSTS OF SHORT-TERM FINANCING

1. **Spontaneous Financing -- Trade Credit**

    a. If a supplier offers an early payment discount (e.g., terms of 2/10, n/30, meaning a 2% discount is given if the invoice is paid within 10 days or the entire balance is due in 30 days), it is usually to the entity's advantage to avail itself of the discount. The annualized cost of not taking a discount can be calculated with the following formula:

    Cost of Not Taking a Discount

    $$\frac{Discount\ \%}{100\% - Discount\ \%} \times \frac{Days\ in\ year}{Total\ payment\ period - Discount\ period}$$

    ### EXAMPLE

    A vendor has delivered goods and invoiced the company on terms of 2/10, net 30. The company has chosen to pay on day 30. The effective annual rate the company paid by forgoing the discount is calculated as follows (using a 360-day year):

    Cost of not taking discount = [2% ÷ (100% − 2%)] × [360 days ÷ (30 days − 10 days)]
    = (2% ÷ 98%) × (360 days ÷ 20 days)
    = 2.0408% × 18
    = 36.73%

    Only entities in dire cash flow situations would incur a 36.73% cost of funds.

    ---

2. **Formal Financing Arrangements**

    a. Commercial banks offer short-term financing in the form of term loans and lines of credit.

        1) A **term loan**, such as a note, must be repaid by a definite time.

        2) A **line of credit** allows the company to continuously reborrow amounts up to a certain ceiling, as long as certain minimum payments are made each month (similar to a consumer's credit card).

3. Simple Interest Short-Term Loans

a. A simple interest loan is one in which the interest is paid at the end of the loan term. The amount of interest to be paid is based on the nominal (stated) rate and the principal of the loan (amount needed).

$$Interest\ expense = Principal\ of\ loan \times Stated\ rate$$

> ### EXAMPLE
>
> A company obtained a short-term bank loan of $15,000 at an annual interest rate of 8%. The interest expense on the loan is $1,200 ($150,000 × 8%).
>
> The stated rate of 8% is also the effective rate.

b. The **effective rate** on any financing arrangement is the ratio of the amount the company must pay to the amount the company gets use of.

$$Effective\ interest\ rate = \frac{Interest\ expense\ (interest\ to\ be\ paid)}{Usable\ funds\ (net\ proceeds)}$$

> ### EXAMPLE
>
> A company obtained a short-term bank loan of $15,000 at an annual interest rate of 8%. The bank charges a loan origination fee of $500.
>
> $$\begin{aligned} Effective\ rate\ &= Interest\ paid \div Net\ proceeds \\ &= (\$15,000 \times 8\%) \div (\$15,000 - \$500) \\ &= \$1,200 \div \$14,500 \\ &= 8.27\% \end{aligned}$$
>
> The effective interest rate (8.27%) is higher than the stated interest rate (8%) because the net proceeds are lower than the principal.

4. Discounted Loans

a. A discounted loan is one in which the interest and finance charges are paid at the beginning of the loan term.

$$Total\ borrowings = \frac{Amount\ needed}{(1.0 - Stated\ rate)}$$

> ### EXAMPLE
>
> A company needs to pay a $90,000 invoice. Its bank has offered to extend this amount at an 8% nominal rate on a discounted basis.
>
> $$\begin{aligned} Total\ borrowings\ &= Amount\ needed \div (1.0 - Stated\ rate) \\ &= \$90,000 \div (100\% - 8\%) \\ &= \$90,000 \div 92\% \\ &= \$97,826 \end{aligned}$$

b. Because the borrower gets the use of a smaller amount, the effective rate on a discounted loan is higher than its nominal rate.

> ### EXAMPLE
>
> $$\begin{aligned} Effective\ rate\ &= Net\ interest\ expense\ (annualized) \div Usable\ funds \\ &= (\$97,826 \times 8\%) \div \$90,000 \\ &= \$7,826 \div \$90,000 \\ &= 8.696\% \end{aligned}$$

c. As with all financing arrangements, the effective rate can be calculated without reference to dollar amounts.

$$\text{Effective rate on discounted loan} = \frac{\textit{Stated rate}}{(1.0 - \textit{Stated rate})}$$

EXAMPLE

The entity calculates the effective rate on this loan without using dollar amounts.

$$
\begin{aligned}
\text{Effective rate} &= \text{Stated rate} \div (1.0 - \text{Stated rate}) \\
&= 8\% \div (100\% - 8\%) \\
&= 8\% \div 92\% \\
&= 8.696\%
\end{aligned}
$$

---

5. **Loans with Compensating Balances**

a. To reduce risk, banks sometimes require borrowers to maintain a compensating balance during the term of a financing arrangement.

$$\text{Total borrowings} = \frac{\textit{Amount needed}}{(1.0 - \textit{Compensating balance} \%)}$$

EXAMPLE

A company has received an invoice for $120,000 with terms of 2/10, net 30. The entity's bank will lend it the necessary amount for 20 days so the discount can be taken on the 10th day at a nominal annual rate of 6% with a compensating balance of 10%.

$$
\begin{aligned}
\text{Total borrowings} &= \text{Amount needed} \div (1.0 - \text{Compensated balance} \%) \\
&= (\$120{,}000 \times 98\%) \div (100\% - 10\%) \\
&= \$117{,}600 \div 90\% \\
&= \$130{,}667
\end{aligned}
$$

---

b. As with a discounted loan, the borrower has access to a smaller amount than the face amount of the loan and so pays an effective rate higher than the nominal rate.

EXAMPLE

$$
\begin{aligned}
\text{Effective rate} &= \text{Net interest expense (annualized)} \div \text{Usable funds} \\
&= (\$130{,}667 \times 6\%) \div \$117{,}600 \\
&= \$7{,}840 \div \$117{,}600 \\
&= 6.667\%
\end{aligned}
$$

---

c. Once again, the dollar amounts involved are not needed to determine the effective rate.

$$\text{Effective rate with comp. balance} = \frac{\textit{Stated rate}}{(1.0 - \textit{Compensating balance} \%)}$$

EXAMPLE

$$
\begin{aligned}
\text{Effective rate} &= \text{Stated rate} \div (1.0 - \text{Compensating balance} \%) \\
&= 6\% \div (100\% - 10\%) \\
&= 6\% \div 90\% \\
&= 6.667\%
\end{aligned}
$$

Stop and review! You have completed the outline for this subunit. Study multiple-choice questions 1 through 5 beginning on page 264.

9.2 CAPITAL BUDGETING -- BASICS

1. **Capital Budgeting**

   a. Capital budgeting is the process of planning and controlling investments for long-term projects. It is the long-term aspect of capital budgeting that presents the accountant with specific challenges.

       1) Most financial and management accounting topics, such as calculating allowance for doubtful accounts or accumulating product costs, concern tracking and reporting activity for a single accounting or reporting cycle, such as 1 month or 1 year.

       2) By their nature, capital projects affect multiple accounting periods and will constrain the organization's financial planning well into the future. Once made, capital budgeting decisions tend to be relatively inflexible.

   b. A capital project usually involves substantial expenditures. Planning is crucial because of uncertainties about capital markets, inflation, interest rates, and the money supply.

   c. Capital budgeting applications include

       1) Buying equipment
       2) Building facilities
       3) Acquiring a business
       4) Developing a product or product line
       5) Expanding into new markets
       6) Replacement of equipment

2. **Relevant Cash Flows**

   a. The first step in assessing the desirability of a potential capital project is to identify the relevant cash flows.

       1) Relevant cash flows do not include sunk costs, i.e., those that have already been paid or are irrevocably committed to be paid. No matter which alternative is selected, sunk costs are already spent and are thus irrelevant to a decision.

   b. The relevant cash flows for capital budgeting are

       1) Cost of new equipment
       2) Annual after-tax cash savings or inflows
       3) Proceeds from disposal of old equipment/residual (salvage) value
       4) Adjustment for depreciation expense on new equipment (called the depreciation tax shield) since it reduces taxable income and thereby reduces cash outflow for tax expense

---

EXAMPLE

A company's annual recurring operating cash income from a new machine is $100,000. The annual depreciation expense on this machine is $20,000. The effective tax rate is 40%. To calculate the company's after-tax annual cash flows from the new machine, the annual depreciation expense must be taken into account.

Operating cash inflow	$100,000	Taxable income	$80,000
Depreciation expense	(20,000)	Effective tax rate	× 40%
Annual taxable income	$ 80,000	Income tax payment	$32,000
Operating cash inflow	$100,000		
Income tax payment	(32,000)		
After-tax cash flow	$ 68,000		

After-tax cash flow can also be calculated as follows:

Operating cash flow net of taxes [$100,000 × (1.0 − .40)]	$60,000
Depreciation tax shield [$20,000 × 40%]	8,000
Annual after-tax cash flow	$68,000

Note: Depreciation expense affects cash inflow only through income tax considerations.

3. **Accounting Rate of Return**

    a.   The accounting rate of return is a technique for assessing potential capital projects that ignores the time value of money.

$$\text{Accounting rate of return} = \frac{\text{Annual increase in GAAP net income}}{\text{Required investment}} = \frac{\text{Annual cash inflow} - \text{Depreciation}}{\text{Initial investment}}$$

        1)   Shareholders and financial analysts prefer the accounting rate of return because GAAP-based numbers are readily available.

EXAMPLE

A manufacturer is considering the purchase of a new piece of machinery that would cost $250,000 and would decrease annual after-tax cash costs by $40,000. The machine is expected to have a 10-year useful life, no salvage value, and would be depreciated on the straight-line basis. The firm calculates the accounting rate of return on this machine as follows:

Annual cash savings	$ 40,000
Less: annual depreciation expense ($250,000 ÷ 10 years)	(25,000)
Annual increase in accounting net income	$ 15,000
Divided by: purchase price of new equipment	÷ 250,000
Accounting rate of return	6%

---

        2)   However, certain aspects of the accounting rate of return create definite limitations on its usefulness as a guide to selecting capital projects.

    b.   Accounting rate of return is affected by the company's choices of accounting methods.

        1)   Accountants must choose which expenditures to capitalize versus which to expense immediately. They also choose how quickly to depreciate capitalized assets.

        2)   A project's true rate of return cannot be dependent on such bookkeeping decisions.

    c.   Another distortion inherent in comparing a single project's book rate of return to the current one for the company as a whole is that the latter is an average of all of an entity's capital projects.

        1)   It reveals nothing about the performance of individual investment choices. Embedded in that number may be a handful of good projects making up for a large number of poor investments.

The AICPA has tested accounting (book) rate of return by asking for its calculation. Questions have also asked for the components that make up the accounting rate of return.

Stop and review! You have completed the outline for this subunit. Study multiple-choice questions 6 through 9 beginning on page 265.

9.3 CAPITAL BUDGETING -- NET PRESENT VALUE THEORY

1. **Discounted Cash Flow Analysis**

   a. A far more sophisticated method for evaluating potential capital projects than accounting rate of return is discounted cash flow analysis, which involves discounting the relevant cash flows (listed in item 2.b. in Subunit 9.2) using the required rate of return as the discount rate (this rate is also called the hurdle rate or opportunity cost of capital).

2. **Net Present Value**

   a. A capital project's net present value is the difference between the present value of the net cash savings or inflows expected over the life of the project and the required dollar investment.

      1) If the difference is positive, the project should be undertaken. If the difference is negative, it should be rejected.

EXAMPLE

The Juan Fangio Co. is planning to invest $100,000 in new equipment. The equipment is expected to create savings in cash operating expenses of $80,000 in the first year and $60,000 in the second year. The equipment's estimated useful life is 2 years, and the firm expects to resell it at the end of its useful life (salvage value) for $15,000. For simplicity, assume that the equipment will be fully depreciated for tax purposes 50% each year. Fangio's internal rate of return is 12%, and its effective tax rate is 40%. The present value of $1 for one period at 12% is 0.893, and the present value of $1 for two periods at 12% is 0.8. Fangio calculates the net present value of this potential investment as follows:

Annual depreciation shield for Year 1 and Year 2:

Asset's cost	$100,000
Depreciation percent	× 50%
Annual depreciation charge	$ 50,000
Tax rate	× 40%
Depreciation tax shield	$ 20,000

Resale of the new equipment (salvage value):

Expected inflow from the proceeds	$ 15,000
Tax basis of equipment	-- (since it is fully depreciated)
Gain on expected disposal	$ 15,000
Taxes ($15,000 × 40%)	(6,000)
Expected cash inflow	$ 9,000

Net annual cash savings:	Year 1	Year 2
Net annual savings/cash inflow	$ 80,000	$60,000
Tax expense	× 40%	× 40%
Net cash inflow/savings	$ 48,000	$36,000

Net present value:	Year 0	Year 1	Year 2
Initial investment in equipment	$(100,000)		
Net annual savings/cash inflow		$ 48,000	$36,000
Depreciation tax shield		20,000	20,000
Inflow from resale (salvage value)			9,000
After-tax net expected cash flows	$(100,000)	$ 68,000	$65,000
Discount rate	× 1	× 0.893	× 0.8
Net present value	$(100,000) +	$ 60,724 +	$52,000 = $12,724

The positive net present value indicates that the project should be undertaken.

EXAMPLE

The Juan Fangio Co. is considering the purchase of a machine for $250,000 that will have a useful life of 10 years with no residual (salvage) value. The machine is expected to generate an annual operating cash savings of $60,000 over its useful life and would be depreciated on the straight-line basis, resulting in annual depreciation expense of $25,000 ($250,000 ÷ 10 years). Fangio's internal rate of return is 12%, and its effective tax rate is 40%.

The present value of $1 for 10 periods at 12% is 0.322, and the present value of an ordinary annuity of $1 for 10 periods at 12% is 5.650. Fangio calculates the net present value of this potential investment as follows:

Present value of cash savings		
Annual operating cash savings/inflows		$ 60,000
Annual tax expense:		
Tax expense on annual cash savings		
(60,000 × 40%)	$(24,000)	
Depreciation tax shield (25,000 × 40%)	10,000	(14,000)
After-tax net annual cash savings		$ 46,000
Times: PV factor for an ordinary annuity		× 5.650
Present value of net cash savings		$259,900
Required investment		
Cost of new equipment		$250,000
Net present value of investment		
Present value of net cash savings		$259,900
Less: required investment		(250,000)
Net present value of investment		$ 9,900

The positive net present value indicates that the project should be undertaken.

---

   b.   Use of the net present value method involves the implicit assumption that cash flows are reinvested at the entity's minimum required rate of return.

3. **Selecting the Appropriate Hurdle Rate**

   a.   Adjusting for Inflation

      1)   In an inflationary environment, future cash inflows will consist of inflated dollars. To compensate for this decline in purchasing power, hurdle rates must be adjusted upward.

   b.   Adjusting for Risk

      1)   Particularly risky projects may be assigned higher hurdle rates to ensure that only those whose potential returns are commensurate with their risks are considered acceptable.

   c.   Division-Specific Rates of Return

      1)   When the divisions of a large, complex firm have their own specific risk attributes and capital costs, using a single company-wide hurdle rate may lead to suboptimal decisions.

         a)   The managers of a high-risk division will be tempted to over-invest in new projects and those of low-risk divisions will tend to under-invest.

      2)   Thus, potential investments in inherently risky divisions should be required to clear somewhat higher hurdle rates, and those being considered by divisions with risks lower than the company average can be assigned slightly lower hurdle rates.

Stop and review! You have completed the outline for this subunit. Study multiple-choice questions 10 through 14 beginning on page 266.

9.4 CAPITAL BUDGETING -- NET PRESENT VALUE CALCULATIONS

This subunit consists entirely of questions that require the student to execute the detailed calculations involved in applying the net present value technique. Please review Subunit 9.3 thoroughly before attempting to answer the questions in this subunit.

Stop and review! You have completed the outline for this subunit. Study multiple-choice questions 15 through 18 beginning on page 268.

9.5 CAPITAL BUDGETING -- INTERNAL RATE OF RETURN

1. **Internal Rate of Return (IRR)**

    a. The internal rate of return of a project is the discount rate at which the investment's net present value equals zero.   In other words, it is the rate that equates the present value of the expected cash inflows with the present value of the expected cash outflows.

    1) If the internal rate of return is higher than the company's hurdle rate, the investment is desirable. If the internal rate of return is lower, the project should be rejected.

    > IRR > Hurdle rate: Accept project
    >
    > IRR < Hurdle rate: Reject project

EXAMPLE

Niki Lauda, Inc., has a hurdle rate of 12% for all capital projects. The firm is considering a project that calls for a cash outlay of $200,000 that will create savings in after-tax cash costs of $52,000 for each of the next 5 years. The applicable present value factor is 3.846 ($200,000 ÷ $52,000). Consulting a table of present value factors for an ordinary annuity for five periods places this factor somewhere between 9% and 10%. Since this is less than Lauda's hurdle rate, the project will be rejected.

---

2. **Comparing Cash Flow Patterns**

    a. Often a decision maker must choose between two mutually exclusive projects: one whose inflows are higher in the early years but fall off drastically later and one whose inflows are steady throughout the project's life.

    1) The higher an entity's hurdle rate, the more quickly a project must pay off.
    2) Entities with low hurdle rates prefer a slow and steady payback.

EXAMPLE

Consider the net cash flows of these two projects with identical initial investments.

	Initial Investment	Year 1	Year 2	Year 3	Year 4
Project K	$(200,000)	$140,000	$100,000	--	--
Project L	(200,000)	65,000	65,000	$65,000	$65,000

A graphical representation of the two projects at various discount rates helps to illustrate the factors a decision maker must consider in such a situation.

-- Continued on next page --

-- EXAMPLE continued --

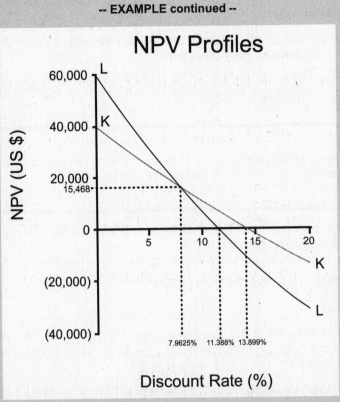

NPV Profiles

Figure 9-1

Project K's internal rate of return is 13.899%. Project L's is 11.388%.

The NPV profile can be of great practical use to managers trying to make investment decisions. It gives the manager a clear insight into the question, how sensitive is a project's profitability to changes in the discount rate?

- At a hurdle rate of **exactly** 7.9625%, a decision maker is **indifferent** between the two projects. The net present value of both is $15,468 at that discount rate.
- At hurdle rates **below** 7.9625%, the project whose **inflows last longer** into the future is the better investment (L).
- At hurdle rates **above** 7.9625%, the project whose **inflows are "front-loaded"** is the better choice (K).

3. **Comparing Net Present Value (NPV) and Internal Rate of Return (IRR)**

   a. The reinvestment rate becomes critical when choosing between the NPV and IRR methods. NPV assumes the cash flows from the investment can be reinvested at the particular project's discount rate, that is, the desired rate of return.

   b. The NPV and IRR methods give the same accept/reject decision if projects are independent. Independent projects have unrelated cash flows. Hence, all acceptable independent projects can be undertaken.

      1) However, if projects are mutually exclusive, the NPV and IRR methods may rank them differently if

         a) The cost of one project is greater than the cost of another.

         b) The timing, amounts, and directions of cash flows differ among projects.

         c) The projects have different useful lives.

         d) The cost of capital or desired rate of return varies over the life of a project. The NPV can easily be determined using different desired rates of return for different periods. The IRR determines one rate for the project.

         e) Multiple investments are involved in a project. NPV amounts are addable, but IRR rates are not. The IRR for the whole is not the sum of the IRRs for the parts.

2) The IRR method assumes that the cash flows will be reinvested at the internal rate of return.

   a) If the project's funds are not reinvested at the IRR, the ranking calculations obtained may be in error.

   b) The NPV method gives a better grasp of the problem in many decision situations because the reinvestment is assumed to be in the desired rate of return.

For both net present value and internal rate of return, expect to see questions asking you to calculate these values as well as understand the theory behind each method.

Stop and review! You have completed the outline for this subunit. Study multiple-choice questions 19 through 23 beginning on page 270.

9.6 CAPITAL BUDGETING -- PAYBACK METHODS

1. **Payback Period**

   a. The payback period is the number of years required for the net cash savings or inflows to equal the original investment, i.e., the time necessary for an investment to pay for itself.

      1) Companies using the payback method set a maximum length of time within which projects must pay for themselves to be considered acceptable.

   b. If the cash flows are constant, the formula is

$$Payback\ period = \frac{Initial\ investment}{Annual\ after\text{-}tax\ cash\ savings/inflows}$$

      1) Note that no consideration is made for the time value of money under this method.

EXAMPLE with Constant Cash Flows

Niki Lauda also applies a 4-year payback period test on all capital projects.

Payback period = $200,000 ÷ $52,000 = 3.846 years

Judged by this criterion, the project is acceptable because its payback period is less than the company's maximum.

---

   c. If the cash flows are not constant, the calculation must be in cumulative form.

EXAMPLE with Varying Cash Flows

Assume that Niki Lauda's initial investment is $160,000 and that, instead of the smooth inflows predicted on page 260, the project's cash stream is expected to vary. The payback period is calculated as follows:

End of Year	Cash Savings	Remaining Initial Investment
Initial investment	$ --	$160,000
Year 1	48,000	112,000
Year 2	54,000	58,000
Year 3	54,000	4,000
Year 4	60,000	--

The project is acceptable because its payback period is over 3 years and under 4 years and is less than the company's maximum.

    d.   The strength of the payback method is its simplicity.

        1)   To some extent, the payback period measures risk. The longer the period, the more risky the investment.

    e.   The payback method has the following two significant weaknesses:

        1)   It disregards the time value of money. Weighting all cash inflows equally ignores the fact that funds have a time cost.

        2)   It disregards all cash inflows after the payback cutoff date. Applying a single cutoff date to every project results in accepting many marginal projects and rejecting good ones.

2. **Discounted Payback**

    a.   The discounted payback method is sometimes used to overcome the major drawback inherent in the basic payback method.

        1)   The net cash flows in the denominator are discounted to calculate the period required to recover the initial investment.

EXAMPLE

Lauda has a 12% cost of capital.

Period	Cash Savings		12% PV Factor		Discounted Cash Savings	Remaining Initial Investment
Initial investment	$ --		--		$ --	$160,000
Year 1	48,000	×	0.89286	=	42,857	117,143
Year 2	54,000	×	0.79719	=	43,048	74,095
Year 3	54,000	×	0.71178	=	38,436	35,659
Year 4	60,000	×	0.63552	=	38,132	--

The project is acceptable because its discounted payback period is over 3 years and under 4 years and is less than the company's maximum.

EXAMPLE

Lauda wants to determine the discounted payback periods in years and assumes that the cash flows are earned evenly throughout each year. The discounted payback period in years is calculated as follows:

1)   The full payback occurs sometime in Year 4. The remaining investment at the beginning of Year 4 is $35,659.

2)   The following is the percentage of Year 4 until the amount of $35,659 is attained:

$$\frac{\$35,659}{\$38,132} = 0.935\%$$

3)   The discounted payback period in years is **3.935 years** (3 + 0.935).

---

    b.   The breakeven time is the amount of time required for the discounted cash flows of an investment to equal the initial cost of an investment.

    c.   The discounted payback method's advantage is that it acknowledges the time value of money.

        1)   Its drawbacks are that it loses the simplicity of the basic payback method and still ignores cash flows after the arbitrary cutoff date.

Stop and review! You have completed the outline for this subunit. Study multiple-choice questions 24 through 29 beginning on page 272.

QUESTIONS

9.1 Types and Costs of Short-Term Financing

> Questions 1 through 3 are based on the following information. Skilantic Company needs to pay a supplier's invoice of $60,000 and wants to take a cash discount of 2/10, net 40. The firm can borrow the money for 30 days at 11% per annum plus a 9% compensating balance.

1. The amount Skilantic Company must borrow to pay the supplier within the discount period and cover the compensating balance is

A. $60,000

B. $65,934

C. $64,615

D. $58,800

Answer (C) is correct.
REQUIRED: The amount the company must borrow to pay the supplier within the discount period and cover the compensating balance requirement.
DISCUSSION: Skilantic's total borrowings on this loan can be calculated as follows:

$$
\begin{aligned}
\text{Total borrowings} &= \text{Amount needed} \div \\
&\quad (1.0 - \text{Compensating balance \%}) \\
&= (\$60,000 \times 98\%) \div (100\% - 9\%) \\
&= \$58,800 \div 91\% \\
&= \$64,615
\end{aligned}
$$

Answer (A) is incorrect. The amount of $60,000 is the invoice amount. Answer (B) is incorrect. The amount of $65,934 assumes the amount paid to the supplier is $60,000. Answer (D) is incorrect. The amount of $58,800 is the amount to be paid to the supplier.

2. Assuming Skilantic Company borrows the money on the last day of the discount period and repays it 30 days later, the effective interest rate on the loan is

A. 11%

B. 10%

C. 12.09%

D. 9.90%

Answer (C) is correct.
REQUIRED: The effective interest rate when a company borrows to take a discount when the terms are 2/10, net 40.
DISCUSSION: Skilantic's effective rate on this loan can be calculated as follows:

$$
\begin{aligned}
\text{Effective rate} &= \text{Stated rate} \div (1.0 - \text{Compensating balance \%}) \\
&= 11\% \div (100\% - 9\%) \\
&= 11\% \div 91\% \\
&= 12.09\%
\end{aligned}
$$

Answer (A) is incorrect. This percentage is the contract rate. Answer (B) is incorrect. The effective rate is greater than the contract rate. The usable funds are less than the face amount of the note. Answer (D) is incorrect. The effective rate is greater than the contract rate. The usable funds are less than the face amount of the note.

3. If Skilantic fails to take the discount and pays on the 40th day, what effective rate of annual interest is it paying the vendor?

A. 2%

B. 24%

C. 24.49%

D. 36.73%

Answer (C) is correct.
REQUIRED: The effective interest rate paid when a discount is not taken.
DISCUSSION: By failing to take the discount, Skilantic is essentially borrowing $58,800 for 30 days. Thus, at a cost of $1,200, the company acquires the use of $58,800, resulting in a rate of 2.0408% ($1,200 ÷ $58,800) for 30 days. Assuming a 360-day year, the effective annual rate is 24.49% [2.0408% × (360 days ÷ 30 days)].
Answer (A) is incorrect. The discount rate for a 30-day period is 2%. Answer (B) is incorrect. This percentage assumes that the available funds equal $60,000. Answer (D) is incorrect. This percentage assumes a 20-day discount period.

4. A company obtained a short-term bank loan of $250,000 at an annual interest rate of 6%. As a condition of the loan, the company is required to maintain a compensating balance of $50,000 in its checking account. The checking account earns interest at an annual rate of 2%. Ordinarily, the company maintains a balance of $25,000 in its account for transaction purposes. What is the effective interest rate of the loan?

A. 6.44%

B. 7.00%

C. 5.80%

D. 6.66%

Answer (A) is correct.
　　REQUIRED: The effective interest rate on a loan that requires a compensating balance of $25,000 above the company's normal working balance.
　　DISCUSSION: The $50,000 compensating balance requirement is partially satisfied by the company's practice of maintaining a $25,000 balance for transaction purposes. Thus, only $25,000 of the loan will not be available for current use, leaving $225,000 of the loan usable. At 6% interest, the $250,000 loan would require an interest payment of $15,000 per year. This is partially offset by the 2% interest earned on the $25,000 incremental balance, or $500. Subtracting the $500 interest earned from the $15,000 of expense results in net interest expense of $14,500 for the use of $225,000 in funds. Dividing $14,500 by $225,000 produces an effective interest rate of 6.44%.
　　Answer (B) is incorrect. This percentage fails to consider that the $25,000 currently being maintained counts toward the compensating balance requirement. Answer (C) is incorrect. This percentage fails to consider the compensating balance requirement. Answer (D) is incorrect. This percentage fails to consider the interest earned on the incremental balance being carried.

5. If a firm purchases raw materials from its supplier on a 2/10, net 40, cash discount basis, the equivalent annual interest rate (using a 360-day year) of forgoing the cash discount and making payment on the 40th day is

A. 2%

B. 18.36%

C. 24.49%

D. 36.72%

Answer (C) is correct.
　　REQUIRED: The equivalent annual interest charge for not taking the discount.
　　DISCUSSION: The buyer could satisfy the $100 obligation by paying $98 on the 10th day. By choosing to wait until the 40th day, the buyer is effectively paying a $2 interest charge for the use of $98 for 30 days (40-day credit period – 10-day discount period). The annualized cost of not taking this discount can be calculated as follows:

$$\frac{Discount\ \%}{100\% - Discount\ \%} \times \frac{Days\ in\ year}{Total\ payment\ period - Discount\ period}$$

Cost of not taking discount = [2% ÷ (100% – 2%)] ×
　　　　　　　　　　　　[360 days ÷ (40 days – 10 days)]
　　　　　　　　= (2% ÷ 98%) × (360 days ÷ 30 days)
　　　　　　　　= 2.0408% × 12
　　　　　　　　= 24.49%

　　Answer (A) is incorrect. This percentage is the discount rate. Answer (B) is incorrect. This percentage is based on the 40-day credit period. Answer (D) is incorrect. This percentage is based on a 20-day credit period.

9.2 Capital Budgeting -- Basics

6. Of the following decisions, capital budgeting techniques would **least** likely be used in evaluating the

A. Acquisition of new aircraft by a cargo company.

B. Design and implementation of a major advertising program.

C. Trade for a star quarterback by a football team.

D. Adoption of a new method of allocating nontraceable costs to product lines.

Answer (D) is correct.
　　REQUIRED: The decision least likely to be evaluated using capital budgeting techniques.
　　DISCUSSION: Capital budgeting is the process of planning expenditures for investments on which the returns are expected to occur over a period of more than 1 year. Thus, capital budgeting concerns the acquisition or disposal of long-term assets and the financing ramifications of such decisions. The adoption of a new method of allocating nontraceable costs to product lines has no effect on a company's cash flows, does not concern the acquisition of long-term assets, and is not concerned with financing. Hence, capital budgeting is irrelevant to such a decision.
　　Answer (A) is incorrect. A new aircraft represents a long-term investment in a capital good. Answer (B) is incorrect. A major advertising program is a high cost investment with long-term effects. Answer (C) is incorrect. A star quarterback is a costly asset who is expected to have a substantial effect on the team's long-term profitability.

7. The relevance of a particular cost to a decision is determined by

   A. Riskiness of the decision.

   B. Number of decision variables.

   C. Amount of the cost.

   D. Potential effect on the decision.

Answer (D) is correct.
   REQUIRED: The determinant of relevance of a particular cost to a decision.
   DISCUSSION: Relevance is the capacity of information to make a difference in a decision by helping users of that information to predict the outcomes of events or to confirm or correct prior expectations. Thus, relevant costs are those expected future costs that vary with the action taken. All other costs are constant and therefore have no effect on the decision.
   Answer (A) is incorrect. The ultimate determinant of relevance is the ability to influence the decision. Answer (B) is incorrect. The ultimate determinant of relevance is the ability to influence the decision. Answer (C) is incorrect. The ultimate determinant of relevance is the ability to influence the decision.

8. Which of the following is irrelevant in projecting the cash flows of the final year of a capital project?

   A. Cash devoted to use in project.

   B. Disposal value of equipment purchased specifically for project.

   C. Depreciation tax shield generated by equipment purchased specifically for project.

   D. Historical cost of equipment disposed of in the project's first year.

Answer (D) is correct.
   REQUIRED: The irrelevant information in projecting the cash flows for the final year of a capital project.
   DISCUSSION: Once an old piece of equipment has been disposed of, its historical cost no longer has an impact on a firm's cash flows.
   Answer (A) is incorrect. The recovery of working capital devoted to a capital project is a relevant cash flow in the final year. Answer (B) is incorrect. The disposal value of equipment acquired for the project is relevant in the final year. Answer (C) is incorrect. The depreciation tax shield generated by equipment acquired for the project is relevant to the final year.

9. The accounting rate of return

   A. Is synonymous with the internal rate of return.

   B. Focuses on income as opposed to cash flows.

   C. Is inconsistent with the divisional performance measure known as return on investment.

   D. Recognizes the time value of money.

Answer (B) is correct.
   REQUIRED: The true statement about the accounting rate of return.
   DISCUSSION: The accounting rate of return is a capital budgeting technique that ignores the time value of money. It is calculated by dividing the increase in average annual accounting net income by the required investment. This method focuses on income rather than cash flows.
   Answer (A) is incorrect. The internal rate of return is the rate at which the net present value is zero. Thus, it incorporates time value of money concepts, whereas the accounting rate of return does not. Answer (C) is incorrect. The accounting rate of return is similar to the divisional performance measure of return on investment. Answer (D) is incorrect. The accounting rate of return ignores the time value of money.

9.3 Capital Budgeting -- Net Present Value Theory

10. A depreciation tax shield is

   A. An after-tax cash outflow.

   B. A reduction in income taxes.

   C. The cash provided by recording depreciation.

   D. The expense caused by depreciation.

Answer (B) is correct.
   REQUIRED: The definition of a depreciation tax shield.
   DISCUSSION: A tax shield is something that will protect income against taxation. Thus, a depreciation tax shield is a reduction in income taxes due to a company being allowed to deduct depreciation against otherwise taxable income.
   Answer (A) is incorrect. A tax shield is not a cash flow but a means of reducing outflows for income taxes. Answer (C) is incorrect. Cash is not provided by recording depreciation; the shield is a result of deducting depreciation from taxable revenues. Answer (D) is incorrect. Depreciation is recognized as an expense even if it has no tax benefit.

11. The NPV of a project has been calculated to be $215,000. Which one of the following changes in assumptions would decrease the NPV?

A. Decrease the estimated effective income tax rate.

B. Decrease the initial investment amount.

C. Extend the project life and associated cash inflows.

D. Increase the discount rate.

Answer (D) is correct.
REQUIRED: The change in assumption that would decrease the net present value (NPV).
DISCUSSION: An increase in the discount rate would lower the net present value, as would a decrease in cash flows or an increase in the initial investment.
Answer (A) is incorrect. A decrease in the tax rate would decrease tax expense, thus increasing cash flows and the NPV. Answer (B) is incorrect. A decrease in the initial investment amount would increase the NPV. Answer (C) is incorrect. An extension of the project life and associated cash inflows would increase the NPV.

12. Assume that the interest rate is greater than zero. Which of the following cash-inflow streams should you prefer?

	Year 1	Year 2	Year 3	Year 4
A.	$400	$300	$200	$100
B.	$100	$200	$300	$400
C.	$250	$250	$250	$250

D. Any of these, since they each sum to $1,000.

Answer (A) is correct.
REQUIRED: The cash-flow stream that would be most advantageous.
DISCUSSION: The concept of present value gives greater value to inflows received earlier in the stream. Thus, the declining inflows would be superior to increasing inflows, or even inflows.
Answer (B) is incorrect. The cash flow shown does not produce the greatest present value. Answer (C) is incorrect. The cash flow shown does not produce the greatest present value. Answer (D) is incorrect. Present value of the cash flows must be considered.

13. The net present value of an investment project represents the

A. Total actual cash inflows minus the total actual cash outflows.

B. Excess of the discounted cash inflows over the discounted cash outflows.

C. Total after-tax cash flow including the tax shield from depreciation.

D. Cumulative accounting profit over the life of the project.

Answer (B) is correct.
REQUIRED: The meaning of net present value.
DISCUSSION: The net present value of an investment project represents the excess of the discounted cash inflows over the discounted cash outflows.
Answer (A) is incorrect. Actual cash inflows minus actual cash outflows ignores the time value of money. Answer (C) is incorrect. Total after-tax cash flow including the tax shield from depreciation ignores the time value of money. Answer (D) is incorrect. Accounting profit ignores the time value of money.

14. For capital budgeting purposes, management would select a high hurdle rate of return for certain projects because management

A. Wants to use equity funding exclusively.

B. Believes too many proposals are being rejected.

C. Believes bank loans are riskier than capital investments.

D. Wants to factor risk into its consideration of projects.

Answer (D) is correct.
REQUIRED: The reason for selecting a high hurdle rate for certain projects.
DISCUSSION: Risk analysis attempts to measure the likelihood of the variability of future returns from the proposed investment. Risk can be incorporated into capital budgeting decisions in a number of ways, one of which is to use a hurdle rate (desired rate of return) higher than the firm's cost of capital, that is, a risk-adjusted discount rate. This technique adjusts the interest rate used for discounting upward as an investment becomes riskier. The expected flow from the investment must be relatively larger or the increased discount rate will generate a negative net present value, and the proposed acquisition will be rejected.
Answer (A) is incorrect. The nature of the funding may not be a sufficient reason to use a risk-adjusted rate. The type of funding is just one factor affecting the risk of a project.
Answer (B) is incorrect. A higher hurdle will result in rejection of more projects. Answer (C) is incorrect. A risk-adjusted high hurdle rate is used for capital investments with greater risk.

9.4 Capital Budgeting -- Net Present Value Calculations

15. Salem Co. is considering a project that yields annual net cash inflows of $420,000 for Years 1 through 5 and a net cash inflow of $100,000 in Year 6. The project will require an initial investment of $1,800,000. Salem's cost of capital is 10%. Present value information is presented below:

Present value of $1 for 5 years at 10% is .62.

Present value of $1 for 6 years at 10% is .56.

Present value of an annuity of $1 for 5 years at 10% is 3.79.

What was Salem's expected net present value for this project?

A. $83,000

B. $(108,200)

C. $(152,200)

D. $(442,000)

Answer (C) is correct.
REQUIRED: The expected net present value for the project.
DISCUSSION: A capital project's net present value is the difference between the present value of the net cash inflows and the required investment. The present value of the payments for Years 1 through 5 is $1,591,800 ($420,000 × 3.79), and the present value of the Year 6 payment is $56,000 ($100,000 × .56). The initial investment is $1,800,000. Thus, the present value of the project is $(152,200) ($1,591,800 + $56,000 – $1,800,000).
Answer (A) is incorrect. The amount of $83,000 is not Salem's expected net present value for the project. Answer (B) is incorrect. The amount of $(108,200) results from not discounting the cash flow in Year 6. Answer (D) is incorrect. The amount of $(442,000) results from multiplying the total amount of the first five annual inflows by .62.

16. Jackson Corporation uses net present value techniques in evaluating its capital investment projects. The company is considering a new equipment acquisition that will cost $100,000, fully installed, and have a zero salvage value at the end of its 5-year productive life. Jackson will depreciate the equipment on a straight-line basis for both financial and tax purposes. Jackson estimates $70,000 in annual recurring operating cash income and $20,000 in annual recurring operating cash expenses. Jackson's desired rate of return is 12% and its effective income tax rate is 40%.

The present value factors for 12% are as follows:

Present value of $1 at the end of five periods   .567
Present value of an ordinary annuity of $1 for
 five periods   3.605

What is the net present value of this investment on an after-tax basis?

A. $28,840

B. $8,150

C. $36,990

D. $80,250

Answer (C) is correct.
REQUIRED: The net present value on an after-tax basis.
DISCUSSION: Annual cash outflow for taxes is $12,000 {[$70,000 inflows – $20,000 cash operating expenses – ($100,000 ÷ 5) depreciation] × 40%}. The annual net cash inflow is therefore $38,000 ($70,000 – $20,000 – $12,000). The present value of these net inflows for a 5-year period is $136,990 ($38,000 × 3.605 present value of an ordinary annuity for 5 years at 12%), and the NPV of the investment is $36,990 ($136,990 – $100,000 investment).
Answer (A) is incorrect. The amount of $28,840 is the present value of the depreciation tax savings. Answer (B) is incorrect. The amount of $8,150 ignores the depreciation tax savings. Answer (D) is incorrect. The amount of $80,250 ignores taxes.

17. The Hopkins Company has estimated that a proposed project's 10-year annual net cash benefit, received each year end, will be $2,500 with an additional terminal benefit of $5,000 at the end of the 10th year.

Information on present value factors is as follows:

Present value of $1 at 8% at the end of
  10 periods .463
Present value of an ordinary annuity of $1
  at 8% for 10 periods 6.710

Assuming that these cash inflows satisfy exactly Hopkins' required rate of return of 8%, what is the initial cash outlay?

  A. $16,775

  B. $19,090

  C. $25,000

  D. $30,000

Answer (B) is correct.
  REQUIRED: The initial cash outlay.
  DISCUSSION: If the 8% return exactly equals the present value of the future flows (i.e., the NPV is zero), then simply determine the present value of the future inflows. Thus, Hopkins Company's initial cash outlay is $19,090 [($2,500)(present value of an ordinary annuity at 8% for 10 periods) + ($5,000)(present value of a single amount at 8% for 10 periods = ($2,500)(6.710) + ($5,000)(.463)].
  Answer (A) is incorrect. The amount of $16,775 failed to include the present value of the $5,000 terminal benefit. Answer (C) is incorrect. This amount is not a result of using present value analysis. Answer (D) is incorrect. This amount is not a result of using present value analysis.

Question 18 is based on the following information. Jorelle Company's financial staff has been requested to review a proposed investment in new capital equipment. Applicable financial data is presented below. There will be no salvage value at the end of the investment's life and, due to realistic depreciation practices, it is estimated that the salvage value and net book value are equal at the end of each year. All cash flows are assumed to take place at the end of each year. For investment proposals, Jorelle uses a 12% after-tax target rate of return.

Investment Proposal

Year	Purchase Cost and Book Value	Annual Net After-Tax Cash Flows	Annual Net Income
0	$250,000	$ 0	$ 0
1	168,000	120,000	35,000
2	100,000	108,000	39,000
3	50,000	96,000	43,000
4	18,000	84,000	47,000
5	0	72,000	51,000

Discounted Factors for a 12% Rate of Return

Year	Present Value of $1.00 Received at the End of Each Period	Present Value of an Annuity of $1.00 Received at the End of Each Period
1	.89	.89
2	.80	1.69
3	.71	2.40
4	.64	3.04
5	.57	3.61
6	.51	4.12

18. The net present value for the investment proposal is

  A. $106,160

  B. $(97,970)

  C. $356,160

  D. $96,560

Answer (A) is correct.
  REQUIRED: The net present value (NPV).
  DISCUSSION: The NPV is the sum of the present values of all cash inflows and outflows associated with the proposal. If the NPV is positive, the proposal should be accepted. The NPV is determined by discounting each expected cash flow using the appropriate 12% interest factor for the present value of $1. Thus, the NPV is $106,160 [(.89 × $120,000) + (.80 × $108,000) + (.71 × $96,000) + (.64 × $84,000) + (.57 × $72,000) – (1.00 × $250,000)].
  Answer (B) is incorrect. The amount of $(97,970) is based on net income instead of cash flows. Answer (C) is incorrect. The amount of $356,160 excludes the purchase cost. Answer (D) is incorrect. The amount of $96,560 equals average after-tax cash inflow times the interest factor for the present value of a 5-year annuity, minus $250,000.

9.5 Capital Budgeting -- Internal Rate of Return

19. What is the approximate IRR for a project that costs $50,000 and provides cash inflows of $20,000 for 3 years?

Rate of Return	Present Value of an Annuity of $1 Received at the End of 3 Years
6%	2.673
8%	2.577
10%	2.487
12%	2.402

A. 10%

B. 12%

C. 22%

D. 27%

Answer (A) is correct.
   REQUIRED: The approximate IRR.
   DISCUSSION: The factor to use is 2.5, which is found at a little under 10% on the 3-year line of an annuity table.
   Answer (B) is incorrect. Discounting the cash inflows at 12% would not produce a NPV of zero. Answer (C) is incorrect. Discounting the cash inflows at 22% would not produce a NPV of zero. Answer (D) is incorrect. Discounting the cash inflows at 27% would not produce a NPV of zero.

20. Pena Company is considering a project that calls for an initial cash outlay of $50,000. The expected net cash inflows from the project are $7,791 for each of 10 years.

Rate of Return	Present Value of an Annuity of $1 Received at the End of 10 Years
6%	7.360
8%	6.710
9%	6.418
10%	6.145
12%	5.650

What is the IRR of the project?

A. 6%

B. 7%

C. 8%

D. 9%

Answer (D) is correct.
   REQUIRED: The internal rate of return.
   DISCUSSION: The IRR can be calculated by equating the initial cash outlay with the present value of the net cash inflows:

$7,791 × PV at i for 10 periods   = $50,000
                                  =   6.418

Using the PV table, 6.418 is PV at 9% for 10 periods.
   Answer (A) is incorrect. Discounting the cash inflows at 6% would not produce a NPV of zero. Answer (B) is incorrect. Discounting the cash inflows at 7% would not produce a NPV of zero. Answer (C) is incorrect. Discounting the cash inflows at 8% would not produce a NPV of zero.

21. Wilkinson, Inc., which has a cost of capital of 12%, invested in a project with an internal rate of return (IRR) of 14%. The project is expected to have a useful life of 4 years, and it will produce net cash inflows as follows:

Year	Net Cash Inflows
1	$1,000
2	2,000
3	4,000
4	4,000

The present value of $1 is as follows:

	Present Value	
No. of Periods	12%	14%
1	0.893	0.877
2	0.797	0.769
3	0.712	0.675
4	0.636	0.592

The initial cost of this project amounted to

A. $7,483

B. $9,647

C. $11,000

D. $12,540

Answer (A) is correct.

REQUIRED: The net present value of the cash inflows from a capital project.

DISCUSSION: The internal rate of return (IRR) of a capital project is the rate at which the net present value (NPV) of its future cash flows equals zero. To find this project's NPV, therefore, it is necessary to discount the cash flows at the appropriate rate (14%) as follows:

Year	Net Cash Inflows	PV Factor	Present Value
1	$1,000	0.877	$ 877
2	2,000	0.769	1,538
3	4,000	0.675	2,700
4	4,000	0.592	2,368
			$7,483

Answer (B) is incorrect. The amount of $9,647 results from treating the cash inflows as occurring at the beginning of the year instead of at year end. Answer (C) is incorrect. The amount of $11,000 results from failing to take the time value of money into account. Answer (D) is incorrect. The amount of $12,540 results from multiplying times the 14% rate rather than discounting by that rate.

22. Brown and Company uses the internal rate of return (IRR) method to evaluate capital projects. Brown is considering four independent projects with the following IRRs:

Project	IRR
I	10%
II	12%
III	14%
IV	15%

Brown's cost of capital is 13%. Which one of the following project options should Brown accept based on IRR?

A. Projects I and II only.

B. Projects III and IV only.

C. Project IV only.

D. Projects I, II, III and IV.

Answer (B) is correct.

REQUIRED: The acceptable projects given a certain cost of capital.

DISCUSSION: When sufficient funds are available, any capital project whose internal rate of return (IRR) exceeds the company's cost of capital should be accepted.

Answer (A) is incorrect. Projects I and II have rates of return lower than the company's cost of capital. Answer (C) is incorrect. The rate of return for Project III also exceeds the company's cost of capital. Answer (D) is incorrect. Projects I and II should be rejected; their rates of return are lower than the company's cost of capital.

23. The net present value of a proposed investment is negative; therefore, the discount rate used must be

A. Greater than the project's internal rate of return.

B. Less than the project's internal rate of return.

C. Greater than the firm's cost of equity.

D. Less than the risk-free rate.

Answer (A) is correct.

REQUIRED: The true statement about the discount rate when the net present value (NPV) is negative.

DISCUSSION: The higher the discount rate, the lower the NPV. The IRR is the discount rate at which the NPV is zero. Consequently, if the NPV is negative, the discount rate used must exceed the IRR.

Answer (B) is incorrect. If the discount rate is less than the IRR, the NPV is positive. Answer (C) is incorrect. The NPV measures the difference between a company's discount rate and the IRR. Answer (D) is incorrect. The relationship between the discount rate and the risk-free rate is not a factor in investment analysis under the NPV method.

9.6 Capital Budgeting -- Payback Methods

24. A characteristic of the payback method (before taxes) is that it

A. Incorporates the time value of money.

B. Neglects total project profitability.

C. Uses accrual accounting inflows in the numerator of the calculation.

D. Uses the estimated expected life of the asset in the denominator of the calculation.

Answer (B) is correct.
REQUIRED: The characteristic of the payback method.
DISCUSSION: The payback method calculates the number of years required to complete the return of the original investment. This measure is computed by dividing the net investment required by the average expected cash flow to be generated, resulting in the number of years required to recover the original investment. Payback is easy to calculate but has two principal problems: It ignores the time value of money, and it gives no consideration to returns after the payback period. Thus, it ignores total project profitability.
Answer (A) is incorrect. The payback method does not incorporate the time value of money. Answer (C) is incorrect. The payback method uses the net investment in the numerator of the calculation. Answer (D) is incorrect. Payback uses the net annual cash inflows in the denominator of the calculation.

25. Jasper Company has a payback goal of 3 years on new equipment acquisitions. A new sorter is being evaluated that costs $450,000 and has a 5-year life. Straight-line depreciation will be used; no salvage is anticipated. Jasper is subject to a 40% income tax rate. To meet the company's payback goal, the sorter must generate reductions in annual cash operating costs of

A. $60,000

B. $100,000

C. $150,000

D. $190,000

Answer (D) is correct.
REQUIRED: The cash savings that must be generated to achieve a targeted payback period.
DISCUSSION: Given a periodic constant cash flow, the payback period is calculated by dividing cost by the annual cash inflows, or cash savings. To achieve a payback period of 3 years, the annual increment in net cash inflow generated by the investment must be $150,000 ($450,000 ÷ 3-year targeted payback period). This amount equals the total reduction in cash operating costs minus related taxes. Depreciation is $90,000 ($450,000 ÷ 5 years). Because depreciation is a noncash deductible expense, it shields $90,000 of the cash savings from taxation. Accordingly, $60,000 ($150,000 – $90,000) of the additional net cash inflow must come from after-tax net income. At a 40% tax rate, $60,000 of after-tax income equals $100,000 ($60,000 ÷ 60%) of pre-tax income from cost savings, and the outflow for taxes is $40,000. Thus, the annual reduction in cash operating costs required is $190,000 ($150,000 additional net cash inflow required + $40,000 tax outflow).

26. Whatney Co. is considering the acquisition of a new, more efficient press. The cost of the press is $360,000, and the press has an estimated 6-year life with zero salvage value. Whatney uses straight-line depreciation for both financial reporting and income tax reporting purposes and has a 40% corporate income tax rate. In evaluating equipment acquisitions of this type, Whatney uses a goal of a 4-year payback period. To meet Whatney's desired payback period, the press must produce a minimum annual before-tax operating cash savings of

A. $90,000

B. $110,000

C. $114,000

D. $150,000

Answer (B) is correct.
REQUIRED: The minimum annual before-tax operating cash savings yielding a specified payback period.
DISCUSSION: Payback is the number of years required to complete the return of the original investment. Given a periodic constant cash flow, the payback period equals net investment divided by the constant expected periodic after-tax cash flow. The desired payback period is 4 years, so the constant after-tax annual cash flow must be $90,000 ($360,000 ÷ 4). Assuming that the company has sufficient other income to permit realization of the full tax savings, depreciation of the machine will shield $60,000 ($360,000 ÷ 6) of income from taxation each year, an after-tax cash savings of $24,000 ($60,000 × 40%). Thus, the machine must generate an additional $66,000 ($90,000 – $24,000) of after-tax cash savings from operations. This amount is equivalent to $110,000 [$66,000 ÷ (1.0 – .4)] of before-tax operating cash savings.
Answer (A) is incorrect. The amount of $90,000 is the total desired annual after-tax cash savings. Answer (C) is incorrect. The amount of $114,000 results from adding, not subtracting, the $24,000 of tax depreciation savings to determine the minimum annual after-tax operating savings. Answer (D) is incorrect. The amount of $150,000 assumes that depreciation is not tax deductible.

27. If the present value of expected cash inflows from a project equals the present value of expected cash outflows, the discount rate is the

A. Payback rate.

B. Internal rate of return.

C. Accounting rate of return.

D. Net present value rate.

Answer (B) is correct.
REQUIRED: The relationship of net present value to the discount rate.
DISCUSSION: The definition of the internal rate of return is the discount rate at which the net present value of a project's cash flows equals zero.
Answer (A) is incorrect. "Payback rate" is not a meaningful term in this context. Answer (C) is incorrect. The accounting rate of return is arrived at without reference to present value. Answer (D) is incorrect. The net present value rate is the rate under discussion.

28. The following methods are used to evaluate capital investment projects:

Internal rate of return
Average rate of return
Payback
Net present value

Which one of the following correctly identifies the methods that utilize discounted cash-flow (DCF) techniques?

	Internal Rate of Return	Average Rate of Return	Payback	Net Present Value
A.	Yes	Yes	No	No
B.	No	No	Yes	Yes
C.	Yes	No	Yes	No
D.	Yes	No	No	Yes

Answer (D) is correct.
REQUIRED: The capital budgeting methods that use discounted cash flows.
DISCUSSION: The internal rate of return (IRR) is the discount rate at which a capital investment's net present value (NPV) equals zero. Both IRR and NPV, therefore, require the use of discounted cash flows. The average rate of return and payback methods use accrual-basis figures and thus are not DCF methods.
Answer (A) is incorrect. Average rate of return does not use DCF, and net present value does. Answer (B) is incorrect. Internal rate of return is a DCF method, and payback is not. Answer (C) is incorrect. Payback is not a DCF method, and net present value is.

29. Which one of the following methods for evaluating capital projects is the **least** useful from an investment analysis point of view?

A. Accounting rate of return.

B. Internal rate of return.

C. Net present value.

D. Payback.

Answer (A) is correct.
REQUIRED: The least useful capital budgeting technique.
DISCUSSION: The accounting, or book, rate of return is an unsatisfactory means of evaluating capital projects for two major reasons. Because the accounting rate of return uses accrual-basis numbers, the calculation is subject to such accounting judgments as how quickly to depreciate capitalized assets. Also, the accounting rate of return is an average of all of a firm's capital projects; it reveals nothing about the performance of individual investment choices.
Answer (B) is incorrect. Internal rate of return, which uses discounted cash flows, can be a useful method for evaluating capital projects. Answer (C) is incorrect. Net present value, which uses discounted cash flows, is generally the most useful method for evaluating capital projects. Answer (D) is incorrect. The payback method can be useful for those firms that have set a minimum length of time within which projects must pay for themselves.

Use the additional questions in Gleim **CPA Test Prep Online** to create Test Sessions that emulate Prometric!

9.7 PRACTICE WRITTEN COMMUNICATION TASK

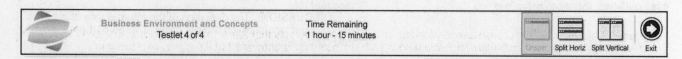

Business Environment and Concepts
Testlet 4 of 4

Time Remaining
1 hour - 15 minutes

Unsplit　Split Horiz　Split Vertical　Exit

DIRECTIONS

Note: If you believe you have encountered a software malfunction, report it to the test center staff immediately.

Navigation

To navigate from task to task, use the controls at the bottom of the screen. Click on the **Next** button to advance to the next task, or the **Previous** button to go to the previous task. To go directly to any task, click on its number.

If you would like a reminder to revisit a task, or want to indicate that you are finished with it, click on the reminder flag below the task number. To clear the flag, click on it again. Reminder flags are for your use only – they do not contribute to your score.

Tabs

In this part of the examination, you will be asked to complete various tasks. Every task has one or more **Work Tabs**. Every task also has a **Help** tab.

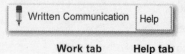

Work tab　　　Help tab

Work Tabs:

- **Work Tabs** are identified with a pencil icon. This is where your responses are expected.
- Each task has one or more **Work Tabs**.
- **Work Tabs** contain directions for completing the task - be sure to read these directions carefully.
- The **Work Tab** name in the example above is for illustration only - yours will differ.
- You must complete all of the **Work Tabs** in each task to receive full credit.

Help Tab:

- The **Help Tab** provides assistance with the exam software that is used in this task. For example, if the task is to compose a memorandum, **Help** will provide information about the word processor.

The Toolbar

The toolbar at the top of the screen shows the amount of time remaining for you to complete the tasks. In addition, the following tools are available. Note that only the **Exit** button is displayed when Directions are visible - the others will appear when you begin the tasks.

Click on these buttons to split or unsplit the screen. You can split the screen vertically or horizontally.

Click on this button to go on to the next part of the examination. You must complete all of the tasks to receive full credit. Once you click on **Exit** and confirm the action, you will NOT be able to return to this testlet.

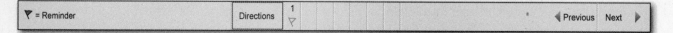

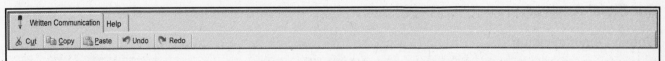

The CFO of Alachua Corporation asked your firm to analyze two projects that Alachua is considering. The CFO knows only the payback period technique for evaluating capital projects and is unaware that it may have drawbacks.

Prepare a memo to the CFO of Alachua Corporation describing the net present value, internal rate of return, and payback period methods of evaluating capital projects.

Type your communication below the line in the response area below.

REMINDER: Your response will be graded for both technical content and writing skills. Technical content will be evaluated for information that is helpful to the intended reader and clearly relevant to the issue. Writing skills will be evaluated for development, organization, and the appropriate expression of ideas in professional correspondence. Use a standard business memorandum or letter format with a clear beginning, middle, and end. Do not convey information in the form of a table, bullet point list, or other abbreviated presentation.

To: CFO, Alachua Corporation
Re: Evaluation methods for capital projects

Unofficial Answer

Written Communication

To: CFO, Alachua Corporation
Re: Evaluation methods for capital projects

In order for management to effectively make an investment decision when choosing between two projects, the benefit value of each project must first be determined. The project with the higher benefit value to the company should be selected. Common methods used for evaluating capital projects include the net present value, the internal rate of return, and the payback period methods.

The net present value (NPV) method expresses a project's returns in dollar terms. It involves netting the expected cash streams (inflows and outflows) related to a project and then discounting them at the desired rate of return. If the NPV of the project is positive, the project is desirable because it has a higher rate of return than the company's desired rate.

The internal rate of return (IRR) method expresses a project's return in percentage terms. The IRR of an investment is the discount rate at which the investment's NPV equals zero. In other words, it is the rate that makes the present value of the expected cash inflows equal the present value of the expected cash outflows. If the IRR is higher than the company's desired rate of return, then the project is desirable.

The payback period method calculates the number of years required to return the original investment, that is, the time necessary for the new project to pay for itself. Companies using the payback period method set a maximum length of time within which the projects must pay for themselves to be considered acceptable. If the project's payback period is less than the company's maximum, then the project is acceptable. The strength of the payback method is its simplicity and, to some extent, it also measures risk. The longer the payback period, the more risky the investment. Weaknesses of the payback period are that it disregards the time value of money and disregards all cash flows after the payback cutoff date.

The above depicts a Level 5 answer. See page 16 in the Introduction for a description of the three grading criteria.

Self-Grade

Evaluate each of the following by selecting a 0, 1, 2, 3, 4, or 5. An average response is 3. Use 4 for better than average and 5 for outstanding. Use 2 for less than average and 1 for quite poor. Use zero for no response, if you did not address the topic, or if you gave advice that is clearly illegal.

Organization	o 0	o 1	o 2	o 3	o 4	o 5
Development	o 0	o 1	o 2	o 3	o 4	o 5
Expression	o 0	o 1	o 2	o 3	o 4	o 5

Your grade for the written communication as a whole is the average of the scores for the three criteria.

Use **CPA Gleim Online** and **Simulation Wizard** to practice more written communication tasks in a realistic environment.

STUDY UNIT TEN
CAPITAL BUDGETING II
AND CORPORATE PERFORMANCE

(8 pages of outline)

Because investment capital is a scarce resource, potential projects must be ranked (Subunit 1). Accountants must be able to recognize the differences between the various capital budgeting techniques (Subunit 2).

The success or failure of an entity in achieving the desired return for its stakeholders is the subject of corporate performance measures (Subunits 3 and 4). A firm's ability to remain in business in the long run is termed solvency, and it can be measured (Subunit 5).

10.1 RANKING CAPITAL PROJECTS

1. **Profitability Index**

    a. When sufficient resources are available, every project with a positive NPV should be undertaken.

        1) However, few entities have the resources to undertake every desirable capital project. In such situations, called capital rationing, management needs a tool to determine which investments provide not necessarily the highest total return, but the highest per dollar invested.

    b. The **profitability index** (or excess present value index) is a method for ranking projects to ensure that limited resources are placed with the investments that will generate the highest return per dollar invested.

$$\text{Profitability index} = \frac{\text{PV of future net cash flows or NPV of project}}{\text{Initial investment}}$$

EXAMPLE

The corporation has $200,000 to invest. It can therefore invest either in Project F below or in Projects G and H:

	Project F	Project G	Project H
Initial investment	$(200,000)	$(150,000)	$(50,000)
Year 1	140,000	50,000	40,000
Year 2	140,000	50,000	30,000
Year 3		50,000	10,000
Year 4		77,453	

The first step in ranking these projects is to calculate their NPVs. The company uses a 6% hurdle rate.

	Project F		Project G		Project H	
	Undiscounted Cash Flows	Discounted Cash Flows	Undiscounted Cash Flows	Discounted Cash Flows	Undiscounted Cash Flows	Discounted Cash Flows
Year 1	$140,000	$132,076	$ 50,000	$ 47,170	$40,000	$37,736
Year 2	140,000	124,600	50,000	44,500	30,000	26,700
Year 3			50,000	41,980	10,000	8,396
Year 4			77,453	61,350		
PV of cash inflows		$256,676		$195,000		$72,832
Initial investment	(200,000)	(200,000)	(150,000)	(150,000)	(50,000)	(50,000)
Net present value		$ 56,676		$ 45,000		$22,832

Each project's profitability index can now be calculated. Note that choice of numerator has no effect on the decision.

PV of cash inflows in numerator	Net present value in numerator
Project F: $256,676 ÷ $200,000 = 1.283	**Project F:** $56,676 ÷ $200,000 = 0.283
Project G: $195,000 ÷ $150,000 = 1.300	**Project G:** $45,000 ÷ $150,000 = 0.300
Project H: $72,832 ÷ $50,000 = 1.457	**Project H:** $22,832 ÷ $50,000 = 0.457

Project H provides the highest profitability index and Project G has the next highest, so the initial decision is to undertake Projects G and H.

---

    c.   When the initial investment is the same, the independent project with the higher NPV is the project with the higher profitability index.

Stop and review! You have completed the outline for this subunit. Study multiple-choice questions 1 through 5 beginning on page 284.

10.2 COMPARING CAPITAL BUDGETING TECHNIQUES

Some CPA exam questions involve selecting the correct capital budgeting method for a given situation rather than the mechanics of calculating the measure itself. This subunit consists entirely of this type of question. Please review Study Unit 9, Subunits 3 through 6, and Subunit 10.1 before attempting to answer these questions.

Stop and review! You have completed the outline for this subunit. Study multiple-choice questions 6 through 10 beginning on page 286.

10.3 RETURN ON INVESTMENT AND RESIDUAL INCOME

    1.   **Asset Effectiveness/Asset Efficiency**

        a.   The return generated for a corporation's owners is most often assessed with one of two measures:

            1)   Return on investment, stated in percentage terms
            2)   Residual income, stated in dollar terms

        b.   These measures allow an investor to assess how effectively (efficiently) the firm is deploying assets in the pursuit of a return.

2. **Return on Investment -- Basic Version**

a. Return on investment (ROI) is calculated as follows:

$$Return\ on\ investment\ (ROI)\ =\ \frac{Operating\ income}{Average\ invested\ capital}$$

If the firm's ROI is higher than its cost of capital, the firm's activities are adding to shareholders' value.

EXAMPLE

A corporation had the following information for the year just ended:

Sales	$100,000
Operating expenses	58,000
Invested capital	800,000

Invested capital at the previous year end was $600,000. ROI for the year can be calculated as follows:

Return on investment (ROI) = Operating income ÷ Average invested capital
= ($100,000 − $58,000) ÷ [($800,000 + $600,000) ÷ 2]
= $42,000 ÷ $700,000
= 6%

---

3. **Return on Investment -- Component View**

a. ROI can be viewed as the product of two component ratios.

Return on Investment		**Profit Margin**		**Capital Turnover**
$\dfrac{Operating\ income}{Average\ invested\ capital}$	$=$	$\dfrac{Operating\ income}{Sales}$	$\times$	$\dfrac{Sales}{Average\ invested\ capital}$

EXAMPLE

Invested capital at the previous year end was $600,000. ROI for the year can be calculated as follows:

Profit margin: Operating income ÷ Sales   = $42,000 ÷ $100,000 = 42%
Capital turnover: Sales ÷ Average invested capital = $100,000 ÷ $700,000 = 14.286 times

The calculation can be checked by recombining the two ratios to generate ROI.

Return on investment: Profit margin × Capital turnover = 42% × 14.286 = 6%

---

4. **Residual Income**

a. Residual income is calculated as follows:

Residual income = Operating income − Target return on invested capital

1) The target return amount is derived by weighting average invested capital with an imputed interest rate.

EXAMPLE

The corporation's capital carries an imputed interest rate of 5.5%.

Residual income = Operating income − Target return on invested capital
= $42,000 − ($700,000 × 5.5%)
= $42,000 − $38,500
= $3,500

---

5.   **Comparing the Two Methods**

a.   ROI and residual income can be best understood in relation to net present value and internal rate of return that were introduced in Study Unit 9 for assessing capital projects.

1)   Like internal rate of return, ROI is a percentage measure, and, like net present value, residual income is a monetary measure.

b.   Like internal rate of return, ROI is a very popular tool because it allows quick and easy comparisons with other percentage-based measures such as the firm's cost of capital and the ROIs of competitors.

1)   However (also like internal rate of return), a significant drawback of relying on ROI is the temptation to reject capital projects that would decrease the ROI percentage in spite of the fact that they would increase shareholder wealth.

2)   Consider a corporation that judges divisional performance solely on ROI. If a division with a current ROI of 12% is presented with a project that is estimated to return only 10%, management would reject it out of hand because it would lower divisional ROI.

a)   Yet, if the project has a positive net present value, it should be accepted because it would increase the company's bottom line.

c.   From this example, it is clear why monetary residual income is often considered a superior assessment tool to percentage return on investment.

1)   Dealing with absolute dollars rather than percentages forces management to consider all decisions in the light of increasing shareholder wealth, not just historical percentage returns.

The AICPA has frequently asked questions regarding the determination of both ROI and residual income, as well as questions requiring comparison of the two.

Stop and review! You have completed the outline for this subunit. Study multiple-choice questions 11 through 25 beginning on page 287.

10.4 OTHER CORPORATE PERFORMANCE MEASURES

1.   **Return on Assets**

a.   Return on assets (ROA) is an alternative ratio to return on investment.

$$Return\ on\ assets\ (ROA) = \frac{Net\ income}{Average\ total\ assets}$$

EXAMPLE

The corporation had the following information about the year just ended:

Operating income	$ 90,000
Income taxes	27,000
Total assets	400,000

Total assets at the previous year end were $500,000. ROA for the year can be calculated as follows:

Return on assets (ROA) = Net income ÷ Average total assets
= ($90,000 − $27,000) ÷ [($400,000 + $500,000) ÷ 2]
= $63,000 ÷ $450,000
= 14%

2.   **Earnings per Share and Return on Common Equity**

   a.   Earnings per share (EPS) is a ratio of particular interest to the corporation's common shareholders. It is a profitability ratio that measures the amount of current-period earnings that can be associated with a single share of a corporation's common stock.

$$EPS = \frac{Net\ income\ -\ Preferred\ dividends}{Common\ shares\ outstanding}$$

   1)   The numerator is often called income available to common shareholders.

   b.   Return on common equity (ROCE) measures the amount of income a company earns per dollar invested by the common shareholders.

$$ROCE = \frac{Net\ income\ -\ Preferred\ dividends}{Average\ common\ equity}$$

   c.   The price-earnings ratio measures the amount that investors are willing to pay for $1 of the company's earnings.

$$Price\text{-}Earnings = \frac{P}{E} = \frac{Market\ price\ of\ share}{Earnings\ per\ share\ (EPS)}$$

   1)   Generally, the higher the ratio, the more confidence the market has in the company's ability to grow and produce higher returns for the investors.

3.   **Economic Rate of Return on Common Stock**

   a.   The economic rate of return on common stock measures the amount of shareholder wealth generated during a period of time relative to the amount invested.

$$\frac{Dividends\ paid\ +\ Change\ in\ stock\ price}{Beginning\ stock\ price}$$

4.   **Economic Value Added**

   a.   Economic value added (EVA) is the formula for residual income adjusted for the opportunity cost of capital.

   b.   The basic formula can be stated as follows:

After-tax operating income	$ xxx,xxx
Investment (capital used) × Cost of capital (WACC*)	(xx,xxx)
Economic value added	$ xx,xxx

   *WACC defined in Study Unit 7, Subunit 5

EXAMPLE

A company invested $200,000 in a new operating segment. The current-year net income of the segment was $21,000. The company's cost of capital is 9%.

Net income	$21,000
Investment × Cost of capital ($200,000 × 9%)	(18,000)
Economic value added	$ 3,000

The economic value is positive. Thus, the investment in a new operating segment increased shareholder value.

---

   c.   EVA represents a business unit's true economic profit primarily because a charge for the cost of equity capital is implicit in the cost of capital.

   1)   The cost of equity is an opportunity cost, that is, the return that could have been obtained on the best alternative investment of similar risk.

   2)   Hence, EVA measures the marginal benefit obtained by using resources in a particular way. It is useful for determining whether a segment of a business is increasing shareholder value.

d.   EVA differs from accounting income not only because it subtracts the cost of equity but also because it makes certain other adjustments.

1)   For example, R&D costs may be capitalized and amortized over 5 years for EVA purposes, and true economic depreciation rather than the amount used for accounting or tax purposes may be recognized. Adjustments will vary from firm to firm.

Stop and review! You have completed the outline for this subunit. Study multiple-choice questions 26 through 28 beginning on page 291.

10.5 MEASURES OF CORPORATE SOLVENCY

1.   **Solvency**

a.   Solvency is a firm's ability to pay its noncurrent obligations as they come due and thus remain in business in the long run (contrast with liquidity). The key ingredients of solvency are the firm's capital structure (discussed here) and degree of leverage (defined in item 5.a. in Study Unit 7, Subunit 1).

2.   **Capital Structure**

a.   A firm's capital structure includes its sources of financing, both long- and short-term. These sources can be in the form of debt (external sources) or equity (internal sources).

b.   **Debt** is the creditor interest in the firm.

1)   The firm is contractually obligated to repay debtholders. The terms of repayment (i.e., timing of interest and principal) are specified in the debt agreement.

2)   As long as the return on debt capital exceeds the amount of interest paid, the use of debt financing is advantageous to a firm. The return is often enhanced due to the fact that interest payments on debt are tax-deductible.

3)   The tradeoff is that an increased debt load makes a firm riskier (since debt must be paid regardless of whether or not the company is profitable). At some point, either a firm will have to pay a higher interest rate than its return on debt or creditors will simply refuse to lend any more money.

c.   **Equity** is the ownership interest in the firm.

1)   Equity is the permanent capital of an entity, contributed by the firm's owners in the hopes of earning a return.

2)   However, a return on equity is uncertain because equity embodies only a residual interest in the firm's assets (residual because it is the claim left over after all debt has been satisfied).

3)   Periodic returns to owners of excess earnings are referred to as dividends. The firm may be contractually obligated to pay dividends to preferred stockholders but not to common stockholders.

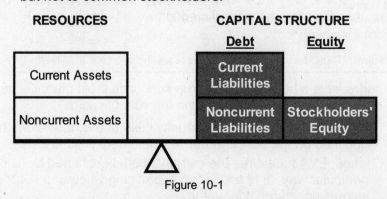

Figure 10-1

    d.   Capital structure decisions affect the risk profile of a firm. For example, a company with a higher percent of debt capital will be riskier than a firm with a high percentage of equity capital.

        1)   Thus, when the relative amount of debt is high, equity investors will demand a higher rate of return on their investments to compensate for the risk brought about by the high degree of financial leverage.

        2)   Alternatively, a company with a relatively larger proportion of equity capital will be able to borrow at lower rates because debt holders will accept lower interest in exchange for the lower risk indicated by the equity cushion.

3.   Capital Structure Ratios

    a.   Capital structure ratios report the relative proportions of debt and equity in a firm's capital structure.

    b.   The total-debt-to-total-capital ratio measures the percentage of the firm's capital structure provided by creditors.

$$Total\ debt\ to\ total\ capital\ = \frac{Total\ debt}{Total\ capital}$$

EXAMPLE

See the sample balance sheet on page 227.

        Current year: $1,000,000 ÷ $1,800,000 = 0.556
        Prior year: $950,000 ÷ $1,600,000 = 0.594

The company became slightly less reliant on debt in its capital structure during the current year. Although total debt rose, equity rose by a greater percentage. The company is thus less leveraged than before.

---

        1)   When total debt to total capital is low, it means more of the firm's capital is supplied by the stockholders. Thus, creditors prefer this ratio to be low as a cushion against losses.

    c.   The debt-to-equity ratio is a direct comparison of the firm's debt load to its equity stake.

$$Debt\ to\ equity = \frac{Total\ debt}{Stockholders'\ equity}$$

EXAMPLE

        Current year: $1,000,000 ÷ $800,000 = 1.25
        Prior year: $950,000 ÷ $650,000 = 1.46

The amount by which the company's debts exceed its equity stake declined in the current year.

---

        1)   Like the previous ratio, the debt-to-equity ratio reflects long-term debt-payment ability. Again, a low ratio means a lower relative debt burden and thus better chances of repayment of creditors.

d.   The long-term-debt-to-total-equity ratio reports the long-term debt burden carried by a company per dollar of equity.

$$\text{Long-term debt to total equity} = \frac{\text{Long-term debt}}{\text{Stockholder's equity}}$$

EXAMPLE

Current year: $610,000 ÷ $800,000 = 0.763
Prior year: $675,000 ÷ $650,000 = 1.038

The company has greatly improved its long-term debt burden. It now carries less than one dollar of long-term debt for every dollar of equity.

1)   A low ratio means a firm will have an easier time raising new debt capital (since its low current debt load makes it a good credit risk).

e.   The debt-to-total-assets ratio (also called the debt ratio) reports the total debt burden carried by a company per dollar of assets.

$$\text{Debt to total assets} = \frac{\text{Total debt}}{\text{Total assets}}$$

EXAMPLE

Current year: $1,000,000 ÷ $1,800,000 = 0.556
Prior year: $950,000 ÷ $1,600,000 = 0.594

Although total liabilities increased in absolute terms, this ratio improved because total assets increased even more.

1)   Numerically, this ratio is identical to the total-debt-to-total-capital ratio since total capital equals total assets.

Stop and review! You have completed the outline for this subunit. Study multiple-choice questions 29 and 30 on page 293.

QUESTIONS

10.1 Ranking Capital Projects

1. Woods, Inc., is considering four independent investment proposals. Woods has $3 million available for investment during the present period. The investment outlay for each project and its projected net present value (NPV) is presented below.

Project	Investment Cost	NPV
I	$ 500,000	$ 40,000
II	900,000	120,000
III	1,200,000	180,000
IV	1,600,000	150,000

Which of the following project options should be recommended to Woods's management?

A.   Projects I, II, and III only.

B.   Projects I, II, and IV only.

C.   Projects II, III, and IV only.

D.   Projects III and IV only.

Answer (A) is correct.
   REQUIRED: The acceptable capital projects given net present value.
   DISCUSSION: When available funds are limited, potential projects should be ranked by profitability index. The indexes for Woods' potential projects can thus be calculated as follows:

Project	Net Present Value		Investment Cost		Profitability Index
I	$ 40,000	÷	$ 500,000	=	0.080
II	120,000	÷	900,000	=	0.133
III	180,000	÷	1,200,000	=	0.150
IV	150,000	÷	1,600,000	=	0.094

Ranked in order of desirability, they are III, II, IV, and I. Since only $3 million is available for funding, only III, II, and I will be selected.
   Answer (B) is incorrect. Project III is more desirable than Project IV. Answer (C) is incorrect. While Project IV is more desirable than Project I, insufficient funding is available to engage Project IV. Answer (D) is incorrect. Projects I and II are also desirable and sufficient funding is available.

2. The profitability index approach to investment analysis

A. Fails to consider the timing of project cash flows.

B. Considers only the project's contribution to net income and does not consider cash flow effects.

C. Always yields the same accept/reject decisions for independent projects as the net present value method.

D. Always yields the same accept/reject decisions for mutually exclusive projects as the net present value method.

Answer (C) is correct.
    REQUIRED: The true statement about the profitability index.
    DISCUSSION: The profitability index is the ratio of a discounted cash flow amount to the initial investment. It is a variation of the net present value (NPV) method and facilitates the comparison of different-sized investments. Because it is based on the NPV method, the profitability index will yield the same decision as the NPV for independent projects. However, decisions may differ for mutually exclusive projects of different sizes.
    Answer (A) is incorrect. The profitability index, like the NPV method, discounts cash flows based on the cost of capital. Answer (B) is incorrect. The profitability index is cash based. Answer (D) is incorrect. The NPV and the profitability index may yield different decisions if projects are mutually exclusive and of different sizes.

3. The profitability index (present value index)

A. Represents the ratio of the discounted net cash outflows to cash inflows.

B. Is the relationship between the net discounted cash inflows less the discounted cash outflows divided by the discounted cash outflows.

C. Is calculated by dividing the discounted profits by the cash outflows.

D. Is the ratio of the discounted net cash flows to initial investment.

Answer (D) is correct.
    REQUIRED: The true statement about the profitability index.
    DISCUSSION: The profitability index, also known as the excess present value index, is the ratio of discounted net cash flows to the initial investment. This tool is a variation of the NPV method that facilitates comparison of different-sized investments.
    Answer (A) is incorrect. The cash inflows are also discounted in the profitability index. Answer (B) is incorrect. The denominator is the initial investment. Answer (C) is incorrect. The profitability index is based on cash flows, not profits.

4. Mesa Company is considering an investment to open a new banana processing division. The project in question would entail an initial investment of $45,000, and cash inflows of $20,000 can be expected in each of the next 3 years. The hurdle rate is 10%. What is the profitability index for the project? The present value of an ordinary annuity of 1 discounted at 10% for 3 periods is 2.487. The present value of 1 due in 3 periods discounted at 10% is .751.

A. 1.0784

B. 1.1053

C. 1.1379

D. 1.1771

Answer (B) is correct.
    REQUIRED: The profitability index.
    DISCUSSION: At a 10% hurdle rate, the present value of the future cash inflows is $49,740 (20,000 × 2.487), yielding a net present value for the project of $4,740 ($49,740 – $45,000). The profitability index is thus 1.1053 ($49,740 ÷ $45,000).

5. Future, Inc., is in the enviable situation of having unlimited capital funds. The best decision rule, in an economic sense, for it to follow would be to invest in all projects in which the

A. Accounting rate of return is greater than the earnings as a percent of sales.

B. Payback reciprocal is greater than the internal rate of return.

C. Internal rate of return is greater than zero.

D. Net present value is greater than zero.

Answer (D) is correct.
    REQUIRED: The investment rule given unlimited capital funds.
    DISCUSSION: Given unlimited funds, all projects with a net present value greater than zero should be invested in. Thus, it would be profitable to invest in any company where the rate of return is greater than the cost of capital.
    Answer (A) is incorrect. Neither the accounting rate of return nor the earnings as a percent of sales is useful in capital budgeting. The accounting rate of return is accounting net income over the required investment; it ignores the time value of money. Earnings as a percent of sales ignores the amount of required investment. Answer (B) is incorrect. The payback criterion for capital budgeting is not efficient or effective. Answer (C) is incorrect. The problem states that there are unlimited capital funds but does not indicate what the cost of capital is. Accordingly, projects can only be invested in when the internal rate of return is greater than cost of capital; i.e., the net present value is greater than zero.

10.2 Comparing Capital Budgeting Techniques

6. Which of the following limitations is common to the calculations of payback period, discounted payback, internal rate of return, and net present value?

A. They do **not** consider the time value of money.

B. They require multiple trial and error calculations.

C. They require knowledge of a company's cost of capital.

D. They rely on the forecasting of future data.

Answer (D) is correct.
REQUIRED: The limitation that is common to the calculations of the given capital budgeting selection models.
DISCUSSION: It is the long-term aspect of capital budgeting that presents the accountant with specific challenges. An entity must accurately forecast future changes in demand in order to have the necessary production capacity when demand for its product is strong without having excess idle capacity when demand slackens. Because capital budgeting requires choosing among investment proposals, a ranking procedure for such decisions is needed. The ranking procedure also requires reliable estimates of future cost savings or revenues in order to calculate the estimated cash flows.
Answer (A) is incorrect. Discounted cash flow, internal rate of return, and net present value all consider the time value of money in their calculations. Answer (B) is incorrect. Multiple trial and error calculations are only required for determining the internal rate of return. Answer (C) is incorrect. The payback period calculation does not require knowledge of a company's cost of capital.

7. The method that divides a project's annual after-tax net income by the average investment cost to measure the estimated performance of a capital investment is the

A. Internal rate of return method.

B. Accounting rate of return method.

C. Payback method.

D. Net present value (NPV) method.

Answer (B) is correct.
REQUIRED: The capital budgeting method that divides annual after-tax net income by the average investment cost.
DISCUSSION: The accounting rate of return uses undiscounted net income (not cash flows) to determine a rate of profitability. Annual after-tax net income is divided by the average carrying amount (or the initial value) of the investment in assets.
Answer (A) is incorrect. The internal rate of return is the rate at which the project's NPV is zero. The minimum desired rate of return is not used in the discounting. Answer (C) is incorrect. The payback period is the time required to complete the return of the original investment. This method gives no consideration to the time value of money or to returns after the payback period. Answer (D) is incorrect. The NPV method computes the discounted present value of future cash inflows to determine whether it is greater than the initial cash outflow.

8. The technique that recognizes the time value of money by discounting the after-tax cash flows for a project over its life to time period zero using the company's minimum desired rate of return is called the

A. Net present value method.

B. Payback method.

C. Average rate of return method.

D. Accounting rate of return method.

Answer (A) is correct.
REQUIRED: The capital budgeting technique that discounts the after-tax cash flows to their present value using the company's minimum desired rate of return.
DISCUSSION: The net present value method discounts future cash flows to the present value using some arbitrary rate of return, which is presumably the firm's cost of capital.
Answer (B) is incorrect. The payback method does not recognize the time value of money. Answer (C) is incorrect. The average rate of return method does not use the firm's cost of capital as a discount rate. Answer (D) is incorrect. The accounting rate of return method does not recognize the time value of money.

9. The technique that measures the number of years required for the after-tax cash flows to recover the initial investment in a project is called the

A. Net present value method.

B. Payback method.

C. Profitability index method.

D. Accounting rate of return method.

Answer (B) is correct.

   REQUIRED: The capital budgeting technique that measures the number of years required for the after-tax cash flows to recover the initial investment.

   DISCUSSION: The usual payback formula divides the initial investment by the constant net annual cash inflow. The payback method is unsophisticated in that it ignores the time value of money, but it is widely used because of its simplicity and emphasis on recovery of the initial investment.

   Answer (A) is incorrect. The net present value method first discounts the future cash flows to their present value. Answer (C) is incorrect. The profitability index method divides the present value of the future net cash inflows by the initial investment. Answer (D) is incorrect. The accounting rate of return divides the annual net income by the average investment in the project.

10. The technique that reflects the time value of money and is calculated by dividing the present value of the future net after-tax cash inflows that have been discounted at the desired cost of capital by the initial cash outlay for the investment is called the

A. Capital rationing method.

B. Average rate of return method.

C. Profitability index method.

D. Accounting rate of return method.

Answer (C) is correct.

   REQUIRED: The technique that divides the present value of future net cash inflows by the initial cash outlay.

   DISCUSSION: The profitability index, also called the excess present value index, measures the ratio of the present value of a project's future net cash inflows to the original investment. If capital rationing is necessary, the profitability index allows management to identify the projects with the highest return per investment dollar.

   Answer (A) is incorrect. Capital rationing is not a technique but rather a condition that characterizes capital budgeting when insufficient capital is available to finance all profitable investment opportunities. Answer (B) is incorrect. The average rate of return method does not divide the future cash flows by the cost of the investment. Answer (D) is incorrect. The accounting rate of return does not recognize the time value of money.

10.3 Return on Investment and Residual Income

11. The following information pertains to Quest Co.'s Gold Division for the year just ended:

Sales	$311,000
Variable cost	250,000
Traceable fixed costs	50,000
Average invested capital	40,000
Imputed interest rate	10%

Quest's return on investment was

A. 10.00%

B. 13.33%

C. 27.50%

D. 30.00%

Answer (C) is correct.

   REQUIRED: The return on investment.

   DISCUSSION: Quest's return on investment can be calculated as follows:

ROI = Operating income ÷ Average invested capital
     = ($311,000 − $250,000 − $50,000) ÷ $40,000
     = $11,000 ÷ $40,000
     = 27.5%

   Answer (A) is incorrect. The imputed interest rate is 10.00%. Answer (B) is incorrect. A 13.33% ROI would result from a net income of $5,332. Answer (D) is incorrect. A 30.00% ROI would result from a net income of $12,000.

12. The following selected data pertain to the Darwin Division of Beagle Co. for the year just ended:

Sales	$400,000
Operating income	$ 40,000
Capital turnover	4
Imputed interest rate	10%

What was Darwin's residual income for the year?

A. $0

B. $4,000

C. $10,000

D. $30,000

Answer (D) is correct.

REQUIRED: The residual income for Darwin.

DISCUSSION: Residual income equals operating income minus a target return on invested capital. Since the capital turnover equals sales divided by average invested capital, average invested capital is $100,000 ($400,000 sales ÷ 4 capital turnover). Residual income can now be calculated as follows:

Residual income = Operating income – Target return on invested capital
= $40,000 – ($100,000 × 10%)
= $40,000 – $10,000
= $30,000

Answer (A) is incorrect. Residual income is $30,000. Answer (B) is incorrect. Operating income times the imputed interest rate is $4,000. Answer (C) is incorrect. The target return on invested capital is $10,000.

13. A company has two divisions. Division A has operating income of $500 and total assets of $1,000. Division B has operating income of $400 and total assets of $1,600. The required rate of return for the company is 10%. The company's residual income would be which of the following amounts?

A. $0

B. $260

C. $640

D. $900

Answer (C) is correct.

REQUIRED: The company's residual income.

DISCUSSION: The company's total residual income can be calculated as follows:

Residual income = Operating income – Target return on invested capital
= ($500 + $400) – [($1,000 + $1,600) × 10%]
= $900 – $260
= $640

Answer (A) is incorrect. Operating income exceeds residual income. Answer (B) is incorrect. The required return is $260. Answer (D) is incorrect. Operating income is $900.

14. Minon, Inc., purchased a long-term asset on the last day of the current year. What are the effects of this purchase on return on investment and residual income?

	Return on Investment	Residual Income
A.	Increase	Increase
B.	Decrease	Decrease
C.	Increase	Decrease
D.	Decrease	Increase

Answer (B) is correct.

REQUIRED: The effects of the long-term asset purchase.

DISCUSSION: ROI equals operating income divided by average invested capital. The purchase of a long-term asset on the last day of the fiscal year has little or no effect on net income but causes an increase in average invested capital, thereby decreasing ROI. Residual income is operating income minus a target return on average invested capital. Given no change in operating income or the required rate of return, an increase in invested capital decreases residual income.

15. Vested, Inc., made some changes in operations and provided the following information:

	Year 2	Year 3
Operating revenues	$ 900,000	$1,100,000
Operating expenses	650,000	700,000
Operating assets	1,200,000	2,000,000

What percentage represents the return on investment for Year 3?

A. 22.5%

B. 10%

C. 20.83%

D. 25%

Answer (D) is correct.

REQUIRED: The return on investment for Year 3.

DISCUSSION: Vested's Year 3 return on investment can be calculated as follows:

ROI = Operating income ÷ Average invested capital
= ($1,100,000 – $700,000) ÷ [($2,000,000 + $1,200,000) ÷ 2]
= $400,000 ÷ $1,600,000
= 25%

Answer (A) is incorrect. This figure is based on Year 2 expenses. Answer (B) is incorrect. This figure is based on Year 2 revenues. Answer (C) is incorrect. This figure is the ROI for Year 2.

Questions 16 and 17 are based on the following information.

Oslo Co.'s industrial photo-finishing division, Rho, incurred the following costs and expenses during the year just ended:

	Variable	Fixed
Direct materials	$200,000	
Direct labor	150,000	
Factory overhead	70,000	$42,000
General, selling, and administrative	30,000	48,000
Totals	$450,000	$90,000

During the year, Rho produced 300,000 units of industrial photo-prints, which were sold for $2.00 each. Oslo's investment in Rho was $500,000 and $700,000 at January 1 and December 31, respectively. Oslo normally imputes interest on investments at 15% of average invested capital.

---

16. Assume that net operating income was $60,000 and that average invested capital was $600,000. For the year ended December 31, Rho's residual income (loss) was

A. $150,000

B. $60,000

C. $(45,000)

D. $(30,000)

Answer (D) is correct.
 REQUIRED: The residual income (loss).
 DISCUSSION: Rho's residual income can be calculated as follows:

Residual income = Operating income – Target return on invested capital
= $60,000 – ($600,000 × 15%)
= $60,000 – $90,000
= $30,000 loss

Answer (A) is incorrect. The imputed interest should not be added to net operating income. Answer (B) is incorrect. The imputed interest needs to be deducted from net operating income. Answer (C) is incorrect. The imputed interest is not 15% of the year-end invested capital.

---

17. For the year ended December 31, Rho's return on average investment was

A. 15.0%

B. 10.0%

C. 8.6%

D. (5.0%)

Answer (B) is correct.
 REQUIRED: The return on average investment.
 DISCUSSION: Rho's return on average investment can be calculated as follows:

ROI = Operating income ÷ Average invested capital
= [(300,000 units × $2) – $450,000 – $90,000] ÷ [($500,000 + $700,000) ÷ 2]
= $60,000 ÷ $600,000
= 10%

Answer (A) is incorrect. Fifteen percent is the imputed rate. Answer (C) is incorrect. Net income should not be divided by the year-end invested capital of $700,000. Answer (D) is incorrect. This percentage equals the residual loss ($30,000) divided by average invested capital.

---

18. What is the primary disadvantage of using return on investment (ROI) rather than residual income (RI) to evaluate the performance of investment center managers?

A. ROI is a percentage, while RI is a dollar amount.

B. ROI may lead to rejecting projects that yield positive cash flows.

C. ROI does not necessarily reflect the company's cost of capital.

D. ROI does not reflect all economic gains.

Answer (B) is correct.
 REQUIRED: The primary disadvantage of using ROI rather than RI to evaluate investment center performance.
 DISCUSSION: A serious drawback of relying on ROI is the temptation to reject capital projects that would decrease the ROI percentage in spite of the fact that they would increase shareholder wealth. Management tends to reject any capital project that would decrease current ROI even if it would add to the company's bottom line. Residual income is often considered superior because dealing with absolute dollars rather than percentages forces management to consider all decisions in the light of increasing shareholder wealth, not just historical percentage returns.
 Answer (A) is incorrect. Expressing ROI as a percentage is not in itself a primary disadvantage. For example, RI is based on an imputed ROI. Answer (C) is incorrect. ROI may reflect the company's cost of capital. For example, using net income as the numerator takes into account interest expense from debt incurred to purchase assets. Answer (D) is incorrect. Failing to use an income measure that reflects all economic gains also is a possible disadvantage of RI.

19. The following information pertains to Bala Co. for the year ended December 31:

Sales	$600,000
Income	100,000
Capital investment	400,000

Which of the following equations should be used to compute Bala's return on investment?

   A. (4/6) × (6/1) = ROI.

   B. (6/4) × (1/6) = ROI.

   C. (4/6) × (1/6) = ROI.

   D. (6/4) × (6/1) = ROI.

Answer (B) is correct.
   REQUIRED: The equation used to compute ROI.
   DISCUSSION: ROI equals capital turnover (sales ÷ investment) times the profit margin (income ÷ sales). Thus, Bala's ROI can be represented by [($600,000 ÷ $400,000) × ($100,000 ÷ $600,000)].
   Answer (A) is incorrect. The ROI yielded is 400%, which is the reciprocal of the true ROI of 25%. ROI equals capital turnover (sales ÷ investment) times the profit margin (income ÷ sales). Answer (C) is incorrect. Capital turnover is sales divided by investment, not investment divided by sales. Answer (D) is incorrect. Profit margin is income divided by sales, not sales divided by income.

20. Galax, Inc., had operating income of $5,000,000 before interest and taxes. Galax's net book value of plant assets at January 1 and December 31 were $22,000,000 and $18,000,000, respectively. Galax achieved a 25% return on investment for the year, with an investment turnover of 2.5. What were Galax's sales for the year?

   A. $55,000,000

   B. $50,000,000

   C. $45,000,000

   D. $20,000,000

Answer (B) is correct.
   REQUIRED: The sales for the year.
   DISCUSSION: The capital (investment) turnover ratio equals sales divided by average invested capital. Sales equals the capital turnover ratio (2.5) times average invested capital ($20,000,000). Galax's sales are therefore $50,000,000.
   Answer (A) is incorrect. The amount of $55,000,000 equals investment turnover times beginning plant assets. Answer (C) is incorrect. The amount of $45,000,000 equals investment turnover times ending plant assets. Answer (D) is incorrect. The amount of $20,000,000 equals the average plant assets.

21. Wexford Co. has a subunit that reported the following data for Year 1:

Asset (investment) turnover	1.5 times
Sales	$750,000
Return on sales	8%

The imputed interest rate is 12%. What is the division residual income for Year 1?

   A. $60,000

   B. $30,000

   C. $20,000

   D. $0

Answer (D) is correct.
   REQUIRED: The residual income.
   DISCUSSION: Residual income is the excess of operating income over a target return on invested capital. Since return on sales is the ratio of operating income to sales, Wexford has operating income of $60,000 ($750,000 sales × 8% return on sales). The target return on invested capital equals invested capital times the imputed interest rate. Invested capital is $500,000 ($750,000 sales ÷ 1.5 asset turnover), so the target return on capital is $60,000 ($500,000 capital × 12% imputed interest). Thus, Wexford's residual income is $0 ($60,000 operating income – $60,000 target return on capital).
   Answer (A) is incorrect. The amount of $60,000 is the operating income. Answer (B) is incorrect. The amount of $30,000 is the difference between sales and investments, times the imputed interest rate. Answer (C) is incorrect. The amount of $20,000 is the difference between sales and investments multiplied by the percentage return on sales.

22. SkyBound Airlines provided the following information about its two operating divisions:

	Passenger	Cargo
Operating profit	$40,000	$50,000
Investment	$250,000	$500,000
External borrowing rate	6%	8%

Measuring performance using return on investment (ROI), which division performed better?

   A. The Cargo division, with an ROI of 10%.

   B. The Passenger division, with an ROI of 16%.

   C. The Cargo division, with an ROI of 18%.

   D. The Passenger division, with an ROI of 22%.

Answer (B) is correct.
   REQUIRED: The division that performed better based on ROI.
   DISCUSSION: ROI is equal to operating profit divided by the investment. The ROI for the Passenger division is 16% ($40,000 ÷ $250,000). The ROI for the Cargo division is 10% ($50,000 ÷ $500,000). Thus, the Passenger division performed better.
   Answer (A) is incorrect. The Cargo division did not perform better. Answer (C) is incorrect. The external borrowing rate must not be added to ROI. Answer (D) is incorrect. The external borrowing rate must not be added to ROI.

23. Which of the following ratios would be used to evaluate a company's profitability?

A. Current ratio.

B. Inventory turnover ratio.

C. Debt-to-total assets ratio.

D. Gross margin ratio.

Answer (D) is correct.
REQUIRED: The ratio used to evaluate profitability.
DISCUSSION: The gross margin ratio is the ratio of sales minus cost of goods sold to sales. It is a profitability ratio that measures the percentage of sales earned after incurring direct costs of goods and services.
Answer (A) is incorrect. The current ratio measures liquidity.
Answer (B) is incorrect. The inventory turnover ratio measures the efficiency of the entity's management of inventory.
Answer (C) is incorrect. The debt-to-total assets ratio reports the total debt burden carried by a company per dollar of asset. It measures solvency.

24. The basic objective of the residual income approach to performance measurement and evaluation is to have a division maximize its

A. Return on investment rate.

B. Imputed interest rate charge.

C. Cash flows.

D. Income in excess of a desired minimum return.

Answer (D) is correct.
REQUIRED: The basic objective of the residual income approach to performance measurement and evaluation.
DISCUSSION: Residual income is the excess of the return on an investment over the targeted amount. This amount may be defined as the imputed interest on invested capital. Some firms prefer to measure managerial performance in terms of the amount of residual income rather than the percentage ROI. The principle is that the firm is expected to benefit from expansion as long as residual income is earned. Using a percentage ROI approach, expansion might be rejected if it lowered ROI even though residual income would increase.
Answer (A) is incorrect. ROI does not have to be maximized under the residual income approach. Answer (B) is incorrect. Maximizing the imputed interest rate charge would diminish the residual return. Answer (C) is incorrect. The residual income method is based on net income rather than cash flows.

25. After investing in a new project, a company discovered that its residual income remained unchanged. Which one of the following must be true about the new project?

A. The net present value of the new project must have been negative.

B. The return on investment of the new project must have been less than the firm's cost of capital.

C. The return on investment of the new project must have been equal to the firm's cost of capital.

D. The net present value of the new project must have been positive.

Answer (C) is correct.
REQUIRED: The true statement about residual income given a set of circumstances.
DISCUSSION: Residual income is the excess of the return on an investment over the firm's cost of capital. If residual income remained unchanged, then the return on the project must have been the same as the firm's cost of capital.
Answer (A) is incorrect. A negative NPV would have decreased residual income. Answer (B) is incorrect. A return less than the cost of capital would have decreased residual income. Answer (D) is incorrect. A positive NPV would increase residual income.

10.4 Other Corporate Performance Measures

26. Assume Avionics Industrials reported at year end that operating income before taxes for the year equaled $2,400,000. The company's weighted-average cost of capital (WACC) is 7.24%. The book value of debt is $1,300,000, and the book value of equity capital is $8,800,000. The income tax rate for Avionics is 30%. What is the economic value added (EVA)?

A. $731,240

B. $948,760

C. $1,668,760

D. $1,680,000

Answer (B) is correct.
REQUIRED: The economic value added (EVA).
DISCUSSION: EVA equals after-tax operating income minus the product of the weighted-average cost of capital (WACC) and the investment base. After-tax operating income equals operating income multiplied by 1 minus the tax rate, or $1,680,000. The investment base is $10,100,000, consisting of $1,300,000 of debt and $8,800,000 of equity. Hence, EVA is equal to $948,760 {($1,680,000) – [$10,100,000 × (0.0724)]}.
Answer (A) is incorrect. The cost of capital is $731,240. Answer (C) is incorrect. Income taxes must be deducted from operating income to compute EVA. Answer (D) is incorrect. The after-tax operating income is $1,680,000.

Questions 27 and 28 are based on the following information. The information below pertains to Devlin Company.

Statement of Financial Position as of May 31 (in thousands)	Year 2	Year 1
Assets		
Current assets		
Cash	$ 45	$ 38
Trading securities	30	20
Accounts receivable (net)	68	48
Inventory	90	80
Prepaid expenses	22	30
Total current assets	$255	$216
Investments, at equity	38	30
Property, plant, and equipment (net)	375	400
Intangible assets (net)	80	45
Total assets	$748	$691
Liabilities		
Current liabilities		
Notes payable	$ 35	$ 18
Accounts payable	70	42
Accrued expenses	5	4
Income taxes payable	15	16
Total current liabilities	$125	$ 80
Long-term debt	35	35
Deferred taxes	3	2
Total liabilities	$163	$117
Equity		
Preferred stock, 6%, $100 par value, cumulative	$150	$150
Common stock, $10 par value	225	195
Additional paid-in capital -- common stock	114	100
Retained earnings	96	129
Total equity	$585	$574
Total liabilities and equity	$748	$691

Income Statement for the year ended May 31 (in thousands)	Year 2	Year 1
Net sales	$480	$460
Costs and expenses		
Costs of goods sold	330	315
Selling, general, and administrative	52	51
Interest expense	8	9
Income before taxes	$ 90	$ 85
Income taxes	36	34
Net income	$ 54	$ 51

27. Assuming there are no preferred stock dividends in arrears, Devlin Company's return on common equity for the year ended May 31, Year 2, was

A. 6.3%

B. 7.5%

C. 7.8%

D. 10.5%

Answer (D) is correct.
REQUIRED: The return on common equity.
DISCUSSION: The return on common equity equals income available to common shareholders divided by average common equity. Net income available to common shareholders is $45 [$54 – ($150 par value of preferred stock × 6%)]. Average common equity is $429.5 {[($574 – $150 preferred stock) + ($585 – $150 preferred stock)] ÷ 2}. Thus, the return is 10.5% ($45 ÷ $429.5).
Answer (A) is incorrect. Average total assets are based on 6.3%. Answer (B) is incorrect. Net income divided by average total assets equals 7.5%. Answer (C) is incorrect. Net income divided by beginning total assets equals 7.8%.

28. Devlin Company's rate of return on assets for the year ended May 31, Year 2, was

A. 7.2%

B. 7.5%

C. 7.8%

D. 11.2%

Answer (B) is correct.
REQUIRED: The rate of return on assets.
DISCUSSION: The rate of return on assets equals net income divided by average total assets. Accordingly, the rate of return is 7.5% {$54 ÷ [($748 + $691) ÷ 2]}.
Answer (A) is incorrect. The figure of 7.2% uses ending total assets instead of average total assets. Answer (C) is incorrect. Net income divided by beginning total assets equals 7.8%. Answer (D) is incorrect. The return on sales is 11.2%.

10.5 Measures of Corporate Solvency

Question 29 is based on the following information.

Selected data from Ostrander Corporation's financial statements for the years indicated are presented in thousands.

Year 2 Operations				December 31	
				Year 2	Year 1
Net credit sales	$4,175				
Cost of goods sold	2,880	Cash		$ 32	$ 28
Interest expense	50	Trading securities		169	172
Income tax	120	Accounts receivable (net)		210	204
Gain on disposal of a segment		Merchandise inventory		440	420
(net of tax)	210	Tangible fixed assets		480	440
Administrative expense	950	Total assets		1,397	1,320
Net income	385	Current liabilities		370	368
		Total liabilities		790	750
		Common stock outstanding		226	210
		Retained earnings		381	360

29. The total debt-to-equity ratio for Ostrander Corporation in Year 2 is

A. 3.49

B. 0.77

C. 2.07

D. 1.30

Answer (D) is correct.

REQUIRED: The total debt-to-equity ratio for Year 2.

DISCUSSION: Total equity consists of the $226 of capital stock and $381 of retained earnings, or $607. Debt is given as the $790 of total liabilities. Thus, the ratio is 1.30 ($790 ÷ $607).

Answer (A) is incorrect. Total liabilities divided by common stock outstanding equals 3.49. Answer (B) is incorrect. Equity divided by debt equals 0.77. Answer (C) is incorrect. Total liabilities divided by retained earnings equals 2.07.

Question 30 is based on the following information. The data presented below show actual figures for selected accounts of McKeon Company for the fiscal year ended May 31, Year 1, and selected budget figures for the Year 2 fiscal year. McKeon's controller is in the process of reviewing the Year 2 budget and calculating some key ratios based on the budget. McKeon Company monitors yield or return ratios using the average financial position of the company. (Round all calculations to three decimal places if necessary.)

	5/31/Year 2	5/31/Year 1
Current assets	$210,000	$180,000
Noncurrent assets	275,000	255,000
Current liabilities	78,000	85,000
Long-term debt	75,000	30,000
Common stock ($30 par value)	300,000	300,000
Retained earnings	32,000	20,000

	Year 2 Operations
Sales*	$350,000
Cost of goods sold	160,000
Interest expense	3,000
Income taxes (40% rate)	48,000
Dividends declared and paid in Year 2	60,000
Administrative expense	67,000

*All sales are credit sales.

	Current Assets	
	5/31/Year 2	5/31/Year 1
Cash	$ 20,000	$10,000
Accounts receivable	100,000	70,000
Inventory	70,000	80,000
Prepaid expenses	20,000	20,000

30. McKeon Company's debt ratio for Year 2 is

A. 0.352

B. 0.315

C. 0.264

D. 0.237

Answer (B) is correct.

REQUIRED: The debt ratio.

DISCUSSION: The debt ratio is equal to the total debt at year end divided by total assets at year end. Total debt at year end is $153,000 ($78,000 current liabilities + $75,000 long-term debt). Total assets equal $485,000 ($210,000 current assets + $275,000 noncurrent assets). Thus, the debt ratio is .315 ($153,000 ÷ $485,000).

10.6 PRACTICE WRITTEN COMMUNICATION TASK

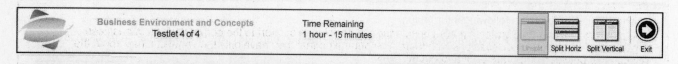

Business Environment and Concepts
Testlet 4 of 4

Time Remaining
1 hour - 15 minutes

Unsplit   Split Horiz   Split Vertical   Exit

DIRECTIONS

Note: If you believe you have encountered a software malfunction, report it to the test center staff immediately.

Navigation

To navigate from task to task, use the controls at the bottom of the screen. Click on the **Next** button to advance to the next task, or the **Previous** button to go to the previous task. To go directly to any task, click on its number.

If you would like a reminder to revisit a task, or want to indicate that you are finished with it, click on the reminder flag below the task number. To clear the flag, click on it again. Reminder flags are for your use only – they do not contribute to your score.

Tabs

In this part of the examination, you will be asked to complete various tasks. Every task has one or more **Work Tabs**. Every task also has a **Help** tab.

Work tab   Help tab

Work Tabs:

- **Work Tabs** are identified with a pencil icon. This is where your responses are expected.
- Each task has one or more **Work Tabs**.
- **Work Tabs** contain directions for completing the task - be sure to read these directions carefully.
- The **Work Tab** name in the example above is for illustration only - yours will differ.
- You must complete all of the **Work Tabs** in each task to receive full credit.

Help Tab:

- The **Help Tab** provides assistance with the exam software that is used in this task. For example, if the task is to compose a memorandum, **Help** will provide information about the word processor.

The Toolbar

The toolbar at the top of the screen shows the amount of time remaining for you to complete the tasks. In addition, the following tools are available. Note that only the **Exit** button is displayed when Directions are visible - the others will appear when you begin the tasks.

Click on these buttons to split or unsplit the screen. You can split the screen vertically or horizontally.

Click on this button to go on to the next part of the examination. You must complete all of the tasks to receive full credit. Once you click on **Exit** and confirm the action, you will NOT be able to return to this testlet.

Written Communication | Help

Cut | Copy | Paste | Undo | Redo

The partners of Packitup Partnership are considering the decision to convert to the corporate form of business organization. During your discussions with them, you determine that they have only the vaguest ideas about the relationship between corporate debt and equity.

Prepare a memo to the partners of Packitup Partnership describing the concept of solvency, the two main components of corporate capital, and how capital structure decisions affect the risk profile of a firm.

Type your communication below the line in the response area below.

REMINDER: Your response will be graded for both technical content and writing skills. Technical content will be evaluated for information that is helpful to the intended reader and clearly relevant to the issue. Writing skills will be evaluated for development, organization, and the appropriate expression of ideas in professional correspondence. Use a standard business memorandum or letter format with a clear beginning, middle, and end. Do not convey information in the form of a table, bullet point list, or other abbreviated presentation.

To: Packitup Partnership
Re: Solvency and capital structure

= Reminder　　　　　　　　　Directions　1　　　　　　　　　◀ Previous　Next ▶

Unofficial Answer

Written Communication

To: Packitup Partnership
Re: Solvency and capital structure

Solvency is a firm's ability to pay its noncurrent obligations as they come due and thus remain in business in the long run (this is in contrast to liquidity, which is the ability to remain in business in the short-run). The key ingredients of solvency are the firm's capital structure and degree of leverage. A firm's capital structure includes its sources of financing, both long- and short-term. These sources can be in the form of debt (external sources) or equity (internal sources).

Debt is the creditor interest in the firm. The firm is contractually obligated to repay debtholders. The terms of repayment (i.e., timing of interest and principal) are specified in the debt agreement. As long as the return on debt capital exceeds the amount of interest paid, the use of debt financing is advantageous to a firm. The return is often enhanced due to the fact that interest payments on debt are tax-deductible. The tradeoff is that an increased debt load makes a firm riskier (since debt must be paid regardless of whether or not the company is profitable). At some point, either a firm will have to pay a higher interest rate than its return on debt or creditors will simply refuse to lend any more money.

Equity is the ownership interest in the firm. Equity is the permanent capital of an entity, contributed by the firm's owners in the hopes of earning a return. However, a return on equity is uncertain because equity embodies only a residual interest in the firm's assets (residual because it is the claim left over after all debt has been satisfied). Periodic returns to owners of excess earnings are referred to as dividends. The firm may be contractually obligated to pay dividends to preferred stockholders but not to common stockholders.

Capital structure decisions affect the risk profile of a firm. For example, a company with a higher percent of debt capital will be riskier than a firm with a high percentage of equity capital. Thus, when the relative amount of debt is high, equity investors will demand a higher rate of return on their investments to compensate for the risk brought about by the high degree of financial leverage. Alternatively, a company with a relatively larger proportion of equity capital will be able to borrow at lower rates because debt holders will accept lower interest in exchange for the lower risk indicated by the equity cushion.

The above depicts a Level 5 answer. See page 16 in the Introduction for a description of the three grading criteria.

Self-Grade

Evaluate each of the following by selecting a 0, 1, 2, 3, 4, or 5. An average response is 3. Use 4 for better than average and 5 for outstanding. Use 2 for less than average and 1 for quite poor. Use zero for no response, if you did not address the topic, or if you gave advice that is clearly illegal.

Organization	○ 0	○ 1	○ 2	○ 3	○ 4	○ 5
Development	○ 0	○ 1	○ 2	○ 3	○ 4	○ 5
Expression	○ 0	○ 1	○ 2	○ 3	○ 4	○ 5

Your grade for the written communication as a whole is the average of the scores for the three criteria.

Use **CPA Gleim Online** and **Simulation Wizard** to practice more written communication tasks in a realistic environment.

STUDY UNIT ELEVEN
IT ROLES, SYSTEMS, AND PROCESSING

(12 pages of outline)

Where once the use of information technology (IT) was restricted to financial applications, over the last 40 years it has permeated every area of the modern organization. No entity, whether for-profit or not-for-profit, can fulfill its mission without the use of sophisticated electronic technologies and their accompanying procedures.

This study unit describes the various broad categories of information systems and the functions they perform (Subunits 1, 4, and 5). The standardized modes of processing transactions and standardized phases of processing are covered in Subunits 2 and 3.

11.1 ROLE OF INFORMATION SYSTEMS IN THE MODERN ORGANIZATION

1.   **Overview**

   a.   Information technology (IT) is an all-encompassing term that refers to the electronic storage, retrieval, and manipulation of data; its conversion into human-usable form (i.e., information); and its transmission from one point to another.

      1)   The Information Technology Association of America has defined IT as "the study, design, development, application, implementation, support or management of computer-based information systems."

   b.   For the purposes of the CPA exam, IT is a synonym for computers, computer networks, and the use of computer programs (i.e., software).

Block Diagram of Information Technology

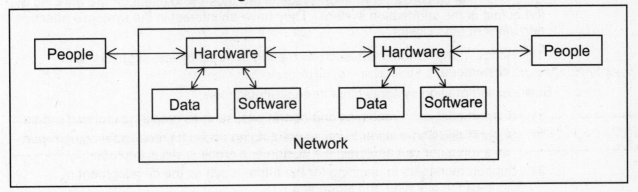

Figure 11-1

2.   **Definitions**

   a.   **Hardware** is any physical item that comprises a computer system. This could refer to the monitor, keyboard, mouse, microchips, or disk drives. In other words, hardware is anything in information technology that can be touched.

b.   **Software** is a combination of computer programs that manipulate data and instruct the hardware on what to do. Software provides instructions to the computer hardware and may also serve as input to other pieces of software. Software is intangible and is anything in the computer system that is NOT hardware. Examples are Microsoft Word or CCH's TaxWise.

c.   **Network** is a collection of hardware devices that are interconnected so they can communicate among themselves. This allows different hardware to share software and communicate data. The Internet is an example of a network, but many offices have intranets where office computers can communicate with other office computers.

d.   **Data** are information, not instructions, that are stored in hardware. Data may be the financial sales data or could be calculations provided by a software program.

e.   **People** refers to anyone who uses hardware (i.e., a computer). This could be an IT professional, an accountant, or a young adult who is surfing the Internet.

f.   Any information system performs four major tasks:

1)   **Input.** The system must acquire (capture) data from within or outside of the entity.

2)   **Transformation.** Raw materials (data) are converted into knowledge useful for decision making (information).

3)   **Output.** The ultimate purpose of the system is communication of results to internal or external users.

4)   **Storage.** Before, during, and after processing, data must be temporarily or permanently stored, for example, in files or databases.

3.   **Business Information Systems (BIS)**

a.   A business information system is any combination of hardware, software, data, people, and procedures employed to pursue an organizational objective.

1)   The first generation of business information systems served the finance and accounting functions, since computing lends itself so readily to quantitative tasks.

2)   Business information systems have evolved to serve the needs of users at all levels of the organizational hierarchy and, with the advent of fast telecommunications, even users outside the organization.

b.   Stakeholders in business information systems are those who affect, or are affected by, the output of the information system. They have an interest in the system's effective and efficient functioning.

1)   Hence, they include users such as managers, employees, suppliers, and customers.

c.   Business information systems have three strategic roles:

1)   Support business processes and operations, such as creating purchase orders.

2)   Support decision making, such as creating an accounts receivable aging report so a manager can ascertain if a customer's credit is still acceptable.

3)   Support managers in planning for the future, such as the development of long-range planning and strategies.

EXAMPLE

All four tasks can be identified in the following description:

A firm collects sales and expense data in its automated accounting system. At year end, adjusting and closing entries are added to the system, and the data are processed into a special format from which the annual report is produced. The firm owns a database server on which all of its transactions and formatted financial statements are kept.

4. **Growing Prevalence of Electronic Communication (Networks)**

    a. Computer-based systems have been woven into almost every facet of the modern organization, from back-office functions, such as human resources and payroll, to instantaneous customer order placement over the Internet.

    b. The use of high-speed communications networks, such as the Internet, has enabled the growth of the truly global organization.

        1) Markets can be tapped on any part of the globe.

        2) Customer support and supply chain functions can be performed around the clock by personnel located on different continents.

    c. Organizations can make use of social networking sites, such as **Facebook** and **Twitter**, to disseminate information and gather customer feedback.

    d. **RSS**, which stands for rich site summary, allows the content of a website that changes often to be pulled and fed automatically to a user's computer. This saves the user the need to constantly revisit the site to get the latest information.

    e. The next stage of evolution is **cloud computing**, where organizations are relieved of the need to manage the storage of both applications and data.

        1) All the software and data they need are located on the Internet.

Stop and review! You have completed the outline for this subunit. Study multiple-choice questions 1 and 2 on page 309.

11.2 TRANSACTION PROCESSING

1. **Overview**

    a. The most common type of system used in the business information systems (BIS) environment is a **transaction processing system (TPS)**.

        1) A transaction is a single discrete event that can be stored in an information system.

        2) Examples include the movement of raw materials from storage to production, the issuance of a purchase order, the recording of a new employee's personal data, or the sale of merchandise.

    b. A TPS captures the fundamental data that reflect the economic life of an organization. An example of a TPS is an **accounting information system (AIS)**.

2. **Two Modes of Transaction Processing**

    a. The phrase "transaction processing modes" refers to the way in which a system is updated with new data. The methods in use can be classified into one of two categories: batch or online.

    b. **Batch Processing**

        1) In this mode, transactions are accumulated and submitted to the computer as a single "batch." In the early days of computers, this was the only way a set of transactions could be processed.

        2) Inherent in batch processing is a time delay between the batching of the transactions and the updating of the records. Sometimes this delay can be as long as overnight.

            a) Thus, errors in a batch processing system caused by incorrect programs or data may not be detected immediately.

   c. **Online Processing**

      1) In this mode, the computer processes each transaction individually as the user enters it. The user is in direct communication with the computer and gets immediate feedback on whether the transaction was accepted or not.

         a) For this reason, this mode is also called **interactive processing**.

      2) A common example is an accounts payable system in which a payables clerk can enter each individual invoice as (s)he verifies the paperwork.

   d. Many applications use combined batch and online modes.

      1) In such systems, users continuously enter transactions in online mode throughout the workday, collecting them in batches. The computer can then take advantage of the efficiencies of batch mode overnight when there are fewer users logged on to the system.

   e. The use of batch processing tends to be restricted to TPSs and systems that get their input from TPSs. Systems that support decision making are almost always of the online type.

   f. In some online systems, having the latest information available at all times is crucial so that users can make immediate decisions. A common example is an airline reservation system, which is constantly updated from moment to moment and must be available all the time.

      1) These are called **real-time systems**. A thermostat is another example, constantly monitoring the temperature in the room and engaging the heating or cooling system accordingly.

3. **IT Infrastructure**

   a. Centralization. During the early days of computer processing, computers were very large and expensive, and only organizations such as large banks and governmental agencies could afford them.

      1) Of necessity, all processing and systems development were done at a single, central location. Users connected to the mainframe via "dumb terminals," i.e., simple monitor-and-keyboard combinations with no processing power of their own.

      2) Since hardware, information security, and data integrity functions were located in one office, economies of scale were achieved and controls were strong.

   b. Decentralization. As the data processing industry evolved, computers became smaller (so-called minicomputers), and branch offices of large organizations could have their own.

      1) Each branch could store and process its data onsite, transmitting the results overnight to the mainframe at the home office. This was an early form of distributed processing in which parts of an organization's computer operations could be performed in separate physical locations.

Centralization Advantages	Decentralization Advantages
• Better and more efficient security	• Remote locations have increased accountability over their data and processes
• Consistent processing because it occurs at a set time in one location	• Remote locations can get data without concern of bottlenecks of traffic over networks

Stop and review! You have completed the outline for this subunit. Study multiple-choice questions 3 through 11 beginning on page 309.

11.3 APPLICATION PROCESSING PHASES

 This subunit explains how data is entered into a transaction processing system (TPS), specifically the accounting information system (AIS). As a future CPA who will hold a license with the ability to perform an audit, you will need to understand how data is entered into a TPS (especially the AIS) as well as how the data in a TPS is processed.

1. **Data Capture**

   a. Data capture is the process of entering data into an information system. Two methods of capture are identical to their respective processing modes, discussed in item 2. in the previous subunit.

      1) **Batch entry** involves loading a group of records at one time.

      2) **Online entry** involves entering single records, usually in an interactive environment where the user gets immediate feedback.

   b. One type of online entry for capturing input is the optical scanner, such as that used in retail checkout lines (called point-of-sale, or POS, transactions). Besides instant updating of accounting and inventory records, POS transaction systems can help management

      1) Identify and respond to trends,

      2) Make sales forecasts,

      3) Determine which products are or are not in demand,

      4) Improve customer service,

      5) Target products and promotions to customers with different demographic traits, and

      6) Evaluate the effects of promotions, including coupons.

2. **Processing**

   a. Processing is the act of converting raw data into usable information. This is performed by the combination of hardware and software that makes up the organization's IT infrastructure.

3. **Types of Data Files**

   a. An understanding of the application processing phases requires an explanation of the two types of computer data files, **master files** and **transaction files**. These types are applicable whether the files are stored on tape, disk, flash drive, or other media and whether they are "flat" files or structured databases.

   b. A master file may be fairly static or very volatile.

      1) An example of a fairly static master file is an authorized vendor file containing each vendor's number, name, and address.

EXAMPLE

Authorized Vendor Master File

vendor_num	vendor_name	address_1	city	state	zip	credit_limit	last_updated
0187634	Neyland's Nuts	101 Dandridge Av	Knoxville	TN	37915	$10,000	07/19/2010
1264428	Basic Barbecue	2224 Blossom St	Columbia	SC	29201	$50,000	06/25/2008
4552170	Bayou Bakery	10118 Florida St	Baton Rouge	LA	70801	$15,000	03/04/2008
5006321	Bulldog Barcoding	9085 Old West Point Rd	Starkville	MS	39759	$5,000	10/01/2007
8981463	Razorback Restaurant Supply	3510 West Maple St	Fayetteville	AR	72701	$20,000	07/01/2009

2)   An example of a volatile master file is a general ledger file, which at any given moment holds the balances of all accounts in the ledger.

EXAMPLE

General Ledger Master File

account_num	account_name	balance	last_transaction_posted
A1209	Cash	$89,580.22	06/10/2011
G6573	Accounts Receivable	$72,024.57	06/10/2011
J0226	Accounts Payable	$(15,156.89)	06/10/2011
K4411	Sales	$(100,558.60)	06/10/2011
M2020	Cost of Goods Sold	$70,005.64	06/10/2011
Y3577	Administrative Expenses	$21,110.33	06/10/2011

---

3)   Volatility is the relative frequency with which the records in a file are added, deleted, or changed during a period.

c.   A transaction file contains the data that reflect ongoing business activity, such as individual purchases from vendors or general journal entries.

EXAMPLE

General Journal Transaction File

transaction	transaction_date	debit_acct	debit_amt	credit_acct	credit_amt
GL5261904	06/10/2011	A1209	$1,001.56	G6573	$(1,001.56)
GL5261905	06/10/2011	G6573	$660.48	K4411	$(660.48)
GL5261906	06/10/2011	G6573	$898.15	K4411	$(898.15)
GL5261907	06/10/2011	Y3577	$150.75	J0226	$(150.75)

---

d.   Transaction files and master files are constantly interacting.

1)   Before an invoice can be paid, the payables transaction file must be matched against the vendor master file to see whether the vendor really exists.

2)   The general ledger balance file must be updated every day by posting from the general journal transaction file.

4.   **Reporting**

a.   Reporting in General

1)   The term "report" in this context does not necessarily refer to a printed hardcopy. Advances in technology allow for report viewing on a computer screen or personal data assistant with the option of printing granted to the user.

b.   Periodic Routine Reports

1)   Certain reports are required at regular intervals. Examples are monthly trial balances and ledger summaries to assist in closing the books.

c.   On-Demand and Ad Hoc Reports

1)   Systems can be designed so that users can generate reports at times they specify. An on-demand report is one whose design is programmed into the system. The user specifies the date and time the report is run.

      2) Advances in processing power and software have given users the ability to design their own reports "on the fly."

         a) These ad hoc (sometimes called "quick-and-dirty") reports can be designed to the user's own specifications without the involvement of IT personnel. Database queries are a common example.

d. Exception Reports

    1) It is a common practice after daily processing to generate reports of transactions or activities that lie outside predefined boundaries. The appropriate personnel can then follow up and determine the reasons for these exceptions.

    2) Examples are batches whose debits and credits do not match and instances of multiple unsuccessful attempts to access the network (which may indicate hacking).

e. Electronic Distribution of Reports

    1) The advent of email and other forms of digital communication has greatly enhanced the ability of organizations to distribute reports. Rather than wait for paper copies to be hand delivered, reports can be sent digitally to the appropriate personnel. This is sometimes referred to as push reporting.

f. Audit Trail

    1) An audit trail of activities is a crucial part of monitoring security over a system. The audit trail includes not only the reports described above and on the previous page, but also such reports as logs of system sign-in and sign-out times to monitor who was doing what on the system.

Stop and review! You have completed the outline for this subunit. Study multiple-choice questions 12 through 16 beginning on page 312.

11.4 SYSTEMS THAT SUPPORT ROUTINE PROCESSES

 This subunit will acquaint you with other types of business information systems (BISs) used in the corporate environment to perform transaction type processes. As a CPA candidate, your knowledge level is most likely highest with the accounting information systems (AIS). However, there are many other types of information systems that comprise the BIS and help corporations perform their day-to-day activities. As a future CPA who will hold a license with the ability to perform an audit, you will need to understand how each of these transaction information systems work and how they interrelate to each other and BISs.

1. **Management Information System (MIS)**

a. A MIS typically receives input from a TPS, aggregates it, then reports it in a format useful by middle management in running the business. For this reason, MISs are often classified by function or activity, such as the following:

    1) Accounting: general ledger, accounts receivable, accounts payable, payroll processing, fixed asset management, and tax accounting; other aspects of accounting information systems are described in item 2. on the next page.

    2) Finance: capital budgeting, operational budgeting, cash management

    3) Manufacturing: production planning, cost control, quality control

    4) Logistics: inventory management, transportation planning

    5) Marketing: sales analysis, forecasting

    6) Human resources: projecting payroll, projecting benefits obligations, employment-level planning, employee evaluation tracking

b.   These single-function systems, often called stovepipe systems because of their limited focus, are gradually being replaced by integrated systems that link multiple business activities across the enterprise. The most comprehensive integrated system is termed an enterprise resource planning (ERP) system (see item 3. below).

2.   **Accounting Information System (AIS)**

a.   An AIS is a subsystem of a MIS that processes routine, highly structured financial and transactional data relevant to managerial as well as financial accounting. An AIS is concerned with

1)   Transactions with external parties (e.g., customers, suppliers, governments, owners, and creditors) reflected in financial statements prepared in conformity with GAAP, and

2)   The internal activities recorded in the cost accounting system and the preparation of related reports and analyses (e.g., production reports, pro forma financial statements, budgets, and cost-volume-profit analyses).

3.   **Enterprise Resource Planning (ERP)**

a.   ERP is the latest phase in the development of computerized systems for managing organizational resources. ERP is intended to integrate enterprise-wide information systems by creating one database linked to all of an organization's applications.

1)   ERP subsumes traditional MISs.

2)   Figure 11-2 contrasts the less integrated MIS with the more integrated ERP system.

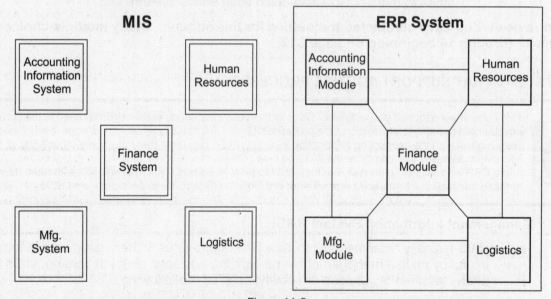

Figure 11-2

b.   In the traditional ERP system, subsystems share data and coordinate their activities. Thus, if marketing receives an order, it can quickly verify that inventory is sufficient to notify shipping to process the order.

1)   Otherwise, production is notified to manufacture more of the product, with a consequent automatic adjustment of output schedules.

2)   If materials are inadequate for this purpose, the system will issue a purchase order.

3)   If more labor is needed, human resources will be instructed to reassign or hire employees.

4)   The foregoing business processes (and others) should interact seamlessly in an ERP system.

c.   The subsystems in a traditional ERP system are internal to the organization. Hence, they are often called **back-office functions**. The information produced is principally (but not exclusively) intended for internal use by the organization's managers.

d.   The current generation of ERP software has added **front-office functions**. These connect the organization with customers, suppliers, owners, creditors, and strategic allies (e.g., the members of a trading community or other business association).

1)   Moreover, the current generation of ERP software also provides the capability for smooth (and instant) interaction with the business processes of external parties.

2)   A newer ERP system's integration with the firm's back-office functions enables supply-chain management (SCM), customer relationship management (CRM), and partner relationship management (PRM).

e.   The disadvantages of ERP are its extent and complexity, which make implementation difficult and costly.

Background

Because ERP software is costly and complex, it is usually installed only by the largest enterprises, although mid-size organizations are increasingly likely to buy ERP software. Major ERP packages include R/3 from SAP AG and Oracle e-Business Suite, PeopleSoft, and JD Edwards EnterpriseOne, all from Oracle Corp.

Background

The tremendous variety of forms that information systems can take and the diverse needs of users have led to the concept of information resources management (IRM), which takes a global view of the information holdings and needs of an organization. This view is promoted by the Information Resources Management Association of Hershey, PA (www.irma-international.org).

Stop and review! You have completed the outline for this subunit. Study multiple-choice questions 17 through 22 beginning on page 313.

11.5 SYSTEMS THAT SUPPORT DECISION MAKING

 This subunit will acquaint you with information systems that support the decision-making process. In contrast to transaction type processes, these types of programs assist humans with making decisions. As a future CPA who will hold a license with the ability to perform an audit, you will need to understand how these decision-making systems work.

1.   **Data Warehouse**

a.   A data warehouse is a central database for transaction-level data from more than one of the organization's TPSs. A data warehouse is strictly a query-and-reporting system. It is not used to carry on the enterprise's routine operations. Rather, a data warehouse gets its input from the various TPSs in the organization.

1)   Data warehouses store a large quantity of data and require that the transaction records be converted to a standard format. The ability of the data warehouse to relate data from multiple systems makes it a very powerful tool for ad hoc queries. The data warehouse can also be accessed using analytical and graphics tools, a technique called **online analytical processing** (OLAP).

a)   An important component of OLAP is drill-down analysis, in which the user is first presented with the data at an aggregate level and then can display successive levels of detail for a given date, region, product, etc., until finally reaching the original transactions.

b. A data warehouse enables **data mining**, i.e., the search for unexpected relationships among data.

1) The classic example of the use of data mining was the discovery by convenience stores that diapers and beer often appeared on the same sales transaction in the late evening.

Data Warehouse and Data Mining

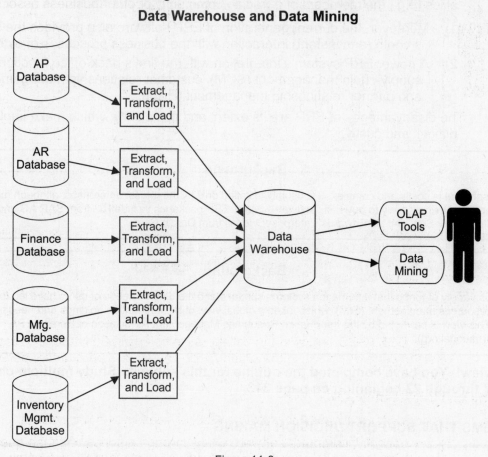

Figure 11-3

2. **Decision Support System (DSS)**

a. A DSS is an interactive system that is useful in solving semistructured problems, that is, those with a structured portion (which the computer can solve) and an unstructured portion (which requires the manager's insight and judgment).

1) This point requires emphasis: A DSS does not automate a decision. It examines the relevant data and presents a manager with choices between alternative courses of action.

b. A DSS has three basic components:

1) The **database** consists of the raw data that are relevant to the decision. In this context, a data warehouse is very useful. The data can come from both within and outside of the organization.

2) The **model** is the set of equations, comparisons, graphs, conditions, assumptions, etc., into which the data will be fed.

3) The **dialog** is the user interface that allows the user to specify the appropriate model and the particular set of data to which the model should be applied.

Decision Support System

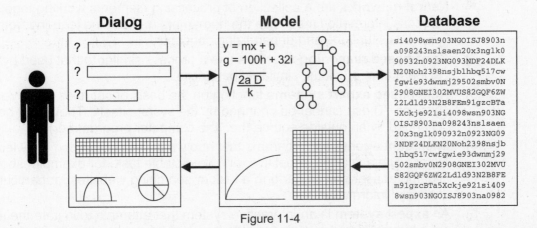

Figure 11-4

EXAMPLE

A manufacturer wishes to improve its inventory management.

- The firm creates a database of the past 5 years of inventory and purchasing history, along with projections for future production, transportation costs, and forecasts of the prices of raw materials.
- The firm creates a model containing the formula for economic order quantity, an algorithm for calculating safety stock, and graphs of inventory levels over time.
- The firm creates a dialog screen allowing the decision maker to specify time periods, particular products, and the variables for displaying on graphs.

---

    c.   A group DSS (GDSS) aids in the collaborative solution of unstructured problems. Users in separate areas of the organization can specify parameters pertinent to their functions.

3. **Artificial Intelligence (AI)**

    a.   AI is computer software designed to perceive, reason, and understand.

        1)   Historically, computer software works through a series of if/then questions in which every operation has exactly two possible outcomes (yes/no, on/off, true/false, one/zero).

            a)   Human reasoning, on the other hand, is extremely complex, based on deduction, induction, intuition, emotion, and biochemistry, resulting in a range of possible outcomes.

        2)   AI attempts to imitate human decision making, which hinges on this combination of knowledge and intuition (i.e., remembering relationships between variables based on experience).

        3)   The advantage of AI in a business environment is that IT systems

            a)   Can work 24 hours a day

            b)   Will not become ill, die, or be hired away

            c)   Are extremely fast processors of data, especially if numerous rules (procedures) must be evaluated

b.   There are several types of AI:

1)   **Neural networks** are a collection of processing elements working together to process information much like the human brain, including learning from previous situations and generalizing concepts.

2)   **Case-based reasoning systems** use a process similar to that used by humans to learn from previous, similar experiences.

3)   **Rule-based expert systems** function on the basis of set rules to arrive at an answer. These cannot be changed by the system itself. They must be changed by an outside source (i.e., the computer programmer).

4)   **Intelligent agents** are programs that apply a built-in or learned knowledge base to execute a specific, repetitive, and predictable task, for example, showing a computer user how to perform a task or searching websites for particular financial information.

5)   An **expert system** is an interactive system that attempts to imitate the reasoning of a human expert in a given field. It is useful for addressing unstructured problems when there is a local shortage of human experts.

4.   **Executive Support System (ESS)**

a.   At the strategic level, high-level decision makers get the information they need to set, and monitor progress toward, the organization's long-term objectives from an ESS, also called an executive information system (EIS).

1)   An ESS assists senior management in making nonroutine decisions, such as identifying problems and opportunities.

2)   An ESS also provides information about the activities of competitors.

b.   The information in an ESS comes from sources both within and outside the organization, including information from nontraditional computer sources.

1)   An ESS should have the ability to provide overviews, often in graphical format, or to drill down to the detailed data.

2)   An ESS can be used on computers of all sizes.

5.   **Business Intelligence (BI)**

a.   Business intelligence is what gives upper management the information it needs to know where the organization is and how to steer it in the intended direction. BI gives an executive immediate information about an organization's critical success factors.

1)   BI is replacing the older ESS model.

b.   BI tools display information about the organization as bar graphs, pie charts, columnar reports, or any other format considered appropriate to upper management's decision making. These displays are sometimes grouped by a particular executive's needs into what is termed a **digital dashboard**.

1)   Stock price trend, sales by region and date, on-time delivery performance, instantaneous cash balances, and profitability by customer are possible metrics to be included.

c.   BI tools use data both from within and outside the organization.

Stop and review! You have completed the outline for this subunit. Study multiple-choice questions 23 through 27 beginning on page 315.

QUESTIONS

11.1 Role of Information Systems in the Modern Organization

1. In business information systems, the term "stakeholder" is best described by which of the following?

- A. The management team responsible for the security of the documents and data stored on the computers or networks.

- B. Information technology personnel responsible for creating the documents and data stored on the computers or networks.

- C. Authorized users who are granted access rights to the documents and data stored on the computers or networks.

- D. Anyone in the organization who has a role in creating or using the documents and data stored on the computers or networks.

Answer (D) is correct.

REQUIRED: The stakeholders in business information systems.

DISCUSSION: Stakeholders are those who affect, or are affected by, the output of the information system. They have an interest in the system's effective and efficient functioning. Hence, they include users such as managers, employees, IT personnel, suppliers, and customers.

Answer (A) is incorrect. Stakeholders are not limited to the management team responsible for the security of the documents and data stored on the computers or networks. Answer (B) is incorrect. Stakeholders are not limited to information technology personnel responsible for creating the documents and data stored on the computers or networks. Answer (C) is incorrect. Stakeholders are not limited to authorized users who are granted access rights to the documents and data stored on the computers or networks.

2. The four major tasks that any system must perform are

- A. Input, transformation, output, and storage.

- B. Input, backup, output, and storage.

- C. Input, transformation, output, and maintenance.

- D. Input, transformation, storage, and feedback.

Answer (A) is correct.

REQUIRED: The four major tasks that any system must perform.

DISCUSSION: The four major tasks that any system must perform are input, transformation, output, and storage.

11.2 Transaction Processing

3. Batch processing

- A. Is not used by most businesses because it reduces the audit trail.

- B. Allows users to inquire about groups of information contained in the system.

- C. Accumulates transaction records into groups for processing against the master file on a delayed basis.

- D. Can only be performed on a centralized basis.

Answer (C) is correct.

REQUIRED: The true statement about batch processing.

DISCUSSION: Batch processing is the accumulation and grouping of transactions for processing on a delayed basis. The batch approach is suitable for applications that can be processed against the master file at intervals and involve large volumes of similar items, such as payroll, sales, inventory, and billing.

Answer (A) is incorrect. Batch processing provides as much of an audit trail as any computerized operation. Answer (B) is incorrect. Batch processing refers to the input of data, not inquiry. Answer (D) is incorrect. Batch processing can also be performed on a decentralized basis.

4. Information processing made possible by a network of computers dispersed throughout an organization is called

- A. Online processing.

- B. Interactive processing.

- C. Time sharing.

- D. Distributed data processing.

Answer (D) is correct.

REQUIRED: The method of information processing by dispersed computers.

DISCUSSION: Distributed processing is characterized by a merger of computer and telecommunications technology. Distributed systems permit not only remote access to a computer but also the performance of local processing at local sites. The result is greater flexibility in systems design and the possibility of an optimal distribution of processing tasks.

Answer (A) is incorrect. Online processing is a method of processing data that permits both immediate posting (updating) and inquiry of master files as transactions occur. Answer (B) is incorrect. Interactive processing is a method of processing data immediately upon input. Answer (C) is incorrect. Time sharing is the processing of a program by the CPU until an input or output operation is required. In time sharing, the CPU spends a fixed amount of time on each program.

5. A new purchasing system for just-in-time production requirements has been proposed. Users want access to current master file information at all times. To satisfy user needs, master file changes should be implemented with

    A. Periodic entry with subsequent batch processing.

    B. Periodic entry with immediate batch processing.

    C. Online entry with subsequent batch processing.

    D. Online entry with immediate processing.

Answer (D) is correct.
    REQUIRED: The appropriate system for JIT production.
    DISCUSSION: JIT production attempts to minimize inventory by more closely coordinating deliveries of needed materials and production. Thus, inventory data must be current. Online entry with immediate (real-time) processing gives users current master file information because changes are entered and applied to the master file as they occur. However, check printing can still occur in batch mode.
    Answer (A) is incorrect. Periodic entry and batch processing do not permit the immediate updating required by JIT production. Answer (B) is incorrect. Periodic entry does not permit immediate updating, and "immediate batch processing" is a contradiction in terms. Answer (C) is incorrect. Online entry and subsequent batch processing do not permit the immediate updating required by JIT production.

6. The concept of timeliness of data availability is most relevant to

    A. Computerized systems.

    B. Payroll systems.

    C. Manual systems.

    D. Online systems.

Answer (D) is correct.
    REQUIRED: The relevance of the concept of timeliness of data availability.
    DISCUSSION: An online processing system is in direct communication with the computer, giving it the capability to handle transactions as they are entered. An online system permits both immediate posting (updating) and inquiry of master files as transactions occur. In an online system, data are immediately available to users upon entry.
    Answer (A) is incorrect. Timeliness is not necessarily an element of a computerized system. Answer (B) is incorrect. Timeliness is not necessarily an element of a payroll system. Answer (C) is incorrect. Timeliness is not necessarily an element of a manual system.

7. The relationship between online, real-time database systems and batch processing systems is that

    A. A firm will have only one processing mode because a single computer cannot do both.

    B. A firm will not use batch processing if it has a large computer.

    C. A firm may use both processing modes concurrently.

    D. A firm will always prefer an online, real-time processing system because batch processing is slow.

Answer (C) is correct.
    REQUIRED: The relationship between online, real-time database systems and batch processing systems.
    DISCUSSION: Firms may find it beneficial to incorporate both processing modes into one system. A database may be established for information that must be obtained quickly, for instance, a sales processing system in which credit information must be available to sales personnel on an ongoing basis. However, other processing requirements may take advantage of the speed and control provided in a batch processing system. For example, payroll transactions may be processed quickly and efficiently in a batch mode.
    Answer (A) is incorrect. One computer can operate in both modes. Answer (B) is incorrect. Firms with large computers find it both cost effective and efficient to group transactions and process them periodically. Answer (D) is incorrect. A firm will not automatically prefer an online, real-time system. When transactions, e.g., payroll, can be conveniently grouped, processing is extremely fast and efficient in a batch mode.

8. Devices that are used only to perform sequential file processing will **not** permit

    A. The use of a database structure.

    B. Data to be edited in an offline mode.

    C. Batch processing to be initiated from a terminal.

    D. Data to be edited on a real-time basis.

Answer (D) is correct.
    REQUIRED: The activity not permitted by devices used only for sequential file processing.
    DISCUSSION: In an online, real-time system, direct (random), not sequential, access to files is required. As each transaction is entered, it is edited (validated). Files can then be immediately updated to reflect that transaction. Sequential file access is typical of (but not required in) batch processing.
    Answer (A) is incorrect. A database can be used with direct or sequential file access. Answer (B) is incorrect. Separate conversion and editing runs are usually performed in an offline mode when sequential processing is used. Answer (C) is incorrect. Remote batch processing of sequential files is not unusual.

9. Remote batch processing avoids the need for having

    A. Terminals at each user location.

    B. Printers at each user location.

    C. File updating at each user location.

    D. Input controls at each user location.

Answer (C) is correct.
    REQUIRED: The true statement about remote batch processing.
    DISCUSSION: Batch processing is the accumulation and grouping of transactions for processing on a delayed basis. The batch approach is suitable for applications involving large volumes of similar items, e.g., payroll, sales, and inventory transactions. Remote batch processing (remote job entry) entails collection and entry of data from places other than the location of the file updating.
    Answer (A) is incorrect. Terminals will be required. Answer (B) is incorrect. Printers will be required. Answer (D) is incorrect. Input/output controls will be required.

10. An insurance company that has adopted cooperative processing is planning to implement new standard software in all its local offices. The new software has a fast response time, is very user friendly, and was developed with extensive user involvement. The new software captures, consolidates, edits, validates, and finally transfers standardized transaction data to the headquarters server. Local managers, who were satisfied with existing locally written personal computer applications, opposed the new approach because they anticipated

    A. Increased workloads.

    B. Centralization of all processing tasks.

    C. More accountability.

    D. Less computer equipment.

Answer (C) is correct.
    REQUIRED: The reason for opposing introduction of new software.
    DISCUSSION: Cooperative processing implies a tighter coupling than previously existed between the personal computers and the server. The result may threaten the managers' perceived autonomy by increasing the control exercised by headquarters and therefore the accountability of local managers.
    Answer (A) is incorrect. Given that only existing systems would be converted, the transaction volume would likely remain relatively constant. Answer (B) is incorrect. In a cooperative processing environment, different computers execute different parts of an application. Answer (D) is incorrect. Compared with mainframe-only processing, cooperative processing typically requires more computer equipment at distributed locations.

11. A firm is considering two possible computer configurations. System I would have a mainframe computer tied to 16 time-sharing terminals. System II would have a minicomputer tied to 16 intelligent workstations. Which of these two systems could be termed a "distributed system"?

    A. System I only.

    B. System II only.

    C. Both Systems I and II.

    D. Neither System I nor II.

Answer (B) is correct.
    REQUIRED: The system(s) that can be described as a distributed system.
    DISCUSSION: The advent of cheaper and smaller computers has permitted the development of a somewhat different alternative to centralization or decentralization: distributed data processing. In a distributed data processing system, the organization's processing needs are examined in their totality. The decision is not whether an application should be done centrally or locally, but rather which parts of the application are better performed by small local computers as intelligent terminals and which parts are better performed at some other, possibly centralized, site. In essence, the best distribution of processing tasks within application areas is sought. The key distinction between decentralized and distributed systems is the interconnection among the nodes (sites) in the latter kind of network. Hence, System I is a traditional system, and System II is a distributed system.
    Answer (A) is incorrect. System I is a traditional centralized system. Answer (C) is incorrect. Only System II is a distributed system. Answer (D) is incorrect. System II is a distributed system.

11.3 Application Processing Phases

12. A file containing relatively long-term information used as a source of reference and periodically updated with detail is termed a

A. Transaction file.

B. Record layout.

C. Master file.

D. Dump.

Answer (C) is correct.
    REQUIRED: The file containing relatively long-term information.
    DISCUSSION: A master file containing relatively long-term information, such as an inventory file listing the part number, description, quantities on hand, quantities on order, etc., is used in a file processing run. Transactions are processed against the master file, thus periodically updating it.
    Answer (A) is incorrect. A transaction file (detail file) contains current transaction information used to update the master file, such as the number of items shipped to be removed from inventory. Answer (B) is incorrect. A record layout is a representation of the format of the records on the file. It shows the position and length of the fields in the file. Answer (D) is incorrect. A dump is a listing of the contents of memory.

13. At a remote computer center, management installed an automated scheduling system to load data files and execute programs at specific times during the day. The best approach for verifying that the scheduling system performs as intended is to

A. Analyze job activity with a queuing model to determine workload characteristics.

B. Simulate the resource usage and compare the results with actual results of operations.

C. Use library management software to track changes to successive versions of applications programs.

D. Audit job accounting data for file accesses and job initiation/termination messages.

Answer (D) is correct.
    REQUIRED: The best approach for verifying that the scheduling system performs as intended.
    DISCUSSION: Job accounting data analysis permits programmatic examination of job initiation and termination, record counts, and processing times. Auditing job accounting data for file accesses and job initiation/termination messages will reveal whether the right data files were loaded/dismounted at the right times and the right programs were initiated/terminated at the right times.
    Answer (A) is incorrect. Analyzing job activity with a queuing model to determine workload characteristics gives information about resource usage but does not verify that the system actually functioned as intended. Answer (B) is incorrect. A simulation helps management characterize the workload but does not verify that the system actually functioned as intended. Answer (C) is incorrect. Using library management software to track changes to successive versions of application programs permits control of production and test versions but does not verify that the system actually functioned as intended.

14. Management is concerned that data uploaded from a personal computer to the company's server may be erroneous. Which of the following controls would best address this issue?

A. Server data should be backed up on a regular basis.

B. Two persons should be present at the personal computer when it is uploading data.

C. The data uploaded to the server should be subject to the same edits and validation routines that online data entry would require.

D. The users should be required to review a random sample of processed data.

Answer (C) is correct.
    REQUIRED: The best control to prevent uploading erroneous data from a personal computer to the company's mainframe system in batch processing.
    DISCUSSION: Data that are uploaded or downloaded are subject to significant risk. Personal computers are more vulnerable than servers to unauthorized access, and uploaded or downloaded data are subject to alteration on the personal computer. Furthermore, an uploaded file may replace an existing file without being subjected to standard edit and validation procedures.
    Answer (A) is incorrect. This practice is a good control, but it does not address the issue of data-upload integrity. Backups cannot prevent or detect data-upload problems. They can only help correct data errors caused by a poor upload. Answer (B) is incorrect. This control may be somewhat helpful in preventing fraud in data uploads, but it is of little use in preventing errors. Answer (D) is incorrect. The error already could have caused erroneous reports and management decisions. Having users try to find errors in uploaded data is costly.

15. Using standard procedures developed by information center personnel, staff members download specific subsets of financial and operating data as they need it. The staff members analyze the data on their own personal computers and share results with each other. Over time, the staff members learn to modify the standard procedures to get subsets of financial and operating data that were not accessible through the original procedures. The greatest risk associated with this situation is that

A. The data obtained might be incomplete or lack currency.

B. The data definition might become outdated.

C. The server data might be corrupted by staff members' updates.

D. Repeated downloading might fill up storage space on staff members' personal computers.

Answer (A) is correct.

REQUIRED: The risk associated with downloading additional subsets of financial data.

DISCUSSION: Staff members may not be aware of how often they need to download data to keep it current, or whether their queries, especially the ones they modified, obtain all the necessary information. Users may employ faulty parameters or logic. Poorly planned queries may also use computing resources inefficiently.

Answer (B) is incorrect. Downloading data does not affect the data definitions. Answer (C) is incorrect. Staff members are downloading, not uploading, so the staff members are unlikely to corrupt server data. Answer (D) is incorrect. The downloading procedures could replace previously downloaded files on the staff members' personal computers.

16. Advanced electronic point-of-sale (POS) systems allow instant capture and transmission of information for which purposes?

I. Instant updating of accounting records
II. Accumulation of marketing information
III. Tracking of information about specific customers
IV. Facilitation of warehousing

A. I and II only.

B. III and IV only.

C. I, II, and III only.

D. I, II, III, and IV.

Answer (D) is correct.

REQUIRED: The functions of an electronic POS system.

DISCUSSION: An electronic POS system may update and analyze the perpetual inventory records for each outlet. It may also perform other accounting tasks, such as crediting revenue accounts and debiting cash, accounts receivable, and cost of goods sold. Moreover, a POS system may (1) provide marketing information to identify and respond to trends; (2) make sales forecasts; (3) determine which products are in demand; (4) improve customer service; (5) target products and promotions to customers with different demographic traits; and (6) evaluate the effects of promotions, including coupons. Another function of a POS system is to record personal and transactional information about specific customers, including tracking of warranties, deposits, rentals, progressive discounts, and special pricing. Still another function is use of bar coding in association with the stocking and warehousing functions to reduce the costs of data entry, including the effects of human error.

11.4 Systems that Support Routine Processes

17. An accounting information system (AIS) must include certain source documents in order to control purchasing and accounts payable. For a manufacturing organization, the best set of documents should include

A. Purchase requisitions, purchase orders, inventory reports of goods needed, and vendor invoices.

B. Purchase orders, receiving reports, and inventory reports of goods needed.

C. Purchase orders, receiving reports, and vendor invoices.

D. Purchase requisitions, purchase orders, receiving reports, and vendor invoices.

Answer (D) is correct.

REQUIRED: The best set of documents to be included in an AIS to control purchasing and accounts payable.

DISCUSSION: An AIS is a subsystem of a management information system that processes financial and transactional data relevant to managerial and financial accounting. The AIS supports operations by collecting and sorting data about an organization's transactions. An AIS is concerned not only with external parties but also with the internal activities needed for management decision making at all levels. An AIS is best suited to solve problems when reporting requirements are well defined. A manufacturer has well-defined reporting needs for routine information about purchasing and payables. Purchase requisitions document user department needs, and purchase orders provide evidence that purchase transactions were appropriately authorized. A formal receiving procedure segregates the purchasing and receiving functions and establishes the quantity, quality, and timeliness of goods received. Vendor invoices establish the liability for payment and should be compared with the foregoing documents.

Answer (A) is incorrect. Receiving reports should be included. Answer (B) is incorrect. Requisitions and vendor invoices should be included. Answer (C) is incorrect. Purchase requisitions should be included.

18. Which one of the following statements about an accounting information system (AIS) is **false**?

    A. AIS supports day-to-day operations by collecting and sorting data about an organization's transactions.

    B. The information produced by AIS is made available to all levels of management for use in planning and controlling an organization's activities.

    C. AIS is best suited to solve problems where there is great uncertainty and ill-defined reporting requirements.

    D. AIS is often referred to as a transaction processing system.

Answer (C) is correct.
    REQUIRED: The false statement about an accounting information system (AIS).
    DISCUSSION: An AIS is a subsystem of a management information system that processes financial and transactional data relevant to managerial and financial accounting. The AIS supports operations by collecting and sorting data about an organization's transactions. An AIS is concerned not only with external parties, but also with the internal activities needed for management decision making at all levels. An AIS is best suited to solve problems when reporting requirements are well defined. A decision support system is a better choice for problems in which decision making is less structured.

19. An enterprise resource planning (ERP) system integrates the organization's computerized subsystems and may also provide links to external parties. An advantage of ERP is that

    A. The reengineering needed for its implementation should improve business processes.

    B. Customizing the software to suit the unique needs of the organization will facilitate upgrades.

    C. It can be installed by organizations of all sizes.

    D. The comprehensiveness of the system reduces resistance to change.

Answer (A) is correct.
    REQUIRED: The advantage of ERP.
    DISCUSSION: The benefits of ERP may significantly derive from the business process reengineering that is needed for its implementation. Using ERP software that reflects industry best practices forces the linked subunits in the organization not only to redesign and improve their processes but also to conform to one standard.
    Answer (B) is incorrect. The disadvantages of ERP are its extent and complexity, which make customization of the software difficult and costly. Answer (C) is incorrect. ERP software is costly and complex. It usually is installed only by the largest enterprises. Answer (D) is incorrect. Implementing an ERP system is likely to encounter significant resistance because of its comprehensiveness.

20. In a traditional ERP system, the receipt of a customer order may result in

I. Customer tracking of the order's progress

II. Automatic replenishment of inventory by a supplier

III. Hiring or reassigning of employees

IV. Automatic adjustment of output schedules

    A. I, II, and IV only.

    B. I and III only.

    C. III and IV only.

    D. I, II, III, and IV.

Answer (C) is correct.
    REQUIRED: The possible effects of receipt of a customer order by a traditional ERP system.
    DISCUSSION: The traditional ERP system is one in which subsystems share data and coordinate their activities. Thus, if marketing receives an order, it can quickly verify that inventory is sufficient to notify shipping to process the order. Otherwise, production is notified to manufacture more of the product, with a consequent automatic adjustment of output schedules. If materials are inadequate for this purpose, the system will issue a purchase order. If more labor is needed, human resources will be instructed to reassign or hire employees. However, the subsystems in a traditional ERP system are internal to the organization. Hence, they are often called back-office functions. The information produced is principally (but not exclusively) intended for internal use by the organization's managers.
    The current generation of ERP software (ERP II) has added front-office functions. Consequently, ERP II but not traditional ERP is capable of customer tracking of the order's progress and automatic replenishment of inventory by a supplier.

21. A principal advantage of an ERP system is

A. Program-data dependence.

B. Data redundancy.

C. Separate data updating for different functions.

D. Centralization of data.

Answer (D) is correct.

REQUIRED: The principal advantage of an ERP system
DISCUSSION: An advantage of an ERP system is the elimination of data redundancy through the use of a central database. In principle, information about an item of data is stored once, and all functions have access to it. Thus, when the item (such as a price) is updated, the change is effectively made for all functions. The result is reliability (data integrity).

Answer (A) is incorrect. An ERP system uses a central database and a database management system. A fundamental characteristic of a database is that applications are independent of the physical structure of the database. Writing programs or designing applications to use the database requires only the names of desired data items, not their locations. Answer (B) is incorrect. An ERP system eliminates data redundancy. Answer (C) is incorrect. An ERP system is characterized by one-time data updating for all organizational functions.

22. The current generation of ERP software (ERP II) may include an advanced planning and scheduling system that

A. Determines the location of retail outlets.

B. Connects the organization with other members of a joint venture.

C. Controls the flow of a manufacturer's materials and components through the supply chain.

D. Permits tracking of orders by customers.

Answer (C) is correct.

REQUIRED: The function of an advanced planning and scheduling system.
DISCUSSION: An advanced planning and scheduling system may be an element of a supply chain management application for a manufacturer. It controls the flow of materials and components within the chain. Schedules are created given projected costs, lead times, and inventories.

Answer (A) is incorrect. Customer relationship management applications in ERP II extend to customer service, finance-related matters, sales, and database creation and maintenance. Integrated data are helpful in better understanding customer needs, such as product preference or location of retail outlets. Answer (B) is incorrect. Partner relationship management applications connect the organization not only with such partners as customers and suppliers but also with owners, creditors, and strategic allies (for example, other members of a joint venture). Answer (D) is incorrect. An advanced planning scheduling system is used by a manufacturer to control flows through the supply chain. Other software permits customers to obtain information about order availability.

11.5 Systems that Support Decision Making

23. Which of the following is the best example of the use of a decision support system (DSS)?

A. A manager uses a personal-computer-based simulation model to determine whether one of the company's ships would be able to satisfy a particular delivery schedule.

B. An auditor uses a generalized audit software package to retrieve several purchase orders for detailed vouching.

C. A manager uses the query language feature of a database management system (DBMS) to compile a report showing customers whose average purchase exceeds $2,500.

D. An auditor uses a personal-computer-based word processing software package to modify an internal control questionnaire for a specific audit engagement.

Answer (A) is correct.

REQUIRED: The best example of the use of a decision support system.
DISCUSSION: A decision support system (DSS) assists middle- and upper-level managers in long-term, nonroutine, and often unstructured decision making. The system contains at least one decision model, is usually interactive, dedicated, and time-shared, but need not be real-time. It is an aid to decision making, not the automation of a decision process. The personal-computer-based simulation model is used to provide interactive problem solving (i.e., scheduling) assistance, the distinguishing feature of a DSS.

Answer (B) is incorrect. The generalized audit software package does not provide interactive problem solving assistance in retrieving the purchase orders and thus is not a DSS. Answer (C) is incorrect. The query feature of a DBMS does not provide interactive problem solving assistance in compiling the report and thus is not a DSS. Answer (D) is incorrect. The word processing software package does not provide interactive problem solving assistance to the auditor and thus is not a DSS.

24. Which one of the following terms best describes a decision support system (DSS)?

    A. Management reporting system.

    B. Formalized system.

    C. Interactive system.

    D. Accounting information system.

Answer (C) is correct.

REQUIRED: The best description of a DSS.

DISCUSSION: A decision support system is an interactive system that is useful in solving semistructured and unstructured problems, that is, those requiring a top-management or middle-management decision maker to exercise judgment and to control the process. A DSS does not automate a decision or provide structured information flows but rather provides tools for an end user to employ in applying insight and judgment. The system must be interactive to permit the user to explore the problem by using the computational capacities, models, assumptions, data resources, and display graphics of the DSS.

Answer (A) is incorrect. A management reporting system provides structured, routine information flows. Answer (B) is incorrect. The required flexibility of a DSS means that it cannot be highly formalized or structured. Answer (D) is incorrect. An accounting information system processes routine, highly structured financial and transactional data relevant for accounting purposes.

25. The processing in expert systems is characterized by

    A. Algorithms.

    B. Deterministic procedures.

    C. Heuristics.

    D. Simulations.

Answer (C) is correct.

REQUIRED: The characteristic of processing in knowledge-based systems.

DISCUSSION: Knowledge-based (expert) systems contain a knowledge base for a limited domain of human expertise and inference procedures for the solution of problems. They use symbolic processing based on heuristics rather than algorithms. A heuristic procedure is an exploratory problem-solving technique that uses self-education methods, e.g., the evaluation of feedback, to improve performance. These systems are often very interactive and provide explanations of their problem-solving behavior.

Answer (A) is incorrect. Algorithms are defined procedures used in typical computer programs. Answer (B) is incorrect. Deterministic procedures are procedures used in computer programs that permit no uncertainty in outcomes. Answer (D) is incorrect. Simulations are computer programs that permit experimentation with logical and mathematical models.

26. For which of the following applications would the use of a fuzzy logic system be the most appropriate artificial intelligence (AI) choice?

    A. Assigning airport gates to arriving airline flights.

    B. Forecasting demand for spare auto parts.

    C. Performing indoor climate control.

    D. Diagnosing computer hardware problems.

Answer (C) is correct.

REQUIRED: The most appropriate use for fuzzy logic.

DISCUSSION: Fuzzy logic is a superset of conventional (Boolean) logic that has been extended to handle the concept of partial truth. Because they use nonspecific terms (membership functions) characterized by well-defined imprecision, fuzzy logic systems can create rules to address problems with many solutions. For example, applying fuzzy logic to indoor climate control may require defining in impressionistic terms and weighting functions such as indoor and outdoor temperature, humidity, and wind conditions. Thus, definitions (e.g., hot, warm, normal, cool, or cold, stated in temperature ranges) may overlap. The resulting rules describe actions to be taken when certain combinations of conditions exist. Fuzzy logic can be used when values are approximate or subjective, objects belong to multiple sets, membership in a set is a matter of degree, and data are incomplete or ambiguous.

Answer (A) is incorrect. Assigning airport gates to arriving airline flights requires an expert system that uses precise data for quick and consistent decisions. Answer (B) is incorrect. Neural networks provide the technology to undertake sophisticated forecasting and analysis. They emulate the processing patterns of the brain and therefore can learn from experience. Answer (D) is incorrect. Diagnosing problems with computer hardware could be accomplished by an expert system.

27. Business intelligence (BI) has all of the following characteristics **except**

- A. Focusing on strategic objectives.

- B. Giving immediate information about an organization's critical success factors.

- C. Displaying information in graphical format.

- D. Providing advice and answers to top management from a knowledge-based system.

Answer (D) is correct.

REQUIRED: The item that is not a characteristic of business intelligence (BI).

DISCUSSION: BI serves the needs of top management for managerial control and strategic planning. BI focuses on strategic (long-range) objectives and gives immediate information about a firm's critical success factors. BI is not a program for providing top management with advice and answers from a knowledge-based (expert) system.

Answer (A) is incorrect. BI does focus on strategic objectives. Answer (B) is incorrect. BI gives immediate information about an organization's critical (strategic) success factors. Answer (C) is incorrect. BI often displays information in graphical format.

Use the additional questions in Gleim **CPA Test Prep Online** to create Test Sessions that emulate Prometric!

Success stories!

I have used Gleim CPA Review and I am glad I did. The benefits of using Gleim were that it was an online program hence accessible anywhere and anytime, the break down of topics made it easier to manage study and focus, and there were sufficient questions coupled with a good format. I will recommend CPA to my friends. I have used Gleim CIA Review and passed three parts.

- Mohamed Abdullahi, CPA

I used Gleim Review materials to prepare for the CPA Exam. I'm happy to report I was able to pass the four sections on the first try. I couldn't have done that without the Gleim products. They were extremely helpful. The guides were well written and organized, and addressed virtually every topic I faced on the actual exams. Also, on the rare occasion I encountered trouble with the software, your technical support staff provided a quick solution. And they were pleasant to deal with on the phone.

- Dave Loverude

11.6 PRACTICE WRITTEN COMMUNICATION TASK

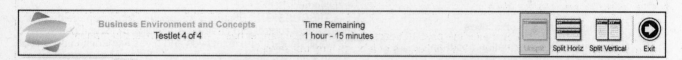

Business Environment and Concepts	Time Remaining
Testlet 4 of 4	1 hour - 15 minutes

Unsplit Split Horiz Split Vertical Exit

DIRECTIONS

Note: If you believe you have encountered a software malfunction, report it to the test center staff immediately.

Navigation

To navigate from task to task, use the controls at the bottom of the screen. Click on the **Next** button to advance to the next task, or the **Previous** button to go to the previous task. To go directly to any task, click on its number.

▽ = Reminder		Directions	1 2 3 4 5 6 7		◀ Previous	Next ▶

If you would like a reminder to revisit a task, or want to indicate that you are finished with it, click on the reminder flag below the task number. To clear the flag, click on it again. Reminder flags are for your use only – they do not contribute to your score.

Tabs

In this part of the examination, you will be asked to complete various tasks. Every task has one or more **Work Tabs**. Every task also has a **Help** tab.

Written Communication   Help

Work tab   Help tab

Work Tabs:

- **Work Tabs** are identified with a pencil icon. This is where your responses are expected.
- Each task has one or more **Work Tabs**.
- **Work Tabs** contain directions for completing the task - be sure to read these directions carefully.
- The **Work Tab** name in the example above is for illustration only - yours will differ.
- You must complete all of the **Work Tabs** in each task to receive full credit.

Help Tab:

- The **Help Tab** provides assistance with the exam software that is used in this task. For example, if the task is to compose a memorandum, **Help** will provide information about the word processor.

The Toolbar

The toolbar at the top of the screen shows the amount of time remaining for you to complete the tasks. In addition, the following tools are available. Note that only the **Exit** button is displayed when Directions are visible - the others will appear when you begin the tasks.

Unsplit   Split Horiz   Split Vertical

Click on these buttons to split or unsplit the screen. You can split the screen vertically or horizontally.

Exit

Click on this button to go on to the next part of the examination. You must complete all of the tasks to receive full credit. Once you click on **Exit** and confirm the action, you will NOT be able to return to this testlet.

▽ = Reminder		Directions	1		◀ Previous	Next ▶

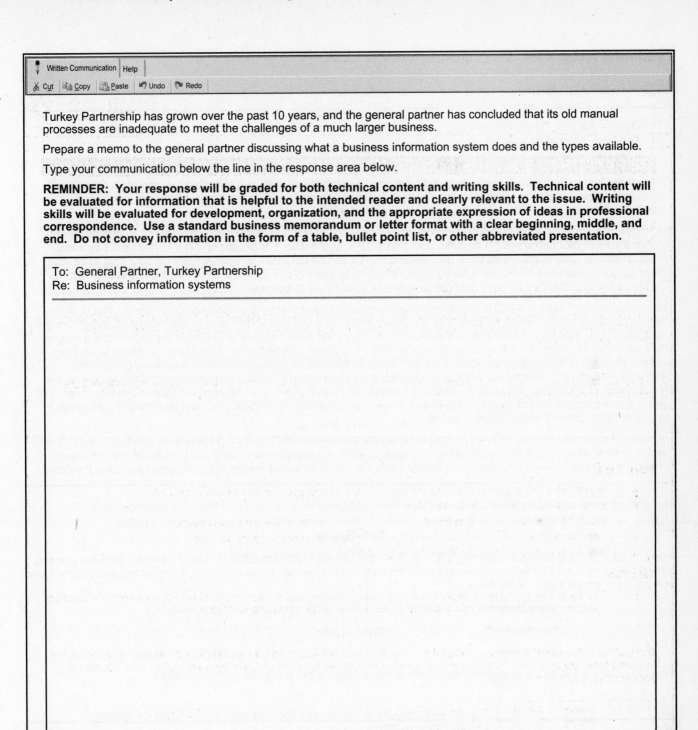

Turkey Partnership has grown over the past 10 years, and the general partner has concluded that its old manual processes are inadequate to meet the challenges of a much larger business.

Prepare a memo to the general partner discussing what a business information system does and the types available.

Type your communication below the line in the response area below.

REMINDER: Your response will be graded for both technical content and writing skills. Technical content will be evaluated for information that is helpful to the intended reader and clearly relevant to the issue. Writing skills will be evaluated for development, organization, and the appropriate expression of ideas in professional correspondence. Use a standard business memorandum or letter format with a clear beginning, middle, and end. Do not convey information in the form of a table, bullet point list, or other abbreviated presentation.

To: General Partner, Turkey Partnership
Re: Business information systems

Unofficial Answer

Written Communication

To: General Partner, Turkey Partnership
Re: Business information systems

A business information system is any combination of people, procedures, data, and computing equipment employed to pursue a business objective. Any information system performs four major tasks: input, transformation, output, and storage. There are many different kinds of business information systems.

A transaction processing system (TPS) captures the fundamental data that reflect the economic life of an organization. A management information system receives input from a TPS, aggregates it, then reports it in a format useful by middle management in running the business. A data warehouse is a central database for transaction-level data from more than one of the organization's TPSs. Data warehouses store a large quantity of data and require that the transaction records be converted to a standard format. They can be powerful tools for ad hoc queries.

A decision support system (DSS) is an interactive system that is useful in solving semistructured problems, that is, those with a structured portion (which the computer can solve) and an unstructured portion (which requires the manager's insight and judgment). However, a DSS does not automate a decision. An expert system is an interactive system that attempts to imitate the reasoning of a human expert in a given field. It is useful for addressing unstructured problems when there is a local shortage of human experts. Even more sophisticated than expert systems is computer software designed to perceive, reason, and understand. Artificial intelligence attempts to imitate human decision making, which hinges on this combination of knowledge and intuition. Business intelligence is what gives upper management the information it needs to know where the organization is and how to steer it in the intended direction. It gives an executive immediate information about an organization's critical success factors.

Enterprise resource planning (ERP) is intended to integrate enterprise-wide information systems by creating one database linked to all of an organization's applications. In traditional ERP, subsystems share data and coordinate their activities. Thus, if marketing receives an order, it can quickly verify that inventory is sufficient to notify shipping to process the order.

The above depicts a Level 5 answer. See page 16 in the Introduction for a description of the three grading criteria.

Self-Grade

Evaluate each of the following by selecting a 0, 1, 2, 3, 4, or 5. An average response is 3. Use 4 for better than average and 5 for outstanding. Use 2 for less than average and 1 for quite poor. Use zero for no response, if you did not address the topic, or if you gave advice that is clearly illegal.

Organization	o 0	o 1	o 2	o 3	o 4	o 5
Development	o 0	o 1	o 2	o 3	o 4	o 5
Expression	o 0	o 1	o 2	o 3	o 4	o 5

Your grade for the written communication as a whole is the average of the scores for the three criteria.

Use **CPA Gleim Online** and **Simulation Wizard** to practice more written communication tasks in a realistic environment.

STUDY UNIT TWELVE
IT SOFTWARE AND DATA ORGANIZATION

(15 pages of outline)

A computer's software consists of the sets of instructions, often called programs, that are executed by the hardware (Subunit 1). Programs and data are stored in a computer in a series of ones and zeros, called binary code (Subunit 2). The binary code is grouped into larger units of fields, records, and files (Subunit 3). Files can be integrated into a database (Subunit 4). When an organization acquires a new system, either by buying it or by creating it internally, a series of steps must be carefully followed to ensure that the system is stable and cost-effective (Subunit 5). The study unit concludes with a discussion of the standardized roles and responsibilities performed by personnel within the IT function (Subunit 6).

12.1 SOFTWARE

1. **Overview**

   a. Software refers to the programs (i.e., sets of computer instructions) that are executed by the hardware.

   b. Software can be described from two perspectives: (1) systems vs. application software and (2) the programming language in which the software is written.

2. **Two Major Types of Software**

   a. **Systems software** performs the fundamental tasks needed to manage computer resources. The two most common pieces of systems software are

      1) The **operating system**, which is the "traffic cop" of any computer system

         a) The operating system negotiates the conversation between the computer's hardware, the application the user is running, and the data that the application is working with.

         b) Examples are Linux and Windows.

      2) **Utility programs**, which perform basic functions that are not particular to a certain application, such as file manipulation (copying, deleting, merging, and sorting data files) and file access control

   b. **Application software** consists of programs that tell the computer what steps the user wants carried out. It may be purchased from vendors or developed internally.

      1) Examples of applications found on personal computers include word processors, spreadsheets, graphics, and small databases.

      2) Applications found on dedicated servers are payroll, human resources, purchasing, accounts payable, general ledger, treasury, etc.

   c. Software is written in languages that can be processed by the computer. The following is a description of types and development of computer languages.

3. **Programming Languages**

   a. First-generation languages (also called machine languages) are written in binary code (a combination of ones and zeros discussed in detail in Subunit 12.2) unique to each type of computer. Because they are in binary code, first generation languages are understood directly by the computer.

   b. Third-generation languages (many of which are termed procedural or programming languages) consist of English-like words and phrases that represent multiple machine language instructions, making these languages much easier to learn. These languages must be converted to machine language either by compilation (the whole program is converted at once, then executed) or interpretation (the program is converted and executed one line at a time). Third-generation languages have been deployed for decades with tremendous success. The following is a list of some of the better-known ones:

      1) COBOL (COmmon Business Oriented Language) was designed in 1959 to be easy to read and maintain, and the standard has been extensively revised and updated over the years. Vast quantities of lines of COBOL are still in use.

      2) BASIC (Beginner's All-purpose Symbolic Instruction Code) was developed to teach programming but is not used in large business application processing. Visual BASIC provides a graphical user interface to develop Microsoft Windows applications from code written in BASIC.

      3) C and C++ have been very popular languages since their introduction. C++ enhances C by adding features like support for object-oriented programming.

      4) Java is a high-level, object-oriented programming language developed by Sun Microsystems that, among other things, is used to write programs embedded in World Wide Web documents.

         a) Thus, software is stored on the network, and the user need not be concerned about compatibility of the software with the computer platform.

         b) Java is platform independent because if each computer has it incorporated into a browser, it can run on the platform. Java programs that run in a web browser are called **applets**, and Java programs that run on a web server are called **servlets**.

   c. Fourth-generation languages (also called problem-oriented or nonprocedural languages) provide still further simplification of programming. These interactive, English-like languages permit a nonspecialized user to describe the problem to, and receive guidance from, the computer instead of specifying a procedure.

      1) Generalized audit software (GAS), also known as computer-assisted audit techniques (CAAT), involves the use of computer software packages that may allow not only parallel simulation but also a variety of other processing functions, such as extracting sample items, verifying totals, developing file statistics, and retrieving specified data fields. Audit Command Language (ACL®) and Interactive Data Extraction and Analysis (IDEA™) are the leading CAAT packages.

      2) Hypertext markup language (HTML) is the authoring software language commonly used to create and link websites.

      3) Extensible markup language (XML) is an open standard usable with many programs and platforms.

      4) Extensible business reporting language (XBRL) is the specification developed by an AICPA-led consortium for commercial and industrial entities that report in accordance with U.S. GAAP. It is a variation of XML that is expected to decrease the costs of generating financial reports, reformulating information for different uses, and sharing business information using electronic media. The SEC allows firms to report using XBRL.

Stop and review! You have completed the outline for this subunit. Study multiple-choice questions 1 through 6 beginning on page 336.

12.2 NATURE OF BINARY DATA STORAGE

1. **Binary Storage**

   a. Digital computers store all information in binary format, that is, as a pattern of ones and zeros. This makes arithmetic operations and true/false decisions on the lowest level extremely straightforward.

   b. A **bit** is either 0 or 1 (off or on) in binary code. Bits can be strung together to form a binary (i.e., base 2) number.

EXAMPLE of a Bit

0

---

   c. A **byte** is a group of bits. A byte can be used to signify a character (a number, letter of the alphabet, or symbol, such as a question mark or asterisk).

EXAMPLE of a 7-Bit ASCII Byte Representing the Letter P

1010000

---

   1) Quantities of bytes are measured with the following units:

$$1{,}024 \ (2^{10}) \text{ bytes} = \textbf{1 kilobyte} = 1 \text{ KB}$$
$$1{,}048{,}576 \ (2^{20}) \text{ bytes} = \textbf{1 megabyte} = 1 \text{ MB}$$
$$1{,}073{,}741{,}824 \ (2^{30}) \text{ bytes} = \textbf{1 gigabyte} = 1 \text{ GB}$$
$$1{,}099{,}511{,}627{,}776 \ (2^{40}) \text{ bytes} = \textbf{1 terabyte} = 1 \text{ TB}$$

   Author's Note: Please do not memorize these numbers. Our intent is to demonstrate the difference in size for each unit to help you better grasp these terms.

   d. A **field** is a group of bytes. The field contains a unit of data about some entity, e.g., a composer's name.

EXAMPLE of a Field

Paul Hindemith

---

   e. A **record** is a group of fields. All the fields contain information pertaining to an entity, e.g., a specific performance of an orchestral work.

EXAMPLE of a Record

Paul Hindemith	Violin Concerto	Chicago Symphony	Claudio Abbado	Josef Suk

---

   1) Some field or combination of fields on each record is designated as the **key**. The essence of a key is that it contains enough information to uniquely identify each record; i.e., there can be no two records with the same key.

      a) The designation of a key allows records to be sorted and managed with much greater efficiency. If all the records are sorted in the order of the key, searching for a particular one becomes much easier.

b) In the example on the previous page, the key is the combination of the first two fields.

  i) The first field alone is not enough because there could be several works by each composer. The second field alone is likewise not enough since there could be many pieces with the same title.

  ii) The combination of the composer's name and title uniquely identify each piece of music.

f. A **file** is a group of records. All the records in the file contain the same pieces of information about different occurrences, e.g., performances of several orchestral works.

EXAMPLE of a File				
Paul Hindemith	Violin Concerto	Chicago Symphony	Claudio Abbado	Josef Suk
Gustav Mahler	Das Lied von der Erde	New York Philharmonic	Leonard Bernstein	Dietrich Fischer-Dieskau
Bela Bartok	Piano Concerto No. 2	Chicago Symphony	Sir Georg Solti	Etsko Tazaki
Arnold Schoenberg	Gurrelieder	Boston Symphony	Seiji Ozawa	James McCracken
Leos Janacek	Sinfonietta	Los Angeles Philharmonic	Simon Rattle	None
Dmitri Shostakovich	Symphony No. 6	San Francisco Symphony	Kazuhiro Koizumi	None
Carl Orff	Carmina Burana	Berlin Radio Symphony	Eugen Jochum	Gundula Janowitz

Stop and review! You have completed the outline for this subunit. Study multiple-choice questions 7 through 9 beginning on page 337.

12.3 FILE ORGANIZATION AND DATABASES

1. **Flat Files**

  a. The oldest file structure is the flat file, in which all the records are stored continuously, one after the other, as on a reel of magnetic tape.

    1) To find a certain record, every record on the tape has to be searched until the desired one is found.

    2) Also, the ways in which a user can perform a search on a flat file are extremely limited.

  b. As computers became more powerful, new ways of storing data became possible that permitted much more flexibility in searching and updating.

    1) Databases allow companies to save information in one place instead of having hundreds of specific files with similar information.

2. **Hierarchical Databases**

  a. The hierarchical, or tree, database model was a major development in file organization. Instead of the records being strung out one after the other, they form "branches" and "leaves" extending from a "root."

    1) Note that the customer's address is stored only once; in a flat file, the address had to be stored every time the customer placed an order.

2) Another feature of the tree file structure is that every "parent" record can have multiple "child" records, but each child can have only one parent.

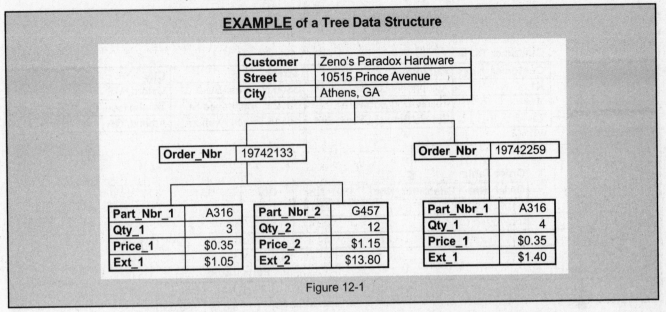

EXAMPLE of a Tree Data Structure

Customer	Zeno's Paradox Hardware
Street	10515 Prince Avenue
City	Athens, GA

Order_Nbr	19742133

Order_Nbr	19742259

Part_Nbr_1	A316
Qty_1	3
Price_1	$0.35
Ext_1	$1.05

Part_Nbr_2	G457
Qty_2	12
Price_2	$1.15
Ext_2	$13.80

Part_Nbr_1	A316
Qty_1	4
Price_1	$0.35
Ext_1	$1.40

Figure 12-1

b. One customer has many orders, but each order can only be assigned to one customer.

1) The tree structure improves speed and storage efficiency for related data; for example, a parent record consisting of a customer may directly index the child records containing the customer's orders.

2) However, adding new records is much more difficult than with a flat file. In a flat file, a new record is simply inserted whole in the proper place. In a tree structure, the relationships between the parent and child records must be maintained.

3. **Relational Databases**

a. When a relational database is used, a file like the one depicted in the example on the next page is stored with every record in a single row and every column containing a value that pertains to that record.

1) In database terminology, a file stored this way is called a table, and the columns are called attributes.

b. Each data element is stored as few times as necessary. This reduction in data redundancy is accomplished through a process called **normalization**.

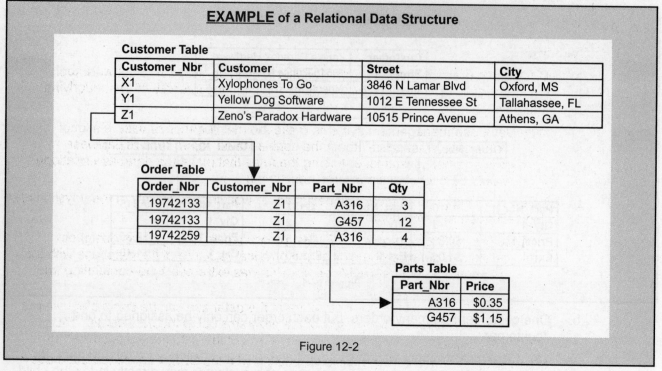

EXAMPLE of a Relational Data Structure

Customer Table

Customer_Nbr	Customer	Street	City
X1	Xylophones To Go	3846 N Lamar Blvd	Oxford, MS
Y1	Yellow Dog Software	1012 E Tennessee St	Tallahassee, FL
Z1	Zeno's Paradox Hardware	10515 Prince Avenue	Athens, GA

Order Table

Order_Nbr	Customer_Nbr	Part_Nbr	Qty
19742133	Z1	A316	3
19742133	Z1	G457	12
19742259	Z1	A316	4

Parts Table

Part_Nbr	Price
A316	$0.35
G457	$1.15

Figure 12-2

c. Two features that make the relational data structure stand out are cardinality and referential integrity.

   1) **Cardinality** refers to how close a given data element is to being unique.

      a) A data element that can only exist once in a given table has high cardinality. In Figure 12-2, Customer_Nbr has high cardinality in the Customer Table.

      b) A data element that is not unique in a given table but that has a restricted range of possible values is said to have normal cardinality. Order_Nbr in the Order Table is an example.

      c) A data element that has a very small range of values is said to have low cardinality. A field that can contain only male/female or true/false is an example.

   2) **Referential integrity** means that for a record to be entered in a given table, there must already be a record in some other table(s).

      a) For example, the Order Table in Figure 12-2 cannot contain a record where the part number is not already present in the Parts Table.

d. The tremendous advantage of a relational data structure is that searching for records is greatly facilitated.

   1) For example, a user can specify a customer and see all the parts that customer has ordered, or the user can specify a part and see all the customers who have ordered it. Such queries were extremely resource-intensive, if not impossible, under older data structures.

e. A group of tables built following the principles of relational data structures is referred to as a **relational database**.

   1) If the rules of cardinality, referential integrity, etc., are not enforced, a database will no longer be relational. To aid in the exceedingly challenging task of enforcing these rules, database management systems have been developed.

Stop and review! You have completed the outline for this subunit. Study multiple-choice questions 10 through 13 beginning on page 338.

12.4 DATABASE MANAGEMENT SYSTEMS

1. **Overview**

    a. A **database management system** (DBMS) is an integrated set of software tools superimposed on the data files that helps maintain the integrity of the underlying database.

        1) Database management systems make the maintenance of vast relational databases practical. Without the sophisticated capabilities of database management systems, enforcing the rules that make the database relational would be overwhelmingly time-consuming.

    b. A DBMS allows programmers and designers to work independently of the physical and logical structure of the database.

        1) Before the development of DBMSs, programmers and systems designers needed to consider the logical and physical structure of the database with the creation of every new application. This was extremely time-consuming and therefore expensive.

        2) With a DBMS, the physical structure of the database can be completely altered without having to change any of the programs using the data items. Thus, different users may define their own views of the data (called subschemas).

    c. Those in the IT function responsible for dealing with the DBMS are called database administrators (see item 1.a. in Subunit 12.6).

EXAMPLE

The three most prominent commercial relational database management systems are Oracle, IBM DB2, and Microsoft Access. A well-known open-source DBMS is MySQL.

---

2. **Aspects of a DBMS**

    a. A particular database's design, called its **schema**, consists of the layouts of the tables and the constraints on entering new records. To a great extent, a DBMS automates the process of enforcing the schema.

    b. Two vital parts of any DBMS are

        1) A **data definition language**, which allows the user to specify how the tables will look and what kinds of data elements they will hold

        2) A **data manipulation language**, with which the DBMS retrieves, adds, deletes, or modifies records and data elements

            a) Both of these roles are commonly fulfilled in the current generation of database management systems by Structured Query Language (SQL) or one of its many variants.

    c. The **data dictionary** contains the physical and logical characteristics of every data element in a database. The data dictionary contains the size, format, usage, meaning, and ownership of every data element as well as what persons, programs, reports, and functions use the data element.

    d. A DBMS can maintain a **distributed database**, meaning one that is stored in two or more physical sites.

        1) In the **replication**, or **snapshot**, technique, the DBMS duplicates the entire database and sends it to multiple locations. Changes are periodically copied and similarly distributed.

2)   In the **fragmentation**, or **partitioning**, method, specific records are stored where they are most needed. For example, a financial institution may store a particular customer's data at the branch where (s)he usually transacts his/her business. If the customer executes a transaction at another branch, the pertinent data are retrieved via communications lines.

Stop and review! You have completed the outline for this subunit. Study multiple-choice questions 14 and 15 beginning on page 339.

12.5 APPLICATION DEVELOPMENT AND MAINTENANCE

1.   **Organization Needs Assessment**

a.   The organizational needs assessment is a detailed process of study and evaluation of how information systems can be deployed to help the organization meet its goals. The steps in the assessment are as follows:

1)   Determine whether current systems support organizational goals
2)   Determine needs unmet by current systems
3)   Determine capacity of current systems to accommodate projected growth
4)   Propose path for information systems deployment to achieve organizational goals within budgetary constraints

2.   **Business Process Design**

a.   A business process is a flow of actions performed on goods and/or information to accomplish a discrete objective.

1)   Examples include hiring a new employee, recruiting a new customer, and filling a customer order.

b.   Some business processes are contained entirely within a single functional area; e.g., hiring a new employee is performed by the human resources function.

1)   Other processes cross functional boundaries. Filling a customer order requires the participation of the sales department, the warehouse, and accounts receivable.

c.   In the early days of automated system deployment, hardware and software were very expensive. Systems tended to be designed to serve a single process or even a single functional area.

1)   These single-purpose systems are commonly referred to now as "stovepipe" systems, since using one is akin to looking down an old-fashioned stovepipe -- the perspective is very limited.

d.   Tremendous gains in processing power and storage capacity have made integrated systems, i.e., those that combine multiple processes, the norm.

1)   The most advanced of these are enterprise resource planning (ERP) systems, described in Study Unit 11, Subunit 4.

e.   The automation of a process, or the acquisition of an integrated system, presents the organization with an opportunity for business process reengineering.

1)   Business process reengineering involves a complete rethinking of how business functions are performed to provide value to customers, that is, radical innovation instead of mere improvement and a disregard for current jobs, hierarchies, and reporting relationships.

3. **Participants in Business Process Design**

    a.   The everyday functioning of a business process affects multiple stakeholder groups.

        1)   At the least, input from each group should be considered in the design of the process. Some stakeholders will be active participants.

    b.   End users are generally the drivers of a new or redesigned process.

        1)   For example, the customers of a multi-division business may have open accounts with several of the divisions. Whenever a customer calls, the customer relations department would like the most up-to-date customer balance information for all divisions to be accessible at once.

        2)   Although the motivation for the new process begins with the customer service department, personnel in the various divisions as well as the central IT function will be affected.

    c.   Because IT pervades every aspect of operations in a modern organization, the IT steering committee must study each request for a new process and either approve or deny it.

        1)   Typical members of the steering committee include, from the IT function, the CIO and the head of systems development. Executive management from each division is also represented.

        2)   The committee members have an understanding of the interactions of the organization's current systems and how they will affect and be affected by new or redesigned business processes.

    d.   Once a new process or system has been approved, a project team is assembled, consisting of representatives of the end users who requested it and the IT personnel who will design and build the software components that will support it.

    e.   Upper management supports process design by making sufficient resources available to ensure successful implementation of the new process.

    f.   If the new process or system crosses organizational boundaries, as is the case with EDI systems (discussed in a later study unit), external parties, such as representatives of the vendor or customer businesses, are participants.

4. **Build or Buy**

    a.   When an organization acquires a new system by purchasing from an outside vendor, contract management personnel oversee the process. The future end-users of the system as well as IT personnel are also involved, drawing up specifications and requirements.

        1)   However, when a new system is to be created in-house, planning and managing the development process is one of the IT function's most important tasks.

        2)   The needs of the end users must be balanced with budget and time constraints; the decision to use existing hardware vs. the purchase of new platforms must be weighed.

    b.   Because so much time and so many resources are devoted to the creation of a new application (and because, generally, the more important the business function being automated, the more complex the application is), having a well-governed methodology for overseeing the development process is vital.

    c.   Both the end users who specified the new system's functionality and IT management who are overseeing the development process must approve progress toward the completion of the system at the end of each of the stages described on the following pages. This requirement for ongoing review and approval of the project is a type of implementation control.

5.   Systems Development Life Cycle (SDLC)

The AICPA asks questions concerning SDLC and specific cycles.

a.   The systems development life-cycle approach is the traditional methodology applied to the development of large, highly structured application systems. A major advantage of the life-cycle approach is enhanced management and control of the development process.

b.   Once the need for a new system has been recognized, the five phases (each with multiple steps) of the SDLC proceed as depicted in the diagram below (portions of the phases can overlap).

Systems Development Life Cycle

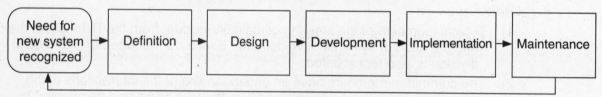

Figure 12-3

c.   Note that the feedback gathered during the maintenance of a system provides information for developing the next generation of systems, hence the name life **cycle**.

6.   The **phases and component steps of the traditional SDLC** can be described as follows:

a.   **Definition**

   1)   A proposal for a new system is submitted to the IT steering committee, describing the need for the application and the business function(s) that it will affect.

   2)   Feasibility studies are conducted to determine

   a)   What technology the new system will require
   b)   What economic resources must be committed to the new system
   c)   How the new system will affect current operations

   3)   The steering committee gives its go-ahead for the project.

b.   **Design**

   1)   Logical design consists of mapping the flow and storage of the data elements that will be used by the new system and the new program modules that will constitute the new system.

   a)   Data flow diagrams (DFDs) and structured flowcharts are commonly used in this step.
   b)   Some data elements may already be stored in existing databases. Good logical design ensures that they are not duplicated.

   2)   Physical design involves planning the specific interactions of the new program code and data elements with the hardware platform (existing or planned for purchase) on which the new system will operate.

   a)   Systems analysts are heavily involved in these two steps.

c.   **Development**

   1)   The actual program code and database structures that will be used in the new system are written.

2) Testing is the most crucial step of the process.

    a) The programmers thoroughly test each new program module of the system, both alone and in concert with other modules.

        i) The data used in testing new programs is never the organization's actual production data; such testing would be far too risky to the organization's business.

        ii) Instead, a carefully designed test database is filled with both good and bad data to test how well the new system deals with bad input.

3) User acceptance testing is the final step before placing the system in live operation.

    a) IT must demonstrate to the user department that submitted the original request that the system performs the desired functionality.

    b) Once the user department is satisfied with the new system, they acknowledge formal acceptance and implementation begins.

d. **Implementation**

1) Four strategies for converting to the new system can be used.

    a) With **parallel** operation, the old and new systems both are run at full capacity for a given period.

        i) This strategy is the safest since the old system is still producing output (in case there are major problems with the new system), but it is also the most expensive and time-consuming.

    b) With **cutover** conversion, the old system is shut down and the new one takes over processing at once.

        i) This is the least expensive and least time-consuming strategy, but it is also the riskiest.

    c) Under **pilot** conversion, one branch, department, or division at a time is fully converted to the new system.

        i) Experience gained from each installation is used to benefit the next one. One disadvantage of this strategy is the extension of the conversion time.

    d) In some cases, **phased** conversion is possible. Under this strategy, one function of the new system at a time is placed in operation.

        i) For instance, if the new system is an integrated accounting application, accounts receivable could be installed, then accounts payable, cash management, materials handling, etc.

        ii) The advantage of this strategy is allowing the users to learn one part of the system at a time.

2) Training and documentation are critical.

    a) The users must be made to feel comfortable with the new system and have plenty of guidance available, either hardcopy or online.

    b) Documentation consists of more than just operations manuals for the users. Layouts of the program code and database structures must also be available for the programmers who must modify and maintain the system.

3) Systems follow-up or post-audit evaluation is a subsequent review of the efficiency and effectiveness of the system after it has operated for a substantial time (e.g., 1 year).

e. **Maintenance**

    1) The final phase of the SDLC is discussed in item 8. below.

7. **Application Development Tools**

a. **Prototyping** is an alternative approach to application development. Prototyping involves creating a working model of the system requested, demonstrating it for the user, obtaining feedback, and making changes to the underlying code.

    1) This process repeats through several iterations until the user is satisfied with the system's functionality.

    2) Formerly, this approach was derided as being wasteful of resources and tending to produce unstable systems, but with vastly increased processing power and high-productivity development tools, prototyping can, in some cases, be an efficient means of systems development.

b. **Computer-aided software engineering (CASE)** applies the computer to software design and development.

    1) It provides the capacity to maintain on the computer all of the system documentation, e.g., data flow diagrams, data dictionaries, and pseudocode (structured English); to develop executable input and output screens; and to generate program code in at least skeletal form.

    2) Thus, CASE facilitates the creation, organization, and maintenance of documentation and permits some automation of the coding process.

8. **Program Change Control**

a. Over the life of an application, users are constantly asking for changes. The process of managing these changes is referred to as systems maintenance, and the relevant controls are called **program change controls**.

b. Once a change to a system has been approved, the programmer should save a copy of the production program in a test area of the computer, sometimes called a "sandbox."

    1) Only in emergencies, and then only under close supervision, should a change be made directly to the production version of a computer program.

c. The programmer makes the necessary changes to this copy of the program's source code.

d. The programmer transforms the changed program into a form that the computer can execute. The resulting machine-ready program is referred to as object code, or more precisely, executable code.

e. Once the programmer has the executable version of the changed program, (s)he tests it to see if it performs the new task as expected.

    1) This testing process absolutely must not be run against production data. A special set of test data must be available for running test programs against.

f. The programmer demonstrates the new functionality for the user who made the request.

    1) Either the user accepts the new program or the programmer goes back and makes further changes.

g. Once the program is in a form acceptable to the user, the programmer moves it to a holding area.

    1) Programmers (except in emergencies) should never be able to put programs directly into production.

h. The programmer's supervisor reviews the new program, approves it, and authorizes its move into production, generally carried out by operations personnel.

1) The compensating control is that operators generally lack the programming knowledge to put fraudulent code into production.

Stop and review! You have completed the outline for this subunit. Study multiple-choice questions 16 through 20 beginning on page 340.

12.6 ROLES AND RESPONSIBILITIES WITHIN THE IT FUNCTION

1. **Typical IT Personnel**

a. **Database administrators** (DBAs) are responsible for developing and maintaining the organization's databases and for establishing controls to protect their integrity.

b. **Network technicians** maintain the bridges, hubs, routers, switches, cabling, and other devices that interconnect the organization's computers. They are also responsible for maintaining the organization's connection to other networks, such as the Internet.

c. The **webmaster** is responsible for the content of the organization's website. (S)he works closely with programmers and network technicians to ensure that the appropriate content is displayed and that the site is reliably available to users.

d. **Computer (console) operators** are responsible for the moment-to-moment running of the organization's medium- and large-scale computers, i.e., servers and mainframes.

1) Computers of this size, unlike personal computers, require 24-hour monitoring. Operators respond to messages received from the system by consulting run manuals that detail the steps for processing.

e. **Librarians** maintain control over and accountability for documentation, programs, and data storage media.

f. **Systems programmers** maintain and fine-tune the operating systems on the organization's medium- and large-scale computers. The operating system is the core software that performs three of a computer's four basic tasks, i.e., input, output, and storage (the transformation task is generally handled by application software, defined in item 2.b. in Subunit 12.1).

g. **Applications programmers** design, write, test, and document computer programs according to specifications provided by the end users.

h. A **systems analyst** uses his/her detailed knowledge of the organization's databases and applications programs to determine how an application should be designed to best serve the users' needs. These duties are often combined with those of applications programmers.

i. **Help desk personnel** log problems reported by users, resolve minor difficulties, and forward more difficult problems to the appropriate person, such as a database administrator or the webmaster. Help desk personnel are often called on to resolve such issues as desktop computers crashing or problems with email.

2. **Segregation of Duties within the IT Function**

Recent CPA exams have contained questions regarding the duties and responsibilities of various IT personnel as well as the segregation of duties within the IT function. Understand the responsibilities of IT personnel from the standpoint of duty segregation.

a. Information Security

1) Information systems pervade every part of a modern organization's operations. Therefore, the area of security over information systems is a distinct function within the larger IT function.

2) The IT security officer is responsible for formulating and enforcing a formal information security policy for all employees and outside parties, such as EDI partners, who have access to the organization's systems.

3) Such a policy should, among other things, inform all those with access to the organization's systems that the organization's hardware, software, and network connections are purely for the benefit of the organization and not to be used for personal reasons.

4) In addition, the IT security function is responsible for ensuring that persons both inside and outside the organization can gain access only to those programs and data elements that are appropriate for their job duties. This requires that the IT security officer and his/her subordinates are well trained in the use of the organization's security software.

b. Systems Development and Maintenance

1) Users within the organization are constantly requesting the creation of new systems to help manage business processes and changes and enhancements to existing systems.

2) Systems analysts and applications programmers are responsible for designing, building, and maintaining the organization's applications.

3) Analysts and programmers should never be able to make changes directly to programs that are used in "live" production. A separate processing area devoted to development and testing should be set up and dedicated to the use of analysts and programmers.

4) In addition, analysts and programmers should never have access to live production data; the data used to test new or altered programs should be stored in the separate development area along with the programs.

c. Computer Operations

1) Console operators are responsible only for the smooth running of the organization's medium- and large-scale computers, i.e., the scheduling of jobs and production of output.

2) Console operators should therefore have no access to make changes to applications programs. Ideally, computer operators should have no programming knowledge or access to documentation not strictly necessary for their work ("ignorance is a good internal control").

3) Librarians are responsible for "checking out" applications programs to analysts and programmers for modification and testing and for ensuring that the properly tested version gets "checked in" to production. Ideally, they too should have no programming knowledge.

d. Data Administration

1) The totality of an organization's data is an extremely valuable asset. Hardware can be replaced for a price, but each organization's data bundle is unique and is indispensable to carrying on business. In large organizations, the task of organizing and storing data is often divided into two subfunctions.

2) Data administrators determine how the organization's data should be stored and what relationships among the data best achieve the organization's business objectives.

   a) Confusingly, this function is also called database analyst.

3) Database administrators (DBAs) keep the organization's databases running efficiently.

   a) Every database is a unique combination of

      i) The relationships among the data (the schema),
      ii) The database management system (the software), and
      iii) The equipment on which the database is stored (the hardware).

   b) Keeping a complex database "tuned" is a demanding task requiring a great deal of technical knowledge.

4) Depending on the size of the organization, the functions of data administrator and database administrator are often combined in a single job.

   a) Because they have unfettered access to the organization's production data, employees in these functions should have no access to the application programs that process the data.

e. End Users

1) In an organizational sense, the "owners" of data are the end user department (the accounting function is responsible for the accuracy of accounting data, the marketing function is responsible for the accuracy of marketing data, etc.). The IT function is merely the custodian of the data.

2) User departments should be able to access and alter only the data pertaining to their job duties; e.g., credit managers should not be able to alter accounts payable data. End users should never be able to access the code underlying applications programs.

Stop and review! You have completed the outline for this subunit. Study multiple-choice questions 21 through 27 beginning on page 341.

QUESTIONS

12.1 Software

1. XML

A. Is focused on the content of the data.

B. Has become less important as new languages on the Internet are developed.

C. Uses standardized tags.

D. Is useful to display highly unstructured data.

Answer (A) is correct.

REQUIRED: The true statement about XML.

DISCUSSION: XML (eXtensible Markup Language) is useful for putting structured data into a text file. It can be used to extract and tag structured information from a database for transmission and subsequent use in other applications, e.g., display on the Internet or importation into a spreadsheet.

Answer (B) is incorrect. XML has become very popular for use on the Internet. Information tagged in XML can be integrated into HTML and other presentations. Answer (C) is incorrect. XML is very flexible and allows the user to design customized (extensible) tags. Answer (D) is incorrect. The data must conform to a structure to be properly tagged.

2. Which of the following is a **false** statement about XBRL?

A. XBRL is freely licensed.

B. XBRL facilitates the automatic exchange of information.

C. XBRL is used primarily in the U.S.

D. XBRL is designed to work with a variety of software applications.

Answer (C) is correct.

REQUIRED: The false statement about XBRL.

DISCUSSION: XBRL (eXtensible Business Reporting Language) was developed for business and accounting applications. It is an XML-based application used to create, exchange, and analyze financial reporting information that was developed for worldwide use.

Answer (A) is incorrect. The AICPA-led consortium that developed XBRL has promoted the language as a freely licensed product. Answer (B) is incorrect. XBRL facilitates the exchange of information, for example, for reporting to the SEC. Answer (D) is incorrect. XBRL allows exchange of data across many platforms and is being integrated into accounting software applications and products.

3. C++, BASIC, FORTRAN, and COBOL are all examples of

A. Application programs.

B. Machine languages.

C. Procedural languages.

D. Operating systems.

Answer (C) is correct.

REQUIRED: The proper classification of C++, BASIC, FORTRAN, and COBOL.

DISCUSSION: A procedure-oriented or higher-level language allows specification of processing steps in terms of highly aggregated operations. They are ordinarily user-friendly. Translation to an object program is performed by a compiler program. COBOL (COmmon Business Oriented Language) consists of a series of English-like statements. FORTRAN (FORmula TRANslation) is very effective for solving mathematics and engineering problems but is less so for business applications. BASIC (Beginner's All-purpose Symbolic Instruction Code) is a widely used language for personal computers but not for large business application processing. C++ is used extensively in the software industry.

Answer (A) is incorrect. C++, BASIC, FORTRAN, and COBOL are languages, not application programs. Answer (B) is incorrect. Machine language is a programming language made up of instructions that a computer can directly recognize and execute. Answer (D) is incorrect. An operating system is a set of programs and routines to control the operations of the computer and its peripheral equipment.

4. A computer program processes payrolls. The program is a(n)

A. Operating system.

B. Application program.

C. Report generator.

D. Utility program.

Answer (B) is correct.

REQUIRED: The term associated with a computer program used to perform a business function.

DISCUSSION: Application programs are written to solve specific user problems; that is, they perform the ultimate computer functions required by system users. Thus, a program designed to process payroll is an application program.

Answer (A) is incorrect. An operating system is a set of programs used by the CPU to control operations. Answer (C) is incorrect. A report generator is a component of a database management system that produces customized reports using data stored in the database. Answer (D) is incorrect. Utility programs are standardized subroutines that can be incorporated into other programs.

5. Which of the following programming languages supports object-oriented programming?

   A. Pascal.

   B. FORTRAN.

   C. XBRL.

   D. C++.

Answer (D) is correct.

   REQUIRED: The programming language that supports object-oriented programming.

   DISCUSSION: C++ was originally called "C with classes." As the name implies, C is its foundation. Classes provide a means of encapsulating the logical entities used by the program (which ordinarily represent the program's data) into a well-organized, modular format that is easy to reuse and maintain. Through a process called inheritance, new classes can be derived from existing classes by adding new elements to the existing class design. C++ was specifically designed with these features in mind. Because code segments can be reused in other programs, the time and cost of writing software is reduced.

   Answer (A) is incorrect. Pascal traditionally emphasizes procedures rather than objects. Answer (B) is incorrect. FORTRAN traditionally emphasizes procedures rather than objects. Answer (C) is incorrect. XBRL is a problem-oriented or nonprocedural language. This is a type of language designed for use by non-technical individuals (i.e., not computer programmers). Object-oriented programming languages are what career computer programmers who have IT backgrounds use to program complex software applications.

6. Fourth-generation computer programming languages are represented by

   A. Procedure-oriented languages, which describe processing procedures.

   B. Query languages, which allow direct access to a computer database.

   C. Symbolic languages, which allow direct access to a stored database.

   D. Machine languages, which describe processing procedures.

Answer (B) is correct.

   REQUIRED: The fourth-generation computer programming languages.

   DISCUSSION: Fourth-generation languages are intended to simplify programming. They are not intended to express a procedure as a specific algorithm. These interactive, English-like languages permit the user to describe the problem to and receive guidance from the computer. Query languages are most often used with databases. They permit reading and reorganization of data but not its alteration.

   Answer (A) is incorrect. Procedure-oriented languages are third-generation languages that require translation into multiple machine-level instructions. Fourth-generation languages are **non**procedural languages. Answer (C) is incorrect. Symbolic languages are second-generation languages. Answer (D) is incorrect. Machine (first-generation) languages are far from the fourth-generation software development stage.

12.2 Nature of Binary Data Storage

7. Computers understand codes that represent letters of the alphabet, numbers, or special characters. These codes require that data be converted into predefined groups of binary digits. Such chains of digits are referred to as

   A. Registers.

   B. ASCII code.

   C. Input.

   D. Bytes.

Answer (D) is correct.

   REQUIRED: The term for the chains of digits that a computer is capable of understanding.

   DISCUSSION: A byte is a grouping of bits that can define one unit of data, such as a letter or an integer.

   Answer (A) is incorrect. A register is a location within the CPU where data and instructions are temporarily stored. Answer (B) is incorrect. ASCII (American Standard Code for Information Interchange) is the coding convention itself. Answer (C) is incorrect. Input is the data placed into processing (noun) or the act of placing the data into processing (verb).

8. Based only on the database file excerpt presented below, which one of the fields or combinations of fields is eligible for use as a key?

Column I	Column II	Column III	Column IV	Column V	Column VI
Florida	Sopchoppy	G9441	6	02/06/2009	$1823.65
Georgia	Hahira	H5277	2	02/06/2009	$412.01
Iowa	Clear Lake	B2021	1	02/06/2009	$6606.53
Iowa	Clear Lake	C2021	14	02/06/2009	$178.90
Kansas	Lawrence	A1714	2	02/06/2009	$444.28
Georgia	Milledgeville	A1713	1	02/06/2009	$195.60

    A. Column I and Column II in combination.

    B. Column I and Column V in combination.

    C. Column III alone.

    D. Column IV and Column V in combination.

Answer (C) is correct.
    REQUIRED: The field or combination thereof that could be used as a key.
    DISCUSSION: Some field or combination of fields on each record is designated as the key. The essence of a key is that it contains enough information to uniquely identify each record; i.e., there can be no two records with the same key. Of the choices presented, only Column III by itself uniquely identifies each record.
    Answer (A) is incorrect. Column I and Column II in combination do not uniquely identify each record. Answer (B) is incorrect. Column I and Column V in combination do not uniquely identify each record. Answer (D) is incorrect. Column IV and Column V in combination do not uniquely identify each record.

9. Which one of the following correctly depicts the hierarchy of storage commonly found in computerized databases, from least complex to most complex?

    A. Byte, field, file, record.

    B. Byte, field, record, file.

    C. Field, byte, record, file.

    D. Field, byte, file, record.

Answer (B) is correct.
    REQUIRED: The correct hierarchy in computerized databases.
    DISCUSSION: A byte is a group of bits (binary 1s and 0s). A field is a group of bytes. A record is a group of fields. A file is a group of records.
    Answer (A) is incorrect. A record is less complex than a file. Answer (C) is incorrect. A byte is less complex than a field. Answer (D) is incorrect. A byte is less complex than a field, and a record is less complex than a file.

12.3 File Organization and Databases

10. In an inventory system on a database, one stored record contains part number, part name, part color, and part weight. These individual items are called

    A. Fields.

    B. Stored files.

    C. Bytes.

    D. Occurrences.

Answer (A) is correct.
    REQUIRED: The term for the data elements in a record.
    DISCUSSION: A record is a collection of related data items (fields). A field (data item) is a group of characters representing one unit of information.
    Answer (B) is incorrect. A file is a group or set of related records ordered to facilitate processing. Answer (C) is incorrect. A byte is a group of bits (binary digits). It represents one character. Answer (D) is incorrect. Occurrences is not a meaningful term in this context.

11. In a database, there are often conditions that constrain database records. For example, a sales order cannot exist unless the corresponding customer exists. This kind of constraint is an example of

    A. Normalization.

    B. Entity integrity.

    C. Internal schema.

    D. Referential integrity.

Answer (D) is correct.
    REQUIRED: The constraint exemplified by prohibiting preparation of a sales order unless it references an existing customer.
    DISCUSSION: The data in a database are subject to the constraint of referential integrity. Thus, if data are collected about something, e.g., a payment voucher, all reference conditions regarding it must be met. Thus, for a voucher to exist, a vendor must also exist.
    Answer (A) is incorrect. Normalization is the practice of decomposing database relations to remove data field redundancies and thus reduce the likelihood of update anomalies. Answer (B) is incorrect. In a database, entity integrity means that each item or relationship in the database is uniquely identified by a single key value. Answer (C) is incorrect. In a database, the internal schema describes the ways the data are physically organized.

12. Of the following, the greatest advantage of a database (server) architecture is that

   A. Data redundancy can be reduced.

   B. Conversion to a database system is inexpensive and can be accomplished quickly.

   C. Multiple occurrences of data items are useful for consistency checking.

   D. Backup and recovery procedures are minimized.

Answer (A) is correct.

   REQUIRED: The greatest advantage of a database architecture.

   DISCUSSION: Data organized in files and used by the organization's various application programs are collectively known as a database. In a database system, storage structures are created that render the applications programs independent of the physical or logical arrangement of the data. Each data item has a standard definition, name, and format, and related items are linked by a system of pointers. The programs therefore need only specify data items by name, not by location. A database management system handles retrieval and storage. Because separate files for different application programs are unnecessary, data redundancy can be substantially reduced.

   Answer (B) is incorrect. Conversion to a database is often costly and time consuming. Answer (C) is incorrect. A traditional flat-file system, not a database, has multiple occurrences of data items. Answer (D) is incorrect. Given the absence of data redundancy and the quick propagation of data errors throughout applications, backup and recovery procedures are just as critical in a database as in a flat-file system.

13. The primary purpose of a database system is to have a single storage location for each

   A. File.

   B. Record.

   C. Database.

   D. Data item.

Answer (D) is correct.

   REQUIRED: The primary purpose of a database system.

   DISCUSSION: Data organized in files and used by the organization's various applications are collectively known as a database. In a database system, storage structures are created that render the applications independent of the physical or logical arrangement of the data. Each data item has a standard definition, name, and format, and related items are linked by a system of pointers. The programs therefore only need to specify data items by name, not by location. A database management system handles retrieval and storage. Because separate files for different applications are unnecessary, data redundancy (multiple storage locations for a data item) can be substantially reduced.

   Answer (A) is incorrect. Databases are not organized by file. Answer (B) is incorrect. Databases are not organized by records. Answer (C) is incorrect. The database is the collective result of organizing data in this way.

12.4 Database Management Systems

14. One advantage of a database management system (DBMS) is

   A. Each organizational unit takes responsibility and control for its own data.

   B. The cost of the data processing department decreases as users are now responsible for establishing their own data handing techniques.

   C. A decreased vulnerability as the database management system has numerous security controls to prevent disasters.

   D. The independence of the data from the application programs, which allows the programs to be developed for the user's specific needs without concern for data capture problems.

Answer (D) is correct.

   REQUIRED: The advantage of a DBMS.

   DISCUSSION: A fundamental characteristic of databases is that applications are independent of the database structure; when writing programs or designing applications to use the database, only the name of the desired item is necessary. Programs can be developed for the user's specific needs without concern for data capture problems. Reference can be made to the items using the data manipulation language, after which the DBMS takes care of locating and retrieving the desired items. The physical or logical structure of the database can be completely altered without having to change any of the programs using the data items. Only the schema requires alteration.

   Answer (A) is incorrect. Each organizational unit develops programs to use the elements of a broad database. Answer (B) is incorrect. Data handling techniques are still the responsibility of the data processing department. It is the use of the data that is departmentalized. Answer (C) is incorrect. The DBMS is not necessarily safer than any other database system.

15. An overall description of a database, including the names of data elements, their characteristics, and their relationship to each other, is defined by using a

    A. Data definition language.

    B. Data control language.

    C. Data manipulation language.

    D. Data command interpreter language.

Answer (A) is correct.

    REQUIRED: The language used to define a database.

    DISCUSSION: The data definition language defines the database structure and content, especially the schema (the description of the entire database) and subschema (logical views of the database). The schema specifies characteristics such as the names of the data elements contained in the database and their relationship to each other. The subschema defines the logical data views required for applications, which limits the data elements and functions available to each application.

    Answer (B) is incorrect. The data control language specifies the privileges and security rules governing database users. Answer (C) is incorrect. Data manipulation language provides application programs with a means of interacting with the database to add, retrieve, modify, or delete data or relationships. Answer (D) is incorrect. Data command interpreter languages are symbolic character strings used to control the current state of database management system operations.

12.5 Application Development and Maintenance

16. Ordinarily, the analysis tool for the systems analyst and steering committee to use in selecting the best system alternative is

    A. Pilot testing.

    B. User selection.

    C. Decision tree analysis.

    D. Cost-benefit analysis.

Answer (D) is correct.

    REQUIRED: The analysis tool to use in selecting the best system alternative.

    DISCUSSION: Feasibility studies should include an analysis of the cost-benefit ratio of any system alternatives. In many cases, the best possible system may not be cost effective. Thus, once the decision makers have determined that two or more systems alternatives are acceptable, the cost-benefit relationship should be used to select the best system for a particular application.

    Answer (A) is incorrect. Pilot testing typically occurs after development of a system. Answer (B) is incorrect. Users may not have the necessary systems knowledge to make a decision. Answer (C) is incorrect. Decision tree analysis is probably more sophisticated than is necessary in choosing between a few systems alternatives.

17. Two phases of systems planning are project definition and project initiation. All of the following are steps in the project initiation phase **except**

    A. Preparing the project proposal.

    B. Informing managers and employees of the project.

    C. Assembling the project team.

    D. Training selected personnel.

Answer (A) is correct.

    REQUIRED: The step not a part of the project initiation phase of systems planning.

    DISCUSSION: The project initiation phase includes promptly informing managers and employees about the project, assembling the project team (possibly including systems analysts, programmers, accountants, and users), training selected personnel to improve necessary skills and enhance communication among team members, and establishing project controls (e.g., by implementing a project scheduling technique such as PERT). Preparing the project proposal is a part of the project definition phase, as are conducting feasibility studies, determining project priority, and submitting the proposal for approval.

    Answer (B) is incorrect. Informing managers and employees of the project is a component of the project initiation phase. Answer (C) is incorrect. Assembling the project team is a component of the project initiation phase. Answer (D) is incorrect. Training selected personnel is a component of the project initiation phase.

18. The **least** risky strategy for converting from a manual to a computerized accounts receivable system would be a

- A. Direct conversion.
- B. Parallel conversion.
- C. Pilot conversion.
- D. Database conversion.

Answer (B) is correct.
REQUIRED: The least risky strategy for converting from a manual to a computerized accounts receivable system.
DISCUSSION: The least risky strategy for converting from a manual to a computerized system is a parallel conversion in which the old and new systems are operated simultaneously until satisfaction is obtained that the new system is operating as expected. Slightly more risky is a pilot conversion in which the new system is introduced by module or segment.
Answer (A) is incorrect. A direct conversion is more risky than a parallel conversion. Answer (C) is incorrect. A pilot conversion is more risky than a parallel conversion. Answer (D) is incorrect. A database conversion is more risky than a parallel conversion.

19. The process of monitoring, evaluating, and modifying a system as needed is referred to as

- A. Systems analysis.
- B. Systems feasibility study.
- C. Systems maintenance.
- D. Systems implementation.

Answer (C) is correct.
REQUIRED: The term for the process of monitoring, evaluating, and modifying a system.
DISCUSSION: Systems maintenance must be undertaken by systems analysts and applications programmers continuously throughout the life of a system. Maintenance is the redesign of the system and programs to meet new needs or to correct design flaws. Ideally, these changes should be made as part of a regular program of preventive maintenance.
Answer (A) is incorrect. Systems analysis is the process of determining user problems and needs, surveying the organization's present system, and analyzing the facts.
Answer (B) is incorrect. A feasibility study determines whether a proposed system is technically, operationally, and economically feasible. Answer (D) is incorrect. Systems implementation involves training and educating system users, testing, conversion, and follow-up.

20. An information system (IS) project manager is currently in the process of adding a systems analyst to the IS staff. The new systems analyst will be involved with testing the new computerized system. At which stage of the systems development life cycle will the analyst be primarily used?

- A. Cost-benefit analysis.
- B. Requirements definition.
- C. Flowcharting.
- D. Development.

Answer (D) is correct.
REQUIRED: The stage of the systems development life cycle involving testing of a new system.
DISCUSSION: The systems development life-cycle approach is the oldest methodology applied to the development of medium or large information systems. The cycle is analytically divisible into stages: definition, design, development, implementation, and maintenance. Testing is the most crucial step in the development stage of the life cycle.
Answer (A) is incorrect. Cost-benefit analysis is a part of the feasibility study conducted early in the life cycle. Answer (B) is incorrect. Requirements are defined during the analysis or systems study stage. Answer (C) is incorrect. Flowcharting is a necessary activity in all early stages of the life cycle.

12.6 Roles and Responsibilities within the IT Function

21. Which of the following internal control procedures would prevent an employee from being paid an inappropriate hourly wage?

- A. Having the supervisor of the data entry clerk verify that each employee's hours worked are correctly entered into the system.
- B. Using real-time posting of payroll so there can be **no** after-the-fact data manipulation of the payroll register.
- C. Giving payroll data entry clerks the ability to change any suspicious hourly pay rates to a reasonable rate.
- D. Limiting access to employee master files to authorized employees in the personnel department.

Answer (D) is correct.
REQUIRED: The control procedure that would prevent an inappropriate hourly wage.
DISCUSSION: Only personnel department employees should have access to employee master files where pay rates, hire dates, etc., are stored.
Answer (A) is incorrect. The setting of hourly wages should only be performed by personnel department employees.
Answer (B) is incorrect. Real-time posting of payroll will not prevent improper wage rates from being set. Answer (C) is incorrect. Only personnel department employees should be able to change hourly pay rates.

22. Which one of the following represents a **lack** of internal control in a computer-based system?

    A. The design and implementation is performed in accordance with management's specific authorization.

    B. Any and all changes in application programs have the authorization and approval of management.

    C. Provisions exist to ensure the accuracy and integrity of computer processing of all files and reports.

    D. Programmers have access to change programs and data files when an error is detected.

Answer (D) is correct.

    REQUIRED: The example of a lack of internal control in a computer system.

    DISCUSSION: A functional separation of computer activities is necessary for internal control. A programmer designs program flowcharts and writes the computer programs as required by the system. Once the program has been debugged and the documentation prepared, the programmer should have no further access to it or to data files. A librarian is responsible for permitting only computer operators, not programmers, to have access to programs.

    Answer (A) is incorrect. The design and implementation should be authorized by management to maintain effective internal controls. Answer (B) is incorrect. Activities that involve making changes in application programs should be authorized and approved by management to maintain effective internal controls. Answer (C) is incorrect. Effective internal control ensures the reliability of records. A control group (clerk) should continuously supervise and monitor input, operations, and distribution of output.

23. In the organization of the information systems function, the most important separation of duties is

    A. Not allowing the data librarian to assist in data processing operations.

    B. Assuring that those responsible for programming the system do not have access to data processing operations.

    C. Having a separate information officer at the top level of the organization outside of the accounting function.

    D. Using different programming personnel to maintain utility programs from those who maintain the application programs.

Answer (B) is correct.

    REQUIRED: The most important separation of duties.

    DISCUSSION: Separation of duties is a general control that is vital in a computerized environment. Some separation of duties common in noncomputerized environments may not be feasible in a computer environment. However, certain tasks should not be combined. Systems analysts and programmers should be separate from computer operators. Both programmers and analysts may be able to modify programs, files, and controls, and should therefore have no access to those programs nor to computer equipment. Operators should not be assigned programming duties or responsibility for systems design, and should have no opportunity to make changes in programs and systems.

    Answer (A) is incorrect. Librarians maintain control over documentation, programs, and data files; they should have no access to equipment, but they can assist in data processing operations. Answer (C) is incorrect. A separate information officer outside of the accounting function would not be as critical a separation of duties as that between programmers and processors Answer (D) is incorrect. Programmers usually handle all types of programs.

24. Which of the following should **not** be the responsibility of a database administrator?

    A. Design the content and organization of the database.

    B. Develop applications to access the database.

    C. Protect the database and its software.

    D. Monitor and improve the efficiency of the database.

Answer (B) is correct.

    REQUIRED: The choice not a responsibility of a database administrator.

    DISCUSSION: The database administrator (DBA) is the person who has overall responsibility for developing and maintaining the database. One primary responsibility is for designing the content of the database. Another responsibility of the DBA is to protect and control the database. A third responsibility is to monitor and improve the efficiency of the database. The responsibility of developing applications to access the database belongs to systems analysts and programmers.

    Answer (A) is incorrect. Designing the content and organization of the database is a responsibility of the database administrator. Answer (C) is incorrect. Protecting the database and its software is a responsibility of the database administrator. Answer (D) is incorrect. Monitoring and improving the efficiency of the database is a responsibility of the database administrator.

25. To maintain effective segregation of duties within the information technology function, an application programmer should have which of the following responsibilities?

A. Modify and adapt operating systems software.

B. Correct detected data entry errors for the cash disbursement system.

C. Code approved changes to a payroll program.

D. Maintain custody of the billing program code and its documentation.

Answer (C) is correct.

REQUIRED: The responsibility that an application programmer should have, in order to maintain effective duty segregation.

DISCUSSION: Applications programmers design, write, test, and document computer programs according to specifications provided by the end users. The programmers are responsible for designing, building, and maintaining the organization's applications. Under no circumstances should programmers be able to make changes directly to programs that are used in "live" production. A separate processing area devoted to development and testing should be set up and dedicated to the use of programmers.

Answer (A) is incorrect. Systems programmers maintain and fine-tune the operating systems on the organization's medium- and large-scale computers. The operating system is the core software that performs the computer's basic tasks of input, output, and storage. Answer (B) is incorrect. The end users of the cash disbursement system should be able to access and alter the data pertaining to their job duties. Answer (D) is incorrect. Maintaining custody of the billing program code and its documentation is the responsibility of the IT librarians.

26. In a large multinational organization, which of the following job responsibilities should be assigned to the network administrator?

A. Managing remote access.

B. Developing application programs.

C. Reviewing security policy.

D. Installing operating system upgrades.

Answer (A) is correct.

REQUIRED: The job responsibility that should be assigned to the network administrator.

DISCUSSION: Database administrators (DBAs), also called network administrators, are responsible for developing and maintaining the organization's databases and for establishing controls to protect their integrity. Managing remote access would be one method used by DBAs to protect the integrity of the organization's databases.

Answer (B) is incorrect. Systems analysts and applications programmers develop application programs. Answer (C) is incorrect. The IT security officer is responsible for formulating and enforcing a formal information security policy for all employees and outside parties who have access to the organization's systems. Answer (D) is incorrect. Installing operating systems upgrades is accomplished by the organization's systems programmers.

27. Which of the following information technology (IT) departmental responsibilities should be delegated to separate individuals?

A. Network maintenance and wireless access.

B. Data entry and antivirus management.

C. Data entry and application programming.

D. Data entry and quality assurance.

Answer (C) is correct.

REQUIRED: The information technology (IT) departmental responsibilities that should be delegated to separate individuals.

DISCUSSION: Application programmers design, write, test, and document computer programs according to specifications provided by the end users. End user departments should be able to access and alter only the data pertaining to their job duties. They should never be able to access the code underlying application programs.

Answer (A) is incorrect. Network technicians maintain the bridges, hubs, routers, switches, cabling, and other devices that interconnect the organization's computers. They are also responsible for maintaining the organization's connection to other networks. Answer (B) is incorrect. Data entry and antivirus management are unrelated activities and can be assigned to the same person. Answer (D) is incorrect. Data entry and quality assurance are unrelated activities and can be assigned to the same person.

12.7 PRACTICE WRITTEN COMMUNICATION TASK

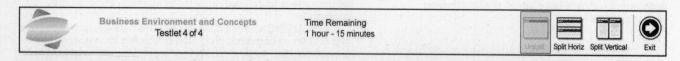

Business Environment and Concepts
Testlet 4 of 4

Time Remaining
1 hour - 15 minutes

Unsplit   Split Horiz   Split Vertical   Exit

DIRECTIONS

Note: If you believe you have encountered a software malfunction, report it to the test center staff immediately.

Navigation

To navigate from task to task, use the controls at the bottom of the screen. Click on the **Next** button to advance to the next task, or the **Previous** button to go to the previous task. To go directly to any task, click on its number.

▽ = Reminder   Directions   1 2 3 4 5 6 7   ◀ Previous   Next ▶

If you would like a reminder to revisit a task, or want to indicate that you are finished with it, click on the reminder flag below the task number. To clear the flag, click on it again. Reminder flags are for your use only – they do not contribute to your score.

Tabs

In this part of the examination, you will be asked to complete various tasks. Every task has one or more **Work Tabs**. Every task also has a **Help** tab.

Written Communication   Help

Work tab   Help tab

Work Tabs:

- **Work Tabs** are identified with a pencil icon. This is where your responses are expected.
- Each task has one or more **Work Tabs**.
- **Work Tabs** contain directions for completing the task - be sure to read these directions carefully.
- The **Work Tab** name in the example above is for illustration only - yours will differ.
- You must complete all of the **Work Tabs** in each task to receive full credit.

Help Tab:

- The **Help Tab** provides assistance with the exam software that is used in this task. For example, if the task is to compose a memorandum, **Help** will provide information about the word processor.

The Toolbar

The toolbar at the top of the screen shows the amount of time remaining for you to complete the tasks. In addition, the following tools are available. Note that only the **Exit** button is displayed when Directions are visible - the others will appear when you begin the tasks.

Unsplit   Split Horiz   Split Vertical

Click on these buttons to split or unsplit the screen. You can split the screen vertically or horizontally.

Exit

Click on this button to go on to the next part of the examination. You must complete all of the tasks to receive full credit. Once you click on **Exit** and confirm the action, you will NOT be able to return to this testlet.

▽ = Reminder   Directions   1   ◀ Previous   Next ▶

The CEO and CIO of Skyburg, Inc., are complaining within your hearing that their information systems, which once made business so much easier, are now a drain on the organization. As you explore this topic, you learn that Skyburg has always acquired its information systems either through their in-house staff of programmers or from contract programmers hired temporarily. Both groups took a "build-on-the-fly" approach to creating the systems. The CIO tells you that whenever users request a change, her programmers spend a great deal of time just digging through the existing code trying to figure out where the change should go.

Prepare a memo to the CEO and CIO of Skyburg describing the appropriate steps in developing an information system.

Type your communication below the line in the response area below.

REMINDER: Your response will be graded for both technical content and writing skills. Technical content will be evaluated for information that is helpful to the intended reader and clearly relevant to the issue. Writing skills will be evaluated for development, organization, and the appropriate expression of ideas in professional correspondence. Use a standard business memorandum or letter format with a clear beginning, middle, and end. Do not convey information in the form of a table, bullet point list, or other abbreviated presentation.

To: CEO and CIO, Skyburg, Inc.
Re: Systems development life cycle (SDLC)

Unofficial Answer

Written Communication

To: CEO and CIO, Skyburg, Inc.
Re: Systems development life cycle (SDLC)

The systems development life-cycle (SDLC) approach is the traditional methodology applied to the development of large, highly structured application systems. A major advantage of the life-cycle approach is enhanced management and control of the development process. Once the need for a new system has been recognized, the five phases (each with multiple steps) of the SDLC proceed in this order: definition, design, development, implementation, and maintenance.

In the definition phase, a proposal for a new system is submitted to the IT steering committee describing the need for the application and the business function(s) that it will affect. Feasibility studies are then conducted, and the steering committee gives its go-ahead for the project.

The design phase consists of two subphases: Logical design consists of mapping the flow and storage of the data elements that will be used by the new system and the new program modules that will constitute the new system. Physical design involves planning the specific interactions of the new program code and data elements with the hardware platform (existing or planned for purchase) on which the new system will operate.

In the development phase, the actual program code and database structures that will be used in the new system are written. Testing is the most crucial step of the process. The programmers thoroughly test each new program module of the system, both alone and in concert with other modules. User acceptance testing is the final step before placing the system in live operation.

Four rollout strategies can be used in the implementation phase: parallel operation, cutover conversion, pilot conversion, and phased conversion. Training and documentation are critical. Systems follow-up or post-audit evaluation is a subsequent review of the efficiency and effectiveness of the system after it has operated for a substantial time (e.g., 1 year).

The final phase of the SDLC is maintenance. Over the life of an application, users are constantly asking for changes. The process of managing these changes is referred to as systems maintenance, and the relevant controls are called program change controls.

The above depicts a Level 5 answer. See page 16 in the Introduction for a description of the three grading criteria.

Self-Grade

Evaluate each of the following by selecting a 0, 1, 2, 3, 4, or 5. An average response is 3. Use 4 for better than average and 5 for outstanding. Use 2 for less than average and 1 for quite poor. Use zero for no response, if you did not address the topic, or if you gave advice that is clearly illegal.

Organization	○ 0	○ 1	○ 2	○ 3	○ 4	○ 5
Development	○ 0	○ 1	○ 2	○ 3	○ 4	○ 5
Expression	○ 0	○ 1	○ 2	○ 3	○ 4	○ 5

Your grade for the written communication as a whole is the average of the scores for the three criteria.

Use **CPA Gleim Online** and **Simulation Wizard** to practice more written communication tasks in a realistic environment.

STUDY UNIT THIRTEEN
IT NETWORKS AND ELECTRONIC COMMERCE

(14 pages of outline)

Huge gains in productivity have resulted from the networking of computers (Subunits 1 and 2). The traditional ways of carrying on business have found new channels through electronic networking (Subunits 3 and 4). The use of encryption is required to make messages sent electronically secure (Subunit 5). As a licensed CPA, you will need to know how computers communicate over networks so you can ascertain their vulnerability. This study unit introduces you to the types of communications between computers. The next study unit focuses on how to assess and quantify information risks.

13.1 NETWORKS AND THE INTERNET

1. **Mainframe Communication**

   a. Large mainframe computers dominated the electronic data processing field in its first decades. Mainframes were arranged so that all processing and data storage were done in a single, central location.

   b. Communication with the mainframe was accomplished with the use of dumb terminals, simple keyboard-and-monitor combinations with no processing power (i.e., no CPU) of their own.

2. **Increasing Decentralization**

   a. Improvements in technology have led to increasing decentralization of information processing.

      1) The mainframe-style computer was the only arrangement available in the early days of data processing. International Business Machines (now called IBM) dominated the marketplace.

      2) Mainframes are still in use at large institutions, such as governments, banks, insurance companies, and universities. However, remote connections to them are usually through personal computers rather than through dumb terminals. This is known as terminal emulation.

      3) As minicomputers evolved, the concept of distributed processing arose.

         a) **Distributed processing** involves the decentralization of processing tasks and data storage and assigning these functions to multiple computers, often in separate locations.

         b) This allowed for a drastic reduction in the amount of communications traffic because data needed locally could reside locally.

   b. During the 1980s, personal computers, and the knowledge needed to build information systems, became widespread throughout the organization.

      1) In the early part of this period, the only means of moving data from one computer to another was through the laborious process of copying the data to a diskette and physically carrying it to the destination computer.

      2) It was clear that a reliable way of wiring office computers together would lead to tremendous gains in productivity.

Be able to describe distributed processing and the types of networks. Recent exams have included questions on this topic.

3. Local Area Networks (LANs)

a. The need to increase productivity led to the development of the local area network (LAN). A LAN is any interconnection between devices in a single office or building.

    1) Very small networks with few devices can be connected using a peer-to-peer arrangement, where every device is connected directly to every other. Peer-to-peer networks become increasingly difficult to administer with each added device.

b. The most cost-effective and easy-to-administer arrangement for LANs uses the client-server model.

    1) Client-server networks differ from peer-to-peer networks in that the devices play more specialized roles. Client processes (initiated by the individual user) request services from server processes (maintained centrally).

    2) In a client-server arrangement, servers are centrally located and devoted to the functions that are needed by all network users.

        a) Examples include mail servers (to handle electronic mail), application servers (to run application programs), file servers (to store databases and make user inquiries more efficient), Internet servers (to manage access to the Internet), and web servers (to host websites).

        b) Whether a device is classified as a server is not determined by its hardware configuration, but rather by the function it performs. A simple personal computer can be a server.

    3) Technically, a client is any object that uses the resources of another object. Thus, a client can be either a device or a software program.

        a) In common usage, however, client refers to a device that requests services from a server. This understanding of the term encompasses anything from a powerful graphics workstation to a personal mobile device.

        b) A client device normally displays the user interface and enables data entry, queries, and the receipt of reports. Moreover, many applications, e.g., word processing and spreadsheet software, run on the client computer.

    4) The key to the client-server model is that it runs processes on the platform most appropriate to that process while attempting to minimize traffic over the network.

        a) This is commonly referred to as the three-tiered architecture of client, application, and database.

        b) Because of the specialized roles, client-server systems are often assembled with equipment from multiple vendors.

    5) Security for client-server systems may be more difficult than in a highly centralized system because of the numerous access points.

c. Along with the increased convenience and flexibility of decentralization came new security risks.

    1) Unauthorized software can be easily installed on the network from a desktop computer. This exposes the organization to both viruses and liability for copyright violation.

    2) Important files stored on a local computer may not be backed up properly by the user.

    3) Applications written by users of local computers may not adhere to the standards of the organization, making data sharing difficult.

4. **Classifying Networks by Geographical Extent and Function**

   a. The range of networking has expanded from the earliest form (two computers in the same room) to the global reach of the Internet.

   b. A **local area network (LAN)** connects devices within a single office or home or among buildings in an office park. The key aspect here is that a LAN is owned entirely by a single organization.

      1) The LAN is the network familiar to office workers all over the world. In its simplest conception, it can consist of a few personal computers and a printer.

   c. A **wide area network (WAN)** consists of a conglomerate of LANs over widely separated locations. The key aspect here is that a WAN can be either publicly or privately owned.

      1) One advantage of a WAN is the possibility of spreading the cost of ownership among multiple organizations.

         a) WANs come in many configurations. In its simplest conception, it can consist of a lone personal computer using a slow dial-up line to connect to an Internet service provider.

      2) Publicly owned WANs, such as the public telephone system and the Internet, are available to any user with a compatible device. The assets of these networks are paid for by means other than individually imposed user fees.

         a) Public-switched networks use public telephone lines to carry data. This arrangement is economical, but the quality of data transmission cannot be guaranteed and security is highly questionable.

      3) Privately owned WANs are profit-making enterprises. They offer fast, secure data communication services to organizations that do not wish to make their own large investments in the necessary infrastructure.

         a) **Value-added networks** (VANs) are private networks that provide their customers with reliable, high-speed secure transmission of data.

            i) To compete with the Internet, these third-party networks add value by providing their customers with error detection and correction services, electronic mailbox facilities for EDI purposes, EDI translation, and security for email and data transmissions.

         b) **Virtual private networks** (VPNs) emerged as a relatively inexpensive way to solve the problem of the high cost of leased lines.

            i) A company connects each office or LAN to a local Internet service provider and routes data through the shared, low-cost public Internet.

            ii) The success of VPNs depends on the development of secure encryption products that protect data while in transit.

      4) Intranets and extranets are types of WANs.

         a) An **intranet** permits sharing of information throughout an organization by applying Internet connectivity standards and Web software (e.g., browsers) to the organization's internal network.

            i) An intranet addresses the connectivity problems faced by organizations that have many types of computers. Its use is restricted to those within the organization.

         b) An **extranet** consists of the linked intranets of two or more organizations, for example, of a supplier and its customers. It typically uses the public Internet as its transmission medium but requires a password for access.

5. **The Internet**

   a. The Internet is a network of networks all over the world.

   > ### Background
   >
   > The Internet is descended from the original ARPANet, a product of the Defense Department's Advanced Research Projects Agency (ARPA), introduced in 1969. The idea was to have a network that could not be brought down during an enemy attack by bombing a single central location. ARPANet connected computers at universities, corporations, and government. In view of the growing success of the Internet, ARPANet was retired in 1990.

   b. The Internet facilitates inexpensive communication and information transfer among computers, with gateways allowing servers to interface with personal computers.

      1) Very high-speed Internet connections (termed the Internet backbone) carry signals around the world and meet at network access points.

   c. Most Internet users obtain connections through **Internet service providers** (ISPs) that in turn connect either directly to a gateway or to a larger ISP with a connection to a gateway.

      1) The topology of the backbone and its interconnections may once have resembled a spine with ribs connected along its length, but it is now more like a fishing net wrapped around the world with many circular paths.

   d. TCP/IP (Transmission Control Protocol/Internet Protocol) is a term candidates should be familiar with. It is defined as a suite of communications protocols (rules or standards) used to connect computers to the Internet. It is also built into network operating systems.

6. **Aspects and Terminology of the Internet**

   a. The Internet was initially restricted to email and text-only documents. **Hypertext markup language** (HTML) allows users to click on a word or phrase (a hyperlink) on their screens and have another document automatically be displayed.

   b. **Hypertext transfer protocol** (HTTP) allows hyperlinking across the Internet rather than on just a single computer. A browser allows users to read HTML from any brand of computer. This system became known as the World Wide Web (often simply called "the Web").

      1) As the use of HTML and its successor languages spread, it became possible to display rich graphics and streaming audio and video in addition to text.

      2) **Extensible markup language** (XML) was developed by an international consortium and released in 1998 as an open standard (e.g., not owned or controlled by any one entity) usable with many programs and platforms.

         a) XML codes all information in such a way that a user can determine not only how it should be presented but also what it is; i.e., all computerized data may be tagged with identifiers.

         b) Unlike HTML, XML uses extensible codes. Thus, if an industry can agree on a set of codes, software for that industry can be written that incorporates those codes.

   c. Every resource on the Web has a unique address, made up of alphanumeric characters, periods, and forward slashes, called a **uniform resource locator** (URL). A URL is recognizable by any web-enabled device. An example is http://www.gleim.com/.

      1) However, just because the address is recognizable does not mean its content is accessible to every user—security is a major feature of any organization's website.

    d.   The Internet provides a wealth of resources to entities. **Cloud computing** is a popular term relating to on-demand access to resources that are accessed on the Internet and shared by others. The entity has the ability to choose and pay for only the applications needed from the array (cloud) of resources, reducing the need for a large investment in IT infrastructure.

Stop and review! You have completed the outline for this subunit. Study multiple-choice questions 1 through 7 beginning on page 360.

13.2 EQUIPMENT AND PROTOCOLS OF NETWORKS

    1.   **Network Equipment -- Client Devices**

        a.   Devices of all sizes and functions (mainframes, laptop computers, personal digital assistants, MP3 players, printers, scanners, point-of-sale terminals, ATMs, etc.) can be connected to networks.

        b.   Connecting a device to a network requires a **network interface card** (NIC). The NIC allows the device to speak that particular network's "language," that is, its protocol (protocols are discussed in depth beginning on page 352). The function of the NIC may be built into some devices, e.g., a cable modem.

    2.   **Network Equipment -- Connecting Media**

        a.   The medium that connects the devices on a network can take many forms.

        b.   **Bandwidth** is the signal-carrying capacity of a transmission medium, such as a fiber-optic cable or copper wire. It is a rough indication of the highest speed that data can attain when traveling through it.

            1)   A medium that can carry only one signal is called **baseband**. A medium that can carry multiple signals is called **broadband**.

        c.   Wired LANs depend on two basic types of networking devices to connect the cabling between devices.

            1)   **Hubs** are, in computing terms, very simple (dumb) and serve only to broadcast messages to every other device on the network.

               a)   The device for which the message is intended will keep it and process it. The other devices will discard it.

            2)   **Bridges** improve traffic flow by dividing LANs into segments. Bridges are more intelligent than hubs.

               a)   Instead of simply broadcasting messages as hubs do, bridges read the destination address and isolate the message to the segment where the destination device is located, greatly reducing unnecessary traffic on the network.

            3)   **Gateways** are devices that manage the flow of data between networks. Contrast this with hubs and bridges that connect parts of a single network.

        d.   WANs, with their greater traffic requirements, need higher-capacity media.

            1)   **Fiber-optic cable** consists of extremely fine threads of glass or plastic.

               a)   The fiber is encased in a special cladding that turns the interior wall into a continuous mirror. The electrical signal is converted to pulses of light, which then bounce from wall to wall as they move down the fiber.

                   i)   These light pulses move at much higher speeds than electrical signals can travel through copper wire.

b)   Fiber optics has three major advantages over wire in addition to drastically greater bandwidth.

  i)   The light pulses used in fiber optics are not subject to electromagnetic interference.

  ii)   Interception by unauthorized parties is impossible because the light pulses cannot be "tapped" as electrical signals can.

  iii)   If an optical fiber breaks, the mirrored end immediately sends the transmitted signal back to the source, alerting the administrator of the distance to the break.

2)   **Microwave transmission** involves propagating electrical signals through air and space instead of through metal wire or optical fiber.

  a)   Satellite relay involves transmitting the microwave signal to a satellite in orbit, which retransmits the signal to the destination back on Earth. This medium offers very high speeds and wide geographic coverage.

e.   Electronic communication networks require protocol. A protocol is a set of standards for message transmission among the devices on the network.

3.   **Transmission Protocols -- LANs**

a.   **Ethernet** has been the most successful protocol for LAN transmission. The Ethernet (capitalized because it is a trademark) design breaks up the flow of data between devices into discrete groups of data bits called "frames."

ANALOGY

Ethernet follows the "polite conversation" method of communicating. Each device "listens" to the network to determine whether another conversation is taking place, that is, whether the network is busy moving another device's message. Once the network is determined to be free of traffic, the device sends its message.

---

1)   Inevitably, frames collide on Ethernet networks constantly. When this happens, the two contending devices wait a random (and extremely brief) length of time, then transmit again. Eventually, both messages will hit the network at a moment when it is free.

2)   This design, while seemingly inefficient in accepting such a high number of collisions and retransmissions, has been extraordinarily successful. Over the years, Ethernet has proven to be secure, adaptable, and expandable.

4.   **Transmission Protocols -- Switched Networks**

a.   In a LAN, all the devices and all the transmission media belong to one organization.

  1)   This single ownership of infrastructure assets plus the ability to unify all communication on a single protocol make for great efficiency and security.

b.   When communication must cross organizational boundaries or travel beyond a limited geographical range, this single ownership principle no longer applies. A WAN is the applicable model.

  1)   A WAN, with its hundreds of users and much greater distances, could never function using the collision-detection-and-retransmission method of Ethernet. To overcome this, the technique called switching is used.

c.   In **packet switching**, the data bits making up a message are broken up into packets of predefined length. Each packet has a header containing the electronic address of the device for which the message is intended.

  1)   A switch is a hardware device that reads the address on each packet and sends it along the appropriate path to its destination.

ANALOGY

The machinery for a new plant is mounted on several 18-wheelers for transport to the plant site. The trucks leave the machinery vendor's factory headed to the destination. As each truck arrives at a traffic light, it stops while vehicles going in other directions pass through the intersection. As the trucks arrive at the plant site, they are unloaded and the machinery is installed.

---

5. **Transmission Protocols -- Routed Networks**

    a. **Routers** have more intelligence than hubs, bridges, or switches.

        1) Routers have tables stored in memory that tell them the most efficient path along which each packet should be sent.

ANALOGY

The trucks leave the machinery vendor's factory with the same destination. As the trucks stop at each intersection, traffic cops redirect them down different routes depending on traffic conditions. As the trucks arrive in unknown sequence at the plant site, they are held until the machinery can be unloaded in the correct order.

---

    b. Routing is what makes the Internet possible.

        1) **Transmission Control Protocol/Internet Protocol (TCP/IP)** is the suite of routing protocols that makes it possible to interconnect many thousands of devices from dozens of manufacturers all over the world through the Internet.

        2) **IP addressing** (also called dotted decimal addressing) is the heart of Internet routing. It allows any device anywhere in the world to be recognized on the Internet through the use of a standard-format IP address.

            a) Each of the four decimal-separated elements of the IP address is a numeral between 0 and 255.

            b) EXAMPLE: 128.67.111.25

        3) **Dynamic host configuration protocol** (DHCP) allows tremendous flexibility on the Internet by enabling the constant reuse of IP addresses.

            a) Routers generally have their IP addresses hardcoded when they are first installed. However, the individual client devices on most organizational networks are assigned an IP address by DHCP from a pool of available addresses every time they connect to the network.

6. **Transmission Protocols -- Wireless Networks**

    a. The **Wi-Fi** family of protocols supports client devices within a radius of about 300 feet around a wireless router. This usable area is called a **hotspot**.

        1) Wi-Fi avoids the collisions inherent in Ethernet by constantly searching for the best frequency within its assigned range to use.

        2) Security was a problem in early incarnations of Wi-Fi. Later versions alleviated some of these concerns with encryption.

    b. The **Bluetooth** standard operates over a much smaller radius than Wi-Fi, about 30 feet. This distance permits the creation of what has come to be called the personal area network or PAN (i.e., a network of devices for a single user).

        1) A prominent example is the in-ear device that allows the wearer to make telephone calls hands-free or to listen to a personal music player in wireless mode. Wireless keyboards and mice also employ the Bluetooth standard.

        2) Bluetooth is considerably slower than Wi-Fi.

Stop and review! You have completed the outline for this subunit. Study multiple-choice questions 8 through 12 beginning on page 362.

13.3 ELECTRONIC COMMERCE

1. **Overview**

   a. **E-business** is an umbrella term referring to all methods of conducting business electronically.

      1) This can include strictly internal communications as well as nonfinancial dealings with outside parties (e.g., contract negotiations).

   b. **E-commerce** is a narrower term referring to the conduct of financial transactions with outside parties electronically (e.g., the purchase and sale of goods and services).

      1) E-commerce introduces a new set of efficiencies into business relationships. Where orders previously were placed using a combination of phone calls and either mailed or faxed hardcopy documents, e-commerce allows such transactions to take place entirely over the Internet.

      2) E-commerce comes in two basic varieties: business-to-business (B2B) and business-to-consumer (B2C).

         a) Consumer-to-consumer (C2C) e-commerce, such as Internet auction sites, makes up a smaller proportion of overall e-commerce.

      3) E-business and e-commerce are sometimes considered to be synonymous.

   c. An extranet, defined in item 4.c.4) in Subunit 13.1, is one means of carrying on e-commerce.

      1) Extranets rely on the established communications protocols of the Internet. Thus, the expensive, specialized equipment needed for EDI is unnecessary (EDI is discussed in detail in Subunit 13.4).

      2) Firewalls, which can be hardware- or software-based, provide security (firewalls are described in Study Unit 14).

      3) The extranet approach is based on less formal agreements between the trading partners than in EDI and requires the sending firm to format the documents into the format of the receiving firm.

2. **Security and Reliability of E-Commerce**

   a. Because of the reduced level of human involvement in e-commerce, new security and reliability concerns arise.

   b. Specific concerns include the following (each issue is of greater or lesser relative importance depending on whether the application is B2B, B2C, or C2C):

      1) The transacting parties must be correctly identified, a process known as authentication. IDs and passwords are the most common tools for authentication.

      2) The circumstances in which a binding agreement can be made must be agreed to; in other words, who (or what system) is authorized to place (or promise to fill) an order? This is especially important in B2B applications, when entire production runs and large amounts of money are at stake.

      3) The confidentiality and integrity of information transmitted electronically must be maintained. Encryption (described in detail later in this study unit) is the most useful tool for this purpose.

      4) A reliable record of the transaction must be preserved such that disputes can be resolved and audits can be performed.

      5) Potential customers must be able to trust listed prices and discounts.

      6) Payment data must be verifiable.

      7) Both parties' systems must be robust; i.e., they are up and running at all times.

3. **Business-to-Business (B2B) E-Commerce**

    a. B2B can be used to speed up the order and fulfillment process.

        1) A manufacturer in need of raw materials can initiate the transaction with an email or by using the vendor's extranet.

        2) The process can be further automated by establishing an EDI arrangement, in which the buyer's purchasing system automatically places an order with the vendor when inventories reach a predetermined level.

           a) The partners must have (1) a common electronic document format and (2) a pre-existing agreement under which such orders will be accepted and filled without human intervention.

    b. **Benefits of B2B** include

        1) Reduced purchasing costs.

           a) Purchasing products online saves time, and electronically processing an order simplifies the ordering process.

        2) Increased market efficiency.

           a) By using the Internet, companies have easy access to price quotes from various suppliers. Buyers are more likely to get a better price, given the increased number of suppliers.

        3) Greater market intelligence.

           a) B2B provides producers with better insights into the demand levels in any given market.

        4) Decreased inventory levels.

           a) Companies can make better use of their inventory and raw materials. The Internet allows companies using just-in-time (JIT) manufacturing techniques to achieve better control of their operations, for example, by more precise coordination of delivery of raw materials. It also allows companies to use less working capital to do the same amount of work, which allows those funds to be invested elsewhere.

    c. The overriding principle of online B2B is that it can make companies more efficient.

        1) Increased efficiency means lower costs, which is a goal that interests every company. Thus, the potential of B2B online commerce is enormous.

4. **Business-to-Consumer (B2C) E-Commerce**

    a. B2C is one of the fastest growing segments of the economy. Consumers can order a vast array of merchandise from the comfort of their homes or from mobile devices.

        1) B2C is almost exclusively conducted via the Internet.

        2) Traditional retailers have expanded their reach with B2C, and some firms, notably Amazon.com, use the Internet as their sole communication channel with customers.

    b. Many of the same benefits accrue to businesses as in the B2B model with reduced costs and increased efficiency.

        1) Many of the same security issues, such as authorization, also apply, but on a smaller scale. Also, the vendor need not concern itself with the IT infrastructure on the customer's end.

5. **Electronic Funds Transfer (EFT)**

a. EFT is an e-commerce application provided by financial institutions worldwide that enables the transfer of funds via an access device, i.e., an electronic terminal (e.g., ATM or POS terminal), telephone, computer, or magnetic stripe (e.g., credit, debit, and check cards).

1) A typical consumer application of EFT is the direct deposit of payroll checks in employees' accounts or the automatic withdrawal of payments for cable and telephone bills, mortgages, etc.

2) EFT transaction costs are lower than for manual systems because documents and human intervention are eliminated from the transaction process. Moreover, transfer customarily requires less than a day.

3) Another significant advantage is that the opportunities for clerical errors are greatly reduced.

b. The most important application of EFT is check collection. To reduce the enormous volume of paper involved, the check-collection process has been computerized.

1) The result has been to reduce the significance of paper checks because EFT provides means to make payments and deposit funds without physical transfer of negotiable instruments. Thus, wholesale EFTs among financial institutions and businesses (commercial transfers) are measured in the trillions of dollars.

2) The two major systems for these "wire" or nonconsumer transfers are Fedwire (Federal Reserve wire transfer network) and CHIPS (Clearing House Interbank Payment System). Private systems also are operated by large banks.

6. **EFT vs. Electronic Money**

a. EFT differs from the use of electronic money, which may someday supplant traditional currency and coins.

b. **Smart cards** contain computer chips rather than magnetized stripes. A smart card therefore can store data and security programs. It not only stores value but also authenticates transactions, such as by means of its digital signature.

c. A disadvantage of electronic money is that most types are not covered by the insurance offered by the Federal Deposit Insurance Corporation (FDIC). Federal Reserve rules concerning EFT also do not extend to electronic money.

d. Methods other than providing a credit card number or using electronic money may be used to make electronic payments.

1) One such method is an online payment system, such as PayPal. A buyer makes a payment by a customary method to the online payment system, which then notifies the seller that payment has been made. The final step is to transfer the money to the seller's account.

Stop and review! You have completed the outline for this subunit. Study multiple-choice questions 13 through 18 beginning on page 363.

13.4 ELECTRONIC DATA INTERCHANGE (EDI)

1. **Overview**

a. Electronic data interchange (EDI) is the leading method of carrying on B2B e-commerce.

1) EDI involves the communication of data in a format agreed to by the parties directly from a computer in one entity to a computer in another entity, for example, to order goods from a supplier or to transfer funds.

b. EDI was the first step in the evolution of e-business.

1) Successful EDI implementation begins with mapping the work processes and flows that support achievement of the organization's objectives.

2) EDI was developed to enhance JIT inventory management.

    c.   Advantages of EDI include the following:

        1)   Reduction of clerical errors

        2)   Increased speed of transactions

        3)   Elimination of repetitive clerical tasks, such as document preparation, processing, and mailing

        4)   Use of digital rather than physical record storage

    d.   Disadvantages of EDI include the following:

        1)   Information may be insecure.

           a)   Thus, end-to-end data encryption should be used to protect data during EDI.

        2)   Data may be lost.

        3)   Transmissions to trading partners may fail.

        4)   EDI is more complex and more costly than simpler B2B arrangements.

           a)   In simpler B2B, each transaction is initiated over the Internet, with XML as the mediating language.

           b)   EDI requires programming expertise and leased telephone lines or the use of a value-added or third-party network, whereas XML is simple and easy to understand.

2. **Costs of EDI**

    a.   Specialized Software

        1)   The software needed to convert data into the agreed-upon EDI format must be either purchased or developed in-house.

    b.   Dedicated Hardware

        1)   High-availability servers and high-speed communications devices must be installed. Another solution is to contract with a third party known as a VAN (see item 4.b. on the following page) to provide this service, but this alternative has its own set of costs.

    c.   Legal Costs

        1)   Contracts with current trading partners must be renegotiated when entering into an EDI arrangement.

    d.   Process Reengineering

        1)   Since existing procedures are being replaced, EDI arrangements may require significant changes to current internal processes. This also involves the cost of employee retraining.

    e.   Enhanced Security and Monitoring

        1)   EDI transactions are subject to the same risks as all electronic communications that cross organizational boundaries.

3. **Terms and Components of EDI**

    a.   Standards concern procedures to convert written documents into a standard electronic document-messaging format to facilitate EDI.

        1)   The current standards are ANSI X.12 in the U.S. or UN/EDIFACT in Europe and most of the rest of the world.

    b.   Conventions are the procedures for arranging data elements in specified formats for various accounting transactions, e.g., invoices, materials releases, and advance shipment notices.

    c.   A data dictionary prescribes the meaning of data elements, including specification of each transaction structure.

    d.   Transmission protocols are rules used to determine how each electronic envelope is structured and processed by the communications devices.

        1)   Normally, a group of accounting transactions is combined in an electronic envelope and transmitted into a communications network.

        2)   Rules are required for the separation and transmission of envelopes.

    e.   A crucial element of any EDI arrangement is the exchange of network and sender/recipient acknowledgment messages.

        1)   Acknowledgments serve as a nonrepudiation tool; i.e., one party cannot claim that a particular message was not received by a certain time or date.

4.   **Methods of Communication between EDI Computers**

    a.   A point-to-point system requires the use of dedicated computers by all parties.

        1)   Each computer must be designed to be compatible with the other(s). This system is very similar to a network within one company. Dedicated lines or modems are used.

    b.   Value-added networks (VANs) are private, third-party providers of common interfaces between organizations.

        1)   Subscribing to a VAN eliminates the need for one organization to establish direct computer communication with a trading partner. VANs also eliminate the need for dedicated computers waiting for incoming messages.

        2)   Although companies must acquire their own software to translate their data to one of the EDI standard protocols, once the data are in the standard format, the VAN handles all aspects of the communication.

5.   **EDI Implications for Control**

    a.   EDI eliminates the paper documents, both internal and external, that are the traditional basis for many controls, including internal and external auditing.

    b.   Moreover, an organization that has reengineered its processes to take full advantage of EDI may have eliminated even the electronic equivalents of paper documents.

        1)   For example, the buyer's point-of-sale (POS) system may directly transmit information to the seller, which delivers on a JIT basis. Purchase orders, invoices, and receiving reports are eliminated and replaced with

            a)   A long-term contract establishing quantities, prices, and delivery schedules;

            b)   Evaluated receipts settlements (authorizations for automatic periodic payment);

            c)   Production schedules;

            d)   Advance ship notices; and

            e)   Payments by EFT.

The AICPA has frequently tested the topic of EDI on recent exams. Questions have addressed such areas as the advantages of EDI and internal control and security for EDI transactions.

Stop and review! You have completed the outline for this subunit. Study multiple-choice questions 19 through 24 beginning on page 364.

13.5 ELECTRONIC TRANSMISSION SECURITY

1. **Encryption Technology**

    a. Encryption technology is vital for the security and therefore the success of electronic commerce, especially with regard to transactions carried out over public networks.

        1) The sender's encryption program encodes the data prior to transmission. The recipient's program decodes it at the other end. Unauthorized users may be able to intercept the data, but without the encryption key, they will be unable to decode it.

    b. Encryption performed by physically secure hardware is inherently more secure than encryption performed by software.

    c. The use of encryption increases system overhead. A certain amount of system resources must be used to execute the machine instructions necessary to encrypt and decrypt data.

2. **Public-Key vs. Symmetric Encryption**

    a. With public-key (asymmetric) encryption, the communicating parties create mathematically related pairs of keys. One of the keys in the pair is made public, and the other is kept secret.

        1) The sending party uses the public key to encrypt the message. Since only the intended recipient has access to the private key that relates to that public key, only that party will be able to decrypt the message.

    b. With symmetric encryption, the communicating parties agree on a single (private) key for use in that session.

        1) Its strength comes from its length. The longer the key (measured in bits), the more resistant it is to decrypting by unauthorized parties.

        2) However, the parties must have a secure way of sharing the key.

3. **Digital Certificates**

    a. Digital certificates are data files created by trusted third parties called certificate authorities (e.g., VeriSign, Thawte, GoDaddy).

        1) An entity who wishes to engage in e-commerce first establishes a relationship with a certificate authority, who verifies that party's identity.

        2) The certificate authority then creates a coded electronic certificate that contains (a) the holder's name, (b) its public key, (c) a serial number, and (d) an expiration date. The certificate authority makes its own public key widely available.

        3) A party wishing to do business over the Internet with the certificate holder seeks the holder's certificate on the authority's server and uses the authority's public key to decrypt it.

        4) The sender obtains the recipient's public key from the certificate, encodes the message, and sends it. The recipient uses its private key to decrypt the message.

    b. This system, called the public-key infrastructure, relieves the parties from the need to establish their own pairs of keys when they want to communicate securely.

        1) The public-key infrastructure allows buyers to securely exchange credit card numbers with Internet vendors.

4. **Digital Signatures**

    a.   A digital signature is a means of authenticating an electronic document such as a purchase order, acceptance of a contract, or financial information.

        1)   The sender uses its private key to encode all or part of the message, and the recipient uses the sender's public key to decode it. Hence, if that key decodes the message, the sender must have written it.

Stop and review! You have completed the outline for this subunit. Study multiple-choice questions 25 through 29 beginning on page 366.

QUESTIONS

13.1 Networks and the Internet

1. The most distinguishing feature of the use of a client-server processing model over an old mainframe configuration is

    A. Digital processing over analog.

    B. Less need for data backup.

    C. Decentralization over centralization.

    D. Ability to connect remote locations.

Answer (C) is correct.
    REQUIRED: The distinguishing feature of a client-server system over a mainframe system.
    DISCUSSION: Mainframes were arranged so that all processing and data storage were done in a single, central location. Improvements in technology have led to increasing decentralization of information processing. The most cost-effective and easy-to-administer arrangement for local area networks (LANs) uses the client-server model.
    Answer (A) is incorrect. Both client-server configurations and mainframes use digital processing. Answer (B) is incorrect. Both client-server configurations and mainframes must employ data backup. Answer (D) is incorrect. Mainframes were able to connect to users in remote locations.

2. Which one of the following network configurations is distinguished by the possibility of spreading the cost of ownership among multiple organizations?

    A. Value-added network.

    B. Baseband network.

    C. Wide area network.

    D. Local area network.

Answer (C) is correct.
    REQUIRED: The network configuration that spreads its cost among multiple organizations.
    DISCUSSION: Wide area networks consist of a conglomerate of local area networks (LANs) over widely separated locations. The key aspect here is that a WAN can be either publicly or privately owned.
    Answer (A) is incorrect. A value-added network is a private network. Answer (B) is incorrect. Baseband refers to the signal-carrying capacity of a network, not the ownership of its hardware devices. Answer (D) is incorrect. All the equipment in a local area network (LAN) is owned by one organization.

3. Which of the following control risks is more likely with personal computers than in a mainframe environment with dedicated terminals?

    A. Copyright violations due to the use of unauthorized copies of purchased software.

    B. Applications written by one department that cannot share data with existing organization-wide systems.

    C. Lack of data availability due to inadequate data retention policies.

    D. All of the answers are correct.

Answer (D) is correct.
    REQUIRED: The environmental control risk(s) likely in a personal computer environment.
    DISCUSSION: When personal computers are used, likely control risks include copyright violations that occur when unauthorized copies of software are made or software is installed on multiple computers; locally written applications that do not adhere to the organization's standards; and inadequate backup, recovery, and contingency planning.
    Answer (A) is incorrect. Copyright violations are a common risk with personal computers. Answer (B) is incorrect. Locally written applications that do not adhere to the organization's standards are a common risk with personal computers. Answer (C) is incorrect. Failure to follow proper backup procedures is a common risk with personal computers.

4. Which of the following networks provides the **least** secure means of data transmission?

   A. Value-added.

   B. Public-switched.

   C. Local area.

   D. Private.

Answer (B) is correct.
   REQUIRED: The network that provides the least secure means of data transmission.
   DISCUSSION: Public-switched networks are wide area networks that use public telephone lines. This arrangement may be the most economical, but data transmission may be of lower quality, no connection may be available, and security measures may be ineffective.
   Answer (A) is incorrect. Value-added carriers provide data security and error detection and correction procedures. Answer (C) is incorrect. Local area networks inherently limit data transmission exposures. Answer (D) is incorrect. Private networks provide security through limited access and dedicated facilities.

5. Kelly Corporation needs an internal communication network that provides high speed communication among nodes. Which of the following is appropriate for Kelly?

   A. Wide area network (WAN).

   B. Local area network (LAN).

   C. File server.

   D. Value-added network (VAN).

Answer (B) is correct.
   REQUIRED: The network that provides the fastest communication.
   DISCUSSION: Local area networks are privately owned networks that provide high-speed communication among nodes. They are usually restricted to limited areas, such as a particular floor of an office building.
   Answer (A) is incorrect. Wide area networks provide lower-speed communication, owing to them being spread out among larger areas than LANs. Answer (C) is incorrect. A file server is hardware that acts as an access control mechanism in a local area network. Answer (D) is incorrect. A VAN is a privately owned telecommunications carrier that provides capacity to outside users. It does not provide high-speed communication among nodes.

6. Appropriate uses of an organization's internal communications network, or intranet, include all of the following **except**

   A. Making the human resources policy manual available to employees.

   B. Informing potential investors about company operations and financial results.

   C. Providing senior management with access to the executive support system.

   D. Enabling a project team that crosses departments to collaborate.

Answer (B) is correct.
   REQUIRED: The item not one of the basic purposes of an organization's internal communications network.
   DISCUSSION: An intranet permits sharing of information throughout an organization by applying Internet connectivity standards and Web software (e.g., browsers) to the organization's internal network. An intranet addresses the connectivity problems faced by organizations that have many types of computers. Its use is restricted to those within the organization.
   Answer (A) is incorrect. Making the human resources policy manual available to employees is an appropriate use of an organization's internal communications network. Answer (C) is incorrect. Providing senior management with access to the executive support system is an appropriate use of an organization's internal communications network. Answer (D) is incorrect. Enabling a project team that crosses departments to collaborate is an appropriate use of an organization's internal communications network.

7. Large organizations often have their own telecommunications networks for transmitting and receiving voice, data, and images. Small organizations, however, also can have remote locations that need to communicate. Such organizations are more likely to use

   A. Public switched lines.

   B. Fast packet switches.

   C. Internet.

   D. A WAN.

Answer (C) is correct.
   REQUIRED: The telecommunications networks likely to be used by small organizations.
   DISCUSSION: Widespread use of the Internet has led to its becoming an efficient, low-cost transmission network.
   Answer (A) is incorrect. Public switched lines have been eclipsed in efficiency by the Internet. Answer (B) is incorrect. Fast packet switching networks are typically installed by telecommunication utility companies and other large companies that have their own networks. Answer (D) is incorrect. Small organizations lack the capital necessary for investment in a wide area network (WAN).

13.2 Equipment and Protocols of Networks

8. Which of the following statements is true regarding Transmission Control Protocol and Internet Protocol (TCP/IP)?

A. Every TCP/IP-supported transmission is an exchange of funds.

B. TCP/IP networks are limited to large mainframe computers.

C. Every site connected to a TCP/IP network has a unique address.

D. The actual physical connections among the various networks are limited to TCP/IP ports.

Answer (C) is correct.
REQUIRED: The true statement regarding TCP/IP.
DISCUSSION: TCP/IP is a suite of communications protocols used to connect computers to the Internet. It is also built into network operating systems. It is the foundation of the Internet protocol as well as numerous other commercial protocols. Every site connected to a TCP/IP network has a unique address.
Answer (A) is incorrect. TCP/IP supports numerous transmissions, not just those involving the exchange of funds. Answer (B) is incorrect. TCP/IP networks can be accessed from both personal computers and large mainframe computers. Answer (D) is incorrect. The physical connections are accessed by the data link connections, which in turn are accessible by numerous network and transport protocols.

9. The Internet consists of a series of networks that include

A. Gateways to allow networks to connect to each other.

B. Bridges to direct messages through the optimum data path.

C. Repeaters to physically connect separate local area networks (LANs).

D. Routers to strengthen data signals between distant computers.

Answer (A) is correct.
REQUIRED: The composition of the Internet.
DISCUSSION: The Internet facilitates information transfer among computers. Gateways are hardware or software products that allow translation between two different protocol families. For example, a gateway can be used to exchange messages between different email systems.
Answer (B) is incorrect. Bridges are used to connect segments of a LAN. Answer (C) is incorrect. Repeaters are used to strengthen data signals. Answer (D) is incorrect. Routers are used to determine the best path for data across the Internet.

10. Which one of the following transmission media is impervious to electromagnetic interference?

A. Category 1 cabling.

B. Category 5 cabling.

C. Fiber optics.

D. Line-of-sight microwave transmission.

Answer (C) is correct.
REQUIRED: The transmission medium not subject to electromagnetic interference.
DISCUSSION: In fiber optic cabling, the electrical signal is converted to pulses of light, which are not subject to electromagnetic interference.
Answer (A) is incorrect. Category 1 cabling uses copper wire to transmit electrical signals and is thus subject to electromagnetic interference. Answer (B) is incorrect. Category 5 cabling uses copper wire to transmit electrical signals and is thus subject to electromagnetic interference. Answer (D) is incorrect. Microwave transmission, being a form of electromagnetic radiation, is subject to electromagnetic interference.

11. The term referring to the volume of electronic traffic that a transmission medium can carry is

A. Protocol.

B. Interface.

C. Routing rate.

D. Bandwidth.

Answer (D) is correct.
REQUIRED: The term referring to the volume of electronic traffic that a transmission medium can carry.
DISCUSSION: Bandwidth is the signal-carrying capacity of a transmission medium. It is a rough indication of the highest speed that data can attain when traveling through it.
Answer (A) is incorrect. A protocol is a set of standards for message transmission among the devices on a network.
Answer (B) is incorrect. An interface is the electronic connection between two devices or a device and a transmission medium.
Answer (C) is incorrect. Routing rate is not a meaningful term in this context.

12. The network signaling technology that makes the Internet possible is

A. Switching.

B. Routing.

C. Bridging.

D. Ethernet.

Answer (B) is correct.
  REQUIRED: The network signaling technology that makes the Internet possible.
  DISCUSSION: Routers are highly intelligent networking devices that have tables stored in memory that tell them the most efficient path along which each transmitted data packet should be sent. Routing is what makes the Internet possible.
  Answer (A) is incorrect. Switching does not have the addressing sophistication to support the kind of global traffic required by the Internet. Answer (C) is incorrect. Bridges are networking devices that improve traffic flow on local area networks (LANs) by dividing the network into segments. Answer (D) is incorrect. Ethernet is a LAN transmission protocol.

13.3 Electronic Commerce

13. A customer places an order for a sweater over the Internet using a mobile phone. This is an example of

A. Authentication.

B. Business intelligence.

C. Electronic funds transfer.

D. E-commerce.

Answer (D) is correct.
  REQUIRED: The term for the transaction described.
  DISCUSSION: E-commerce refers to the conduct of financial transactions with outside parties electronically, e.g., the purchase and sale of goods and services.
  Answer (A) is incorrect. Authentication is a necessary step to completing this transaction but does not describe the transaction itself. Answer (B) is incorrect. Business intelligence is a system that provides executive management immediate information about an organization's critical success factors. Answer (C) is incorrect. Electronic funds transfer is the electronic movement of monies from one financial institution to another.

14. An employee uses her company-issued ID and password to log into her employer's human resources system from home and change her choices of benefits. This is an example of

A. E-business.

B. Data warehouse.

C. Transmission protocol.

D. Extensible markup language.

Answer (A) is correct.
  REQUIRED: The term for the transaction described.
  DISCUSSION: E-business is an umbrella term referring to all methods of conducting business electronically. This can include strictly internal communications as well as nonfinancial dealings with outside parties (e.g., contract negotiations).
  Answer (B) is incorrect. A data warehouse is a central database for transaction-level data from more than one of the organization's transaction processing systems. Answer (C) is incorrect. A transmission protocol is a necessary component of this transaction but does not describe the transaction itself. Answer (D) is incorrect. Extensible markup language (XML) is a way of coding information in such a way that a user can determine not only how it should be presented but also what it is; i.e., all computerized data may be tagged with identifiers.

15. Which of the following is normally a benefit of using electronic funds transfer (EFT)?

A. Improvement of the audit trail for cash receipts and disbursements.

B. Creation of self-monitoring access controls.

C. Reduction of the frequency of data entry errors.

D. Off-site storage of source documents for cash transactions.

Answer (C) is correct.
  REQUIRED: The benefit of using EFT for cash transactions.
  DISCUSSION: The processing and transmission of electronic transactions, such as EFTs, virtually eliminates human interaction. This process not only helps eliminate errors but also allows for the rapid detection and recovery from errors when they do occur.
  Answer (A) is incorrect. The audit trail is typically less apparent in an electronic environment than in a manual environment. Answer (B) is incorrect. A key control is management's establishment and monitoring of access controls. Answer (D) is incorrect. Source documents are often eliminated in EFT transactions.

16. Which of the following risks is **not** greater in an electronic funds transfer (EFT) environment than in a manual system using paper transactions?

   A. Unauthorized access and activity.

   B. Duplicate transaction processing.

   C. High cost per transaction.

   D. Inadequate backup and recovery capabilities.

Answer (C) is correct.
   REQUIRED: The risk not greater in an EFT environment than in a manual system using paper transactions.
   DISCUSSION: EFT is a service provided by financial institutions worldwide that is based on EDI technology. EFT transaction costs are lower than for manual systems because documents and human intervention are eliminated from the transaction process.
   Answer (A) is incorrect. Unauthorized access and activity is a risk specific to EFT. Answer (B) is incorrect. Inaccurate transaction processing (including duplication) is a risk specific to EFT. Answer (D) is incorrect. Inadequate backup and recovery capabilities is a risk specific to EFT.

17. Which one of the following is **not** a reason for a company to use EFT with an EDI system?

   A. To take advantage of the time lag associated with negotiable instruments.

   B. To allow the company to negotiate discounts with EDI vendors based upon prompt payment.

   C. To improve its cash management program.

   D. To reduce input time and input errors.

Answer (A) is correct.
   REQUIRED: The item not a reason for using EFT.
   DISCUSSION: The time lag between transmittal of a check (a negotiable instrument) and its clearance through regular banking channels is called float. Float is eliminated by EFT.
   Answer (B) is incorrect. Payment schedules may be based on the time required to process invoices, prepare checks, and transmit checks. Using EFT, payment is instantaneous, and payment schedules can be based on other criteria, e.g., discounts for prompt payment. Answer (C) is incorrect. EFT allows for more effective control of payments and transfers among accounts. Answer (D) is incorrect. Integration of EDI and EFT eliminates manual input of transaction data, a process that introduces errors into the accounting system.

18. Which of the following significantly encouraged the development of electronic funds transfer (EFT) systems?

I.   Response to competition
II. Cost containment
III. Advances in information technology

   A. I and II.

   B. I and III.

   C. II only.

   D. I, II, and III.

Answer (D) is correct.
   REQUIRED: The items that most significantly encouraged the development of EFTs.
   DISCUSSION: Competition has been a strong motivator in the financial services industry in the development of EFT systems, which are an application of EDI. Furthermore, containing costs in a highly competitive industry can be aided by leveraging information technology. Finally, advances in information technology, especially the wide acceptance of telecommunications standards and protocols, have made EFT systems possible.
   Answer (A) is incorrect. Advances in information technology also significantly encouraged the development of EFT. Answer (B) is incorrect. Cost containment also significantly encouraged the development of EFT. Answer (C) is incorrect. Competitive forces and advances in information technology also significantly encouraged the development of EFT.

13.4 Electronic Data Interchange (EDI)

19. Which of the following are essential elements of the audit trail in an electronic data interchange (EDI) system?

   A. Network and sender/recipient acknowledgments.

   B. Message directories and header segments.

   C. Contingency and disaster recovery plans.

   D. Trading partner security and mailbox codes.

Answer (A) is correct.
   REQUIRED: The essential element in an EDI audit trail.
   DISCUSSION: An audit trail allows for the tracing of a transaction from initiation to conclusion. Network and sender/recipient acknowledgments relate to the transaction flow and provide for the tracking of transactions.
   Answer (B) is incorrect. Message directories and header segments provide information controlling the message, such as originating and destination stations, message type and priority level, which are part of the message and not the audit trail. Answer (C) is incorrect. Although contingency and disaster recovery plans are important controls, they do not relate to the audit trail. Answer (D) is incorrect. Although maintaining control over security and mailbox codes is an important control, it does not relate to the audit trail.

20. Which of the following statements is true concerning internal control in an electronic data interchange (EDI) system?

A. Preventive controls generally are more important than detective controls in EDI systems.

B. Control objectives for EDI systems generally are different from the objectives for other information systems.

C. Internal controls in EDI systems rarely permit control risk to be assessed at below the maximum.

D. Internal controls related to the segregation of duties generally are the most important controls in EDI systems.

Answer (A) is correct.

REQUIRED: The true statement about EDI controls.

DISCUSSION: In general, preventive controls are more important than detective controls because the benefits typically outweigh the costs. In electronic processing, once a transaction is accepted, there is often little opportunity to apply detective controls. Thus, it is important to prevent errors or frauds before they happen.

Answer (B) is incorrect. The basic control objectives are the same regardless of the nature of the processing: to ensure the integrity of the information and to safeguard the assets. Answer (C) is incorrect. To gather sufficient evidence in a sophisticated computer system, it is often necessary to rely on the controls. Control risk may be assessed at below the maximum if relevant controls are identified and tested and if the resulting evidential matter provides the degree of assurance necessary to support the assessed level of control risk. Answer (D) is incorrect. The level of segregation of duties achieved in a manual system is usually not feasible in a computer system.

21. After a company implements electronic data interchange (EDI) to communicate with its customers, an appropriate control for ensuring authenticity of the electronic orders it receives is to

A. Encrypt sensitive messages such as electronic payments for raw materials received.

B. Perform reasonableness checks on quantities ordered before filling orders.

C. Verify the identity of senders and determine whether orders correspond to contract terms.

D. Acknowledge receipt of electronic payments with a confirming message.

Answer (C) is correct.

REQUIRED: The control for ensuring the authenticity of the electronic orders the company receives.

DISCUSSION: An EDI system is subject not only to the usual risk exposures for computer systems but also to those arising from the potential ineffectiveness of control on the part of the trading partner and the third-party service provider. Accordingly, authentication of users and messages received is a major security concern.

Answer (A) is incorrect. Encrypting sensitive messages sent is an appropriate step but does not necessarily authenticate the transaction. Answer (B) is incorrect. Performing reasonableness checks on quantities ordered before placing orders is a control for ensuring the correctness of the company's own orders, not the authenticity of its customers' orders. Answer (D) is incorrect. Acknowledging receipt of electronic payments with a confirming message is good practice but will not authenticate orders from customers.

22. Which of the following is usually a benefit of transmitting transactions in an electronic data interchange (EDI) environment?

A. A compressed business cycle with lower year-end receivables balances.

B. A reduced need to test computer controls related to sales and collections transactions.

C. An increased opportunity to apply statistical sampling techniques to account balances.

D. No need to rely on third-party service providers to ensure security.

Answer (A) is correct.

REQUIRED: The benefit of EDI.

DISCUSSION: EDI transactions are typically transmitted and processed in real time. Thus, EDI compresses the business cycle by eliminating delays. The time required to receive and process an order, ship goods, and receive payment is greatly reduced compared with that of a typical manual system. Accordingly, more rapid receipt of payment minimizes receivables and improves cash flow.

Answer (B) is incorrect. Use of a sophisticated processing system would increase the need to test computer controls. Answer (C) is incorrect. Computer technology allows all transactions to be tested rather than just a sample. Answer (D) is incorrect. EDI often uses a VAN (value-added network) as a third-party service provider, and reliance on controls provided by the VAN may be critical.

23. Before sending or receiving electronic data interchange (EDI) messages, a company should

    A. Execute a trading partner agreement with each of its customers and suppliers.

    B. Reduce inventory levels in anticipation of receiving shipments.

    C. Demand that all its suppliers implement EDI capabilities.

    D. Evaluate the effectiveness of its use of EDI transmissions.

Answer (A) is correct.

    REQUIRED: The process to be performed before sending or receiving EDI messages.

    DISCUSSION: Before sending or receiving EDI messages, a company should execute a trading partner agreement with its customers and suppliers. All parties should understand their responsibilities, the messages each will initiate, how they will interpret messages, the means of authenticating and verifying the completeness and accuracy of messages, the moment when the contract between the parties is effective, the required level of security, etc.

    Answer (B) is incorrect. The company may intend to reduce inventory levels, but that intention is unrelated to the timing of its first EDI messages. Answer (C) is incorrect. The company may want to demand or encourage all its customers and suppliers to implement EDI capabilities, but that request is independent of sending and receiving messages. Answer (D) is incorrect. It is not possible to evaluate the effectiveness of EDI transmissions until after they occur.

24. Which of the following is an accepted example of electronic data interchange (EDI)?

    A. Request for an airline reservation by a travel agent.

    B. Withdrawal of cash from an automated teller by a bank's customer.

    C. Transfer of summary data from a local area network to a centralized mainframe.

    D. Placement of order entry transactions from a customer to its supplier.

Answer (D) is correct.

    REQUIRED: The accepted example of electronic data interchange.

    DISCUSSION: EDI is the communication of electronic documents directly from a computer in one entity to a computer in another entity. Placement of order entry transactions from a customer to its supplier is an accepted use of EDI between trading partners.

    Answer (A) is incorrect. A request for an airline reservation requires an online, real-time reservations system. Answer (B) is incorrect. Withdrawal of cash from an automated teller is accomplished via online transactions to copies of master files. Answer (C) is incorrect. The transfer of summary data to headquarters may be accomplished with point-to-point communications, known as distributed computing.

13.5 Electronic Transmission Security

25. A client communicates sensitive data across the Internet. Which of the following controls will be most effective to prevent the use of the information if it were intercepted by an unauthorized party?

    A. A firewall.

    B. An access log.

    C. Passwords.

    D. Encryption.

Answer (D) is correct.

    REQUIRED: The most effective control for preventing the use of intercepted information.

    DISCUSSION: Encryption technology converts data into a code. Encoding data before transmission over communications lines makes it more difficult for someone with access to the transmission to understand or modify its contents.

    Answer (A) is incorrect. A firewall prevents access from specific types of traffic to an internal network. After an unauthorized user has obtained information from the site, a firewall cannot prevent its use. Answer (B) is incorrect. An access log only records attempted usage of a system. Answer (C) is incorrect. Passwords prevent unauthorized users from accessing the system. If information has already been obtained, a password cannot prevent its use.

26. The use of message encryption software

    A. Guarantees the secrecy of data.

    B. Requires manual distribution of keys.

    C. Increases system overhead.

    D. Reduces the need for periodic password changes.

Answer (C) is correct.

    REQUIRED: The effect of message encryption software.

    DISCUSSION: The machine instructions necessary to encrypt and decrypt data constitute system overhead. As a result, processing speed may be slowed.

    Answer (A) is incorrect. No encryption approach absolutely guarantees the secrecy of data. Answer (B) is incorrect. Keys may also be distributed electronically via secure key transporters. Answer (D) is incorrect. Periodic password changes are needed. Passwords are the typical means of validating users' access to unencrypted data.

27. Which of the following IT developments poses the **least** risk to organizational security?

    A. Adoption of wireless technology.

    B. Use of public-key encryption.

    C. Outsourcing of the IT infrastructure.

    D. Enterprise-wide integration of functions.

Answer (B) is correct.
    REQUIRED: The least risky IT developments.
    DISCUSSION: Encryption is essential when electronic commerce is conducted over public networks, such as the Internet. Thus, the use of public-key encryption is a response to risk, not a source of risk.
    Answer (A) is incorrect. Adoption of wireless technology increases the risk that communications will be intercepted. Answer (C) is incorrect. Outsourcing of the IT infrastructure means that ineffective controls over the outside service provider's operations could compromise the security of the organization's information. Answer (D) is incorrect. Enterprise-wide integration of functions, for example, in an ERP system with an organization-wide database, increases the difficulty of assuring the integrity of information. In an organization with discrete, closed functional subsystems, compromising one subsystem does not affect the others. In an ERP system, however, a breach of security may affect the entire organization.

28. To ensure privacy in a public-key encryption system, knowledge of which of the following keys is(are) required to decode the received message?

  I.   Private
  II. Public

    A. I.

    B. II.

    C. Both I and II.

    D. Neither I nor II.

Answer (A) is correct.
    REQUIRED: The key(s) required to decode messages in a public-key system to ensure privacy.
    DISCUSSION: In a public-key system, the public key is used to encrypt the message prior to transmission. The private key is needed to decrypt (decode) the message.
    Answer (B) is incorrect. The private key, not the public key, is needed to decrypt (decode) the message. Answer (C) is incorrect. The public key is needed to encode, not decode, the message. Answer (D) is incorrect. The private key is needed to decrypt (decode) the message.

29. Which improvement in IT control specifically addresses the authentication issue?

    A. A digital certificate.

    B. A firewall.

    C. An intelligent router.

    D. Encryption.

Answer (A) is correct.
    REQUIRED: The improvement in IT control that specifically addresses the authentication issue
    DISCUSSION: A digital certificate is a data file created by trusted third parties called certificate authorities that verify an e-commerce participant's identity.
    Answer (B) is incorrect. A firewall is a configuration of hardware and software that intercepts and examines message packets sent to an internal network from an external network. Messages or access attempts that do not meet specified criteria are rejected. Answer (C) is incorrect. A router sends data packets from one LAN or WAN to another. It decides how to send packets based on the most expedient routine. Answer (D) is incorrect. Encryption converts data into a code that cannot be read by an unauthorized party who does not have the key required for decoding.

Use the additional questions in Gleim **CPA Test Prep Online** to create Test Sessions that emulate Prometric!

13.6 PRACTICE WRITTEN COMMUNICATION TASK

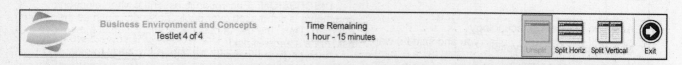

Business Environment and Concepts
Testlet 4 of 4

Time Remaining
1 hour - 15 minutes

Unsplit   Split Horiz   Split Vertical   Exit

DIRECTIONS

Note: If you believe you have encountered a software malfunction, report it to the test center staff immediately.

Navigation

To navigate from task to task, use the controls at the bottom of the screen. Click on the **Next** button to advance to the next task, or the **Previous** button to go to the previous task. To go directly to any task, click on its number.

| ▽ = Reminder | | Directions | 1 ▽ | 2 ▽ | 3 ▽ | 4 ▽ | 5 ▽ | 6 ▽ | 7 ▽ | | ◀ Previous | Next ▶ |

If you would like a reminder to revisit a task, or want to indicate that you are finished with it, click on the reminder flag below the task number. To clear the flag, click on it again. Reminder flags are for your use only – they do not contribute to your score.

Tabs

In this part of the examination, you will be asked to complete various tasks. Every task has one or more **Work Tabs**. Every task also has a **Help** tab.

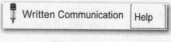

Written Communication   Help

Work tab   Help tab

Work Tabs:

- **Work Tabs** are identified with a pencil icon. This is where your responses are expected.
- Each task has one or more **Work Tabs**.
- **Work Tabs** contain directions for completing the task - be sure to read these directions carefully.
- The **Work Tab** name in the example above is for illustration only - yours will differ.
- You must complete all of the **Work Tabs** in each task to receive full credit.

Help Tab:

- The **Help Tab** provides assistance with the exam software that is used in this task. For example, if the task is to compose a memorandum, **Help** will provide information about the word processor.

The Toolbar

The toolbar at the top of the screen shows the amount of time remaining for you to complete the tasks. In addition, the following tools are available. Note that only the **Exit** button is displayed when Directions are visible - the others will appear when you begin the tasks.

Unsplit   Split Horiz   Split Vertical

Click on these buttons to split or unsplit the screen. You can split the screen vertically or horizontally.

Exit

Click on this button to go on to the next part of the examination. You must complete all of the tasks to receive full credit. Once you click on **Exit** and confirm the action, you will NOT be able to return to this testlet.

| ▽ = Reminder | | Directions | 1 ▽ | | | ◀ Previous | Next ▶ |

The CEO of Popular, Inc., called you and said he wants to immediately become an e-business. After some discussion with him, you realize he keeps repeating certain buzz words and does not understand what an e-business means technically.

Prepare a memo to the CEO of Popular distinguishing e-business from e-commerce, explaining the risks inherent in e-commerce and the potential benefits that may be gained from B2B (business-to-business) e-commerce.

Type your communication below the line in the response area below.

REMINDER: Your response will be graded for both technical content and writing skills. Technical content will be evaluated for information that is helpful to the intended reader and clearly relevant to the issue. Writing skills will be evaluated for development, organization, and the appropriate expression of ideas in professional correspondence. Use a standard business memorandum or letter format with a clear beginning, middle, and end. Do not convey information in the form of a table, bullet point list, or other abbreviated presentation.

To: CEO, Popular, Inc.
Re: E-business

Unofficial Answer

Written Communication

To: CEO, Popular, Inc.
Re: E-business

An e-business is a business conducting its operations electronically. The electronic portion of the business is not strictly relegated to sales, although this may certainly be a component of the overall e-business; it can also include internal communications and non-financial dealings with outside parties. The narrower term pertaining specifically to the financial transactions with third parties is e-commerce. Two widely used forms of e-commerce are business-to-business (B2B) and business-to-consumer (B2C), each version with its risks and benefits.

The security issues inherent with e-commerce need to be considered and evaluated any time a decision is made to enter into this method of transaction processing. Some of the risks include, but are not limited to, correct identification of the transacting parties; determination of who may rightfully make binding agreements; protecting the confidentiality and integrity of information; assuring the trustworthiness of listed prices and discounts; providing evidence of the transmission and receipt of documents; guarding against repudiation by the sender or recipient; the proper extent of verification of payment data; and the nature of the audit trail.

B2B e-commerce most often takes the form of a business' purchases from other businesses (or sales to other businesses). Four benefits of B2B can be identified. First, purchasing online reduces costs by saving time and simplifying the ordering process. Second, by using the Internet, companies have easy access to price quotes from various suppliers, i.e., increased market efficiency. Buyers are more likely to get a better price, given the increased number of suppliers. Third, market intelligence is increased by B2B, and producers get better insights into the demand levels in any given market. Lastly, inventory levels can be decreased. Companies can make better use of their inventory and raw materials. Such techniques as just-in-time inventory can be deployed.

The above depicts a Level 5 answer. See page 16 in the Introduction for a description of the three grading criteria.

Self-Grade

Evaluate each of the following by selecting a 0, 1, 2, 3, 4, or 5. An average response is 3. Use 4 for better than average and 5 for outstanding. Use 2 for less than average and 1 for quite poor. Use zero for no response, if you did not address the topic, or if you gave advice that is clearly illegal.

Organization	O 0	O 1	O 2	O 3	O 4	O 5
Development	O 0	O 1	O 2	O 3	O 4	O 5
Expression	O 0	O 1	O 2	O 3	O 4	O 5

Your grade for the written communication as a whole is the average of the scores for the three criteria.

Use **CPA Gleim Online** and **Simulation Wizard** to practice more written communication tasks in a realistic environment.

STUDY UNIT FOURTEEN
IT SECURITY

(15 pages of outline)

The goals of a business information system are the same regardless of whether the system is manual or computerized; the risks of a computer-based system, however, are quite different (Subunit 1). Proper control over information security requires the enactment of a comprehensive, entity-wide information security plan (Subunit 2). In addition to the controls that affect an entity's overall information processing environment, every individual computer application has its own set of controls to ensure that the data entering and exiting the system are the right data (Subunit 3). Business information systems are crucial to the continued existence of the modern organization; therefore, every entity must plan how it will continue processing in the case of an interruption to normal processing (Subunit 4).

14.1 RISKS ASSOCIATED WITH BUSINESS INFORMATION SYSTEMS

1. **Principle**

   a. The goals of a business information system are the same regardless of whether it is manual or computer-based. The risks, on the other hand, can be quite different.

2. **System Availability**

   a. The ability to make use of any computer-based system is dependent on

      1) An uninterrupted flow of electricity
      2) Protection of computer hardware from environmental hazards (e.g., fire and water)
      3) Protection of software and data files from unauthorized alteration
      4) Preservation of functioning communications channels between devices

3. **Volatile Transaction Trails**

   a. In any computer-based environment, a complete trail useful for audit purposes might exist for only a short time or in only computer-readable form. In online and real-time systems, data are entered directly into the computer, eliminating portions of the audit trail traditionally provided by source documents.

4. **Decreased Human Involvement**

   a. Because employees who enter transactions may never see the final results, the potential for detecting errors is reduced. Also, output from a computer system often carries a mystique of infallibility, reducing the incentive of system users to closely examine reports and transaction logs.

5. **Uniform Processing of Transactions**

   a. Computer processing uniformly subjects like transactions to the same processing instructions, therefore virtually eliminating clerical error. Thus, it permits consistent application of predefined business rules and the performance of complex calculations in high volume.

   b. However, programming errors (or other similar systematic errors in either the hardware or software) will result in all like transactions being processed incorrectly.

6. **Unauthorized Access**

   a. When accounting records were kept in pen-and-ink format, physical access to them was the only way to carry out an alteration. Once they are computer-based, however, access may be gained by parties both internal and external to the organization.

   b. Security measures, such as firewalls and user ID-and-password combinations, are thus vital to maintaining security over data in an automated environment.

7. **Data Vulnerability**

   a. Destruction of a few hardware devices or units of storage media could have disastrous consequences if they contain the only copies of crucial data files or application programs.

   b. For this reason, it is vital that an organization's computer files be duplicated and stored offsite periodically.

8. **Reduced Segregation of Duties**

   a. Many functions once performed by separate individuals may be combined in an automated environment.

   b. For example, receiving cash, issuing a receipt to the payor, preparing the deposit slip, and preparing the journal entry may once have been performed by separate individuals. In a computer-based system, the receipt, deposit slip, and journal entry may be automatically generated by the computer. If the same employee who receives the cash is also responsible for entering the relevant data into the system, the potential for error or fraud is increased.

9. **Reduced Individual Authorization of Transactions**

   a. Certain transactions may be initiated automatically by a computer-based system. This is becoming ever more widespread as an increasing number of business processes become automated.

   b. For example, an ERP system at a manufacturing company may automatically generate a purchase order when raw materials inventory reaches a certain level. If the company shares an EDI system with the vendor, the purchase order may be sent to the vendor electronically without any human intervention.

   c. This reduced level of oversight for individual transactions requires careful coding to ensure that computer programs accurately reflect management's goals for business processes.

      1) Independent verification of transactions is an important compensating control in the absence of segregation of duties and reduced individual authorization. A third party performs the verification to ensure that the transactions were appropriately processed.

10. **Specialized Knowledge**

   a. From the beginning of the computer era in the 1950s, the ability to operate computer-based systems has depended on a high level of specialization and training among computer professionals.

   b. Even as computing has become more "democratized" by the prevalence of personal computers and the Internet, organizations require groups of employees dedicated to keeping their automated systems running.

   c. Attracting and retaining employees with the necessary skillsets can be time-consuming and expensive. This situation has led to the practice of outsourcing, the hiring of an outside firm to take over all or part of an organization's computer operations.

      1) Advantages of outsourcing include access to expertise, superior service quality, avoidance of changes in the organization's IT infrastructure, cost predictability, the freeing of human and financial capital, and avoidance of fixed costs.

      2) Risks of outsourcing include the inflexibility of the relationship, the loss of control, the vulnerability of important information, and often dependency on a single vendor.

11. **Malicious Software (Malware)**

   a. Malware is a term describing any program code that enters a computer system that has the potential to degrade that system. Common forms of malware include the following:

      1) A **Trojan horse** is an apparently innocent program (e.g., a spreadsheet) that includes a hidden function that may do damage when activated.

      2) A **virus** is a program that copies itself from file to file. The virus may destroy data or programs. A common way of spreading a virus is by email attachments and downloads.

      3) A **worm** copies itself not from file to file but from computer to computer, often very rapidly. Repeated replication overloads a system by depleting memory or overwhelming network traffic capacity.

      4) A **denial-of-service (DOS) attack** is an attempt to overload a system (e.g., a network or Web server) with messages so that it cannot function (a system crash).

         a) A distributed DOS attack comes from multiple sources, for example, the machines of innocent parties infected by Trojan horses. When activated, these programs send messages to the target and leave the connection open.

      5) **Phishing** is a method of electronically obtaining confidential information, such as a password or credit card number, through deceit. The perpetrator sets up a website that appears to be legitimate but actually serves no other purpose than to obtain the victim's information.

         a) Phishing scams are often initiated through email spoofing, in which the perpetrator sends out emails that appear to be from a real financial institution. When the victim clicks on the link to what (s)he thinks is the institution's website, the victim is unknowingly redirected to the perpetrator's website.

12.   **COBIT -- A Framework for IT Governance and Management**

a.   COBIT is the best-known control and governance framework that addresses information technology.

1)   In its original version, COBIT was focused on controls for specific IT processes.

2)   Over the years, information technology has gradually come to pervade every facet of the organization's operations. IT can no longer be viewed as a function distinct from other aspects of the organization.

a)   The evolution of COBIT has reflected this change in the nature of IT within the organization.

Background

When originally published in 1996, COBIT was an acronym for *Control Objectives for Information and Related Technology*. COBIT 5, the most recent version, was published in April 2012 by ISACA (formerly known as the Information Systems Audit and Control Association), located in Rolling Meadows, Illinois. The COBIT 5 framework document, which describes the five key principles for IT governance and management, is available as a free download at www.isaca.org/COBIT/Pages/Product-Family.aspx.

---

13.   **COBIT 5 -- Five Key Principles**

a.   **Principle 1: Meeting Stakeholder Needs**

1)   COBIT 5 asserts that value creation is the most basic stakeholder need. Thus, the creation of stakeholder value is the fundamental goal of any enterprise, commercial or not.

a)   Value creation in this model is achieved by balancing three components:

i)   Realization of benefits
ii)   Optimization (not minimization) of risk
iii) Optimal use of resources

2)   COBIT 5 also recognizes that stakeholder needs are not fixed. They evolve under the influence of both internal factors (e.g., changes in organizational culture) and external factors (e.g., disruptive technologies).

a)   These factors are collectively referred to as stakeholder drivers.

3)   In response to the identified stakeholder needs, enterprise goals are established.

a)   COBIT 5 supplies 17 generic enterprise goals that are tied directly to the balanced scorecard model.

4)   Next, IT-related goals are drawn up to address the enterprise goals.

a)   COBIT 5 translates the 17 generic enterprise goals into IT-related goals.

5)   Finally, enablers are identified that support pursuit of the IT-related goals. An enabler is broadly defined as anything that helps achieve objectives.

a)   The seven categories of enablers are listed in item 13.d. on page 376.

6) COBIT 5 refers to the process described on the previous page as the goals cascade. It can be depicted graphically as follows:

COBIT 5 Goals Cascade

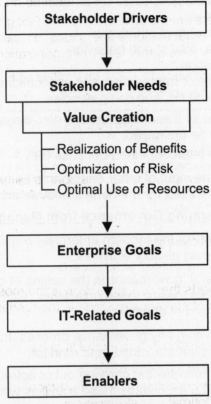

Figure 14-1

b. **Principle 2: Covering the Enterprise End-to-End**

1) COBIT 5 takes a comprehensive view of all of the enterprise's functions and processes. Information technology pervades them all; it cannot be viewed as a function distinct from other enterprise activities.

a) Thus, IT governance must be integrated with enterprise governance.

2) IT must be considered enterprise-wide and end-to-end, i.e., all functions and processes that govern and manage information "wherever that information may be processed."

c. **Principle 3: Applying a Single, Integrated Framework**

1) In acknowledgment of the availability of multiple IT-related standards and best practices, COBIT 5 provides an overall framework for enterprise IT within which other standards can be consistently applied.

2) COBIT 5 was developed to be an overarching framework that does not address specific technical issues; i.e., its principles can be applied regardless of the particular hardware and software in use.

d. **Principle 4: Enabling a Holistic Approach**

1) COBIT 5 describes seven categories of enablers that support comprehensive IT governance and management:

a) Principles, policies, and frameworks
b) Processes
c) Organizational structures
d) Culture, ethics, and behavior
e) Information
f) Services, infrastructure, and applications
g) People, skills, and competencies

2) The last three of these enablers are also classified as resources, the use of which must be optimized.

3) Enablers are interconnected because they

a) Need the input of other enablers to be fully effective and
b) Deliver output for the benefit of other enablers.

e. **Principle 5: Separating Governance from Management**

1) The complexity of the modern enterprise requires governance and management to be treated as distinct activities.

a) In general, governance is the setting of overall objectives and monitoring progress toward those objectives. COBIT 5 associates governance with the board of directors.

   i) Within any governance process, three practices must be addressed: evaluate, direct, and monitor.

b) Management is the carrying out of activities in pursuit of enterprise goals. COBIT 5 associates these activities with executive management under the leadership of the CEO.

   i) Within any management process, four responsibility areas must be addressed: plan, build, run, and monitor.

Background

The entire COBIT product family includes, besides the framework itself, three other documents that can be purchased separately: enabler guides, which describe enabling processes (i.e., anything that can help to achieve enterprise objectives); professional guides, which provide guidance for the implementation of COBIT, as well as for such specific topics as information security, assurance, and risk; and an online environment allowing simultaneous participation and collaboration by interested parties.

---

14. **Role of Technology Systems in Control Monitoring**

a. While the use of automated systems introduces some new risks to the organization (discussed in items 1.-11. of this subunit), IT can also help mitigate other risks.

1) A common example is the automated verification of requests for vendor payment against the authorized vendor file. If the vendor number is not on the authorized list, a payment is not issued.

2) The increased speed and consistency of this operation over those of the manual process are evident.

15. **Operational Effectiveness**

    a.   Operational effectiveness is the degree to which a system (automated or not) serves its intended purpose.

        1)   A system may gather large amounts of data and generate extensive reports, but if the reports do not help the users carry out business processes and make decisions, the system is not effective.

16. **Policies**

    a.   All organizations should have policies in place regarding the proper consideration of cross-functional business processes when a new system procurement or design is undertaken.

Stop and review! You have completed the outline for this subunit. Study multiple-choice questions 1 through 11 beginning on page 386.

14.2 INFORMATION SECURITY

1.   **Overview**

    a.   Information security encompasses not only computer hardware and software but all of an organization's information, no matter what medium it resides on. It involves far more than just user IDs and passwords.

        1)   The importance of a broad definition of information security becomes clear in light of recent incidents of firms accidentally disposing of documents containing confidential customer information with their regular trash.

    b.   Organizations have three principal goals for their information security programs: data confidentiality, data availability, and data integrity.

        1)   **Confidentiality** is protecting data from disclosure to unauthorized persons.

        2)   **Availability** is assuring that the organization's information systems are up and running so that employees and customers are able to access the data they need.

        3)   **Integrity** is assuring that data accurately reflect the business events underlying them and are not subject to tampering or destruction.

2.   **Steps in Creating an Information Security Plan**

    a.   Identify the threats to the organization's information, i.e., events that can potentially compromise an organization's information infrastructure.

        1)   Threats to confidentiality include the previously mentioned improper disposal of customer records, threats to availability include viruses and denial-of-service attacks, and threats to integrity include employee errors and disgruntled employee sabotage.

    b.   Identify the risks that these threats entail.

        1)   Risk analysis has two phases: determining the likelihood of the identified threats and the level of damage that could potentially be done should the threats materialize.

        2)   For example, an organization may conclude that, while the potential damage from sabotage is very high, its likelihood may be quite low.

    c.   Design the controls that will compensate for the risks.

        1)   Controls are designed based on the combination of likelihood and potential damage determined in the risk analysis.

        2)   Controls are of three major types: physical, logical, and policy.

d.   Incorporate the controls into a coherent, enterprise-wide information security plan.

1)   The plan lists the controls that will be put in place and how they will be enforced.

e.   Policies set forth expectations of all persons, both employees and external users, with access to the organization's systems.

1)   The single most important policy is that which governs the information resources to which individuals have access and how the level of access will be tied to their job duties.

a)   Carrying out such a policy requires the organization's systems to be able to tie data and program access to individual system IDs.

b)   One provision of the policy must be for the immediate removal of access to the system by terminated employees.

3.   **Three Generic Types of Controls**

a.   IT controls can also be classified according to the traditional three-way division of internal controls.

b.   **Preventive controls** prevent errors from entering the system. Preventive controls are often highly visible and are considered better than other forms of control because they stop problems before they occur.

1)   Examples of physical preventive controls include fences, locked doors, security guards, and a separation of duties policy.

2)   Examples of logical preventive controls are the input controls described later in this study unit.

c.   **Detective controls** call attention to errors that have already entered the system before an error causes a negative outcome.

1)   Examples of detective accounting controls are petty cash counts and physical inventories.

a)   An important detective control in IT is examination of system logs. These logs are reports automatically generated by the system of actions that require scrutiny, such as repeated failed login attempts and the use of powerful utility programs.

2)   Examples in an automated systems context are the output controls described later in this study unit.

d.   **Corrective controls** correct errors after they have been detected.

1)   Examples include correcting errors reported on error listings, isolating and removing viruses, and restarting from system crashes.

4.   **General Controls**

a.   The classic division of controls in information systems is between general controls and application controls.

1)   General controls relate to the organization's IT environment as a whole. They sustain the conditions under which application controls can function properly.

b.   IT Administration

1)   A modern organization should recognize information technology as a separate function with its own set of management and technical skills. An organization that allows every functional area to acquire and administer its own systems in isolation is not serious about proper control.

2) Treating IT as a separate functional area of the organization involves the designation of a chief information officer (CIO) or chief technology officer (CTO) and the establishment of an information systems steering committee to set a coherent direction for the organization's systems and prioritize information technology projects.

c.   Segregation of duties within the IT function is discussed in Study Unit 12, Subunit 6.

d.   Controls over systems development are discussed in Study Unit 12, Subunit 5.

e.   **Hardware controls** are built into the equipment by the manufacturer. They ensure the proper internal handling of data as they are moved and stored.

1) They include parity checks, echo checks, read-after-write checks, and any other procedure built into the equipment to assure data integrity.

f.   **Physical controls** limit physical access and environmental damage to computer equipment, data, and important documents.

1) **Access Controls**

a) No persons except operators should be allowed unmonitored access to the processing facility. This can be accomplished through the use of a guard desk, a keypad, or a magnetic card reader.

b) The distribution of printed reports must be controlled so that unauthorized persons are not able to view data that are not connected with their job duties. This encompasses the proper disposal of documents in such a way that the disclosure of confidential customer or company data is prevented (e.g., shredding).

2) **Environmental Controls**

a) The processing facility should be equipped with both a cooling and heating system (to maintain a year-round constant level of temperature and humidity) and a fire-suppression system.

g.   **Logical controls** are established to limit access in accordance with the principle that all persons should have access only to those elements of the organization's information systems that are necessary to perform their job duties. Logical controls have a double focus, authentication and authorization.

1) Authentication is the act of assuring that the person attempting to access the system is in fact who (s)he says (s)he is. The most widespread means of achieving this is through the use of IDs and passwords.

2) The elements of user account management are as follows:

a) Anyone attempting access to one of the organization's systems must supply a unique identifier (e.g., the person's name or other series of characters) and a password that is known only to that person and is not stored anywhere in the system in unencrypted format.

i) Not even information security personnel should be able to view unencrypted passwords. Security personnel can change passwords, but the policy should require that the user immediately changes it to something secret.

b) The organization's systems should force users to change their passwords periodically, e.g., every 90 days.

c) The policy should prohibit employees from leaving their IDs and passwords written down in plain view.

3) Authorization is the practice of ensuring that, once in the system, the user can only access those programs and data elements necessary for his/her job duties.

    a) In many cases, users should be able to view the contents of some data fields but not be able to change them.

    b) An example is an accounts receivable clerk who can view customers' credit limits but cannot change them. This same clerk can, however, change a customer's outstanding balance by entering or adjusting an invoice.

    c) To extend the example, only the head of the accounts receivable department should be able to execute the program that updates the accounts receivable master balance file. An individual clerk should have no such power.

h. A **firewall** is a combination of hardware and software that separates an internal network from an external network (e.g., the Internet) and prevents passage of traffic deemed suspicious. Two principal types of firewalls are network firewalls and application firewalls.

1) Network firewalls regulate traffic to an entire network, such as an organization's LAN. They accomplish this with a technique known as packet filtering (packets are described in item 4. in Study Unit 13, Subunit 2).

    a) The firewall examines the header of each packet. Depending on the rules set up by the network security administrator, packets can be denied entry to the network based on their source, destination, or other data in the header.

    b) Packets from a particular source address that repeatedly fail to gain access to the network might indicate a penetration attempt. The firewall can notify network security personnel who can then investigate.

2) Application firewalls regulate traffic to a specified application, such as email or file transfer.

    a) An application firewall is based on proxy server technology. The firewall becomes a proxy, or intermediary, between the computer actually sending the packet and the application in question. This arrangement allows for a high level of security over the application, but at the cost of slowing down communications.

    b) Since an application firewall only provides security for a single application, it is not a substitute for a network firewall.

3) A firewall alone is not an adequate defense against computer viruses. Specialized antivirus software is a must.

i. Backup and contingency planning will be discussed later in this study unit.

5. **Application controls** are built into each application (payroll, accounts payable, inventory management, etc.)

a. Application controls are designed to ensure that only correct, authorized data enter the system and that the data are processed and reported properly.

1) Lists of widely-used application controls are provided in the next subunit.

Stop and review! You have completed the outline for this subunit. Study multiple-choice questions 12 through 19 beginning on page 389.

14.3 APPLICATION CONTROLS

 CPA exam questions concerning application controls often give a description of a control, then ask for the name of it.

1. **Input Controls**

   a. Input controls are designed to prevent unauthorized, invalid, or duplicate data from entering the system.

      1) The most basic input control is thus authorization; e.g., a batch of accounts payable transactions must be authorized by the AP supervisor before being submitted for recording.

   b. Many input controls take the form of edit routines, i.e., controls programmed into the software that prevent certain types of errors from ever getting into the system.

      1) Preformatting

         a) To avoid data entry errors in online systems, a preformatted screen may be designed to look exactly like the corresponding paper document.

      2) Field Checks

         a) Some data elements can only contain certain characters, and any transaction that attempts to use an invalid character is halted. A typical example is a Social Security number, which is not allowed to contain letters.

      3) Limit (Reasonableness) and Range Checks

         a) Based on known limits for given information, certain entries can be rejected by the system. For example, hours worked per week cannot exceed 80 without a special override by management, date of birth cannot be any date within the last 15 years, etc.

      4) Validity Checks

         a) In order for a transaction to be processed, some other record must already exist in another file. For example, for the system to accept a transaction requesting payment of a vendor invoice, the vendor must already have a record on the vendor master file.

      5) Sequence Checks

         a) Processing efficiency is greatly increased when files are sorted on some designated field(s), called the "key," before operations such as matching. For instance, the accounts payable transaction file and master file should both be sorted according to vendor number before the matching operation is attempted. If the system discovers a record out of order, it may indicate that the files were not properly prepared for processing.

6) Check Digit Verification (Self-Checking Digits)

    a) An algorithm is applied to, for instance, a product number and incorporated into the number. This reduces keying errors such as dropped and transposed digits.

EXAMPLE

A box of detergent has the product number 4187604. The last digit is actually a derived number, arrived at by applying the check-digit algorithm to the other digits.

The check digit is calculated by starting with the last position of the base product number and multiplying each successive digit to the left by 2, then by 1, then by 2, etc., and adding the results: $(0 \times 2) + (6 \times 1) + (7 \times 2) + (8 \times 1) + (1 \times 2) + (4 \times 1) = 0 + 6 + 14 + 8 + 2 + 4 = 34$. The last digit of this result becomes the check digit.

When the clerk enters 4187604 into the terminal, the system performs an immediate calculation and determines that this is a valid product number.

---

7) Zero-Balance Checks

    a) The system will reject any transaction or batch thereof in which the sum of all debits and credits does not equal zero.

2. **Processing Controls**

    a. Processing controls provide reasonable assurance that processing has been performed as intended for the particular application.

    b. Some processing controls repeat the steps performed during input, such as limit or range checks and validity checks. Others include the following:

        1) Completeness

            a) Any record that does not match to a master file record is identified and rejected.

        2) Arithmetic Controls

            a) Cross-footing compares an amount to the sum of its components.

        3) Zero-Balance Checking

            a) This control adds the debits and credits in a transaction or batch to ensure they sum to zero.

        4) Key Integrity

            a) A record's "key" is the group of values in designated fields that uniquely identify the record. No application process should be able to alter the data in these key fields.

3. **Output Controls**

    a. Output controls provide assurance that the processing result (such as account listings or displays, reports, files, invoices, or disbursement checks) is accurate and that only authorized personnel receive the output.

    b. These procedures are performed at the end of processing to ensure that all transactions the user expected to be processed were actually processed.

        1) Transaction Logs

            a) Every action performed in the application is logged along with the date, time, and ID in use when the action was taken.

2) Error Listings

    a) All transactions rejected by the system are printed and distributed to the appropriate user department for resolution.

3) Record Counts

    a) The total number of records processed by the system is compared to the number the user expected to be processed.

4) Run-to-Run Control Totals

    a) The new financial balance should be the sum of the old balance plus the activity that was just processed.

5) Hash Totals

    a) The arithmetic sum of a numeric field, which has no meaning by itself, can serve as a check that the same records that should have been processed were processed. An example is the sum of all Social Security numbers.

Stop and review! You have completed the outline for this subunit. Study multiple-choice questions 20 through 25 beginning on page 391.

14.4 DISASTER RECOVERY AND BUSINESS CONTINUITY

1. **Overview**

    a. The information security goal of data availability is primarily the responsibility of the IT function. **Contingency planning** is the name commonly given to this activity.

        1) **Business continuity** is the continuation of business by other means during the period in which computer processing is unavailable or less than normal.

        2) **Disaster recovery** is the process of resuming normal information processing operations after the occurrence of a major interruption.

    b. Two major types of contingencies must be planned for: those in which the data center is physically available and those in which it is not.

        1) Examples of the first type of contingency are power failure, random intrusions such as viruses, and deliberate intrusions such as hacking incidents. The organization's physical facilities are sound, but immediate action is required to keep normal processing going.

        2) The second type of contingency is much more serious. This type is caused by disasters such as floods, fires, hurricanes, earthquakes, etc. An occurrence of this type necessitates the existence of an alternate processing facility, described later in this subunit.

2. **File Backup and Rotation**

    a. Periodic backup and offsite rotation of computer files is the most basic part of any disaster recovery/business continuity plan.

        1) A truth seldom grasped by those who are not computer professionals is that an organization's data is more valuable than its hardware. Hardware can be replaced for a price, but each organization's data bundle is unique and is indispensable to carrying on business. If it is destroyed, it cannot be replaced. For this reason, periodic backup and rotation are essential.

b. A typical backup routine involves duplicating all data files and application programs periodically (e.g., once a month). Incremental changes are then backed up and taken to the offsite location (e.g., once a week). (Application programs must be backed up in addition to data since programs change too.)

   1) The offsite location must be temperature- and humidity-controlled and guarded against physical intrusion. Just as important, it must be geographically remote enough from the site of the organization's main operations that it would not be affected by the same natural disaster. It does the organization no good to have adequate backup files if the files are not accessible or have been destroyed.

   2) In case of an interruption of normal processing, the organization's systems can be restored such that, at most, 7 days of business information is lost. This is not an ideal situation, but it is better than a complete loss of a company's files, which could essentially put it out of business.

3. **IT Risk Assessment**

   a. Identifying and prioritizing the organization's critical applications

      1) Not all of an organization's systems are equally important. The firm must decide which vital applications it simply cannot do business without and in what order they should be brought back into operation.

   b. Determining the minimum recovery time frames and minimum hardware requirements

      1) How long will it take to reinstall each critical application, and what platform is required? If the interruption has been caused by an attack, such as a virus or hacker, how long will it take to isolate the problem and eliminate it from the system?

   c. Developing a recovery plan

      1) The tasks that must be performed in the event of a disaster are enumerated, along with identification of the parties responsible for each.

         a) The names and contact information for key vendors and a description of the current hardware configuration should also be included.

      2) Each type of contingency requires its own specific recovery procedures.

4. **Dealing with Specific Types of Contingencies**

   a. Power failures can be guarded against by the purchase of backup electrical generators. These can be programmed to automatically begin running as soon as a dip in the level of electric current is detected.

      1) This is a widespread practice in settings such as hospitals where 24-hour system availability is crucial.

   b. Attacks such as viruses and denial-of-service call for a completely different response. The system must be brought down "gracefully" to halt the spread of the infection.

      1) The IT staff must be well trained in the nature of the latest virus threats to know how to isolate the damage and bring the system back to full operation.

c.   The most extreme contingency is when the organization's main facility is rendered uninhabitable by flood, fire, earthquake, etc. It is to prepare for these cases that organizations contract for alternate processing facilities.

1)   An alternate processing facility is a physical location maintained by an outside contractor for the express purpose of providing processing facilities for customers in case of disaster.

a)   The recovery center, like the offsite storage location for backup files, must be far enough away that it will likely be unaffected by the same natural disaster that forced the abandonment of the main facility. Usually, companies contract for backup facilities in another city.

b)   Once the determination is made that processing is no longer possible at the principal site, the backup files are retrieved from the secure storage location and taken to the recovery center.

 Be able to describe the three types of recovery centers. This may help you on a multiple-choice or essay question.

---

c)   Recovery centers can take many forms. Organizations determine which facility is best by calculating the tradeoff between the cost of the contract and the cost of downtime.

i)   A **hot site** is a fully operational processing facility that is immediately available. A flying-start site is a hot site with the latest data and software that permit startup within a few minutes or even a few seconds.

ii)   A **warm site** is a facility with limited hardware, such as communications and networking equipment, that is already installed but is lacking the necessary servers and client terminals.

iii)   A **cold site** is a shell facility lacking most infrastructure but is readily available for the quick installation of hardware and software.

5.   Other Technologies

a.   Fault-tolerant computer systems have additional hardware and software as well as a backup power supply. A fault-tolerant computer has additional chips and disk storage. This technology is used for mission-critical applications that cannot afford to suffer downtime.

1)   The enabling technology for fault-tolerance is the redundant array of inexpensive discs, or RAID. It is a grouping of multiple hard drives with special software that allows for data delivery along multiple paths. If one drive fails, the other discs can compensate for the loss.

b.   High-availability computing is used for less-critical applications because it provides for a short recovery time rather than the elimination of recovery time.

Stop and review! You have completed the outline for this subunit. Study multiple-choice questions 26 through 30 beginning on page 392.

QUESTIONS

14.1 Risks Associated with Business Information Systems

1. Which of the following control activities should be taken to reduce the risk of incorrect processing in a newly installed computerized accounting system?

- A. Segregation of duties.
- B. Ensure proper authorization of transactions.
- C. Adequately safeguard assets.
- D. Independently verify the transactions.

Answer (D) is correct.
    REQUIRED: The control activity that should be taken to reduce the risk of incorrect processing in a newly installed computerized accounting system.
    DISCUSSION: Independent verification is an important compensating control in the absence of segregation of duties and reduced individual authorization of transactions. A third party performs the verification to ensure that the transactions were appropriately processed.
    Answer (A) is incorrect. Segregation of duties is an important internal control, but it does not reduce the risk of incorrect computer processing. Answer (B) is incorrect. Authorization of transactions is an important internal control, but it does not reduce the risk of incorrect computer processing. Answer (C) is incorrect. Adequate safeguarding of assets is an important internal control, but it does not reduce the risk of incorrect computer processing.

2. Which of the following is an advantage of a computer-based system for transaction processing over a manual system? A computer-based system

- A. Does not require as stringent a set of internal controls.
- B. Will produce a more accurate set of financial statements.
- C. Will be more efficient at producing financial statements.
- D. Eliminates the need to reconcile control accounts and subsidiary ledgers.

Answer (C) is correct.
    REQUIRED: The advantage of computer processing.
    DISCUSSION: Computer processing permits consistent application of predefined business rules and the performance of complex calculations in high volume. Hence, computer processing of the accounting transactions reported in financial statements is more efficient than in a manual system.
    Answer (A) is incorrect. Many functions once performed by separate individuals may be concentrated in computer systems. As a result, other controls may be necessary to achieve the control objectives ordinarily accomplished by segregation of functions. Answer (B) is incorrect. Greater accuracy is not necessarily a result of greater efficiency. Answer (D) is incorrect. Reconciliations must be performed regardless of the processing method.

3. Which of the following is most likely a disadvantage for an entity that keeps data files prepared by personal computers rather than manually prepared files?

- A. Attention is focused on the accuracy of the programming process rather than errors in individual transactions.
- B. It is usually easier for unauthorized persons to access and alter the files.
- C. Random error associated with processing similar transactions in different ways is usually greater.
- D. It is usually more difficult to compare recorded accountability with physical count of assets.

Answer (B) is correct.
    REQUIRED: The disadvantage of personal-computer-prepared data files.
    DISCUSSION: In a manual system, one individual is assigned responsibility for maintaining and safeguarding the records. However, in a personal computer environment, the data files may be subject to change by others without documentation or indication of who made the changes.
    Answer (A) is incorrect. The focus on programming is an advantage of using the computer. A program allows transactions to be processed uniformly. Answer (C) is incorrect. An advantage of the computer is that it processes similar transactions in the same way. Answer (D) is incorrect. The method of maintaining the files is independent of the ability to compare this information in the file with the physical count of assets.

4. Which of the following risks are greater in computerized systems than in manual systems?

- I. Erroneous data conversion
- II. Erroneous source document preparation
- III. Repetition of errors
- IV. Concentration of data

- A. I and II.
- B. II and III.
- C. I, III, and IV.
- D. I, II, III, and IV.

Answer (C) is correct.
    REQUIRED: The risks that are greater in computerized systems than in manual systems.
    DISCUSSION: Unlike a manual system, a computer system converts data to machine-readable form so that transactions can be processed. This additional step increases the risk of input error. Moreover, if an error exists in the program, systematic, repetitive errors will occur in processing transactions. Finally, data are typically stored magnetically or optically on disks. This concentration of data increases the risk of loss from natural and other disasters. Source document preparation either precedes processing or is eliminated altogether in a computerized system. Thus, the risk of erroneous source document preparation in computerized systems is the same as or less than the equivalent risk in manual systems.

5. Your firm has recently converted its purchasing cycle from a manual process to an online computer system. Which of the following is a probable result associated with conversion to the new automatic system?

A. Processing errors are increased.

B. The firm's risk exposures are reduced.

C. Processing time is increased.

D. Traditional duties are less segregated.

Answer (D) is correct.

REQUIRED: The probable result associated with conversion to the new automatic system.

DISCUSSION: In a manual system with appropriate internal control, separate individuals are responsible for authorizing transactions, recording transactions, and having custody of assets. These checks and balances prevent fraud and detect inaccurate or incomplete transactions. In a computer environment, however, this segregation of duties is not always feasible. For example, a computer may print checks, record disbursements, and generate information for reconciling the account balance.

Answer (A) is incorrect. A computer system decreases processing errors. Answer (B) is incorrect. The conversion to a new system does not reduce the number of risk exposures. Answer (C) is incorrect. Processing time is decreased.

6. Matthews Corp. has changed from a system of recording time worked on clock cards to a computerized payroll system in which employees record time in and out with magnetic cards. The computer system automatically updates all payroll records. Because of this change,

A. A generalized computer audit program must be used.

B. Part of the audit trail is altered.

C. The potential for payroll-related fraud is diminished.

D. Transactions must be processed in batches.

Answer (B) is correct.

REQUIRED: The effect of changing to a computerized payroll system.

DISCUSSION: In a manual payroll system, a paper trail of documents is created to provide audit evidence that controls over each step in processing are in place and functioning. One element of a computer system that differentiates it from a manual system is that a transaction trail useful for auditing purposes might exist only for a brief time or only in computer-readable form.

Answer (A) is incorrect. Use of generalized audit software is only one of many ways of auditing through a computer. Answer (C) is incorrect. Conversion to a computer system may increase the chance of fraud by eliminating segregation of incompatible functions and other controls. Answer (D) is incorrect. Automatic updating indicates that processing is not in batch mode.

7. Which of the following statements most accurately describes the impact that automation has on the controls normally present in a manual system?

A. Transaction trails are more extensive in a computer-based system than in a manual system because a one-for-one correspondence always exists between data entry and output.

B. Responsibility for custody of information assets is more concentrated in user departments in a computer-based system than it is in a manual system.

C. Controls must be more explicit in a computer-based system because many processing points that present opportunities for human judgment in a manual system are eliminated.

D. The quality of documentation becomes less critical in a computer-based system than it is in a manual system because data records are stored in machine-readable files.

Answer (C) is correct.

REQUIRED: The impact that automation has on the controls normally present in a manual system.

DISCUSSION: Using a computer does not change the basic concepts and objectives of control. However, the use of computers may modify the control techniques used. The processing of transactions may be combined with control activities previously performed separately, or control functions may be combined within the information system activity.

Answer (A) is incorrect. The audit trail is less extensive in an information system. Combining processing and controls within the system reduces documentary evidence. Answer (B) is incorrect. Information assets are more likely to be under the control of the information system function. Answer (D) is incorrect. Documentation is more important in an information system. Information is more likely to be stored in machine-readable form than in hard copy.

8. Which of the following is a key difference in controls when changing from a manual system to a computer system?

A. Internal control principles change.

B. Internal control objectives differ.

C. Control objectives are more difficult to achieve.

D. Methodologies for implementing controls change.

Answer (D) is correct.
REQUIRED: The key difference in controls when changing from a manual system to a computer system.
DISCUSSION: The controls in a manual and in a computerized system are geared toward the same control objectives. Only the design and implementation are different.
Answer (A) is incorrect. Sound internal control principles apply to both manual and computerized systems. Though they differ in design and implementation, the controls are geared toward the same objectives. Answer (B) is incorrect. Though they differ in design and implementation, the controls in a manual and in a computerized system are geared toward the same objectives. Answer (C) is incorrect. Achieving internal control objectives can be quite challenging in a manual environment.

9. Which of the following statements is **inconsistent** with the key principles of the COBIT 5 framework?

A. Enterprise governance and management are treated as the same activity.

B. The needs of stakeholders are the focus of all organizational activities.

C. Information technology controls are considered to be intertwined with those of the organization's everyday operations.

D. COBIT 5 can be applied even when other IT-related standards have been adopted.

Answer (A) is correct.
REQUIRED: The statement inconsistent with the key principles of the COBIT 5 framework.
DISCUSSION: Under the COBIT 5 framework, the complexity of the modern enterprise requires governance and management to be treated as distinct activities.
Answer (B) is incorrect. COBIT 5 asserts that the creation of stakeholder value is the fundamental goal of any enterprise. Answer (C) is incorrect. COBIT 5 takes a comprehensive view of all of the enterprise's functions and processes. Information technology pervades them all; it cannot be viewed as a function distinct from other enterprise activities. Answer (D) is incorrect. In acknowledgment of the availability of multiple IT-related standards and best practices, COBIT 5 provides an overall framework for enterprise IT within which other standards can be applied.

10. Which of the following statements is true concerning the COBIT 5 framework?

A. Governance and management are synonyms for the activities of upper management.

B. Information technology controls are most effectively designed and executed in isolation from other business processes.

C. Minimization of risk and resource use are among the major goals of COBIT 5.

D. Information and organizational structures are among the enablers identified in COBIT 5.

Answer (D) is correct.
REQUIRED: The true statement regarding the COBIT 5 framework.
DISCUSSION: COBIT 5 describes seven categories of enablers that support comprehensive IT governance and management, among them information and organizational structures.
Answer (A) is incorrect. Under the COBIT 5 framework, the complexity of the modern enterprise requires governance and management to be treated as distinct activities. Answer (B) is incorrect. COBIT 5 takes a comprehensive view of all of the enterprise's functions and processes. Information technology pervades them all; it cannot be viewed as a function distinct from other enterprise activities. Answer (C) is incorrect. COBIT 5 asserts that the creation of stakeholder value is the fundamental goal of any enterprise. Value creation is achieved by balancing the realization of benefits with the optimization (note that it is not minimization) of risk and the use of resources.

11. Which of the following is a computer program that appears to be legitimate but performs some illicit activity when it is run?

A. Hoax virus.

B. Web crawler.

C. Trojan horse.

D. Killer application.

Answer (C) is correct.
REQUIRED: The apparently legitimate computer program that performs an illicit activity.
DISCUSSION: A Trojan horse is a computer program that appears friendly, for example, a game, but that actually contains an application destructive to the computer system.
Answer (A) is incorrect. A hoax virus is a false notice about the existence of a computer virus. Answer (B) is incorrect. A web crawler (a spider or bot) is a computer program created to access and read information on websites. The results are included as entries in the index of a search engine. Answer (D) is incorrect. A killer application is one that is so useful that it may justify widespread adoption of a new technology.

14.2 Information Security

12. Review of the audit log is an example of which of the following types of security control?

- A. Governance.
- B. Detective.
- C. Preventive.
- D. Corrective.

Answer (B) is correct.
REQUIRED: The type of security control a review of the audit log is an example of.
DISCUSSION: Detective controls call attention to errors that have already entered the system before an error causes a negative outcome. A review of the audit log would show errors entered into the system and would hopefully catch the error before it causes a negative outcome.
Answer (A) is incorrect. Governance controls include ensuring the firm adheres to corporate policy and procedure. Answer (C) is incorrect. Preventive controls prevent errors from entering the system. Answer (D) is incorrect. Corrective controls correct errors after they have been detected.

13. Which of the following is a true statement regarding security over an entity's IT?

- A. Controls should exist to ensure that users have access to and can update only the data elements that they have been authorized to access.
- B. Controls over data sharing by diverse users within an entity should be the same for every user.
- C. The employee who manages the computer hardware should also develop and debug the computer programs.
- D. Controls can provide assurance that all processed transactions are authorized but cannot verify that all authorized transactions are processed.

Answer (A) is correct.
REQUIRED: The true statement regarding security over an entity's IT.
DISCUSSION: Authorization is the practice of ensuring that, once in a particular system, a user can only access those programs and data elements necessary for his/her job duties.
Answer (B) is incorrect. Certain data should not be accessed by all individuals, and those who do have access may have different levels of authority. Thus, the controls should vary among users regardless of whether the environment includes a database. Answer (C) is incorrect. These duties should be segregated. Answer (D) is incorrect. Controls can play multiple roles in a database or nondatabase environment by comparing authorized transactions with processed transactions and reporting anomalies.

14. Controls in the information technology area are classified into the preventive, detective, and corrective categories. Which of the following is a preventive control?

- A. Contingency planning.
- B. Hash total.
- C. Echo check.
- D. Access control software.

Answer (D) is correct.
REQUIRED: The preventive control.
DISCUSSION: Access control software prevents entry into a system by unauthorized personnel and prevents access by authorized personnel to data elements that are unnecessary to the performance of their job duties.
Answer (A) is incorrect. Contingency planning is a corrective control. Answer (B) is incorrect. A hash total is a detective control. Answer (C) is incorrect. An echo check is a detective control.

15. An organization relied heavily on e-commerce for its transactions. Evidence of the organization's security awareness manual would be an example of which of the following types of controls?

- A. Preventive.
- B. Detective.
- C. Corrective.
- D. Compliance.

Answer (A) is correct.
REQUIRED: The control evidenced by a security awareness manual.
DISCUSSION: Preventive controls are measures taken in advance so that anticipated problems associated with performance of an activity will not occur. Creating a security awareness manual involves anticipating problems.
Answer (B) is incorrect. Detective controls are not applied in advance. They provide post-performance feedback about whether deviations from standards have occurred. Answer (C) is incorrect. Corrective controls are not applied in advance. They solve problems identified by detective controls. Answer (D) is incorrect. Compliance relates to abiding by laws, regulations, contracts, etc.

16. Which of the following statements best characterizes the function of a physical access control?

A. Protects systems from the transmission of Trojan horses.

B. Provides authentication of users attempting to log into the system.

C. Separates unauthorized individuals from computer resources.

D. Minimizes the risk of incurring a power or hardware failure.

Answer (C) is correct.
REQUIRED: The function of a physical access control.
DISCUSSION: Physical security controls limit physical access and protect against environmental risks and natural catastrophes, such as fire and flood. For example, keypad devices and magnetic card readers can be used to deny unauthorized persons access to the computer center.
Answer (A) is incorrect. An organization-wide network security policy that includes protections against viruses and other malicious software protects systems from the transmission of Trojan horses. Physical access control does not. Answer (B) is incorrect. Logical security control (e.g., passwords and ID numbers) provides authentication of users attempting to log into the system. Answer (D) is incorrect. A disaster recovery and business continuity plan minimizes the risk of incurring a power or hardware failure. For example, it may provide for fully protected or fault-tolerant systems.

17. An auditor was examining a client's network and discovered that the users did not have any password protection. Which of the following would be the best example of the type of network password the users should have?

A. trjunpqs.

B. 34787761.

C. tr34ju78.

D. tR34ju78.

Answer (D) is correct.
REQUIRED: The best network password.
DISCUSSION: The password tR34ju78 should be effective because it has at least eight characters consisting of random uppercase and lowercase letters and numbers. Furthermore, it does not contain words or phrases.
Answer (A) is incorrect. The password trjunpqs does not contain random uppercase and lowercase letters or numbers. Answer (B) is incorrect. The password 34787761 does not contain any letters. Answer (C) is incorrect. The password tr34ju78 does not contain both random uppercase and lowercase letters.

18. Authentication is the process by which the

A. System verifies that the user is entitled to enter the transaction requested.

B. System verifies the identity of the user.

C. User identifies him/herself to the system.

D. User indicates to the system that the transaction was processed correctly.

Answer (B) is correct.
REQUIRED: The definition of authentication.
DISCUSSION: Identification is the process of uniquely distinguishing one user from all others. Authentication is the process of determining that individuals are who they say they are. For example, a password may identify but not authenticate its user if it is known by more than one individual.
Answer (A) is incorrect. Authentication involves verifying the identity of the user. This process does not necessarily confirm the functions the user is authorized to perform. Answer (C) is incorrect. User identification to the system does not imply that the system has verified the identity of the user. Answer (D) is incorrect. This procedure is an application control for accuracy of the transaction.

19. Which of the following activities would most likely detect computer-related fraud?

A. Using data encryption.

B. Performing validity checks.

C. Conducting fraud-awareness training.

D. Reviewing the systems-access log.

Answer (D) is correct.
REQUIRED: The activity most likely to detect computer fraud.
DISCUSSION: A system access log records all attempts to access the system. The date and time, codes used, mode of access, data involved, and interventions by operators are recorded. Thus, reviewing the systems-access log may detect improper access related to fraud.
Answer (A) is incorrect. Encryption is a preventive control that codes information before transmission so that it cannot be read by someone who does not have the key. Answer (B) is incorrect. Performing validity checks is a preventive control. These checks test whether transaction codes or identification numbers are authorized. Answer (C) is incorrect. Conducting fraud-awareness training is a preventive control.

14.3 Application Controls

20. Which of the following is a validity check?

A. The computer ensures that a numerical amount in a record does not exceed some predetermined amount.

B. As the computer corrects errors and data are successfully resubmitted to the system, the causes of the errors are printed out.

C. The computer flags any transmission for which the control field value did not match that of an existing file record.

D. After data are entered, the computer sends certain data back to the terminal for comparison with data originally sent.

Answer (C) is correct.
REQUIRED: The validity check.
DISCUSSION: Validity checks test identification numbers or transaction codes for validity by comparison with items already known to be correct or authorized. For example, a validity check may identify a transmission for which the control field value did not match a pre-existing record in a file.
Answer (A) is incorrect. A limit check determines whether a numerical amount exceeds a predetermined amount. Answer (B) is incorrect. An error log or error listing identifies errors that were previously detected and subsequently corrected. Answer (D) is incorrect. This action describes an older technology referred to as closed-loop verification.

21. A customer's order was never filled because an order entry clerk transposed the customer identification number while entering the sales transaction into the system. Which of the following controls would most likely have detected the transposition?

A. Sequence test.

B. Completeness test.

C. Validity check.

D. Limit test.

Answer (C) is correct.
REQUIRED: The control that would most likely have detected the transposition.
DISCUSSION: Validity checks are tests of identification numbers or transaction codes for validity by comparison with items already known to be correct or authorized.
Answer (A) is incorrect. Sequence tests determine whether records are in proper order. Answer (B) is incorrect. Completeness checks of transmission of data determine whether all necessary information has been sent. Answer (D) is incorrect. Limit tests are based on known limits for given information. For example, hours worked per week cannot exceed 168.

22. Which one of the following input validation routines is **not** likely to be appropriate in a real-time operation?

A. Sign check.

B. Reasonableness check.

C. Sequence check.

D. Field check.

Answer (C) is correct.
REQUIRED: The input validation routine not appropriate in a real-time operation.
DISCUSSION: A sequence check tests to determine that records are in proper order. For example, a payroll input file can be sorted into Social Security number order. A sequence check can then be performed to verify record order. This control would not apply in a real-time operation because records are not processed sequentially.
Answer (A) is incorrect. Sign checks test data for the appropriate arithmetic sign. For instance, hours worked in a payroll should always be a positive number. Answer (B) is incorrect. Reasonableness tests verify that amounts fall within predetermined limits. Answer (D) is incorrect. A field check tests a data item to determine if it has the expected type of characters; for example, a name field should have all alphabetic characters.

23. A customer intended to order 100 units of product Z96014 but incorrectly ordered nonexistent product Z96015. Which of the following controls most likely would detect this error?

A. Check digit verification.

B. Record count.

C. Hash total.

D. Redundant data check.

Answer (A) is correct.
REQUIRED: The control that would detect a nonexistent product number.
DISCUSSION: Check digit verification is used to identify incorrect identification numbers. The digit is generated by applying an algorithm to the ID number. During input, the check digit is recomputed by applying the same algorithm to the entered ID number.
Answer (B) is incorrect. A record count is a control total of the number of transactions in a batch. Answer (C) is incorrect. A hash total is a control total that is the sum of a field without a defined meaning. Answer (D) is incorrect. A redundant data check searches for duplicate information in a database.

24. Able Co. uses an online sales order processing system to process its sales transactions. Able's sales data are electronically sorted and subjected to edit checks. A direct output of the edit checks most likely would be a

A. Report of all missing sales invoices.

B. File of all rejected sales transactions.

C. Printout of all user code numbers and passwords.

D. List of all voided shipping documents.

Answer (B) is correct.

REQUIRED: The output of edit checks.

DISCUSSION: Edit checks are applied to transactions to test for completeness, reasonableness, validity, and other related issues prior to acceptance. Rejected transactions should be recorded in a file for evaluation, correction, and resubmission.

25. Which of the following input controls would prevent an incorrect state abbreviation from being accepted as legitimate data?

A. Reasonableness test.

B. Field check.

C. Digit verification check.

D. Validity check.

Answer (D) is correct.

REQUIRED: The input control that will detect an incorrect abbreviation.

DISCUSSION: Validity checks are tests of identification numbers or transaction codes for validity by comparison with items already known to be correct or authorized.

Answer (A) is incorrect. Reasonableness (relationship) checks consider the logical correctness of relationships among the values of data items on an input and the corresponding master file record. For example, it may be known that employee John Smith works only in departments A, C, or D. Thus, a reasonableness check could be performed to determine that the payroll record contains one of the likely department numbers. Answer (B) is incorrect. Field checks are tests of the characters in a field to verify that they are of an appropriate type for that field. For example, the field for a Social Security number cannot contain alphabetic characters. Answer (C) is incorrect. Check digit verification is used to identify incorrect identification numbers. The digit is generated by applying an algorithm to the ID number.

14.4 Disaster Recovery and Business Continuity

26. Which of the following procedures should be included in the disaster recovery plan for an Information Technology department?

A. Replacement of personal computers for user departments.

B. Identification of critical applications.

C. Physical security of warehouse facilities.

D. Cross-training of operating personnel.

Answer (B) is correct.

REQUIRED: The disaster recovery procedure.

DISCUSSION: The first step in preparing a business continuity/disaster recovery plan is to identify and prioritize the entity's critical applications.

Answer (A) is incorrect. Replacement of personal computers is a procedure for upgrading computers, not disaster recovery. Answer (C) is incorrect. Physical security may prevent a disaster but is not a specific recovery procedure. Answer (D) is incorrect. Cross-training of operating personnel is not a specific recovery procedure.

27. In which of the following locations should a copy of the accounting system data backup of year-end information be stored?

A. Secure off-site location.

B. Data backup server in the network room.

C. Fireproof cabinet in the data network room.

D. Locked file cabinet in the accounting department.

Answer (A) is correct.

REQUIRED: The storage location of a copy of the accounting system data backup of year-end information.

DISCUSSION: The IT function should have a business continuity/disaster recovery plan that will allow it to resume normal processing in the event of a disaster. The plan should include the creation of backup (duplicate) copies of data files, databases, programs, and documentation. It should also mandate storage of backup copies off-site and plan for auxiliary processing at another site.

28. Which of the following best describes the primary reason that organizations develop contingency plans for their computer-based information systems operations?

A. To ensure that they will be able to process vital transactions in the event of a disaster.

B. To ensure the safety of important records.

C. To help hold down the cost of insurance.

D. To plan for sources of capital for recovery from any type of disaster.

Answer (A) is correct.
    REQUIRED: The primary reason that organizations develop contingency plans for their IS operations.
    DISCUSSION: Contingency plans must be drafted so that the organization will be able to resume normal processing following a disaster.
    Answer (B) is incorrect. The safety of records is a secondary reason. Answer (C) is incorrect. The reduction of insurance costs is a secondary reason. Answer (D) is incorrect. Planning for sources of capital is seldom included in disaster recovery planning.

29. Which of the following best describes a hot site?

A. Location within the company that is most vulnerable to a disaster.

B. Location where a company can install data processing equipment on short notice.

C. Location that is equipped with a redundant hardware and software configuration.

D. Location that is considered too close to a potential disaster area.

Answer (C) is correct.
    REQUIRED: The best description of a hot site.
    DISCUSSION: A hot site is a fully operational processing facility that is immediately available.
    Answer (A) is incorrect. The hot site must be located where the company is least vulnerable to disaster. Answer (B) is incorrect. A location where a company can install data processing equipment on short notice is the definition of a cold site. Answer (D) is incorrect. A location deemed too close to a potential disaster area cannot be designated a hot site.

30. Which of the following procedures would an entity most likely include in its computer disaster recovery plan?

A. Develop an auxiliary power supply to provide uninterrupted electricity.

B. Store duplicate copies of critical files in a location away from the processing facility.

C. Maintain a listing of all entity passwords with the network manager.

D. Translate data for storage purposes with a cryptographic secret code.

Answer (B) is correct.
    REQUIRED: The most likely procedure to follow in a computer disaster recovery plan.
    DISCUSSION: Off-site storage of duplicate copies of critical files protects them from a fire or other disaster at the computing facility. The procedure is part of an overall disaster recovery plan.
    Answer (A) is incorrect. The use of an uninterruptible power supply ensures continued processing rather than recovery from a disaster. Answer (C) is incorrect. Maintaining a safeguarded copy of passwords protects against loss of passwords by personnel. Answer (D) is incorrect. Encrypting stored data files protects them from unauthorized use.

Use the additional questions in Gleim **CPA Test Prep Online** to create Test Sessions that emulate Prometric!

14.5 PRACTICE WRITTEN COMMUNICATION TASK

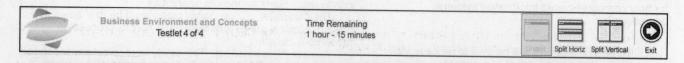

| | | Business Environment and Concepts
Testlet 4 of 4 | Time Remaining
1 hour - 15 minutes | | | | |

Unsplit   Split Horiz   Split Vertical   Exit

DIRECTIONS

Note: If you believe you have encountered a software malfunction, report it to the test center staff immediately.

Navigation

To navigate from task to task, use the controls at the bottom of the screen. Click on the **Next** button to advance to the next task, or the **Previous** button to go to the previous task. To go directly to any task, click on its number.

▼ = Reminder   Directions | 1 | 2 | 3 | 4 | 5 | 6 | 7 | ◀ Previous   Next ▶

If you would like a reminder to revisit a task, or want to indicate that you are finished with it, click on the reminder flag below the task number. To clear the flag, click on it again. Reminder flags are for your use only – they do not contribute to your score.

Tabs

In this part of the examination, you will be asked to complete various tasks. Every task has one or more **Work Tabs**. Every task also has a **Help** tab.

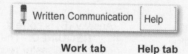

Written Communication   Help

Work tab   **Help tab**

Work Tabs:

- **Work Tabs** are identified with a pencil icon. This is where your responses are expected.
- Each task has one or more **Work Tabs**.
- **Work Tabs** contain directions for completing the task - be sure to read these directions carefully.
- The **Work Tab** name in the example above is for illustration only - yours will differ.
- You must complete all of the **Work Tabs** in each task to receive full credit.

Help Tab:

- The **Help Tab** provides assistance with the exam software that is used in this task. For example, if the task is to compose a memorandum, **Help** will provide information about the word processor.

The Toolbar

The toolbar at the top of the screen shows the amount of time remaining for you to complete the tasks. In addition, the following tools are available. Note that only the **Exit** button is displayed when Directions are visible - the others will appear when you begin the tasks.

Unsplit   Split Horiz   Split Vertical

Click on these buttons to split or unsplit the screen. You can split the screen vertically or horizontally.

Exit

Click on this button to go on to the next part of the examination. You must complete all of the tasks to receive full credit. Once you click on **Exit** and confirm the action, you will NOT be able to return to this testlet.

▼ = Reminder   Directions | 1 | ◀ Previous   Next ▶

Written Communication | Help

✂ Cut | 🖿 Copy | 🖿 Paste | ↶ Undo | ↷ Redo

During your review of the information systems of Cornweed Corporation, the CEO said, "We have the best system. There are no risks with our technologically advanced system."

Prepare a memo to the CEO of Cornweed about how risks are inherent in all business information systems.

Type your communication below the line in the response area below.

REMINDER: Your response will be graded for both technical content and writing skills. Technical content will be evaluated for information that is helpful to the intended reader and clearly relevant to the issue. Writing skills will be evaluated for development, organization, and the appropriate expression of ideas in professional correspondence. Use a standard business memorandum or letter format with a clear beginning, middle, and end. Do not convey information in the form of a table, bullet point list, or other abbreviated presentation.

To: CEO, Cornweed Corporation
Re: Risks inherent in all business information systems

Unofficial Answer

Written Communication

To: CEO, Cornweed Corporation
Re: Risks inherent in all business information systems

Although the goals of a business information system do not change between manual and computer-based systems, the risks certainly do. A highly automated electronic system may appear to be faultless at first glance, but certain risks are inherent and need to be considered whenever one is implementing a computer-based information system.

First, it cannot be taken for granted that there are no physical risks associated with an electronic system. Power sources can be compromised, computer hardware can be damaged by fire or flood, and communications channels between devices may fail. Another risk is in data maintenance of "paper trails." Since data may be entered in real-time into a computer system (frequently without a physical output), the ease of information-gathering for audit purposes is hindered significantly. This leads to another risk: the potential for human error. When information systems were manual, the possibility of catching an input error was far easier (as a user was able to see all products of the information input and output); with a computer-based system, routine entries are entered without context, and the risk of error is increased significantly if effective controls are not in place.

Additionally, some risks are associated with the data security itself. If data are kept on only a few hardware components, the data loss could be disastrous should those components become damaged. Also, the threat of unauthorized access needs to be considered; before the electronic transmission of information, it was easier to keep track of the users of paper accounting records. However, with advanced information technology, it is possible to access information from hardware devices almost anywhere, given the appropriate know-how. Finally, there is an issue inherent in the speed of information processing, and it relates to the reality that authorization of individual transactions becomes less and less realistic given an expanding quantity of transactions. System designers will have to ensure proper coding to verify that management goals are being carried out when the possibility of viewing each transaction becomes impossible.

The above depicts a Level 5 answer. See page 16 in the Introduction for a description of the three grading criteria.

Self-Grade

Evaluate each of the following by selecting a 0, 1, 2, 3, 4, or 5. An average response is 3. Use 4 for better than average and 5 for outstanding. Use 2 for less than average and 1 for quite poor. Use zero for no response, if you did not address the topic, or if you gave advice that is clearly illegal.

Organization	o 0	o 1	o 2	o 3	o 4	o 5
Development	o 0	o 1	o 2	o 3	o 4	o 5
Expression	o 0	o 1	o 2	o 3	o 4	o 5

Your grade for the written communication as a whole is the average of the scores for the three criteria.

Use **CPA Gleim Online** and **Simulation Wizard** to practice more written communication tasks in a realistic environment.

STUDY UNIT FIFTEEN
STRATEGIC PLANNING AND BUDGETING CONCEPTS

(16 pages of outline)

All organizations have a mission, that is, a reason for existing. Likewise, all organizations must have a plan for achieving that mission. Planning and managing progress toward the objectives stated in the resulting plans are the essence of strategic management (Subunits 1 and 2).

Corporate objectives must be stated in concretely measurable terms. Thus, budgets are an essential part of any strategic plan. Budgeting has many purposes in the organization (one of which is motivating managers and employees), and a successful budgeting process requires careful planning. The appropriate budgeting method for an organization depends upon that organization's situation (Subunits 3 and 4).

15.1 STRATEGIC MANAGEMENT

1. **Strategic Management**

   a. Strategic management sets overall objectives for an entity and guides the process of reaching those objectives. It is the responsibility of upper management.

      1) Strategic planning is the design and implementation of the specific steps and processes necessary to reach the overall objectives.

   b. Strategic management and strategic planning are thus closely linked. By their nature, strategic management and strategic planning have a long-term planning horizon.

2. **Steps in the Strategic Management Process**

   a. Strategic management is a five-stage process:

      1) The board of directors drafts the organization's mission statement.
      2) The organization performs a situational analysis, also called a SWOT analysis.
      3) Based on the results of the situational analysis, upper management develops a group of strategies describing how the mission will be achieved.
      4) Strategic plans are implemented through the execution of component plans at each level of the entity.
      5) Strategic controls and feedback are used to monitor progress, isolate problems, and take corrective action. Over the long term, feedback is the basis for adjusting the original mission and objectives.

Strategic Management

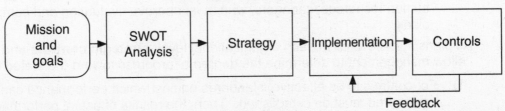

Figure 15-1

b. The **mission statement** summarizes the entity's reason for existing. It provides the framework for formulation of the company's strategies.

   1) Missions tend to be most effective when they consist of a single sentence.

      a) For example, the mission of Starbucks Coffee Company is "to inspire and nurture the human spirit – one person, one cup and one neighborhood at a time."

   2) Missions tend to be stated in general terms. Setting specific objectives in the mission statement can limit an entity's ability to respond to a changing marketplace.

c. The **situational analysis** is most often called a SWOT analysis because it identifies the entity's strengths, weaknesses, opportunities, and threats.

   1) **Strengths and weaknesses** are usually identified by considering the entity's capabilities and resources (its internal environment).

      a) What the entity does particularly well or has in greater abundance are its core competencies. But many entities may have the same core competencies (cutting-edge IT, efficient distribution, etc.).

      b) An entity gains a competitive advantage in the marketplace by developing one or more distinctive competencies, i.e., competencies that are unlike those of its competitors.

   2) **Opportunities and threats** exist in the entity's external environment. They are identified by considering

      a) Macroenvironment factors (economic, demographic, political, legal, social, cultural, and technical) and

      b) Microenvironment factors (suppliers, customers, distributors, competitors, and other competitive factors in the industry).

d. Based on the results of the situational analysis, upper management develops a **group of strategies** describing how the mission will be achieved. The strategies answer such questions as

   1) "Which lines of business will we be in?"
   2) "How do we penetrate and compete in the international marketplace?"
   3) "How will this line of business reach its objectives that contribute to achievement of the overall entity's mission?"
   4) "How do we perform each strategic business unit's basic processes (materials handling, assembly, shipping, human resources, customer relations, etc.) as efficiently as possible?"

e. **Implementing** the chosen strategies involves every employee at every level of the entity. Incentive systems and employee performance evaluations must be designed so that they encourage employees to focus their efforts on achieving the entity's objectives.

   1) This approach requires communication among senior managers, who devise strategies; middle managers, who supervise and evaluate employees; and human resources managers, who must approve evaluation and compensation plans.

f. As plans are executed at each organizational level, **strategic controls and feedback** allow management to determine the degree of progress toward the stated objectives.

   1) For controls to be effective, standards against which performance can be measured must be established. Then, the results of actual performance must be measured against the standards and reported to the appropriate managers. If performance is unsatisfactory, managers take corrective action.

2) Results are sent to higher-level management for continual refinement of the strategies.

3. **Porter's Five Competitive Forces**

a. Business theorist Michael E. Porter has developed a model of the structure of industries and competition. It includes an analysis of the five competitive forces that determine long-term profitability as measured by long-term return on investment.

1) This analysis includes an evaluation of the basic economic and technical characteristics that determine the strength of each force and the attractiveness of the industry. The competitive forces are depicted in the following diagram and discussed in detail below and on the following pages:

Porter's Five Competitive Forces

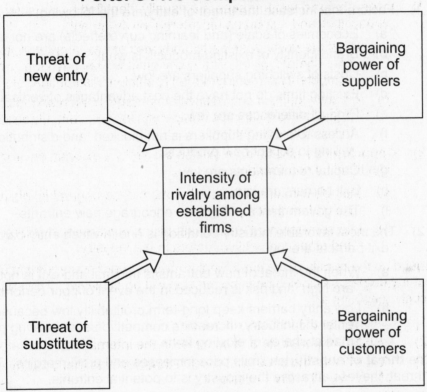

Figure 15-2

b. **Rivalry among existing firms** will be intense when an industry contains many strong competitors. Price-cutting, large advertising budgets, and frequent introduction of new products are typical. The intensity of rivalry and the threat of entry vary with the following factors:

1) The stage of the industry life cycle, e.g., rapid growth, growth, maturity, decline, or rapid decline.

a) Thus, growth is preferable to decline. In a declining or even a stable industry, a firm's growth must come from winning other firms' customers, thereby strengthening competition.

2) The distinctions among products (product differentiation) and the costs of switching from one competitor's product to another.

a) Less differentiation tends to heighten competition based on price, with price cutting leading to lower profits. But high costs of switching suppliers weaken competition.

        3)   Whether fixed costs are high in relation to variable costs.

              a)   High fixed costs indicate that rivalry will be intense. The greater the cost to generate a given amount of sales revenues, the greater the investment intensity and the need to operate at or near capacity. Hence, price cutting to sustain demand is typical.

        4)   Capacity expansion.

              a)   If the size of the expansion must be large to achieve economies of scale, competition will be more intense. The need for large-scale expansion to achieve production efficiency may result in an excess of industry capacity over demand.

  c.   The prospects of long-term profitability depend on the industry's **barriers to entry**.

        1)   Factors that increase the threat of entry are the following:

              a)   Economies of scale (and learning curve effects) are not significant.

              b)   Brand identity of existing products is weak.

              c)   Costs of switching suppliers are low.

              d)   Existing firms do not have the cost advantages of vertical integration.

              e)   Product differences are few.

              f)   Access to existing suppliers is not blocked, and distribution channels are willing to accept new products.

              g)   Capital requirements are low.

              h)   Exit barriers are low.

              i)   The government's policy is to encourage new entrants.

        2)   The most favorable industry condition is one in which entry barriers are high and exit barriers are low.

              a)   When the threat of new entrants is minimal and exit is not difficult, returns are high, and risk is reduced in the event of poor performance.

              b)   Low entry barriers keep long-term profitability low because new firms can enter the industry, increasing competition and lowering prices and the market shares of existing firms.

  d.   The **threat of substitutes** limits price increases and profit margins. The greater the threat, the less attractive the industry is to potential entrants.

        1)   Substitutes are types (not brands) of goods and services that have the same purposes, for example, plastic and metal or minivans and SUVs. Hence, a change in the price of one such product (service) causes a change in the demand for its substitutes.

        2)   Structural considerations affecting the threat of substitutes are

              a)   Relative prices,

              b)   Costs of switching to a substitute, and

              c)   Customers' inclination to use a substitute.

  e.   As the **threat of buyers' bargaining power** increases, the appeal of an industry to potential entrants decreases. Buyers seek lower prices, better quality, and more services. Moreover, they use their purchasing power to obtain better terms, possibly through a bidding process. Thus, buyers affect competition.

        1)   Buyers' bargaining power varies with the following factors:

              a)   When purchasing power is concentrated in a few buyers or when buyers are well organized, their bargaining power is greater. This effect is reinforced when sellers are in a capital-intensive industry.

b) High (low) switching costs decrease (increase) buyers' bargaining power.

c) The threat of backward (upstream) vertical integration, that is, the acquisition of a supply capacity, increases buyers' bargaining power.

d) Buyers are most likely to bargain aggressively when their profit margins are low and a supplier's product accounts for a substantial amount of their costs.

e) Buyers are in a stronger position when the supplier's product is undifferentiated.

f) The more important the supplier's product is to buyers, the less bargaining power they have.

f. As the **threat of suppliers' bargaining power** increases, the appeal of an industry to potential entrants decreases. Accordingly, suppliers affect competition through pricing and the manipulation of the quantity supplied.

1) Suppliers' bargaining power is greater when

a) Switching costs are substantial.

b) Prices of substitutes are high.

c) They can threaten forward (downstream) vertical integration.

d) They provide something that is a significant input to the value added by the buyer.

e) Their industry is concentrated, or they are organized.

2) Buyers' best responses are to develop favorable, mutually beneficial relationships with suppliers or to diversify their sources of supply.

4. **Generic Competitive Strategies Model**

a. Strategies with a Broad Competitive Scope

1) **Cost leadership** is the generic strategy of entities that seek competitive advantage through lower costs and that have a broad competitive scope.

2) **Differentiation** is the generic strategy of entities that seek competitive advantage through providing a unique product and that have a broad competitive scope.

b. Strategies with a Narrow Competitive Scope

1) **Cost focus** is the generic strategy of entities that seek competitive advantage through lower costs and that have a narrow competitive scope (a regional or smaller market).

2) **Focused differentiation** is the generic strategy of entities that seek competitive advantage through providing a unique product and that have a narrow competitive scope (a regional or smaller market).

Competitive Advantage

Competitive Scope	Low Cost	Product Uniqueness
Broad (Industry wide)	Cost Leadership Strategy	Differentiation Strategy
Narrow (Market segment)	Focused Strategy: Cost	Focused Strategy: Differentiation

Figure 15-3

5. **Five Operations Strategies**

    a. A **cost strategy** is successful when the entity is the low-cost producer. However, the product (e.g., a commodity) tends to be undifferentiated in these cases, the market is often very large, and the competition tends to be intense because of the possibility of high-volume sales.

    b. A **quality strategy** involves competition based on product quality or process quality. Product quality relates to design, for example, the difference between a luxury car and a subcompact. Process quality concerns the degree of freedom from defects.

    c. A **delivery strategy** may permit an entity to charge a higher price when the product is consistently delivered rapidly and on time. An example company is UPS.

    d. A **flexibility strategy** involves offering many different products. This strategy also may reflect an ability to shift rapidly from one product line to another. An example company is a publisher that can write, edit, print, and distribute a book within days to exploit the public's short-term interest in a sensational event.

    e. A **service strategy** seeks to gain a competitive advantage and maximize customer value by providing services, especially post-purchase services such as warranties on automobiles and home appliances.

6. **Strategies for Product Life Cycle Stages**

    a. The strategy in the **precommercialization** (product development) stage is to innovate by conducting R&D, marketing research, and production tests. During product development, the entity has no sales, but it has high investment costs.

    b. The **introduction stage** is characterized by slow sales growth and lack of profits because of the high expenses of promotion and selective distribution to generate awareness of the product and encourage customers to try it. Thus, the per-customer cost is high.

        1) Competitors are few, basic versions of the product are produced, and higher-income customers (innovators) are usually targeted. Cost-plus prices are charged. They may initially be high to permit cost recovery when unit sales are low.

        2) The strategy is to infiltrate the market, plan for financing to cope with losses, build supplier relations, increase production and marketing efforts, and plan for competition.

    c. In the **growth stage**, sales and profits increase rapidly, cost per customer decreases, customers are early adopters, new competitors enter an expanding market, new product models and features are introduced, and promotion spending declines or remains stable.

        1) The entity enters new market segments and distribution channels and attempts to build brand loyalty and achieve the maximum share of the market. Thus, prices are set to penetrate the market, distribution channels are extended, and the mass market is targeted through advertising.

        2) The strategy is to advance by these means and by achieving economies of productive scale.

    d. In the **maturity stage**, sales peak but growth declines, competitors are most numerous but may begin to decline in number, and per-customer cost is low.

        1) Profits are high for large market-share entities. For others, profits may fall because of competitive price-cutting and increased R&D spending to develop improved versions of the product.

        2) The strategy is to defend market share and maximize profits through diversification of brands and models to enter new market segments; still more intensive distribution, cost cutting, advertising and promotions to encourage brand switching; and emphasizing customer service.

e.   During the **decline stage**, sales and profits drop as prices are cut, and some entities leave the market. Customers include late adopters (laggards), and per-customer cost is low.

1)   Weak products and unprofitable distribution media are eliminated, and advertising budgets are pared to the level needed to retain the most loyal customers. The strategy is to withdraw by reducing production, promotion, and inventory.

f.   **Graphical Depiction**

Product Life Cycle

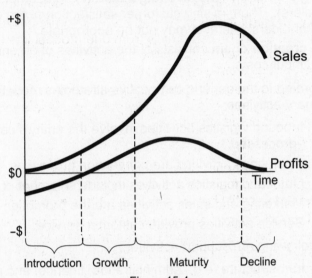

Figure 15-4

7.   **Customer Value and Satisfaction as Strategic Issues**

a.   A market analysis must identify potential customers and determine their needs. A marketer responds to customer needs by stating a **value proposition**, that is, the benefits offered to satisfy those needs. The value proposition is an attempt to affect customer wants (needs focused on particular satisfiers). It becomes tangible in an offering, which may consist of products, services, and other things that are intended to satisfy the needs of target buyers.

1)   Value is a combination of the elements of the **customer value triad**: quality, service, and price. Value increases as quality and service increase and price decreases.

b.   **Customer satisfaction** is the relation between the offering's perceived performance and the customer's expectations. High customer satisfaction tends to create high customer loyalty that results in repurchases. However, at lower satisfaction levels, customers are more likely to switch when a superior alternative becomes available.

1)   Expectations are a function of a customer's experience, marketing information, and other factors. Marketers should not raise expectations above the level at which they can be satisfied. However, some superior entities have had great success by adopting a total customer satisfaction approach, that is, by elevating expectations and then satisfying them.

2)   **High customer loyalty** is an emotional as well as rational bond that develops when an entity provides high customer value. To obtain such loyalty, the entity needs to develop a value proposition that has superior competitiveness in the target market segment. Crucially, it must be supported by an effective value delivery system, the accumulation of all the experiences the customer has with the offering. Thus, brand value must be supported by core business processes that actually deliver the promised customer value.

3) Customer satisfaction information is gathered by

    a) Complaint and suggestion systems, such as websites and hotlines

    b) Customer surveys

    c) Lost customer analysis (e.g., exit interviews and determination of the customer loss rate)

    d) Testing of the treatment customers receive when purchasing the entity's (or competitors') products (ghost shopping)

4) Customer satisfaction must be balanced against the satisfaction level of the entity's other stakeholders (e.g., shareholders, employees, suppliers, and retailers). Thus, raising customer satisfaction at the expense of profit or other stakeholders' interests may not be appropriate.

c. The **value creation chain** consists of the activities of an entity that create customer value and incur costs.

1) According to the generic competitive strategies model, the following are the primary activities:

    a) Inbound logistics activities involve the entity's capture of materials to be processed.

    b) Operations activities are conversion processes.

    c) Outbound logistics activities include shipment of products.

    d) Marketing and sales activities are the promotion and sale of final products.

    e) Service activities provide customer service.

2) The following are support activities:

    a) Infrastructure (e.g., administration, finance, and planning),

    b) Procurement,

    c) Human resources, and

    d) Technology development.

d. To sustain customer value, the entity must seek continuous improvement of value-creating activities. **Benchmarking** the best performance attributes of top entities and adopting their best practices is a key continuous improvement technique.

e. Effective coordination of the following core business processes is crucial:

1) Market sensing consists of obtaining, distributing, and acting upon market intelligence.

2) New offering realization should be timely and efficient. It involves R&D and the launch of products, services, and other elements of offerings.

3) Customer acquisition defines target markets and researches customers.

4) Customer relationship management seeks to increase the value of the customer base by developing long-term relationships with individual customers by such methods as customer service, customized (if not personalized) offerings, and choice of marketing messages and media.

5) Fulfillment management relates to order processing, on-time delivery, and collection.

f. The value-delivery network is another source of competitive advantage. Partner relationship management involves coordinating with suppliers and distributors in this network (the supply chain) to provide better customer value.

8. **Customer Relationship Management (CRM)**

a. Customer relationship management can be defined as "the process of managing detailed information about individual customers and carefully managing all the customer 'touchpoints' with the aim of maximizing customer loyalty." Its purpose is to create optimal customer equity. CRM is an attempt to tie together three traditionally separate functions: marketing, sales, and service. It employs large databases and integrated information systems to link the three customer relationship functions.

   1) Marketing seeks out unfulfilled customer needs and customer groups who might be interested in the entity's existing products.

   2) Sales brings the products to the attention of the targeted customers and closes the sale.

   3) Customer service provides after-the-sale support, such as product help and account information.

b. **Customer retention** through customer satisfaction is a key to profitability. Thus, the entity should seek to minimize customer churn (customer loss).

   1) High customer satisfaction means a longer relationship with the entity, repeat purchases of new offerings and upgrades, favorable word-of-mouth, and less concern about price and competitors' offerings.

      a) Moreover, the highly satisfied repeat customer is less costly than a new customer and is more likely to provide helpful feedback.

   2) The listening process plays a major role in customer retention. Accordingly, the entity should measure customer satisfaction frequently, facilitate complaints and suggestions, and act rapidly on the results.

   3) The entity should emphasize customer retention because the customer base is an important intangible asset.

      a) Loss of some customers is unavoidable. For example, a customer may cease operations.

      b) Customer retention is far less costly than customer attraction.

      c) Increasing the retention rate increases profits exponentially.

      d) The longer the customer relationship, the more profitable it is.

c. An entity should estimate **customer lifetime value**, the net present value of the cash flows (purchases – costs of acquiring, selling to, and serving the customer) related to a particular customer.

d. An entity may be able to regain lost customers more cheaply than it could attract new ones using existing information and the results of surveys and exit interviews. An entity must determine the appropriate investment in building customer relationships.

e. Customer profitability analysis determines all revenues and all costs assignable to specific customers. The following classification of customers is possible:

   1) Platinum – most profitable (highest investment)

   2) Gold – profitable (high investment, with objective of converting to platinum)

   3) Iron – low profit but desirable (lower investment with objective of converting to gold)

   4) Lead – not profitable or desirable (drop or provide low investment while raising prices or lowering costs of serving)

Stop and review! You have completed the outline for this subunit. Study multiple-choice questions 1 through 9 beginning on page 413.

15.2 STRATEGIC PLANNING

1. **Planning**

   a. Planning is the determination of what is to be done and of how, when, where, and by whom it is to be done. Plans serve to direct the activities that all organizational members must undertake and successfully perform to move the organization from where it is to where it wants to be (accomplishment of its objectives).

      1) However, no transactions occur during the planning cycle that must be recorded in the general ledger.

   b. Planning must be completed before undertaking any other managerial function.

      1) Forecasting is the basis of planning because it projects the future.

   c. Planning establishes the means to reach organizational ends (objectives).

      1) This means-end relationship extends throughout the organizational hierarchy and ties together the parts of the organization so that the various means all focus on the same end.

      2) One organizational level's ends provide the next higher level's means.

EXAMPLE

Management by objectives (MBO) identifies relationships between an individual's job objectives (ends) and the immediate superior's objectives (ends). Thus, the subordinate can understand how his/her job is the means by which the superior's job is accomplished. This will be discussed in more detail later in this subunit.

---

2. **The Planning Process**

   a. Long-range (strategic) planning includes **strategic budgeting**. It has a horizon of 1 to 10 years or more. Such planning is difficult because of uncertainty about future events and conditions.

      1) Thus, strategic plans tend to be general and exclude operational detail.

      2) An entity must complete its strategic plan before any specific budgeting can begin. The strategic plan states the means by which an entity expects to achieve its stated mission.

   b. Strategic planning embodies the concerns of senior management. It is based on a strategic analysis that includes the following:

      1) Identifying and specifying organizational objectives.

      2) Evaluating the strengths (competitive advantages) and weaknesses of the organization and its competitors.

      3) Assessing risk levels.

      4) Identifying and forecasting the effects of external (environmental) factors relevant to the organization. For example, market trends, changes in technology, international competition, and social change may provide opportunities, impose limitations, or represent threats.

         a) Forecasting is the basis of planning because it projects the future. A variety of quantitative methods are used in forecasting.

      5) Deriving the best strategy for reaching the objectives, given the organization's strengths and weaknesses and the relevant future trends.

      6) Capital budgeting, a planning process for choosing and financing long-term projects and programs.

      7) Capacity planning, an element of planning closely related to capital budgeting that includes, among other things, consideration of business combinations or divestitures.

    c.   Strategic plans are translated into measurable and achievable intermediate and operational plans. Thus, intermediate and operational plans must be consistent with, and contribute to achieving, strategic objectives.

3. **Premises**

    a.   Premises are the underlying assumptions about the expected environment in which the strategic plan will be carried out. Thus, the next step in planning is premising, or the generation of planning assumptions. Premises should be limited to those crucial to the success of the plans.

    b.   Managers should ask, "What internal and external factors would influence the actions planned for this organization (division, department, program)?" Premises must be considered at all levels of the organization.

        1)   Thus, capital budgeting plans should be premised on assumptions (forecasts) about economic cycles, price movements, etc.

        2)   The inventory department's plans might be premised on stability of parts prices or on forecasts that prices will rise.

EXAMPLES

- The general economy will suffer an 11% decline next year.
- Our closest competitor's new model will provide greater competition for potential sales.
- Union negotiations will result in a general wage increase of 8%.
- Over the next 5 years, the cost of our raw materials will increase by 30%.
- The elasticity of demand for the company's products is 1.2.

---

4. **Organizational Objectives**

    a.   Organizations may have multiple objectives that are contradictory.

        1)   The objective of maximizing profit and the objective of growth could be mutually exclusive within a given year. Maximizing short-term profit might hamper or preclude future growth.

        2)   Conflict among an organization's objectives is common.

    b.   Objectives vary with the organization's type and stage of development.

5. **Management Objectives**

    a.   The primary task of management is to carry on operations effectively and efficiently. This is, in fact, one of the three control objectives of the COSO model described in item 3. in Study Unit 1, Subunit 4.

        1)   **Effectiveness** is the degree to which the objective is accomplished. **Efficiency** is maximizing the output for a given quantity of input.

        2)   Effectiveness is sometimes called "doing the right things," and efficiency is known as "doing things right."

           a)   Trade-offs are frequently made between efficiency and effectiveness.

    b.   Objectives should be clearly and specifically stated, communicated to all concerned parties, and accepted by those affected.

6. **Means-End Hierarchy**

    a. Objectives should be established at the top and retranslated in more specific terms as they are communicated downward in the means-end hierarchy.

EXAMPLE

- An entity has a socioeconomic purpose, such as providing food.
- The entity's mission is the accomplishment of its socioeconomic purpose through the production of breakfast cereal.
- The entity develops long-range or strategic objectives with regard to profitability, growth, or survival.
- A more specific overall objective might be to provide investors with an adequate return on their investment.
- Divisional objectives can be developed, e.g., to increase the sales of a certain kind of cereal.
- Departmental objectives are developed, e.g., to reduce waste in the packaging department.
- Low-level managers and supervisors then develop personal performance and development objectives.

---

7. **Policies, Procedures, and Rules**

    a. After premises and objectives are formulated, the next step in the planning process is the development of policies, procedures, and rules. These elements are necessary at all levels of the organization and overlap both in definition and in practice.

        1) Intermediate and operational plans are translated into policies, procedures, and rules, which are standing plans for repetitive situations.

    b. Policies and procedures provide feedforward control because they anticipate and prevent problems and provide guidance on how an activity should be performed to best ensure that an objective is achieved.

        1) **Policies** are general statements that guide thinking and action in decision making. Policies may be explicitly published by, or implied by the actions of, management.

            a) A strong organizational culture means that the organization's key values are intensely held and widely shared. In this case, the need for formal written policies is minimized.

        2) **Procedures** are specific directives that define how work is to be done.

        3) **Rules** are specific, detailed guides that restrict behavior.

8. **Management by Objectives (MBO)**

    a. MBO is a behavioral, communications-oriented, responsibility approach to management and employee self-direction. It is a comprehensive management approach and therefore is relevant to planning and control.

    b. MBO is based on the philosophy that employees

        1) Want to work hard if they know what is expected
        2) Like to understand what their jobs actually entail
        3) Are capable of self-direction and self-motivation

    c. MBO requires

        1) Senior management participation and commitment to the program. These managers must

            a) Determine the overall direction and objectives for the organization
            b) Communicate these effectively in operational or measurable terms
            c) Coordinate subordinates' objectives with overall objectives
            d) Follow up at the end of the MBO cycle period to reward performance and review problems

2) Integration of objectives for all subunits into a compatible, balanced system directed toward accomplishment of the overall objectives.

3) Provisions for regular periodic reporting of performance toward attainment of the objectives.

4) Free and honest communication between supervisor and subordinate.

5) A commitment to taking the ideas of subordinates seriously on the part of supervisors.

6) An organizational climate that encourages mutual trust and respect.

d. Steps necessary to implement an MBO program include establishing objectives and action plans (the planning steps) and periodic review and final appraisal (the control steps).

Stop and review! You have completed the outline for this subunit. Study multiple-choice questions 10 through 16 beginning on page 415.

15.3 ASPECTS OF SUCCESSFUL BUDGETING

1. **Four Uses of a Budget**

   a. **The budget is a planning tool.**

      1) A budget is a written plan for the future that forces management to evaluate the assumptions used and the objectives identified in the budgetary process.

      2) Companies that prepare budgets anticipate problems before they occur.

EXAMPLE

If a company runs out of a critical raw material, it may have to shut down. At best, it will incur high freight costs to have the needed materials rushed in. The company with a budget will have anticipated the shortage and planned around it.

---

   b. **The budget is a control tool.**

      1) A budget helps an entity control costs by setting cost guidelines.

      2) Guidelines reveal the efficient or inefficient use of company resources.

      3) Budgets also can reveal the progress of highly effective managers. Consequently, employees should not view budgets negatively.

         a) Managers may use a budget as a personal self-evaluation tool.

      4) For the budgetary process to serve effectively as a control function, it must be integrated with the accounting system and the organizational structure. Such integration enhances control by transmitting data and assigning variances to the proper organizational subunits.

   c. **The budget is a motivational tool.**

      1) A budget must be seen as realistic by employees before it can become a good motivational tool.

      2) Unfortunately, the budget is not always viewed in a positive manner. Some managers view a budget as a restriction.

      3) Employees are more apt to have a positive feeling toward a budget if some degree of flexibility is allowed.

   d.   **The budget is a means of communication and coordination.**

   1)   A budget can help tell employees what objectives the entity is attempting to achieve.

   2)   A budget functions as an aid to planning, coordination, and control. Thus, a budget helps management to allocate resources efficiently and to ensure that subunit objectives are consistent with those of other subunits and of the organization.

   3)   For the budget to function in these roles, senior management must be involved in the process. This involvement does not extend to dictating the exact numerical contents of the budget because senior management lacks a detailed knowledge of daily operations.

EXAMPLE

The sales department may want to keep as much inventory as possible so that no sales will be lost, but the company CFO may want to keep the inventory as low as possible so that cash need not be spent any sooner than necessary. If the budget specifies the amount of inventory, all employees can work toward the same objectives.

---

2. **The Budget as a Formal Quantification of Management's Plans**

   a.   Corporations have objectives for market share, profitability, growth, dividend payout, etc. Not-for-profit organizations also have objectives, such as increased number of free meals served or money raised for medical research.

   1)   These objectives cannot be achieved without careful planning about the allocation of resources and the expected results.

   b.   A budget quantifies an organization's expectations about the consumption of resources and the resulting outcomes.

   c.   An organizational budget requires a significant commitment of internal resources. The most important factor in ensuring its success is for senior managers to demonstrate that they take the project seriously and consider it vital to the organization's future.

3. **Budgeting's Role in the Overall Planning and Evaluation Process**

   a.   Planning is the process by which an organization sets specific objectives for itself. Planning is an organization's response to the expression, "If you don't know where you're going, any path will take you there."

   b.   To evaluate progress toward achievement of the organization's objectives, quantification is necessary. This is the role of the various types of budgets.

   1)   The budget is therefore a strategic control.

4. **Effects of External Factors on the Budgeting Process**

   a.   Decisions about an entity's strategy and its budget are dependent on general economic conditions and their expected trends and the availability of financial resources.

EXAMPLE

If the economy is entering a period of lower demand, a manufacturer will not project increased sales. If costs are not changeable, the company may budget losses for the short-term to hold on to market share.

---

   b.   The industry's situation includes the company's current market share, governmental regulatory measures, the labor market, and the activities of competitors.

EXAMPLE

If input costs are rising in an entity's industry, the budget must reflect that reality; profit margins and cash flows will not be the same as in prior years. Also, a company in or near bankruptcy will face a different financial situation than would the market leader.

---

5. **Budgeting's Role in Formulating and Controlling Short-Term Objectives**

   a. The budget states the specific revenue targets and expense limitations for each functional area and department of the organization on a month-by-month basis.

      1) A budget cannot simply be a lump-sum total for a year. Incremental objectives must be achieved each month or week. This is especially true in seasonal businesses, such as agricultural supply.

6. **Characteristics of a Successful Budgeting Process**

   a. **Sufficient lead time.** For a budget to be useful, it must be finalized when the fiscal year begins.

      1) The preparation of a complete organizational budget usually takes several months. An entity with a calendar year end may start the budget process in September, anticipating its completion by the first of December.

      2) The **budget planning calendar** is the schedule of activities for the development and adoption of the budget. It includes a list of dates indicating when specific information is to be provided to others by each information source.

         a) Because all of the individual departmental budgets are based on forecasts prepared by others and the budgets of other departments, it is essential to have a planning calendar to integrate the entire process.

      3) The budget department is responsible for compiling the budget and managing the budget process. However, the budget director and department are not responsible for actually developing the estimates on which the budget is based.

   b. **Budget manual.** Everyone involved in preparing the budget at all levels must be educated on the detailed procedures for preparing and submitting their part of the overall budget.

      1) Because budgets have many components, they must be prepared in a standard format.

      2) Distribution instructions are vital because the components of the organizational budget are interrelated and must be coordinated.

         a) One department's budget may be dependent on another's, and functional areas must be aggregated from their constituent departmental budgets.

   c. **Buy-in at all levels.**

      1) Participative budgeting has a much greater chance of acceptance by those affected and thus of achieving ultimate success than does a budget that is imposed from above.

      2) The single most important factor in ensuring the success of a budget process is for senior management to demonstrate that they take the project seriously and consider it vital to the organization's future.

7. **Revisions of the Budget**

   a. Often, an organization will find that the assumptions under which the budget was prepared undergo significant change during the year. A policy must be in place to accommodate revisions to the budget resulting from these changes.

      1) Accommodation of change is a key characteristic of successful budgeting. If such a policy is not in place, managers can come to believe they are being held to a budget that is no longer possible to achieve, and morale can suffer.

    b.   Information gained during the year as actual results and variances are reported can be used to help the company take corrective action. The following steps are a control loop:

        1)   Establishing standards of performance (the budget)
        2)   Measuring actual performance
        3)   Analyzing and comparing performance with standards
        4)   Devising and implementing corrective actions
        5)   Reviewing and revising the standards

Stop and review! You have completed the outline for this subunit. Study multiple-choice questions 17 through 23 beginning on page 417.

15.4 BUDGETING AND MOTIVATION

1.   **Role of Budgets in Measuring Performance**

    a.   One of the most important reasons for adopting a budget is to provide standards for the assessment of success or failure of individual managers and functional areas.

    b.   As the fiscal year progresses, revenues, expenses, and other measures can be compared with the budget to determine whether organizational performance is meeting expectations.

2.   **Authoritative vs. Participative Budgeting**

    a.   A purely top-down (authoritative) approach to budgeting has the apparent advantage of ensuring total consistency across all functional areas. It is also far less complex and time-consuming than coordinating input from the middle and lower levels.

    b.   Participative (grass-roots or bottom-up) budgeting uses input from middle- and lower-level employees.

        1)   Participation encourages employees to have a sense of ownership of the output of the process. The result is an acceptance of, and commitment to, the objectives expressed in the budget.

        2)   An imposed budget is much less likely to promote this sense of commitment.

    c.   Participation also enables employees to relate performance to rewards or penalties.

        1)   A further advantage of participation is that it provides a broader information base. Middle- and lower-level managers often are far better informed about operational realities than senior managers.

    d.   Disadvantages of participative budgeting include its cost in time and money. In addition, the quality of participation is affected by the objectives, values, beliefs, and expectations of those involved.

        1)   A manager who expects his/her request to be reduced may inflate the amount. If a budget is to be used as a performance evaluator, a manager asked for an estimate may provide one that is easily attained.

        2)   This creation of **budgetary slack** (overestimation of expenses or underestimation of revenues) must be avoided if a budget is to have its desired effects. The natural tendency of a manager is to negotiate for a less stringent measure of performance so as to avoid unfavorable variances from expectations.

Stop and review! You have completed the outline for this subunit. Study multiple-choice questions 24 through 29 beginning on page 419.

QUESTIONS

15.1 Strategic Management

1. A firm's statement of broad objectives or mission statement should accomplish all of the following **except**

    A. Outlining strategies for technological development, market expansion, and product differentiation.

    B. Defining the purpose of the company.

    C. Providing an overall guide to those in high-level, decision-making positions.

    D. Stating the moral and ethical principles that guide the actions of the firm.

Answer (A) is correct.

    REQUIRED: The purpose not achieved by a mission statement.

    DISCUSSION: The determination of organizational objectives is the first step in the planning process. A mission statement is a formal, written document that defines the organization's purpose in society, for example, to produce and distribute certain goods of high quality in a manner beneficial to the public, employees, shareholders, and other constituencies. Thus, a mission statement does not announce specific operating plans. It does not describe strategies for technological development, market expansion, or product differentiation because these are tasks for operating management.

    Answer (B) is incorrect. A mission statement defines the purpose of the company (some writers differentiate between purpose and mission). Answer (C) is incorrect. Broad objectives provide guidance to those in high-level positions who are responsible for long-range planning. Answer (D) is incorrect. Mission statements increasingly are concerned with ethical principles.

2. Intensity of rivalry among existing firms in an industry increases when

    I.   Products are relatively undifferentiated
    II. Consumer switching costs are low

    A. I only.

    B. II only.

    C. Both I and II.

    D. Neither I nor II.

Answer (C) is correct.

    REQUIRED: The condition(s), if any, that increase(s) the intensity of rivalry in an industry.

    DISCUSSION: The degree of product differentiation and the costs of switching from one competitor's product to another increase the intensity of rivalry and competition in an industry. Less differentiation tends to heighten competition based on price, with price cutting leading to lower profits. Low costs of switching products also increase competition.

    Answer (A) is incorrect. Low consumer switching costs also increase rivalry. Answer (B) is incorrect. A low degree of product differentiation also increases rivalry. Answer (D) is incorrect. Both low consumer switching costs and a low degree of product differentiation increase rivalry.

3. Structural considerations affecting the threat of substitutes include all of the following **except**

    A. Relative prices.

    B. Brand identity.

    C. Cost of switching to substitutes.

    D. Customers' inclination to use a substitute.

Answer (B) is correct.

    REQUIRED: The structural consideration that does not affect the threat of substitutes.

    DISCUSSION: Substitutes are types of goods and services that serve the same purpose. All products that can replace a good or service should be considered substitutes. For example, bicycles and cars are substitutes for public transportation. Structural considerations determine the effect substitutes have on one another. However, because substitutes are types (not brands) of goods and services that have the same purposes, brand identity is not a structural consideration affecting the threat of substitutes.

    Answer (A) is incorrect. Relative price is a structural consideration affecting the threat of substitutes. Answer (C) is incorrect. The cost of switching is a structural consideration affecting the threat of substitutes. Answer (D) is incorrect. Customers' inclination to use a substitute is a structural consideration affecting the threat of substitutes.

4. A manufacturing company produces plastic utensils for a particular segment at the lowest possible cost. The company is pursuing a cost

    A. Leadership strategy.

    B. Focus strategy.

    C. Differentiation strategy.

    D. Containment strategy.

Answer (B) is correct.

    REQUIRED: The cost strategy pursued by the manufacturing company.

    DISCUSSION: Cost focus is the generic strategy that seeks competitive advantage through lower costs but with a narrow competitive scope (e.g., a regional market or a specialized product line). The reason for a cost-focus strategy is that the narrower market can be better served because the firm knows it well.

    Answer (A) is incorrect. A cost leader is the lowest cost producer in the industry as a whole. Answer (C) is incorrect. Cost differentiation aims at providing a product at different costs in different market segments. Answer (D) is incorrect. Cost containment aims at controlling costs related to a particular product/market but not necessarily producing at the lowest possible cost.

5. What operations strategy is most likely to be adopted when the product sold by an organization is a commodity and the market is very large?

    A. Flexibility strategy.

    B. Quality strategy.

    C. Service strategy.

    D. Cost strategy.

Answer (D) is correct.

    REQUIRED: The strategy most likely to be adopted when the product sold by an organization is a commodity and the market is very large.

    DISCUSSION: An operations strategy formulates a long-term plan for using entity resources to reach strategic objectives. A cost strategy is successful when the entity is the low-cost producer. However, the product (e.g., a commodity) tends to be undifferentiated in these cases, the market is often very large, and the competition tends to be intense because of the possibility of high-volume sales.

    Answer (A) is incorrect. A flexibility strategy involves offering many different products. Answer (B) is incorrect. A quality strategy involves competition based on product quality or process quality. Answer (C) is incorrect. Service is not an issue in a sale of commodities.

6. In the <List A> stage of the product life cycle, <List B> tend to be highest.

	List A	List B
A.	Introduction	Sales
B.	Growth	Profits
C.	Maturity	Profits
D.	Decline	Cash flows

Answer (C) is correct.

    REQUIRED: The stages in the product life cycle.

    DISCUSSION: The product life cycle has five stages: product development, introduction, growth, maturity, and decline. In the maturity stage, profits level off or begin to decline.

    Answer (A) is incorrect. In the introduction stage, sales are low. Answer (B) is incorrect. In the growth stage, profits are increasing, but they do not usually peak until the maturity stage. Answer (D) is incorrect. In the decline stage, sales and profits drop, and cash flows are low.

7. In the value creation chain model, the primary activities include

    A. Logistics, operations, marketing and sales, and service.

    B. Procurement, infrastructure, operations, and service.

    C. Procurement, infrastructure, operations, and technology development.

    D. Procurement, infrastructure, human resources, and technology development.

Answer (A) is correct.

    REQUIRED: The primary activities in the value creation chain.

    DISCUSSION: The model consists of primary and supporting activities. The primary activities are inbound logistics, operations, outbound logistics, marketing and sales, and service. Inbound logistics activities involve the firms' capture of materials to be processed. Operations activities are conversion processes. Outbound logistics activities include shipment of products. Marketing and sales activities are the promotion and sale of final products. Service activities provide customer service. The four support activities are infrastructure (e.g., administration, finance, and planning), procurement, human resources, and technology development.

8. Customer relationship management is best defined as

A. Coordination with members of the firm's supply chain.

B. Maximizing short-term sales to customers.

C. Market sensing.

D. Maximizing customer loyalty by managing customer "touchpoints."

Answer (D) is correct.

REQUIRED: The best definition of customer relationship management.

DISCUSSION: Customer relationship management can be defined as "the process of managing detailed information about individual customers and carefully managing all the customer 'touchpoints' with the aim of maximizing customer loyalty." Its purpose is to create optimal customer equity. Thus, the process involves more than merely attracting customers (through media advertising, direct mail, etc.) and satisfying them (something competitors also may do).

Answer (A) is incorrect. Coordination with members of the firm's supply chain is partner relationship management. Answer (B) is incorrect. Customer relationship management seeks to increase the value of the customer base by developing long-term relationships with individual customers by such methods as customer service, customized (if not personalized) offerings, and choice of marketing messages and media. Answer (C) is incorrect. Market sensing consists of obtaining, distributing, and acting upon market intelligence.

9. The firm should emphasize customer retention

A. By creating low switching costs.

B. By maximizing customer churn.

C. Although new customers are less costly than old customers.

D. Because the customer base is an intangible asset.

Answer (D) is correct.

REQUIRED: The true statement about customer retention.

DISCUSSION: Customer retention through customer satisfaction is a key to profitability. The firm should emphasize customer retention because the customer base is an important intangible asset.

Answer (A) is incorrect. High switching costs tend to increase customer retention. Answer (B) is incorrect. The firm should minimize customer churn (customer loss). Answer (C) is incorrect. Customer retention is less costly than customer attraction.

15.2 Strategic Planning

10. The budget that describes the long-term position and objectives of an entity within its environment is the

A. Capital budget.

B. Operating budget.

C. Cash management budget.

D. Strategic budget.

Answer (D) is correct.

REQUIRED: The budget that describes the long-term position and objectives of an entity.

DISCUSSION: Strategic budgeting is a form of long-range planning based on identifying and specifying organizational objectives. The strengths and weaknesses of the organization are evaluated and risk levels are assessed. The influences of environmental factors are forecast to derive the best strategy for reaching the organization's objectives.

Answer (A) is incorrect. Capital budgeting involves evaluating specific long-term investment decisions. Answer (B) is incorrect. The operating budget is a short-range management tool. Answer (C) is incorrect. Cash management is a short-range consideration related to liquidity.

11. Which of the following is an example of an outcome of strategic planning?

A. A formal statement of the organization's definition of the fundamental truths that guide its actions.

B. A broad statement of concepts that emphasizes the implementation of organizational objectives over the long term.

C. A set of general guides for action that channel thinking and allow a certain amount of discretion in execution.

D. A document specifying a sequence of steps detailing the exact manner in which a certain activity must be accomplished.

Answer (B) is correct.

REQUIRED: The outcome of strategic planning.

DISCUSSION: The strategic plan states the means by which an entity expects to achieve its stated mission. Achieving the mission is predicated on implementing long-term objectives.

Answer (A) is incorrect. Truths that guide an organization's actions are principles. Answer (C) is incorrect. General guides for action are policies. Answer (D) is incorrect. A detailed sequence of steps for accomplishing a certain activity is a procedure.

12. Which one of the following management considerations is usually addressed first in strategic planning?

   A. Outsourcing.

   B. Overall objectives of the firm.

   C. Organizational structure.

   D. Recent annual budgets.

Answer (B) is correct.

   REQUIRED: The management consideration usually addressed first in strategic planning.

   DISCUSSION: Strategic planning is the process of setting overall organizational objectives and drafting strategic plans. Setting ultimate objectives for the firm is a necessary prelude to developing strategies for achieving those objectives. Plans and budgets are then needed to implement those strategies.

   Answer (A) is incorrect. Outsourcing is an operating decision of a more short-term nature. Answer (C) is incorrect. Organizational structure, although important in strategic planning, is based upon the firm's overall objectives. Answer (D) is incorrect. Recent annual budgets are a basis for short-term planning.

13. Strategy is a broad term that usually means the selection of overall objectives. Strategic analysis ordinarily **excludes** the

   A. Trends that will affect the entity's markets.

   B. Target product mix and production schedule to be maintained during the year.

   C. Forms of organizational structure that would best serve the entity.

   D. Best ways to invest in research, design, production, distribution, marketing, and administrative activities.

Answer (B) is correct.

   REQUIRED: The item ordinarily excluded from the process of strategic analysis.

   DISCUSSION: Strategic analysis is the process of long-range planning. Such tasks as setting the target product mix and production schedule for the current year are short-term activities.

   Answer (A) is incorrect. Strategic analysis includes examining marketing trends. Answer (C) is incorrect. Strategic analysis evaluates organizational structure. Answer (D) is incorrect. Strategic analysis includes evaluation of the best ways to invest in research, design, etc.

14. All of the following are characteristics of the strategic planning process **except** the

   A. Emphasis on long run.

   B. Analysis of external economic factors.

   C. Review of the attributes and behavior of the organization's competition.

   D. Analysis and review of departmental budgets.

Answer (D) is correct.

   REQUIRED: The item that is not a characteristic of the strategic planning process.

   DISCUSSION: Strategic planning is the process of setting the overall organizational objectives and involves the drafting of strategic plans. Analysis and review of departmental budgets is an aspect of operational management.

   Answer (A) is incorrect. Emphasis on the long run is an aspect of strategic planning. Answer (B) is incorrect. Analysis of external economic factors is an aspect of strategic planning. Answer (C) is incorrect. Consideration of competitive factors and analysis of consumer demand are all aspects of strategic planning.

15. Strategic planning, as practiced by most modern organizations, includes all of the following **except**

   A. Top-level management participation.

   B. A long-term focus.

   C. Strategies that will help in achieving long-range goals.

   D. Analysis of the current month's actual variances from budget.

Answer (D) is correct.

   REQUIRED: The item not an element of strategic planning.

   DISCUSSION: Strategic planning is the process of setting overall organizational objectives. It is a long-term process aimed at determining the future course of the organization. Analysis of the current month's budget variances is a short-term activity.

   Answer (A) is incorrect. Top-level management participation is an element of strategic planning. Answer (B) is incorrect. A long-term focus is an element of strategic planning. Answer (C) is incorrect. Strategies that will help in achieving long-range goals are elements of strategic planning.

16. An organization's policies and procedures are part of its overall system of internal controls. The control function performed by policies and procedures is

A. Feedforward control.

B. Implementation control.

C. Feedback control.

D. Application control.

Answer (A) is correct.
    REQUIRED: The control function of policies and procedures.
    DISCUSSION: Feedforward control anticipates and prevents problems. Policies and procedures serve as feedforward controls because they provide guidance on how an activity should be performed to best ensure that an objective is achieved.
    Answer (B) is incorrect. Implementation controls are controls applied during systems development. Answer (C) is incorrect. Policies and procedures provide primary guidance before and during the performance of some task rather than give feedback on its accomplishment. Answer (D) is incorrect. Application controls apply to specific applications, e.g., payroll or accounts payable.

15.3 Aspects of Successful Budgeting

17. Each organization plans and budgets its operations for slightly different reasons. Which one of the following is **not** a significant reason for budgeting?

A. Providing a basis for controlling operations.

B. Forcing managers to consider expected future trends and conditions.

C. Ensuring profitable operations.

D. Checking progress toward the objectives of the organization.

Answer (C) is correct.
    REQUIRED: The item that is not a significant reason for budgeting.
    DISCUSSION: A budget is a realistic plan for the future that is expressed in quantitative terms. It is a planning, control, motivational, and communications tool. A budget promotes consistency of objectives at all levels of the organization and coordination among operating units. Unfortunately, a budget does not ensure profitable operations.
    Answer (A) is incorrect. Control of operations is a goal of planning. Answer (B) is incorrect. Forcing managers to consider expected future trends and conditions is a goal of planning. Answer (D) is incorrect. Checking progress toward objectives is a goal of planning.

18. One of the primary advantages of budgeting is that it

A. Does not take the place of management and administration.

B. Bases the profit plan on estimates.

C. Is continually adapted to fit changing circumstances.

D. Requires departmental managers to make plans in conjunction with the plans of other interdependent departments.

Answer (D) is correct.
    REQUIRED: The primary advantage of budgeting.
    DISCUSSION: A budget is a quantitative model of a plan of action developed by management. A budget functions as an aid to planning, coordination, and control. Thus, a budget helps management to allocate resources efficiently and to ensure that subunit objectives are consistent with those of other subunits and of the organization.
    Answer (A) is incorrect. Budgeting, far from taking the place of management and administration, makes them even more important. Answer (B) is incorrect. Basing the profit plan on estimates is a necessity, not an advantage. Answer (C) is incorrect. Adaptation to changing circumstances is a commitment that upper management must make; it is not inherent in a budget.

19. All of the following are advantages of the use of budgets in a management control system **except** that budgets

A. Force management planning.

B. Provide performance criteria.

C. Promote communication and coordination within the organization.

D. Limit unauthorized expenditures.

Answer (D) is correct.
    REQUIRED: The item not an advantage of using budgets in a management control system.
    DISCUSSION: Budgets force management to plan ahead, communicate organizational goals throughout the organization, and provide criteria for future performance evaluations. However, they cannot prevent departments from overspending.
    Answer (A) is incorrect. Forcing management planning is an advantage of using budgets. Answer (B) is incorrect. Providing performance criteria is an advantage of using budgets. Answer (C) is incorrect. Promoting communication and coordination within the organization is an advantage of using budgets.

20. When developing a budget, an external factor to consider in the planning process is

A. A change to a decentralized management system.

B. The implementation of a new bonus program.

C. New product development.

D. The merger of two competitors.

Answer (D) is correct.
REQUIRED: The external factor that should be considered during the budget planning process.
DISCUSSION: External factors that must be considered in the planning process include (1) general economic conditions and their expected trend; (2) the company's current market share; (3) governmental regulatory measures; (4) the labor market in the locale of the company's facilities; and (5) activities of competitors, including the effects of mergers.
Answer (A) is incorrect. A change in management is an internal factor. Answer (B) is incorrect. Employee compensation is an internal factor. Answer (C) is incorrect. A new product line is an internal factor.

21. A planning calendar in budgeting is the

A. Calendar period covered by the budget.

B. Schedule of activities for the development and adoption of the budget.

C. Calendar period covered by the annual budget and the long-range plan.

D. Sales forecast by months in the annual budget period.

Answer (B) is correct.
REQUIRED: The definition of a budget planning calendar.
DISCUSSION: The preparation of a master budget usually takes several months. The budget planning calendar is the schedule of activities for the development and adoption of the budget. It should include a list of dates indicating when specific information is to be provided by each information source to others.
Answer (A) is incorrect. The period covered by the budget precedes the events in the planning calendar. Answer (C) is incorrect. The period covered by the budget precedes the events in the planning calendar. Answer (D) is incorrect. The planning calendar is not associated with sales.

22. A budget manual, which enhances the operation of a budget system, is most likely to include

A. A chart of accounts.

B. Distribution instructions for budget schedules.

C. Employee hiring policies.

D. Documentation of the accounting system software.

Answer (B) is correct.
REQUIRED: The item normally included in a budget manual.
DISCUSSION: A budget manual describes how a budget is to be prepared. Items usually included in a budget manual are a planning calendar and distribution instructions for all budget schedules.
Answer (A) is incorrect. A chart of accounts is included in the accounting manual. Answer (C) is incorrect. Employee hiring policies are not needed for budget preparation. They are already available in the human resources manual. Answer (D) is incorrect. Software documentation is not needed in the budget preparation process.

23. Which one of the following is most important to a successful budgeting effort?

A. Experienced analysts.

B. Integrated budget software.

C. Reliable forecasts and trend analyses.

D. Top management support.

Answer (D) is correct.
REQUIRED: The most important factor to a successful budgeting effort.
DISCUSSION: An organizational budget requires a significant commitment of internal resources. The single most important factor in ensuring its success is for senior management to demonstrate that they take the project seriously and consider it vital to the organization's future.
Answer (A) is incorrect. Experienced analysts are not crucial to success of a budget; "knowing your business" is as important as training in budget preparation. Answer (B) is incorrect. Integrated budget software is not the most important factor in budget success; fairly large and sophisticated budgets can be prepared with ordinary spreadsheets. Answer (C) is incorrect. While they are important, reliable forecasts and trend analyses are not the most important factor; a budget must be flexible enough to adapt to changing circumstances.

15.4 Budgeting and Motivation

24. All of the following are advantages of top-down budgeting as opposed to participatory budgeting **except** that it

A. Increases coordination of subunit objectives.

B. Reduces the time required for budgeting.

C. May limit the acceptance of proposed objectives.

D. Facilitates implementation of strategic plans.

Answer (C) is correct.
    REQUIRED: The item that is not an advantage of top-down budgeting as opposed to participatory budgeting.
    DISCUSSION: Because a top-down budget is imposed by upper management, it has less chance of acceptance (also called buy-in) by those on whom the budget is imposed.
    Answer (A) is incorrect. A top-down budget is imposed by upper management, so coordinating the objectives of separate divisions is simplified. Answer (B) is incorrect. A top-down budget is coordinated from above. Therefore, it is less time-consuming than obtaining lower-level input. Answer (D) is incorrect. Because a top-down budget is coordinated from above, the implementation of strategic plans is centralized and thus simplified.

25. The following sequence of steps is employed by a company to develop its annual profit plan:

- Planning guidelines are disseminated downward by upper-level management after receiving input from all levels of management.

- A sales budget is prepared by individual sales units reflecting the sales targets of the various segments. This provides the basis for departmental production budgets and other related components by the various operating units. Communication is primarily lateral with some upward communication possible.

- A profit plan is submitted to upper-level management for coordination and review. Upper-level management's recommendations and revisions are acted upon by middle management. A revised profit plan is resubmitted for further review to upper-level management.

- Upper-level management grants final approval and distributes the formal plan downward to the various operating units.

This outline of steps best describes which one of the following approaches to budget development?

A. Imposed budgeting by upper-level management.

B. Participative approach.

C. Top-down approach.

D. Total justification of all activities by operating units.

Answer (B) is correct.
    REQUIRED: The described approach to budget development.
    DISCUSSION: A participative approach is characterized by general guidance from the highest levels of management, followed by extensive input from middle and lower management. This sequence of steps aptly describes this process.
    Answer (A) is incorrect. Upper-level management has received extensive input and cooperation from lower levels through performing these steps. Answer (C) is incorrect. These steps describe the opposite of a top-down approach. Answer (D) is incorrect. Upper-level management is not demanding justification of all activities in the steps described; such a demand would be consistent with a system known as zero-based budgeting.

26. All of the following are disadvantages of top-down budgeting as opposed to participatory budgeting **except** that it

A. May result in a budget that is not possible to achieve.

B. May limit the acceptance of proposed objectives.

C. Reduces the communication between employees and management.

D. Reduces the time required for budgeting.

Answer (D) is correct.
    REQUIRED: The item not a disadvantage of top-down budgeting.
    DISCUSSION: Because a top-down budget is coordinated from above, it is less time-consuming than obtaining lower-level input.
    Answer (A) is incorrect. A budget established without lower-level input may set unrealistic objectives. Answer (B) is incorrect. Because a top-down budget is imposed by upper management, it has less chance of acceptance (also called buy-in) by those on whom the budget is imposed. Answer (C) is incorrect. Reduced communication between employees and management is a disadvantage of top-down budgeting.

27. In developing the budget for the next year, which approach is most likely to produce positive motivation and consistency of objectives?

A. Permit the subunit manager to develop the objectives for the subunit that, in the manager's view, will generate the greatest profit.

B. Have senior management develop overall objectives and permit the subunit manager to determine how they will be met.

C. Have the subunit manager and senior management jointly develop objectives and operational plans.

D. Have the subunit manager and senior management jointly develop objectives and the subunit manager develop operational plans.

Answer (D) is correct.
REQUIRED: The approach that is most likely to produce positive motivation and consistency of objectives.
DISCUSSION: Participative development of objectives has a positive effect on motivation because lower-level managers are more likely to accept and be committed to the result.
Answer (A) is incorrect. Allowing subunit managers to develop their objectives does not promote consistency of the entity's overall objectives with those of all levels of the entity. Answer (B) is incorrect. Allowing the subunit manager to participate in the development of objectives has a positive effect on motivation. Answer (C) is incorrect. A further advantage of participation is that it provides a broader information base. Middle- and lower-level managers often are far better informed about operational realities than senior managers.

28. Marietta Thomas, Amador Corporation's vice president of planning, has seen and heard it all. She has told the corporate controller that she is "....very upset with the degree of slack that veteran managers have in the budgets they prepare." Thomas has considered implementing some of the following activities during the budgeting process:

1. Develop the budgets by top management and issue them to lower-level operating units.

2. Study the actual revenues and expenses of previous periods in detail.

3. Have the budgets developed by operating units and accept them as submitted by a company-wide budget committee.

4. Share the budgets with all employees as a means to reach company objectives.

5. Use a budgeting process that proceeds through several stages with changes initiated by operating units or senior managers.

Which of these activities should Amador implement to best remedy Thomas's concerns, help eliminate the problems experienced by Amador, and motivate personnel?

A. 1 only.

B. 2 and 3.

C. 2 and 4.

D. 2, 4, and 5.

Answer (D) is correct.
REQUIRED: The activity or activities Amador should implement during the budgeting process.
DISCUSSION: Steps 2, 4, and 5 are appropriate for alleviating Amador's budget problems. Step 1 should not be performed because a budget imposed from the top is more likely to encounter resistance. Step 3 should not be performed because operating units will tend to consider only their own interests when preparing budgets.
Answer (A) is incorrect. A budget imposed from the top is more likely to encounter resistance. Answer (B) is incorrect. Operating units will tend to consider only their own interests when preparing budgets. Answer (C) is incorrect. While studying previous periods and sharing the budget with all employees are important steps to correcting Amador's problems, incrementally improving the budget through a multistage process is also crucial.

29. The budgeting process should motivate managers and employees to work toward organizational objectives. Which one of the following is **least** likely to motivate managers?

A. Setting budget targets at attainable levels.

B. Participation by subordinates in the budgetary process.

C. Use of management by exception.

D. Having upper-level management set budget levels.

Answer (D) is correct.

REQUIRED: The item least likely to motivate managers.

DISCUSSION: A budget is potentially a good motivational tool. If lower-level managers have participated in preparing the budget instead of simply receiving a budget imposed by upper-level management, they are more likely to understand and share the objectives of upper-level management and to work to keep costs within the budget. Participation and understanding also are likely to result in budgets that are reasonably attainable and viewed as realistic. However, a budget is also a motivator in the sense that managers are accountable for variances in controllable costs but are rewarded for good performance. Moreover, budgeting coupled with analysis of variances tends to improve motivation by allowing upper-level managers to concentrate on problems (exceptions) rather than engaging in routine supervision of subordinates, which may be viewed as unnecessarily intrusive and unwelcome.

Answer (A) is incorrect. Setting budget targets at attainable levels is a means of increasing manager motivation. Answer (B) is incorrect. Participation by subordinates in the budgetary process is a means of increasing manager motivation. Answer (C) is incorrect. Use of management by exception is a means of increasing manager motivation.

Use the additional questions in Gleim **CPA Test Prep Online** to create Test Sessions that emulate Prometric!

15.5 PRACTICE WRITTEN COMMUNICATION TASK

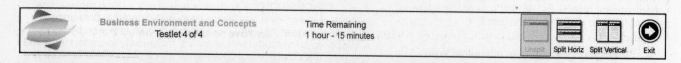

Business Environment and Concepts	Time Remaining
Testlet 4 of 4	1 hour - 15 minutes

Unsplit   Split Horiz   Split Vertical   Exit

DIRECTIONS

Note: If you believe you have encountered a software malfunction, report it to the test center staff immediately.

Navigation

To navigate from task to task, use the controls at the bottom of the screen. Click on the **Next** button to advance to the next task, or the **Previous** button to go to the previous task. To go directly to any task, click on its number.

▼ = Reminder   Directions   1 2 3 4 5 6 7   ◀ Previous   Next ▶

If you would like a reminder to revisit a task, or want to indicate that you are finished with it, click on the reminder flag below the task number. To clear the flag, click on it again. Reminder flags are for your use only – they do not contribute to your score.

Tabs

In this part of the examination, you will be asked to complete various tasks. Every task has one or more **Work Tabs**. Every task also has a **Help** tab.

✏ Written Communication   Help

Work tab   Help tab

Work Tabs:

- **Work Tabs** are identified with a pencil icon. This is where your responses are expected.
- Each task has one or more **Work Tabs**.
- **Work Tabs** contain directions for completing the task - be sure to read these directions carefully.
- The **Work Tab** name in the example above is for illustration only - yours will differ.
- You must complete all of the **Work Tabs** in each task to receive full credit.

Help Tab:

- The **Help Tab** provides assistance with the exam software that is used in this task. For example, if the task is to compose a memorandum, **Help** will provide information about the word processor.

The Toolbar

The toolbar at the top of the screen shows the amount of time remaining for you to complete the tasks. In addition, the following tools are available. Note that only the **Exit** button is displayed when Directions are visible - the others will appear when you begin the tasks.

Unsplit   Split Horiz   Split Vertical

Click on these buttons to split or unsplit the screen. You can split the screen vertically or horizontally.

Exit

Click on this button to go on to the next part of the examination. You must complete all of the tasks to receive full credit. Once you click on **Exit** and confirm the action, you will NOT be able to return to this testlet.

▼ = Reminder   Directions   1   ◀ Previous   Next ▶

Written Communication | **Help**

✂ Cut | 🗐 Copy | 🗐 Paste | ↩ Undo | ↪ Redo

During a tax planning meeting with Family Partnership, you learned that they have no plans for marketing and business strategy.

Prepare a memo to Family Partnership discussing strategic management and the steps to enact it.

Type your communication below the line in the response area below.

REMINDER: Your response will be graded for both technical content and writing skills. Technical content will be evaluated for information that is helpful to the intended reader and clearly relevant to the issue. Writing skills will be evaluated for development, organization, and the appropriate expression of ideas in professional correspondence. Use a standard business memorandum or letter format with a clear beginning, middle, and end. Do not convey information in the form of a table, bullet point list, or other abbreviated presentation.

To: Family Partnership
Re: Steps for enacting effective strategic management

Unofficial Answer

Written Communication

To: Family Partnership
Re: Steps for enacting effective strategic management

Strategic management is the setting of overall objectives for an entity and guiding the process of reaching those objectives. It is thus the purview of upper management. Strategic management is a five-stage process.

First, the board of directors drafts the organization's mission statement, which summarizes the entity's reason for existing. Missions tend to be most effective when they consist of a single sentence. Missions tend to be stated in general terms; setting a specific goal in the mission statement can limit an entity's ability to respond to a changing marketplace.

Second, the organization performs a situational analysis, also called a SWOT analysis, in reference to its purpose of identifying the entity's strengths, weaknesses, opportunities, and threats. Strengths and weaknesses refer to the entity's internal environment. Opportunities and threats refer to the entity's external environment.

Third, based on the results of the situational analysis, upper management develops a group of strategies describing how the mission statement will be fulfilled. The strategies answer such questions as, "Which lines of business will we be in?" and "How do we penetrate and compete in the international marketplace?"

Fourth, strategic plans are implemented through the execution of component plans at each level of the entity. Incentive systems and employee performance evaluations must be structured such that they encourage employees to focus their efforts on pursuing the entity's goals. This obviously calls for communication between upper management, who devise the strategies; middle managers, who supervise and evaluate employees; and human resources, who must approve evaluation and compensation plans.

Lastly, strategic controls and feedback are used to monitor progress, isolate problems, and take corrective action. Over the long term, feedback can be used to adjust the original mission and goals. For controls to be effective, targets or benchmarks against which performance can be measured must be established. Then, the results of actual performance must be measured against the standards and reported to the appropriate manager.

The above depicts a Level 5 answer. See page 16 in the Introduction for a description of the three grading criteria.

Self-Grade

Evaluate each of the following by selecting a 0, 1, 2, 3, 4, or 5. An average response is 3. Use 4 for better than average and 5 for outstanding. Use 2 for less than average and 1 for quite poor. Use zero for no response, if you did not address the topic, or if you gave advice that is clearly illegal.

Organization	o 0	o 1	o 2	o 3	o 4	o 5
Development	o 0	o 1	o 2	o 3	o 4	o 5
Expression	o 0	o 1	o 2	o 3	o 4	o 5

Your grade for the written communication as a whole is the average of the scores for the three criteria.

Use **CPA Gleim Online** and **Simulation Wizard** to practice more written communication tasks in a realistic environment.

STUDY UNIT SIXTEEN
BUDGET COMPONENTS

(12 pages of outline)

A modern organization needs an integrated, entity-wide budget (Subunit 1). To be effective, a budget must be based on carefully chosen standards (Subunit 2). The preparation of a comprehensive budget has two stages: the operating budget (Subunit 3) and the financial budget (Subunit 4). A flexible budget is prepared for better analysis of the budget variances (Subunit 5).

16.1 THE MASTER BUDGET AND ITS COMPONENTS

1. **The Master Budget Process -- Sequence**

    a. The master budget, also called the comprehensive budget, static budget, or annual profit plan, encompasses the organization's operating and financial plans for a specified period (ordinarily a year or single operating cycle).

    b. The master budget consists of the operating budget and the financial budget. Both consist of interrelated sub-budgets.

        1) The information contained in the lower-numbered budgets are inputs to the higher-numbered budgets. For example, the production budget cannot be prepared until after completion of the sales budget. The direct materials budget and the direct labor budget cannot be prepared until after completion of the production budget.

2. **The Operating Budget**

    a. In the operating budget, the emphasis is on obtaining and using current resources. It contains the following components:

        1) Sales budget
        2) Production budget
        3) Direct materials budget
        4) Direct labor budget
        5) Manufacturing overhead budget
        6) Cost of goods sold budget
        7) Nonmanufacturing budget

            a) Research and development budget
            b) Selling and administrative budget

                i) Design budget
                ii) Marketing budget
                iii) Distribution budget
                iv) Customer service budget
                v) Administrative budget

        8) Pro forma income statement

3.   **The Financial Budget**

   a.   In the financial budget, the emphasis is on obtaining the funds needed to purchase operating assets. It contains the following components:

   1)   Capital budget (completed before operating budget is begun)
   2)   Cash budget

      a)   Projected cash disbursement schedule
      b)   Projected cash collection schedule

   3)   Pro forma balance sheet
   4)   Pro forma statement of cash flows

4.   **Master Budget Process -- Graphical Depiction**

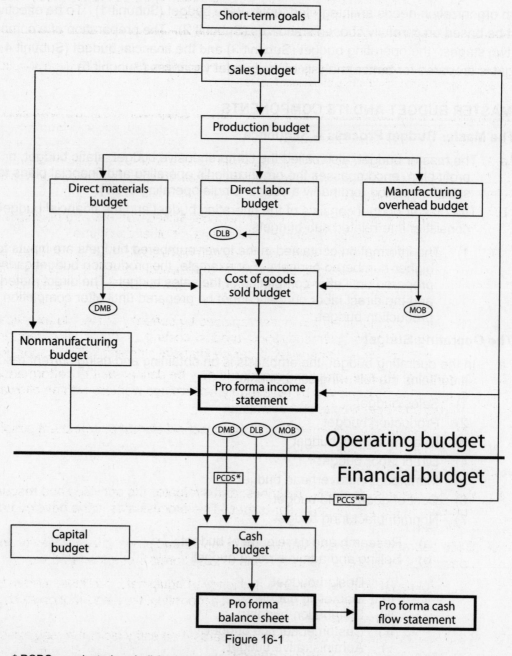

Figure 16-1

   * PCDS = projected cash disbursements schedule
   ** PCCS = projected cash collection schedule

Stop and review! You have completed the outline for this subunit. Study multiple-choice questions 1 through 9 beginning on page 436.

16.2 STANDARD SETTING

1. **Standard Costs**

   a. Standard costs are predetermined expectations about how much a unit of input, a unit of output, or a given activity should cost.

      1) The use of standard costs in budgeting allows the standard-cost system to alert management when the actual costs of production differ significantly from the standard.

   Standard cost of input = Units of input per single unit of output × Price per unit of input

   b. A standard cost is not just an average of past costs but an objectively determined estimate of what a cost should be. Standards may be based on accounting, engineering, or statistical quality control studies.

   Standard costs have been tested by asking for the calculation of a cost for a standard unit of input. You may be asked to explain the use of standard costs.

2. **Theoretical vs. Practical Standards**

   a. Ideal (theoretical) standards are standard costs that are set for production under optimal conditions. For this reason, they also are called perfection or maximum efficiency standards.

      1) They are based on the work of the most skilled workers with no allowance for spoilage, waste, machine breakdowns, or other downtime.

      2) Often called "tight" standards, they can have positive behavioral implications if workers are motivated to strive for excellence. However, they are not in wide use because they can have negative behavioral effects if the standards are impossible to attain.

      3) Ideal standards ordinarily are replaced by currently attainable (practical) standards for cash budgeting, product costing, and budgeting departmental performance. Otherwise, accurate financial planning will be impossible.

   b. Currently attainable (practical) standards may be defined as the performance that is expected to be achieved by reasonably well-trained workers with an allowance for normal spoilage, waste, and downtime.

      1) An alternative interpretation is that practical standards represent possible but difficult-to-attain results.

3. **Activity Analysis**

   a. Activity analysis identifies, describes, and evaluates the activities and resources needed to produce a particular output. This process aids in the development of standard costs.

   b. Each operation requires a unique set of inputs and preparations. Activity analysis describes what these inputs are and who performs these preparations.

      1) Inputs include the amounts and kinds of equipment, facilities, materials, and labor. Engineering analysis, cost accounting, time-and-motion study, and other approaches may be useful.

   c. Historical data may be used to set standards if an entity lacks the resources to engage in the complex task of activity analysis.

Stop and review! You have completed the outline for this subunit. Study multiple-choice questions 10 through 12 beginning on page 438.

16.3 THE OPERATING BUDGET

1. **Sales Budget**

    a. The sales budget, also called the revenue budget, is the starting point for the cycle that produces the annual profit plan (the master budget).

    b. The sales budget is based on the sales forecast. The forecast reflects recent sales trends, overall conditions in the economy and industry, market research, activities of competitors, and credit and pricing policies.

    c. The sales budget must specify both projected unit sales and dollar revenues.

EXAMPLE of a sales budget

	April	Ref.
Projected sales in units	1,000	SB1
Selling price	× $400	
Projected total sales	$400,000	SB2

---

2. **Production Budget**

    a. The production budget follows directly from the sales budget. The production budget is concerned with units only. Product pricing is ignored because the purpose is only to plan output and inventory levels and the necessary manufacturing activity.

    b. To minimize finished goods carrying costs and obsolescence, the levels of production are dependent upon the projections contained in the sales budget.

EXAMPLE of a production budget

The company's finished goods beginning inventory is 100 units at $125 cost per unit, for a total of $12,500.

	Source	April	Ref.
Projected sales in units	SB1	1,000	
Plus: desired ending inventory (10% of next month's sales)		120	
Minus: beginning inventory		(100)	
Units to be produced		1,020	PB

---

    c. The **purchases budget** for a retailer is prepared after projected sales are estimated.

    1) It is prepared on a monthly or even a weekly basis.
    2) Purchases can be planned so that stockouts are avoided.
    3) Inventory should be at an appropriate level to avoid unnecessary carrying costs.
    4) It is similar to the production budget example above. However, the units are purchased rather than produced.

Questions asked by the AICPA about budgeting often require calculations. Always read and think through the scenario very carefully. For example, you may encounter a question regarding budgeted materials required for a time period. If it asks for the budgeted number of legs necessary for tables produced, be sure to calculate the amount using four legs per table.

3. Direct Materials Budget

a.   The direct materials budget is concerned with both units and input prices.

   1)   Two dollar amounts are calculated in the direct materials budget: the cost of raw materials actually used in production and the total cost of raw materials purchased.

EXAMPLE of a direct materials budget

The company's raw material beginning inventory is 1,000 units at $18 cost per unit, and the desired raw material ending inventory is 980 units.

Raw Materials Used (Quantity)	Source	April	Ref.
Finished units to be produced	PB	1,020	
Times: raw material per finished product		× 4	
Total units needed for production		4,080	DMB1

Raw Materials Purchased	Source	April	Ref.
Units needed for production	DMB1	4,080	
Plus: desired units in ending inventory (20% of next month's need)		980	
Minus: beginning inventory		(1,000)	
Raw materials to be purchased		4,060	
Times: raw material cost per unit		× $20	
Cost of raw materials to be purchased		$81,200	DMB2

Raw Materials Used ($)	Source	April	Ref.
Beginning inventory (1,000 × $18)		$18,000	
Plus: purchases of raw material	DMB2	81,200	
Minus: desired ending inventory (980 × $20)		(19,600)	
Cost of raw materials used in production		$79,600	DMB3

---

4. Direct Labor Budget

a.   The direct labor budget depends on wage rates, amounts and types of production, numbers and skill levels of employees to be hired, etc.

b.   In addition to the regular wage rate, the total direct labor cost per hour may also include employer FICA taxes, health insurance, life insurance, and pension contributions.

EXAMPLE of a direct labor budget

The company's Human Resources department has determined that benefits amount to 25% of direct labor wages.

	Source	April	Ref.
Units to be produced	PB	1,020	
Times: direct labor hours per unit		× 2	
Projected total direct labor hours		2,040	DLB1
Times: direct labor cost per hour		× $18	
Total projected direct labor cost		$36,720	DLB2

5. **Manufacturing Overhead Budget**

   a. The manufacturing overhead budget reflects the nature of overhead as a mixed cost, i.e., one that has a variable component and a fixed component (mixed costs are defined in Study Unit 18).

   b. Variable overhead contains those elements that vary with the level of production.

       1) Indirect materials
       2) Some indirect labor
       3) Variable factory operating costs (e.g., electricity)

EXAMPLE of a variable overhead budget

The company applies variable overhead to production on the basis of direct labor hours.

	Source	April	Ref.
Projected total direct labor hours	DLB1	2,040	
Variable OH rate per direct labor hour		× $3	
Projected variable overhead		$6,120	MOB1

---

   c. Fixed overhead contains those elements that remain the same regardless of the level of production.

       1) Real estate taxes
       2) Insurance
       3) Depreciation

EXAMPLE of a fixed overhead budget

	April	Ref.
Projected fixed overhead	$9,000	MOB2

---

6. **Cost of Goods Sold Budget**

   a. The cost of goods sold budget combines the projections for the three major inputs (materials, labor, and overhead). The result directly affects the pro forma income statement. Cost of goods sold is the largest cost for a manufacturer.

EXAMPLE of a cost of goods sold budget

	Source	April		Ref.
Beginning finished goods inventory			$ 12,500	
Manufacturing costs:				
Direct materials used	DMB3	$79,600		
Direct labor employed	DLB2	36,720		
Variable overhead	MOB1	6,120		
Fixed overhead	MOB2	9,000		
Cost of goods manufactured			131,440	
Cost of goods available for sale			$143,940	
Ending finished goods inventory				
(120 units @ $130)			(15,600)	
Cost of goods sold			$128,340	CGSB

7. **Nonmanufacturing Budget**

   a. The nonmanufacturing budget consists of the individual budgets for R&D, design, marketing, distribution, customer service, and administrative costs. The development of separate budgets for these functions reflects a value chain approach.

      1) An alternative is to prepare a single budget for selling and administrative (S&A) costs of nonproduction functions.

   b. The variable and fixed portions of selling and administrative costs must be treated separately.

      1) Some S&A costs vary directly and proportionately with the level of sales. As more product is sold, sales representatives must travel more miles and serve more customers.

      2) Other S&A expenses, such as sales support staff, are fixed. They must be paid at any level of sales.

8. **Pro Forma Income Statement**

   a. The pro forma income statement is the end of the operating budget process.

      1) Financial statements are pro forma when they reflect projected results rather than actual ones.

   b. The pro forma income statement is used to decide whether the budgeted activities will result in an acceptable level of income. If the initial projection is a loss or an unacceptable level of income, adjustments can be made to the components of the master budget.

EXAMPLE of a pro forma income statement

Manufacturing Company
Pro Forma Statement of Income
Month of April

Sales		$400,000
Beginning finished goods inventory	$ 12,500	
Plus: cost of goods manufactured	131,440	
Goods available for sale	$143,940	
Minus: ending finished goods inventory	(15,600)	
Cost of goods sold		(128,340)
Gross margin		$271,660
Minus: selling and administrative expenses		(82,000)
Operating income		$189,660
Minus: other revenues/expenses/gains/losses		(15,000)
Earnings before interest and taxes		$174,660
Minus: interest expense		(45,000)
Earnings before income taxes		$129,660
Minus: income taxes (40%)		(49,200)
Net income		$ 80,460

Stop and review! You have completed the outline for this subunit. Study multiple-choice questions 13 through 22 beginning on page 439.

16.4 THE FINANCIAL BUDGET

1. **Capital Budget**

   a. The preparation of the capital budget is separate from the operating budget cycle. The capital budget, which often must be approved by the board of directors, concerns financing of major expenditures for long-term assets. It must therefore have a multi-year perspective. Productive assets must be acquired to enable the entity to achieve its projected levels of output.

   b. A procedure for ranking projects according to their risk and return characteristics is necessary because every organization has finite resources. [These procedures (net present value, internal rate of return, payback method, etc.) were discussed in Study Unit 9, Subunits 3 through 6.]

   c. The capital budget is a direct input to the cash budget and the pro forma balance sheet and statement of cash flows.

      1) Principal and interest on debt acquired to finance capital purchases require regular cash outflows. The acquired debt also appears in the liabilities section of the pro forma balance sheet.

      2) The output produced by the new productive assets generates regular cash inflows. In addition, the new assets appear in the assets section of the pro forma balance sheet.

2. **Cash Budget**

   a. The cash budget is the part of the financial budget cycle that connects all the schedules from the operating budget. A cash budget projects cash flows for planning and control purposes. Hence, it helps prevent not only cash emergencies but also excessive idle cash.

      1) A cash budget is vital because an organization must have adequate cash at all times. Almost all organizations, regardless of size, prepare a cash budget.

         a) Even with plenty of other assets, an organization with a temporary shortage of cash can become bankrupt.

      2) Proper planning can help forestall financial difficulty. Thus, cash budgets are prepared not only for annual and quarterly periods but also for monthly and weekly periods.

         a) They are particularly important for organizations operating in seasonal industries.

         b) The factors needed to prepare a cash forecast include all other elements of the budget preparation process plus consideration of collection policies, bad debt estimates, and changes in the economy.

      3) Credit and purchasing policies directly affect the cash budget.

         a) Loose customer credit policies delay cash receipts.
         b) Use of purchase discounts accelerates cash payments.

b.   The cash budget process begins with preparation of a **projected cash collection schedule**. It forecasts the inflows of cash from customer payments.

EXAMPLE of a cash collection schedule for April

The company's sales are made on credit.

	February Sales (Actual)	March Sales (Actual)	Source	April Sales (Projected)	Totals	Ref.
Sales	$180,000	$220,000	SB2	$400,000		
Projection of collection in April	× 30%	× 50%		× 15%		
From 2nd prior-month sales	$ 54,000				$ 54,000	
From prior-month sales		$110,000			110,000	
From current-month sales				$ 60,000	60,000	
Total cash collections from sales					$224,000	PCCS

---

c.   The next step is preparation of a **projected cash disbursements schedule**.

EXAMPLE of a cash disbursements schedule for April

For clarity, raw materials purchases are the only purchases that are made on credit.

	March Purchases (Actual)	Source	April Purchases (Projected)	Totals	Ref.
Cost of raw materials purchased	$72,000	DMB2	$81,200		
Projection of payments in April	× 40%		× 60%		
For prior-month purchases	$28,800			$28,800	
For current-month purchases			$48,720	48,720	
Total cash disbursements for raw materials				$77,520	PCDS

---

d.   The **cash budget** is the key element of the financial budget.

1)   It combines the operating budget with the cash flow schedules to produce a comprehensive statement of the sources and uses of the entity's cash flows.

2)   The cash budget can be used to plan financing activities. For example, if the budget projects a cash deficit, the entity can plan to borrow the necessary funds or sell stock.

3)   Dividend policy also can be planned using the cash budget. For instance, dividend payment dates should correspond to a time when the entity has excess cash.

EXAMPLE of a cash budget

The bottom line is the expected cash surplus or the financing required.

	Source	April
Beginning cash balance		$100,000
Cash collections from sales	PCCS	224,000
Cash available for disbursement		$324,000
Cash disbursements:		
For raw materials	PCDS	$ 77,520
For direct labor	DLB2	36,720
For variable overhead	MOB1	6,120
For fixed overhead	MOB2	9,000
For nonmanufacturing costs		26,000
For equipment purchases		110,000
Total disbursements		(265,360)
Excess of cash available over disbursements		$ 58,640
Desired ending cash balance		100,000
Short-term financing required		$ 41,360

3.   **Pro Forma Balance Sheet and Cash Flow Statement**

a.   The **pro forma balance sheet** is prepared using the cash and capital budgets and the pro forma income statement.

1)   The pro forma balance sheet is the beginning-of-the-period balance sheet updated for projected changes in cash, receivables, payables, inventory, etc.

2)   If the balance sheet indicates that a contractual agreement may be violated, the budgeting process must be repeated.

a)   For example, some loan agreements require that owners' equity be maintained at some percentage of total debt or that current assets be maintained at a given multiple of current liabilities.

b.   The **pro forma statement of cash flows** classifies cash flows depending on whether they are from operating, investing, or financing activities.

c.   The pro forma statements are interrelated; e.g., the pro forma cash flow statement includes anticipated borrowing. The interest on this borrowing appears in the pro forma income statement.

Stop and review! You have completed the outline for this subunit. Study multiple-choice questions 23 through 29 beginning on page 444.

16.5 FLEXIBLE BUDGETING

1.   **Flexible Budget**

a.   A flexible budget is an annual profit plan prepared for various levels of production or sales. It reports the operating income for each level.

1)   A flexible budget can be used for any component of the budget process that varies with the level of activity, for example, sales revenue, direct labor and materials, marketing expenses, and sales and administrative expenses.

2.   **Static vs. Flexible Budgeting**

a.   The **static (master) budget** is prepared before the period begins and is left unchanged. The static budget is based on only one level of expected activity (output that was planned at the beginning of the period).

EXAMPLE of a static budget

A company has the following static (master) budget for the upcoming month based on production and sales of 1,000 units:

Sales revenue ($400 per unit)	$400,000
Minus: variable costs ($160 per unit)	(160,000)
Contribution margin	$240,000
Minus: fixed costs	(200,000)
Operating income	$ 40,000

b. A flexible budget is prepared by using the same drivers (direct labor cost per hour, direct material cost per pound, etc.) that were used to prepare the static budget but for different levels of production.

EXAMPLE of a flexible budget

	Flexible Budget Based on 800 Units	Static Budget Based on 1,000 Units	Flexible Budget Based on 1,200 Units
Sales revenue ($400 per unit)	$320,000	$400,000	$480,000
Minus: variable costs ($160 per unit)	(128,000)	(160,000)	(192,000)
Contribution margin	$192,000	$240,000	$288,000
Minus: fixed costs	(200,000)	(200,000)	(200,000)
Operating income	$ (8,000)	$ 40,000	$ 88,000

---

3. **Variance Analysis Using Flexible Budgeting**

   a. The most common use of the flexible budget is for analysis of budget variances.

      1) Variance analysis helps management in monitoring and measuring a company's performance.

   b. A variance is the difference between the actual results for the period and a budget amount for the period.

      1) A favorable variance (F) occurs when actual revenues are greater than standard (budgeted) or actual costs are less than standard (budgeted).

      2) An unfavorable variance (U) occurs when actual revenues are less than standard (budgeted) or actual costs are greater than standard (budgeted).

EXAMPLE of budget variances

The company's actual results for the month were as follows:

Sales revenue of $342,000 (800 units × $427.50 price per unit)
Variable costs of $153,000
Fixed costs of $220,000

	Actual Results	Budget Variances		Master Budget
Sales revenue	$342,000	$(58,000)	U	$400,000
Minus: variable costs	(153,000)	7,000	F	(160,000)
Contribution margin	$189,000	$(51,000)	U	$240,000
Minus: fixed costs	(220,000)	(20,000)	U	(200,000)
Operating income (loss)	$ (31,000)	$(71,000)	U	$ 40,000

---

   c. To analyze the company's performance for the period, the budget variances should be subdivided into sales-volume variances and flexible budget variances.

      1) Sales-volume variances arise from inaccurate forecasting of the output sold for the period. They are measured as the difference between the flexible budget and the static (master) budget.

      2) Flexible budget variances report the differences between the actual revenues and costs for the period and the amounts that should have been earned and expended given the achieved level of production.

         a) Flexible budget variances are measured as the difference between the actual results and the flexible budget. More extensive analysis of flexible budget variances can be made by using standard costing (covered in detail in Study Unit 20).

d. To make this subdivision, the flexible budget must be prepared.

1) The flexible budget is prepared based on the actual output sold/produced during the period and on the same drivers that were used in the preparation of the master budget.

2) The flexible budget is prepared after the end of the period when all the actual results are known.

EXAMPLE of a flexible budget and sales-volume variances

	Actual Results	Flexible Budget Variances	Flexible Budget Based on Actual Sales of 800 Units	Sales-Volume Variances	Master (Static) Budget
Sales revenue	$342,000	$ 22,000 F	$320,000	$(80,000) U	$400,000
Minus: variable costs	(153,000)	(25,000) U	(128,000)	32,000 F	(160,000)
Contribution margin	$189,000	$ (3,000) U	$192,000	$(48,000) U	$240,000
Minus: fixed costs	(220,000)	(20,000) U	(200,000)	– –	(200,000)
Operating income (loss)	$ (31,000)	$(23,000) U	$ (8,000)	$(48,000) U	$ 40,000

Note that the net of the two variances equals the difference between the master budget and the actual results, called the static budget variance.

Flexible budget variance	$(23,000) U		Actual results	$(31,000)
Sales volume variance	(48,000) U		Master (static) budget	40,000
Static budget variance	$(71,000) U		Static budget variance	$(71,000) U

Stop and review! You have completed the outline for this subunit. Study multiple-choice questions 30 through 34 beginning on page 446.

QUESTIONS

16.1 The Master Budget and Its Components

1. In an organization that plans by using comprehensive budgeting, the master budget is

A. A compilation of all the separate operational and financial budget schedules of the organization.

B. The booklet containing budget guidelines, policies, and forms to use in the budgeting process.

C. The current budget updated for operations for part of the current year.

D. A budget of a not-for-profit organization after it is approved by the appropriate authoritative body.

Answer (A) is correct.
REQUIRED: The nature of the master budget.
DISCUSSION: A company's overall budget, often called the master or comprehensive budget, encompasses the organization's operating and financial plans for a specified period (ordinarily a year). Thus, all other budgets are subsets of the master budget.
Answer (B) is incorrect. The booklet containing budget guidelines, policies, and forms to use in the budgeting process is the budget manual. Answer (C) is incorrect. The current budget updated for operations for part of the current year is a continuous budget. Answer (D) is incorrect. A master budget may be prepared by a for-profit entity.

2. Pro forma financial statements are part of the budgeting process. Normally, the **last** pro forma statement prepared is the

A. Capital expenditure plan.

B. Income statement.

C. Statement of cost of goods sold.

D. Statement of cash flows.

Answer (D) is correct.
REQUIRED: The last pro forma financial statement prepared.
DISCUSSION: The statement of cash flows is usually the last of the listed items prepared. All other elements of the budget process must be completed before it can be developed.
Answer (A) is incorrect. The capital expenditure plan must be prepared before the cash budget. Cash may be needed to pay for capital purchases. Answer (B) is incorrect. The income statement must be prepared before the statement of cash flows, which reconciles net income and net operating cash flows. Answer (C) is incorrect. Cost of goods sold is included in the income statement, which is an input to the statement of cash flows.

3. The preparation of a comprehensive master budget culminates with the preparation of the

    A. Production budget.

    B. Capital investment budget.

    C. Cash budget.

    D. Strategic budget.

Answer (C) is correct.
    REQUIRED: The final step in the preparation of the comprehensive master budget.
    DISCUSSION: Apart from the pro forma balance sheet and statement of cash flows, the cash budget is the culmination of the master budget process.
    Answer (A) is incorrect. The production budget must precede the capital investment and cash budgets. Answer (B) is incorrect. A capital investment budget is prepared before a cash budget. Answer (D) is incorrect. A strategic budget is a long-range planning tool that is prepared before the master budget.

4. Wilson Company uses a comprehensive planning and budgeting system. The proper order for Wilson to prepare certain budget schedules would be

    A. Cost of goods sold, balance sheet, income statement, and statement of cash flows.

    B. Income statement, balance sheet, statement of cash flows, and cost of goods sold.

    C. Statement of cash flows, cost of goods sold, income statement, and balance sheet.

    D. Cost of goods sold, income statement, balance sheet, and statement of cash flows.

Answer (D) is correct.
    REQUIRED: The proper order in which budget schedules should be prepared.
    DISCUSSION: The cost of goods sold budget feeds the pro forma income statement. The entire operating budget process must be completed before the pro forma balance sheet and statement of cash flows can be prepared.
    Answer (A) is incorrect. The balance sheet should not precede the income statement. Answer (B) is incorrect. The income statement cannot precede cost of goods sold. Answer (C) is incorrect. The statement of cash flows cannot precede the cost of goods sold. The latter is an input of the former.

5. Which one of the following best describes the order in which budgets should be prepared when developing the annual master operating budget?

    A. Production budget, direct material budget, revenue budget.

    B. Production budget, revenue budget, direct material budget.

    C. Revenue budget, production budget, direct material budget.

    D. Revenue budget, direct material budget, production budget.

Answer (C) is correct.
    REQUIRED: The order in which budgets should be prepared when developing the annual master operating budget.
    DISCUSSION: The components of the operating budget are prepared in the following order: sales (revenue) budget, production budget, direct materials budget, direct labor budget, manufacturing overhead budget, ending finished goods inventory budget, cost of goods sold budget, and nonmanufacturing budget.
    Answer (A) is incorrect. The revenue budget must be completed before the other two can be prepared. Answer (B) is incorrect. The revenue budget must be completed before the production budget can be prepared. Answer (D) is incorrect. The production budget must be completed before the direct material budget can be prepared.

6. Many companies use comprehensive budgeting in planning for the next year's activities. When both an operating budget and a financial budget are prepared, which one of the following is correct concerning the financial budget?

	Included in the Financial Budget		
	Capital Budget	Pro-forma Balance Sheet	Cash Budget
A.	Yes	No	Yes
B.	No	Yes	No
C.	Yes	Yes	Yes
D.	No	No	No

Answer (C) is correct.
    REQUIRED: The true statement concerning the financial budget.
    DISCUSSION: In the financial budget, the emphasis is on obtaining the funds needed to purchase operating assets. It contains the capital budget, projected cash disbursement schedule, projected cash collection schedule, cash budget, pro forma balance sheet, and pro forma statement of cash flows.
    Answer (A) is incorrect. The pro forma balance sheet is part of the financial budget. Answer (B) is incorrect. The capital budget and cash budget are part of the financial budget. Answer (D) is incorrect. All three of these items are part of the financial budget.

7. The operating budget process usually begins with the

A. Financial budget.

B. Balance sheet.

C. Income statement.

D. Sales budget.

Answer (D) is correct.

REQUIRED: The budget that begins the operating budget process.

DISCUSSION: For most companies, the starting point for the annual budget is the sales forecast. All other aspects of the budget, including production, costs, and inventory levels, rely on the sales figures.

Answer (A) is incorrect. A financial budget cannot be prepared until after the sales budget has been completed. Answer (B) is incorrect. A balance sheet cannot be prepared until after the sales budget has been completed. Answer (C) is incorrect. An income statement cannot be prepared until after the sales budget has been completed.

8. The cash budget must be prepared before completing the

A. Capital expenditure budget.

B. Sales budget.

C. Forecasted balance sheet.

D. Production budget.

Answer (C) is correct.

REQUIRED: The budget element prepared after the cash budget.

DISCUSSION: The pro forma balance sheet is the balance sheet for the beginning of the period updated for projected changes in cash, receivables, inventories, payables, etc. Accordingly, it cannot be prepared until after the cash budget is completed because cash is a current asset reported on the balance sheet.

Answer (A) is incorrect. The capital expenditure budget is an input necessary for the preparation of a cash budget. Answer (B) is incorrect. The sales budget is usually the first budget prepared. Answer (D) is incorrect. A production budget is normally prepared before the cash budget is started.

9. Which of the following is normally included in the financial budget of a firm?

A. Direct materials budget.

B. Selling expense budget.

C. Budgeted balance sheet.

D. Sales budget.

Answer (C) is correct.

REQUIRED: The item normally included in the financial budget.

DISCUSSION: The financial budget normally includes the capital budget, the cash budget, the budgeted balance sheet, and the budgeted statement of cash flows.

Answer (A) is incorrect. The direct materials budget is included in the production budget. Answer (B) is incorrect. The selling expense budget is included in the operating budget. Answer (D) is incorrect. The sales budget is included in the operating budget.

16.2 Standard Setting

10. In connection with a standard cost system being developed by Flint Co., the following information is being considered with regard to standard hours allowed for output of one unit of product:

	Hours
Average historical performance for the past 3 years	1.85
Production level to satisfy average consumer demand over a seasonal time span	1.60
Engineering estimates based on attainable performance	1.50
Engineering estimates based on ideal performance	1.25

To measure controllable production inefficiencies, what is the best basis for Flint to use in establishing standard hours allowed?

A. 1.25

B. 1.50

C. 1.60

D. 1.85

Answer (B) is correct.

REQUIRED: The best basis for establishing standard hours allowed.

DISCUSSION: A standard cost system separates the expected cost from the actual cost. Thus, deviations from expected results are identified. The best standards are based on attainable performance so that any deviation identifies inefficiencies that have a reasonable probability of correction. Attainable standards also motivate employees. Accordingly, the engineering estimate based on attainable performance (1.50) is the best basis for establishing standard hours allowed.

Answer (A) is incorrect. Ideal standards are seldom attainable. Answer (C) is incorrect. Standard hours should be lower than the production level to satisfy average customer demand. Answer (D) is incorrect. Average historical performance standard hours are higher than the attainable standard.

11. The following direct labor information pertains to the manufacture of product Glu:

Time required to make one unit	2 direct labor hours
Number of direct workers	50
Number of productive hours per week, per worker	40
Weekly wages per worker	$500
Workers' benefits treated as direct labor costs	20% of wages

What is the standard direct labor cost per unit of product Glu?

A. $30

B. $24

C. $15

D. $12

Answer (A) is correct.

REQUIRED: The standard direct labor cost per unit.

DISCUSSION: The hourly wage per worker is $12.50 ($500 ÷ 40 hrs.). The direct labor cost per hour is $15 [$12.50 × (1.0 + benefits equal to 20% of wages)]. Consequently, the standard direct labor cost per unit is $30 ($15 × 2 hrs.).

12. Companies in what type of industry may use a standard cost system for cost control?

	Mass Production Industry	Service Industry
A.	Yes	Yes
B.	Yes	No
C.	No	No
D.	No	Yes

Answer (A) is correct.

REQUIRED: The types of industry that may use a standard cost system.

DISCUSSION: A standard cost system assigns a predetermined unit amount to output. It is applicable to both job-order and process costing systems and to service as well as mass production industries. For example, a standard labor cost may be developed for the labor involved in a service activity.

16.3 The Operating Budget

13. The following table contains Emerald Corp.'s quarterly revenues, in thousands, for the past 3 years. During that time, there were no major changes to Emerald's selling strategies and total capital investment.

Year	1st Qtr.	2nd Qtr.	3rd Qtr.	4th Qtr.
Year 1	500	500	550	750
Year 2	525	550	600	800
Year 3	550	525	625	850

Which of the following statements best describes the likely cause of the fluctuations in Emerald's revenues and the best response to those fluctuations?

A. The fluctuations are from changes in the economy, and Emerald should examine its cost structure for potential changes.

B. The fluctuations are from changes in the economy, and Emerald should manage its inventories and cash flow to match the cycle.

C. The fluctuations are from the seasonal demand for Emerald's products, and Emerald should examine its cost structure for potential changes.

D. The fluctuations are from the seasonal demand for Emerald's products, and Emerald should manage its inventories and cash flow to match the cycle.

Answer (D) is correct.

REQUIRED: The statement best describing the likely cause of the revenue fluctuations and the best response.

DISCUSSION: Seasonal fluctuations correspond with cycles within a year that repeat over multiple years. The routine increase in revenues in the third and fourth quarters indicates a seasonal cycle.

Answer (A) is incorrect. Economic fluctuations would preclude such repetitive similarities among Years 1, 2, and 3. Also, altering the cost structure is not indicated given only revenue data. Answer (B) is incorrect. Economic fluctuations would preclude such repetitive similarities among Years 1, 2, and 3. Answer (C) is incorrect. Altering the cost structure is not indicated given only revenue data.

14. Superior Industries' sales budget shows quarterly sales for the next year as follows:

Quarter	Units
1	10,000
2	8,000
3	12,000
4	14,000

Company policy is to have a finished goods inventory at the end of each quarter equal to 20% of the next quarter's sales. Budgeted production for the second quarter of the next year would be

A. 7,200 units.

B. 8,000 units.

C. 8,800 units.

D. 8,400 units.

Answer (C) is correct.

REQUIRED: The budgeted production for the second quarter given ending inventory for each quarter.

DISCUSSION: The finished units needed for sales (8,000), plus the units desired for ending inventory (12,000 units to be sold in the third quarter × 20% = 2,400), minus the units in beginning inventory (8,000 units to be sold in the second quarter × 20% = 1,600), equals budgeted production for the second quarter of 8,800 units.

Answer (A) is incorrect. Subtracting the beginning inventory twice results in 7,200 units. Answer (B) is incorrect. Assuming no change in inventory results in 8,000 units. Answer (D) is incorrect. Including the beginning inventory for the first quarter, not the second quarter, in the calculation results in 8,400 units.

Questions 15 and 16 are based on the following information. Paradise Company budgets on an annual basis for its fiscal year. The following beginning and ending inventory levels (in units) are planned for the fiscal year of July 1 through June 30:

	July 1	June 30
Raw material*	40,000	50,000
Work-in-process	10,000	20,000
Finished goods	80,000	50,000

* Two (2) units of raw material are needed to produce each unit of finished product.

---

15. If Paradise Company plans to sell 480,000 units during the fiscal year, the number of units it will have to manufacture during the year is

A. 440,000 units.

B. 480,000 units.

C. 510,000 units.

D. 450,000 units.

Answer (D) is correct.

REQUIRED: The number of units to be manufactured at a given sales level.

DISCUSSION: If the company sells 480,000 units with an ending finished goods inventory of 50,000 units, 530,000 units must be available. Given 80,000 units are in beginning inventory, production will have to be 450,000 units (530,000 – 80,000).

Answer (A) is incorrect. The calculation need not be adjusted for the change in work-in-process. Only finished goods are being discussed. Answer (B) is incorrect. The amount to be sold is 480,000 units. Answer (C) is incorrect. The number of 510,000 units equals sales, plus beginning inventory, minus ending inventory.

---

16. If 500,000 complete units were to be manufactured during the fiscal year by Paradise Company, the number of units of raw materials to be purchased is

A. 1,000,000 units.

B. 1,020,000 units.

C. 1,010,000 units.

D. 990,000 units.

Answer (C) is correct.

REQUIRED: The number of units of raw materials to be purchased at a given production level.

DISCUSSION: The total raw materials needed for production will be 1,000,000 units (500,000 units × 2 units of raw materials). In addition, raw materials inventory is expected to increase by 10,000 units. Thus, raw materials purchases will be 1,010,000.

Answer (A) is incorrect. The total needed for production is 1,000,000 units. Answer (B) is incorrect. The number of units in raw materials is not doubled. Answer (D) is incorrect. The number of 990,000 units is less than the amount used in production.

Questions 17 and 18 are based on the following information. Superflite expects April sales of its deluxe model airplane, the C-14, to be 402,000 units at $11 each. Each C-14 requires three purchased components shown below.

	Purchase Cost	Number Needed for Each C-14 Unit
A-9	$ .50	1
B-6	.25	2
D-28	1.00	3

Factory direct labor and variable overhead per unit of C-14 totals $3.00. Fixed factory overhead is $1.00 per unit at a production level of 500,000 units. Superflite plans the following beginning and ending inventories for the month of April and uses standard absorption costing for valuing inventory.

Part No.	Units at April 1	Units at April 30
C-14	12,000	10,000
A-9	21,000	9,000
B-6	32,000	10,000
D-28	14,000	6,000

17. Superflite's C-14 production budget for April should be based on the manufacture of

A. 390,000 units.

B. 400,000 units.

C. 402,000 units.

D. 424,000 units.

Answer (B) is correct.
REQUIRED: The number of units upon which the production budget should be based.
DISCUSSION: Sales are expected to be 402,000 units in April. The beginning inventory is 12,000 units, and the ending inventory is expected to be 10,000 units, a decline in inventory of 2,000 units. Thus, the budget should be based on production of 400,000 units (402,000 units to be sold – 12,000 units BI + 10,000 units EI).
Answer (A) is incorrect. Not considering the need to produce for ending inventory results in 390,000 units. Answer (C) is incorrect. Sales for the month equals 402,000 units; a portion of these sales will come from the beginning inventory. Answer (D) is incorrect. The sum of sales and beginning and ending inventories is 424,000 units.

18. Assume Superflite plans to manufacture 400,000 units in April. Superflite's April budget for the purchase of A-9 should be

A. 379,000 units.

B. 388,000 units.

C. 402,000 units.

D. 412,000 units.

Answer (B) is correct.
REQUIRED: The purchases budget for component A-9.
DISCUSSION: Each of the 400,000 units to be produced in April will require one unit of A-9, a total requirement of 400,000 units. In addition, ending inventory is expected to be 9,000 units. Hence, 409,000 units must be supplied during the month. Of these, 21,000 are available in the beginning inventory. Subtracting the 21,000 beginning inventory from 409,000 leaves 388,000 to be purchased.
Answer (A) is incorrect. The number of 379,000 units fails to consider the 9,000 units in the ending inventory. Answer (C) is incorrect. Sales for the month equals 402,000 units. Answer (D) is incorrect. Adding the decline in inventory of 12,000 to production needs instead of subtracting it results in 412,000.

Questions 19 and 20 are based on the following information. Simpson, Inc., is in the process of preparing its annual budget. The following beginning and ending inventory levels (in units) are planned for the year ending December 31.

	Beginning Inventory	Ending Inventory
Raw material*	40,000	50,000
Work-in-process	10,000	10,000
Finished goods	80,000	50,000

*Two units of raw material are needed to produce each unit of finished product.

19. If Simpson, Inc., plans to sell 480,000 units during the year, the number of units it would have to manufacture during the year would be

A. 440,000 units.

B. 480,000 units.

C. 510,000 units.

D. 450,000 units.

Answer (D) is correct.
REQUIRED: The units to be manufactured for the given annual sales level.
DISCUSSION: The finished units needed for sales (480,000), plus the units desired for ending inventory (50,000), minus beginning inventory (80,000), equals the necessary production of 450,000 units.
Answer (A) is incorrect. Treating beginning work-in-process as beginning finished goods results in 440,000 units. Answer (B) is incorrect. The figure of 480,000 units assumes no change in finished goods inventory. Answer (C) is incorrect. Reversing the beginning and ending inventories results in 510,000 units.

20. If 500,000 finished units were to be manufactured for the year by Simpson, Inc., the units of raw material that must be purchased would be

A. 1,000,000 units.

B. 1,020,000 units.

C. 1,010,000 units.

D. 990,000 units.

Answer (C) is correct.
REQUIRED: The units of raw materials to be purchased given the units of finished goods.
DISCUSSION: The 500,000 finished units to be manufactured require 1,000,000 units of raw material (2 × 500,000). In addition, the inventory of raw material is planned to increase by 10,000 units. Consequently, 1,010,000 units of raw material should be purchased.
Answer (A) is incorrect. Raw material needed for production only equals 1,000,000 units. Answer (B) is incorrect. The figure of 1,020,000 units is based on an erroneous doubling of the difference between beginning and ending inventory of raw material. Answer (D) is incorrect. Reversing the beginning and ending inventories results in 990,000 units.

Questions 21 and 22 are based on the following information. Berol Company plans to sell 200,000 units of finished product in July and anticipates a growth rate in sales of 5% per month. The desired monthly ending inventory in units of finished product is 80% of the next month's estimated sales. There are 150,000 finished units in inventory on June 30. Each unit of finished product requires 4 pounds of direct materials at a cost of $1.20 per pound. There are 800,000 pounds of direct materials in inventory on June 30.

21. Berol Company's production requirement in units of finished product for the 3-month period ending September 30 is

    A. 712,025 units.

    B. 630,500 units.

    C. 638,000 units.

    D. 665,720 units.

Answer (D) is correct.
    REQUIRED: The unit production requirement for the next quarter.
    DISCUSSION: Sales are expected to increase at the rate of 5% per month. Given that July sales are estimated to be 200,000 units, August, September, and October sales are expected to be 210,000 units (200,000 × 1.05), 220,500 units (210,000 × 1.05), and 231,525 units (220,500 × 1.05), respectively. Moreover, September ending inventory must be 80% of October's estimated sales, or 185,220 units (231,525 × 80%). Consequently, the production requirement for the 3-month period is 665,720 units (200,000 + 210,000 + 220,500 + 185,220 September EI – 150,000 July BI).
    Answer (A) is incorrect. The total estimated sales for the next 4 months, minus beginning inventory for July, equals 712,025 units. Answer (B) is incorrect. The total sales for 3 months equals 630,500 units. Answer (C) is incorrect. The number of 638,000 units assumes that each succeeding month's sales are 105% of July's.

22. Assume Berol Company plans to produce 600,000 units of finished product in the 3-month period ending September 30 and to have direct materials inventory on hand at the end of the 3-month period equal to 25% of the use in that period. The estimated cost of direct materials purchases for the 3-month period ending September 30 is

    A. $2,200,000

    B. $2,400,000

    C. $2,640,000

    D. $2,880,000

Answer (C) is correct.
    REQUIRED: The estimated cost of direct materials purchases for the next quarter.
    DISCUSSION: Production of 600,000 units will require 2,400,000 pounds of direct materials (600,000 units × 4 lbs.). In addition, ending inventory will be 25% of the period's usage, or 600,000 pounds (2,400,000 × 25%). Thus, 3,000,000 total pounds will be needed. However, given 800,000 pounds in inventory, purchases will be only 2,200,000 pounds. At $1.20 per pound, the cost will be $2,640,000.
    Answer (A) is incorrect. The number of pounds needed to be purchased is 2,200,000. Answer (B) is incorrect. The number of pounds that will be used is 2,400,000. Answer (D) is incorrect. The $2,880,000 is obtained by multiplying the total usage times the cost per pound without considering the change in inventory.

16.4 The Financial Budget

23. A company forecast first quarter sales of 10,000 units, second quarter sales of 15,000 units, third quarter sales of 12,000 units, and fourth quarter sales of 9,000 units at $2 per unit. Past experience has shown that 60% of the sales will be in cash and 40% will be on credit. All credit sales are collected in the following quarter, and none are uncollectible. What amount of cash is forecasted to be collected in the second quarter?

A. $8,000

B. $18,000

C. $26,000

D. $30,000

Answer (C) is correct.
REQUIRED: The estimated cash collected in the second quarter.
DISCUSSION: The credit sales from the first quarter are collected in the second. The amount of cash forecasted to be collected in the second quarter is calculated as follows:

First quarter: 10,000 units × $2 per unit × 40% = $ 8,000
Second quarter: 15,000 units × $2 per unit × 60% = $18,000
Total cash collected in second quarter $26,000

Answer (A) is incorrect. The amount of $8,000 is the cash collected in the second quarter from sales in the first quarter. Answer (B) is incorrect. The amount of $18,000 is the cash collected in the second quarter from sales made in the first quarter. Answer (D) is incorrect. The amount of $30,000 is the revenue from sales made during the second quarter.

24. Which of the following inputs would be most beneficial to consider when management is developing the capital budget?

A. Supply/demand for the company's products.

B. Current product sales prices and costs.

C. Wage trends.

D. Profit center equipment requests.

Answer (D) is correct.
REQUIRED: The most beneficial input to the capital budget.
DISCUSSION: The capital budget is part of the financial budget, so its emphasis is on obtaining the funds needed to acquire operating assets. It may be prepared more than a year in advance to allow time to plan financing of major expenditures for such long-term assets as equipment, buildings, and land. Thus, profit center equipment requests are directly relevant to development of the capital budget.
Answer (A) is incorrect. Future supply/demand for the company's products is more relevant than current supply/demand for the company's products. Furthermore, even expected unfavorable future conditions are less useful a factor than profit center requests for equipment that may be needed regardless of an economic downturn. Answer (B) is incorrect. Current product sales prices and costs are less critical than future prices and costs. Answer (C) is incorrect. Wage trends have an effect on a capital budget that may have less direct impact than profit center equipment requests.

25. Lon Co.'s budget committee is preparing its master budget on the basis of the following projections:

Sales	$2,800,000
Decrease in inventories	70,000
Decrease in accounts payable	150,000
Gross margin	40%

What are Lon's estimated cash disbursements for inventories?

A. $1,040,000

B. $1,200,000

C. $1,600,000

D. $1,760,000

Answer (D) is correct.
REQUIRED: The estimated cash disbursements for inventory.
DISCUSSION: Projected cost of sales is 60% of $2,800,000 of sales, which is $1,680,000. Projected purchases is the $1,680,000 cost of sales minus the $70,000 projected decrease in inventory, which is $1,610,000. Projected cash payments equal the projected purchases of $1,610,000 plus the $150,000 projected decrease in A/P, which is $1,760,000.

26. A cash budget is being prepared for the purchase of Toyi, a merchandise item. Budgeted data are

Cost of goods sold for upcoming year	$300,000
Accounts payable, beginning of upcoming year	20,000
Inventory, beginning of upcoming year	30,000
Inventory, end of upcoming year	42,000

Purchases will be made in 12 equal monthly amounts and paid for in the following month. What is the budgeted cash payment for purchases of Toyi?

A. $295,000

B. $300,000

C. $306,000

D. $312,000

Answer (C) is correct.

REQUIRED: The budgeted cash payment for purchases.

DISCUSSION: Purchases equal cost of goods sold, plus ending inventory, minus beginning inventory, or $312,000 ($300,000 + $42,000 – $30,000). Purchases are made evenly throughout the year at a rate of $26,000 per month ($312,000 ÷ 12). Given that 11 payments will be made in the upcoming year for that year's purchases, the total cash payment will be $306,000 [(11 × $26,000) + $20,000 beginning accounts payable balance].

Answer (A) is incorrect. The budgeted cash payment is $306,000. Answer (B) is incorrect. The cost of goods sold is $300,000. Answer (D) is incorrect. The amount of purchases is $312,000.

27. Ryan Co. projects the following monthly revenues for next year:

January	$100,000	July	$250,000
February	500,000	August	275,000
March	425,000	September	300,000
April	450,000	October	350,000
May	575,000	November	400,000
June	300,000	December	525,000

Ryan's terms are net 30 days. The company typically receives payment on 80% of sales the month following the sale, and 17% is collected 2 months after the sale. Approximately 3% of sales are deemed bad debt. What amount represents the expected cash collection in the second calendar quarter of next year?

A. $1,450,000

B. $1,393,750

C. $1,325,000

D. $1,234,250

Answer (B) is correct.

REQUIRED: The expected cash collection in the second calendar quarter of next year.

DISCUSSION: April collections will total 17% of February sales, or $85,000 ($500,000 × 17%), and 80% of March sales, or $340,000 ($425,000 × 80%). May collections will total 17% of March sales, or $72,250 ($425,000 × 17%), and 80% of April sales, or $360,000 ($450,000 × 80%). Finally, June collections will total 17% of April sales, or $76,500 ($450,000 × 17%), and 80% of May sales, or $460,000 ($575,000 × 80%). The total cash collected during the second calendar quarter of next year will equal $1,393,750 ($85,000 + $340,000 + $72,250 + $360,000 + $76,500 + $460,000).

Answer (A) is incorrect. The amount of $1,450,000 assumes 100% of sales are collected the following month. Answer (C) is incorrect. The amount of $1,325,000 is the total sales collected for the second quarter. Answer (D) is incorrect. The amount of $1,234,250 understates actual sales collections for the second calendar quarter of next year.

28. Which of the following budgets provides information for preparation of the owner's equity section of a budgeted balance sheet?

A. Sales budget.

B. Cash budget.

C. Capital expenditures budget.

D. Budgeted income statement.

Answer (D) is correct.

REQUIRED: The budget that provides information for preparation of the equity section of a budgeted balance sheet.

DISCUSSION: The pro forma balance sheet is prepared using the cash and capital budgets and the pro forma income statement. The statement of retained earnings, which flows through to the equity section of the balance sheet, is increased by net income and decreased by a net loss.

Answer (A) is incorrect. The sales budget projects sales and revenues, and although revenues will flow through to the budgeted income statement, the sales budget does not have an immediate effect on the owner's equity section of a budgeted balance sheet. Answer (B) is incorrect. The cash budget has no effect on income or retained earnings and no residual effect on equity. Answer (C) is incorrect. The capital budget affects the cash budget and is a tool for capital budgeting and long-term projects.

29. On June 30, a company is preparing the cash budget for the third quarter. The collection pattern for credit sales has been 60% in the month of sale, 30% in the first month after sale, and the rest in the second month after sale. Uncollectible accounts are negligible. There are cash sales each month equal to 25% of total sales. The total sales for the quarter are estimated as follows: July, $30,000; August, $15,000; September, $35,000. Accounts receivable on June 30 were $10,000. What amount would be the projected cash collections for September?

A. $21,375

B. $28,500

C. $30,125

D. $40,125

Answer (C) is correct.

REQUIRED: The projected cash collections for September.

DISCUSSION: September's total projected cash collections can be calculated as follows:

	Total Sales	Minus: Cash Sales (25%)	Equals: Credit Sales	Times: Percent Collected	Equals: Total
July	$30,000	$7,500	$22,500	10%	$ 2,250
August	15,000	3,750	11,250	30%	3,375
September	35,000	8,750	26,250	60%	15,750
September collections on credit sales					$21,375
September cash sales					8,750
Total September cash collections					$30,125

Answer (A) is incorrect. The amount of $21,375 results from neglecting to add back the cash sales collected in September. Answer (B) is incorrect. The amount of $28,500 results from applying the credit collection pattern to all sales for the 3 months instead of applying it to just the credit sales. Answer (D) is incorrect. The amount of $40,125 includes the accounts receivable at the end of the previous period.

16.5 Flexible Budgeting

30. A flexible budget is appropriate for a

	Marketing Budget	Direct Materials Usage Budget
A.	No	No
B.	No	Yes
C.	Yes	Yes
D.	Yes	No

Answer (C) is correct.

REQUIRED: The type(s) of budget, if any, for which a flexible budget is appropriate.

DISCUSSION: A flexible budget approach is appropriate for both a materials budget and a marketing budget because each contains elements that vary with the activity level.

Answer (A) is incorrect. A flexible budget can be used for either marketing or direct materials. Direct materials is inherently a variable cost, and marketing contains variable elements. Any cost that varies with the level of production can benefit from being compared on a flexible budget basis. Answer (B) is incorrect. Because flexible budgeting is based on the actual quantity of outputs produced, the variable portion of marketing can be budgeted on a flexible basis. Answer (D) is incorrect. Direct materials, being a variable cost, can be budgeted on a flexible basis. The flexible budget reports the costs that should have been incurred given the achieved level of production.

31. A flexible budget is appropriate for a(n)

	Administrative Budget	Marketing Budget
A.	No	No
B.	No	Yes
C.	Yes	No
D.	Yes	Yes

Answer (D) is correct.

REQUIRED: The situation(s) in which a flexible budget is appropriate.

DISCUSSION: A flexible budget is a budget adjusted for the actual level of activity. Thus, it is appropriate for any level of activity. A flexible budget approach is appropriate for both an administrative budget and a marketing budget because each contains some elements that vary with the activity level and some that do not.

Answer (A) is incorrect. A flexible budget is appropriate for both an administrative budget and a marketing budget. Answer (B) is incorrect. A flexible budget is also appropriate for an administrative budget. Answer (C) is incorrect. A flexible budget is also appropriate for a marketing budget.

32. The flexible budget for a company may include

	Direct Material Costs	Variable Selling Costs
A.	Yes	No
B.	Yes	Yes
C.	No	Yes
D.	No	No

Answer (B) is correct.
REQUIRED: The costs included in a flexible budget.
DISCUSSION: Any variable cost component, such as direct materials or variable selling costs, can be budgeted on a flexible basis. A flexible budget, prepared after the budget period has ended, consists of the costs that should have been incurred given the actual level of production achieved.
Answer (A) is incorrect. Flexible budgeting is appropriate for any variable cost component, including selling costs. Answer (C) is incorrect. Direct material costs are variable and thus appropriate for budgeting on a flexible basis. Answer (D) is incorrect. Both direct material and variable selling costs are variable; the assessment of performance for any variable cost can benefit from flexible budgeting.

33. Which of the following is a characteristic of a flexible budget?

A. Provides budgeted numbers for various activity levels.

B. Allows for modification during the budgeted period.

C. Isolates the impact of variable costs on the overall budget.

D. Can be utilized by several product divisions.

Answer (A) is correct.
REQUIRED: The choice that is a characteristic of a flexible budget.
DISCUSSION: A flexible budget consists of the costs that should have been incurred given the actual level of production achieved. It captures the complexity of the relationships among input, output, and resource prices.
Answer (B) is incorrect. Modification during the budgeted period is not relevant to the use of a flexible budget. Answer (C) is incorrect. Isolating the impact of variable costs on an overall budget is the goal of variance analysis, not flexible budgeting. Answer (D) is incorrect. A flexible budgeting system can be used by multiple product divisions.

34. The basic difference between a master budget and a flexible budget is that a master budget is

A. Prepared before the period begins, while a flexible budget is prepared after it ends.

B. Reporting the costs that should have been incurred given the achieved level of production.

C. Based on a fixed standard, but a flexible budget allows management latitude in meeting goals.

D. For an entire production facility, but a flexible budget is applicable to single departments only.

Answer (A) is correct.
REQUIRED: The basic difference between a master budget and a flexible budget.
DISCUSSION: The master budget, prepared before the next accounting period, is management's best estimate of sales, production levels, and costs. The flexible budget, prepared after actual output is known, consists of the costs that should have been incurred based on the actual level of production.
Answer (B) is incorrect. The budget that reports the costs that should have been incurred given the achieved level of production is the flexible budget. Answer (C) is incorrect. A flexible budget is prepared based on the same drivers (fixed standards) as the master budget. Answer (D) is incorrect. Flexible budgets can be prepared at the departmental level or at the production facility level.

Use the additional questions in Gleim **CPA Test Prep Online** to create Test Sessions that emulate Prometric!

16.6 PRACTICE WRITTEN COMMUNICATION TASK

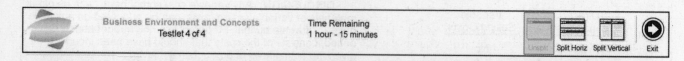

Business Environment and Concepts
Testlet 4 of 4

Time Remaining
1 hour - 15 minutes

Unsplit Split Horiz Split Vertical Exit

DIRECTIONS

Note: If you believe you have encountered a software malfunction, report it to the test center staff immediately.

Navigation

To navigate from task to task, use the controls at the bottom of the screen. Click on the **Next** button to advance to the next task, or the **Previous** button to go to the previous task. To go directly to any task, click on its number.

If you would like a reminder to revisit a task, or want to indicate that you are finished with it, click on the reminder flag below the task number. To clear the flag, click on it again. Reminder flags are for your use only – they do not contribute to your score.

Tabs

In this part of the examination, you will be asked to complete various tasks. Every task has one or more **Work Tabs**. Every task also has a **Help** tab.

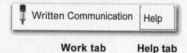

Work tab   Help tab

Work Tabs:

- **Work Tabs** are identified with a pencil icon. This is where your responses are expected.
- Each task has one or more **Work Tabs**.
- **Work Tabs** contain directions for completing the task - be sure to read these directions carefully.
- The **Work Tab** name in the example above is for illustration only - yours will differ.
- You must complete all of the **Work Tabs** in each task to receive full credit.

Help Tab:

- The **Help Tab** provides assistance with the exam software that is used in this task. For example, if the task is to compose a memorandum, **Help** will provide information about the word processor.

The Toolbar

The toolbar at the top of the screen shows the amount of time remaining for you to complete the tasks. In addition, the following tools are available. Note that only the **Exit** button is displayed when Directions are visible - the others will appear when you begin the tasks.

Click on these buttons to split or unsplit the screen. You can split the screen vertically or horizontally.

Click on this button to go on to the next part of the examination. You must complete all of the tasks to receive full credit. Once you click on **Exit** and confirm the action, you will NOT be able to return to this testlet.

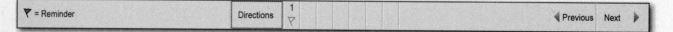

Written Communication | Help

✂ Cut | 📋 Copy | 📋 Paste | ↩ Undo | ↪ Redo

Aquinas Company, which started in a storefront 5 years ago, has grown in size and complexity. The owner has finally realized that controlling the organization requires the use of budgeting.

Prepare a memo to the owner of Aquinas Company describing the master budget and its components.

Type your communication below the line in the response area below.

REMINDER: Your response will be graded for both technical content and writing skills. Technical content will be evaluated for information that is helpful to the intended reader and clearly relevant to the issue. Writing skills will be evaluated for development, organization, and the appropriate expression of ideas in professional correspondence. Use a standard business memorandum or letter format with a clear beginning, middle, and end. Do not convey information in the form of a table, bullet point list, or other abbreviated presentation.

To: Aquinas Company
Re: The master budget and its components

Unofficial Answer

Written Communication

To: Aquinas Company
Re: The master budget and its components

A master budget is a comprehensive, annual budget plan. It consists of the operating budget and the financial budget. Each of these sub-budgets consists of several interrelated component budgets. Thus, it is necessary to identify the elements of the operating and financial budgets and to understand their relationships.

The operating budget focuses on obtaining and using current resources. The budgets that track this use are the sales, production, direct materials, direct labor, manufacturing overhead, ending finished goods inventory, cost of goods sold, and nonmanufacturing budgets. The data provided by these budgets are inputs to the pro forma income statement.

The financial budget emphasizes the process of obtaining the funds needed to purchase operating assets. It contains the capital budget, the projected cash disbursement schedule, the projected cash collection schedule, and the cash budget. These items are inputs to the pro forma balance sheet and statement of cash flows.

Identifying the components of the master budget is required to establish the budget calendar. In other words, a higher-level budget must be created before work can begin on the next level. For example, the production budget cannot be prepared until the sales budget is completed. Likewise, a projected cash collection schedule needs to be completed prior to the development of a cash budget. For this reason, the individual parts of the operating and financial budgets must be understood before a master budget is prepared.

The above depicts a Level 5 answer. See page 16 in the Introduction for a description of the three grading criteria.

Self-Grade

Evaluate each of the following by selecting a 0, 1, 2, 3, 4, or 5. An average response is 3. Use 4 for better than average and 5 for outstanding. Use 2 for less than average and 1 for quite poor. Use zero for no response, if you did not address the topic, or if you gave advice that is clearly illegal.

Organization	○ 0	○ 1	○ 2	○ 3	○ 4	○ 5
Development	○ 0	○ 1	○ 2	○ 3	○ 4	○ 5
Expression	○ 0	○ 1	○ 2	○ 3	○ 4	○ 5

Your grade for the written communication as a whole is the average of the scores for the three criteria.

Use **CPA Gleim Online** and **Simulation Wizard** to practice more written communication tasks in a realistic environment.

STUDY UNIT SEVENTEEN
PERFORMANCE MEASUREMENT AND
PROCESS MANAGEMENT

(18 pages of outline)

Responsibility accounting allows each component of the organization to be judged on the achievement of its own goals (Subunit 1). The performance of a responsibility center must be evaluated based on appropriate criteria. Marketing incentives and executive compensation must be designed to inspire improvement in these criteria. The balanced scorecard is a tool for ensuring that the organization does not lose sight of some objectives in the pursuit of others (Subunit 2).

Business processes have been the subject of much practical and theoretical innovation in recent years (Subunit 3), along with tools for monitoring the efficiency of these processes (Subunit 4). Quality has been an area of management scrutiny since the 1980s; its costs can be quantified (Subunit 5), and frameworks have been developed for regularizing the pursuit of quality (Subunit 6).

One of a manager's most important tasks is the monitoring of progress toward the completion of an individual project (Subunit 7).

17.1 RESPONSIBILITY CENTERS

1. **Decision Making and Decentralization**

   a. The primary distinction between centralized and decentralized organizations is in the degree of freedom of decision making by managers at many levels.

      1) In a centralized organization, decision making is consolidated so that activities throughout the organization may be more effectively coordinated from the top.

      2) In a decentralized organization, decision making is at the lowest level possible. The premise is that the local manager can make more informed decisions than a manager further from the decision.

2. **Responsibility Centers**

   a. A decentralized organization is divided into **responsibility centers** (also called **strategic business units**, or SBUs) to facilitate local decision making.

      1) Four types of responsibility centers are generally recognized.

    b.   A **cost center**, e.g., a maintenance department, is responsible for costs only.

        1)   Cost drivers are the relevant performance measures.

        2)   A disadvantage of a cost center is the potential for cost shifting, for example, replacement of variable costs for which a manager is responsible with fixed costs for which (s)he is not.

            a)   Another disadvantage is that long-term issues may be disregarded when the emphasis is on, for example, annual cost amounts.

            b)   Yet another issue is allocation of service department costs to cost centers.

        3)   Service centers exist primarily and sometimes solely to provide specialized support to other organizational subunits. They are usually operated as cost centers.

    c.   A **revenue center**, e.g., a sales department, is responsible for revenues only.

        1)   Revenue drivers are the relevant performance measures. They are factors that influence unit sales, such as changes in prices and products, customer service, marketing efforts, and delivery terms.

    d.   A **profit center**, e.g., an appliance department in a retail store, is responsible for both revenues and expenses.

    e.   An **investment center**, e.g., a branch office, is responsible for revenues, expenses, and invested capital.

        1)   The advantage of an investment center is that it permits an evaluation of performance that can be compared with that of other responsibility centers or other potential investments on a return on investment basis, i.e., on the basis of the effectiveness of asset usage.

3.   **Performance Measures and Manager Motivation**

    a.   Each responsibility center is structured such that a logical group of operations is under the direction of a single manager.

        1)   Measures are designed for every responsibility center to monitor performance.

    b.   **Controllability.** The performance measures on which the manager's incentive package are based must be, as far as practicable, under the manager's direct influence.

        1)   "Controllable" factors can be thought of as those factors that a manager can influence in a given time period.

            a)   Inevitably, some costs, especially common costs such as the costs of central administrative functions, cannot be traced to particular activities or responsibility centers.

        2)   Controllable cost is not synonymous with variable cost. Often, this classification is particular to the level of the organization.

            a)   For instance, the fixed cost of depreciation may not be a controllable cost of the manager of a revenue center, but is controllable by the division vice president to which that manager reports.

    c.   **Goal congruence.** These performance measures must be designed such that the manager's pursuit of them ties directly to accomplishment of the organization's overall goals.

        1)   Suboptimization results when segments of the organization pursue goals that are in that segment's own best interests rather than those of the organization as a whole.

    d.   Along with the responsibility, a manager must be granted sufficient authority to control those factors on which his/her incentive package is based.

4. **Common Costs**

   a. Common costs are the costs of products, activities, facilities, services, or operations shared by two or more cost objects. The term "joint costs" is frequently used to describe the common costs of a single process that yields two or more joint products.

      1) The costs of service centers and headquarters are common examples.

   b. Because common costs are indirect costs, identification of a direct cause-and-effect relationship between a common cost and the actions of the cost object to which it is allocated can be difficult.

      1) Such a relationship promotes acceptance of common cost allocation by managers who perceive the fairness of the procedure.

5. **Management Reporting**

   a. Relevance is the most important attribute of management reporting. Relevance is determined by asking the question, "Does a change to this revenue or cost element depend on my choice?"

Stop and review! You have completed the outline for this subunit. Study multiple-choice questions 1 through 4 beginning on page 468.

17.2 PERFORMANCE MEASURES, INCENTIVES, AND THE BALANCED SCORECARD

1. **Financial vs. Nonfinancial Measures**

   a. Each type of responsibility center described in Subunit 17.1 has its own appropriate financial performance measures.

      1) Cost centers -- Variable costs, total costs.
      2) Revenue centers -- Gross sales, net sales.
      3) Profit centers -- Sales, gross margin, operating income.
      4) Investment Centers

         a) Return on investment, residual income (discussed in Study Unit 10, Subunit 3)

         b) Return on assets, return on common equity, economic rate of return on common stock, economic value added (discussed in Study Unit 10, Subunit 4)

   b. Nonfinancial performance measures are not standardized and thus can take any form appropriate to the SBU under review.

      1) Examples of nonfinancial performance measures are provided as part of the discussion of the balanced scorecard later in this subunit.

2. **Impact of Marketing Practices on Performance**

   a. An appropriate link must be established between SBU performance measurement and corporate marketing goals.

      1) As noted in the previous subunit, sales is the typical performance measure for a revenue center.

      2) For a profit center, sales, gross margin, and operating income should all be subject to evaluation.

Calculation of Profit Center Operating Income

Net sales	$1,000,000
Cost of goods sold	(650,000)
Gross margin	$ 350,000
Controllable expenses	(200,000)
Operating income	$ 150,000

b. If an overall goal to gain market share has been set, prices will likely be cut to such a degree that gross margin is negatively affected. Profit center managers in these situations should be evaluated based on sales results, not margins.

1) By the same token, if profits are of greatest concern to the enterprise, operating income is a more appropriate measure. The manager is held responsible for striking the proper balance between sales, cost of goods sold, and controllable expenses.

c. Choices among marketing practices must be considered in a similar manner.

1) The amount of flexibility granted to salespeople in matters of price affects margin and operating income.

2) Highly centralized marketing, such as advertising to heighten corporate brand awareness, increases the difficulty of tracing marketing costs to profit centers (an example of the common-cost challenge is noted in item 4. in Subunit 17.1).

3. **Incentive Compensation**

a. Executive compensation generally consists of three components:

1) Annual salary
2) Fringe benefits
3) Annual bonus

a) Ideally, these components are structured to motivate the executive toward the goals of his/her responsibility center, which are in turn aligned with those of the enterprise.

b. Salary is base pay, i.e., contractually obligated to be paid for effort and not affected by outcomes.

c. Fringe benefits for almost all employees include such things as medical insurance, life insurance, and paid vacation.

1) Executives, however, must motivate all employees of a responsibility center to pursue the center's goals. The incentive provided to an executive must therefore be commensurate with the effort required.

2) Executive benefits may thus include use of a company vehicle, travel by company airplane, use of a company-owned resort home, etc. These are known as perquisites of upper management (usually shortened to perks).

d. The executive bonus is usually directly tied to the main performance measure for that responsibility center.

1) Bonuses for the highest executives of the enterprise are generally tied to the stock price. Return on investment and residual income may also pay a role.

2) For profit centers, operating income (often called segment contribution for these purposes) is the most appropriate basis for executive bonus.

4. **Balanced Scorecard -- Critical Success Factors (CSFs)**

a. The trend in performance evaluation is the balanced scorecard approach to managing the implementation of the firm's strategy.

1) The balanced scorecard is an accounting report that connects the firm's critical success factors to measurements of its performance.

b. Critical success factors (CSFs) are specific, measurable financial and nonfinancial elements of a firm's performance that are vital to its competitive advantage.

1) Multiple measures of performance permit a determination as to whether a manager is achieving certain objectives at the expense of others that may be equally or more important. For example, an improvement in operating results at the expense of new product development would be apparent using a balanced scorecard approach.

c. The balanced scorecard is a goal congruence tool that informs managers about the nonfinancial factors that top management believes to be important.

    1) Measures on the balanced scorecard may be financial or nonfinancial, internal or external, and short term or long term.

    2) The balanced scorecard facilitates best practice analysis. Best practice analysis determines a method of carrying on a business function or process that is considered to be superior to all other known methods. A lesson learned from one area of a business can be passed on to another area of the business or between businesses.

5. SWOT Analysis

a. A firm identifies its CSFs by means of a SWOT analysis that addresses internal factors (its strengths and weaknesses) and external factors (its opportunities and threats).

    1) The firm's greatest strengths are its core competencies, which are functions the company performs especially well. These are the basis for its competitive advantages and strategy.

    2) For a discussion of the strengths, weaknesses, opportunities, and threats facing a firm, see Study Unit 15, Subunit 1.

b. The SWOT analysis tends to highlight the basic factors of cost, quality, and the speed of product development and delivery.

6. Balanced Scorecard -- Measures

a. Once the firm has identified its CSFs, it must establish specific measures for each CSF that are both relevant to the success of the firm and can be reliably stated.

    1) Thus, the balanced scorecard varies with the strategy adopted by the firm.

    2) For example, product differentiation or cost leadership in either a broad market or a narrowly focused market (a focus strategy). These measures provide a basis for implementing the firm's competitive strategy.

b. The scorecard should include lagging indicators (such as output and financial measures) and leading indicators (such as many types of nonfinancial measures).

    1) The latter should be used only if they are predictors of ultimate financial performance.

c. The scorecard should permit a determination of whether certain objectives are being achieved at the expense of others.

    1) For example, reduced spending on customer service may improve short-term financial results at a significant cost that is revealed by a long-term decline in customer satisfaction measures.

d. By providing measures that are **nonfinancial as well as financial**, long term as well as short term, and internal as well as external, the balanced scorecard de-emphasizes short term financial results and focuses attention on CSFs.

7. Possible CSFs and Measures

a. A typical balanced scorecard classifies objectives into one of four perspectives on the business.

b. **Financial**

    1) CSFs may be sales, fair value of the firm's stock, profits, and liquidity.

    2) Measures may include sales, projected sales, accuracy of sales projections, new product sales, stock prices, operating earnings, earnings trend, revenue growth, gross margin percentage, cost reductions, return on investment (or any of its variants), residual income, cash flow coverage and trends, turnover (assets, receivables, and inventory), and interest coverage.

c.   **Customer Satisfaction**

    1)   **CSFs** may be customer satisfaction, dealer and distributor relationships, marketing and selling performance, prompt delivery, and quality.

    2)   **Measures**

        a)   **Financial.** These may include dollar amount of sales, trends in dollar amount of sales, dollar amount of returns, dollar amount of defects, and warranty expense.

        b)   **Nonfinancial.** These may include unit sales, trends in unit sales, market share, trend in market share, number of returns, rate of returns, customer retention rate, number of defects, rate of defects, number of warranty claims, rate of warranty claims, lead time, survey results, coverage and strength of distribution channels, market research results, training of marketing people, on-time delivery rate, service response time, and service effectiveness.

d.   **Internal Business Processes**

    1)   **CSFs** may be quality, productivity (an input-output relationship), flexibility of response to changing conditions, operating readiness, and safety.

    2)   **Measures**

        a)   **Financial.** These may include such things as quality costs, scrap costs, and level of inventory carrying costs.

        b)   **Nonfinancial.** These may include new products marketed, technological capabilities, rate of scrap and rework, survey results, field service reports, vendor defect rate, cycle time, labor and machine efficiency, setup time, scheduling effectiveness, downtime, capacity usage, maintenance, and accidents and their results.

e.   **Learning and Growth**

    1)   **CSFs** may be development of new products, promptness of their introduction, human resource development, morale, and competence of the work force.

    2)   **Measures**

        a)   **Financial.** These may include financial and operating results, recruiting costs, orientation costs, and training costs.

        b)   **Nonfinancial.** These may include number of design changes, patents and copyrights registered, R&D personnel qualifications, actual versus planned shipping dates, hours of training, skill set levels attained, personnel turnover, personnel complaints and survey results, organizational learning, and industry leadership.

8.   **Functionality**

a.   Each objective is associated with one or more measures that permit the organization to gauge progress toward the objective.

    1)   Achievement of the objectives in each perspective makes it possible to achieve the objectives in the next higher perspective.

    2)   This chaining of objectives and perspectives embodies the implementation of a **strategy map**.

The AICPA has tested the balanced scorecard approach by asking for the perspective described by either the given measures or the given CSFs.

EXAMPLE of a Balanced Scorecard

Each objective is associated with one or more measures that permit the organization to gauge progress toward the objective. Note that achievement of the objectives in each perspective makes it possible to achieve the objectives in the next higher perspective.

Financial Perspective

Objective: Increase shareholder value

Measures: Increase in common stock price
Reliability of dividend payment

Customer Perspective

Objective: Increase customer satisfaction

Measures: Greater market share
Higher customer retention rate
Positive responses to surveys

Internal Business Process Perspective

Objective: Improve product quality

Measures: Achievement of zero defects

Objective: Improve internal processes

Measures: Reduction in delivery cycle time
Smaller cost variances

Learning and Growth Perspective

Objective: Increase employee confidence

Measures: Number of suggestions to
improve processes
Positive responses to surveys

Objective: Increase employee competence

Measures: Attendance at internal and
external training seminars

Stop and review! You have completed the outline for this subunit. Study multiple-choice questions 5 through 8 on page 470.

17.3 PROCESS MANAGEMENT

1. **Performance-Improving Processes**

    a. The Process-Management-Driven Business

        1) In this conception, the management of the organization concerns itself with the effective and efficient carrying out of the predefined business processes.

        2) If the processes have been designed correctly, this should inexorably lead to the accomplishment of the organization's goals.

    b. Shared Services

        1) The concept of shared services represents a return to the old idea of centralization, but with a new focus.

        2) Where centralized service departments in old-line large organizations tended to see themselves as simply efficient bureaucracies detached from the entity's customers, the shared services model involves designing the service center so that its employees are incentivized to be flexible and responsive to customer needs.

        3) The centralization of a firm's internal services into a single location may cause a delay in services provided.

    c. Outsourcing

        1) Some organizations have determined that processes such as human resources, payroll, and information services are not among their core competencies.

        2) By contracting with outside service providers who specialize in these functions, the organization may find that it can gain cost savings and no longer has to worry about knowledge drain when key employees leave.

        3) The potential disadvantages include loss of core knowledge, loss of control over the outsourced function, unexpected costs, and the challenges of contract management.

    d. Off-Shore Operations

        1) Cost advantages (lower taxes, lower wages, and less stringent occupational safety regulations) can be gained by moving operations to foreign countries.

        2) The effects of currency exchange rate fluctuations and the possibility of political instability must be taken into consideration.

2. **Business Process Reengineering (BPR)**

    a. BPR is the complete, bottom-up revision of the way an organization carries out a particular business process.

    b. Organizations undertaking BPR begin with a blank sheet of paper and totally rethink how a particular business function should be carried out, without regard to how it is currently performed.

    c. One way of understanding BPR is by grasping that it is not

        1) Gradual, incremental streamlining of existing procedures (kaizen)
        2) The movement of manual processes to computers (automation)
        3) A change in the nature of the business itself (paradigm shift)

    d. The goals of BPR are usually stated in terms of increased efficiency or redundant jobs eliminated. At some point, these goals should be quantifiable in terms of cost savings.

    e. Experience has shown that BPR initiatives often fail to deliver the promised benefits.

        1) Business processes routinely cross organizational boundaries.

            a) Totally redesigning the process of a single department is often pointless without the cooperation of other departments. Those in other departments can be reluctant to aid in what they may perceive as a project that will reduce their own autonomy.

        2) Upper management may have other strategic initiatives, such as total quality management or Six Sigma, underway that conflict with either the goals of, or the resources necessary for, BPR.

            a) Any BPR program must be closely aligned with the overall organizational strategy in the minds of executive management.

3. **Newer Business Process Types**

    a. Just-in-Time Inventory Management

        1) For a discussion of the benefits and requirements of just-in-time inventory management, see item 6. in Study Unit 8, Subunit 8.

    b. Lean Operation

        1) Lean operation is a closely related concept.

        2) The ultimate goal of lean operation is a smooth, rapid flow of work through the system. To achieve this ultimate goal, three supporting goals are constantly pursued.

            a) Elimination of Disruptions

                i) A disruption is anything that interrupts the smooth flow of work, e.g., line stoppages, raw materials unavailability, and excessive defects.

        b) System Flexibility

           i) A flexible system can be adapted to changes in product mix and/or quantities without creating a disruption.

        c) Elimination of Waste

           i) Waste is any unproductive use of resources. In accord with the just-in-time philosophy, inventory is considered a waste.

  c. Demand Flow Technology

    1) Demand flow technology (DFT) is a mathematically based methodology devised in the 1980s by operations management expert John Costanza.

    2) DFT combines knowledge of raw materials and work-in-process inventory levels with customer demand to maximize use of the firm's productive capacity, i.e., maintain continuous production flow.

        a) In contrast to the forecast-push model used by MRP (described in item 8. in Study Unit 8, Subunit 8), DFT is a pull system driven by customer demand.

  d. Theory of Constraints

    1) The theory of constraints (TOC) is a system to improve human thinking about problems. It has been greatly extended to include manufacturing operations.

        a) The basic premise of TOC as applied to business is that improving any process is best done not by trying to maximize efficiency in every part of the process but by focusing on the slowest part of the process, called the constraint.

EXAMPLE

During the early days of the American Civil War, several units calling themselves legions were formed, consisting of combined infantry, artillery, and cavalry. This arrangement did not last because the entire unit could only maneuver as fast as the slowest part. The artillery was the constraint.

---

        b) Increasing the efficiency of processes that are not constraints merely creates backup in the system.

    2) The steps in a TOC analysis are as follows:

        a) Identify the constraint.
        b) Determine the most profitable product mix given the constraint.
        c) Maximize the flow through the constraint.
        d) Increase capacity at the constraint.
        e) Redesign the manufacturing process for greater flexibility and speed.

    3) A basic principle of TOC analysis is that short-term profit maximization requires maximizing the contribution margin through the constraint, called the throughput margin or throughput contribution.

        a) TOC thus helps managers to recognize that the product they should produce the most of is not necessarily the one with the highest contribution margin per unit, but the one with the highest throughput margin per unit; i.e., managers must make the most profitable use of the bottleneck operation.

    4) To determine the most profitable use of the bottleneck operation, a manager next calculates the throughput margin per unit of time spent in the constraint.

        a) Profitability is maximized by keeping the bottleneck operation busy with the product with the highest throughput margin per unit of time.

e.   Six Sigma

  1)   Six Sigma is a quality improvement methodology. The goal is to reduce the number of defects in a mass-production process.

    a)   The name Six Sigma (sometimes written 6σ) is derived from the fact that, using a normal distribution (i.e., a bell curve), six standard deviations encompass 99.99966% of the items within the distribution.

    b)   Statistical analysis tools obviously play a major role in any Six Sigma program. Thus, accurate and verifiable data are a necessity.

  2)   A Six Sigma program also involves role-filling by specific individuals in the organization.

    a)   The executive level must demonstrate their commitment to the Six Sigma program and must empower those in the other roles with enough authority and resources to successfully implement the program.

    b)   Champions are those whose responsibility it is to oversee the implementation of the Six Sigma program across the enterprise.

    c)   Master black belts assist the champions in implementing the program across the organization.

    d)   Black belts, like champions and master black belts, devote 100% of their time to the Six Sigma program. They spend their time overseeing particular Six Sigma projects.

    e)   Green belts and yellow belts do Six Sigma work in addition to their regular job duties. They are the ones closest to the production processes that are being improved.

Stop and review! You have completed the outline for this subunit. Study multiple-choice questions 9 and 10 on page 471.

17.4 TOOLS FOR PROCESS MEASUREMENT

 Past exam questions have asked for identification of the methods used to measure process performance.

1.   **Statistical Control Charts**

  a.   Statistical control charts are graphic aids for monitoring the status of any process subject to acceptable or unacceptable variations during repeated operations.

    1)   They also have applications of direct interest to auditors and accountants, for example, (a) unit cost of production, (b) direct labor hours used, (c) ratio of actual expenses to budgeted expenses, (d) number of calls by sales personnel, or (e) total accounts receivable.

  b.   A control chart consists of three lines plotted on a horizontal time scale.

    1)   The center line represents the overall mean or average range for the process being controlled. The other two lines are the upper control limit (UCL) and the lower control limit (LCL).

    2)   The processes are measured periodically, and the values (X) are plotted on the chart.

    a)   If the value falls within the control limits, no action is taken.

    b)   If the value falls outside the limits, the result is abnormal, the process is considered out of control, and an investigation is made for possible corrective action.

    c.   Another advantage of the chart is that it makes trends and cycles visible.

        1)   A disadvantage of the chart is that it does not indicate the cause of the variation.

EXAMPLE

The chart below depicts 2 weeks of production by a manufacturer who produces a single precision part each day. To be salable, the part can vary from the standard by no more than +/– 0.1 millimeter.

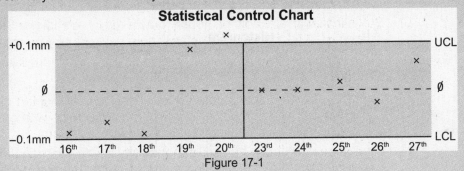

Figure 17-1

The part produced on the 20th had to be scrapped, and changes were made to the equipment to return the process to the controlled state for the following week's production.

---

2.   **Pareto Diagrams**

    a.   A Pareto diagram is a bar chart that assists managers in quality control analysis.

        1)   In the context of quality control, managers optimize their time by focusing their effort on the handful of areas from which most defects arise.

            a)   The independent variable, plotted on the X axis, is the factor selected by the manager as the area of interest: department, time period, geographical location, etc. The frequency of occurrence of the defect (dependent variable) is plotted on the Y axis.

            b)   The occurrences of the independent variable are ranked from highest to lowest, allowing the manager to see at a glance which areas are of most concern.

EXAMPLE

The chief administrative officer wants to know which departments are generating the most travel vouchers that have to be returned to the submitter because of incomplete documentation

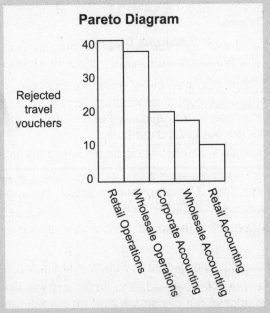

Figure 17-2

3. Histograms

    a.   A histogram is similar in presentation to a Pareto diagram. The major distinction is that histograms display a continuum for the independent variable.

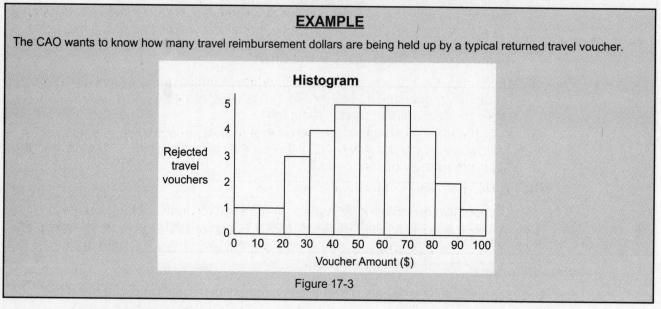

EXAMPLE

The CAO wants to know how many travel reimbursement dollars are being held up by a typical returned travel voucher.

Figure 17-3

4. Fishbone Diagrams

    a.   A fishbone diagram (also called a cause-and-effect diagram) is a total quality management process improvement technique that is useful in studying causation (why the actual and desired situations differ).

        1)   This format organizes the analysis of causation and helps to identify possible interactions among causes.

        2)   The head of the skeleton represents the statement of the problem.

        3)   The principal classifications of causes are represented by lines (bones) drawn diagonally from the heavy horizontal line (the spine).

        4)   Smaller horizontal lines are added in their order of probability in each classification.

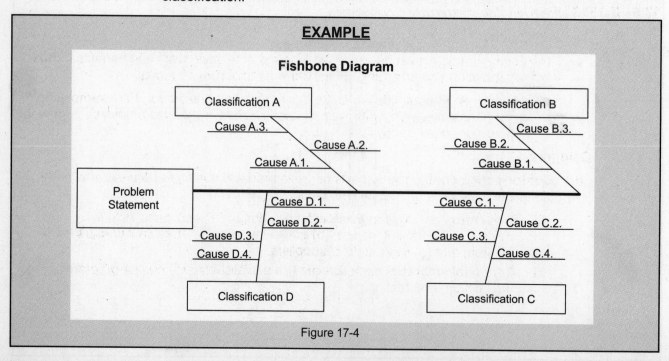

EXAMPLE

Figure 17-4

5. **Benchmarking**

    a. Benchmarking is a primary tool used in quality management. It is a means of helping organizations with productivity management and business process analysis.

        1) Benchmarking involves analysis and measurement of key outputs against those of the best organizations. This procedure also involves identifying the underlying key actions and causes that contribute to the performance difference.

        2) Best practices are recognized by authorities in the field and by customers for generating outstanding results. They are generally innovative technically or in their management of human resources.

        3) Benchmarking is an ongoing process that requires quantitative and qualitative measurement of the difference between the performance of an activity and the performance by the benchmark.

    b. The following are kinds of benchmarking:

        1) Competitive benchmarking studies an organization in the same industry.

        2) Process (function) benchmarking studies operations of organizations with similar processes regardless of industry. Thus, the benchmark need not be a competitor or even a similar entity.

            a) This method may introduce new ideas that provide a significant competitive advantage.

        3) Strategic benchmarking is a search for successful competitive strategies.

        4) Internal benchmarking is the application of best practices in one part of the organization to its other parts.

EXAMPLE

A team from an airline company charged with improving its aircraft ground turnaround time (refueling, maintenance, and service) might consider the benchmark of auto racing's pit stops and determine the applicability of their best practices.

Stop and review! You have completed the outline for this subunit. Study multiple-choice questions 11 through 14 beginning on page 471.

17.5 COSTS OF QUALITY

1. **Costs of Quality**

    a. The costs of quality must be assessed in terms of relative costs and benefits. Thus, an organization should attempt to minimize its total cost of quality.

        1) Moreover, nonquantitative factors also must be considered. For example, an emphasis on quality improves competitiveness, enhances employee expertise, and generates goodwill.

2. **Categories**

    a. **Conformance costs** include costs of prevention and costs of appraisal, which are financial measures of internal performance.

        1) **Prevention** attempts to avoid defective output. These costs include (a) preventive maintenance, (b) employee training, (c) review of equipment design, and (d) evaluation of suppliers.

        2) **Appraisal** embraces such activities as statistical quality control programs, inspection, and testing.

b. **Nonconformance costs** include internal failure costs (a financial measure of internal performance) and external failure costs (a financial measure of customer satisfaction).

    1) **Internal failure costs** occur when defective products are detected before shipment. Examples are scrap, rework, tooling changes, and downtime.

    2) **External failure costs**, e.g., warranty costs, product liability costs, and loss of customer goodwill, arise when problems occur after shipment.

        a) Environmental costs also are external failure costs, e.g., fines for nonadherence to environmental law and loss of customer goodwill.

EXAMPLE

Conformance costs:	
Prevention costs	$35,000
Appraisal costs	5,000
Nonconformance costs:	
Internal failure costs	17,500
External failure costs	9,500
Total costs of quality	**$67,000**

Stop and review! You have completed the outline for this subunit. Study multiple-choice questions 15 through 20 beginning on page 472.

17.6 TQM AND THE ISO FRAMEWORK

1. **Total Quality Management (TQM) Defined**

a. TQM is the continuous pursuit of quality in every aspect of organizational activities through a philosophy of doing it right the first time, employee training and empowerment, promotion of teamwork, improvement of processes, and attention to satisfaction of customers, both internal and external.

    1) TQM emphasizes the supplier's relationship with the customer, identifies customer needs, and recognizes that everyone in a process is at some time a customer or supplier of someone else, either within or without the organization.

    2) Thus, TQM begins with external customer requirements, identifies internal customer-supplier relationships and requirements, and establishes requirements for external suppliers.

    3) Organizations tend to be vertically organized, but TQM requires strong horizontal linkages.

Background

TQM was developed in the mid-1940s by statistician W. Edwards Deming, who aided Japanese industry in its recovery from World War II. The Deming Prize is awarded by the Union of Japanese Scientists and Engineers for outstanding contributions to the study or application of TQM (www.juse.or.jp/e/deming). While Deming was praised and deeply respected in Japan, it took 30 years for his principles to be applied in the U.S.

---

b. TQM treats the pursuit of quality as a basic organizational function that is as important as production or marketing.

    c.   TQM recognizes that quality improvement can increase revenues and decrease costs significantly. The following are TQM's core principles or critical factors:

       1)   Emphasis on the customer

          a)   Satisfaction of external customers
          b)   Satisfaction of internal customers
          c)   Requirements for external suppliers
          d)   Requirements for internal suppliers

       2)   Continuous improvement as a never-ending process, not a destination

       3)   Engaging every employee in the pursuit of total quality because avoidance of defects in products or services and satisfaction of external customers requires that all internal customers be satisfied

    d.   The management of quality is not limited to quality management staff, engineers, and production personnel, but extends to all within the organization.

2.   **Implementation**

    a.   Implementation of TQM cannot be accomplished by application of a formula, and the process is lengthy and difficult. The following phases are typical:

       1)   Establishing an executive-level quality council of senior managers with strong involvement by the CEO.

       2)   Providing quality training programs for senior managers.

       3)   Conducting a quality audit to evaluate the success of the process for gathering background information to develop the strategic quality improvement plan.

          a)   The quality audit also may identify the best improvement opportunities and the organization's strengths and weaknesses compared with its benchmarked competitors.

       4)   Preparing a gap analysis to ascertain what is necessary to bridge the gap between the organization and the quality leaders in its industry and to establish a database for the development of the strategic quality improvement plan.

       5)   Developing strategic quality improvement plans for the short and long term.

       6)   Conducting employee communication and training programs.

       7)   Establishing quality teams, which ensure that goods and services conform to specifications.

       8)   Creating a measurement system and setting goals.

       9)   Revising compensation, appraisal, and recognition systems.

       10) Reviewing and revising the entire effort periodically.

3.   **The ISO Standards**

    a.   In 1987, the International Organization for Standardization (ISO) introduced ISO 9000, a "family" of 11 standards and technical reports that provide guidance for establishing and maintaining a quality management system (QMS). The ISO's rules specify that its standards be revised every 5 years in light of technological and market developments.

Background

ISO is not an acronym. It means equal, suggesting that entities certified under ISO standards have equal quality. For specific and up-to-date information, see the ISO's website (www.iso.org).

---

    b.   The intent of the standards is to ensure the quality of the process, not the product. The marketplace determines whether a product is good or bad.

        1)   For this reason, the ISO deems it unacceptable for phrases referring to ISO certification to appear on individual products or packaging.

    c.   Basic Requirements of an ISO QMS

        1)   Key processes affecting quality must be identified and included.

            a)   A process management approach must be used. It manages the entity as a set of linked processes that are controlled for continuous improvement.

        2)   General requirements. The entity must have a quality policy and quality goals. It also must design a QMS to control process performance. Quality goals are measurable and specific.

            a)   The QMS is documented in the (1) quality policy, (2) quality manual, (3) procedures, (4) work instructions, and (5) records.

        3)   Management responsibility. Management (a) reviews the quality policy, (b) analyzes data about QMS performance, and (c) assesses opportunities for improvement and the need for change.

            a)   Management ensures that systems exist to determine and satisfy customer requirements.

        4)   Resource management. The resources needed to improve the QMS and satisfy customer requirements must be provided.

        5)   Product realization processes result in products or services received by customers. These processes must be planned and controlled. Issues are (a) means of control, (b) objectives, (c) documentation and records needed, and (d) acceptance criteria.

        6)   Measurement, analysis, and improvement. The entity must have processes for (a) inspection, (b) testing, (c) measurement, (d) analysis, and (e) improvement.

Stop and review! You have completed the outline for this subunit. Study multiple-choice questions 21 through 24 on page 474.

17.7 PROJECT MANAGEMENT

1. Project Management

    a.   A project is a temporary undertaking with specified objectives that often involves a cross-functional team and working outside customary organizational lines. Hence, interpersonal skills are at a premium in project management because a manager may not have line authority over some team members.

        1)   Examples include building construction, R&D projects, new product planning, feasibility studies, audit studies, movie production, and conversion to a new computer information system.

        2)   Project management techniques are designed to aid the planning and control of large-scale projects having many interrelated activities.

b. Four distinct roles for those taking part in the project can be identified:

1) The steering committee consists of the executives who decide which projects should be undertaken. Once a project is approved, it becomes the committee's function to demand accountability regarding the project's progress.

2) The project sponsor can also be called the project champion. The sponsor defines the project and makes the business case for it to the steering committee. The project sponsor is vested with sufficient authority by executive management to allocate the resources that will ensure successful completion. The sponsor's mandate includes compelling cooperation across departmental boundaries to achieve the project's goals.

3) The project manager oversees the day-to-day activities of the project team members and ensures that project deliverables are ready for the sponsor to present to the steering committee on time.

4) Project team members often must continue performing their regular job duties while simultaneously committing some portion of their time to the project. Getting buy-in from the project members' immediate supervisors is thus crucial to the success of a project.

c. Project management consists of the following five principal tasks:

1) Authorization -- establishes through the project charter the scope, objectives, and stakeholders in a project and defines the responsibilities and authority of the project manager

2) Planning -- determining goals and their due dates and scheduling available resources

3) Implementation -- putting the plan into effect and directing resources to the proper areas

4) Monitoring -- correcting, meeting expectations, and finishing the project within the time and budgetary limits

5) Closing -- confirming the completion of the project to the satisfaction of the relevant stakeholders

d. The risk of an unsuccessful project can be analyzed in terms of the following four components:

1) Ensuring resources. Resources consist of personnel, equipment, computer processing time, and sometimes cash.

2) Maintaining scope. Experience has shown that a phenomenon known as "scope creep" often affects projects in organizations. The temptation is to continue adding functionality to a new system or process. Keeping project members focused on the approved goals (and timetable) of the project is a crucial role of the project manager.

3) Controlling cost. The cost of a project must be measured in the opportunity cost of employee time and cash spent on new equipment.

4) Providing deliverables. A deliverable may be as simple as a one-page written report or as complex as an installation of enterprise-wide software. Most large-scale projects have deliverables at the completion of each stage of the project to ensure that the project remains on schedule.

e.   Project management is the process of managing the trade-off between the two major inputs (time and cost) and the major output (quality). The project management triangle graphically depicts this relationship.

Project Management Triangle

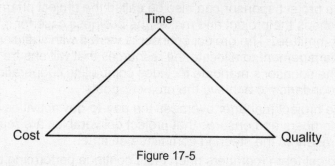

Figure 17-5

1)   The implication is that a high-quality deliverable can only be achieved either by devoting a large number of employee hours to a project or by spending a lot of money.

EXAMPLE

In the days before widespread computer use, old-fashioned job-order print shops used to display signs saying, "You Want It Fast -- Cheap -- Correct. Pick Two."

Designers of submarines often speak of their classic trade-off of depth, speed, and stealth. A vessel with sufficient shielding to be silent and to survive at great depths is too heavy to go very fast.

---

f.   Project management software is available. Among other things, it should

1)   Specify and schedule required activities
2)   Provide the ability to do sensitivity analysis of the effects of changes in plans
3)   Calculate a project's critical path
4)   Establish priorities
5)   Be able to modify or merge plans
6)   Manage all types of project resources
7)   Monitor progress, including adherence to time budgets for activities

Stop and review! You have completed the outline for this subunit. Study multiple-choice questions 25 through 28 on page 475.

QUESTIONS

17.1 Responsibility Centers

1. If a manufacturing company uses responsibility centers, which one of the following items is **least** likely to appear in a performance report for a manager of an assembly line?

A.   Supervisory salaries.

B.   Materials.

C.   Repairs and maintenance.

D.   Equipment depreciation.

Answer (D) is correct.
    REQUIRED: The item least likely to appear in a performance report for the manager of an assembly line.
    DISCUSSION: Responsibility centers hold managers responsible only for factors under their control. The depreciation of equipment will probably not appear on the performance report of an assembly-line manager because the manager usually has no control over the investment in the equipment.
    Answer (A) is incorrect. The manager of an assembly line is likely to be responsible for the salaries of supervisors, which is to some degree controllable by the manager. Answer (B) is incorrect. The manager of an assembly line is likely to be responsible for the materials, which is to some degree controllable by the manager. Answer (C) is incorrect. The manager of an assembly line is likely to be responsible for the repairs and maintenance, which is to some degree controllable by the manager.

2. A segment of an organization is referred to as a profit center if it has

A. Authority to make decisions affecting the major determinants of profit including the power to choose its markets and sources of supply.

B. Authority to make decisions affecting the major determinants of profit including the power to choose its markets and sources of supply and significant control over the amount of invested capital.

C. Authority to make decisions over the most significant costs of operations including the power to choose the sources of supply.

D. Authority to provide specialized support to other units within the organization.

Answer (A) is correct.
REQUIRED: The definition of a profit center.
DISCUSSION: A profit center is responsible for both revenues and expenses. For example, the perfume department in a department store is a profit center. The manager of a profit center usually has the authority to make decisions affecting the major determinants of profit, including the power to choose markets (revenue sources) and suppliers (costs).
Answer (B) is incorrect. An investment center, not a profit center, has control over invested capital. Answer (C) is incorrect. A cost center manager has control over all significant costs but not of revenues or investments. Answer (D) is incorrect. A service center supports other organizational units.

3. The **least** complex segment or area of responsibility for which costs are allocated is a(n)

A. Profit center.

B. Investment center.

C. Contribution center.

D. Cost center.

Answer (D) is correct.
REQUIRED: The least complex segment or area of responsibility for which costs are allocated.
DISCUSSION: A cost center is a responsibility center that is accountable only for costs. The cost center is the least complex type of segment because it has no responsibility for revenues or investments.
Answer (A) is incorrect. A profit center is a segment responsible for both revenues and costs. A profit center has the authority to make decisions concerning markets and sources of supply. Answer (B) is incorrect. An investment center is a responsibility center that is accountable for revenues (markets), costs (sources of supply), and invested capital. Answer (C) is incorrect. A contribution center is responsible for revenues and variable costs, but not invested capital.

4. Managers are most likely to accept allocations of common costs based on

A. Cause and effect.

B. Ability to bear.

C. Percent of revenues earned.

D. Top management decisions.

Answer (A) is correct.
REQUIRED: The criterion most likely to result in acceptable allocations of common costs.
DISCUSSION: The difficulty with common costs is that they are indirect costs whose allocation may be arbitrary. A direct cause-and-effect relationship between a common cost and the actions of the cost object to which it is allocated is desirable. Such a relationship promotes acceptance of the allocation by managers who perceive the fairness of the procedure, but identification of cause and effect may not be feasible.
Answer (B) is incorrect. Allocation using an ability-to-bear criterion punishes successful managers and rewards underachievers. Answer (C) is incorrect. Allocations based on the percent of revenues earned use an ability-to-bear approach. Answer (D) is incorrect. Top management decisions on cost allocation tend to be arbitrary.

17.2 Performance Measures, Incentives, and the Balanced Scorecard

5. Management of a company is attempting to build a reputation as a world-class manufacturer of quality products. Which of the following measures would **not** be used by the firm to measure quality?

A. The percentage of shipments returned by customers because of poor quality.

B. The number of parts shipped per day.

C. The number of defective parts per million.

D. The percentage of products passing quality tests the first time.

Answer (B) is correct.
   REQUIRED: The measure not used for quality measurement.
   DISCUSSION: The number of parts shipped per day would most likely be used as a measure of the effectiveness and efficiency of shipping procedures, not the quality of the product. This measure does not consider how many of the parts are defective.
   Answer (A) is incorrect. The percentage of shipments returned is a very useful direct measure of the number of unacceptable products. Answer (C) is incorrect. The number of defective parts per million, being a simple and direct measure of poor quality, would be used by this company. Answer (D) is incorrect. The percentage of products passing quality tests the first time measures quality by the number of nondefective products.

6. Using the balanced scorecard approach, an organization evaluates managerial performance based on

A. A single ultimate measure of operating results, such as residual income.

B. Multiple financial and nonfinancial measures.

C. Multiple nonfinancial measures only.

D. Multiple financial measures only.

Answer (B) is correct.
   REQUIRED: The nature of the balanced scorecard approach.
   DISCUSSION: The trend in managerial performance evaluation is the balanced scorecard approach. Multiple measures of performance permit a determination as to whether a manager is achieving certain objectives at the expense of others that may be equally or more important. These measures may be financial or nonfinancial and usually include items with four perspectives: financial; customer; internal business processes; and learning, growth, and innovation.

7. The balanced scorecard provides an action plan for achieving competitive success by focusing management attention on critical success factors. Which one of the following is **not** one of the perspectives on the business into which critical success factors are commonly grouped in the balanced scorecard?

A. Competitor business strategies.

B. Financial performance.

C. Internal business processes.

D. Employee innovation and learning.

Answer (A) is correct.
   REQUIRED: The item not a perspective on the business as used on a balanced scorecard.
   DISCUSSION: A typical balanced scorecard classifies critical success factors and measures into one of four perspectives on the business: financial, customer satisfaction, internal business processes, and learning and growth.
   Answer (B) is incorrect. Financial performance measures are among the tools used in a typical balanced scorecard. Answer (C) is incorrect. A typical balanced scorecard contains critical success factors and measures focused on internal business processes. Answer (D) is incorrect. Employee innovation and learning is one of the perspectives on the business commonly used in a balanced scorecard.

8. On a balanced scorecard, which is more of an internal process measure than an external-based measure?

A. Cycle time.

B. Profitability.

C. Customer satisfaction.

D. Market share.

Answer (A) is correct.
   REQUIRED: The measure that is more internal-process related on a balanced scorecard.
   DISCUSSION: Cycle time is the manufacturing time to complete an order. Thus, cycle time is strictly related to internal processes. Profitability is a combination of internal and external considerations. Customer satisfaction and market share are related to how customers perceive a product and how competitors react.
   Answer (B) is incorrect. Profitability is a measure that includes external considerations. Answer (C) is incorrect. Customer satisfaction is a measure that includes external considerations. Answer (D) is incorrect. Market share is a measure that includes external considerations.

17.3 Process Management

9. Champions, yellow belts, and master black belts are associated with which business process?

  A. Business process reengineering.

  B. Six Sigma.

  C. Demand flow technology.

  D. Kanban.

Answer (B) is correct.
  REQUIRED: The business process associated with champions, yellow belts, and master black belts.
  DISCUSSION: A Six Sigma program involves role-filling by specific individuals in the organization. Champions are those whose responsibility it is to oversee the implementation of the Six Sigma program across the enterprise. Master black belts assist the champions in implementing the program across the organization. Green belts and yellow belts are the ones closest to the production processes that are being improved.
  Answer (A) is incorrect. Champions, yellow belts, and master black belts are not associated with business process reengineering. Answer (C) is incorrect. Champions, yellow belts, and master black belts are not associated with demand flow technology. Answer (D) is incorrect. Champions, yellow belts, and master black belts are not associated with kanban.

10. Increasing the efficiency of all phases of a given process is specifically discouraged by which of the following models?

  A. Lean operation.

  B. Theory of constraints.

  C. Six Sigma.

  D. Demand flow technology.

Answer (B) is correct.
  REQUIRED: The business process model that specifically discourages increasing the efficiency of all phases.
  DISCUSSION: Under the theory of constraints, increasing the efficiency of processes that are not constraints (bottlenecks) merely creates backup in the system.
  Answer (A) is incorrect. Lean operation does not specifically discourage increasing the efficiency of all phases. Answer (C) is incorrect. Six Sigma does not specifically discourage increasing the efficiency of all phases. Answer (D) is incorrect. Demand flow technology does not specifically discourage increasing the efficiency of all phases.

17.4 Tools for Process Measurement

11. The director of sales asks for a count of customers grouped in descending numerical rank by (1) the number of orders they place during a single year and (2) the dollar amounts of the average order. The visual format of these two pieces of information is most likely to be a(n)

  A. Fishbone diagram.

  B. Cost of quality report.

  C. Kaizen diagram.

  D. Pareto diagram.

Answer (D) is correct.
  REQUIRED: The appropriate process measurement tool.
  DISCUSSION: A Pareto diagram displays the values of an independent variable such that managers can quickly identify the areas most in need of attention.
  Answer (A) is incorrect. A fishbone diagram is useful for determining the unknown causes of problems, not for stratifying quantifiable variables. Answer (B) is incorrect. The contents of a cost of quality report are stated in monetary terms. This report is not helpful for determining when to adjust machinery.
  Answer (C) is incorrect. Kaizen diagram is not a meaningful term in this context.

12. The management of a company would do which of the following to compare and contrast its financial information to published information reflecting optimal amounts?

  A. Budget.

  B. Forecast.

  C. Benchmark.

  D. Utilize best practices.

Answer (C) is correct.
  REQUIRED: The action that involves comparing and contrasting financial information with optimal amounts.
  DISCUSSION: Benchmarking is an ongoing process that requires quantitative and qualitative measurement of the difference between the performance of an activity and the performance by the benchmark.
  Answer (A) is incorrect. A budget is a plan for the future. Answer (B) is incorrect. A forecast is a prediction about future events and circumstances. Answer (D) is incorrect. Best practices are recognized by authorities in the field and by customers for generating outstanding results.

13. An example of an internal nonfinancial benchmark is

A. The labor rate of comparably skilled employees at a major competitor's plant.

B. The average actual cost per pound of a specific product at the company's most efficient plant.

C. A $50,000 limit on the cost of employee training programs at each of the company's plants.

D. The percentage of customer orders delivered on time at the company's most efficient plant.

Answer (D) is correct.
REQUIRED: The internal nonfinancial benchmark.
DISCUSSION: Benchmarking is a continuous evaluation of the practices of the best organizations in their class and the adaptation of processes to reflect the best of these practices. It requires analysis and measurement of key outputs against those of the best organizations. This procedure also involves identifying the underlying key actions and causes that contribute to the performance difference. The percentage of orders delivered on time at the company's most efficient plant is an example of an internal nonfinancial benchmark.
Answer (A) is incorrect. The labor rate of a competitor is a financial benchmark. Answer (B) is incorrect. The cost per pound of a product at the company's most efficient plant is a financial benchmark. Answer (C) is incorrect. The cost of a training program is a financial benchmark.

14. A company, which has many branch stores, has decided to benchmark one of its stores for the purpose of analyzing the accuracy and reliability of branch store financial reporting. Which one of the following is the most likely measure to be included in a financial benchmark?

A. High turnover of employees.

B. High level of employee participation in setting budgets.

C. High amount of bad debt write-offs.

D. High number of suppliers.

Answer (C) is correct.
REQUIRED: The most likely measure to be included in a financial benchmark.
DISCUSSION: A high level of bad debt write-offs could indicate fraud, which would compromise the accuracy and reliability of financial reports. Bad debt write-offs may result from recording fictitious sales.
Answer (A) is incorrect. Turnover of employees is not a financial benchmark. Answer (B) is incorrect. Employee participation in setting budgets is not a financial benchmark. Answer (D) is incorrect. The number of suppliers is not a financial benchmark.

17.5 Costs of Quality

15. An example of an internal failure cost is

A. Maintenance.

B. Inspection.

C. Rework.

D. Product recalls.

Answer (C) is correct.
REQUIRED: The example of an internal failure cost.
DISCUSSION: In a quality management system, one of the costs of product nonconformance is internal failure cost, which is the cost of discovering, after appraisal but before shipment, that a completed product does not meet quality standards. An example is the cost of reworking the product.
Answer (A) is incorrect. A maintenance cost is a prevention cost. Answer (B) is incorrect. Inspection is an appraisal cost. Answer (D) is incorrect. Product recalls are external failure costs.

16. The cost of statistical quality control in a product quality cost system is categorized as a(n)

A. Internal failure cost.

B. Training cost.

C. External failure cost.

D. Appraisal cost.

Answer (D) is correct.
REQUIRED: The cost category that includes statistical quality control.
DISCUSSION: The four categories of quality costs are prevention, appraisal, internal failure, and external failure (lost opportunity). Appraisal costs include quality control programs, inspection, and testing. However, some authorities regard statistical quality and process control as preventive activities because they not only detect faulty work but also allow for adjustment of processes to avoid future defects.
Answer (A) is incorrect. Internal failure costs arise after poor quality has been found before shipment; statistical quality control is designed to detect quality problems. Answer (B) is incorrect. Statistical quality control is not a training cost. Answer (C) is incorrect. External failure costs are incurred after the product has been shipped, including the costs associated with warranties, product liability, and customer ill will.

17. The cost of scrap, rework, and tooling changes in a product quality cost system are categorized as a(n)

A. External failure cost.

B. Internal failure cost.

C. Prevention cost.

D. Appraisal cost.

Answer (B) is correct.

REQUIRED: The cost category that includes scrap, rework, and tooling changes.

DISCUSSION: The four categories of quality costs are prevention, appraisal, internal failure, and external failure (lost opportunity). Internal failure costs are incurred when detection of defective products occurs before shipment. Examples include scrap, rework, tooling changes, and downtime.

Answer (A) is incorrect. External failure costs are those incurred for quality reasons after the product has reached the customer; for example, warranty and product liability costs would be classified as external failure costs. Answer (C) is incorrect. Scrap and rework costs are incurred after a product has been manufactured; they are not prevention costs. Answer (D) is incorrect. Appraisal costs are those incurred to discover quality problems; scrap and rework occur after the discovery of a quality problem.

18. Listed below are selected line items from the cost of quality report for Watson Products for last month.

Category	Amount
Rework	$ 725
Equipment maintenance	1,154
Product testing	786
Product repair	695

What is Watson's total prevention and appraisal cost for last month?

A. $786

B. $1,154

C. $1,940

D. $2,665

Answer (C) is correct.

REQUIRED: The total prevention and appraisal costs.

DISCUSSION: The costs of prevention and appraisal are conformance costs that serve as financial measures of internal performance. Prevention costs are incurred to prevent defective output. These costs include preventive maintenance, employee training, review of equipment design, and evaluation of suppliers. Appraisal costs are incurred to detect nonconforming output. They embrace such activities as statistical quality control programs, inspection, and testing. The equipment maintenance cost of $1,154 is a prevention cost. The product testing cost of $786 is an appraisal cost. Their sum is $1,940.

Answer (A) is incorrect. This amount is the appraisal cost. Answer (B) is incorrect. This amount is the prevention cost. Answer (D) is incorrect. This amount includes rework, an internal failure cost.

19. The four categories of costs associated with product quality costs are

A. External failure, internal failure, prevention, and carrying.

B. External failure, internal failure, prevention, and appraisal.

C. Warranty, product liability, training, and appraisal.

D. Warranty, product liability, prevention, and appraisal.

Answer (B) is correct.

REQUIRED: The categories of product quality costs.

DISCUSSION: The four categories of quality costs are prevention, appraisal, internal failure, and external failure (lost opportunity). Costs of prevention include attempts to avoid defective output, including employee training, review of equipment design, preventive maintenance, and evaluation of suppliers. Appraisal costs include quality control programs, inspection, and testing. Internal failure costs are incurred when detection of defective products occurs before shipment, including scrap, rework, tooling changes, and downtime. External failure costs are incurred after the product has been shipped, including the costs associated with warranties, product liability, and customer ill will.

Answer (A) is incorrect. Carrying cost is an inventory cost. Answer (C) is incorrect. All training costs are not quality control related. Also, internal failure costs should be included. Answer (D) is incorrect. Internal failure costs should be included.

20. Which of the following quality costs are nonconformance costs?

A. Systems development costs.

B. Costs of inspecting in-process items.

C. Environmental costs.

D. Costs of quality circles.

Answer (C) is correct.

REQUIRED: The nonconformance costs.

DISCUSSION: Nonconformance costs include internal and external failure costs. External failure costs include environmental costs, e.g., fines for violations of environmental laws and loss of customer goodwill.

Answer (A) is incorrect. Systems development costs are prevention (conformance) costs. Answer (B) is incorrect. Costs of inspecting in-process items are appraisal (conformance) costs. Answer (D) is incorrect. Costs of quality circles are prevention (conformance) costs.

17.6 TQM and the ISO Framework

21. Which statement best describes total quality management (TQM)?

    A. TQM emphasizes reducing the cost of inspection.

    B. TQM emphasizes participation by all employees in the decision-making process.

    C. TQM implementation is quick and easy.

    D. TQM is the continuous pursuit of quality.

Answer (D) is correct.
    REQUIRED: The best description of total quality management (TQM).
    DISCUSSION: TQM is the continuous pursuit of quality in every aspect of organizational activities through a philosophy of doing it right the first time, employee training and empowerment, promotion of teamwork, improvement of processes, and attention to satisfaction of customers, both internal and external.
    Answer (A) is incorrect. Reducing the cost of inspection helps achieve the lowest overall business cost. Answer (B) is incorrect. This statement describes participative management. Answer (C) is incorrect. TQM implementation is often lengthy and difficult.

22. One of the main reasons that implementation of a total quality management program works better through the use of teams is

    A. Teams are more efficient and help an organization reduce its staffing.

    B. Employee motivation is always higher for team members than for individual contributors.

    C. Teams are a natural vehicle for sharing ideas, which leads to process improvement.

    D. The use of teams eliminates the need for supervision, thereby allowing a company to reduce staffing.

Answer (C) is correct.
    REQUIRED: The reason that implementation of a TQM program works better through the use of teams.
    DISCUSSION: TQM promotes teamwork by modifying or eliminating traditional (and rigid) vertical hierarchies and instead forming flexible groups of specialists. Quality circles, cross-functional teams, and self-managed teams are typical formats. Teams are an excellent vehicle for encouraging the sharing of ideas and removing process improvement obstacles.
    Answer (A) is incorrect. Teams are often inefficient and costly. Answer (B) is incorrect. High motivation does not directly affect the process improvement that is the key to quality improvement. Answer (D) is incorrect. The use of teams with less supervision and reduced staffing may be by-products of TQM, but they are not ultimate objectives.

23. Which statement best describes the emphasis of total quality management (TQM)?

    A. Reducing the cost of inspection.

    B. Implementing better statistical quality control techniques.

    C. Doing each job right the first time.

    D. Encouraging cross-functional teamwork.

Answer (C) is correct.
    REQUIRED: The emphasis of TQM.
    DISCUSSION: The basic principles of TQM include doing each job right the first time, being customer oriented, committing the company culture to continuous improvement, and building teamwork and employee empowerment.
    Answer (A) is incorrect. Reducing the cost of inspection is a detail of the TQM emphasis. Answer (B) is incorrect. Implementing better statistical quality control techniques is a detail of the TQM emphasis. Answer (D) is incorrect. Encouraging cross-functional teamwork is a detail of the TQM emphasis.

24. Which of the following statements is **not** true regarding ISO 9000 standards?

    A. Compliance with the standards is voluntary.

    B. The ISO 9000 standards are revised every 5 years to account for technological and market developments.

    C. The objective of ISO 9000 standards is to ensure high quality products and services.

    D. ISO 9000 is a set of generic standards for establishing and maintaining a quality system within a company.

Answer (C) is correct.
    REQUIRED: The false statement regarding ISO 9000 standards.
    DISCUSSION: The objective of ISO 9000 standards is to ensure consistent quality even if the quality is poor. The market will determine the quality of the end result.
    Answer (A) is incorrect. Compliance is voluntary, but many companies are adopting the standards for competitive reasons or out of fear that the standards will become a requirement in foreign markets. Answer (B) is incorrect. The ISO rules specify that standards are periodically revised every 5 years in light of technological and market developments. Answer (D) is incorrect. ISO 9000 standards are generic in nature and only ensure consistent quality in the product being produced.

17.7 Project Management

25. Which of the following personnel has primary responsibility for allocating sufficient resources to ensure successful completion of a project?

- A. Project manager.
- B. Project sponsor.
- C. Project team members.
- D. Steering committee.

Answer (B) is correct.
REQUIRED: The person charged with the responsibility to allocate resources to a project.
DISCUSSION: The project sponsor is vested with sufficient authority by executive management to allocate the resources that will ensure successful completion.
Answer (A) is incorrect. The project manager typically is not vested with sufficient authority to allocate resources. Answer (C) is incorrect. Project team members rarely have sufficient authority to allocate organizational resources. Answer (D) is incorrect. The steering committee provides guidance and demands accountability; allocating resources is a day-to-day management function in which the steering committee would not normally participate.

26. Which of the following personnel has primary responsibility for ensuring that project deliverables are ready on time?

- A. Project manager.
- B. Project sponsor.
- C. Project team members.
- D. Steering committee.

Answer (A) is correct.
REQUIRED: The person charged with the responsibility for project deliverables.
DISCUSSION: The project manager oversees the day-to-day activities of the project team members and ensures that project deliverables are ready for the sponsor to present to the steering committee on time.
Answer (B) is incorrect. The project sponsor is not responsible for such day-to-day oversight activities as monitoring progress on project deliverables. Answer (C) is incorrect. Project team members must exert the required effort to complete the deliverables, but they are not responsible for day-to-day oversight of the project as a whole. Answer (D) is incorrect. The steering committee reviews and approves the project deliverables; it does not present them.

27. The project management triangle depicts

- A. The degree of shared responsibility between the participants in a project.
- B. The decision process used to determine which projects should be undertaken.
- C. The interrelation of the component tasks that make up the overall project.
- D. The tradeoff between the time spent on a project, the cost of the project, and the quality of the final deliverable.

Answer (D) is correct.
REQUIRED: The contents of the project management triangle.
DISCUSSION: The project management triangle depicts the tradeoff between the time spent on a project, the cost of the project, and the quality of the final deliverable.

28. During which of the following tasks of a project is the satisfaction of the stakeholders confirmed?

- A. Authorization.
- B. Implementation.
- C. Monitoring.
- D. Closing.

Answer (D) is correct.
REQUIRED: The project task that includes stakeholder satisfaction.
DISCUSSION: The closing phase consists of confirming that completion of the project to the satisfaction of the stakeholders.
Answer (A) is incorrect. This task is carried out at the beginning of the project. Answer (B) is incorrect. During this task, the detailed steps to achieve the project's goals are carried out. Answer (C) is incorrect. This ongoing task, which runs parallel with implementation, ensures that efforts are directed toward achieving the project's goals.

Use the additional questions in Gleim **CPA Test Prep Online** to create Test Sessions that emulate Prometric!

17.8 PRACTICE WRITTEN COMMUNICATION TASK

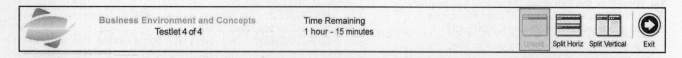

Business Environment and Concepts
Testlet 4 of 4

Time Remaining
1 hour - 15 minutes

Unsplit   Split Horiz   Split Vertical   Exit

DIRECTIONS

Note: If you believe you have encountered a software malfunction, report it to the test center staff immediately.

Navigation

To navigate from task to task, use the controls at the bottom of the screen. Click on the **Next** button to advance to the next task, or the **Previous** button to go to the previous task. To go directly to any task, click on its number.

▽ = Reminder   Directions   1 2 3 4 5 6 7   ◀ Previous   Next ▶

If you would like a reminder to revisit a task or want to indicate that you are finished with it, click on the reminder flag below the task number. To clear the flag, click on it again. Reminder flags are for your use only – they do not contribute to your score.

Tabs

In this part of the examination, you will be asked to complete various tasks. Every task has one or more **Work Tabs**. Every task also has a **Help** tab.

Written Communication   Help

Work tab   Help tab

Work Tabs:

- **Work Tabs** are identified with a pencil icon. This is where your responses are expected.
- Each task has one or more **Work Tabs**.
- **Work Tabs** contain directions for completing the task - be sure to read these directions carefully.
- The **Work Tab** name in the example above is for illustration only - yours will differ.
- You must complete all of the **Work Tabs** in each task to receive full credit.

Help Tab:

- The **Help Tab** provides assistance with the exam software that is used in this task. For example, if the task is to compose a memorandum, **Help** will provide information about the word processor.

The Toolbar

The toolbar at the top of the screen shows the amount of time remaining for you to complete the tasks. In addition, the following tools are available. Note that only the **Exit** button is displayed when Directions are visible - the others will appear when you begin the tasks.

Unsplit   Split Horiz   Split Vertical

Click on these buttons to split or unsplit the screen. You can split the screen vertically or horizontally.

Exit

Click on this button to go on to the next part of the examination. You must complete all of the tasks to receive full credit. Once you click on **Exit** and confirm the action, you will NOT be able to return to this testlet.

▽ = Reminder   Directions   1   ◀ Previous   Next ▶

Written Communication | Help

✂ Cut | 📋 Copy | 📋 Paste | ↺ Undo | ↻ Redo

Your client, who owns a clothing factory, has just told you that her daughter called her from college and asked whether they use balanced scorecard at the factory.

Prepare a memo to your client concerning the balanced scorecard and how it can help achieve strategic objectives.

Type your communication below the line in the response area below.

REMINDER: Your response will be graded for both technical content and writing skills. Technical content will be evaluated for information that is helpful to the intended reader and clearly relevant to the issue. Writing skills will be evaluated for development, organization, and the appropriate expression of ideas in professional correspondence. Use a standard business memorandum or letter format with a clear beginning, middle, and end. Do not convey information in the form of a table, bullet point list, or other abbreviated presentation.

To: Client
Re: The balanced scorecard and its benefits

⚑ = Reminder

Directions

1

Previous   Next

Unofficial Answer

Written Communication

To: Client
Re: The balanced scorecard and its benefits

Even if the current quality of products is high, evaluative measures of one's business and production will help to increase some aspect of a business. The most effective overarching measure currently in use is the balanced scorecard approach. The balanced scorecard is an accounting report that connects the firm's critical success factors (CSFs) determined in a strategic analysis to measurements of its performance. The first step in creating an effective balanced scorecard is to determine the critical success factors by means of a SWOT analysis. Next, it will be important to understand the four basic components of a strong balanced scorecard.

A firm identifies its CSFs by means of a SWOT analysis, which addresses internal factors (strengths and weaknesses) and external factors (opportunities and threats). The firm's strengths and weaknesses are internal resources or a lack of them. Opportunities and threats arise from such externalities as government regulation, advances in technology, and demographic conditions. This SWOT analysis and identification of CSFs helps the firm to determine its competitive strategy. The next step in the firm's identification of critical success factors is to establish specific measures for each CSF that are both relevant to the success of the firm and reliably stated. Thus, the balanced scorecard varies with the strategy adopted by the firm.

A typical balanced scorecard includes measures in four categories: financial, customer, internal business processes, and learning and growth. The measures within each category are dependent on the CSFs identified. For example, the financial category may include the CSFs of sales, fair value of the firm's stock, profits, and liquidity. As another example, the internal business processes category should include such CSFs as quality, productivity, flexibility of response to changing conditions, and safety. The measures organized by these categories permit the organization to gauge progress toward the objective. An example of a learning and growth category measure is the number of patents and copyrights registered, which will gauge the success the organization has achieved toward the objective of developing new products (a critical success factor recognized by the organization). These elements of organizational evaluation will bring to light many aspects of a business that otherwise might not be thoroughly explored. Traveling down these new avenues may tremendously enhance a business's operations.

The above depicts a Level 5 answer. See page 16 in the Introduction for a description of the three grading criteria.

Self-Grade

Evaluate each of the following by selecting a 0, 1, 2, 3, 4, or 5. An average response is 3. Use 4 for better than average and 5 for outstanding. Use 2 for less than average and 1 for quite poor. Use zero for no response, if you did not address the topic, or if you gave advice that is clearly illegal.

Organization	○ 0	○ 1	○ 2	○ 3	○ 4	○ 5
Development	○ 0	○ 1	○ 2	○ 3	○ 4	○ 5
Expression	○ 0	○ 1	○ 2	○ 3	○ 4	○ 5

Your grade for the written communication as a whole is the average of the scores for the three criteria.

Use **CPA Gleim Online** and **Simulation Wizard** to practice more written communication tasks in a realistic environment.

STUDY UNIT EIGHTEEN
COSTING FUNDAMENTALS

(12 pages of outline)

The core of management accounting is its specialized terminology, and how an understanding of this terminology can improve marginal decision making. Cost-volume-profit analysis allows an entity to identify the level of production at which all its fixed costs are covered.

18.1 COST MEASUREMENT TERMINOLOGY

1. **Manufacturing vs. Nonmanufacturing**

    a. The costs of manufacturing a product can be classified as one of three types:

    1) **Direct materials** are tangible inputs to the manufacturing process that can practicably be traced to the product, e.g., sheet metal welded together for a piece of heavy equipment.

        a) All costs of bringing raw materials to the production line, e.g., transportation-in, are included in the cost of direct materials.

    2) **Direct labor** is the cost of human labor that can feasibly be traced to the product, e.g., the wages of the welder.

    3) **Manufacturing overhead** consists of all costs of manufacturing that are not direct materials or direct labor.

        a) Indirect materials are tangible inputs to the manufacturing process that cannot practicably be traced to the product, e.g., the welding compound used to put together a piece of heavy equipment.

        b) Indirect labor is the cost of human labor connected with the manufacturing process that cannot practicably be traced to the product, e.g., the wages of assembly line supervisors and janitorial staff.

        c) Factory operating costs, such as utilities expense, real estate taxes, insurance, and depreciation on factory equipment.

    b. Manufacturing costs are often grouped into the following classifications:

    1) **Prime cost** equals **direct materials plus direct labor**, i.e., those costs directly attributable to a product.

    2) **Conversion cost** equals **direct labor plus manufacturing overhead**, i.e., the costs of converting raw materials into the finished product.

    c. A manufacturer also incurs nonmanufacturing costs.

    1) Selling (marketing) costs are incurred in getting the product from the factory to the consumer, e.g., sales personnel salaries and product transportation.

    2) Administrative expenses are not directly related to producing or marketing the product, e.g., executive salaries and depreciation on the headquarters building.

2.   **Direct vs. Indirect**

   a.   Costs can be classified by how they are assigned to cost objects.

   1)   Direct costs can be traced to a particular cost object in an economically feasible way.

      a)   Examples are direct materials and direct labor inputs to a manufacturing process.

   2)   Indirect costs cannot be traced to a particular cost object in an economically feasible way. Thus, they must be allocated to that object.

      a)   Examples are indirect materials and indirect labor inputs to a manufacturing process.

      b)   To simplify the allocation process, indirect costs often are collected in cost pools.

         i)   A cost pool is an account in which similar cost elements with a common cause are accumulated.

         ii)   Manufacturing overhead is a commonly used cost pool in which various untraceable costs of manufacturing are accumulated prior to being allocated.

3.   **Product vs. Period**

   a.   An important issue in management accounting is whether to capitalize costs in finished goods inventory or to expense them as incurred.

   1)   Product costs (inventoriable costs) are capitalized as part of finished goods inventory. They eventually become components of cost of goods sold.

   2)   Period costs are expensed as incurred and are therefore excluded from cost of goods sold.

   b.   This distinction is crucial because of the required treatment of manufacturing costs for external financial reporting purposes.

   1)   Under GAAP, all manufacturing costs (direct materials, direct labor, variable overhead, and fixed overhead) must be recognized as product costs. All selling and administrative (S&A) costs are period costs.

      a)   This approach is **absorption costing** (full costing).

   2)   For internal reporting, operational planning and control may be facilitated by treating only variable manufacturing costs as product costs. All other costs (variable S&A and the fixed portion of both production and S&A expenses) are period costs.

      a)   This approach is **variable costing** (direct costing).
      b)   See Study Unit 19, Subunit 1.

   3)   The following table summarizes absorption and variable costing:

	Absorption Costing (Required under GAAP)	Variable Costing (For Internal Reporting Only)
Product Costs (Included in Cost of Goods Sold)	Variable production costs	
	Fixed production costs	
Period Costs		Fixed production costs
	Variable S&A expenses	
(Excluded from Cost of Goods Sold)	Fixed S&A expenses	

c. **Gross margin** is an intermediate component of operating income under absorption (full) costing. It is the excess of sales over cost of goods sold that consists of variable and fixed manufacturing costs.

    1) Only costs directly associated with manufacturing the product may be subtracted.

    2) This is the only acceptable calculation under GAAP.

d. **Contribution margin** is the intermediate component when variable costing is used. It is the excess of sales over the sum of variable manufacturing and selling and administrative costs.

    1) Contribution margin is the amount available to the firm to cover fixed costs.

    2) This calculation is often used for internal (managerial) reporting purposes.

Stop and review! You have completed the outline for this subunit. Study multiple-choice questions 1 through 4 on page 491.

18.2 BASIC COST CALCULATIONS

1. **Cost of Goods Sold and Cost of Goods Manufactured**

   a. Cost of goods sold is a straightforward computation for retailers because they have only one class of inventory.

Beginning inventory	$XX,XXX
Plus: purchases	X,XXX
Minus: ending inventory	(X,XXX)
Cost of goods sold	**$XX,XXX**

   b. The calculation is more complex for manufacturers because they have three classes of inventory.

       1) Cost of goods sold contains an additional component called cost of goods manufactured, which is similar to a retailer's purchases account.

Beginning work-in-process inventory	$XX,XXX
Plus: total manufacturing costs	X,XXX
Minus: ending work-in-process inventory	(X,XXX)
Cost of goods manufactured	**$XX,XXX**

   c. A comparison of these computations in full is as follows:

Cost of goods sold for a manufacturer:

Beginning direct materials inventory		$ xxx,xxx
Plus: purchases	$x,xxx,xxx	
Minus: returns and discounts	(xx,xxx)	
Net purchases	x,xxx,xxx	
Plus: freight-in	xx,xxx	x,xxx,xxx
Direct materials available for use		x,xxx,xxx
Minus: ending direct materials inventory		(xxx,xxx)
Direct materials used in production		$ x,xxx,xxx
Direct labor costs		x,xxx,xxx
Manufacturing overhead costs		xxx,xxx
Total manufacturing costs for the period		**$x,xxx,xxx**
Plus: beginning work-in-process inventory		xxx,xxx
Minus: ending work-in-process inventory		(xxx,xxx)
Costs of goods manufactured		**x,xxx,xxx**
Plus: beginning finished goods inventory		xxx,xxx
Goods available for sale		**x,xxx,xxx**
Minus: ending finished goods inventory		(xxx,xxx)
Costs of goods sold		**$x,xxx,xxx**

Cost of goods sold for a retailer:

Beginning inventory		$ xxx,xxx
Plus: purchases	$x,xxx,xxx	
Minus: returns and discounts	(xx,xxx)	
Net purchases	x,xxx,xxx	
Plus: freight-in	xx,xxx	x,xxx,xxx
Goods available for sale		x,xxx,xxx
Minus: ending inventory		(xxx,xxx)
Costs of goods sold		**$x,xxx,xxx**

2.   **Relevant vs. Sunk**

    a.   Relevant costs are future costs that vary depending on the action taken. All other costs are assumed to be constant and thus are irrelevant to the decision.

        1)   An example is tuition that must be spent to attend a fourth year of college.

    b.   Sunk costs already have been incurred or irrevocably committed to be incurred. Because they are unavoidable and do not vary with the option chosen, they are not relevant to future decisions.

        1)   An example is 3 years of tuition already paid. The previous 3 years of tuition do not affect the decision to attend a fourth year.

3.   **Additional Cost Concepts**

    a.   **Value-adding costs** cannot be eliminated without reducing the quality, responsiveness, or quantity of the output required by a customer or by an organization.

    b.   **Incremental (differential) cost** is the difference in total cost between two decisions. Incremental cost never includes fixed costs or sunk costs.

    c.   **Opportunity cost** is the maximum benefit forgone by using a scarce resource for a given purpose.

Stop and review! You have completed the outline for this subunit. Study multiple-choice questions 5 through 9 beginning on page 492.

18.3 OTHER COST MEASUREMENT CONCEPTS

1.   **Variable vs. Fixed**

    a.   Variable cost per unit remains constant in the short run regardless of the level of production. But variable costs in total vary directly and proportionally with changes in volume. Typical variable costs are direct materials, direct labor, and manufacturing supplies.

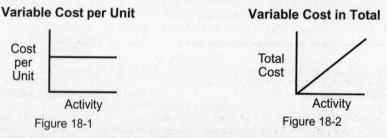

Variable Cost per Unit	Variable Cost in Total
Figure 18-1	Figure 18-2

EXAMPLE

A company requires one unit of direct material to be used in each finished good it produces.

Number of Units Produced		Cost per Unit		Total Cost of Units
0	×	$10	=	$0
100	×	$10	=	$1,000
1,000	×	$10	=	$10,000
5,000	×	$10	=	$50,000
10,000	×	$10	=	$100,000

b. Fixed costs in total remain unchanged in the short run regardless of production level. Accordingly, the amount paid for an assembly line is the same even if production is halted entirely. But fixed cost per unit varies indirectly with the activity level. Typical fixed costs are rent, depreciation, and insurance.

Fixed Costs in Total

Figure 18-3

Fixed Cost per Unit

Figure 18-4

EXAMPLE

The historical cost of the assembly line is fixed, but its cost per unit decreases as production increases.

Cost of Assembly Line		Number of Units Produced		Per-Unit Cost of Assembly Line
$1,000,000	÷	1	=	$1,000,000
$1,000,000	÷	100	=	$10,000
$1,000,000	÷	1,000	=	$1,000
$1,000,000	÷	5,000	=	$200
$1,000,000	÷	10,000	=	$100

---

c. **Mixed (semivariable) costs** combine fixed and variable elements, e.g., rental of a car for a flat fee per month plus an additional fee for each mile driven.

Mixed Cost

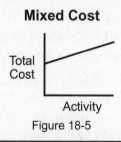

Figure 18-5

EXAMPLE

The company rents a piece of machinery to make its production line more efficient. The rental is $150,000 per year plus $1 for every unit produced.

Number of Units Produced	Fixed Cost of Extra Machine		Variable Cost of Extra Machine		Total Cost of Extra Machine
0	$150,000	+	$0	=	$150,000
100	$150,000	+	$100	=	$150,100
1,000	$150,000	+	$1,000	=	$151,000
5,000	$150,000	+	$5,000	=	$155,000
10,000	$150,000	+	$10,000	=	$160,000

---

1) The fixed and variable portions of a mixed cost can be estimated using the high-low method (see Study Unit 6, Subunit 1 for an explanation of the high-low method).

2. **Relevant Range**

    a. Within the relevant range, per-unit variable costs and fixed costs do not change. It is synonymous with the **short run** because all costs are variable in the long run.

        1) The relevant range is established by the efficiency of a company's current manufacturing plant, its agreements with labor unions and suppliers, etc.

            a) Investment in more efficient equipment may result in higher total fixed costs and lower total and per-unit variable costs.

3. **Spoilage and Scrap**

    a. **Normal spoilage** occurs under normal operating conditions. It is essentially uncontrollable in the short run. Because it is expected under efficient operations, it is treated as a product cost, that is, absorbed into the cost of the good output.

    b. **Abnormal spoilage** is not expected to occur under normal, efficient operating conditions. It is typically treated as a period cost (a loss).

    c. **Scrap** consists of materials left over from the production process. If scrap is sold, it reduces factory overhead. If it is discarded, it is absorbed into the cost of the good output.

Stop and review! You have completed the outline for this subunit. Study multiple-choice questions 10 through 14 beginning on page 493.

18.4 DECISION COSTING

1. **Relevant vs. Irrelevant Factors**

    a. In decision making, an organization must focus on only relevant revenues and costs. To be relevant, the revenues and costs must

        1) Be made in the future

            a) Costs that have already been incurred or to which the organization is committed, called sunk costs, have no bearing on any future decisions.

            b) EXAMPLE: A manufacturer is considering upgrading its production equipment owing to the obsolescence of its current machinery. The amounts paid for the existing equipment are sunk costs; they make no difference in the decision to modernize.

        2) Differ among the possible alternative courses of action

            a) EXAMPLE: A union contract may require 6 months of wage continuance in case of a plant shutdown. Thus, 6 months of wages must be disbursed, regardless of whether the plant remains open.

    b. Only avoidable costs are relevant.

        1) An avoidable cost may be saved by not adopting a particular option. Avoidable costs might include variable raw material costs and direct labor costs.

        2) An unavoidable cost is one that cannot be avoided if a particular action is taken.

            a) For example, if a company has a long-term lease on a building, closing out the business in that building will not eliminate the need to pay rent. Thus, the rent is an unavoidable cost.

c.   Incremental (marginal or differential) costs are inherent in the concept of relevance.

1)   Throughout the relevant range, the incremental cost of an additional unit of output is the same. Once a certain level of output is reached, however, the current production capacity is insufficient and another increment of fixed costs must be incurred.

EXAMPLE

A firm produces a product for which it incurs the following unit costs:

Direct materials	$2.00
Direct labor	3.00
Variable overhead	.50
Fixed overhead	.50
Total cost	$6.00

The product normally sells for $10 per unit. An application of marginal analysis is necessary if a foreign buyer, who has never before been a customer, offers to pay $5.60 per unit for a special order of the firm's product. The immediate reaction might be to refuse the offer because the selling price is less than the average cost of production.

However, marginal analysis results in a different decision. Assuming that the firm has idle capacity, only the additional costs should be considered. In this example, the only marginal costs are for direct materials, direct labor, and variable overhead. No additional fixed overhead costs would be incurred. Because marginal revenue (the $5.60 selling price) exceeds marginal costs ($2 materials + $3 labor + $.50 variable OH = $5.50 per unit), accepting the special order will be profitable.

If a competitor bids $5.80 per unit, the firm can still profitably accept the special order while underbidding the competitor by setting a price below $5.80 per unit but above $5.50 per unit.

---

2.   **Add-or-Drop-a-Segment Decisions**

a.   Disinvestment decisions are the opposite of capital budgeting decisions, i.e., to terminate an operation, product or product line, business segment, branch, or major customer rather than start one.

1)   In general, if the marginal cost of a project exceeds the marginal revenue, the firm should disinvest.

b.   Four steps should be taken in making a disinvestment decision:

1)   Identify fixed costs that will be eliminated by the disinvestment decision, e.g., insurance on equipment used.

2)   Determine the revenue needed to justify continuing operations. In the short run, this amount should at least equal the variable cost of production or continued service.

3)   Establish the opportunity cost of funds that will be received upon disinvestment (e.g., salvage value).

4)   Determine whether the carrying amount of the assets is equal to their economic value. If not, re-evaluate the decision using current fair value rather than the carrying amount.

c.   When a firm disinvests, excess capacity exists unless another project uses this capacity immediately. The cost of idle capacity should be treated as a relevant cost.

3. Special Orders When Excess Capacity Exists

a. When a manufacturer has excess production capacity, there is no opportunity cost involved when accepting a special order.

1) The company should accept the order if the minimum price for the product is equal to the variable costs.

EXAMPLE

Granton Fabricators produces two models of pump for natural gas pipelines. The following price and cost data are available for these products:

	Small Pump		Large Pump	
Selling price		$250		$300
Variable costs:				
Direct materials	$110		$125	
Direct labor	20		25	
Variable overhead	55		50	
Variable S&A	5	(190)	5	(205)
Contribution margin		$ 60		$ 95

Granton has just received a special, one-time order for 2,000 units of its small pump and has enough unused capacity to produce them. Granton can accept the order if it requires at least a minimum price of $190 (unit variable cost) per pump.

---

4. Special Orders in the Absence of Excess Capacity

a. When a manufacturer lacks excess production capacity, the differential (marginal or incremental) costs of accepting the order must be considered.

1) Besides the variable costs of the production run, the firm must consider the opportunity cost of redirecting productive capacity away from (possibly more profitable) products.

EXAMPLE

Granton has received another special order for 2,000 small pumps, but this month the production line is committed to running at its full capacity. Granton is using all of the 24,000 machine hours available to produce its large pump.

Each small pump requires 4 hours to produce, and each large pump requires 6 hours. Granton will need to divert 8,000 hours (2,000 small pumps × 4 hours per unit) to run the special order.

The opportunity cost of these hours is the contribution margin (CM) that would be earned by devoting them to the higher-margin large pump [the small pump generates a CM of $15 per machine hour ($60 ÷ 4 hours), while the large pump produces a CM of $15.83 per machine hour ($95 ÷ 6 hours)].

Hours needed	8,000	Large pump UCM	$ 95
Hours per large pump	÷ 6	Large pumps forgone	× 1,333
Large pumps forgone	1,333	Opportunity cost	$126,635

For the special order to be profitable, Granton must recover (1) the opportunity cost of not producing the large pump and (2) the variable costs of the production run itself.

Large pump margin forgone	$ 126,635
Variable costs of special order (2,000 units × $190)	380,000
Total cost to be recovered	$ 506,635
Size of special order	÷ 2,000
Minimum price per unit	$253.3175

Stop and review! You have completed the outline for this subunit. Study multiple-choice questions 15 through 19 beginning on page 495.

18.5 COST-VOLUME-PROFIT ANALYSIS -- BASICS

1. Cost-volume-profit (CVP) analysis (also called breakeven analysis) is a tool for understanding the interaction of revenues with fixed and variable costs.

    a. It explains the effects of changes in assumptions about cost behavior and the relevant ranges in which those assumptions are valid. These changes may affect the relationships among revenues, variable costs, and fixed costs at various production levels.

    b. Thus, CVP analysis allows management to determine the probable effects of changes in sales volume, sales price, product mix, etc.

2. **Simplifying Assumptions**

    a. Cost and revenue relationships are predictable and linear. These relationships are true over the relevant range of activity and specified time span.

    b. Unit selling prices and market conditions are constant.

    c. Changes in inventory are insignificant in amount, so production equals sales.

    d. Total variable costs change proportionally with volume, but unit variable costs are constant over the relevant range. Direct materials and direct labor are typically variable costs.

    e. Fixed costs remain constant over the relevant range of volume, but unit fixed costs vary indirectly with volume. The classification of fixed versus variable can be affected by the time frame being considered.

3. **Determining the Breakeven Point in Units**

    a. The **breakeven point** is the level of output at which all fixed costs and cumulative variable costs have been covered. It is the output at which operating income is zero.

        1) Each additional unit produced above the breakeven point generates operating profit.

    b. The simplest calculation for breakeven in units is to divide fixed costs by the unit contribution margin (UCM). UCM equals unit selling price minus unit variable cost.

$$\text{Breakeven point in units} = \frac{\text{Fixed costs}}{\text{UCM}}$$

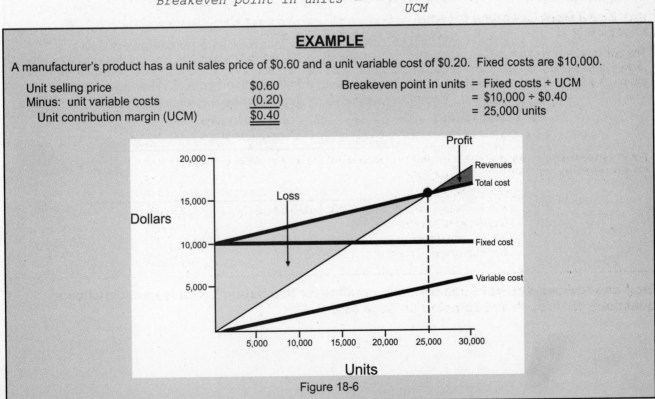

EXAMPLE

A manufacturer's product has a unit sales price of $0.60 and a unit variable cost of $0.20. Fixed costs are $10,000.

Unit selling price	$0.60	
Minus: unit variable costs	(0.20)	
Unit contribution margin (UCM)	$0.40	

Breakeven point in units = Fixed costs ÷ UCM
= $10,000 ÷ $0.40
= 25,000 units

Figure 18-6

4. **Determining the Breakeven Point in Dollars**

a. The breakeven point in sales dollars equals fixed costs divided by the contribution margin ratio (CMR). CMR is the ratio of contribution margin to sales price on either a total or per-unit basis.

$$Breakeven\ point\ in\ dollars\ =\ \frac{Fixed\ costs}{CMR}$$

b. The breakeven point in sales dollars also equals the breakeven point in units multiplied by the selling price.

EXAMPLE

The manufacturer's contribution margin ratio is 66.667% ($0.40 ÷ $0.60).

Breakeven point in dollars = Fixed costs ÷ CMR
= $10,000 ÷ .66667
= $15,000

Stop and review! You have completed the outline for this subunit. Study multiple-choice questions 20 through 23 on page 497.

18.6 COST-VOLUME-PROFIT ANALYSIS -- APPLICATIONS

1. **Margin of Safety**

a. The margin of safety is the excess of sales over breakeven sales. It is the amount by which sales can decline before losses occur.

b. The margin of safety can be expressed as either a dollar amount or a percentage of sales.

$$Margin\ of\ safety\ in\ dollars\ =\ Total\ sales\ in\ dollars\ -\ Breakeven\ point\ in\ dollars$$

$$Margin\ of\ safety\ (\%)\ =\ \frac{Margin\ of\ safety\ (in\ dollars)}{Total\ sales\ (in\ dollars)}$$

2. **Target Operating Income**

a. An amount of operating income, either in dollars or as a percentage of sales, is frequently required.

1) By treating target income as an additional fixed cost, CVP analysis can be applied. The necessary level of sales can be expressed as either unit volume or dollars.

$$Target\ unit\ volume\ =\ \frac{Fixed\ costs\ +\ Target\ operating\ income}{UCM}$$

$$Target\ sales\ in\ dollars\ =\ \frac{Fixed\ costs\ +\ Target\ operating\ income}{Contribution\ margin\ ratio}$$

b.   Other target income situations call for the application of the standard formula for operating income.

Sales – Variable costs – Fixed costs = Operating income

EXAMPLE

A company with fixed costs of $150,000 and variable costs of 85% would like to project the level of sales needed to achieve a 10% return on sales.

$$
\begin{aligned}
\text{Sales} - \text{Variable costs} - \text{Fixed costs} &= \text{Operating income} \\
\text{Sales} - (.85)\text{Sales} - \$150,000 &= (.1)\text{Sales} \\
(.15)\text{Sales} - \$150,000 &= (.1)\text{Sales} \\
(.05)\text{Sales} &= \$150,000 \\
\text{Sales} &= \$3,000,000
\end{aligned}
$$

---

1)   Note that the unit selling price is not necessary to perform this calculation.

EXAMPLE

The manufacturer wants to generate $25,000 of operating income.

$$
\begin{aligned}
\text{Target unit volume} &= (\text{Fixed costs} + \text{Target operating income}) \div \text{UCM} \\
&= (\$10,000 + \$25,000) \div \$0.40 \\
&= \$35,000 \div \$.40 \\
&= 87,500 \text{ units}
\end{aligned}
$$

---

3.   **Target Net Income**

a.   A variation of this problem asks for net income (an after-tax amount) instead of operating income (a pretax amount).

$$
\begin{aligned}
\text{Net income} &= \text{Operating income} - (\text{Operating income} \times \text{Tax rate}) \\
&= \text{Operating income} \times (1 - \text{Tax rate}) \\
\text{Operating income} &= \text{Net income} \div (1 - \text{Tax rate})
\end{aligned}
$$

1)   The calculation of the unit volume or sales dollars needed to produce a target net income is based on the same formulas used for target operating income. The only difference is that the target operating income is expressed in terms of related net income.

$$
Target\ unit\ volume = \frac{Fixed\ costs + [Target\ net\ income \div (1.0 - tax\ rate)]}{UCM}
$$

EXAMPLE

The manufacturer wants to generate $30,000 of net income. The effective tax rate is 40%.

$$
\begin{aligned}
\text{Target unit volume} &= \{\text{Fixed costs} + [\text{Target net income} \div (1.0 - .40)]\} \div \text{UCM} \\
&= [\$10,000 + (\$30,000 \div .60)] \div \$.40 \\
&= 150,000 \text{ units}
\end{aligned}
$$

---

4. **Multiple Products**

   a. When adapting CVP analysis to a multiproduct situation with variable costing, it is assumed that the product mix is maintained throughout the relevant range.

      1) The UCM in a multiproduct setting is the weighted average of the UCMs of the individual products.

EXAMPLE

Warbler, Inc., manufactures and sells two products, Skand and Tunster, with the following selling prices and variable costs:

	Skand	Tunster
Unit selling price	$100.00	$130.00
Unit variable cost	85.00	95.00

Warbler sells five units of Skand for every four units of Tunster. Warbler's total annual fixed costs are $80,600. Warbler wishes to determine how many units of each product must be sold to generate $100,000 of operating income.

The unit contribution margins of the two products are $15 ($100 – $85) and $35 ($130 – $95), respectively. The sales mix consists of a composite unit of five units of Skand and four units of Tunster. Thus, the number of composite units that must be sold is calculated using the composite (weighted-average) UCM.

$$\text{Target unit volume} = (\text{Target operating income} + \text{Fixed costs}) \div \text{Composite (weighted-average) UCM}$$
$$= (\$100,000 + \$80,600) \div [(5 \times \$15) + (4 \times \$35)]$$
$$= \$180,600 \div (\$75 + \$140)$$
$$= \$180,600 \div \$215$$
$$= 840 \text{ composite units}$$

         840 total units sold × 9 = 7,560
         Skand: 7,560 × (5 ÷ 9) = 4,200 units
         Tunster: 7,560 × (4 ÷ 9) = 3,360 units

Total contribution margin of $180,600 [(4,200 × $15) + (3,360 × $35)] is exactly equal to the sum of fixed costs ($80,600) and targeted operating income ($100,000).

 Be proficient in your ability to rearrange the equations used in CVP analysis to determine the information required by the question. The multiple-choice questions in the Gleim materials give you the opportunity to practice and improve your proficiency in working with these equations.

Stop and review! You have completed the outline for this subunit. Study multiple-choice questions 24 through 28 beginning on page 498.

QUESTIONS

18.1 Cost Measurement Terminology

1. Which one of the following best describes direct labor?

    A. A prime cost.

    B. A period cost.

    C. A product cost.

    D. Both a product cost and a prime cost.

Answer (D) is correct.
    REQUIRED: The best description of direct labor.
    DISCUSSION: Direct labor is both a product cost and a prime cost. Product costs are incurred to produce units of output and are deferred to future periods to the extent that output is not sold. Prime costs are the direct cost of manufacturing, for example, direct materials and direct labor.
    Answer (A) is incorrect. Direct labor is also a product cost. Answer (B) is incorrect. A period cost is expensed when incurred. Direct labor cost is inventoriable. Answer (C) is incorrect. Direct labor is also a prime cost.

2. Inventoriable costs

    A. Include only the prime costs of manufacturing a product.

    B. Include only the conversion costs of manufacturing a product.

    C. Are expensed when products become part of finished goods inventory.

    D. Are regarded as assets before the products are sold.

Answer (D) is correct.
    REQUIRED: The true statement about inventoriable costs.
    DISCUSSION: Product (inventoriable) costs are capitalized as part of finished goods inventory. In contrast, period costs are expensed as they are incurred and are not capitalized as assets. Under an absorption costing system, inventoriable costs include both variable and fixed costs of production; under variable costing, inventoriable costs include only variable production costs.
    Answer (A) is incorrect. Overhead costs as well as prime costs (direct materials and labor) are included in inventory. Answer (B) is incorrect. Materials costs are also included. Answer (C) is incorrect. Inventory costs are expensed when the goods are sold, not when they are transferred to finished goods.

3. In cost terminology, conversion costs consist of

    A. Direct and indirect labor.

    B. Direct labor and direct materials.

    C. Direct labor and factory overhead.

    D. Indirect labor and variable factory overhead.

Answer (C) is correct.
    REQUIRED: The components of conversion costs.
    DISCUSSION: Conversion costs consist of direct labor and manufacturing overhead. These are the costs of converting raw materials into a finished product.
    Answer (A) is incorrect. All manufacturing overhead is included in conversion costs, not just indirect labor. Answer (B) is incorrect. Direct materials are not an element of conversion costs; they are a prime cost. Answer (D) is incorrect. Direct labor is also an element of conversion costs.

4. The unit costs for direct materials, machining, and assembly of a manufactured product represent

    A. Conversion costs.

    B. Separable costs.

    C. Committed costs.

    D. Prime costs.

Answer (D) is correct.
    REQUIRED: The type of cost represented by raw materials, machining, and assembly.
    DISCUSSION: Prime costs are a manufacturer's direct cost. Direct materials and direct labor (such as machining and assembly) are examples.
    Answer (A) is incorrect. Conversion costs consist of direct labor and overhead. Answer (B) is incorrect. Separable costs are incurred beyond the point at which jointly produced items become separately identifiable. Answer (C) is incorrect. Committed costs result when an entity holds fixed assets. Examples of committed costs include long-term lease payments and depreciation.

18.2 Basic Cost Calculations

5. The following is selected information from the records of Ray, Inc.:

Purchases of raw materials	$ 6,000
Raw materials, beginning	500
Raw materials, ending	800
Work-in-process, beginning	0
Work-in-process, ending	0
Cost of goods sold	12,000
Finished goods, beginning	1,200
Finished goods, ending	1,400

What is the total amount of conversion costs?

    A. $5,500

    B. $5,900

    C. $6,100

    D. $6,500

Answer (D) is correct.

    REQUIRED: The conversion costs.

    DISCUSSION: Conversion costs are direct labor plus manufacturing overhead, i.e., the costs of converting direct materials into finished goods. The cost of goods manufactured equals all manufacturing costs (DM + DL + OH) adjusted for the change in WIP ($0 in this case). COGS equals COGM adjusted for the change in FG. Accordingly, COGM equals $12,200 ($12,000 COGS – $1,200 + $1,400). Materials used equaled $5,700 ($6,000 purchased + $500 – $800). Given no BWIP or EWIP, conversion costs (DL + OH) must be $6,500 ($12,200 COGM – $5,700 DM used).

    Answer (A) is incorrect. Purchases of materials minus beginning materials equals $5,500. Answer (B) is incorrect. Purchases of materials, plus the increase in finished goods, minus the increase in materials equals $5,900. Answer (C) is incorrect. Purchases of materials, plus the increase in materials, minus the increase in finished goods equals $6,100.

Questions 6 and 7 are based on the following information. The estimated unit costs for Cole Co. using absorption (full) costing and planning to produce and sell at a level of 12,000 units per month are as follows:

Cost Item	Estimated Unit Cost
Direct materials	$32
Direct labor	20
Variable manufacturing overhead	15
Fixed manufacturing overhead	6
Variable selling	3
Fixed selling	4

6. Cole's estimated conversion costs per unit are

    A. $35

    B. $41

    C. $48

    D. $67

Answer (B) is correct.

    REQUIRED: The estimated conversion costs per unit.

    DISCUSSION: Conversion costs are incurred in transforming raw materials into finished products. They include direct labor and manufacturing overhead. Thus, unit conversion costs equal $41 ($20 direct labor + $15 variable overhead + $6 fixed overhead).

    Answer (A) is incorrect. Direct labor plus variable manufacturing overhead equals $35. It does not include $6 fixed overhead. Answer (C) is incorrect. Including $3 in variable selling costs and $4 in fixed selling costs results in $48. Answer (D) is incorrect. The amount of $67 includes $32 in direct materials and excludes $6 fixed overhead.

7. Cole's estimated direct manufacturing costs per unit are

    A. $73

    B. $32

    C. $67

    D. $52

Answer (D) is correct.

    REQUIRED: The estimated prime costs per unit.

    DISCUSSION: The direct costs of manufacturing, also called prime costs, are the costs of direct materials and direct labor. They are costs that can be directly associated with the finished product. Hence, direct manufacturing costs per unit are $52 ($32 direct materials + $20 direct labor).

    Answer (A) is incorrect. The amount of $73 includes $15 variable manufacturing overhead and $6 fixed manufacturing overhead. Answer (B) is incorrect. Not including $20 direct labor results in $32. Answer (C) is incorrect. Including $15 variable manufacturing overhead results in $67.

Questions 8 and 9 are based on the following information.

Jackson Products
Schedule of Cost of Goods Manufactured
For the Year Ended December 31 (in thousands)

Direct materials:		
Beginning inventory	$17,000	
Purchases of direct materials	70,000	
Cost of direct materials available for use	$87,000	
Ending inventory	(9,000)	
Direct materials used		$ 78,000
Direct manufacturing labor		9,000
Indirect manufacturing costs:		
Indirect manufacturing labor	$ 8,000	
Supplies	1,000	
Heat, light, and power	4,000	
Depreciation -- plant building	2,000	
Depreciation -- plant equipment	3,000	
Miscellaneous	2,000	20,000
Manufacturing costs incurred during the period		$107,000
Add beginning work-in-process inventory		11,000
Total manufacturing costs to account for		$118,000
Deduct ending work-in-process inventory		(7,000)
Cost of goods manufactured (to Income Statement)		$111,000

8. What are Jackson's direct manufacturing costs for the year?

A. $20,000

B. $79,000

C. $87,000

D. $98,000

Answer (C) is correct.
    REQUIRED: The total of prime costs.
    DISCUSSION: Prime costs are all direct manufacturing costs; in this case, direct materials cost ($78,000) plus direct manufacturing labor cost ($9,000), or $87,000.
    Answer (A) is incorrect. The $20,000 is overhead. Answer (B) is incorrect. Using the cost of material purchases instead of materials used results in $79,000. Answer (D) is incorrect. Using overhead instead of labor results in $98,000.

9. What are Jackson's conversion costs for the year?

A. $4,000

B. $20,000

C. $29,000

D. $98,000

Answer (C) is correct.
    REQUIRED: The total conversion costs.
    DISCUSSION: Conversion costs are all manufacturing costs other than direct material costs. In this case, conversion costs are equal to the direct manufacturing labor cost ($9,000) plus indirect manufacturing costs ($20,000), or $29,000.
    Answer (A) is incorrect. The difference between the beginning and ending work-in-process inventories is $4,000. Answer (B) is incorrect. The amount of $20,000 excludes direct labor. Answer (D) is incorrect. Erroneously including materials and excluding labor results in $98,000.

18.3 Other Cost Measurement Concepts

10. A delivery company is implementing a system to compare the costs of purchasing and operating different vehicles in its fleet. Truck 415 is driven 125,000 miles per year at a variable cost of $0.13 per mile. Truck 415 has a capacity of 28,000 pounds and delivers 250 full loads per year. What amount is the truck's delivery cost per pound?

A. $0.00163 per pound.

B. $0.00232 per pound.

C. $0.58036 per pound.

D. $1.72000 per pound.

Answer (B) is correct.
    REQUIRED: The truck's delivery cost per pound.
    DISCUSSION: The truck's variable delivery cost per pound equals the total variable cost divided by the total pounds delivered by the truck. The truck's mileage cost is $16,250 (125,000 miles × $0.13 per mile). The truck delivered 7,000,000 pounds (28,000 pounds × 250 loads). The truck's variable delivery cost per pound is therefore $0.00232 per pound ($16,250 ÷ 7,000,000 pounds).
    Answer (A) is incorrect. A per-pound cost of $0.00163 is not the truck's delivery cost per pound. Answer (C) is incorrect. A per-pound cost of $0.58036 results from dividing the total variable cost by the truck's capacity. Answer (D) is incorrect. A per-pound cost of $1.72000 results from dividing the truck's capacity by the total variable cost.

11. Data from the duplicating department of a company for the last 2 months are as follows:

	Number of Copies Made	Duplicating Department's Costs
January	100,000	$8,500
February	150,000	9,500

What is total variable cost at 110,000 copies?

A. $1,100

B. $2,200

C. $5,500

D. $7,920

Answer (B) is correct.
REQUIRED: The total variable cost.
DISCUSSION: The fixed and variable portion of mixed costs can be estimated using the high-low method. Unit variable cost can be determined by dividing the $1,000 cost increase for the additional copies made in February by the increase in copies made. Hence, total variable cost for 110,000 copies is $2,200 {110,000 × [$1,000 ÷ (150,000 – 100,000)]}.
Answer (A) is incorrect. Total variable cost would be $1,100 if 200,000 copies were made in February. Answer (C) is incorrect. Variable cost per unit would have to be $.05 to total $5,500. Answer (D) is incorrect. Calculating an average cost per copy for January and February and then multiplying by 110,000 copies results in $7,920.

Questions 12 and 13 are based on the following information. The estimated unit costs for Cole Co. using absorption (full) costing and planning to produce and sell at a level of 12,000 units per month are as follows:

Cost Item	Estimated Unit Cost
Direct materials	$32
Direct labor	20
Variable manufacturing overhead	15
Fixed manufacturing overhead	6
Variable selling	3
Fixed selling	4

12. Cole's estimated total variable costs per unit are

A. $38

B. $70

C. $52

D. $18

Answer (B) is correct.
REQUIRED: The estimated total variable costs per unit.
DISCUSSION: Variable costs vary in direct proportion to production. Total unit variable costs are $70 ($32 direct materials + $20 direct labor + $15 variable overhead + $3 variable selling costs).
Answer (A) is incorrect. The amount of $38 does not include $32 direct materials. Answer (C) is incorrect. The amount of $52 does not include $15 variable overhead and $3 variable selling costs. Answer (D) is incorrect. The amount of $18 does not include $32 direct materials and $20 direct labor.

13. Estimated total costs that Cole would incur during a month with a production level of 12,000 units and a sales level of 8,000 units are

A. $692,000

B. $960,000

C. $948,000

D. $932,000

Answer (C) is correct.
REQUIRED: The estimated total costs incurred during a month with given production and sales levels.
DISCUSSION: Manufacturing costs at a production level of 12,000 units are $73 per unit ($32 + $20 + $15 + $6). Total estimated manufacturing costs are therefore $876,000 (12,000 units × $73). Fixed selling costs are expected to be $48,000 (12,000 units × $4). The anticipated total variable selling costs are $24,000 (8,000 units × $3). Thus, the total estimated costs are $948,000 ($876,000 + $48,000 + $24,000).
Answer (A) is incorrect. Total estimated costs are $948,000 [(12,000 × $73) + (12,000 × $4) + (8,000 × $3)]. Answer (B) is incorrect. Using 12,000 units to determine variable selling costs instead of 8,000 results in $960,000. Answer (D) is incorrect. Using 8,000 units to determine fixed selling costs instead of 12,000 results in $932,000.

14. Dahl Co. uses a standard costing system in connection with the manufacture of a "one size fits all" article of clothing. Each unit of finished product contains 2 yards of direct materials. However, a 20% direct materials spoilage calculated on input quantities occurs during the manufacturing process. The cost of the direct materials is $3 per yard. The standard direct materials cost per unit of finished product is

A. $4.80

B. $6.00

C. $7.20

D. $7.50

Answer (D) is correct.
REQUIRED: The standard direct materials cost per unit of finished product.
DISCUSSION: If 2 yards remain in each unit after spoilage of 20% of the direct materials input, the total per unit input must have been 2.5 yards (2.0 ÷ 80%). The standard unit direct materials cost is therefore $7.50 (2.5 yards × $3).
Answer (A) is incorrect. The 2 yards of good output should be divided (not multiplied) by 80% to determine the standard yards of material per unit. Answer (B) is incorrect. The cost per unit before spoilage is added is $6.00. Answer (C) is incorrect. Adding 20% of the materials of the finished product as spoilage and then multiplying by the $3.00 cost per yard results in $7.20 [(2.00 × 1.20) × $3.00].

18.4 Decision Costing

15. Clay Co. has considerable excess manufacturing capacity. A special job order's cost sheet includes the following applied manufacturing overhead costs:

Fixed costs	$21,000
Variable costs	33,000

The fixed costs include a normal $3,700 allocation for in-house design costs, although no in-house design will be done. Instead, the job will require the use of external designers costing $7,750. What is the total amount to be included in the calculation to determine the minimum acceptable price for the job?

A. $36,700

B. $40,750

C. $54,000

D. $58,050

Answer (B) is correct.
REQUIRED: The total amount to be included in the calculation to determine the minimum acceptable price.
DISCUSSION: Given that Clay has excess capacity, it will incur neither increased fixed costs nor opportunity costs if it accepts the special order. Thus, the incremental cost of the order (the minimum acceptable price) will be $40,750 ($33,000 variable costs + $7,750 cost of external design).
Answer (A) is incorrect. The amount of $36,700 equals variable costs plus the in-house design costs. Answer (C) is incorrect. The amount of $54,000 equals the fixed costs plus the variable costs. Answer (D) is incorrect. The amount of $58,050 equals the fixed costs, plus the variable costs, minus the in-house design costs, plus the external design costs.

16. A company's target gross margin is 40% of the selling price of a product that costs $89 per unit. The product's selling price should be

A. $124.60

B. $142.40

C. $148.33

D. $222.50

Answer (C) is correct.
REQUIRED: The product's selling price.
DISCUSSION: The gross margin is calculated as [1 – (Unit cost ÷ Unit selling price)]. The question gives a company's target gross margin as 40%. Rearranging the gross margin equation, the unit selling price equals [Unit cost ÷ (1 – Gross margin)]. Thus, the product's selling price is $148.33 [$89 ÷ (1 – .40)].
Answer (A) is incorrect. The amount of $124.60 equals the product's cost plus the target gross margin percentage [$89 + ($89 × .4)]. Answer (B) is incorrect. The amount of $142.40 equals the product's cost plus the cost percentage [($89 + ($89 × .6)]. Answer (D) is incorrect. The product's cost divided by gross margin equals $222.50.

17. A company that produces 10,000 units has fixed costs of $300,000, variable costs of $50 per unit, and a sales price of $85 per unit. After learning that its variable costs will increase by 20%, the company is considering an increase in production to 12,000 units. Which of the following statements is correct regarding the company's next steps?

A. If production is increased to 12,000 units, profits will increase by $50,000.

B. If production is increased to 12,000 units, profits will increase by $100,000.

C. If production remains at 10,000 units, profits will decrease by $50,000.

D. If production remains at 10,000 units, profits will decrease by $100,000.

Answer (D) is correct.
REQUIRED: The true statement about maintaining or increasing the production level given an increase in variable costs.
DISCUSSION: Variable costs will increase by $10 per unit ($50 × 20%). If production remains at 10,000 units, the additional cost is $100,000 (10,000 units × $10). Thus, profits will decrease by $100,000 assuming (1) the sales price and fixed costs do not change and (2) all units are sold for that sales price. The new unit contribution margin (UCM) is $25 ($85 sales price – $50 original unit VC – $10 increase in unit VC). The contribution margin given production and sale of 10,000 units is $250,000 (10,000 units × $25 UCM). The result is a $50,000 loss ($300,000 FC – $250,000 contribution margin). The original UCM was $35 ($85 sales price – $50 unit VC). Given production and sale of 10,000 units, the contribution margin is $35,000 (10,000 × $35 UCM), a gross profit of $50,000 ($350,000 contribution margin – $300,000 FC).
Answer (A) is incorrect. Production and sale of 12,000 units is the breakeven point. The contribution margin (12,000 units × $25 UCM = $300,000) equals fixed costs. Thus, profits decrease by $50,000 despite the increase in output. Given the original assumptions, the contribution margin is $350,000 (10,000 units × $35 UCM), a gross profit of $50,000 ($350,000 – $300,000 FC). Answer (B) is incorrect. Profits decrease relative to those earned given the original costs, sales price, and output. Answer (C) is incorrect. Profits decrease by $10,000 if production remains at 10,000 units.

18. Egan Co. owns land that could be developed in the future. Egan estimates it can sell the land for $1,200,000, net of all selling costs. If it is not sold, Egan will continue with its plans to develop the land. As Egan evaluates its options for development or sale of the property, what type of cost would the potential selling price represent in Egan's decision?

A. Sunk.

B. Opportunity.

C. Future.

D. Variable.

Answer (B) is correct.
REQUIRED: The cost classification of the potential selling price of land.
DISCUSSION: Opportunity cost is the maximum benefit forgone by using a resource for a given purpose and not for the best alternative. If Egan develops the land, it will not receive the revenue from the selling price.
Answer (A) is incorrect. Sunk costs have already been incurred. Answer (C) is incorrect. The potential selling price is not a future cost. Answer (D) is incorrect. Variable costs are production costs that vary in relation to production volume.

19. A company is offered a one-time special order for its product and has the capacity to take this order without losing current business. Variable costs per unit and fixed costs in total will be the same. The gross profit for the special order will be 10%, which is 15% less than the usual gross profit. What impact will this order have on total fixed costs and operating income?

A. Total fixed costs increase, and operating income increases.

B. Total fixed costs do **not** change, and operating income increases.

C. Total fixed costs do **not** change, and operating income does **not** change.

D. Total fixed costs increase, and operating income decreases.

Answer (B) is correct.
REQUIRED: The effect of a special order on total fixed costs and operating income.
DISCUSSION: Variable costs per unit and fixed costs in total do not change. Because the company has excess capacity, accepting a project with a positive gross profit margin increases operating income.
Answer (A) is incorrect. Total fixed costs do not change. Answer (C) is incorrect. Operating income increases. Answer (D) is incorrect. Total fixed costs do not change, and operating income increases.

18.5 Cost-Volume-Profit Analysis -- Basics

20. Breakeven analysis assumes over the relevant range that

A. Total costs are linear.

B. Fixed costs are nonlinear.

C. Variable costs are nonlinear.

D. Selling prices are nonlinear.

Answer (A) is correct.
    REQUIRED: The assumption underlying cost-volume-profit analysis.
    DISCUSSION: Breakeven analysis assumes that the cost and revenue factors used in the formula are linear and do not fluctuate with volume. Hence, fixed costs are deemed to be fixed over the relevant range of volume, and variable cost per unit remains constant as volume changes within the relevant range.
    Answer (B) is incorrect. Fixed costs are assumed to be constant in breakeven analysis. Answer (C) is incorrect. Variable costs per unit are constant and therefore linear in breakeven analysis. Answer (D) is incorrect. The selling price is assumed to be linear in breakeven analysis.

21. The following information pertains to a manufacturing company:

Total sales	$80,000
Total variable costs	20,000
Total fixed costs	30,000

What is the breakeven level in sales dollars?

A. $30,000

B. $40,000

C. $50,000

D. $80,000

Answer (B) is correct.
    REQUIRED: The breakeven level in sales dollars.
    DISCUSSION: The breakeven point in sales dollars equals fixed costs divided by the contribution margin ratio (CMR). The CMR equals .75 [($80,000 sales – $20,000 variable costs) ÷ $80,000 sales]. Thus, the breakeven level in sales dollars is $40,000 ($30,000 ÷ .75).
    Answer (A) is incorrect. The amount of $30,000 is the total fixed cost. Answer (C) is incorrect. The amount of $50,000 is the total cost. Answer (D) is incorrect. The amount of $80,000 equals total sales.

22. Snyder Co. manufactures fans with direct material costs of $10 per unit and direct labor of $7 per unit. A local carrier charges Snyder $5 per unit to make deliveries. Sales commissions are paid at 10% of the selling price. Fans are sold for $100 each. Indirect factory costs and administrative costs are $6,800 and $37,200 per month, respectively. How many fans must Snyder produce to break even?

A. 1,375

B. 648

C. 564

D. 530

Answer (B) is correct.
    REQUIRED: The output needed to break even.
    DISCUSSION: The breakeven point in units is derived by dividing fixed costs by the unit contribution margin. Snyder has fixed costs of $44,000 per month ($6,800 indirect factory + $37,200 administrative). The unit contribution margin is $100 – $10 – $7 – $5 – ($100 × 10%) = $68. The breakeven point is therefore $44,000 ÷ $68 = 647.06 units.
    Answer (A) is incorrect. Improperly dividing by variable costs instead of by contribution margin results in 1,375. Answer (C) is incorrect. Failing to deduct sales commissions in arriving at unit contribution margin results in 564. Answer (D) is incorrect. Failing to deduct the delivery charge and sales commissions in arriving at unit contribution margin results in 530.

23. The breakeven point in units sold for Tierson Corporation is 44,000. If fixed costs for Tierson are equal to $880,000 annually and variable costs are $10 per unit, what is the contribution margin per unit for Tierson Corporation?

A. $0.05

B. $20.00

C. $44.00

D. $88.00

Answer (B) is correct.
    REQUIRED: The contribution margin per unit.
    DISCUSSION: The breakeven point in units is equal to the fixed costs divided by the unit contribution margin (UCM).

$$\text{Fixed costs} \div \text{UCM} = \text{Breakeven point in units}$$
$$\$880,000 \div \text{UCM} = 44,000 \text{ units}$$
$$\text{UCM} = \$20$$

18.6 Cost-Volume-Profit Analysis -- Applications

24. Lake Co. has just increased its direct labor wage rates. All other budgeted costs and revenues were unchanged. How did this increase affect Lake's budgeted breakeven point and budgeted margin of safety?

	Budgeted Breakeven Point	Budgeted Margin of Safety
A.	Increase	Increase
B.	Increase	Decrease
C.	Decrease	Decrease
D.	Decrease	Increase

Answer (B) is correct.
REQUIRED: The effect on the breakeven point and margin of safety of an increase in direct labor cost.
DISCUSSION: The BEP is the sales volume at which total revenue equals total cost. The margin of safety is the excess of budgeted sales over the breakeven volume. Given that all other costs and revenues are constant, an increase in direct labor cost will increase the BEP and decrease the margin of safety.
Answer (A) is incorrect. The margin of safety will decrease. Answer (C) is incorrect. The BEP will increase. Answer (D) is incorrect. The BEP will increase and the margin of safety will decrease.

25. During Year 1, Thor Lab supplied hospitals with a comprehensive diagnostic kit for $120. At a volume of 80,000 kits, Thor had fixed costs of $1 million and a profit before income taxes of $200,000. Because of an adverse legal decision, Thor's Year 2 liability insurance increased by $1.2 million over Year 1. Assuming the volume and other costs are unchanged, what should the Year 2 price be if Thor is to make the same $200,000 profit before income taxes?

A. $120.00

B. $135.00

C. $150.00

D. $240.00

Answer (B) is correct.
REQUIRED: The price charged to earn a specified pretax profit.
DISCUSSION: CVP analysis can be used to restate the formula for operating income to determine the required level of unit sales:

$$Target\ unit\ volume = \frac{Fixed\ costs\ +\ Target\ operating\ income}{UCM}$$

Thor's Year 1 unit variable cost (UVC) can thus be calculated as follows:

$$80,000\ units = (\$1,000,000 + \$200,000) \div (\$120 - UVC)$$
$$80,000 \times (\$120 - UVC) = \$1,200,000$$
$$\$120 - UVC = \$15$$
$$UVC = \$105$$

The Year 2 unit selling price (USP) can now be derived:

$$80,000\ units = (\$1,000,000 + \$200,000 + \$1,200,000) \div (USP - \$105)$$
$$80,000 \times (USP - \$105) = \$2,400,000$$
$$USP - \$105 = \$30$$
$$USP = \$135$$

Answer (A) is incorrect. The Year 1 unit price was $120.00. Answer (C) is incorrect. This amount assumes that the unit variable cost is $120. Answer (D) is incorrect. This amount assumes that the price must double, given that the sum of fixed costs and targeted profit has doubled.

26. In using cost-volume-profit analysis to calculate expected unit sales, which of the following should be added to fixed costs in the numerator?

A. Predicted operating loss.

B. Predicted operating income.

C. Unit contribution margin.

D. Variable costs.

Answer (B) is correct.
REQUIRED: The addition to fixed costs when calculating expected unit sales.
DISCUSSION: CVP analysis can be used to restate the formula for target net income to determine the required level of unit sales.

$$Target\ unit\ volume = \frac{Fixed\ costs\ +\ Target\ operating\ income}{UCM}$$

Answer (A) is incorrect. Predicted operating loss would be subtracted from fixed costs, not added. Answer (C) is incorrect. Unit contribution margin is the denominator. Answer (D) is incorrect. Variable costs are a component of unit contribution margin.

Question 27 is based on the following information. Oradell Company sells its single product at a price of $60 per unit and incurs the following variable costs per unit of product:

Direct material	$16
Direct labor	12
Manufacturing overhead	7
Variable manufacturing costs	$35
Selling expenses	5
Total variable costs	$40

Oradell's annual fixed costs are $880,000, and Oradell is subject to a 30% income tax rate.

27. The annual sales revenue required by Oradell Company in order to achieve after-tax net income of $224,000 for the year is

A. $3,600,000

B. $3,312,000

C. $1,656,000

D. $3,110,400

Answer (A) is correct.
    REQUIRED: The annual sales revenue needed to achieve a given after-tax net income.
    DISCUSSION: CVP analysis can be used to restate the formula for net income and determine the required level of unit sales.

$$
\begin{aligned}
\text{Target unit volume} &= \{\text{Fixed costs} + [\text{Target net income} \div \\
&\quad (1.0 - \text{tax rate})]\} \div \text{UCM} \\
&= [\$880,000 + (\$224,000 \div .70)] \div (\$60 - \$40) \\
&= \$1,200,000 \div \$20 \\
&= 60,000 \text{ units}
\end{aligned}
$$

At a unit selling price of $60, the total revenue is $3,600,000 (60,000 units × $60).

28. Wren Co. manufactures and sells two products with selling prices and variable costs as follows:

	A	B
Selling price	$18.00	$22.00
Variable costs	12.00	14.00

Wren's total annual fixed costs are $38,400. Wren sells four units of A for every unit of B. If operating income last year was $28,800, what was the number of units Wren sold?

A. 5,486

B. 6,000

C. 9,600

D. 10,500

Answer (D) is correct.
    REQUIRED: The number of units Wren sold.
    DISCUSSION: The contribution margins of the two products are $6 and $8, respectively ($18 – $12 and $22 – $14). The units sold can be calculated as follows:

$$
\begin{aligned}
\text{Target unit volume} &= (\text{Fixed costs} + \text{Target operating income}) \div \\
&\quad \text{Weighted UCM} \\
&= (\$38,400 + \$28,800) \div (\$6A + \$8B) \\
\$6A + \$8B &= \$67,200 \\
\$6(4B) + \$8B &= \$67,200 \\
\$32B &= \$67,200 \\
B &= 2,100 \text{ units}
\end{aligned}
$$

Since 4 units of A are sold for every unit of B, the volume of A was 8,400 units (2,100 × 4). Thus, the total number of units sold was 10,500 (8,400A + 2,100B).
    Answer (A) is incorrect. The amount of 5,486 units equals the fixed costs divided by the contribution margin from product B. Answer (B) is incorrect. The amount of 6,000 units does not include the operating income of $28,800 in the calculation. Answer (C) is incorrect. The operating income plus the fixed costs are divided by the contribution margin for product B, giving the number of units sold of 9,600.

Use the additional questions in Gleim **CPA Test Prep Online** to create Test Sessions that emulate Prometric!

18.7 PRACTICE WRITTEN COMMUNICATION TASK

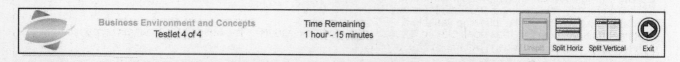

| | Business Environment and Concepts
Testlet 4 of 4 | Time Remaining
1 hour - 15 minutes | Unsplit   Split Horiz   Split Vertical   Exit |

DIRECTIONS

Note: If you believe you have encountered a software malfunction, report it to the test center staff immediately.

Navigation

To navigate from task to task, use the controls at the bottom of the screen. Click on the **Next** button to advance to the next task, or the **Previous** button to go to the previous task. To go directly to any task, click on its number.

| ▼ = Reminder | | Directions | 1 2 3 4 5 6 7 | | ◀ Previous   Next ▶ |

If you would like a reminder to revisit a task, or want to indicate that you are finished with it, click on the reminder flag below the task number. To clear the flag, click on it again. Reminder flags are for your use only – they do not contribute to your score.

Tabs

In this part of the examination, you will be asked to complete various tasks. Every task has one or more **Work Tabs**. Every task also has a **Help** tab.

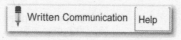

Work tab   Help tab

Work Tabs:

- **Work Tabs** are identified with a pencil icon. This is where your responses are expected.
- Each task has one or more **Work Tabs**.
- **Work Tabs** contain directions for completing the task - be sure to read these directions carefully.
- The **Work Tab** name in the example above is for illustration only - yours will differ.
- You must complete all of the **Work Tabs** in each task to receive full credit.

Help Tab:

- The **Help Tab** provides assistance with the exam software that is used in this task. For example, if the task is to compose a memorandum, **Help** will provide information about the word processor.

The Toolbar

The toolbar at the top of the screen shows the amount of time remaining for you to complete the tasks. In addition, the following tools are available. Note that only the **Exit** button is displayed when Directions are visible - the others will appear when you begin the tasks.

Click on these buttons to split or unsplit the screen. You can split the screen vertically or horizontally.

Click on this button to go on to the next part of the examination. You must complete all of the tasks to receive full credit. Once you click on **Exit** and confirm the action, you will NOT be able to return to this testlet.

| ▼ = Reminder | | Directions | 1 | | | ◀ Previous   Next ▶ |

Written Communication | Help

Cut | Copy | Paste | Undo | Redo

Bonaparte's Buttons, Inc., has been offered a special order from a customer. The head of Sales wants production on the order to begin immediately, but the CEO is uncertain.

Prepare a memo to the CEO of Bonaparte's Buttons describing the qualities of relevant costs and the factors that should be considered when deciding whether to accept a special order.

Type your communication below the line in the response area below.

REMINDER: Your response will be graded for both technical content and writing skills. Technical content will be evaluated for information that is helpful to the intended reader and clearly relevant to the issue. Writing skills will be evaluated for development, organization, and the appropriate expression of ideas in professional correspondence. Use a standard business memorandum or letter format with a clear beginning, middle, and end. Do not convey information in the form of a table, bullet point list, or other abbreviated presentation.

To: CEO, Bonaparte's Buttons
Re: Relevant costs and special orders

Unofficial Answer

Written Communication

To: CEO, Bonaparte's Buttons
Re: Relevant costs and special orders

In decision making, an organization must focus on only relevant revenues and costs. To be relevant, the revenues and costs under consideration must have two qualities. First, they must be earned or expended in the future. Only future costs are relevant because costs that have already been incurred or to which the organization is committed, called sunk costs, have no bearing on any future decisions. An example is the decision to replace an aging automobile that requires constant repair with a newer, more reliable one. The money already spent on repairs is not relevant.

Second, the revenues and costs must differ among the possible alternative courses of action. Cash flows that do not vary can have no bearing on the decision. An example is a gym membership that is debited every month regardless of usage. The choice of going to a movie or to the gym on a given night depends on the cost of the movie ticket but not that of the gym membership.

Only avoidable costs are relevant. A cost is unavoidable if it is incurred regardless of the action taken. An example is a 12-month lease liability that is due to a landlord, even if a new job in another city is accepted.

When a manufacturer has excess production capacity, there is no opportunity cost involved when accepting a special order. The company should accept the order if the minimum price for the product is equal to the variable costs. When a manufacturer lacks excess production capacity, however, the differential (marginal or incremental) costs of accepting the order must be considered. Besides the variable costs of the production run, the firm must consider the opportunity cost of redirecting productive capacity away from (possibly more profitable) products. management, control, and governance processes.

The above depicts a Level 5 answer. See page 16 in the Introduction for a description of the three grading criteria.

Self-Grade

Evaluate each of the following by selecting a 0, 1, 2, 3, 4, or 5. An average response is 3. Use 4 for better than average and 5 for outstanding. Use 2 for less than average and 1 for quite poor. Use zero for no response, if you did not address the topic, or if you gave advice that is clearly illegal.

Organization	o 0	o 1	o 2	o 3	o 4	o 5
Development	o 0	o 1	o 2	o 3	o 4	o 5
Expression	o 0	o 1	o 2	o 3	o 4	o 5

Your grade for the written communication as a whole is the average of the scores for the three criteria.

Use **CPA Gleim Online** and **Simulation Wizard** to practice more written communication tasks in a realistic environment.

STUDY UNIT NINETEEN
COSTING TECHNIQUES

(10 pages of outline)

One crucial distinction between cost accounting for external reporting and that for internal reporting is the difference between absorption (or full) costing and variable (or direct) costing. When multiple products result from a single process, the appropriate allocation of costs incurred during the single process is critical to making sound pricing decisions.

19.1 ABSORPTION COSTING AND VARIABLE COSTING -- THEORY

1. **Absorption Costing**

    a. Under absorption costing (also called full costing), the fixed portion of manufacturing overhead is included in the cost of each product.

        1) Product cost includes all manufacturing costs, both fixed and variable.

        2) Sales minus absorption-basis cost of goods sold equals **gross margin**.

        3) **Operating income** equals gross margin minus total selling and administrative expenses (fixed and variable).

        4) This method is required under GAAP for external reporting purposes and under the Internal Revenue Code for tax purposes. The justification is that, for external reporting, product cost should include all manufacturing costs.

2. **Variable Costing**

    a. Under variable costing (also called direct costing or contribution costing), product cost includes only variable manufacturing costs. Variable costing is preferable for internal reporting. It better satisfies management's needs for operational planning and control information because it excludes arbitrary allocations of fixed costs.

        1) Furthermore, variable-costing net income varies directly with sales and is not affected by changes in inventory levels.

    b. **Contribution margin** equals sales minus variable cost of goods sold and the variable portion of selling and administrative expenses.

        1) This amount (sales minus total variable costs) is an important element of the variable costing income statement. It is the amount available for covering fixed costs (fixed manufacturing, fixed selling, and administrative). For this reason, some accountants call the method contribution margin reporting.

EXAMPLE

During Manu's first month in business, it produced 100 units and sold 80 while incurring the following costs:

Direct materials	$1,000
Direct labor	2,000
Variable overhead	1,500
Manufacturing costs used in variable costing	$4,500
Fixed overhead	3,000
Manufacturing costs used in absorption costing	$7,500

The following are the effects on the financial statements of using absorption and variable costing:

	Manufacturing costs	Divided by: Units produced	Equals: Per-unit cost	Times: Units in ending inventory	Equals: Cost of ending inventory
Absorption costing	$7,500	100	$75	20	$1,500
Variable costing	$4,500	100	$45	20	$900

The per-unit selling price of the finished goods was $100, and Manu incurred $200 of variable selling and administrative expenses and $600 of fixed selling and administrative expenses.

The following are partial income statements prepared using the two methods:

		Absorption Costing (Required under GAAP)	Variable Costing (For internal reporting only)
	Sales	$ 8,000	$ 8,000
	Beginning inventory	$ 0	$ 0
Product Costs	Plus: variable production costs	4,500 (a)	4,500 (a)
	Plus: fixed production costs	3,000 (b)	
	Goods available for sale	$7,500	$4,500
	Minus: ending inventory	(1,500)	(900)
	Cost of goods sold	$(6,000)	$(3,600)
	Minus: variable S&A expenses		(200) (c)
	Gross margin (abs.) / Contribution margin (var.)	$ 2,000	$ 4,200
Period Costs	Minus: fixed production costs		(3,000) (b)
	Minus: variable S&A expenses	(200) (c)	
	Minus: fixed S&A expenses	(600) (d)	(600) (d)
	Operating income	$ 1,200	$ 600

Given no beginning inventory, the difference in operating income ($1,200 – $600 = $600) is the difference between the ending inventory amounts ($1,500 – $900 = $600).

Under the absorption method, 20% of the fixed overhead costs ($3,000 × 20% = $600) is recorded as an asset because 20% of the month's production (100 units available – 80 units sold = 20 units) is still in inventory.

3. Effects on Operating Income

CPA candidates must know how to calculate the various income statement component amounts under the absorption and variable costing methods. The AICPA has frequently tested this topic, focusing especially on the differences between the amounts, such as operating income, determined by each method.

   a.   As production and sales levels change, the two methods have varying effects on operating income.

   b.   When production and sales are equal for a period, the two methods report the same operating income.

      1)   Total fixed costs for the period are expensed during the period under both methods.

c.   When production and sales are not equal for a period, the two methods report different operating incomes.

1)   This is illustrated in the diagram below:

When production	**When production**
△ △ △ △ △ △ △	△ △ △
exceeds sales,	**is less than sales,**
△ △ △	△ △ △ △ △ △ △
ending inventory expands.	**ending inventory contracts.**
↑↑↑↑↑↑↑↑↑↑↑↑↑↑	↓↓↓↓↓↓
Under absorption costing, some fixed manufacturing costs are still embedded in ending inventory.	**Under absorption costing,** fixed manufacturing costs embedded in beginning inventory get expensed.
Under variable costing, all fixed costs have been expensed.	**Under variable costing,** only the current period's fixed costs are expensed.
Therefore,	Therefore,
operating income is higher under <u>absorption</u> costing.	**operating income is higher under <u>variable</u> costing.**

Figure 19-1

Stop and review! You have completed the outline for this subunit. Study multiple-choice questions 1 through 8 beginning on page 512.

19.2 ABSORPTION COSTING AND VARIABLE COSTING -- CALCULATIONS

The difference between absorption and variable costing is crucial in the practice of accounting, and CPA candidates can expect to encounter questions that require quantifying the difference. This subunit consists entirely of such questions. Please review Subunit 19.1 before answering these questions.

Stop and review! You have completed the outline for this subunit. Study multiple-choice questions 9 through 14 beginning on page 515.

19.3 JOINT PRODUCT AND BY-PRODUCT COSTING

1.   **Joint Product Costing**

a.   Joint products are separate products resulting from a common manufacturing process and common inputs. Joint (common) costs are incurred up to the split-off point where the products become separately identifiable.

1)   Joint costs include direct materials, direct labor, and manufacturing overhead. Because they are not separately identifiable, they must be allocated to the individual joint products.

b. At the split-off point, the joint products become separate. Costs incurred after split-off are separable costs.

1) Separable costs can be identified with a particular joint product and allocated to a specific unit of output.

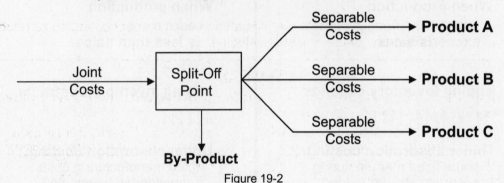

Figure 19-2

c. The decision to **sell or process further** is made based on whether the incremental revenue to be gained by further processing exceeds the incremental cost. The joint cost of the product is irrelevant because it is a sunk cost.

2. **By-Product Costing**

a. By-products are one or more products of relatively small total value that are produced simultaneously from a common manufacturing process with products of greater value and quantity.

1) The entity must determine whether the benefits of further processing and sale exceed the costs.

Selling price	$x,xxx
Minus: additional processing costs	(xxx)
Minus: selling costs	(xxx)
Net realizable value	**$x,xxx**

2) If the net realizable value is zero or negative, the by-products should be sold at the split-off point or discarded as scrap if they cannot be sold.

b. The value of a by-product may be initially recognized either

1) At the time production is completed, for an amount equal to the expected proceeds from its sale (or at its expected NRV if the by-product is subject to further processing in order to be salable); or

2) At the time the by-product is actually sold.

c. Any proceeds (revenue) from the sale of a by-product are recognized either

1) As a reduction of the joint cost, so that the cost of production (cost of sales) of the main products is reduced by the proceeds from the sale of the by-product; or

2) As a miscellaneous revenue.

d. Regardless of the timing of their recognition in the accounts, by-products usually do not receive an allocation of joint costs. The cost of this accounting treatment ordinarily exceeds the benefit.

Stop and review! You have completed the outline for this subunit. Study multiple-choice questions 15 through 22 beginning on page 517.

19.4 JOINT COST ALLOCATION METHODS

1. **Physical-Quantity Method**

    a. The physical-quantity method uses a physical measure such as volume, weight, or length.

        1) Joint production costs are allocated to each product based on its relative proportion of the measure selected.

EXAMPLE

A refinery processes 1,000 barrels of crude oil and incurs $100,000 of processing costs. The process results in the following outputs:

	Barrels	Selling price per barrel at a split-off point	Separable costs	Selling price per barrel after additional process
Asphalt	300	$ 60	$1,000	$ 70
Fuel oil	300	180	1,000	200
Diesel fuel	200	160	1,000	180
Kerosene	100	80	2,000	90
Gasoline	100	180	2,000	190

Under the physical-quantity method, the joint costs up to split-off are allocated as follows:

Asphalt	$100,000 × (300 barrels ÷ 1,000 barrels) =	$ 30,000
Fuel oil	$100,000 × (300 barrels ÷ 1,000 barrels) =	30,000
Diesel fuel	$100,000 × (200 barrels ÷ 1,000 barrels) =	20,000
Kerosene	$100,000 × (100 barrels ÷ 1,000 barrels) =	10,000
Gasoline	$100,000 × (100 barrels ÷ 1,000 barrels) =	10,000
Joint costs allocated		$100,000

---

    b. The physical-quantity method's simplicity makes it appealing, but it does not match costs with the individual products' revenues.

2. **Allocating Joint Costs -- Market-Based Approach**

    a. A market-based approach assigns a proportionate amount of the total cost to each product on a quantitative basis. These allocations are performed using the entire production run for an accounting period, not units sold. This is because the joint costs were incurred for all units produced, not just those sold. Two major methods of allocation are available.

    b. The **sales-value at split-off method** is based on the relative sales values of the separate products at split-off.

EXAMPLE

The refinery estimates that the five outputs can sell for the following prices at split-off:

Asphalt	300 barrels × $ 60 per barrel =	$ 18,000
Fuel oil	300 barrels × $180 per barrel =	54,000
Diesel fuel	200 barrels × $160 per barrel =	32,000
Kerosene	100 barrels × $ 80 per barrel =	8,000
Gasoline	100 barrels × $180 per barrel =	18,000
Total sales value at split-off		$130,000

The total expected sales value for the entire production run at split-off is thus $130,000. Multiply the total joint costs to be allocated by the proportion of the total expected sales of each product:

Asphalt	$100,000 × ($18,000 ÷ $130,000) =	$ 13,846
Fuel oil	$100,000 × ($54,000 ÷ $130,000) =	41,538
Diesel fuel	$100,000 × ($32,000 ÷ $130,000) =	24,616
Kerosene	$100,000 × ($ 8,000 ÷ $130,000) =	6,154
Gasoline	$100,000 × ($18,000 ÷ $130,000) =	13,846
Joint costs allocated		$100,000

---

c. The **estimated net realizable value (NRV) method** allocates joint costs based on the relative market values of the products after an additional process to make the products salable is performed.

1) Net realizable value (NRV) at split-off is equal to the sale price at the point of sale minus the cost to complete after split-off (separable costs).

2) The difference is that, under the estimated NRV method, all separable costs necessary to make the product salable are subtracted before the allocation is made.

EXAMPLE

The refinery estimates final sales prices as follows:

Asphalt	300 barrels × $ 70 per barrel =	$21,000
Fuel oil	300 barrels × $200 per barrel =	60,000
Diesel fuel	200 barrels × $180 per barrel =	36,000
Kerosene	100 barrels × $ 90 per barrel =	9,000
Gasoline	100 barrels × $190 per barrel =	19,000

From these amounts, separable costs are subtracted (these costs are given):

Asphalt	$21,000 – $1,000 =	$ 20,000
Fuel oil	$60,000 – $1,000 =	59,000
Diesel fuel	$36,000 – $1,000 =	35,000
Kerosene	$ 9,000 – $2,000 =	7,000
Gasoline	$19,000 – $2,000 =	17,000
Total net realizable value		$138,000

The total final sales value for the entire production run is thus $138,000. Multiply the total joint costs to be allocated by the proportion of the final expected sales of each product:

Asphalt	$100,000 × ($20,000 ÷ $138,000) =	$ 14,493
Fuel oil	$100,000 × ($59,000 ÷ $138,000) =	42,754
Diesel fuel	$100,000 × ($35,000 ÷ $138,000) =	25,362
Kerosene	$100,000 × ($ 7,000 ÷ $138,000) =	5,072
Gasoline	$100,000 × ($17,000 ÷ $138,000) =	12,319
Joint costs allocated		$100,000

Stop and review! You have completed the outline for this subunit. Study multiple-choice questions 23 through 27 beginning on page 520.

19.5 JOB-ORDER COSTING AND OVERHEAD APPLICATION

1. **Uses of Job-Order Costing**

   a. Job-order costing is used when each end product is unique. Because the end products are so few, tracking their costs is relatively straightforward.

   b. Manufacturing industries that use job-order costing include construction and shipbuilding. Service industries include software creation and plumbing.

2. **Accumulation of Direct Costs**

   a. The accumulation of costs in a job-order system can best be described in terms of the flow of manual documents in the process before computerized record keeping. (These functions are currently performed most often with the help of computers rather than physical documents.)

   b. A sales order is received from a customer. Because products are custom made, no inventory is held. Production cannot begin until an order is placed. Once the sales order is approved, a production order is issued.

   c. The physical inputs required for the production process are obtained from suppliers.

Direct materials	$100,000	
Accounts payable		$100,000

d. A subsidiary account is created within the work-in-process ledger account to track the costs for each job. The accumulation of direct costs (direct materials and direct labor) is straightforward.

e. Materials requisition forms request direct materials to be sent from the warehouse to the production line.

Work-in-process -- Job 1015	$60,000	
Direct materials		$60,000

f. Time tickets track the direct labor by workers on various jobs.

Work-in-process -- Job 1015	$45,000	
Wages payable		$45,000

g. Direct costs are entered into the general ledger at their actual amounts. In job-order costing, tracing the direct costs incurred in a given job is simple.

3. **Accumulation of Indirect Costs**

a. Accounting for overhead costs is more difficult because they are indirect costs. It is either impossible or cost-ineffective to trace them to final products. Thus, they must be accumulated in one or more indirect cost pools and allocated based on an appropriate cost driver.

1) When a single indirect cost pool is used, it is commonly called manufacturing overhead control. (Some manufacturers require a higher degree of accuracy in indirect cost assignment and use two overhead control accounts, one for variable overhead and one for fixed. For simplicity, the following examples will use a single pool.)

b. Manufacturing overhead consists of three main categories of costs:

1) Indirect materials are tangible inputs to the manufacturing process that cannot feasibly be traced to the product, e.g., the welding compound used to assemble a piece of heavy equipment.

Manufacturing overhead control	$4,500	
Indirect materials		$4,500

2) Indirect labor is the cost of human labor connected with the manufacturing process that cannot feasibly be traced to the product, e.g., the wages of assembly line supervisors and janitorial staff.

Manufacturing overhead control	$2,000	
Wages payable		$2,000

3) Factory operating costs include such items as utilities, real estate taxes, insurance, and depreciation on factory equipment. The actual total of these costs is not known until the end of the period.

Manufacturing overhead control	$8,500	
Property taxes payable		$8,500
Manufacturing overhead control	$1,600	
Prepaid insurance		$1,600
Manufacturing overhead control	$12,000	
Accumulated depreciation -- factory equipment		$12,000

c. When an overhead control account is used, actual overhead costs do not affect work-in-process when they are incurred. The total actual overhead incurred is the debit balance in the control account.

4.   **Allocation of Indirect Costs**

a.   Indirect costs are allocated to production using an overhead allocation rate. The first step is to estimate the total indirect costs for the coming period.

1)   The overhead application rate is best derived using estimated totals rather than on a monthly basis. Many overhead costs are fixed and must be incurred every month regardless of the level of production. Calculating a new rate every month may cause large variations in product costs even though the underlying cost structure does not change.

b.   The following is the formula for the rate:

$$\text{Overhead application rate} = \frac{\text{Estimated total overhead costs for year}}{\text{Estimated total units of allocation base}}$$

(If more than one indirect cost pool is used, a different rate is computed for each pool.)

1)   The numerator is estimated from budget data for the year.

2)   The denominator (the allocation base) must be a cost driver that has a direct cause-and-effect relationship with the level of overhead costs. When overhead costs rise or fall, the units of the allocation base also should rise or fall. Among the most common for use with a single indirect cost pool are direct labor hours and machine hours.

Estimated total overhead costs for year	$350,000
Estimated total machine hours for year	10,000

Overhead application rate ($350,000 ÷ 10,000) = $35 per machine hour

c.   At the end of each month, the number of units of the allocation base expended is multiplied by the application rate to determine the amount of overhead that will be applied to that month's production.

Overhead applied = Units of overhead driver × Application rate
                 = 900 machine hours on Job 1015 × $35 per hour
                 = $31,500

1)   This amount ordinarily is not credited to the control account. Instead, it is credited to manufacturing overhead applied (a contra account). The two accounts track actual and applied costs separately.

Work-in-process -- Job 1015	$31,500	
Manufacturing overhead applied		$31,500

2)   Separate tracking retains actual overhead amounts in the debit balance of the control account. It also permits comparison of actual and applied costs. The closer they are, the better the estimate.

5.   **Completion of Job**

a.   When a job order is completed, all costs are transferred to finished goods.

Finished goods	$136,500	
Work-in-process -- Job 1015		$136,500

b.   When the output is sold, the sale is recorded and the appropriate portion of the cost is transferred to cost of goods sold.

Accounts receivable	$200,000	
Sales		$200,000
Cost of goods sold	$136,500	
Finished goods		$136,500

6. **Graphical Depiction**

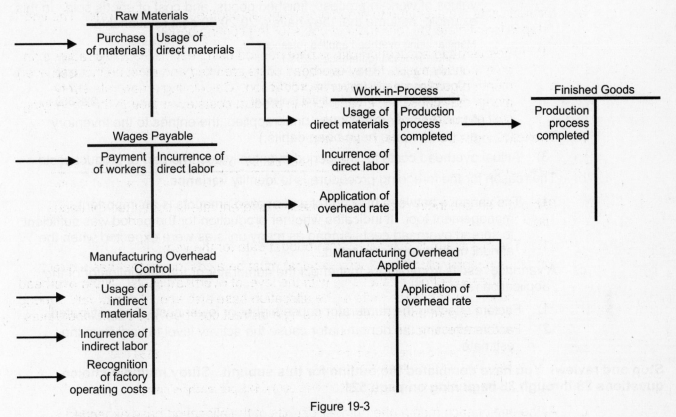

Figure 19-3

7. **Over- and Underapplied Overhead**

a. At the end of the period, if the balance in the overhead control account is less than that in the applied account, overhead was overapplied. If the balance in the applied account is lower, overhead was underapplied.

Manufacturing overhead control	$328,600 Dr.
Manufacturing overhead applied	$331,500 Cr.

1) Total indirect costs were less than expected ($328,600 < $350,000). Furthermore, the number of machine hours was only 9,471.4 ($331,500 ÷ $35) instead of the 10,000 estimated.

2) Given that more overhead was applied than was actually incurred, overhead was overapplied by $2,900.

a) If the variance is immaterial, it may be closed directly to cost of goods sold.

Manufacturing overhead applied (balance)	$331,500	
Cost of goods sold (difference)		$ 2,900
Manufacturing overhead control (balance)		328,600

(Had overhead been underapplied, the entry to cost of goods sold would have been a debit.)

    b)   If the variance is material, it should be allocated based on the relative values of work-in-process, finished goods, and cost of goods sold. In this example, assume that they have a 20:20:60 cost relationship.

Manufacturing overhead applied (balance)	$331,500
Work-in-process (difference × 20%)	$ 580
Finished goods (difference × 20%)	580
Cost of goods sold (difference × 60%)	1,740
Manufacturing overhead control (balance)	328,600

    (Again, had overhead been underapplied, the entries to the inventory accounts would have been debits.)

    3)   Actual overhead costs for the period eventually become part of product costs.

  b.   The reason for the foregoing procedure is to identify **variance**.

    1)   The variance between the control and applied amounts is an important management tool. It indicates whether production for the period was sufficient to spread overhead costs among as many units as were expected when the annual budget was formulated.

  c.   A variance results from factors that affect the numerator or the denominator of the application rate.

    1)   Factors affecting the numerator cause higher or lower costs than estimated.

    2)   Factors affecting the denominator cause the activity level to vary from the estimate.

Stop and review! You have completed the outline for this subunit. Study multiple-choice questions 28 through 33 beginning on page 521.

QUESTIONS

19.1 Absorption Costing and Variable Costing -- Theory

1. Which of the following statements is true for a firm that uses variable costing?

A. The cost of a unit of product changes because of changes in number of units manufactured.

B. Profits fluctuate with sales.

C. An idle facility variation is calculated.

D. Product costs include variable administrative costs.

Answer (B) is correct.
    REQUIRED: The true statement about variable costing.
    DISCUSSION: In a variable costing system, only the variable costs are recorded as product costs. All fixed costs are expensed in the period incurred. Because changes in the relationship between production levels and sales levels do not cause changes in the amount of fixed manufacturing cost expensed, profits more directly follow the trends in sales.
    Answer (A) is incorrect. Changing unit costs based on different levels of production is a characteristic of absorption costing systems. Answer (C) is incorrect. An idle facility variation is calculated in absorption costing. Answer (D) is incorrect. Neither variable nor absorption costing includes administrative costs in inventory.

2. Which method of inventory costing treats direct manufacturing costs and manufacturing overhead costs, both variable and fixed, as inventoriable costs?

A. Direct costing.

B. Variable costing.

C. Absorption costing.

D. Conversion costing.

Answer (C) is correct.
    REQUIRED: The method of inventory costing that treats direct manufacturing costs and all factory overhead as inventoriable.
    DISCUSSION: Absorption (full) costing considers all manufacturing costs to be inventoriable as product costs. These costs include variable and fixed manufacturing costs, whether direct or indirect. The alternative to absorption is known as variable (direct) costing.
    Answer (A) is incorrect. Direct costing does not inventory fixed factory overhead. Answer (B) is incorrect. Variable costing does not inventory fixed factory overhead. Answer (D) is incorrect. Conversion costs include direct labor and factory overhead but not direct materials.

3. When a firm prepares financial reports by using absorption costing,

   A. Profits will always increase with increases in sales.

   B. Profits will always decrease with decreases in sales.

   C. Profits may decrease with increased sales even if there is no change in selling prices and costs.

   D. Decreased output and constant sales result in increased profits.

Answer (C) is correct.
   REQUIRED: The profit relationship between output and sales under absorption costing.
   DISCUSSION: In an absorption costing system, fixed overhead costs are included in inventory. When sales exceed production, more overhead is expensed under absorption costing because fixed overhead is carried over from the prior inventory. If sales exceed production, more than one period's fixed overhead is recognized as expense. Accordingly, if the increase in fixed overhead expensed is greater than the contribution margin of the increased units sold, less profit may result from an increased level of sales.
   Answer (A) is incorrect. Profit is a function of both sales and production, so profit may not increase with increases in sales. Answer (B) is incorrect. Profit is a function of both sales and production, so profit may not decrease with decreases in sales. Answer (D) is incorrect. Decreased output will increase the unit cost of items sold. Fixed overhead per unit will increase.

4. Which one of the following statements is true regarding absorption costing and variable costing?

   A. Overhead costs are treated in the same manner under both costing methods.

   B. If finished goods inventory increases, absorption costing results in higher income.

   C. Variable manufacturing costs are lower under variable costing.

   D. Gross margins are the same under both costing methods.

Answer (B) is correct.
   REQUIRED: The true statement regarding absorption costing and variable costing.
   DISCUSSION: Under variable costing, inventories are charged only with the variable costs of production. Fixed manufacturing costs are expensed as period costs. Absorption costing charges to inventory all costs of production. If finished goods inventory increases, absorption costing results in higher income because it capitalizes some fixed costs that would have been expensed under variable costing. When inventory declines, variable costing results in higher income because some fixed costs capitalized under the absorption method in prior periods are expensed in the current period.
   Answer (A) is incorrect. Fixed factory overhead is treated differently under the two methods. Answer (C) is incorrect. Variable costs are the same under either method. Answer (D) is incorrect. Gross margins will be different. Fixed factory overhead is expensed under variable costing and capitalized under the absorption method.

5. Which one of the following considers the impact of fixed overhead costs?

   A. Full absorption costing.

   B. Marginal costing.

   C. Direct costing.

   D. Variable costing.

Answer (A) is correct.
   REQUIRED: The method of costing that considers the impact of fixed overhead costs.
   DISCUSSION: Full absorption costing treats fixed manufacturing overhead costs as product costs. Thus, inventory and cost of goods sold include (absorb) fixed manufacturing overhead.
   Answer (B) is incorrect. Marginal costing considers only the incremental costs of producing an additional unit of product. In most cases, marginal costs are variable costs. Answer (C) is incorrect. Direct costing treats only variable costs as product costs. Answer (D) is incorrect. Variable costing treats only variable costs as product costs.

6. The change in period-to-period operating income when using variable costing can be explained by the change in the

    A. Unit sales level multiplied by the unit sales price.

    B. Finished goods inventory level multiplied by the unit sales price.

    C. Unit sales level multiplied by a constant unit contribution margin.

    D. Finished goods inventory level multiplied by a constant unit contribution margin.

Answer (C) is correct.
    REQUIRED: The factor explaining the change in period-to-period operating income when using variable costing.
    DISCUSSION: In a variable costing system, only the variable costs are recorded as product costs. All fixed costs are expensed in the period incurred. Because changes in the relationship between production levels and sales levels do not cause changes in the amount of fixed manufacturing cost expensed, profits more directly follow the trends in sales, especially when the UCM (selling price per unit – variable costs per unit) is constant. Unit sales times the UCM equals the total CM, and operating income (a pretax amount) equals the CM minus fixed costs of operations. If the UCM is constant and fixed costs are stable, the change in operating income will approximate the change in the CM (unit sales × UCM).
    Answer (A) is incorrect. Unit sales multiplied by the sales price equals sales revenue, but this amount does not necessarily correlate with operating income. A change in unit variable costs may cause revenue and operating income to move in different directions. Answers (B) and (D) are incorrect. Operating income is not necessarily correlated positively or negatively with finished goods inventory, however valued.

7. The management of a company computes net income using both absorption and variable costing. This year, the net income under the variable-costing approach was greater than the net income under the absorption-costing approach. This difference is most likely the result of

    A. A decrease in the variable marketing expenses.

    B. An increase in the finished goods inventory.

    C. Sales volume exceeding production volume.

    D. Inflationary effects on overhead costs.

Answer (C) is correct.
    REQUIRED: The reason net income is greater under variable costing than under absorption costing.
    DISCUSSION: Absorption costing (full costing) is the accounting method that considers all manufacturing costs as product costs. These costs include variable and fixed manufacturing costs, whether direct or indirect. However, variable costing treats fixed factory overhead as a period cost instead of charging it to the product (inventory). Thus, when sales exceed production, the absorption costing method recognizes fixed factory overhead inventoried in a prior period. Direct costing does not. Accordingly, net income under variable costing will be greater than net income under absorption costing.
    Answer (A) is incorrect. A change in a variable period cost will affect absorption and variable costing in the same way. Answer (B) is incorrect. If the beginning inventory is less than the ending finished goods inventory, absorption costing assigns more fixed overhead costs to the balance sheet and less to the cost of goods sold on the income statement than does variable costing. Answer (D) is incorrect. Inflationary effects will usually affect both absorption and variable costing in the same way.

8. In the application of variable costing as a cost-allocation process in manufacturing,

    A. Variable direct costs are treated as period costs.

    B. Nonvariable indirect costs are treated as product costs.

    C. Variable indirect costs are treated as product costs.

    D. Nonvariable direct costs are treated as product costs.

Answer (C) is correct.
    REQUIRED: The true statement about variable costing.
    DISCUSSION: Variable costing considers only variable manufacturing costs to be product costs. Variable indirect costs included in variable overhead are therefore treated as inventoriable. Fixed costs are considered period costs and are expensed as incurred.
    Answer (A) is incorrect. Variable manufacturing costs, whether direct (direct materials and direct labor) or indirect (variable overhead), are accounted for as product costs, not period costs. Answer (B) is incorrect. Nonvariable indirect costs are treated as period costs in direct costing. Answer (D) is incorrect. In direct costing, nonvariable direct costs are treated as period costs, not product costs.

19.2 Absorption Costing and Variable Costing -- Calculations

Questions 9 and 10 are based on the following information. Osawa, Inc., planned and actually manufactured 200,000 units of its single product during its first year of operations. Variable manufacturing costs were $30 per unit of product. Planned and actual fixed manufacturing costs were $600,000, and selling and administrative costs totaled $400,000. Osawa sold 120,000 units of product at a selling price of $40 per unit.

9. Osawa's operating income using absorption (full) costing is

A. $200,000

B. $440,000

C. $600,000

D. $840,000

Answer (B) is correct.

REQUIRED: The operating income under absorption costing.

DISCUSSION: Because production equaled planned output, and fixed costs equaled the budgeted amount, fixed overhead was not over- or under-applied. Also, planned fixed overhead equaled the actual amount. Thus, no fixed overhead variances had to be accounted for. Osawa applied $600,000 of fixed overhead, or $3 per unit ($600,000 ÷ 200,000 units), to its output. The unit cost of the 80,000 (200,000 – 120,000 sold) units in ending inventory is therefore $33 ($30 VC + $3 FC). Absorption costing net income is computed as follows:

Sales (120,000 units × $40)		$4,800,000
Variable production costs		
(200,000 units × $30)	$6,000,000	
Fixed production costs	600,000	
Total production costs	$6,600,000	
Ending inventory		
(80,000 units × $33)	(2,640,000)	
Cost of goods sold		(3,960,000)
Gross profit		$ 840,000
Selling and administrative expenses		(400,000)
Operating income		$ 440,000

10. Osawa's operating income for the year using variable costing is

A. $200,000

B. $440,000

C. $800,000

D. $600,000

Answer (A) is correct.

REQUIRED: The operating income under variable costing.

DISCUSSION: The contribution margin from manufacturing (sales – variable costs) is $10 ($40 – $30) per unit sold, or $1,200,000 (120,000 units × $10). The fixed costs of manufacturing ($600,000) and selling and administrative costs ($400,000) are deducted from the contribution margin to arrive at an operating income of $200,000. The difference between the absorption income of $440,000 and the $200,000 of variable costing income is attributable to capitalization of the fixed manufacturing costs under the absorption method. Because 40% of the goods produced are still in inventory (80,000 ÷ 200,000), 40% of the $600,000 in fixed costs, or $240,000, was capitalized under the absorption method. That amount was expensed under the variable costing method.

Questions 11 and 12 are based on the following
information. At the end of its fiscal year,
C.G. Manufacturing recorded the data below:

Prime cost	$800,000
Variable manufacturing overhead	100,000
Fixed manufacturing overhead	160,000
Variable selling and other expenses	80,000
Fixed selling and other expenses	40,000

11. If C.G. uses variable costing, the inventoriable
costs for the fiscal year are

A. $800,000

B. $900,000

C. $980,000

D. $1,060,000

Answer (B) is correct.
   REQUIRED: The inventoriable costs using variable costing.
   DISCUSSION: The only costs capitalized are the variable
costs of manufacturing. Prime costs (direct materials and direct
labor) are variable.

Prime costs, direct materials, and direct labor	$800,000
Variable manufacturing overhead	100,000
Total inventoriable costs	$900,000

12. Using absorption (full) costing, C.G.'s
inventoriable costs are

A. $800,000

B. $900,000

C. $1,060,000

D. $1,080,000

Answer (C) is correct.
   REQUIRED: The inventoriable costs using absorption
costing.
   DISCUSSION: Absorption costing is required by GAAP. It
charges all costs of production to inventories. The prime costs
($800,000), variable manufacturing overhead ($100,000), and the
fixed manufacturing overhead ($160,000) are included. They
total $1,060,000.

Questions 13 and 14 are based on the following
information. Presented are Valenz Company's
records for the current fiscal year ended
November 30:

Direct materials used	$300,000
Direct labor	100,000
Variable factory overhead	50,000
Fixed factory overhead	80,000
Selling and admin. costs -- variable	40,000
Selling and admin. costs -- fixed	20,000

13. If Valenz Company uses variable costing, the
inventoriable costs for the fiscal year are

A. $400,000

B. $450,000

C. $490,000

D. $530,000

Answer (B) is correct.
   REQUIRED: The inventoriable costs using the variable
costing.
   DISCUSSION: Under variable costing, the only costs that
are capitalized are the variable costs of manufacturing. These
include

Direct materials used	$300,000
Direct labor	100,000
Variable overhead	50,000
Total inventoriable costs	$450,000

   Answer (A) is incorrect. The amount of $400,000 does not
include $50,000 of variable overhead. Answer (C) is incorrect.
The $40,000 of variable selling and administrative costs should
not be included in the inventoriable costs. Answer (D) is
incorrect. The inventoriable cost under absorption (full) costing is
$530,000.

14. Using absorption (full) costing, inventoriable costs for Valenz are

A. $400,000

B. $450,000

C. $530,000

D. $590,000

Answer (C) is correct.
REQUIRED: The inventoriable costs using the absorption costing.
DISCUSSION: The absorption method is required for financial statements prepared according to GAAP. It charges all costs of production to inventories. The variable cost of materials ($300,000), direct labor ($100,000), variable overhead ($50,000), and the fixed overhead ($80,000) are included. They total $530,000.
Answer (A) is incorrect. Not including $80,000 of fixed overhead and $50,000 of variable overhead results in $400,000. Answer (B) is incorrect. The inventoriable cost under variable costing is $450,000. Answer (D) is incorrect. Selling and administrative costs are not inventoriable using absorption (full) costing.

19.3 Joint Product and By-Product Costing

15. For the purposes of cost accumulation, which of the following are identifiable as different individual products before the split-off point?

	By-Products	Joint Products
A.	Yes	Yes
B.	Yes	No
C.	No	No
D.	No	Yes

Answer (C) is correct.
REQUIRED: The identifiable products before the split-off point.
DISCUSSION: In a joint production process, neither by-products nor joint products are separately identifiable as individual products until the split-off point. This is the definition of the split-off point. Joint costs up to the split-off point are usually related to both joint products and by-products. After split-off, additional (separable) costs can be traced and charged to the individual products. By-products usually do not receive an allocation of joint costs.
Answer (A) is incorrect. Neither by-products nor joint products are separately identifiable until split-off. Answer (B) is incorrect. By-products are also not separately identifiable until split-off. Answer (D) is incorrect. Joint products are also not separately identifiable until split-off

16. Kode Co. manufactures a major product that gives rise to a by-product called May. May's only separable cost is a $1 selling cost when a unit is sold for $4. Kode accounts for May's sales by deducting the $3 net amount from the cost of goods sold of the major product. There are no inventories. If Kode were to change its method of accounting for May from a by-product to a joint product, what would be the effect on Kode's overall gross margin?

A. No effect.

B. Gross margin increases by $1 for each unit of May sold.

C. Gross margin increases by $3 for each unit of May sold.

D. Gross margin increases by $4 for each unit of May sold.

Answer (B) is correct.
REQUIRED: The effect on gross margin of treating a product as a joint product rather than a by-product.
DISCUSSION: Gross margin is the difference between sales and the cost of goods sold. Deducting the $3 net amount from cost of goods sold does not have the same effect on overall gross margin as recording the $4 sales revenue and deducting the $1 cost. In the latter case, the $1 unit selling cost is not deducted in arriving at the gross margin. Thus, gross margin increases by $1 for each unit of May sold.
Answer (A) is incorrect. There is no effect on net income (not gross margin). Answer (C) is incorrect. The amount of $3 is the per-unit increase in net income using either by-product or joint-product costing. Answer (D) is incorrect. The amount of $4 is the per-unit increase in sales when switching to joint-product from by-product costing.

17. In accounting for by-products, the value of the by-product may be recognized at the time of

	Production	Sale
A.	Yes	Yes
B.	Yes	No
C.	No	No
D.	No	Yes

Answer (A) is correct.
REQUIRED: The timing of recognition of by-products.
DISCUSSION: Practice with regard to recognizing by-products in the accounts is not uniform. The most cost-effective method for the initial recognition of by-products is to account for their value at the time of sale as a reduction in the joint cost or as a revenue. The alternative is to recognize the net realizable value at the time of production, a method that results in the recording of by-product inventory.
Answer (B) is incorrect. By-products may also be initially recognized at the time of sale. Answer (C) is incorrect. By-products may be initially recognized at the time of sale or at the time of production. Answer (D) is incorrect. By-products may also be recorded in the accounts when produced.

18. One hundred pounds of raw material W is processed into 60 pounds of X and 40 pounds of Y. Joint costs are $135. X is sold for $2.50 per pound, and Y can be sold for $3.00 per pound or processed further into 30 pounds of Z (10 pounds are lost in the second process) at an additional cost of $60. Each pound of Z can then be sold for $6.00. What is the effect on profits of further processing product Y into product Z?

A. $60 increase.

B. $30 increase.

C. No change.

D. $60 decrease.

Answer (C) is correct.
REQUIRED: The effect on profits of further processing of a product.
DISCUSSION: The joint costs of $135 do not vary with the option chosen. Without further processing of product Y, revenue equals $270 [(60 lbs × $2.50) + (40 lbs × $3.00)], and net revenue equals $135 ($270 – $135). If product Y is processed further into product Z, revenue equals $330 [(60 lbs × $2.50) + (30 lbs × $6.00)]. This additional processing is at an incremental cost of $60, resulting in net revenue of $135 ($330 – $135 – $60). Hence, further processing results in no increase or decrease in net revenue.
Answer (A) is incorrect. The additional cost of $60 must be considered in evaluating the profit effect of processing product Y into product Z. Answer (B) is incorrect. A greater sales amount is obtained by processing product Y into product Z with an additional cost of $60, creating the same profit under each process. Answer (D) is incorrect. The profit effect is the same whether or not product Y is processed into product Z.

19. A joint process is a manufacturing operation yielding two or more identifiable products from the resources employed in the process. The two characteristics that identify a product generated from this type of process as a joint product are that it

A. Is identifiable as an individual product only upon reaching the split-off point, and it has relatively minor sales value when compared to the other products.

B. Is identifiable as an individual product before the production process, and it has relatively significant physical volume when compared with the other products.

C. Is identifiable as an individual product only upon reaching the split-off point, and it has relatively significant sales value when compared with the other products.

D. Has relatively significant physical volume when compared with the other products, and it can be sold immediately without any additional processing.

Answer (C) is correct.
REQUIRED: The two characteristics of a joint product.
DISCUSSION: Joint products are two or more separate products generated by a common process from a common input that are not separable prior to the split-off point. Moreover, in contrast with by-products, they have significant sales values in relation to each other either before or after additional processing.
Answer (A) is incorrect. A joint product has relatively significant sales value when compared with the other products. A by-product is identifiable as an individual product only upon reaching the split-off point, and it has relatively minor sales value when compared to the other products. Answer (B) is incorrect. Products that are separately identifiable before the production process are not classified as joint products. Furthermore, physical volume has nothing to do with determining a joint product. Some joint products with significant physical volume may not have significant sales value. Answer (D) is incorrect. Products do not have to be salable at the split-off point to be considered joint products; in fact, many joint products have to be processed after the split-off point before they can be sold.

20. In joint-product costing and analysis, which one of the following costs is relevant when deciding the point at which a product should be sold to maximize profits?

A. Separable costs after the split-off point.

B. Joint costs to the split-off point.

C. Sales salaries for the period when the units were produced.

D. Purchase costs of the materials required for the joint products.

Answer (A) is correct.
REQUIRED: The cost relevant to deciding when a joint product should be sold.
DISCUSSION: Joint products are created from processing a common input. Joint costs are incurred prior to the split-off point and cannot be identified with a particular joint product. As a result, joint costs are irrelevant to the timing of sale. However, separable costs incurred after the split-off point are relevant because, if incremental revenues exceed the separable costs, products should be processed further, not sold at the split-off point.
Answer (B) is incorrect. Joint costs have no effect on the decision as to when to sell a product. Answer (C) is incorrect. Sales salaries for the production period do not affect the decision. Answer (D) is incorrect. Purchase costs are joint costs.

21. A lumber company produces two-by-fours and four-by-eights as joint products and sawdust as a by-product. The packaged sawdust can be sold for $2 per pound. Packaging costs for the sawdust are $.10 per pound and sales commissions are 10% of sales price. The by-product net revenue serves to reduce joint processing costs for joint products. Joint products are assigned joint costs based on board feet. Cost and production data are:

Joint processing costs	$ 50,000
Two-by-fours produced (board feet)	200,000
Four-by-eights produced (board feet)	100,000
Sawdust produced (pounds)	1,000

What is the cost assigned to two-by-fours?

A. $32,000

B. $32,133

C. $32,200

D. $33,333

Answer (C) is correct.
REQUIRED: The cost assigned to a joint product when joint products and a by-product are produced.
DISCUSSION: The net revenue from sale of the by-product is $1,700 [(1,000 lb. × $2 price) – (1,000 lb. × $.10) – (1,000 lb. × $2 × .1)]. Joint processing costs to be allocated to joint products are therefore $48,300 ($50,000 – $1,700 net by-product revenue). Of this amount, $32,200 should be assigned to the two-by-fours [$48,300 × (200,000 board feet of two-by-fours ÷ 300,000 total board feet)].
Answer (A) is incorrect. The net revenue from the sale of the by-product is $1,700, not $2,000. The costs related to the packaging and selling of the by-product must be deducted. Answer (B) is incorrect. The $.10-per-pound packaging cost for the sawdust must be deducted from the by-product revenue. Answer (D) is incorrect. The net revenue of $1,700 [1,000 lb. × ($2 sale price – $.10 packaging – $.20 sales cost)] from the by-product should be subtracted from the joint processing costs before the joint processing costs are allocated.

22. Copeland, Inc., produces X-547 in a joint manufacturing process. The company is studying whether to sell X-547 at the split-off point or upgrade the product to become Xylene. The following information has been gathered:

I. Selling price per pound of X-547
II. Variable manufacturing costs of upgrade process
III. Avoidable fixed costs of upgrade process
IV. Selling price per pound of Xylene
V. Joint manufacturing costs to produce X-547

Which items should be reviewed when making the upgrade decision?

A. I, II, and IV.

B. I, II, III, and IV.

C. All items.

D. I, II, IV, and V.

Answer (B) is correct.
REQUIRED: The items reviewed for a sell-or-process further decision.
DISCUSSION: Common, or joint, costs cannot be identified with a particular joint product. By definition, joint products have common costs until the split-off point. Costs incurred after the split-off point are separable costs. The decision to continue processing beyond split-off is made separately for each product. The costs relevant to the decision are the separable costs because they can be avoided by selling at the split-off point. They should be compared with the incremental revenues from processing further. Thus, items I (revenue from selling at split-off point), II (variable costs of upgrade), III (avoidable fixed costs of upgrade), and IV (revenue from selling after further processing) are considered in making the upgrade decision.
Answer (A) is incorrect. The affordable fixed costs of the upgrade process also should be considered. Answer (C) is incorrect. The joint manufacturing costs are irrelevant. Answer (D) is incorrect. The affordable fixed costs of the upgrade process should be reviewed, and the joint manufacturing costs should be ignored.

19.4 Joint Cost Allocation Methods

Questions 23 through 25 are based on the following information.

Atlas Foods produces the following three supplemental food products simultaneously through a refining process costing $93,000.

The joint products, Alfa and Betters, have a final selling price of $4 per pound and $10 per pound, respectively, after additional processing costs of $2 per pound of each product are incurred after the split-off point. Morefeed, a by-product, is sold at the split-off point for $3 per pound.

Alfa	10,000 pounds of Alfa, a popular but relatively rare grain supplement having a caloric value of 4,400 calories per pound
Betters	5,000 pounds of Betters, a flavoring material high in carbohydrates with a caloric value of 11,200 calories per pound
Morefeed	1,000 pounds of Morefeed, used as a cattle feed supplement with a caloric value of 1,000 calories per pound

23. Assuming Atlas Foods inventories Morefeed, the by-product, the joint cost to be allocated to Alfa using the net realizable value method is

A. $3,000

B. $30,000

C. $31,000

D. $60,000

Answer (B) is correct.
REQUIRED: The joint cost allocated to Alfa based on net realizable values if the by-product is inventoried.
DISCUSSION: The NRV at split-off for each of the joint products must be determined. Given that Alfa has a $4 selling price and an additional $2 of processing costs, the value at the split-off is $2 per pound. The total value at split-off for 10,000 pounds is $20,000. Betters has a $10 selling price and an additional $2 of processing costs. Thus, the value at split-off is $8 per pound. The total value of 5,000 pounds of Betters is therefore $40,000. The 1,000 pounds of Morefeed has a split-off value of $3 per pound, or $3,000. Assuming that Morefeed (a by-product) is inventoried (recognized in the accounts when produced) and treated as a reduction of joint costs, the allocable joint cost is $90,000 ($93,000 – $3,000). The total net realizable value of the main products is $60,000 ($20,000 Alfa + $40,000 Betters). The allocation to Alfa is $30,000 [$90,000 × ($20,000 ÷ $60,000)].
Answer (A) is incorrect. The value of the by-product is $3,000. Answer (C) is incorrect. Failing to adjust the joint processing cost for the value of the by-product results in $31,000. Answer (D) is incorrect. The amount allocated to Betters is $60,000.

24. Assuming Atlas Foods inventories Morefeed, the by-product, and that it incurs no additional processing costs for Alfa and Betters, the joint cost to be allocated to Alfa using the gross sales value method is

A. $36,000

B. $40,000

C. $41,333

D. $50,000

Answer (B) is correct.
REQUIRED: The joint cost allocated to Alfa using the gross sales value method if the by-product is inventoried.
DISCUSSION: The gross sales value of Alfa is $40,000 (10,000 pounds × $4), Betters has a total gross sales value of $50,000 (5,000 pounds × $10), and Morefeed has a split-off value of $3,000. If the value of Morefeed is inventoried and treated as a reduction in joint cost, the allocable joint cost is $90,000 ($93,000 – $3,000). The total gross sales value of the two main products is $90,000 ($40,000 + $50,000). Of this total, $40,000 should be allocated to Alfa [$90,000 × ($40,000 ÷ $90,000)].
Answer (A) is incorrect. The amount of $36,000 is based on 40%, not 4/9. Answer (C) is incorrect. Failing to adjust the joint cost by the value of the by-product results in $41,333. Answer (D) is incorrect. The joint cost allocated to Betters is $50,000.

25. Assuming Atlas Foods does not inventory Morefeed, the by-product, the joint cost to be allocated to Betters using the net realizable value method is

A. $30,000

B. $31,000

C. $52,080

D. $62,000

Answer (D) is correct.
REQUIRED: The joint cost allocated to Betters based on net realizable values if the by-product is not inventoried.
DISCUSSION: The NRV of Alfa is $20,000, and the NRV of Betters is $40,000. If the joint cost is not adjusted for the value of the by-product, the amount allocated to Betters is $62,000 {$93,000 × [$40,000 ÷ ($20,000 + $40,000)]}.
Answer (A) is incorrect. The amount allocated to Alfa when the by-product is inventoried is $30,000. Answer (B) is incorrect. The amount allocated to Alfa when the by-product is not inventoried is $31,000. Answer (C) is incorrect. Assuming that a weighting method using caloric value is used results in $52,080.

Questions 26 and 27 are based on the following information.

Petro-Chem, Inc., is a small company that acquires high-grade crude oil from low-volume production wells owned by individuals and small partnerships. The crude oil is processed in a single refinery into Two Oil, Six Oil, and impure distillates. Petro-Chem does not have the technology or capacity to process these products further and sells most of its output each month to major refineries. There were no beginning inventories of finished goods or work-in-process on November 1. The production costs and output of Petro-Chem for November are shown in the next column.

Crude oil acquired and placed in production	$5,000,000
Direct labor and related costs	2,000,000
Manufacturing overhead	3,000,000

Production and sales

- Two Oil, 300,000 barrels produced; 80,000 barrels sold at $20 each.
- Six Oil, 240,000 barrels produced; 120,000 barrels sold at $30 each.
- Distillates, 120,000 barrels produced and sold at $15 each.

26. The portion of the joint production costs assigned to Two Oil based upon the relative sales value of output is

A. $4,800,000
B. $4,000,000
C. $2,286,000
D. $2,500,000

Answer (B) is correct.
REQUIRED: The joint production costs assigned to Two Oil based on relative sales value.
DISCUSSION: The total production costs incurred are $10,000,000, consisting of crude oil of $5,000,000, direct labor of $2,000,000, and overhead of $3,000,000. The total value of the output is as follows:

Two Oil (300,000 × $20)	$ 6,000,000
Six Oil (240,000 × $30)	7,200,000
Distillates (120,000 × $15)	1,800,000
Total sales value	$15,000,000

Because Two Oil composes 40% of the total sales value ($6,000,000 ÷ $15,000,000), it will be assigned 40% of the $10,000,000 of joint costs, or $4,000,000.

27. The portion of the joint production costs assigned to Six Oil based upon physical output is

A. $3,636,000
B. $3,750,000
C. $1,818,000
D. $7,500,000

Answer (A) is correct.
REQUIRED: The joint production costs assigned to Six Oil based on physical output.
DISCUSSION: The total production costs incurred are $10,000,000, consisting of crude oil of $5,000,000, direct labor of $2,000,000, and overhead of $3,000,000. The total physical output was 660,000 barrels, consisting of 300,000 barrels of Two Oil, 240,000 barrels of Six Oil, and 120,000 barrels of distillates. Thus, the allocation (rounded) is $3,636,000 {$10,000,000 × [240,000 ÷ (300,000 + 240,000 + 120,000)]}.

19.5 Job-Order Costing and Overhead Application

28. Felicity Corporation manufactures a specialty line of dresses using a job-order cost system. During January, the following costs were incurred in completing job J-1:

Direct materials	$27,400
Direct labor	9,600
Administrative costs	2,800
Selling costs	11,200

Overhead was applied at the rate of $50 per direct labor hour, and job J-1 required 400 direct labor hours. If job J-1 resulted in 4,000 good dresses, the cost of goods sold per unit is

A. $9.25
B. $14.25
C. $14.95
D. $17.75

Answer (B) is correct.
REQUIRED: The cost of goods sold per unit.
DISCUSSION: Cost of goods sold is based on the manufacturing costs incurred in production. It does not include selling or general and administrative expenses. Manufacturing costs consist of direct materials, $27,400; direct labor, $9,600; and overhead, $20,000 (400 direct labor hours × $50 per hour). The total of these three cost elements is $57,000. Dividing the $57,000 of total manufacturing costs by the 4,000 units produced results in a per-unit cost of $14.25.
Answer (A) is incorrect. Failing to include overhead results in $9.25. Answer (C) is incorrect. Including administrative costs results in $14.95. Answer (D) is incorrect. The amount of $17.75 includes selling and administrative costs.

29. Lucy Sportswear manufactures a specialty line of T-shirts using a job-order cost system. During March, the following costs were incurred in completing Job ICU2: direct materials, $13,700; direct labor, $4,800; administrative, $1,400; and selling, $5,600. Overhead was applied at the rate of $25 per machine hour, and Job ICU2 required 800 machine hours. If Job ICU2 resulted in 7,000 good shirts, the cost of goods sold per unit would be

   A. $6.50

   B. $6.30

   C. $5.70

   D. $5.50

Answer (D) is correct.
   REQUIRED: The cost of goods sold per unit.
   DISCUSSION: Cost of goods sold is based on the manufacturing costs incurred in production but does not include selling or general and administrative expenses. Manufacturing costs equal $38,500 [$13,700 DM + $4,800 DL + (800 hours × $25) OH]. Thus, per-unit cost is $5.50 ($38,500 ÷ 7,000 units).
   Answer (A) is incorrect. The amount of $6.50 includes selling and administrative expenses. Answer (B) is incorrect. Including selling costs results in $6.30. Answer (C) is incorrect. Including administrative expenses results in $5.70.

30. Worley Company has underapplied overhead of $45,000 for the year. Before disposition of the underapplied overhead, selected year-end balances from Worley's accounting records were

Sales	$1,200,000
Cost of goods sold	720,000
Direct materials inventory	36,000
Work-in-process inventory	54,000
Finished goods inventory	90,000

Under Worley's cost accounting system, over- or underapplied overhead is assigned to appropriate inventories and COGS based on year-end balances. In its year-end income statement, Worley should report COGS of

   A. $682,500

   B. $684,000

   C. $757,500

   D. $765,000

Answer (C) is correct.
   REQUIRED: The amount of cost of goods sold after allocation of underapplied overhead.
   DISCUSSION: The assignment of underapplied overhead increases COGS. The underapplied overhead of $45,000 for the year should be assigned on a pro rata basis to work-in-process ($54,000), finished goods ($90,000), and COGS ($720,000). The sum of these three items is $864,000. Thus, $37,500 should be assigned to COGS [($720,000 ÷ $864,000) × $45,000]. COGS after assignment is $757,500 ($37,500 + $720,000). The remaining $7,500 should be assigned proportionately to work-in-process and finished goods.
   Answer (A) is incorrect. The appropriate COGS balance if overhead was overapplied by $45,000 and $37,500 was assigned to COGS is $682,500. Answer (B) is incorrect. The COGS balance if overhead was overapplied by $45,000 and direct materials inventory was incorrectly included in the denominator of the ratio used to assign overhead is $684,000. Answer (D) is incorrect. Debiting the full amount of underapplied overhead ($45,000) to COGS results in $765,000.

31. Lucas Co. has a job-order cost system. For the month of April, the following debits (credits) appeared in the general ledger account, work-in-process:

April		
1	Balance	$ 24,000
30	Direct materials	80,000
30	Direct labor	60,000
30	Factory overhead	54,000
30	To finished goods	(200,000)

Lucas applies overhead to production at a predetermined rate of 90% based on direct labor cost. Job No. 100, the only job still in process at the end of April, has been charged with factory overhead of $4,500. The amount of direct materials charged to Job No. 100 was

   A. $18,000

   B. $8,500

   C. $5,000

   D. $4,500

Answer (B) is correct.
   REQUIRED: The amount of direct materials charged to the only job in process at the end of the period.
   DISCUSSION: The ending balance in the WIP account is $18,000 ($24,000 + $80,000 + $60,000 + $54,000 – $200,000). This amount equals the $218,000 sum of all debits to the account minus the $200,000 credit. The $18,000 balance consists of materials, labor, and overhead for Job No. 100. Overhead is given as $4,500 (90% of direct labor cost). Direct labor is thus $5,000 ($4,500 ÷ .90), and the amount of direct materials is $8,500.

$$DM + DL + OH = \$18,000$$
$$DM + DL + .9\ DL =$$
$$DM + \$5,000 + \$4,500 =$$
$$DM = \$\ 8,500$$

   Answer (A) is incorrect. The ending balance in the WIP account is $18,000. Answer (C) is incorrect. The direct labor cost of Job No. 100 is $5,000. Answer (D) is incorrect. The amount of factory overhead charged to Job No. 100 is $4,500.

Questions 32 and 33 are based on the following information. Hamilton Company uses job-order costing. Factory overhead is applied to production at a predetermined rate of 150% of direct labor cost. Any over- or underapplied factory overhead is closed to the cost of goods sold account at the end of each month. Additional information is available as follows:

- Job 101 was the only job in process at January 31, with accumulated costs as follows:

Direct materials	$4,000
Direct labor	2,000
Applied factory overhead	3,000
Total manufacturing costs	$9,000

- Jobs 102, 103, and 104 were started during February.
- Direct materials requisitions for February totaled $26,000.
- Direct labor cost of $20,000 was incurred for February.
- Actual factory overhead was $32,000 for February.
- The only job still in process on February 28 was Job 104, with costs of $2,800 for direct materials and $1,800 for direct labor.

32. The cost of goods manufactured for February was

A. $77,700

B. $78,000

C. $79,700

D. $85,000

Answer (A) is correct.
    REQUIRED: The cost of goods manufactured (COGM).
    DISCUSSION: COGM is the sum of the costs in BWIP and all the costs incurred during the period minus the costs in EWIP. The calculation of COGM uses applied overhead ($30,000 = $20,000 DL cost × 150%). The $7,300 in EWIP includes $2,800 for direct materials, $1,800 for direct labor, and $2,700 for applied overhead (at 150% of DL cost).

BWIP	$ 9,000
Direct labor	20,000
Applied OH	30,000
Direct materials	26,000
EWIP	(7,300)
COGM	$77,700

    Answer (B) is incorrect. The amount of $78,000 does not reflect BWIP and EWIP and is based on actual factory OH. Answer (C) is incorrect. Actual factory OH of $32,000 was used. Answer (D) is incorrect. EWIP was not subtracted.

33. Over- or underapplied factory overhead should be closed to the cost of goods sold account at February 28 in the amount of

A. $700 overapplied.

B. $1,000 overapplied.

C. $1,700 underapplied.

D. $2,000 underapplied.

Answer (D) is correct.
    REQUIRED: The amount of over- or underapplied factory overhead closed to COGS.
    DISCUSSION: The amount of over- or underapplied overhead is the difference between the actual overhead incurred and the overhead applied. The amount of overhead applied was $30,000 ($20,000 DL cost ×150%). The amount of overhead incurred was $32,000. Consequently, underapplied overhead of $2,000 ($32,000 actual – $30,000 applied) should be closed to COGS.
    Answer (A) is incorrect. The amount of $700 overapplied equals applied overhead in EWIP minus the difference between actual February overhead and overhead applied in February. Answer (B) is incorrect. The $3,000 of applied factory overhead in BWIP should not be used in determining the current month's over- or underapplied overhead. Answer (C) is incorrect. The amounts of applied overhead in BWIP and EWIP should not be used in calculating the current month's over- or underapplied overhead.

Use the additional questions in Gleim **CPA Test Prep Online** to create Test Sessions that emulate Prometric!

19.6 PRACTICE WRITTEN COMMUNICATION TASK

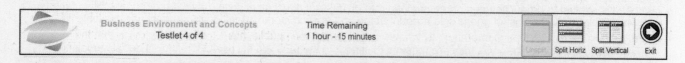

DIRECTIONS

Note: If you believe you have encountered a software malfunction, report it to the test center staff immediately.

Navigation

To navigate from task to task, use the controls at the bottom of the screen. Click on the **Next** button to advance to the next task, or the **Previous** button to go to the previous task. To go directly to any task, click on its number.

▽ = Reminder		Directions	1	2	3	4	5	6	7		◀ Previous	Next ▶
			▽	▽	▽	▽	▽	▽	▽			

If you would like a reminder to revisit a task, or want to indicate that you are finished with it, click on the reminder flag below the task number. To clear the flag, click on it again. Reminder flags are for your use only – they do not contribute to your score.

Tabs

In this part of the examination, you will be asked to complete various tasks. Every task has one or more **Work Tabs**. Every task also has a **Help** tab.

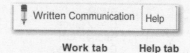

Work tab   Help tab

Work Tabs:

- **Work Tabs** are identified with a pencil icon. This is where your responses are expected.
- Each task has one or more **Work Tabs**.
- **Work Tabs** contain directions for completing the task - be sure to read these directions carefully.
- The **Work Tab** name in the example above is for illustration only - yours will differ.
- You must complete all of the **Work Tabs** in each task to receive full credit.

Help Tab:

- The **Help Tab** provides assistance with the exam software that is used in this task. For example, if the task is to compose a memorandum, **Help** will provide information about the word processor.

The Toolbar

The toolbar at the top of the screen shows the amount of time remaining for you to complete the tasks. In addition, the following tools are available. Note that only the **Exit** button is displayed when Directions are visible - the others will appear when you begin the tasks.

Click on these buttons to split or unsplit the screen. You can split the screen vertically or horizontally.

Click on this button to go on to the next part of the examination. You must complete all of the tasks to receive full credit. Once you click on **Exit** and confirm the action, you will NOT be able to return to this testlet.

Written Communication | Help

Cut | Copy | Paste | Undo | Redo

The management of Wildcat Corporation, which has only recently gone public, has expressed frustration that the GAAP-based financial statements they are required to submit to the SEC are not useful for internal decision making.

Prepare a memo to the CEO and CFO of Wildcat Corporation explaining absorption costing and variable costing and why variable costing may be a more appropriate tool for them to use internally than their GAAP-based financial statements.

Type your communication below the line in the response area below.

REMINDER: Your response will be graded for both technical content and writing skills. Technical content will be evaluated for information that is helpful to the intended reader and clearly relevant to the issue. Writing skills will be evaluated for development, organization, and the appropriate expression of ideas in professional correspondence. Use a standard business memorandum or letter format with a clear beginning, middle, and end. Do not convey information in the form of a table, bullet point list, or other abbreviated presentation.

To: CEO and CFO, Wildcat Corporation
Re: Absorption costing, variable costing; using variable costing in internal reporting

▼ = Reminder   Directions   1 ▽   ◀ Previous   Next ▶

Unofficial Answer

Written Communication

To: CEO and CFO, Wildcat Corporation
Re: Absorption costing, variable costing; using variable costing in internal reporting

Although GAAP require absorption (full) costing for external reporting, and the IRS requires it for tax purposes, variable costing is preferred for internal reporting purposes. First, an understanding of the differences between absorption and variable costing needs to be developed. Next, it is important to understand the benefit of using variable costing in internal reporting despite statutory requirements to use absorption costing for external reporting.

Absorption costing reports unit costs that include the portion of total manufacturing cost attributable to that unit or group of units. It is more inclusive than variable costing, which only includes variable manufacturing costs in the determination of unit costs. Hence, absorption costing is required for external reporting and for tax purposes.

Nevertheless, variable costing, or contribution margin reporting, is an important internal measure because it is an immediate response to the informational needs of management. Management requires a knowledge of cost behavior under various operating conditions. For planning and control, management is more concerned about treating fixed and variable costs separately than with calculating full costs. Full costs are usually of little value because they contain arbitrary allocations of fixed cost. Also, profit planning and decision making are easier under variable costing. It does not require auxiliary records and supplementary analysis for the fixed manufacturing portion of product costs. Thus, although absorption costing responds to the needs of external users, managers within the organization have different informational needs.

The above depicts a Level 5 answer. See page 16 in the Introduction for a description of the three grading criteria.

Self-Grade

Evaluate each of the following by selecting a 0, 1, 2, 3, 4, or 5. An average response is 3. Use 4 for better than average and 5 for outstanding. Use 2 for less than average and 1 for quite poor. Use zero for no response, if you did not address the topic, or if you gave advice that is clearly illegal.

Organization	○ 0	○ 1	○ 2	○ 3	○ 4	○ 5
Development	○ 0	○ 1	○ 2	○ 3	○ 4	○ 5
Expression	○ 0	○ 1	○ 2	○ 3	○ 4	○ 5

Your grade for the written communication as a whole is the average of the scores for the three criteria.

Use **CPA Gleim Online** and **Simulation Wizard** to practice more written communication tasks in a realistic environment.

STUDY UNIT TWENTY
COSTING SYSTEMS AND VARIANCE ANALYSIS

(15 pages of outline)

Process costing is used when relatively homogeneous products are mass produced on a continuous basis (Subunits 1 and 2). Activity-based costing is employed by entities with high levels of indirect costs (Subunit 3).

A standard cost is an estimate of what a cost should be under normal operating conditions based on accounting and engineering studies. Standard costs are used to assign costs to products as well as to control actual costs. Comparing actual and standard costs permits evaluation of managerial performance using variance analysis (Subunits 4 and 5). This analysis can also be applied to revenue amounts (Subunit 6).

20.1 PROCESS COSTING -- PRINCIPLES

1. **Uses of Process Costing**

    a. Process cost accounting assigns costs to inventoriable goods or services. It applies to relatively homogeneous products that are mass produced on a continuous basis (e.g., petroleum products, thread, and computer monitors).

    b. Instead of using subsidiary ledgers to track specific jobs, process costing typically uses a work-in-process account for each department through which the production of output passes.

    c. Process costing calculates the average cost of all units as follows:

        1) Costs are accumulated for a cost object that consists of a large number of similar units of goods or services,

        2) Work-in-process is stated in terms of equivalent units, and

        3) Unit costs are established.

2. **Accumulation of Costs**

    a. The accumulation of costs under a process costing system is by department rather than by project. This reflects the continuous, homogeneous nature of the manufacturing process.

b.   The physical inputs required for the production process are obtained from suppliers.

Direct materials	$XXX	
Accounts payable		$XXX

c.   Direct materials are added by the first department in the process.

Work-in-process -- Department A	$XXX	
Direct materials		$XXX

d.   Conversion costs are the sum of direct labor and manufacturing overhead. The nature of process costing makes this accounting treatment more efficient (see item 4, beginning on the following page for a discussion on equivalent units).

Work-in-process -- Department A	$XXX	
Wages payable (direct and indirect labor)		$XXX
Manufacturing overhead		XXX

e.   The products move from one department to the next.

Work-in-process -- Department B	$XXX	
Work-in-process -- Department A		$XXX

f.   The second department adds more direct materials and more conversion costs.

Work-in-process -- Department B	$XXX	
Direct materials		$XXX

Work-in-process -- Department B	$XXX	
Wages payable (direct and indirect labor)		$XXX
Manufacturing overhead		XXX

g.   When processing is finished in the last department, all costs are transferred to finished goods.

Finished goods	$X,XXX	
Work-in-process -- Department B		$X,XXX

h.   As products are sold, sales are recorded and the costs are transferred to cost of goods sold.

Accounts receivable	$XX,XXX	
Sales		$XX,XXX
Cost of goods sold	$ X,XXX	
Finished goods		$ X,XXX

i.   The changes to these accounts during the period can be summarized as follows:

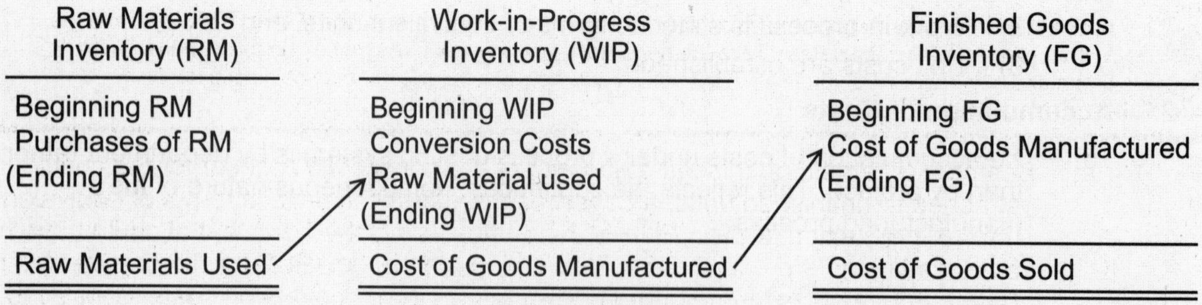

Raw Materials Inventory (RM)	Work-in-Progress Inventory (WIP)	Finished Goods Inventory (FG)
Beginning RM	Beginning WIP	Beginning FG
Purchases of RM	Conversion Costs	Cost of Goods Manufactured
(Ending RM)	Raw Material used	(Ending FG)
	(Ending WIP)	
Raw Materials Used	Cost of Goods Manufactured	Cost of Goods Sold

Figure 20-1

3. Graphical Depiction

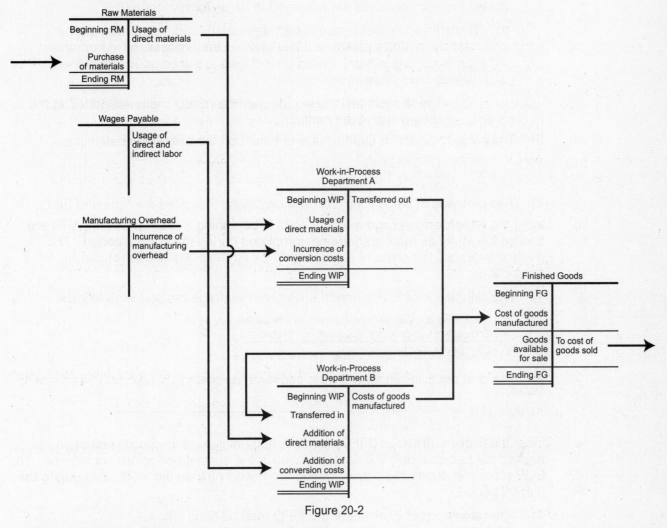

Figure 20-2

4. Equivalent Units of Production (EUP)

The AICPA frequently tests the calculation of equivalent units of production (EUP). This topic may be confusing to CPA candidates. Take the necessary time to work through the questions in the Gleim materials to make sure you thoroughly understand how to accomplish these calculations.

    a.   Some units remain unfinished at the end of the period. To account for the costs attached to unfinished units, a department restates the units in terms of equivalent units of production (EUP). EUP is the number of finished goods that could have been produced using the inputs consumed during the period. EUP for direct materials or conversion costs is the amount of direct materials or conversion costs required to complete one physical unit of production.

EXAMPLE

One thousand work-in-process units, completed 80% for direct materials and 60% for conversion costs, would represent 800 EUP of direct materials (1,000 × 80%) and 600 EUP of conversion costs (1,000 × 60%).

---

        1)   The EUP conversion requires (a) determining the equivalent units and (b) calculating the per-unit cost.

2) The two calculations are made separately for direct materials and conversion costs. Conversion costs are assumed to be uniformly incurred.

a) Transferred-in costs (also called previous-department costs) are by definition 100% complete. The units (costs) transferred in from the previous department should be included in the computation of the EUP of the second department.

i) These costs are treated the same as direct materials added at the beginning of the period.

3) The actual production quantity flow is based on the following relationship:

$$\begin{matrix} Beginning \\ work\text{-}in\text{-}process \end{matrix} + \begin{matrix} Units\ started \\ this\ period \end{matrix} = \begin{matrix} Units\ transferred \\ out\ (completed) \end{matrix} + \begin{matrix} Ending \\ work\text{-}in\text{-}process \end{matrix}$$

4) Two methods of calculating EUP are common: weighted-average and FIFO.

b. Under the **weighted-average** method, units in beginning work-in-process (WIP) are treated the same as units started and completed during the current period. This method averages the costs of beginning WIP with the costs of current-period production.

1) The calculation of EUP under the weighted-average method is as follows:

```
  Total units completed (transferred out) this period
+ Ending work-in-process × Percent completed
  EUP under weighted-average
```

2) The cost per EUP under the weighted-average method is calculated as follows:

$$Cost\ per\ EUP = \frac{Beginning\ WIP\ costs + Current\ period\ costs}{EUP}$$

c. Under the **first-in, first-out (FIFO)** method, beginning work-in-process must be backed out because only the costs incurred in the current period are considered. The EUP produced during the current period are based only on the work done during the current period.

1) The calculation of EUP under the FIFO method is as follows:

```
  Beginning work-in-process (WIP) × Percent left to complete
+ Units started and completed during the current period
+ Ending work-in-process (WIP) × Percent completed
  EUP under FIFO
```

NOTE: Units started and completed during the current period are equal to units started minus ending WIP.

Another version of this equation is presented below:

```
  Total units completed this period
+ Ending work-in-process (WIP) × Percent completed
  (Beginning work-in-process × Percent completed in previous periods)
  EUP FIFO
```

2) The cost per EUP under FIFO is calculated as follows:

$$Cost\ per\ EUP = \frac{Current\ period\ costs}{EUP}$$

EXAMPLE

The first step is to prepare a quantity schedule. A department of a manufacturer is preparing its cost reports for the month.

	Units	Completed for Direct Materials	Completed for Conversion Costs
Beginning work-in-process	2,000	80%	40%
Units started during period	8,000		
Units to account for	10,000		
Units completed	9,000		
Ending work-in-process	1,000	90%	70%
Units accounted for	10,000		

The next step is to calculate the equivalent units of production. This table illustrates the different outcomes of the two methods. Note that beginning work-in-process is not backed out in the weighted-average computation but is under FIFO.

	Weighted-Average		FIFO	
	Direct Materials	Conversion Costs	Direct Materials	Conversion Costs
Units completed	9,000	9,000	9,000	9,000
Plus: ending work-in-process EUP				
Direct materials: 1,000 units × 90%	900		900	
Conversion costs: 1,000 units × 70%		700		700
Minus: beginning work-in-process EUP				
Direct materials: 2,000 units × 80%			(1,600)	
Conversion costs: 2,000 units × 40%				(800)
Equivalent units of production	9,900	9,700	8,300	8,900

The costs to be allocated are presented in this table:

	Direct Materials	Conversion Costs
Beginning work-in-process	$25,000	$10,000
Added during the month	55,000	50,000
Totals	$80,000	$60,000

d. Once the equivalent units have been calculated, the per-unit costs under each of the two methods can be derived.

1) Under the weighted-average method, all direct materials and conversion costs incurred in the current period and in beginning work-in-process are averaged.

EXAMPLE

Direct materials cost per EUP: $\dfrac{\$80,000}{9,900 \text{ EUP}}$ = $ 8.08

Conversion costs per EUP: $\dfrac{\$60,000}{9,700 \text{ EUP}}$ = $ 6.19

Total unit cost under weighted-average $14.27

2) Under the FIFO method, only the costs incurred in the current period are included in the calculation.

EXAMPLE

Direct materials cost per EUP: $\dfrac{\$55,000}{8,300 \text{ EUP}}$ = $ 6.63

Conversion costs per EUP: $\dfrac{\$50,000}{8,900 \text{ EUP}}$ = $ 5.62

Total unit cost under FIFO $12.25

e. When beginning work-in-process is zero, the two methods yield the same results.

Reminder: Only when applying FIFO is beginning inventory subtracted from the EUP calculation. The weighted-average method treats units in beginning inventory as if they were started and completed during the current period.

Stop and review! You have completed the outline for this subunit. Study multiple-choice questions 1 through 4 on page 542.

20.2 PROCESS COSTING -- CALCULATIONS

Process costing questions on the CPA exam will test both the understanding of principles and the ability to perform the detailed computations. This subunit consists entirely of the second type of question. Please review Subunit 20.1 before answering these questions.

Stop and review! You have completed the outline for this subunit. Study multiple-choice questions 5 through 10 beginning on page 543.

20.3 ACTIVITY-BASED COSTING (ABC)

1. **Drawbacks of Volume-Based Systems**

   a. ABC is a response to the significant increase in the incurrence of indirect costs resulting from the rapid advance of technology. ABC is a refinement of an existing costing system (job-order or process).

      1) Under a traditional (volume-based) costing system, overhead is simply dumped into a single cost pool and spread evenly across all end products.

      2) Under ABC, indirect costs are attached to activities that are then rationally allocated to end products.

      3) ABC may be used by manufacturing, service, or retailing entities.

      4) ABC may be used in a job-order system or a process cost system.

   b. The inaccurate averaging or spreading of indirect costs over products or service units that use different amounts of resources is called **peanut-butter costing**. Peanut-butter costing results in product-cost cross-subsidization, the condition in which the miscosting of one product causes the miscosting of other products.

   c. The peanut-butter effect of using a traditional (i.e., volume-based) costing system can be summarized as follows:

      1) Direct labor and direct materials are traced to products or service units.

      2) A single pool of indirect costs (overhead) is accumulated for a given organizational unit.

      3) Indirect costs from the pool are assigned using an allocative (rather than a tracing) procedure, such as using a single overhead rate for an entire department, e.g., $3 of overhead for every direct labor hour.

         a) The effect is an averaging of costs that may result in significant inaccuracy when products or service units do not use similar amounts of resources.

EXAMPLE

The effect of product-cost cross-subsidization can be illustrated as follows:

1. A company produces two products. Both products require 1 unit of direct material and 1 hour of direct labor. Raw materials costs are $14 per unit, and direct labor is $70 per hour.

2. During the month just ended, the company produced 1,000 units of Product A and 100 units of Product B. Manufacturing overhead for the month totaled $20,000.

3. Using direct labor hours as the overhead allocation base, per-unit costs and profits are calculated as follows:

	Product A	Product B	Total
Direct materials	$ 14,000	$ 1,400	
Direct labor	70,000	7,000	
Overhead {$20,000 × [1,000 ÷ (1,000 + 100)]}	18,182		
Overhead {$20,000 × [1,000 ÷ (1,000 + 100)]}		1,818	
Total costs	$102,182	$ 10,218	$112,400
Selling price	$ 119.99	$ 139.99	
Cost per unit	(102.18)	(102.18)	
Profit per unit	$ 17.81	$ 37.81	

4. The company's management accountants have determined that overhead consists almost entirely of production line setup costs and that the two products require equal setup times. Allocating overhead on this basis yields vastly different results.

	Product A	Product B	Total
Direct materials	$14,000	$ 1,400	
Direct labor	70,000	7,000	
Overhead ($20,000 × 50%)	10,000		
Overhead ($20,000 × 50%)		10,000	
Total costs	$94,000	$18,400	$112,400
Selling price	$119.99	$139.99	
Cost per unit	(94.00)	(184.00)	
Profit (loss) per unit	$ 25.99	$ (44.01)	

5. Rather than the profit the company believed it was making on both products using peanut-butter costing, it is losing money on every unit of Product B that it sells. The high-volume Product A has been heavily subsidizing the setup costs for the low-volume Product B.

d. The example above assumed a single component of overhead for clarity. In reality, overhead is typically made up of many components. The peanut-butter effect of traditional overhead allocation is illustrated in the following diagram:

Overhead Allocation in a Traditional (Volume-Based) Cost Accumulation System

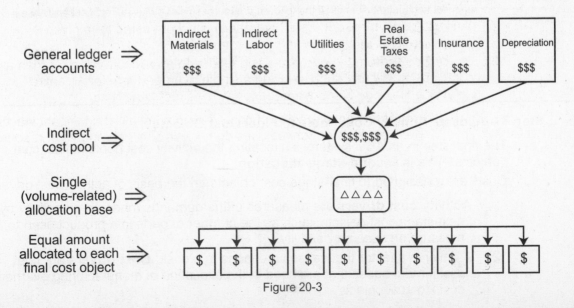

Figure 20-3

2. **Volume-Based vs. Activity-Based**

    a.   Volume-based systems were appropriate when most manufacturing costs were direct. However, overhead costs do not always fluctuate with volume. ABC addresses the increasing complexity and variety of overhead costs.

    b.   Activity-based systems involve

        1)   Identifying organizational activities that result in overhead

        2)   Assigning the costs of resources consumed by the activities

        3)   Assigning the costs of the activities by appropriate cost drivers to final cost objects

3. **Step 1 – Activity Analysis**

    a.   An activity is a set of work actions undertaken within the entity, and a cost pool is established for each activity.

    b.   Analysis identifies value-adding activities, which contribute to customer satisfaction. Nonvalue-adding activities should be reduced or eliminated.

    c.   Activities are classified in a hierarchy according to the level of the production process where they occur.

4. **Step 2 – Assign Resource Costs to Activities**

    a.   Once the activities are designated, the next step in an ABC system is to assign the costs of resources to the activities. This is **first-stage allocation**.

    b.   Identifying resource costs is not as simple as in volume-based overhead allocation, which designates general ledger accounts to be combined in one certain GL cost pool.

        1)   A separate accounting system may be necessary to track resource costs separately from the general ledger.

    c.   Once the resources have been identified, resource drivers are designated to allocate resource costs to the **activity cost pools**.

        1)   **Resource drivers** are measures of the resources consumed by an activity.

EXAMPLE

Fabulous Foundry uses a job-order system to accumulate costs for the custom pipe fittings of all sizes that it produces. With increasing reliance on robots in the production process and computers for monitoring and control, overhead is now a greater percentage of total costs, and direct labor costs have decreased. The company has begun the process of implementing an activity-based costing system.

Fabulous Foundry's management accountants identified the following resources used by its indirect cost processes:

Resource	Driver
Computer processing	CPU cycles
Production line	Machine hours
Materials management	Hours worked
Utilities	Square footage

---

5. **Step 3 – Allocate Activity Cost Pools to Final Cost Objects**

    a.   The final step in an ABC system is allocating the activity cost pools to final cost objects. This is **second-stage allocation**.

    b.   Costs are reassigned to final-stage cost objects on the basis of activity cost drivers.

        1)   **Activity cost drivers** are measures of the demands made on an activity by next-stage cost objects, such as the number of parts in a product used to measure an assembly activity.

        2)   A driver is a factor that causes a change in a cost. **Cost drivers** are cost assignment bases that are used in the allocation of manufacturing overhead costs to cost objects.

c. Drivers (both resource and activity) must be chosen on the basis of a cause-and-effect relationship with the resource or activity cost being allocated, not simply on the basis of a high positive correlation.

EXAMPLE

Fabulous Foundry's management accountants have designated the following cost drivers to associate with their corresponding activities:

Activity	Cost driver
Product design	Number of products
Production setup	Number of setups
Machining	Number of units produced
Inspection & testing	Number of units produced
Production orders	Number of orders

EXAMPLE

Knight Company is a manufacturer of pants and coats. The following information pertains to the company's current month activities:

Manufacturing overhead costs		Cost driver
Plant utilities and real estate taxes	$150,000	Square footage
Materials handling	40,000	Pounds of direct material used
Inspection & testing	10,000	Number of units produced
	$200,000	

Current month activity level

	Pants	Coats	Total
Direct labor hours	20,000	5,000	25,000
Plant square footage	400	600	1,000
Pounds of direct material used	10,000	6,000	16,000
Number of units produced	15,000	3,000	18,000

Using direct labor hours as the overhead allocation base (traditional volume-based system), the manufacturing overhead costs are allocated as follows:

Pants: $200,000 × (20,000 ÷ 25,000) = $160,000
Coats: $200,000 × (5,000 ÷ 25,000) = $40,000

Manufacturing overhead costs per pant: $160,000 ÷ 15,000 = $10.67
Manufacturing overhead costs per coat: $40,000 ÷ 3,000 = $13.33

Under an activity-based costing system, the manufacturing overhead costs are allocated as follows:

	Pants		Coats	
Plant utilities and real estate taxes	$150,000 × (400 ÷ 1,000) =	$60,000	$150,000 × (600 ÷ 1,000) =	$ 90,000
Material handling	$40,000 × (10,000 ÷ 16,000) =	$25,000	$40,000 x (6,000 ÷ 16,000) =	$ 15,000
Inspection & testing	$10,000 × (15,000 ÷ 18,000) =	$ 8,333	$10,000 × (3,000 ÷ 18,000) =	$ 1,667
		$93,333		$106,667

Manufacturing overhead costs per pant = $93,333 ÷ 15,000 = $6.22
Manufacturing overhead costs per coat = $106,667 ÷ 3,000 = $35.56

Stop and review! You have completed the outline for this subunit. Study multiple-choice questions 11 through 16 beginning on page 545.

20.4 VARIANCE ANALYSIS -- MATERIALS AND LABOR

> The AICPA frequently tests variance analysis. This is another topic that often confuses CPA candidates. Make sure you understand how to calculate the different variances.

1. **Use of Variance Analysis**

   a. Variance analysis is the basis of performance evaluation using standard costs.

      1) A favorable variance **(F)** occurs when actual costs are less than standard.
      2) An unfavorable variance **(U)** occurs when actual costs are greater than standard.

   b. Variance analysis enables management-by-exception, the practice of giving attention primarily to significant deviations from expectations (whether favorable or unfavorable). When a variance occurs, management is signaled that corrective action may be needed.

2. **Framework for Variance Calculation**

   a. Variable inputs (direct materials and direct labor) can be analyzed in terms of a price (rate) variance and a quantity usage (efficiency) variance.

      1) **Price (rate) variances** arise from a difference between the actual price of resources used in production and the standard prices, holding quantity constant.

      2) **Efficiency (quantity usage) variances** arise from differences in the actual level of resources used in production and the standard level allowed, holding price constant.

   b. The following abbreviations are used to demonstrate the calculation of variances:

      AQP = Actual quantity of materials purchased
      AQ = Actual quantity of materials consumed or hours worked
      AP = Actual price/rate of materials consumed or hours worked
      SQ = Standard quantity of materials consumed or hours allowed
      SP = Standard price/rate of materials consumed or hours worked

3. **Direct Materials**

   a. The **materials price variance** is the actual quantity of input purchased times the difference between the standard price of materials and the actual price.

$$\text{Direct material price variance} = \text{Actual quantity purchased (AQP)} \times \left(\text{Standard material price (SP)} - \text{Actual material price (AP)} \right)$$

   b. The **materials quantity variance** (also called a usage or efficiency variance) is the standard cost times the difference between the standard quantity of materials and the actual quantity used in production.

$$\text{Direct material usage variance} = \left(\text{Standard quantity of input allowed (SQ)} - \text{Actual quantity consumed (AQ)} \right) \times \text{Standard material price (SP)}$$

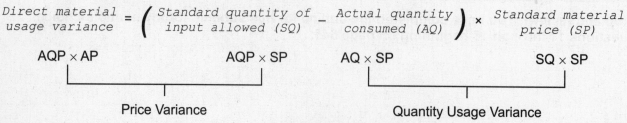

Figure 20-4

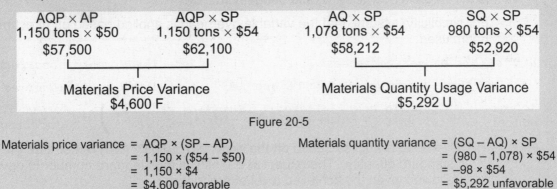

EXAMPLE of direct materials variances

For the month just ended, DV Products budgeted the use of 980 tons of materials at a cost of $54 per ton. The actual amounts purchased and used during the month were 1,150 tons and 1,078 tons, respectively. The actual cost for the period was $50 per ton. The variances for direct materials are calculated as follows:

AQP × AP	AQP × SP	AQ × SP	SQ × SP
1,150 tons × $50	1,150 tons × $54	1,078 tons × $54	980 tons × $54
$57,500	$62,100	$58,212	$52,920

Materials Price Variance
$4,600 F

Materials Quantity Usage Variance
$5,292 U

Figure 20-5

Materials price variance = AQP × (SP − AP)
= 1,150 × ($54 − $50)
= 1,150 × $4
= $4,600 favorable

Materials quantity variance = (SQ − AQ) × SP
= (980 − 1,078) × $54
= −98 × $54
= $5,292 unfavorable

4.   **Direct Labor**

   a.   The **labor rate variance** is the actual number of hours worked times the difference between the standard hourly wage and the actual hourly wage.

$$\text{Direct labor rate variance} = \text{Actual number of hours worked (AQ)} \times \left(\text{Standard hourly rate (SP)} - \text{Actual hourly rate (AP)} \right)$$

   b.   The **labor efficiency variance** is the difference between the standard number of hours and the actual number worked, times standard hourly wage.

$$\text{Direct labor efficiency variance} = \left(\text{Standard number of hours allowed (SQ)} - \text{Actual number of hours worked (AQ)} \right) \times \text{Standard hourly rate (SP)}$$

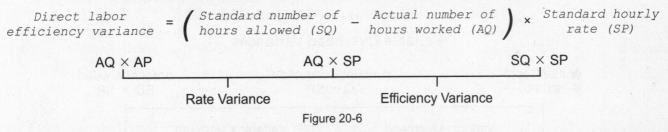

AQ × AP	AQ × SP	SQ × SP

Rate Variance   Efficiency Variance

Figure 20-6

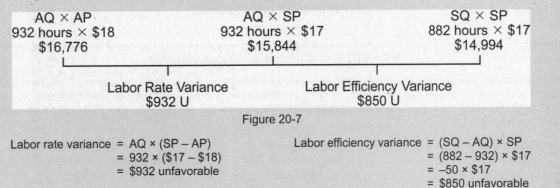

EXAMPLE of direct labor variances

Standard direct labor for the month was 882 hours at $17 per hour. However, 932 direct labor hours were actually worked at a cost of $18 per hour. The variances for direct labor are calculated as follows:

AQ × AP	AQ × SP	SQ × SP
932 hours × $18	932 hours × $17	882 hours × $17
$16,776	$15,844	$14,994

Labor Rate Variance
$932 U

Labor Efficiency Variance
$850 U

Figure 20-7

Labor rate variance = AQ × (SP − AP)
= 932 × ($17 − $18)
= $932 unfavorable

Labor efficiency variance = (SQ − AQ) × SP
= (882 − 932) × $17
= −50 × $17
= $850 unfavorable

Stop and review! You have completed the outline for this subunit. Study multiple-choice questions 17 through 22 beginning on page 548.

20.5 VARIANCE ANALYSIS -- OVERHEAD

1. **Variable Overhead**

   a. The amount of variable overhead (VOH) that was under- or overapplied for the period is the variable overhead flexible budget variance.

       For simplicity, assume that the variable overhead is applied based on direct machine hours used.

       VOH flexible budget variance = (EQ × SP) − Actual VOH costs incurred

       VOH over-/underapplied = VOH applied − Actual VOH costs incurred

       $$\left(\begin{matrix} Actual \\ production \end{matrix} \times \begin{matrix} Standard\ hours\ allowed \\ per\ unit\ of\ production \end{matrix} \times \begin{matrix} Standard\ variable \\ overhead\ rate \end{matrix} \right) - \begin{matrix} Actual\ VOH \\ incurred \end{matrix}$$

       1) Overhead is applied based on the expected quantity (EQ) rather than the standard quantity. The expected quantity is the standard number of driver units allowed given the achieved level of production.

   b. The variable overhead flexible budget variance has a spending component and an efficiency component.

       1) The **VOH spending variance** is equivalent to the materials price/labor rate variance.

           VOH spending variance = (Actual driver level × Standard VOH rate) − Actual VOH

           = (AQ × SP) − Actual VOH

       2) The **VOH efficiency variance** is equivalent to the materials quantity/labor efficiency variance.

           VOH efficiency variance = (EQ − AQ) × SP

Variable Overhead Variances

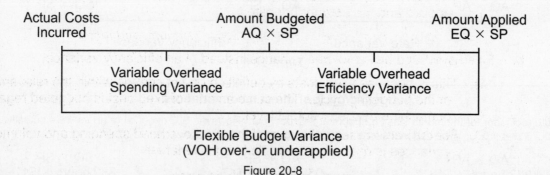

Figure 20-8

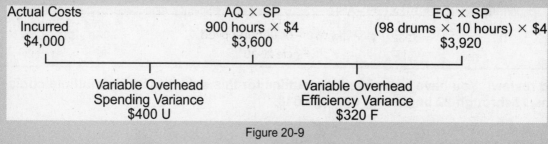

Figure 20-9

-- Continued on next page --

-- EXAMPLE continued --

These calculations can be reconciled with the following equation:

$$\text{Amount applied} - \text{Actual costs incurred} = \text{VOH flexible budget variance}$$
$$= \text{VOH spending variance} + \text{VOH efficiency variance}$$
$$\$3,920 - \$4,000 = \$400 \text{ U} + \$320 \text{ F}$$
$$\$80 \text{ underapplied} = \$80 \text{ U}$$

$$\text{VOH efficiency variance} = \text{Standard VOH rate} \times \left(\begin{matrix} \text{Standard hours allowed} \\ \text{for actual production} \end{matrix} - \begin{matrix} \text{Actual hours} \\ \text{used} \end{matrix} \right)$$
$$= \$ \ 4 \quad \times \quad [(10 \text{ hours} \times 98 \text{ drums}) - \quad 900]$$
$$= \$320 \text{ F}$$

$$\text{VOH spending variance} = (\text{Actual driver level} \times \quad \text{Standard VOH rate}) - \text{Actual VOH}$$
$$= (900 \text{ hours} \quad \times \quad \$4) \quad - \quad \$4,000$$
$$= \$400 \text{ U}$$

---

2. Fixed Overhead

a. The amount of fixed overhead (FOH) that was under- or overapplied for the period consists of a spending component and a volume component.

$$FOH \ over\text{-}/underapplied = FOH \ applied - Actual \ FOH \ incurred$$
$$= \left(\begin{matrix} Actual \\ production \end{matrix} \times \begin{matrix} Standard \ hours \ allowed \\ per \ unit \ of \ production \end{matrix} \times \begin{matrix} Standard \\ FOH \ rate \end{matrix} \right) - \begin{matrix} Actual \ FOH \\ incurred \end{matrix}$$

1) The **FOH spending variance** is the difference between the amount budgeted and the actual costs incurred.

$$FOH \ spending \ variance = Amount \ budgeted - Actual \ FOH \ incurred$$
$$= \left(\begin{matrix} Budgeted \\ production \end{matrix} \times \begin{matrix} Standard \ hours \ allowed \\ per \ unit \ of \ production \end{matrix} \times \begin{matrix} Standard \\ FOH \ rate \end{matrix} \right) - \begin{matrix} Actual \ FOH \\ incurred \end{matrix}$$

2) The **FOH volume variance** is the difference between the amount of overhead applied and the amount budgeted.

$$FOH \ volume \ variance = FOH \ applied - Amount \ budgeted$$

b. Fixed overhead has a volume variance instead of an efficiency variance.

1) This is because fixed costs by definition do not change within the relevant range of the budgeting cycle. The same amount of fixed cost is budgeted regardless of machine usage or output level.

2) For the same reason, the sum of the fixed overhead spending and volume variances is not called a flexible budget variance.

Fixed Overhead Variances

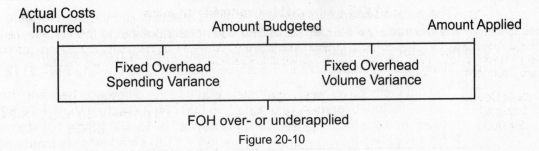

Figure 20-10

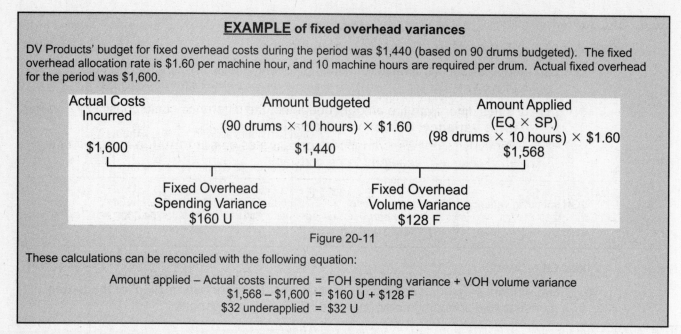

Figure 20-11

These calculations can be reconciled with the following equation:

Amount applied − Actual costs incurred = FOH spending variance + VOH volume variance
$1,568 − $1,600 = $160 U + $128 F
$32 underapplied = $32 U

3. **Integrated Overhead Variance Analysis**

    a. **Three-way overhead variance analysis** combines the variable and fixed spending variances ($400 U + $160 U = $560 U) and reports the other two variances separately.

> **EXAMPLE**
>
> | Three-Way Analysis | Spending Variance | Efficiency Variance | Volume Variance |
> |---|---|---|---|
> | Total overhead | $560 U | $320 F | $128 F |

    b. **Two-way overhead variance analysis** combines the spending and efficiency variances into a single budget variance ($560 U + $320 F = $240 U) and reports the volume variance separately.

> **EXAMPLE**
>
> | Two-Way Analysis | Budget Variance | Volume Variance |
> |---|---|---|
> | Total overhead | $240 U | $128 F |

      1) The budget variance in two-way analysis is also called the **controllable variance**. It is the portion of the total not attributable to the volume variance.

    c. The **net factory overhead variance** (also called one-way overhead variance analysis) combines all the components into a single amount ($240 U + $128 F = **$112 U**).

      1) The net factory overhead variance is equal to the difference between the total actual factory overhead incurred of $5,600 ($4,000 actual VOH + $1,600 actual FOH) and the total factory overhead applied of $5,488 [(98 × 10) standard hours applied to actual production × ($4 + $1.6) standard total overhead rate].

$5,600 − $5,488 = $112 U

Stop and review! You have completed the outline for this subunit. Study multiple-choice questions 23 through 28 beginning on page 549.

20.6 SALES VARIANCES

1. **Sales, Contribution Margin, and Operating Income**

   a. Variance analysis is useful for evaluating not only the production function but also the selling function.

      1) If sales differ from the amount budgeted, the difference could consist of a **sales price variance**, a **sales volume variance**, or both.

      2) The analysis of these variances concentrates on **contribution margins** because fixed costs are assumed to be constant.

EXAMPLE

A firm has budgeted sales of 10,000 units of its sole product at $17 per unit. Variable costs are expected to be $10 per unit, and fixed costs are budgeted at $50,000. The following compares budgeted and actual results:

	Budget Computation	Budget Amount	Actual Computation	Actual Amount
Sales	10,000 units × $17 per unit	$170,000	11,000 units × $16 per unit	$176,000
Variable costs	10,000 units × $10 per unit	(100,000)	11,000 units × $10 per unit	(110,000)
Contribution margin		$ 70,000		$ 66,000
Fixed costs		(50,000)		(50,000)
Operating income		$ 20,000		$ 16,000
Unit contribution margins	$70,000 ÷ 10,000 units	$7	$66,000 ÷ 11,000 units	$6

---

2. **Sales Variances**

   a. Although sales were greater than budgeted, the contribution margin is less than budgeted. The discrepancy can be analyzed in terms of the sales price variance and the sales volume variance.

      1) The **sales price variance** is the change in the contribution margin attributable solely to the change in selling price (holding quantity constant).

$$\text{Sales price variance} = \text{Actual units sold} \times \left(\begin{array}{c} \text{Actual selling} \\ \text{price per unit} \end{array} - \begin{array}{c} \text{Budgeted selling} \\ \text{price per unit} \end{array} \right)$$

      2) In the example, the actual selling price of $16 per unit is $1 less than expected. Thus, the sales price variance is $11,000 U (11,000 actual units sold × $1).

   b. The **sales volume variance** is the change in the contribution margin attributable solely to the difference between the actual and budgeted unit sales (holding price constant).

$$\text{Sales volume variance} = \begin{array}{c} \text{Budgeted contribution} \\ \text{margin per unit} \end{array} \times \left(\begin{array}{c} \text{Actual units} \\ \text{sold} \end{array} - \begin{array}{c} \text{Budgeted units} \\ \text{sold} \end{array} \right)$$

      1) In the example, it equals $7,000 F [$7 × (11,000 − 10,000)].

   c. The sales price variance ($11,000 U) plus the sales volume variance ($7,000 F) equals the total change in the contribution margin ($4,000 U).

Stop and review! You have completed the outline for this subunit. Study multiple-choice question 29 on page 551.

QUESTIONS

20.1 Process Costing -- Principles

1. Purchased direct materials are added in the second department of a three-department process. This addition does **not** increase the number of units produced in the second department and will

A. Not change the dollar amount transferred to the next department.

B. Decrease total ending work-in-process inventory.

C. Increase the factory overhead portion of the ending work-in-process inventory.

D. Increase total unit cost.

Answer (D) is correct.

REQUIRED: The effect of adding direct materials in a subsequent department given constant production.

DISCUSSION: Adding materials to a production process without changing the number of units produced increases the unit cost. The numerator (total cost) increases while the denominator (total units) remains the same.

Answer (A) is incorrect. If purchased materials are added to the process, the cost will be added to the total cost transferred to the next department. Answer (B) is incorrect. The unit cost, and therefore the cost of EWIP, increases when materials are added. Answer (C) is incorrect. Materials cost is separate from overhead.

2. The units transferred in from the first department to the second department should be included in the computation of the equivalent units for the second department under which of the following methods of process costing?

	FIFO	Weighted-Average
A.	Yes	Yes
B.	Yes	No
C.	No	Yes
D.	No	No

Answer (A) is correct.

REQUIRED: The cost flow method(s) that include(s) transferred-in costs in EUP calculations.

DISCUSSION: The units transferred from the first to the second department should be included in the computation of equivalent units for the second department regardless of the cost flow assumption used. The transferred-in units are considered raw materials added at the beginning of the period.

Answer (B) is incorrect. Units transferred in also should be included in the EUP computation under the weighted-average method. Answer (C) is incorrect. Units transferred in also should be included in the EUP computation under the FIFO method. Answer (D) is incorrect. Units transferred in should be included in the EUP computation under both methods.

3. Assuming no beginning work-in-process (BWIP) inventory, and that the ending work-in-process (EWIP) inventory is 50% complete as to conversion costs, the number of equivalent units as to conversion costs would be

A. The same as the units completed.

B. The same as the units placed in process.

C. Less than the units completed.

D. Less than the units placed in process.

Answer (D) is correct.

REQUIRED: The number of EUP as to conversion costs.

DISCUSSION: Given no BWIP, it is immaterial whether FIFO or weighted average is used. Thus, conversion cost EUP equal the units that were started and completed this period plus the EUP in EWIP. Because the units in EWIP are 50% complete as to conversion costs, they will not be fully counted for purposes of determining EUP.

Answer (A) is incorrect. Given no BWIP, the only units completed were those started in the current period. Total EUP include these units plus the EUP in EWIP. Answer (B) is incorrect. Given no BWIP, conversion cost EUP would equal units started if there were no EWIP. Answer (C) is incorrect. Conversion cost EUP include units completed plus work in EWIP.

4. Assuming no beginning work-in-process inventory, and that the ending work-in-process inventory is 100% complete as to materials costs, the number of equivalent units as to materials costs is

A. The same as the units placed in process.

B. The same as the units completed.

C. Less than the units placed in process.

D. Less than the units completed.

Answer (A) is correct.

REQUIRED: The number of EUP as to materials costs.

DISCUSSION: Given no BWIP, whether FIFO or weighted average is used is immaterial. Because EWIP is 100% complete as to materials costs, the EUP for materials costs are equal to the number of units placed in process (units in EWIP + units transferred to finished goods).

Answer (B) is incorrect. The number of equivalent units is equal to the units completed only if there is no EWIP. Answer (C) is incorrect. The number of equivalent units is less than the units placed in process when EWIP is less than 100% complete as to materials costs. Answer (D) is incorrect. The EUP must at least equal the number of units completed.

20.2 Process Costing -- Calculations

Questions 5 and 6 are based on the following information. A sporting goods manufacturer buys wood as a direct material for baseball bats. The Forming Department processes the baseball bats, and the bats are then transferred to the Finishing Department, where a sealant is applied. The Forming Department began manufacturing 10,000 "Casey Sluggers" during the month of May. There was no beginning inventory. Costs for the Forming Department for the month of May were as follows:

Direct materials	$33,000
Conversion costs	17,000
Total	$50,000

A total of 8,000 bats were completed and transferred to the Finishing Department; the remaining 2,000 bats were still in the forming process at the end of the month. All of the Forming Department's direct materials were placed in process, but, on average, only 25% of the conversion cost was applied to the ending work-in-process inventory.

5. The cost of the units transferred to the Finishing Department is

A. $50,000

B. $40,000

C. $53,000

D. $42,400

Answer (D) is correct.
    REQUIRED: The cost of the units transferred to the Finishing Department.
    DISCUSSION: The total equivalent units for materials equals 10,000 because all materials for the ending work-in-process had already been added to production. Hence, the materials cost per unit was $3.30 ($33,000 ÷ 10,000). For conversion costs, the total equivalent units equals 8,500 [8,000 completed + (2,000 in EWIP × 25%)]. Thus, the conversion cost was $2.00 per unit ($17,000 ÷ 8,500). The total cost transferred was therefore $42,400 [8,000 units × ($3.30 + $2.00)].
    Answer (A) is incorrect. A portion of the total costs is still in work-in-process. Answer (B) is incorrect. The amount of $40,000 assumes that work-in-process is 100% complete as to conversion costs. Answer (C) is incorrect. The amount of $53,000 exceeds the actual costs incurred during the period. Given no beginning inventory, the amount transferred out cannot exceed the costs incurred during the period.

6. The cost of the work-in-process inventory in the Forming Department at the end of May is

A. $10,000

B. $2,500

C. $20,000

D. $7,600

Answer (D) is correct.
    REQUIRED: The cost of the work-in-process inventory.
    DISCUSSION: The equivalent units for materials equal 10,000 (8,000 + 2,000) because the work-in-process is 100% complete as to materials. Thus, dividing the $33,000 by 10,000 units results in a unit cost for materials of $3.30. The equivalent units for conversion costs equal 8,500 units [8,000 + (2,000 units × .25)]. Dividing the $17,000 of conversion costs by 8,500 equivalent units results in a unit cost of $2 per bat, and the total cost of goods transferred out is $5.30, consisting of $3.30 for materials and $2 for conversion costs. Multiplying $5.30 by the 8,000 bats completed results in a total transfer of $42,400. Consequently, the cost of the ending work-in-process must have been $7,600 ($50,000 total costs incurred – $42,400).
    Answer (A) is incorrect. The amount of $10,000 assumes that work-in-process inventory is 100% complete as to conversion costs. Answer (B) is incorrect. The amount of $2,500 assumes that work-in-process inventory is 100% complete as to conversion costs and that 500 bats are in inventory. Answer (C) is incorrect. The amount of $20,000 assumes that work-in-process is 100% complete as to conversion costs and that 6,000 units were transferred out.

7. A company employs a process cost system using the first-in, first-out (FIFO) method. The product passes through both Department 1 and Department 2 in order to be completed. Units enter Department 2 upon completion in Department 1. Additional direct materials are added in Department 2 when the units have reached the 25% stage of completion with respect to conversion costs. Conversion costs are added proportionally in Department 2. The production activity in Department 2 for the current month was as follows:

Beginning work-in-process inventory (40% complete with respect to conversion costs)	15,000
Units transferred in from Department 1	80,000
Units completed and transferred to finished goods	85,000
Ending work-in-process inventory (20% complete with respect to conversion costs)	10,000

How many equivalent units for direct materials were added in Department 2 for the current month?

- A. 70,000 units.
- B. 80,000 units.
- C. 85,000 units.
- D. 90,000 units.

Answer (A) is correct.
REQUIRED: The equivalent units for direct materials added in Department 2 for the current month.
DISCUSSION: Beginning inventory is 40% complete. Hence, direct materials have already been added. Ending inventory has not reached the 25% stage of completion, so direct materials have not yet been added to these units. Thus, the equivalent units for direct materials calculated on a FIFO basis are equal to the units started and completed in the current period (85,000 units completed – 15,000 units in BWIP = 70,000 units started and completed).
Answer (B) is incorrect. The amount transferred in from Department 1 was 80,000 total units. Answer (C) is incorrect. The equivalent units for direct materials calculated on a weighted-average basis equals 85,000. Answer (D) is incorrect. The sum of units transferred in from Department 1 and ending work-in-process inventory equals 90,000 units.

8. A company manufactures a product that passes through two production departments: molding and assembly. Direct materials are added in the assembly department when conversion is 50% complete. Conversion costs are incurred uniformly. The activity in units for the assembly department during April is as follows:

	Units
Work-in-process inventory, April 1 (60% complete as to conversion costs)	5,000
Transferred in from molding department	32,000
Defective at final inspection (within normal limits)	2,500
Transferred out to finished goods inventory	28,500
Work-in-process inventory, April 30 (40% complete as to conversion costs)	6,000

The number of equivalent units for direct materials in the assembly department for April calculated on the weighted-average basis is

- A. 26,000 units.
- B. 28,500 units.
- C. 31,000 units.
- D. 34,000 units.

Answer (C) is correct.
REQUIRED: The equivalent units for direct materials on the weighted-average basis.
DISCUSSION: The weighted-average approach averages the costs in beginning work-in-process with those incurred during the period. Accordingly, the degree of completion of the BWIP is ignored in computing the equivalent units for direct materials. Direct materials equivalent units therefore consist of units transferred to finished goods (28,500) and units that failed inspection (2,500), or 31,000. Ending work-in-process inventory has not reached the point at which materials are added.
Answer (A) is incorrect. The number of direct materials equivalent units calculated using the FIFO method is 26,000 (31,000 weighted-average EUP – 5,000 EUP in BWIP). Answer (B) is incorrect. The number of units transferred out to finished goods inventory is 28,500. Answer (D) is incorrect. The number of physical units minus the conversion work previously done on the BWIP is 34,000 [5,000 units in BWIP + 32,000 units transferred in – (5,000 units in BWIP × 60%)].

9. The following data pertain to a company's cracking-department operations in December:

	Units	Completion
Work-in-process, December 1	20,000	50%
Units started	170,000	
Units completed and transferred to the distilling department	180,000	
Work-in-process, December 31	10,000	50%

Materials are added at the beginning of the process, and conversion costs are incurred uniformly throughout the process. Assuming use of the FIFO method of process costing, the equivalent units of production (EUP) with respect to conversion performed during December were

A. 170,000

B. 175,000

C. 180,000

D. 185,000

Answer (B) is correct.
    REQUIRED: The equivalent units of conversion.
    DISCUSSION: Under the FIFO method, equivalent units are determined based only on work performed during the current period. Thus, units in beginning work-in-process must be backed out.

	Conversion
Units transferred out	180,000
Add: EWIP (10,000 × 50%)	5,000
Total completed units	185,000
Less: BWIP (20,000 × 50%)	(10,000)
Equivalent units of production	175,000

    Answer (A) is incorrect. The number of equivalent units of materials for the period is 170,000. Answer (C) is incorrect. The total amount of work done on the completed units is 180,000. Answer (D) is incorrect. The amount determined using the weighted-average method is 185,000.

10. A company uses weighted-average process costing for the product it manufactures. All direct materials are added at the beginning of production, and conversion costs are applied evenly during production. The following data apply to the past month:

Total units in beginning inventory (30% complete as to conversion costs)	1,500
Total units transferred to finished goods inventory	7,400
Total units in ending inventory (60% complete as to conversion costs)	2,300

Assuming no spoilage, equivalent units of production (EUP) with respect to conversion costs total

A. 8,330

B. 8,780

C. 9,230

D. 9,700

Answer (B) is correct.
    REQUIRED: The equivalent units of production for conversion costs.
    DISCUSSION: The weighted-average method averages the work performed in the prior period with the work done in the current period. Thus, beginning work-in-process is left in the calculation (unlike FIFO).

	Conversion
Units transferred out	7,400
Add: EWIP (2,300 × 60%)	1,380
Equivalent units of production	8,780

    Answer (A) is incorrect. The EUP for conversion costs would be 8,330 [8,780 weighted-average EUP − (1,500 units in BWIP × 30%)] if the FIFO method were used. Answer (C) is incorrect. Including 30% of BWIP in the total results in 9,230. Answer (D) is incorrect. The sum of the physical, not equivalent, units completed and in EWIP is 9,700.

20.3 Activity-Based Costing (ABC)

11. A company is considering the implementation of an activity-based costing and management program. The company

A. Should focus on manufacturing activities and avoid implementation with service-type functions.

B. Would probably find a lack of software in the marketplace to assist with the related recordkeeping.

C. Would normally gain added insights into causes of cost.

D. Would likely use fewer cost pools than it did under more traditional accounting methods.

Answer (C) is correct.
    REQUIRED: The most likely result of an ABC and ABM program.
    DISCUSSION: One of the benefits of activity-based costing is the discovery of cost relationships that went unnoticed under traditional accounting methods.
    Answer (A) is incorrect. Activity-based costing is suitable for service-type functions. Answer (B) is incorrect. Software exists to help firms implement activity-based management. Answer (D) is incorrect. Activity-based costing generally results in many more cost pools than under traditional accounting methods.

12. All of the following are likely to be used as a cost allocation base in activity-based costing **except** the

A. Number of different materials used to manufacture the product.

B. Units of materials used to manufacture the product.

C. Number of vendors supplying the materials used to manufacture the product.

D. Cost of materials used to manufacture the product.

Answer (D) is correct.
REQUIRED: The item not an appropriate allocation base in activity-based costing.
DISCUSSION: Activity-based costing is founded on the idea that drivers for indirect cost assignment should be based on some level of activity. Cost of materials does not directly reflect a level of a given activity.
Answer (A) is incorrect. The number of different materials used to manufacture a product can be a cost driver. Different materials often require different setups and thus a proportional amount of employee time. Answer (B) is incorrect. The units of materials used to manufacture a product can be a cost driver. Units of material used directly reflects the amount of employee time spent on the production process. Answer (C) is incorrect. The number of vendors supplying the materials used to manufacture the product can be a cost driver. Each supplier requires servicing by buyers and other personnel, and thus the number of suppliers directly reflects the level of production activity.

13. Pelder Products Company manufactures two types of engineering diagnostic equipment used in construction. The two products are based on different technologies, x-ray and ultrasound, but are manufactured in the same factory. Pelder has computed the manufacturing cost of the x-ray and ultrasound products by adding together direct materials, direct labor, and overhead cost applied based on the number of direct labor hours. The factory has three overhead departments that support the single production line that makes both products. Budgeted overhead spending for the departments is as follows:

Department			
Engineering design	Material handling	Setup	Total
$6,000	$5,000	$3,000	$14,000

Pelder's budgeted manufacturing activities and costs for the period are as follows:

	Product	
Activity	X-Ray	Ultrasound
Units produced and sold	50	100
Direct materials used	$5,000	$8,000
Direct labor hours used	100	300
Direct labor cost	$4,000	$12,000
Number of parts used	400	600
Number of engineering changes	2	1
Number of product setups	8	7

The budgeted cost to manufacture one ultrasound machine using the activity-based costing method is

A. $225

B. $264

C. $293

D. $305

Answer (B) is correct.
REQUIRED: The ABC cost of a single ultrasound machine.
DISCUSSION: Charges for direct materials and direct labor are traceable to each type of machine ($8,000 and $12,000 respectively for the ultrasound). The departmental costs must be allocated based on each machine's proportional driver level. Engineering design costs can be allocated to the ultrasound machine at a rate of 33.3% [1 ÷ (1 + 2)], material handling at a rate of 60% [600 ÷ (600 + 400)], and setup at a rate of 46.7% [7 ÷ (7 + 8)]. Pelder's cost for a single ultrasound machine can thus be calculated as follows:

	For 100 Units
Direct materials ($8,000)	$ 80
Direct labor ($12,000)	120
Engineering changes ($6,000 × 33.3%)	20
Material handling ($5,000 × 60%)	30
Setup ($3,000 × 46.7%)	14
Total	$264

Answer (A) is incorrect. The amount of $225 results from using x-ray direct labor rather than ultrasound direct labor. Answer (C) is incorrect. The amount of $293 results from improperly using the units of production to allocate the engineering, handling, and setup costs. Answer (D) is incorrect. The amount of $305 results from improperly using direct labor hours to allocate the engineering, handling, and setup costs.

14. The Chocolate Baker specializes in chocolate baked goods. The firm has long assessed the profitability of a product line by comparing revenues to the cost of goods sold. However, Barry White, the firm's new accountant, wants to use an activity-based costing system that takes into consideration the cost of the delivery person. Listed below are activity and cost information relating to two of Chocolate Baker's major products.

	Muffins	Cheesecake
Revenue	$53,000	$46,000
Cost of goods sold	26,000	21,000
Delivery activity:		
Number of deliveries	150	85
Average length of delivery	10 minutes	15 minutes
Cost per hour for delivery	$20.00	$20.00

Using activity-based costing, which one of the following statements is correct?

A. The muffins are $2,000 more profitable.

B. The cheesecakes are $75 more profitable.

C. The muffins are $1,925 more profitable.

D. The muffins have a higher profitability as a percentage of sales and therefore are more advantageous.

Answer (C) is correct.

    REQUIRED: The true statement given activity-based costing.

    DISCUSSION: White's first step is to calculate the gross margin on the two products:

	Muffins	Cheesecake
Revenues	$53,000	$46,000
Cost of goods sold	(26,000)	(21,000)
Gross margin	$27,000	$25,000

The next step is to calculate total delivery cost for each product:

	Muffins	Cheesecake
Number of deliveries	150	85
Times: minutes per delivery	× 10	× 15
Total delivery minutes	1,500	1,275
Divided by: minutes per hour	÷ 60	÷ 60
Total delivery hours	25.00	21.25
Times: delivery cost per hour	× $20	× $20
Total delivery cost	$500	$425

The operating profits on these two products, and the difference between them, can now be determined:

Muffins	($27,000 – $500)	$26,500
Cheesecake	($25,000 – $425)	(24,575)
Excess		$ 1,925

    Answer (A) is incorrect. Muffins exceed cheesecake by $2,000 only at the gross margin, not the total profitability, level. Answer (B) is incorrect. The total delivery cost for muffins exceeds that of cheesecake by $75. Answer (D) is incorrect. Muffins ($26,500 ÷ $53,000 = 50.0%) have a lower profitability percentage than cheesecake ($24,575 ÷ $46,000 = 53.4%).

15. Cost allocation is the process of assigning indirect costs to a cost object. The indirect costs are grouped in cost pools and then allocated by a common allocation base to the cost object. The base that is employed to allocate a homogeneous cost pool should

A. Have a cause-and-effect relationship with the cost items in the cost pool.

B. Assign the costs in the pool uniformly to cost objects even if the cost objects use resources in a nonuniform way.

C. Be a nonfinancial measure (e.g., number of setups) because a nonfinancial measure is more objective.

D. Have a high correlation with the cost items in the cost pool as the sole criterion for selection.

Answer (A) is correct.

    REQUIRED: The characteristic of a base used to allocate a homogeneous cost pool.

    DISCUSSION: A cost allocation base is the common denominator for systematically correlating indirect costs and a cost object. The cost driver of the indirect costs is ordinarily the allocation base. In a homogeneous cost pool, all costs should have the same or a similar cause-and-effect relationship with the cost allocation base.

    Answer (B) is incorrect. If an allocation base uniformly assigns costs to cost objects when the cost objects use resources in a nonuniform way, the base is smoothing or spreading the costs. Smoothing can result in undercosting or overcosting of products, with adverse effects on product pricing, cost management and control, and decision making. Answer (C) is incorrect. Financial measures (e.g., sales dollars and direct labor costs) and nonfinancial measures (e.g., setups and units shipped) can be used as allocation bases. Answer (D) is incorrect. High correlation between the cost items in a pool and the allocation base does not necessarily mean that a cause-and-effect relationship exists. Two variables may move together without such a relationship. The perceived relationship between the cost driver (allocation base) and the indirect costs should have economic plausibility and high correlation.

16. A company with three products classifies its costs as belonging to five functions: design, production, marketing, distribution, and customer services. For pricing purposes, all company costs are assigned to the three products. The direct costs of each of the five functions are traced directly to the three products. The indirect costs of each of the five business functions are collected into five separate cost pools and then assigned to the three products using appropriate allocation bases. The allocation base that will most likely be the best for allocating the indirect costs of the distribution function is

A. Number of customer phone calls.

B. Number of shipments.

C. Number of sales persons.

D. Dollar sales volume.

Answer (B) is correct.
   REQUIRED: The allocation base that will most likely be the best for allocating the indirect costs of the distribution function.
   DISCUSSION: The number of shipments is an appropriate cost driver. A cause-and-effect relationship may exist between the number of shipments and distribution costs.
   Answer (A) is incorrect. The number of customer phone calls has little relation to distribution. It is probably more closely related to customer service. Answer (C) is incorrect. The number of sales persons is not related to distribution. It is more closely related to marketing. Answer (D) is incorrect. The dollar sales volume is not necessarily related to distribution. It is more likely related to marketing.

20.4 Variance Analysis -- Materials and Labor

17. In a standard cost system, the materials price variance is obtained by multiplying the

A. Actual price by the difference between actual quantity used and standard quantity used.

B. Actual quantity used by the difference between standard price and actual price.

C. Standard price by the difference between expected quantity and budgeted quantity.

D. Actual quantity purchased by the difference between actual price and standard price.

Answer (B) is correct.
   REQUIRED: The method used to compute the materials price variance.
   DISCUSSION: The materials price variance is that portion of the flexible budget variance attributable entirely to a difference in input unit cost. It is calculated by multiplying the actual quantity used by the difference between standard price and actual price [AQ × (SP – AP)].
   Answer (A) is incorrect. The product of actual price and the difference between actual quantity used and standard quantity used is not a defined variance. Answer (C) is incorrect. The product of standard price and the difference between expected quantity and budgeted quantity is the sales volume variance. Answer (D) is incorrect. The product of actual quantity purchased and the difference between actual price and standard price is the purchase price variance.

18. The standard unit cost is used in the calculation of which of the following variances?

	Materials Price Variance	Materials Usage Variance
A.	No	No
B.	No	Yes
C.	Yes	No
D.	Yes	Yes

Answer (D) is correct.
   REQUIRED: The variance(s) using standard unit costs.
   DISCUSSION: The materials price variance is calculated by multiplying the actual quantity of units used by the difference between actual price and standard price. The materials usage variance is calculated by multiplying the difference between the expected quantity of units (the actual level of output times the standard number of inputs per unit of output) and the actual quantity of units consumed times standard price. Thus, the standard unit cost is used to compute both the materials price variance and the materials usage variance.
   Answer (A) is incorrect. Standard unit cost is used in the calculation of materials price variances and materials usage variances. Answer (B) is incorrect. Standard unit cost also is used in the calculation of the materials price variance. Answer (C) is incorrect. Standard unit cost also is used in the calculation of the materials usage variance.

19. Which of the following unfavorable variances is directly affected by the relative position of a production process on a learning curve?

A. Materials mix.

B. Materials price.

C. Labor rate.

D. Labor efficiency.

Answer (D) is correct.
   REQUIRED: The variance affected by the learning curve.
   DISCUSSION: The efficiency of the employees varies with how long they have been performing the particular task. Thus, more experienced employees are expected to be more efficient, which affects the labor efficiency variance.
   Answer (A) is incorrect. The learning curve has little correlation with materials mix variances. Answer (B) is incorrect. A materials price variance is primarily the result of external factors. Answer (C) is incorrect. The labor rate variance should not be affected by the learning curve.

20. The difference between the actual labor rate multiplied by the actual hours worked and the standard labor rate multiplied by the standard labor hours is the

A. Total labor variance.

B. Labor rate variance.

C. Labor usage variance.

D. Labor efficiency variance.

Answer (A) is correct.

REQUIRED: The variance defined by the difference between total actual labor costs and total standard costs allowed.

DISCUSSION: The total actual labor cost equals the actual labor rate times the actual labor hours. The total standard cost for good output equals the standard rate times the standard hours allowed. The total labor rate variance is the difference between the total actual labor costs and the total standard labor costs.

Answer (B) is incorrect. The labor rate variance is AQ × (SP – AP). Answer (C) is incorrect. The labor usage variance is (SQ – AQ) × SP. Answer (D) is incorrect. The labor efficiency variance is the same as the labor usage variance: (SQ – AQ) × SP.

21. Information on Hanley's direct labor costs for the month of January is as follows:

Actual direct labor rate	$7.50
Standard direct labor hours allowed	11,000
Actual direct labor hours	10,000
Direct labor rate variance -- favorable	$5,500

The standard direct labor rate in January was

A. $6.95

B. $7.00

C. $8.00

D. $8.05

Answer (D) is correct.

REQUIRED: The standard direct labor rate for the month.

DISCUSSION: The labor rate variance, actual hours, and actual rate are given. Thus, the standard rate can be derived by substituting into the following formula:

$$
\begin{aligned}
AQ \times (SP - AP) &= \text{Labor rate variance} \\
10,000 \times (SP - \$7.50) &= \$5,500 \text{ F} \\
10,000SP - \$75,000 &= \$5,500 \\
10,000SP &= \$80,500 \\
SP &= \$8.05
\end{aligned}
$$

Answer (A) is incorrect. The amount of $6.95 treats the $.55 variance per unit as unfavorable. Answer (B) is incorrect. Actual hours, not standard hours, are used to determine the standard rate. Furthermore, the favorable variance should be added, not subtracted, in calculating the standard rate. Answer (C) is incorrect. Actual hours, not standard hours, should be used in determining the standard rate.

22. Relevant information for material A follows:

Quantity purchased	6,500 lbs.
Standard quantity allowed	6,000 lbs.
Actual price	$3.80
Standard price	$4.00

What was the direct materials price variance for material A?

A. $1,300 favorable.

B. $1,200 favorable.

C. $1,200 unfavorable.

D. $1,300 unfavorable.

Answer (A) is correct.

REQUIRED: The direct materials price variance.

DISCUSSION: The materials price variance is the difference between the actual price of materials and the standard price.

$$
\begin{aligned}
\text{Materials price variance} &= AQ \times (SP - AP) \\
&= 6,500 \text{ pounds purchased} \times \\
&\quad (\$4.00 - \$3.80) \\
&= 6,500 \text{ pounds purchased} \times \$0.20 \\
&= \$1,300 \text{ favorable}
\end{aligned}
$$

Answer (B) is incorrect. The amount of $1,200 favorable results from using standard quantity rather than actual quantity. Answer (C) is incorrect. The amount of $1,200 unfavorable results from using standard quantity rather than actual quantity and reversing the order of subtraction. Answer (D) is incorrect. The amount of $1,300 unfavorable results from reversing the proper order of subtraction.

20.5 Variance Analysis -- Overhead

23. Which of the following standard costing variances would be **least** controllable by a production supervisor?

A. Overhead volume.

B. Overhead efficiency.

C. Labor efficiency.

D. Material usage.

Answer (A) is correct.

REQUIRED: The variance least controllable by a production supervisor.

DISCUSSION: The overhead volume variance measures the difference between the amount of fixed overhead applied and the amount of fixed overhead actually incurred. Thus, the overhead volume variance does not depend on the actual level of production during the current period.

Answer (B) is incorrect. The overhead efficiency variance is wholly attributable to variable overhead. Answer (C) is incorrect. The efficiency of employees affects the labor efficiency variance. Answer (D) is incorrect. The material usage variance is typically influenced most by activities within the production department.

24. The following information pertains to Roe Co.'s manufacturing operations for the month just ended:

Standard direct labor hours per unit	2
Actual direct labor hours	10,500
Number of units produced	5,000
Standard variable overhead per standard direct labor hour	$3
Actual variable overhead	$28,000

Roe's unfavorable variable overhead efficiency variance was

A. $0

B. $1,500

C. $2,000

D. $3,500

Answer (B) is correct.
    REQUIRED: The amount of unfavorable variable overhead efficiency variance.
    DISCUSSION: The variable overhead efficiency variance measures the efficiency with which the allocation base was used (holding the application rate constant). It equals the difference between the amount applied and the product of the actual number of units of the overhead cost driver consumed and the application rate. The expected quantity EQ equals the standard hours for the production achieved (5,000 units × hours per unit = 10,000 hours).

Variable overhead
    efficiency variance = (EQ – AQ) × SP
            = (10,000 hours – 10,500 hours) × $3
            = –500 × $3
            = $1,500 unfavorable

    Answer (A) is incorrect. Roe incurred an unfavorable variable overhead efficiency variance. Answer (C) is incorrect. The total overapplied variable overhead is $2,000. Answer (D) is incorrect. The variable overhead spending variance is $3,500 favorable.

25. During the month just ended, a department's fixed overhead standard costing system reported unfavorable spending and volume variances. The activity level selected for allocating overhead to the product was based on 80% of practical capacity. If 100% of practical capacity had been selected instead, how would the reported unfavorable spending and volume variances be affected?

	Spending Variance	Volume Variance
A.	Increased	Unchanged
B.	Increased	Increased
C.	Unchanged	Increased
D.	Unchanged	Unchanged

Answer (C) is correct.
    REQUIRED: The effects on unfavorable spending and volume variances of increasing the budgeted activity level.
    DISCUSSION: The fixed overhead spending variance equals the actual costs incurred minus the budgeted amount. Thus, the spending variance is not affected by the denominator level of the overhead application driver. However, the volume variance equals the budgeted amount minus amount applied. Because the fixed overhead applied depends on the activity level of the driver used for application, a change in the denominator affects the volume variance. If the denominator increases, the application rate and the amount applied decrease, causing the variance to increase.

26. Baby Frames, Inc., evaluates manufacturing overhead in its factory by using variance analysis. The following information applies to the month of May:

	Actual	Budgeted
Number of frames manufactured	19,000	20,000
Variable overhead costs	$4,100	$2 per direct labor hour
Fixed overhead costs	$22,000	$20,000
Direct labor hours	2,100 hours	0.1 hour per frame

What is the fixed overhead spending variance?

A. $1,000 favorable.

B. $1,000 unfavorable.

C. $2,000 favorable.

D. $2,000 unfavorable.

Answer (D) is correct.
    REQUIRED: The fixed overhead spending variance.
    DISCUSSION: The fixed overhead spending variance is the difference between the amount budgeted for fixed manufacturing overhead costs and the actual costs incurred. The fixed overhead spending variance is thus $2,000 unfavorable ($20,000 budgeted – $22,000 actual).
    Answer (A) is incorrect. The fixed overhead spending variance is unfavorable. Answer (B) is incorrect. The fixed overhead spending variance is $2,000. Answer (C) is incorrect. Actual costs exceed budgeted costs, causing the $2,000 variance to be unfavorable.

27. Which of the following variances would be useful in calling attention to a possible short-term problem in the control of overhead costs?

	Spending Variance	Volume Variance
A.	No	No
B.	No	Yes
C.	Yes	No
D.	Yes	Yes

Answer (C) is correct.
REQUIRED: The variance(s) useful for controlling overhead costs.
DISCUSSION: The volume variance is the difference between fixed overhead applied and fixed overhead budgeted. Thus, the volume variance has no relation to cost control because the amount of fixed costs is constant. The variance results only from a change in the level of the application base. However, the spending variance is simply a price variance for factory overhead. Consequently, it is the spending variance, not the volume variance, that is useful in detecting problems in the control of overhead costs.
Answer (A) is incorrect. The spending variance is a price variance. Answer (B) is incorrect. The spending variance, not the volume variance, is useful for calling attention to a possible short-term problem in the control of overhead costs. Answer (D) is incorrect. The volume variance does not indicate whether problems exist in the control of costs.

28. Jones, a department manager, exercises control over the department's costs. The following is selected information relating to the department for July:

Variable factory overhead

Budgeted based on standard hours allowed	$80,000
Actual	85,000

Fixed factory overhead

Budgeted	25,000
Actual	27,000

In a three-way analysis of variance, the department's unfavorable spending variance for July was

A. $7,000

B. $5,000

C. $2,000

D. $0

Answer (A) is correct.
REQUIRED: The amount of unfavorable spending variance.
DISCUSSION: In three-way analysis, the spending variance is the sum of the variable overhead spending variance and the fixed overhead spending variance. The variable overhead spending variance equals the actual number of units of the overhead driver consumed times the application rate minus the amount actually incurred ($80,000 – $85,000 = $5,000 unfavorable). The fixed overhead spending variance equals the budgeted amount minus the actual amount incurred ($25,000 – $27,000 = $2,000 unfavorable). The department's total unfavorable spending variance for July is thus $7,000 ($5,000 + $2,000).
Answer (B) is incorrect. The variable overhead spending variance is $5,000. Answer (C) is incorrect. The fixed overhead spending variance is $2,000. Answer (D) is incorrect. The department incurred an unfavorable spending variance for the month.

20.6 Sales Variances

29. The following data are available for July:

	Budget	Actual
Sales	40,000 units	42,000 units
Selling price	$6 per unit	$5.70 per unit
Variable cost	$3.50 per unit	$3.40 per unit

What is the sales volume variance for July?

A. $5,000 favorable.

B. $4,600 favorable.

C. $12,000 unfavorable.

D. $12,600 unfavorable.

Answer (A) is correct.
REQUIRED: The sales volume variance for a particular month.
DISCUSSION: The sales volume variance is the difference between the actual volume and the budgeted volume in units, times the budgeted contribution margin per unit.

= (Actual Volume – Budgeted Volume) ×
    (Selling Price – Unit Variable Cost)
= (42,000 – 40,000) × ($6 – $3.50)
= $5,000 F

Answer (B) is incorrect. The budgeted selling price and budgeted variable cost must be used to determine the sales volume variance, not the actual selling price and actual variable cost. Answer (C) is incorrect. The budgeted variable cost must be subtracted from the selling price before multiplying by the 2,000 difference in units actually sold from budgeted sales. Answer (D) is incorrect. The sales volume variance is found by multiplying the 2,000 unit difference between actual and budgeted sales by the $2.50 budgeted contribution margin.

20.7 PRACTICE WRITTEN COMMUNICATION TASK

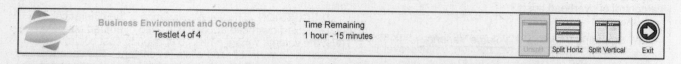

Business Environment and Concepts
Testlet 4 of 4

Time Remaining
1 hour - 15 minutes

Unsplit   Split Horiz   Split Vertical   Exit

DIRECTIONS

Note: If you believe you have encountered a software malfunction, report it to the test center staff immediately.

Navigation

To navigate from task to task, use the controls at the bottom of the screen. Click on the **Next** button to advance to the next task, or the **Previous** button to go to the previous task. To go directly to any task, click on its number.

⚑ = Reminder   Directions | 1 | 2 | 3 | 4 | 5 | 6 | 7 | ◀ Previous   Next ▶

If you would like a reminder to revisit a task, or want to indicate that you are finished with it, click on the reminder flag below the task number. To clear the flag, click on it again. Reminder flags are for your use only – they do not contribute to your score.

Tabs

In this part of the examination, you will be asked to complete various tasks. Every task has one or more **Work Tabs**. Every task also has a **Help** tab.

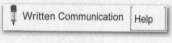

✏ Written Communication   Help

Work tab   Help tab

Work Tabs:

- **Work Tabs** are identified with a pencil icon. This is where your responses are expected.
- Each task has one or more **Work Tabs**.
- **Work Tabs** contain directions for completing the task - be sure to read these directions carefully.
- The **Work Tab** name in the example above is for illustration only - yours will differ.
- You must complete all of the **Work Tabs** in each task to receive full credit.

Help Tab:

- The **Help Tab** provides assistance with the exam software that is used in this task. For example, if the task is to compose a memorandum, **Help** will provide information about the word processor.

The Toolbar

The toolbar at the top of the screen shows the amount of time remaining for you to complete the tasks. In addition, the following tools are available. Note that only the **Exit** button is displayed when Directions are visible - the others will appear when you begin the tasks.

Unsplit   Split Horiz   Split Vertical

Click on these buttons to split or unsplit the screen.   You can split the screen vertically or horizontally.

Exit

Click on this button to go on to the next part of the examination. You must complete all of the tasks to receive full credit. Once you click on **Exit** and confirm the action, you will NOT be able to return to this testlet.

⚑ = Reminder   Directions | 1 | ◀ Previous   Next ▶

Jayhawk Aircraft Corporation currently uses a process costing system. The CFO argues that Jayhawk has a factory line process. After some investigation, you discover that avionics and GPS systems in each aircraft are different.

Prepare a memo to the CFO of Jayhawk Aircraft Corporation explaining the differences between process costing and job-order costing and why job-order costing would be better in Jayhawk's situation.

Type your communication below the line in the response area below.

REMINDER: Your response will be graded for both technical content and writing skills. Technical content will be evaluated for information that is helpful to the intended reader and clearly relevant to the issue. Writing skills will be evaluated for development, organization, and the appropriate expression of ideas in professional correspondence. Use a standard business memorandum or letter format with a clear beginning, middle, and end. Do not convey information in the form of a table, bullet point list, or other abbreviated presentation.

To: CFO, Jayhawk Aircraft Corporation
Re: Differences between process costing and job-order costing

Unofficial Answer

Written Communication

To: CFO, Jayhawk Aircraft Corporation
Re: Differences between process costing and job-order costing

---

Although Jayhawk currently uses a process costing system, its business would be better served by a job-order costing system. Each product produced by the company requires different specifications. Process costing and job-order costing are substantially different, and their differences must be understood before concluding that Jayhawk would be better served by a job-order system.

Cost measurement has two prominent types: job-order and process costing systems. Process costing assigns costs to inventoriable goods or services. It generally applies to relatively homogeneous products that are mass produced on a continuous basis. Job-order costing accumulates costs based on a specific job (product or service) and is best used for major, discrete products, possibly requiring specialization. Each project accounted for under a job-order system has a special set of accounts. In a process-costing system, the units of output are assumed to be indistinguishable from one other, so separate accounting is not needed. In Jayhawk's case, a process costing system will place an undue burden on those required to disclose costs as accurately as possible. The reason is that the likelihood of overlooking costs is greater when discrete costs are common but appear in generalized cost accounts.

The benefit of a job-order costing system for Jayhawk's production of aircraft is that each aircraft requires a degree of specialization not provided by a process costing system. The additional bookkeeping necessary to translate the specifications is far more costly than establishing a job-order costing system that will allow for each project to be individually costed and managed.

The above depicts a Level 5 answer. See page 16 in the Introduction for a description of the three grading criteria.

Self-Grade

Evaluate each of the following by selecting a 0, 1, 2, 3, 4, or 5. An average response is 3. Use 4 for better than average and 5 for outstanding. Use 2 for less than average and 1 for quite poor. Use zero for no response, if you did not address the topic, or if you gave advice that is clearly illegal.

Organization	○ 0	○ 1	○ 2	○ 3	○ 4	○ 5
Development	○ 0	○ 1	○ 2	○ 3	○ 4	○ 5
Expression	○ 0	○ 1	○ 2	○ 3	○ 4	○ 5

Your grade for the written communication as a whole is the average of the scores for the three criteria.

Use **CPA Gleim Online** and **Simulation Wizard** to practice more written communication tasks in a realistic environment.

REVIEW CHECKLIST
BUSINESS

Your objective is to prepare to pass this section of the CPA exam. It is **not** to do a certain amount of work or spend a certain amount of time with this book or other CPA review material/courses. Rather, you **must**

1. Understand the CPA exam thoroughly -- study *CPA Review: A System for Success* and the Introduction in this book.

2. Understand the subject matter in the 20 study units in this book. The list of subunits in each of the 20 study units (presented below and on the following page) should bring to mind core concepts, basic rules, principles, etc.

3. If you have not already done so, prepare a 1- to 2-page summary of each study unit for your final review just before you go to the exam (do not bring notes into the examination room).

Study Unit 1: Corporate Governance

1.1 Roles in the Governance Hierarchy
1.2 The Internal Audit Function
1.3 The Sarbanes-Oxley Act of 2002 (SOX)
1.4 The COSO Model for Internal Control
1.5 The COSO Model for Enterprise Risk Management

Study Unit 2: Microeconomics

2.1 Demand, Supply, and Equilibrium
2.2 Elasticity
2.3 Government Intervention in the Market
2.4 Profits and Costs
2.5 Marginal Analysis
2.6 Market Structures -- Pure Competition
2.7 Market Structures -- Monopoly
2.8 Market Structures -- Monopolistic Competition
2.9 Market Structures -- Oligopoly
2.10 Resource Markets and Labor

Study Unit 3: Macroeconomics

3.1 Domestic Output -- Expenditures Approach
3.2 Domestic Output -- Income Approach
3.3 Business Cycles
3.4 Issues in Macroeconomics -- Growth
3.5 Issues in Macroeconomics -- Inflation
3.6 Issues in Macroeconomics -- Unemployment
3.7 Demand Management through Fiscal Policy
3.8 The Creation of Money
3.9 Monetary Policy

Study Unit 4: Globalization

4.1 Protectionism
4.2 Currency Exchange Rates
4.3 Mitigating Exchange Rate Risk

Study Unit 5: Financial Risk Management

5.1 Risk and Return
5.2 Quantifying Investment Risk
5.3 Capital Asset Pricing Model
5.4 Derivatives

Study Unit 6: Forecasting Analysis

6.1 Linear Regression Analysis
6.2 Correlation Analysis
6.3 Learning Curve Analysis
6.4 Expected Value
6.5 Selecting the Forecasting Technique

Study Unit 7: Corporate Capital Structure

7.1 Bonds
7.2 Equity
7.3 Leasing
7.4 Component Costs of Capital
7.5 Weighted-Average Cost of Capital

Study Unit 8: Working Capital

8.1 Working Capital Management
8.2 Liquidity Ratios -- Calculation
8.3 Liquidity Ratios -- Effects of Transactions
8.4 Cash Management
8.5 Marketable Securities Management
8.6 Receivables Management
8.7 Inventory Management -- Ratios
8.8 Inventory Management -- Techniques
8.9 The Operating Cycle and Cash Conversion Cycle
8.10 Multiple Ratio Analysis

Study Unit 9: Short-Term Financing and Capital Budgeting I

9.1 Types and Costs of Short-Term Financing
9.2 Capital Budgeting -- Basics
9.3 Capital Budgeting -- Net Present Value Theory
9.4 Capital Budgeting -- Net Present Value Calculations
9.5 Capital Budgeting -- Internal Rate of Return
9.6 Capital Budgeting -- Payback Methods

Study Unit 10: Capital Budgeting II and Corporate Performance

10.1 Ranking Capital Projects
10.2 Comparing Capital Budgeting Techniques
10.4 Return on Investment and Residual Income
10.5 Other Corporate Performance Measures
10.6 Measures of Corporate Solvency

556

INDEX

GLEIM CPA REVIEW SYSTEM

Includes: Gleim Online, Review Books, Test Prep Online, Simulation Wizard, Audio Review, Practice Exam, CPA Review: A System for Success booklet, plus bonus Book Bag.

$989.95 x _____ = $_____

Also available by exam section (does not include Book Bag).

GLEIM CMA REVIEW SYSTEM

Includes: Gleim Online, Review Books, Test Prep Software Download, Essay Wizard, Audio Review, Practice Exam, CMA Review: A System for Success booklet, plus bonus Book Bag.

$739.95 x _____ = $_____

Also available by exam part (does not include Book Bag).

GLEIM CIA REVIEW SYSTEM

Includes: Gleim Online, Review Books, Test Prep Software Download, Audio Review, Practice Exam, CIA Review: A System for Success booklet, plus bonus Book Bag.

$824.95 x _____ = $_____

Also available by exam part (does not include Book Bag).

GLEIM EA REVIEW SYSTEM

Includes: Gleim Online, Review Books, Test Prep Software Download, Audio Review, Practice Exam, EA Review: A System for Success booklet, plus bonus Book Bag.

$629.95 x _____ = $_____

Also available by exam part (does not include Book Bag).

GLEIM RTRP REVIEW SYSTEM

Includes: Gleim Online, Question Bank Online, Practice Exam, 15 hours of CE.

$139.95 x _____ = $_____

"THE GLEIM EQE SERIES" EXAM QUESTIONS AND EXPLANATIONS

Includes: 5 Books and Test Prep Software Download.

$112.25 x _____ = $_____

Also available by part.

GLEIM ONLINE CPE

Try a FREE 4-hour course at gleim.com/cpe
• Easy-to-Complete
• Informative
• Effective

Contact
GLEIM PUBLICATIONS
for further assistance:

gleim.com
800.874.5346
sales@gleim.com

SUBTOTAL $_____

Complete your order on the next page

Subject to change without notice.

GLEIM PUBLICATIONS, INC.

P. O. Box 12848   Gainesville, FL 32604

TOLL FREE:	800.874.5346	Customer service is available (Eastern Time):
LOCAL:	352.375.0772	8:00 a.m. - 7:00 p.m., Mon. - Fri.
FAX:	352.375.6940	9:00 a.m. - 2:00 p.m., Saturday
INTERNET:	gleim.com	Please have your credit card ready,
EMAIL:	sales@gleim.com	or save time by ordering online!

SUBTOTAL (from previous page) $_____
Add applicable sales tax for shipments within Florida. _____
Shipping (nonrefundable) 14.00

TOTAL $_____

Email us for prices/instructions on shipments outside the 48 contiguous states, or simply order online.

NAME (please print) _____

ADDRESS _____ Apt. _____
(street address required for UPS/Federal Express)

CITY _____ STATE _____ ZIP _____

____ MC/VISA/DISC/AMEX   ____ Check/M.O.   Daytime Telephone (____) _____

Credit Card No. _____ - _____ - _____ - _____

Exp. ____/____ Signature _____
Month / Year

Email address _____

1. We process and ship orders daily, within one business day over 98.8% of the time. Call by 3:00 pm for same day service.
2. Gleim Publications, Inc. guarantees the immediate refund of all resalable texts, unopened and un-downloaded Test Prep Software, and unopened and un-downloaded audios returned within 30 days. Accounting and Academic Test Prep online courses may be canceled within 30 days if no more than the first study unit or lesson has been accessed. In addition, Online CPE courses may be canceled within 30 days if no more than the Introductory Study Questions have been accessed. Accounting Practice Exams may be canceled within 30 days of purchase if the Practice Exam has not been started. Aviation online courses may be canceled within 30 days if no more than two study units have been accessed. This policy applies only to products that are purchased directly from Gleim Publications, Inc. No refunds will be provided on opened or downloaded Test Prep Software or audios, partial returns of package sets, or shipping and handling charges. Any freight charges incurred for returned or refused packages will be the purchaser's responsibility.
3. Please PHOTOCOPY this order form for others.
4. No CODs. Orders from individuals must be prepaid.

Subject to change without notice. 11/12

For updates and other important information, visit our website.

GLEIM
KNOWLEDGE
TRANSFER
SYSTEMS®

gleim.com